W9-CHS-127

Infants

Second Edition

INFANTS

DEVELOPMENT AND RELATIONSHIPS

Mollie S. Smart and Russell C. Smart

Macmillan Publishing Co., Inc.
NEW YORK

Collier Macmillan Publishers
LONDON

Copyright © 1978, Macmillan Publishing Co., Inc.

Printed in the United States of America

All rights reserved. No part of this book may be reproduced or
transmitted in any form or by any means, electronic or mechanical,
including photocopying, recording, or any information storage and
retrieval system, without permission in writing from the Publisher.

Earlier edition copyright © 1973 by Macmillan Publishing Co., Inc.

Reprinted with modifications from *Children: Development and Relationships,*
Third Edition, by Mollie S. Smart and Russell C. Smart, copyright © 1967,
1972, and 1977 by Macmillan Publishing Co., Inc., and *Readings in Child
Development and Relationships,* by Russell C. Smart and Mollie S. Smart,
copyright © 1972 and 1977 by Macmillan Publishing Co., Inc.

Macmillan Publishing Co., Inc.
866 Third Avenue, New York, New York 10022

Collier Macmillan Canada, Ltd.

Library of Congress Cataloging in Publication Data

Smart, Mollie Stevens.
  Infants : development and relationships.

  "Reprinted with modifications from Children: develop-
ment and relationships, third edition . . . and Readings
in child development and relationships."
  Includes bibliographies and indexes.
  1. Infant psychology—Addresses, essays, lectures.
I.   Smart, Russell Cook, joint author. II. Title.
BF723.I6S54   1978   155.4'22   77–5495
ISBN 0-02-411970-9

Printing: 1 2 3 4 5 6 7 8   Year: 8 9 0 1 2 3 4

Contents

Introduction

Infants, by simply being themselves, evoke all sorts of interesting reactions in other people. A baby always exists in relationship to other persons, influencing others and being influenced by them physically, mentally, and emotionally. This book is concerned with those interactions and with the resources that the infant uses in self development and in relating to family and other people.

An infant is very much a whole organism and person, even though psychologists may study how he sucks, looks, and grasps, while nutritionists consider his utilization of various foods, and sociologists may focus on the baby's impact on his parents' marriage. As child developmentalists, we use findings of research in all these fields and more. Since the study of infant development promotes understanding of human beings and of self, it contributes to one's liberal education. Infant studies also serve as a foundation for students who will later specialize in any of the contributing fields.

The practical applications of studying infancy are of great importance. Parenting skills are no longer taught informally in the North American family to any great extent. Many prospective and many new parents need the help of specialists in infancy in order to give their babies excellent opportunities for development and to help themselves to feel and be competent as parents. Day care centers need the services of workers who know how to promote the health and growth of infants and families. Hospitals need personnel who treat the baby as a person and family member, and not just as a physical body.

From many points of view, infancy is easily seen as a distinctive stage of life. Locomotion and posture are very different from the bodily control of an older child. Infants need very special kinds of food which they ingest through behavior quite unlike adults' eating. They are resistant to certain kinds of disease and very vulnerable to certain other physical insults. Babies learn to talk only as the end of infancy draws near. Their cognitive activities are a mystery to most people. Only recently have infants' cognitive abilities begun to be comprehensible to psychologists, largely those following Piaget's lead. Basic personality growth occurs during infancy. Erikson gives us a fruitful way of thinking about it, in terms of the development of the sense of trust and the sense of autonomy.

Each of the five chapters of the book consists of a text section followed by readings from other authors. Some of the readings report research; others review and discuss topics concerning infants. The last chapter is philosophical and theoretical, concerned with life and development of human beings, and dealing with topics which apply to all ages. We urge the teacher to consider assigning the last chapter first. Some teachers prefer to start the course with the infant, while others like to lay a theoretical groundwork first. The text sections are from our book *Children: Development and Relationships,* Third Edition; the articles by other authors are from the second edition of our *Readings in Child Development and Relationships.*

The first chapter takes the individual from fertilized ovum to newborn infant. The mother is the primary other person in this stage of prenatal life, but father, family, and society are also involved. The first of the readings in this chapter is concerned with genetic endowment and the ethical issues raised by new methods of diagnosis, treatment, and termination. The second article is about a recent development in obstetrical care—the use of nurse-midwives. Stimulation of premature infants is the topic of the last article, which shows that health and growth can be enhanced by new techniques.

Early infancy, or about the first month of life, is discussed in Chapter 2. Newborn infants have many competencies that psychologists investigate by means of new methods and instruments. Interaction with parents and caretakers are discussed in two of the articles. The wholeness of the infant is apparent in its response to inconsistency in the environment provided by caretakers.

The third chapter deals with the period from about one month to about two years of age, discussing physical development, nutrition, and health, as well as cognitive, motor, and language development. The brain and central nervous system are the focus of the first two articles, the second of which analyzes the crying of malnourished infants. The last article shows strong relationships between cognitive functioning and home environment.

Chapter 4 is concerned with social behavior and self-development. Even infants have impulses that result in cooperative and sympathetic behavior when there are opportunities for positive social interaction. Toddlers have been found able to play with each other without much of the conflict that adults may expect. A description of child care in another culture, that of the kibbutz, highlights some aspects of social interaction in infancy.

Suggestions to the Student

TAKING NOTES ON DIFFERENT KINDS OF READINGS

The first part of each chapter, which is from our textbook *Children,* Third Edition, gives basic subject matter. We show you by means of the headings what we think most important. When you are taking notes, we suggest that you use our headings as a framework. Put under them, in your own words, what the section says to you.

The articles in each chapter elaborate on something mentioned much more briefly in the chapter, or they may lay a background for the chapter. You will need to adapt your note taking to the style of the article. Reviews of research and statements of theoretical positions require about the same kinds of notes. There are usually not a great many main points, although some of them may have subsidiary points made in connection with them. Often these points are reiterated in a summary that may come at the beginning or the end of the selection. If there is no summary, the author may have omitted it because he thought he made his points so clearly that they would not be missed. In any case, assume the author had a message and ask yourself, "What does the author want me to learn? Why does he think it important? What evidence does he present for accepting the truth of his statements?"

The selections that are research reports are more specialized kinds of writing and therefore require a different kind or form of note taking. Here is an outline that we have developed over our years of teaching. Students have found it helpful.

HOW TO MAKE AN ABSTRACT OF RESEARCH ARTICLES

Author, Name of. The complete title of the article, as stated in the journal. Name of journal, year, volume, inclusive pages. (Month). For the selections in this book add the bibliographic reference for this book also, in the same form. Note that so far you have been copying, exercising your writing muscles. You should not do much more copying.

Purpose. State the purpose in the author's words if he has not been too verbose. Do you see why copying may be a good idea here? But make an active decision to copy. Do not just keep on writing.

Subjects. Name, ages, sex, socioeconomic status, hereditary factors, environmental factors, all the important identifying material that the author gives. Put it in tabular form if possible.

Apparatus and Procedure. A brief description of any special apparatus, tests, or techniques. If a standard test is used, be sure to mention any deviations from the usual method of presentation or scoring. If the length of time the test continued or the number of determinations is important, be sure to include these facts.

Results. What the investigator found, in terms of scores, and so on. Put these in tabular form also if you can. Keep in mind that you are writing a summary, but do not leave out any important items. Also remember that you usually make abstracts for use over a long period of time, and that later you may want to know the results of this study for a purpose different from your present one.

Conclusions. How the author interprets his findings. Does he think his hypothesis is substantiated? What does he think is the "next step?" Does he tie his results into the main body of knowledge in his field?

Remarks. This is the place, and the *only* place, for you to say what you think. Is it a good study? Are there any points on which you disagree? Can you offer any interpretations other than those given by the author? What are the theoretical implications? Are there implications for practice? What further studies does this one suggest to you?

The following questions are some of the points you should investigate under each of the major headings. All of them, of course, are not applicable to any one study, and there may be others in some instances. A beginning student will not have the background for answering all of them.

Purpose. Does the author state the purpose clearly? Allowing for personal enthusiasms, was the purpose worthwhile?

Subjects. Is the number adequate? Is the sample clearly described as to age, sex, SE status, education, race, and so on? Remember that in different studies different things are important. The two criteria here are whether the sampling is good and whether the sample is reproducible. That is, if you wanted to check the experiment, has the author given you enough information so that you could reproduce the group in all important characteristics?

Apparatus and Procedure. As far as you can tell, did the investigator set up his procedure so that his results are not biased by it? Are factors controlled that might invalidate the results? Is there a better way of testing the same hypothesis? If statistics were used, are they adequate? Why did the investigator use the ones he did? If statistics were not used, why did he handle the data as he did? Do you approve of his methods? Why?

Results. Are the results clearly stated? Are sufficient raw data given so that someone else could rework them? Would the results be different if better methods of handling the data had been used? What effect does the sampling have on the results? Do you know of any other studies that bear on this one, either substantiating it or contradicting it?

Conclusions. Do the author's conclusions follow from the results he has stated? Do they bear any relation to his stated purpose? Do the conclusions as stated take into account any limitations in the sampling or method?

This is not the only way of keeping track of research articles. This outline, however, is as exhaustive as most people will need for ordinary purposes. Only occasionally, when you are engaged in writing a minute analysis of the literature on one topic, will you want to keep a more inclusive record of the details in an article. More often you will want to record less material than this outline requires. It is a lot of work to make a complete abstract, but when you have done it, your thinking becomes clearer and your files are that much more well stocked. Complete abstracts should not be neglected.

A VERY SHORT COURSE IN STATISTICS

Many students who read this book will not have had a course in statistics. Usually the authors of research articles interpret the statistics they use and state the conclusions that follow from them. But because you should not get into the lazy habit of skipping over them, we include this section in order to help you to understand some of the important kinds of statistics. When you come across a statistic (correlation, for instance), refer back to this section. Some that are used only occasionally, like the sign test and the Mann-Whitney test, are not described here. A text on statistics will explain these.

Averages or Measures of Central Tendency. What a nonstatistician calls the average, a statistician calls the *mean* or the *arithmetic mean*. The average (mean) cost of your textbooks for this semester is the sum of what you paid for all the books divided by the number of books. A mean is a number that, mathematically, is most representative of a series of similar numbers.

Another kind of average is the *median*. A median is the middle number when a series of numbers is arranged from small to large. There are two conditions under which it is used. The median is used when some of the numbers are much larger or smaller than the others. If you were able to get four used textbooks for $4, $4.75, $5, and $7, but had to spend $15 for a new edition, the mean cost would be $7.15. The median cost of $5 is more representative of the series of numbers. The median is also used when the unit of measurement is not divisible into smaller units. The mean number of children per family is an incorrect use of the mean, although it is sometimes reported, because there can be no such thing as a fractional child, and means rarely come out as integers. Since a median can be an integer, the average number of children per family should always be stated as a median.

The *mode* and the *harmonic mean* are occasionally used as a measure of central tendency. A statistics textbook will explain them.

Tests of Significance. In most research two or more groups are compared with each other. The important question is, "Are the differences due to chance or to a real difference in condition or treatment of the groups?" The researcher sets up the hypothesis (called the null hypothesis) that there is no true difference. He applies an appropriate statistical test, on the basis of which he decides to accept or reject the null hypothesis. He would accept the null hypothesis that there is no significant difference if the test showed that a difference as large as the one discovered could have arisen by chance. If the test showed that the difference could have arisen by chance less than five times out of 100 repetitions of the study, he rejects the null hypothesis and concludes there *is* a true, or significant, difference. The statistical notation for such a statement is $p < .05$, which is read, "the probability is less than five in 100." Occasionally a more stringent test of significance is used, which is written $p < .01$. This means that the result could be obtained by chance less than 1 per cent of the time. Note that a statistician does not say a difference could *never* occur by chance, but the probability of its occurring by chance is so many in 100.

There are many different kinds of tests of significance, depending on the kind of data being used. Some of the more usual are χ^2 (chi-squared), the *t* test, and the F test of analysis of variance. Always a test of significance gives the basis for deciding whether the difference could have arisen by chance.

The *t* test and analysis of variance (ANOVA) are statistical tests that are similar: In the *t* test two conditions or situations can be compared; in a one-way ANOVA more than two (high, moderate, and no nutritional supplement, for instance) can be compared. A two-way ANOVA makes it possible to compare the effects of two variables (nutritional supplement and sex of subject) and also determine the effect of the interaction between the variables. In such a study, there would be boys and girls in the three nutritional supplement groups. All of them would be measured for height at the beginning of the period of nutritional supplement and again at the end. The gains of all the children, both boys and girls, in each of the nutritional supplement groups would be compared; this would be a one-way ANOVA. Similarly, the gains of all the girls, regardless of level of supplement, would be compared with all the boys' gains, another one-way. The analysis of variance is two-way, because it is possible, also, to find out if there is an interaction between nutritional supplement and sex of subject—do high-level boys react differently from high-level girls *and* from moderate-level and no-level boys. Because there are computers to do the immense number of calculations, there are three-variable and even four-variable ANOVAs reported in the literature, although they are rare, for very large numbers of subjects are necessary in order to make the subgroups big enough.

Correlation. A coefficient of correlation measures the degree to which two measures (height and weight, for instance) vary together—positive correlation if one measure gets bigger as the second one does, and negative correlation if one gets smaller as the other one gets bigger. Zero correlation means that there is no relationship between the two. Note carefully that correlation coefficients do not say anything about causation. Heights and weights are positively correlated, but a person's weight does not cause her height, nor does her height cause her weight.

Coefficients of correlation range in size between +1.00 and −1.00. If the coefficient is .00, there is no relationship between the two measures. The closer it is to 1.00, either positive or negative, the closer is the relationship. If there was discovered to be a correlation of +1.00 between height and weight in a group of children, the tallest child would be the heaviest, the second tallest would be second heaviest, and so on to the shortest, the lightest. If you knew the height of one of these children in relation to the others, you could place him exactly in weight in relation to the others. If a correlation coefficient is −1.00, the relationship is perfectly inverse. Suppose the coefficient between reading and arithmetic scores is .00 or not significantly different from .00. The best prediction of any child's reading test score, knowing what his arithmetic test score is, would be the mean reading score of the group of children. Such a prediction would not be very helpful, unless the score in arithmetic (the independent variable) is itself close to the mean.

Most often the correlation coefficient reported is the Pearson product-moment coefficient (r). Another one often used is the rank-order coefficient (rho, or ρ).

Factor Analysis. As noted above, correlation coefficients are measures of the degree to which pairs of scores vary together. Therefore a set of coefficients can be used to obtain an indication of the *factors* underlying the co-variation of the scores. The method is called *factor analysis*. Although factor analysis was invented before there were computers, the number of calculations involved in the method prevented its wide use. If there are 50 variables to be correlated with each other, 1225 correlation coefficients are necessary, and each coefficient involves several arithmetic calculations. Then many more calculations must be made on those coefficients in order to measure the factors. These kinds of repetitive calculations are what a modern computer does very well. More factor analyses are reported in the research journals now than were reported even five years ago.

A factor analysis yields from two up to nine or ten factors. Each variable (test) in the analysis has a loading on each factor. Loadings range from .00 up to .99. A loading not significantly different from zero means that that factor does not contribute anything to that test. The bigger the loading, the more important is that factor in influencing the variability of the test scores. When several tests or measures all have large loadings on a factor, there is evidence that all of them share something in common. The investigator then sets about naming the factor, by considering what it is that all members of the group have in common, and that the rest of the tests have not at all or in only small amounts. Unlike the calculation of correlation coefficients and factor loadings, the naming of the factors is not precise, since judgments have to be made about what the members of each subset share. Often, perhaps usually, the naming of the factors is obvious when the reader of the research considers what the original measures are. But sometimes an investigator has not considered all the possibilities of the meanings of the factors the computer has extracted from his data.

Chapter 1
Prenatal Development and Birth

PHOTOGRAPH BY LENORE HOLLAND

Although it takes two to make a baby, and the mother's bodily rhythms determine exactly when fertilization can take place, it is the fetus that controls the timing of birth [38]. As an embryo and then a fetus, the new individual influences the mother and is influenced by her. This chapter is concerned with the physical and psychological development of these two individuals, within their family and culture.

Stages of Prenatal Development

FROM FERTILIZATION TO IMPLANTATION

At about the middle of each menstrual cycle (the thirteenth or fourteenth day of a 28-day cycle), a mature ovum reaches the middle of the Fallopian tube in its journey from the ovary to the uterus. Fertilization takes place here, when a sperm penetrates the egg. If the sperm bears an X chromosome, a female is conceived, if a Y, a male. If parents want to choose the sex of their baby-to-be, techniques are available that can give them an 80-to-90 chance of success [42].

1

The ovum is a little ball about the size of a dot that looks a lot like a chicken egg when viewed under a microscope. Figure 1-1 shows a greatly magnified human egg. A tough membrane encloses a layer of whitish fluid, inside which is a yoke-like central portion. The little ball inside the white layer is a polar body, containing unused chromosomes. Unable to move by itself, the ovum is swept down the Fallopian tube by suction, expansion and contraction of the tube, and hair-like parts of the tube that lash back and forth. The sperm that must meet the ovum partway down the tube if fertilization is to take place is one of 500 million, more or less, contributed by the father some time during the past 48 hours. Ever so much smaller than the egg, the sperm swims by lashing its long tail. Figure 1-2 shows several sperm cells. Many sperm will probably bump against the egg before one succeeds in penetrating the egg's tough outer membrane. Although more than one sperm may penetrate the membrane, only one sperm's nucleus unites with the nucleus of the egg. The male and female nucleus lie side by side for a few hours, as seen in Figure 1-3, before they merge to form the *zygote,* the fertilized egg, at the beginning of a new individual. The egg splits into 2 cells, as can be seen in Figure 1-4. The 2 cells form 4 cells and the 4 cells 8. After 72 hours, the ovum has grown into 32 cells, as shown in Figure 1-5, and after four days, it consists of 90 cells and looks like Figure 1-6. Note that there is a cavity in the center, and cells are clustered around it. It is in this state that the organism, now called a *blastocyst,* leaves the Fallopian tube and enters the uterus, where it floats for one or two days before settling itself into the lining of the uterus. The outer layer of cells, the *trophoblast,* produces tendrils, or villi, which burrow into the uterine lining and connect the ovum with the uterine wall. This

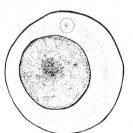

Figure 1-1.   A human egg, about 400 times actual size.

SOURCE: After a photograph by Landrum Shettles in E. H. Havemann, *Birth control.* Time, Inc., 1967.

Figure 1-2.   Male and female sperm cells magnified about 400 times.

SOURCE: After a photograph by Landrum Shettles in E. H. Havemann, *Birth Control.* Time, Inc., 1967.

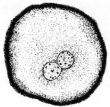

Figure 1-3. A fertilized egg. Male and female nuclei lie side by side for a few hours before uniting.

Source: After a photograph by Landrum Shettles in E. H. Havemann, *Birth control*. Time, Inc., 1967.

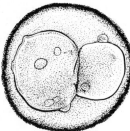

Figure 1-4. A few hours after the male and female nuclei merge, the egg splits into two cells.

Source: After a photograph by Landrum Shettles in E. H. Havemann, *Birth control*. Time, Inc., 1967.

Figure 1-5. During the first 72 hours of life, the ovum grows into 32 cells.

Source: After a photograph by Landrum Shettles in E. H. Havemann, *Birth control*. Time, Inc., 1967.

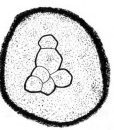

Figure 1-6. At four days of age, the ovum consists of about 90 cells.

Source: After a photograph by Landrum Shettles in E. H. Havemann, *Birth control*. Time, Inc., 1967.

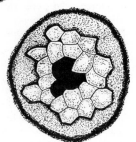

process, called *implantation,* marks the end of the stage of the ovum and the beginning of the stage of the embryo.

The question of when this organism can be considered a human being is an important one, since we have the means of diagnosing many abnormalities *in utero.* A properly performed abortion carries less risk than a tonsillectomy and a great deal less discomfort. In addition, a growing number of people are coming to believe that every woman has a right to decide for herself whether or not she shall bear a child. Until the nineteenth century, abortion was not considered punishable by the Roman Catholic church if it took place early in the pregnancy. St. Thomas Aquinas, in the thirteenth century, taught that life and soul began when the mother first felt the fetus move inside her [23a]. Another interpretation, derived from Aristotle's belief that the soul developed gradually, held that abortion after 40 days was pun-ishable [30a]. In 1869, the Roman Catholic church eliminated distinctions between different levels of development of the soul and declared abortion punishable at any time. More liberal trends concerning abortion are again in evidence. Scholars point out that before implantation, the ovum has no dependence on the mother and that the embryo is not an individual life until it becomes a fetus and produces hormones of its own [7]. Until near the end of the gestation period, the fetus is not an independent organism because it cannot survive outside the mother. Different cultures have varying notions as to when an organism becomes a human being. At one extreme are those who think that a fertilized ovum is a human being; at the other are those who think that a child is not a real person until several months after birth.

None of the events of the period of the ovum can be felt by the mother, not even implantation. Her offspring is well settled into her body before she has any indication of its presence.

THE EMBRYO

The individual is called an embryo during the time that the various organs and tissues are being differentiated and formed, from the end of the second week to

Figure 1-7. From ovum to fetus. These actual-size silhouettes show the rapid growth and development of the embryo. Dot at left represents the egg. Silhouettes show development at 1, 14, 16, 18, 20, 22, 25, 30, 42, and 56 days of age. Highlights of development are: two weeks: flat embryonic disc with three germ layers. Three weeks: Disc arches to form cylinder; beginnings of alimentary canal, kidney, heart, nervous system, and muscles. Four weeks: "C" shape with large head end, tail, limb buds, gill slits, and bulging, beating heart; beginning of eyes, nose pits, ears, lungs, and jaws. Six weeks: Face forming, with lips, eyes on sides, paddle-like limbs; cartilage beginning; brain growing rapidly, bending forward. Eight weeks: Embryo looks human, with jaws, ears, fingers, and toes; tail almost covered; head about half of total length. Fore-head bulges with large brain. Ossification centers. Testes and ovaries distinguishable.

SOURCES: G. S. Dodds. *The essentials of human embryology,* 3rd ed. New York: John Wiley & Sons, 1946. M. S. Gilbert. *Biography of the unborn.* Baltimore: The Williams & Wilkins Co., 1938. B. M. Patten. *Human embryology,* 2nd ed. New York: McGraw-Hill, 1953. E. L. Potter. *Funda-mentals of human reproduction.* New York: McGraw-Hill, Inc., 1948.

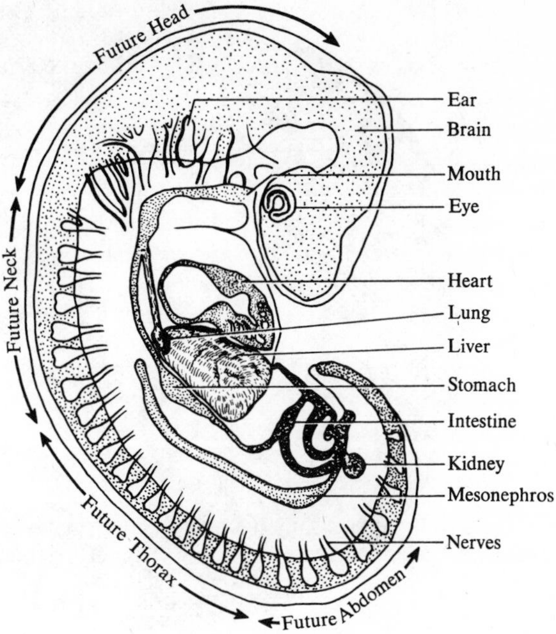

Figure 1-8. The month-old embryo has the foundations of many organs and systems.

SOURCE: After M. S. Gilbert. *Biography of the unborn.* Baltimore: The Williams & Wilkins Co., 1938.

the end of the second month. Mosslike villi extend from the embryo into the blood spaces of the maternal uterus, forming a means of exchanging body fluids. Protective and supportive membranes, the *chorion* and *amnion,* take form. The amniotic sac enclosing the embryo begins to fill with fluid.

The head comes first in the developmental timetable. The head of the embryo is one half of its total length; of the newborn, one quarter; of the adult, one tenth. These ratios illustrate the principle of developmental direction, described in Chapter 5 which holds for lower animals as well as for man and for function as well as for structure—that is, *development proceeds from anterior to posterior.*

The development of the embryo is outlined in Figure 1-7. Note the great speed of increase in height and weight. Figure 1-8 represents the development of the organs and systems at one month, greatly enlarged. The true size of the embryo at one month is shown by the eighth silhouette. From its appearance, a person would have a hard time distinguishing a human embryo from any sort of mammal embryo.

THE FETUS

At eight weeks, the organism is beginning to look human, although changes are gradual. A new name is applied. From the end of the eighth week until birth, the individual is called *fetus* instead of embryo. Complete with face, neck, arms, legs, fingers, toes, some calcification of its bones, and functioning internal organs and muscles, the fetus is ready to build upon the basic form that has been laid down.

Development during the third month includes differentiation between the

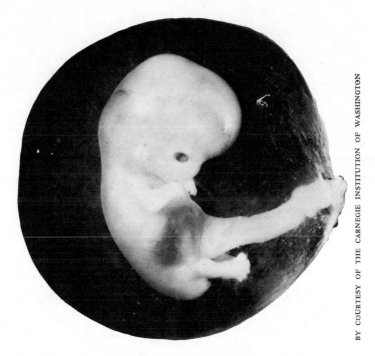

BY COURTESY OF THE CARNEGIE INSTITUTION OF WASHINGTON

Figure 1-9.   The fetus at about nine weeks. This photograph is about four times life size. The face has eyes, ears, nose, and lips. The arms have hands, with fingers and thumbs. The legs have knees, ankles, and toes.

sexes, the formation of tooth buds and sockets for the temporary teeth, the vocal chords, and, of course, growth in size and complexity. The third and fourth months are a time of tremendous growth in size; six or eight inches are added to the length. At 4 months the fetus has reached half of what its length will be at birth. At 6 months the *vernix caseosa,* formed from skin cells and a fatty secretion, protects the thin, delicate skin. The skin is red and wrinkled until subcutaneous fat is deposited under it, during the last three months of prenatal life. The fetus swallows, makes breathing movements along with rapid eye movements, and may suck its thumb. All of these functions indicate the maturing of the nervous system. The surrounding amniotic fluid supports the fetus in an almost weightless state, protecting it from shocks and jarring, and gives the fetus the freedom to move.

By 12 weeks the head of the fetus extends when the trunk flexes, the rump flexes more rapidly, and one arm moves farther back than its opposite. To a lesser degree, the legs also move independently of the trunk and asymmetrically, suggesting the beginning of alternating movements. Thus, the anterior portion shows more behavior than the posterior portion, illustrating again the principle that development proceeds from anterior to posterior. Another principle specified in Chapter 5 is demonstrated also, namely that development proceeds through differentiation and integration. The generalized movement of the fetus at eight weeks, when the limbs move along with the trunk, is differentiated to a unit of movement in which arms and legs are independent of the trunk but coordinated with it.

The fetus is 16 to 20 weeks old when its mother first feels it moving like a butterfly inside her. Before long it will thump her interior instead of tickling it. Already it has a large repertory of movements that includes blinking, sucking, turning the head, and gripping, and a wide variety of movements of limbs, hands, and feet.

The motor behavior of the fetus is related to the behavior of the baby, as might be expected [55]. Thirty-five women kept records of fetal movements during the last three months of pregnancy. Gesell tests done on the babies at 12, 24, and 36 weeks showed positive relationships between amount of fetal activity and motor and total scores at each level.

A "mini-growth spurt" occurs between 12 and 18 weeks, when nerve cells multiply [16a]. By 26 weeks, the six layers of the cerebral cortex are established. The brain is growing very rapidly at this point, with the addition of new cells and

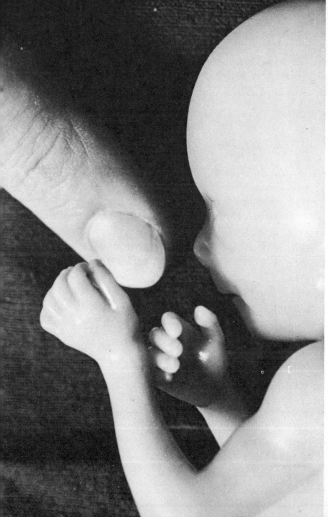

Figure 1-10.   Fetus at about 16 weeks. Its hand is about the size of a woman's fingernail.

ELLEN S. SMART

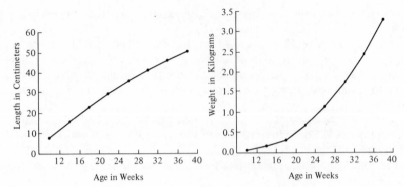

Figure 1-11.   Mean length and weight of the human fetus from 10 weeks to birth.
Highlights of development are:

12th week: Sex distinguishable. Eyelids sealed shut. Buds for deciduous teeth. Vocal
cords. Digestive tract, kidneys and liver secrete.

16th week: Head about one third of total length. Nose plugged. Lips visible. Fine
hair on body. Pads on hands and feet. Skin dark red, loose, wrinkled.

20th week: Body axis straightens. Vernix caseosa covers skin as skin glands
develop. Internal organs move toward mature positions.

24th to 28th week. Eyes open. Taste buds present. If born, can breathe, cry, and
live for a few hours.

28th to 40th week. Fat deposited. Rapid brain growth. Nails develop. Permanent
tooth buds. Testes descend. Fetus becomes viable.

SOURCES: H. V. Meredith. Somatic changes during human prenatal life. *Child Development,*
1975, **46,** 603–610, and references cited in Figure 1-9.

the growth of cells [13]. During the last three months of pregnancy and for about
2 years, after birth, the nervous system is very vulnerable [15]. If seriously malnourished for as long as about four months at the beginning of this period, the
nervous system is unlikely to recover from the deprivation.

The last half of prenatal life is a period of preparation for birth and independent living. Most important is the maturing of the nervous system, which must
organize and coordinate all the other systems. The establishment of breathing, the
most precarious step into the outside world, will be determined largely by the condition of the nervous system.

Figure 1-11 shows growth in length and weight during the prenatal period,
along with some landmarks of development. Male fetuses grow faster than female.
The male's placenta and the male fetus are larger than the female's placenta and
the female fetus [38].

THE PLACENTA AND CORD

The *placenta,* an organ that serves the fetus' growth needs, might be thought
of as a part of the fetus that is discarded at birth. Derived from the *trophoblast,*
which sends tendrils into the *endometrial tissue* (uterine lining) of the mother, the
placenta grows into an inch-thick disc, about seven inches across. One side of it is

attached to the mother's uterus and the other side to the fetus' umbilical cord. In the early stages of pregnancy, the placenta does the work of kidneys, intestine, liver, endocrines, and lungs, adjusting its function as the fetus grows its internal organs. Through the placenta the fetus gets nutrients and oxygen from its mother and sends carbon dioxide and other waste products into her body for disposal. The fetus' and mother's bloodstream do not mix, however, except for the occasional escape of small amounts of the fetus' blood into the mother's. They exchange products through the walls of tiny blood vessels that lie close to each other but do not run into each other. This system is the *placental barrier.* Bodies carrying immunity pass through the barrier from mother to fetus, thus giving the child some protection for several months after birth from the diseases to which the mother is immune. The placenta makes hormones that affect both fetus and mother, directing development of the mother's body in ways that nurture the fetus and prepare her body for birth and lactation. An inadequate placenta is likely to cause poor development in the fetus.

The umbilical cord is derived from the body stalk, which is differentiated out of the trophoblast. Connecting the placenta, the cord in utero looks like a stiff rope or tube, about 20 inches long. Blood flows through the cord at a high rate. Since the cord is under pressure, it is not flexible enough to knot in the uterus. Only during the birth processes, when it becomes slack, is there any possibility of danger from the baby entangling himself in it. At that point, of course, the physician or midwife will take care of such an emergency.

Stages of Maternal Development and Experience

Since the zygote is free-floating and self-contained for about a week, the mother has no reactions to pregnancy until after implantation.

SYMPTOMS AND DIAGNOSIS

Failure to menstruate is usually the first symptom of pregnancy, although it is not a conclusive symptom. Absence of menses can be caused by a variety of reasons, including age, illness, and emotional upset; menstruation during the first two or three months of pregnancy is possible. Breast changes may announce pregnancy: fullness, tingling, and hypersensitivity may occur even before the first missed period.

Nausea or queasiness may begin when the first period is overdue. For those who are nauseated, the common pattern is morning queasiness, which disappears gradually in about eight weeks. Recent studies indicate that about one out of two pregnant women has some nausea during pregnancy. The most common pattern is a mild disturbance, consisting of morning queasiness that disappears during the day. Such symptoms are most likely the result of biochemical changes rather than of psychological maladjustment [22]. Severe, pathological vomiting, which occurs in a small percentage of women, is more likely to have some psychological origins. Research on nausea of pregnancy has yielded conflicting results, however, and these conclusions are only tentative. Fatigue and the need for extra sleep, frequent during the early months of pregnancy, probably represent a protective mechanism for facilitating physical changes. Frequency of urination is another early symptom.

Pregnancy can be diagnosed through laboratory tests soon after the first missed period.

PHYSICAL CHANGES

The whole body is affected by pregnancy. The first stage seems to be one of reorganization. The middle stage is normally one of smooth functioning, when the mother feels and looks blooming and settles into her job of supplying the fetus. Later stages involve more preparations for the birth process.

Foundations for childbearing are laid early in the mother's life, even at her conception, since pregnancy and birth are affected by the whole of her development and health [29]. The woman who begins pregnancy with a normal, fully mature, healthy, well-nourished body, in contrast to one in poor nutritional condition, is less likely to have complications in pregnancy, premature birth, and a baby in poor condition. It is difficult to compensate for inadequacies in certain nutritional elements during pregnancy. For example, if the mother has a good supply of calcium already stored in her bones, she will be more likely to keep herself and her baby well supplied with calcium than will a mother with inadequate stores, even though both have a good diet during pregnancy. Similarly with nitrogen retention and hemoglobin level, a healthy condition in the beginning makes it easier to maintain good levels through pregnancy.

Figure 1-12.   Some of the changes in a woman's body as pregnancy progresses.
SOURCE: M. S. Smart and L. S. Smart. *Families.* New York: Macmillan Publishing Co., Inc., 1976.

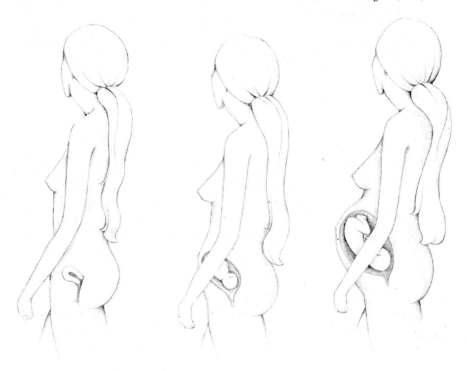

Special diets for the bride-to-be are a feature of some non-Western societies —a very functional feature. Even husbands-to-be have been known to receive nutritional supervision. Where a fat girl is beautiful, as in some African cultures, the standard of beauty may contribute to the nutritional preparation of mothers. In America, where slenderness is beautiful and high-fashion models are scrawny, teenage girls often eat inadequate diets that put them into poor condition for motherhood. Recent evidence pushes the important period for nutrition back into childhood, indicating that the adolescent years are only part of the time when a girl's nutrition has implications for her offspring: ". . . the mother's opportunity to grow during her childhood is perhaps the single strongest determining factor for her obstetrical and reproductive performance" [8].

Reproductive System. The uterus grows in weight from two ounces to over two pounds, in capacity from a half teaspoon to four or five quarts. Muscle fibers grow to ten times their former length. The preparation of the muscular layer of the uterus is extremely important, since it will open the cervix, help to push the baby out, and form ligatures to cut off the blood vessels supplying the lining of the uterus. The lining provides the spot where the blastocyst implants and takes part in forming the placenta. It provides a mucous plug to close the entrance to the uterus. The cervix, or neck of the uterus, softens as its muscle fibers diminish in number and size, connective tissue grows thinner, and blood supply increases. The vagina increases in length and capacity as its muscle fibers hypertrophy, connective tissue loosens, and more blood is supplied. All perineal structures, the tissues surrounding the birth canal, are loosened, becoming more distensible. Vaginal secretions increase in quantity and in bacteriocidal action.

Hormones from the placenta prepare the breasts for lactation. The breasts increase in size. Losing much of their fat, they gain mammary gland tissue and an increased blood supply. *Colostrum,* a clear, yellow, high-protein fluid, may be secreted from the breasts starting in the fourth month.

Preparation for breast-feeding includes care of the nipples during pregnancy. An examination in midpregnancy will reveal any need for treatment to improve protractility [23, pp. 26–32].

Circulatory System. The blood vessels supplying the uterus elongate, dilate, and become tortuous. The blood volume increases by one fifth, but has a progressively lower specific gravity and lower hemoglobin count. Although this condition is not true anemia, good hygiene is important in order to prevent anemia. Because of the changing specific gravity, the ordinary balance of fluids in the lymph system and certain veins may be upset. Balance is encouraged by breathing movements and muscular activity and is upset by inactivity and gravity. When too much blood accumulates in the vessels of the legs and the perineal and anal regions, drainage is improved by resting with the feet up.

Systemic Functions. Changes in the hormonal balance occur. Pregnancy affects various glands, including the thyroid, parathyroid, pituitary, and suprarenals. Metabolism is increased and improved after the third month. The capacity to store essential elements increases. The kidneys must work harder to take care of the products of increased metabolism and excretion of the fetus. The pelvis of the kidney dilates to double its former capacity. Sweat and sebaceous glands become more active.

PSYCHOLOGICAL ASPECTS

Pregnancy is a time of emotional disequilibrium and increased anxiety [47]. New feelings go along with the pervading physical changes and reorganization. The first pregnancy. brings sensations that a woman has not known before. Perhaps there has been something like it, but not exactly in this form. She has been tired before, but not so eager for an afternoon nap. She has experienced an upset stomach, but not the consistent daily cycle of hovering on the brink of nausea and then conquering it. The deep, alive, tingling sensation in the breasts may remind her of premenstrual sensations, but it is more than that. Then, as the pregnancy advances, there is the perception of fetal movements, which is like nothing else. She may describe it first as a fluttering. The spectrum of new bodily experiences demands attention. The pregnant woman, therefore, turns some of her attention inward, thinking about what she is feeling and about what is happening to her body.

The burden of pregnancy is carried easily by some women and not so easily by others. It is a burden in a literal sense. Simply transporting 20 to 25 extra pounds requires additional muscular exertion and more work done by the lungs, heart, kidneys—in fact, all of the body. When some parts of the body are found to be not quite up to carrying their share of the burden, their performance, resulting in discomfort, adds to the perceived burden. Common discomforts of pregnancy include varicose veins (the bulging of loaded blood vessels), heartburn (the product of the stomach's imperfect functioning), and shortness of breath (resulting from squeezed lungs). Such discomforts may be slight or severe, depending on such physical factors as bodily structure, nutrition, and fatigue. Medical care and good hygiene help to alleviate the difficulties. The woman's reactions to pregnancy are also the product of her culture and of her own personality.

Little girls are taught what to anticipate as they look forward to growing up and having babies of their own. Their mothers set an example when carrying baby brothers and sisters. Overheard conversations are influential. So are glances, nuances, and conversations that stop in midair as the child approaches. If mothers tell their children that pregnancy and birth are simple, natural, and beautiful and yet the children hear them exchanging stories with their friends that depict these processes as frightening and agonizing, they will surely not accept the first version confidently. Children also give each other information and misinformation. They may read news items and see films and television programs that contribute to their attitude toward pregnancy and childbirth. The reality of the situation is not lost in those looking forward to pregnancy. They notice how pregnant women are regarded in their culture. The range and variety of attitudes toward pregnancy in the various cultures of the world are quite amazing. Some people regard pregnancy as a time of illness and an abnormal condition, as do certain groups in South, Central, and North America; other tribes in South America and in the Pacific regard pregnancy as very normal and natural; some African tribes think that it is the height of happiness. Birth may be considered defiling and unclean, so that a woman is dirty afterwards and must be purified by a religious ritual. Birth may be thought to be supernatural, a time when a woman hovers between life and death or is especially vulnerable to demons [36].

The wide diversity of cultures in North America results in wide variation in attitudes toward pregnancy. Although today, in contrast to half a century ago, there is no taboo on pregnant women appearing in public and carrying on their ordinary activities, substantial fears, superstitions, and anxieties linger on because of ignorance. Many a young woman in a pretty maternity dress, unembarrassed at her bulge in front, is afraid of the unknown she will have to meet in the labor room. The luckier ones have had a good sex education and preparation for childbirth. An aspect of today's reality is the comparative ease and safety with which human reproduction occurs. Because of medical knowledge and techniques, drugs, nutrition, and health care, young women do not hear very often about women dying in childbirth or of their being almost frightened to death. They do hear, however, of children being born with physical and mental defects. They may be even more aware of these children than their grandmothers were, since there are more of them around. Modern medicine, although doing marvels to correct defects, maintains life in increasing numbers of defective children. Pregnant women commonly fear that their children will not be normal.

The personality of the expectant mother plays a large part in her reactions to pregnancy. If she has coped successfully with the problems of identity and has a marriage in which her sense of intimacy has developed, then, most likely, she welcomes parenthood with a feeling of confidence and happy anticipation. Nobody is unshakable in his or her self-concepts, and nobody has perfect communication and sharing with another. Therefore, even the healthiest pregnant woman will have occasional doubts about herself: her potential as a mother and her ability to cope with the more complicated family that will result from the birth of her baby. The woman who had difficult problems before her pregnancy is likely to find life harder now. The demands upon her would understandably increase fears about sex, modesty, physical adequacy, and family difficulties.

The Expectant Father. Interviews with pregnant couples showed that a husband and wife were likely to have similar emotional responses to pregnancy as compared with other couples [48]. Couples tended to have similar views of social support, labor, and delivery. Husbands' anxiety was more focused than wives'. Husbands generally felt more anxiety over the well-being of their babies.

At the other end of the spectrum of expectant couples are those interviewed in a study of violence between husbands and wives [20]. Indications were that husbands attacked pregnant wives more frequently than anyone had suspected. The attacks seemed to grow out of the stresses of pregnancy, compounded by existing stresses.

There must be stresses on all expectant fathers, but the severity of stress varies with the man's personality integration, the existing pair relationship, the planning and timing of the pregnancy, and the resources available. The father's ability to cope with his own anxieties and problems will affect his offspring. A man can contribute to the well-being of his unborn child through the help and support he gives to his wife. Feeling vulnerable as she does, her confidence in him as provider and protector is constructive in making her relaxed and secure. She appreciates reassurance that she is still attractive in spite of her increasing girth and decreasing agility. She may want some sympathy for the aches, pains, annoyances, and limitations on her activity. If she has fears about the pain of delivery and the well-being of the baby, or fears about her competence as a mother, she may seek reassurance from her husband. A mature man, who has coped successfully with his own personality growth, can give his pregnant wife a great deal of comfort through his understanding, sympathy, and confidence.

With a first pregnancy, the natural turning inward of the woman's attention may constitute the first time in the marriage when the husband feels displaced in her thoughts. He may realize that the worst is yet to come, when the infant will require a great deal of the time and attention that used to belong to him. He may feel deprived sexually. The father will probably feel added financial responsibility, since a new baby costs something even before birth and then costs more and more as the years go by. New, larger, costlier living quarters may be indicated. The thoughts of college expenses may cross his mind. If the pregnancy is an unwanted one, especially if it threatens the mother's health and the family's solvency, then the expectant father is likely to feel guilt.

The husband may find himself being the main, or even only, emotional support of his pregnant wife. When a young North American couple move to another part of the country, leaving family and friends behind, they are dependent, at least for a while, on the resources they have as a pair. In contrast, an extended family offers vast aid and support to a pregnant woman. If not already living with the older generation, the young woman may go home to her mother's house, where she is surrounded with affectionate care until after her baby is born and adjusted to life. Or her mother may come to her, taking authoritative command of what is considered woman's affairs, thus relieving the young father of much of the burden he would have to carry in a nuclear family consisting of husband, wife, and child.

In order to fill in some of the emotional and technical gaps created by the change from extended to nuclear family life, many communities offer education for childbirth. Pregnant mothers learn about the changes taking place within themselves, how delivery takes place, how to care for themselves, and how to care for their babies. Fathers go to classes that focus on what they want to know, what is happening to mother and baby, their own hereditary contribution, what they can do psychologically, and something about infant care and development. They may learn how to help their wives in labor and even how to deliver the baby. Through discussions, both parents clarify their own feelings and share with other expectant parents. Thus, they derive much of the security offered in other cultures by experienced family members, while they enjoy the added advantage of applying knowledge from modern research. The International Childbirth Education Association is a federation of groups and individuals interested in family-centered maternity and infant care. This association holds conferences, sponsors programs, provides educational materials on preparation for childbirth and breast-feeding, and promotes medical and hospital practices that support sound parent–child and husband–wife relationships. (The address of the association is 1840 South Elena, Suite 205, Redondo Beach, California 90277.)

When There Is No Father. Because out-of-wedlock pregnancies are increasing, it is appropriate to wonder how a pregnant woman manages without a partner's help and love. Much depends on the woman's motivation for becoming pregnant and upon her social group's evaluation of illegitimate pregnancies. When the pregnancy represents rebellion against parents and/or society, then obviously the young woman is immature and in serious emotional conflict. When, on the other hand, an unmarried girl is pregnant in a social setting where illegitimate pregnancies are frequent and easily accepted, then she may have little or no psychological trauma. Her own mother may take over much responsibility, giving her protection and security that a married woman would get from her husband. Statistics concerning illegitimate pregnancies are hard to interpret because of the socioeconomic factors involved. However, studies of such pregnancies do show the following: they occur at all social levels, but in greater numbers at lower levels; the women tend to be young, many of them under 20; mothers are more likely to work late in pregnancy, to receive little or no prenatal care, and to live in poor housing; death rates for mothers and babies are higher than in legitimate pregnancies; low birth weights and higher prematurity rates are more frequent [30].

Prenatal Influence

The question of whether and how a woman can influence her unborn baby is one that has intrigued people since the dawn of history. Some societies have maintained that specific thoughts and experiences could mark the baby in specific ways, such as the notion that if a rabbit ran across the pregnant woman's path, she would bear a baby with a harelip, or if she squashed a strawberry, her baby would have a red birthmark. Less specific, but just as unfounded, is the notion that by listening to good music and viewing great paintings, a woman could confer talent upon the child within her. As scientific knowledge about pregnancy and birth became widespread, more and more people realized that the baby's blood system was separate from the mother's, exchanging nutrients and products of excretion through membranes, but not exchanging blood. As the old superstitions, such as those of the harelip and strawberry mark, were swept away, many people got the idea that nutrition was the *only* prenatal influence. It is now known that the fetus is affected by nutrition, stress, drugs, radiation, infections, and blood incompatibilities.

NUTRITION

The woman who starts her pregnancy in good nutritional condition is fortunate, since she can thus provide the optimal environment for her baby right from the beginning. A nutritional defect is difficult to correct when the demands upon the body are increased by pregnancy. The very fact of being well nourished shows that the woman has established a pattern of eating an adequate selection of foods in amounts suited to her. She will not have to change her ways of eating other than to increase the amounts slightly as pregnancy advances.

Although nearly all people in all parts of the world believe that diet during pregnancy is important, the nutritional adaptations prescribed for pregnant women are not always helpful. Meat and fish are often forbidden, as in the tribe which prohibited the eating of owl monkey meat for fear that it would influence the baby to stay awake at night.

Types of Prenatal Malnutrition. The two main sources of fetal malnutrition are a *poor maternal diet* and *placental insufficiency* [51]. Animal studies show that a poor maternal diet before and/or during pregnancy results in fewer brain cells in the fetus and also increases the harmful effects of postnatal malnutrition on later brain growth. Placental insufficiency, according to animal experiments, may produce changes in enzymes and in the protein content of the cerebellum. Placental insufficiency may result from curtailment of cell division, in maternal malnutrition [16]. Frequent pregnancies and closely spaced pregnancies are likely to result in placental insufficiency.

Although calories and protein are most often considered in prenatal nutrition, deficiencies can occur in any of the many nutrients listed in the two parts of Appendix A. Pregnant women need more folacin, iron, and calcium than do nonpregnant women. Although trace elements such as zinc, as indicated by the term, are needed in only minute amounts, they *are* needed for normal development. When pregnant rats were deprived of zinc, 90 per cent of their babies had malformations, including cleft lips, missing limbs, brain anomalies, and curved spines [29]. Analyses of the mothers' bodies showed no loss of zinc from their bones and livers. The zinc was in the mothers' bodies, but the fetuses could not obtain it. Apparently they had to get their supply from zinc in the current diet, not from the mothers' reserves.

Results and Treatment of Malnutrition. Malnutrition of the fetus usually results in low birth weight and poor development [51]. Low birth weight is associated with high mortality. The underdeveloped newborn, compared with a normal one, grows less adequately, may have more illnesses, and may have poorer brain development and behavior difficulties.

Several nutritional supplementation studies have shown that increasing the food intake of poorly fed pregnant women increased the birth weight of their infants [14]. In Taiwan, birth weights increased by an average 150 grams when mothers were given additional proteins, vitamins, and calories. When Guatemalan mothers received an extra 20,000 calories, infant birth weights increased by 20 grams per 1,000 calories, no matter whether the calories were fed to the mother during the final trimester or throughout the pregnancy. Nutritional supplementation improved the condition of mothers and infants in a poverty area of New York City.

In Montreal, clinic patients were given measured amounts of supplementary foods in diets designed to fit each pregnant woman's individual needs, along with nutritional counseling and supervision [25]. Diets were adjusted in terms of pregnancy requirements, age, ideal body weight, actual weight, physical activity, degree of undernutrition, multiple fetuses, and stress. Included under stress were pernicious vomiting, pregnancies spaced less than one year apart, poor obstetrical history, failure to gain enough weight, and extreme anxiety from personal or family matters. For each stress condition, 200 calories and 20 grams of protein were added. The patients in this program had infants whose birth weights averaged 3,284 grams, or 276 grams more than those in a control group. Infants born to private patients in the same hospital averaged 3,276 grams at birth. Thus, the nutrition program erased the usual socioeconomic difference in birth weight. Another benefit to the group in the program was having fewer induced deliveries than did mothers in the control group.

Feeding the Pregnant Woman. Pregnant North American women are often placed in conflict over what they should eat [36]. It is common medical practice to restrict weight gain. Doctors often give out a diet sheet prescribing a diet of good quality while restricting calories. The rationale for limiting weight gain is usually threefold: the mother will have less fat to lose after delivery and hence will look better; chances of toxemia will be decreased; the baby will take what he needs, anyway. Sometimes a fourth reason is added: the baby will be smaller at birth and hence easier to deliver. A report of the Food and Nutrition Board of the National Research Council calls for important changes in the nutritional management of pregnancy [44]. The average optimal gain in pregnancy is 24 pounds, and there is no scientific reason for limiting it to lesser amounts. When well-fed, younger women will tend to gain a little more, thin women more, fat women less, and women having their first babies more. Pregnancy is not a time for fat women to try to reduce. Severe restriction of calories during pregnancy is potentially harmful to both mother and baby. The mother should eat what she wants, as long as her diet is balanced.

Figure 1-13. Normal prenatal weight gain, and tissues in which weight gain occurs during pregnancy.

SOURCE: Reprinted by permission from R. E. Shank. A chink in our armor. *Nutrition Today,* 1970, **5:** 2, p. 6. Copyright © 1970 by Enloe, Stalvey and Associates.

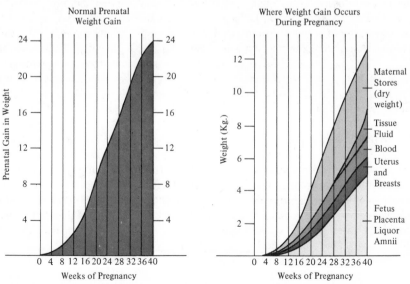

There is no evidence that weight gain due to accumulation of fat is associated with toxemia. The committee also recommends supplements of iron and folic acid and cautions against routine restriction of salt. Normal weight gain and the distribution of the weight are shown in Figure 1-13.

The notion that the baby will somehow draw what he needs out of his mother's body is an old wives' tale. Animal experiments show that calorie and protein restrictions in the mother's diet drastically affect litter size, survival, birth weight, growth patterns, and behavior of offspring [44]. Human studies have shown a strong association between weight gain of mother and birth weight of baby. Birth weight of baby is linked to the survival, normalcy, and health of the infant. A specific example of the baby's inability to get what he needs if the mother does not supply enough is that of eight-month-old babies whose mothers had had low iodine levels in their blood during pregnancies that were otherwise normal [26]. When compared with babies of mothers who had had normal iodine levels, the experimental group scored significantly lower on motor and mental tests and showed higher incidences of cerebral palsy, mental deficiency, visual and hearing loss, and other impairments.

Poverty and Malnutrition. Mental retardation, apathy, and impaired learning ability are serious problems in underdeveloped countries and among the poor people in North America. Although sufficient income does not assure a pregnant woman of an adequate diet, low income means virtual certainty of a poor diet.

A United States nutrition study showed low income groups receiving fewer calories and proteins than women from higher income groups [1]. Among women between 18 and 44, all groups got too little iron, low-income white women received too little vitamin A, and black women at all income levels were low in calcium. The dietary study, *Nutrition Canada*, assessed the percentages of all pregnant women at risk because of inadequate nutrition [43]. Indians and/or Eskimo had more severe dietary deficiencies than the general population in regard to iron, calcium, and several vitamins. A substantial number of pregnant women did not get enough protein, calcium, and vitamin D. Ignorance and maladaptive customs can increase the deprivation of poverty. In India, where the average income is $86 a year, and in much of Asia, for example, the wife eats after her husband and children have eaten. What is more, it is not easy to get enough protein from a vegetarian diet, and most Indians are vegetarians. In parts of Nigeria, pregnant women may not eat vegetables or fruits, and after delivery, they are not supposed to eat soup containing meat or fish [10].

Importance of Nutrition Education. Even when enough good food is available, most women need education and guidance in planning their diets. Probably the best place to begin is in nutrition education for all high school girls. More specific guidance during pregnancy is offered by classes for mothers, often taught as part of a comprehensive maternal care program in a hospital or clinic. Public programs in New Zealand and Sweden, teach and help a large proportion of pregnant women. The lower rates of infant and maternal mortality in these countries reflect the value of such programs (See Figure 1-14).

Dietary requirements vary from one woman to another, and there are a

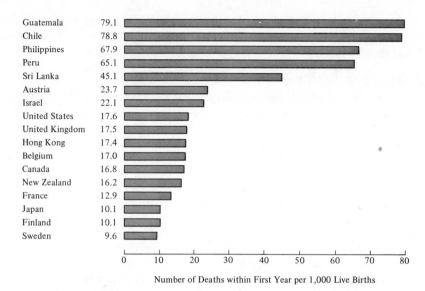

Guatemala	79.1
Chile	78.8
Philippines	67.9
Peru	65.1
Sri Lanka	45.1
Austria	23.7
Israel	22.1
United States	17.6
United Kingdom	17.5
Hong Kong	17.4
Belgium	17.0
Canada	16.8
New Zealand	16.2
France	12.9
Japan	10.1
Finland	10.1
Sweden	9.6

Number of Deaths within First Year per 1,000 Live Births

Figure 1-14. Infant mortality rates in selected nations for the latest available year.

SOURCE: United Nations Department of Economic and Social Affairs. *Demographic Yearbook 1973*. New York: United Nations, 1974.

variety of ways in which requirements can be met. When deficiencies occur, they can harm either mother or baby but they are likely to harm both. Dietary deficiencies can contribute to premature and otherwise abnormal births, stillbirths, death within the first few days of life, congenital defects, small size, and illnesses during infancy. The importance of adequate, individualized prenatal care is emphasized by the role of nutrition in assuring the health and safety of mother and baby.

SENSORY STIMULI

The fetus reacts to a variety of stimuli, including touch, pressure, temperature changes, sound, light, and taste [33]. The fetus gives violent responses to needle punctures and injections of cold or hypertonic solutions. It conditions and habituates to sounds. The sounds of the prenatal environment may be meaningful for postnatal life. The mother's internal organs make noises that in all likelihood her fetus can hear. Her breathing is rhythmic, too, with some tactile and kinesthetic stimulation along with auditory. The fetus surely hears its mother talking, coughing, sneezing, and swallowing. Her heartbeat is a rhythmic sound that may take on important significance at this time, when the fetus receives steady auditory stimulation from it over a long period.

It has been suggested that the mother's heartbeat provides an imprinting stimulus prenatally, resulting in an infant, child, and adult who feels comforted when held in someone's arms, where he feels a heartbeat. A recent experiment failed to show the soothing properties of a heartbeat sound on newborns, but did give an interesting result [47a]. Infants born to mothers with slow heart rates fell asleep sooner, slept longer, and cried less than infants born to mothers with faster heart rates. Thus it seems that the fetus is affected by the rate of the mother's heartbeat and that the effects last at least into the neonatal period.

MATERNAL EMOTIONS

There is little doubt that maternal emotional stress affects the fetus adversely. Depending on the timing and severity of the mother's upset, results may be the death of a fertilized ovum [41], bodily abnormalities [24; 49], physical complications of childbirth [24], and gastrointestinal malfunction and feeding problems in the newborn baby [17]. The health, development, and behavior of school-age children was related to prenatal stress by studying a cohort, all of the 1,300 children born during one year in a Canadian city [49]. Among children who had at least 20 per cent more illness than the cohort as a whole, the following conditions were present in their mothers during their prenatal life. The mothers suffered these conditions at least one and a half times as often as the average: respiratory illnesses; physical stresses such as standing all day or carrying heavy loads; and situational stresses, including fears about marriage, marital discord, money problems, shocks and worries over people or pets, and tensions involving people outside the family. Almost as high in frequency were other family tensions like being upset at moving away from her parents, not settled in her own home, not wanting the pregnancy, wanting an abortion, marital infidelity, out-of-wedlock conception, and having incurred heavy debts. In regard to situational stress, the investigators concluded that it was ongoing stress, or situations in which the pregnant woman felt trapped that resulted in damage to the fetus. They further concluded that the pregnancy conditions that were most noxious were those most likely to occur in a human group threatened with overpopulation. The effects of such noxious conditions would be to reduce the viability of the young and to restore balance between population, food, and space. The value of species survival is thus served. Fortunately, the availability of birth control makes it no longer necessary for human beings to let nature take its course in population control through the cruel method of stressing mothers and thus cutting down on the survival of children.

If a fetus can suffer from its mother's extreme emotional upset, then could the opposite be true? What happens to the fetus whose mother has an unusually happy, safe, secure time? At birth, is the child of a happy mother different from babies whose mothers have had an average or disturbed pregnancy? Definitive answers to these questions are not available. However, the multiplicity of studies on harmful influences makes one very much aware of what can go wrong prenatally. Perhaps a happy, relaxed pregnancy contributes physical and mental health to the baby. There is nothing to lose and possibly much to gain when the father and other family members are understanding, considerate, and affectionate with the expectant mother, not only for her sake but also for the baby's. This is not to say that the pregnant mother cannot safely deal with everyday problems and work, but only that she benefits from having the general tone of her life a positive one.

PHYSICAL AND CHEMICAL AGENTS

Heavy labor during pregnancy constitutes a stress on the fetus as well as on the mother [48]. Extreme summer heat is another kind of stress [40]. Massive X-ray doses are lethal or seriously damaging to the unborn child. After World War II, the effects of atom bomb radiation on children who had been in utero at the time included increased anomalies and morbidity [56].

Many drugs taken by the pregnant mother can affect the fetus, some apparently temporarily and some drastically and permanently. Quinine can cause deafness. The tranquilizer thalidomide caused thousands of tragic births in Germany, England, and Canada, where its prenatal use produced babies lacking limbs or with limbs in early stages of embryonic development. Many other substances, including mild tranquilizers such as meprobamate (Miltown and Equanil), and chlordiazepoxide (Librium) [37] may cause deformities if taken during the period of the embryo, when organs and systems are forming and growing rapidly. These findings illustrate the developmental principle of *critical periods,* described in Chapter 5.

The dangers of cigarette smoking have been well known for over a decade [40]. When pregnant women smoke, they are more likely to have a premature baby and/or a baby small for gestational age. These infants, of course, have a greater risk of dying, being ill, and having defects. Reports of research continue to confirm and extend these findings. A sample of several thousand British children were followed from birth to 11 years [9]. Physical and mental retardation were found more frequently in children whose mothers smoked during their prenatal life. Defects increased with the numbers of cigarettes smoked after the fourth month. Compared with children of nonsmokers, children of smokers of ten or more cigarettes per day were retarded in reading, mathematics, and general ability.

Some of the paths through which maternal smoking affects the fetus have been discovered [57]. Smoking raises the vitamin A level in the mother's blood. Extremely high levels of vitamin A may cause deformities in the embryo. Nicotine reduces peripheral circulation of the blood and probably also reduces placental circulation. Carbon dioxide competes with oxygen for circulation and hence reduces the oxygen going to the fetus, probably decreasing the growth rate of the fetus. Cyanide, another product of smoking, competes with nutrients especially vitamin B12, in the blood of the mother and hence reduces the amounts of nutrients going to the fetus. Luckily, the queasiness of early pregnancy causes many women to stop smoking. If they understood how important it is to the life and health of their future babies to stay off cigarettes, surely they would not start smoking when the nausea clears up.

Evidence against marijuana is also piling up. It has been implicated in birth defects in children [46] and has been demonstrated to cause deformities and still-births in rats [57]. Hard drugs have different harmful effects on the fetus since they localize in different tissues, such as the thyroid, the pigment of the eye, the skeleton, and even in the yolk sac of the embryo [54]. A number of studies have shown withdrawal symptoms in babies born to addicted mothers [50]. Symptoms include irritability, excitability, tremulousness, excessive nervous system reactions, and great sensitivity to light. Death and defects also result from drugs such as heroin and barbiturates [3].

Oral contraceptives pose a threat to the embryo if conception takes place immediately after the woman discontinues her use of the pill. Like cigarette smoking, oral contraceptives induce high vitamin A levels in the blood [57]. The combination of smoking and taking oral contraceptives increases blood levels of vitamin A to greater heights. The interaction of drugs with nutrients is a new area of research that holds promise for giving more understanding of birth defects.

INFECTIONS

When a viral disease is contracted by the mother, it may damage her fetus. Among such infections are rubella, hepatitis, rubeola, syphilis, smallpox, chicken pox, and scarlet fever. Tuberculosis and malaria are also dangerous to the fetus. The severity and type of damage depend upon the stage of development, with the embryo usually being more vulnerable. A worldwide epidemic of rubella in 1964 left 20,000 to 30,000 defective babies in the United States. (European-derived people are more susceptible to rubella than many other ethnic groups [28].) A study performed on a sample of these children found that 40 per cent were premature and many of these were small for their gestational age [9]. Only 20 per cent had no observable defect. Eleven per cent had defects in all major areas, hearing, visual, cardiac, and neurological. Over half of the children had psychiatric disorders, with various combinations of mental retardation and serious mental illness. Efforts are being made to treat these children and to help their families. Immunization campaigns have since reduced the likelihood of pregnant women contracting rubella. Many families choose to terminate a pregnancy that has only a 20 per cent (or even a somewhat larger) chance of producing a normal baby.

DAMAGE FROM HORMONAL AND BLOOD CONDITIONS

Endocrine problems, such as hypothyroidism and Addison's disease in the pregnant woman, require special medical care but can be managed [34, p. 32]. Diabetic women have higher chances of producing infants with defects, including hypoglycemia and heart, respiratory, and blood problems. Good medical care is important here. Administration of sex hormones during pregnancy has various and complex effects on fetal development.

About one pregnancy in 200 results in some disturbance from incompatibility between the blood of the mother and baby. The Rh factor is a substance that occurs in the red blood cells of about 85 per cent of white people, 93 per cent of blacks, and 99 per cent of Mongolian peoples. The remaining minorities are Rh negative [7]. When the mother's blood is Rh negative and the fetus' blood is Rh positive, there is one chance in ten that the infant will have some of his red blood cells destroyed. The way it happens is that the fetus produces antigens that go through the placenta into the mother's blood. Her blood then makes antibodies that go back through the placenta to the baby's bloodstream. Results include miscarriage, stillbirth, death after birth, brain damage, jaundice, and anemia. Adequate prenatal care requires a blood test that will detect negative Rh. The physician discovering it would then determine the husband's blood type and learn the chances of incompatibility arising between fetus and mother. Taking into account the finding that the danger from Rh factors increases with each baby after the first, the doctor would be ready to cope with symptoms likely to arise. Much can be done to alleviate the condition immediately after birth or even before birth. Harm to future babies can be prevented immediately after the birth of an Rh positive baby to an Rh negative mother. She can be given medication that will prevent damage to subsequent babies through blood incompatibility.

AGE AND PARITY OF THE MOTHER

The only time a woman of 35 is considered elderly is when she is having her first baby. In this case, she is called an "elderly primipara" by the medical profession, a logical term in light of the fact that the childbearing period is more than two-thirds over. At age 35 and older, the average length of labor is increased beyond the overall average by an hour and a half, and the risk to mother and baby is increased slightly. Maternal mortality, by age and race, is shown in Figure 1-15. Note that the hazards of age are enormously increased if the woman is black, but only slightly increased if she is white. These figures reflect the depressed economic conditions under which many blacks live.

When risk to the baby is estimated, it makes a difference which portion of the

Figure 1-15. Number of maternal deaths for each 100,000 live births, given for nonwhite and white women (United States, 1971), by age.

Source: Department of Health, Education, and Welfare. *Vital Statistics of the United States.* National Center for Health Statistics. Washington, D.C.: U.S. Government Printing Office, 1975.

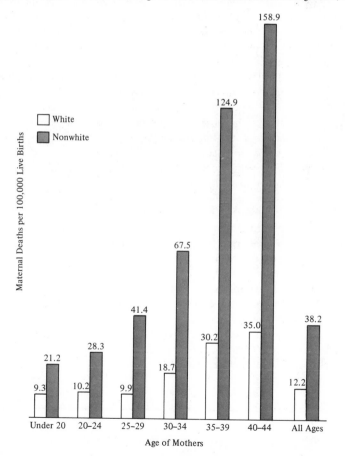

first year of life is considered. Although death rates are stated in terms of the mother's age and parity (number of pregnancies she has had), it must be remembered that both age and parity have different significance in different sociocultural settings. Stillbirths rise with increasing age and fall with parity up to the fourth pregnancy. The lowest rates are in the 20- to 24-year-age group and the highest is in mothers 35 and over. Death within the first month occurs most often with high parity in the youngest age group and next often to mothers of high parity in the oldest age group. The death rate between one month and 11 months rises with increasing parity and falls with increasing age. Prematurity rates are highest in 15- to 19-year-old mothers, with the exception of first babies born to mothers over 35, who have the highest prematurity rate of all [30]. Older mothers are also more likely to produce mongoloid children. Before age 30, the risk of having a mongoloid baby is 1 in 1,000, whereas at age 40 it is 1 in 100, and at age 45, 1 in 45 [18]. When defects of all kinds are counted, very young mothers and older mothers produce more impaired infants than do mothers in the ages in between [40].

From all these findings there follows a generalization that the first birth carries an extra risk and that aging and repeated births also add risk. Frequently repeated births carry a risk to the normalcy of the child, as well as to his life. Babies born within one year of a previous gestation were matched with controls born two to five years after the previous gestation. Matching was done for sex, race, hospital of birth, and socioeconomic status [27]. Their gestation ages were equal, but the babies produced in rapid succession averaged significantly smaller birth weights, lower scores on the Bayley tests at eight months, and lower Stanford–Binet IQs at four years. At one year of age, the average baby in the experimental group had a smaller head and slower motor development than the average control baby.

Effects of family size and birth order on measured intelligence were shown at age 19 in a cohort of 400,000 Dutch men [4]. The more children per family, the lower was the average IQ for all social levels. The trend was clearest in the manual occupational level. For birth order, however, trends were definite in all occupational groups; IQ decreased with birth order.

TEENAGE MOTHERS: A SPECIAL PROBLEM

Of all the prosperous countries in the world, the United States has the largest number of adolescent mothers, who account at least in part for the poor showing of this country in regard to infant mortality rates. During one 12-month period over 600,000 girls under age 19 gave birth [24a]. Among them, 10,000 were 15 years old or younger. At this age of the mother, the baby's growth needs are superimposed upon those of the mother. The impact of pregnancy upon the body of a growing mother has not been determined, but the impact on her baby has been indicated in the likelihood of very young mothers delivering prematurely. Figure 1-16 shows that mothers under the age of 15 are more likely to experience the death of their babies before the babies reach their first birthdays than are mothers of any other age.

PHYSICAL ADEQUACY OF THE MOTHER

Studies from several different countries have shown a relationship between height of mother and reproductive performance. Mothers judged poor in physique

Figure 1-16. Ratio of infant mortality rate of mothers 20 to 39 years old to infant mortality rates of younger and older mothers.

SOURCE: R. J. Armstrong. *A study of infant mortality from linked records by birth weight, period of gestation, and other variables.* National Center for Health Statistics. Data from the National Vital Statistics System. Series 20, No. 12. DHEW Publication No. (HSM) 72-1055. Washington, D.C.: U.S. Government Printing Office, 1972.

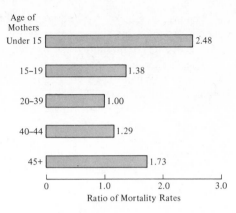

tended to be short and to have flattening of the pelvic brim. Short mothers are more likely to have complications of pregnancy and delivery, and to produce babies with lower birth weights, greater prematurity, more birth trauma, and more stillbirths. The relationship between stature of mother and physical well-being of baby is not thought to be a direct one, but, rather, both conditions are results of a socioeconomic environment. A poor environment, supplying inadequate food, housing, clothing, sanitation, and education, will stunt the physical and mental growth of children living in it. Short stature is thus associated with low education, early marriage, premarital pregnancy, premature delivery, longer labor, absence of family planning, frequent pregnancies, poor diet, poor housing, and poor use of information, health services, and social services [30].

The Birth Process

The developments described thus far occur in the course of about nine months. The obstetrician names the delivery date on the pregnant woman's first visit, by adding 280 days to the first day of her last menstrual period. He will warn her, though, that this date is an approximation. Only 4 per cent of women deliver on the 280th day; 46 per cent deliver within a week of that date; and 74 per cent within two weeks of it. Being born and giving birth are physical crises for the two persons most concerned. The crises are emotional, also, for the two and their family. Thus, birth must be understood in various contexts.

THE PROCESSES AND STAGES OF LABOR

Labor is the work that the mother does in giving birth. Three distinct stages can be described. *The first stage,* requiring the major portion of the duration of labor, is the opening of the cervix or neck of the uterus. It begins with rhythmic uterine contractions, which are usually felt as pains. Two types of muscular forces work to enlarge the cervical openings. The uterus resembles a pear-shaped balloon whose walls are made of very strong muscle fibers. The fibers contract, exerting about 30 pounds of pressure on the fluids surrounding the fetus. The membranes enclosing the fluids press on the tiny opening in the lower end of the uterus. After the membranes break (the mother cannot feel this), the baby presses on the opening. At the same time another set of muscle fibers, which surround the tiny opening, are relaxing to allow the opening to enlarge. As these muscular processes continue, the tissues of the cervix are pulled back into the general roundish shape of the uterus. When the cervix is completely dilated, the diameter of the opening is about four inches.

The muscular processes of the first stage of labor are involuntary. The only way in which a woman can influence them is through relaxation. Although it is still a debatable subject, it is commonly believed that general bodily relaxation, due to the absence of fear, plus confidence, hastens the relaxation of the muscle fibers surrounding the cervix; fear and tension are thought to increase their resistance to stretching and to result in pain. One of the purposes of education for childbirth is to induce this kind of relaxation.

The second stage lasts from the time that the cervix is completely open until the baby emerges from his mother. For a first baby this stage requires an hour and a half on the average; for the second, half as long. The uterus continues to push the baby out. The mother adds a bearing-down action to it, pushing with her diaphragm, but involving her whole body. (See Figure 1-17.) Although she bears down spontaneously, without teaching or conscious thought, a great deal of this activity can be placed under conscious control. Education for childbirth includes teaching the mother to breathe, relax, and bear down in a manner calculated to facilitate the natural labor processes. The confidence factor is just as important in the second stage as in the first in promoting control and either eliminating pain, reducing it, or making it more bearable. The *third stage* is the expelling of the placenta and membranes. It lasts only a few minutes.

When women discuss the length of labor with each other, they often mark its beginning with the trip to the hospital. Or the beginning of labor may be considered the time when labor contractions become severe. To be accurate, labor length has to be measured from the time of the first contraction to the moment when the placenta and membranes are completely expelled. Therefore, the average figures for length of labor may look formidably long to the woman who takes her neighbor's experience as the norm.

An overall average for the length of labor is about 14 hours, divided among the three stages about like this: first stage 12½ hours; second stage 80 minutes; third stage 10 minutes. The second stage requires about 20 contractions for a first baby and 10 or less for subsequent babies. For a first baby, half of the women in a study of nearly 15,000 cases took less than 11 hours; half took more. The most common length of labor was seven hours. Women who had already had at least one baby had shorter labors; half under approximately six hours and half over, with the most common length of labor being four hours [18].

When a normal birth is impossible or dangerous, the baby may be delivered by Caesarian section, a procedure of cutting the mother's abdomen and uterus to remove the baby and then, of course, the placenta. Although this surgical procedure used to be very dangerous, it now carries relatively slight risk. A Caesarian section is much safer for mother and baby than a difficult forceps delivery or a breech birth through a narrowed pelvis. Although there is no limit to the number of Caesarian births that one patient can have, each repetition means that the scar in

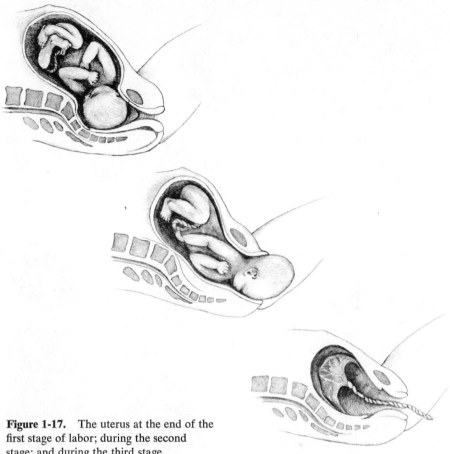

Figure 1-17. The uterus at the end of the first stage of labor; during the second stage; and during the third stage.

SOURCE: M. Smart and L. Smart. *Families.* New York: Macmillan Publishing Co., Inc., 1976.

the uterus is stretched by the pregnancy and hence runs a small risk of rupturing. Many physicians recommend sterilization of the mother with the third Caesarian operation.

EMOTIONAL ASPECTS

The culture in which she has grown up will set the broad outlines of a woman's attitude toward labor. The Judeo-Christian tradition, for example, builds up considerable expectation of pain and tears. According to Mead [52, p. 28],

> in some African tribes, women are expected to shriek, scream, writhe and go through the most terrific expressions of agony, and all the little girl children are brought along to watch, so they will know how to have a baby. In other societies, women are enjoined to the greatest stoicism, and to utter a single cry would be to proclaim yourself not a woman, and again the little girls are brought along to see that they behave like this.

Account of Labor & Delivery
for Hillary C. Adams
by Sara Adams

I suspected I was in labor, with low back-ache and with intermittent mild menstrual-type cramps throughout Saturday morning. By 4 o'clock they were all between 4 and 8 minutes apart. I was beginning to believe that at last, almost two weeks after the due date, I was in labor!

The contractions got gradually sharper, but were easily talked and walked through by supper time. I felt every inch the martyr with my dry toast and tea as I watched Bill and a friend consume quantities of delicious smelling lasagne she had brought. By 10 o'clock I didn't want to finish our game of Scrabble because of the strength of the contractions. It was much nicer to be horizontal when they came, though not necessary. By eleven I had developed a shaking in my arms and legs which I couldn't control and instead of snoozing at home until I really *had* to go to the hospital as I'd planned, we went in then at the advice of the doctor.

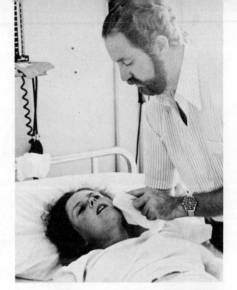

It took a while for the labor pattern to re-establish itself after the ride to the hospital. We set up the gods-eye I'd made to focus on and I did the deep chest breathing and was entirely comfortable except for the distress caused, I thought, by the small enema I'd been given during prep. Later I decided that it wasn't enema-caused but baby-caused pressure pain. This pressure discomfort continued and increased in strength throughout my labor. Because of it I was fooled into continuing whatever breathing technique I was using, long after the actual contraction was over. In late active labor the contractions peaked fast, so I was shallow-chest breathing right away and then could taper off into deep chest breathing to slide down the other side of the contractions. With the pressure pains I found it comfortable, though in retrospect tiring, just to keep deep chest breathing until the next peak.

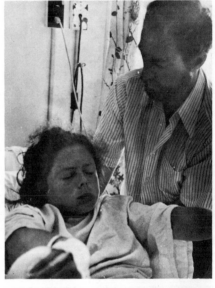

I remember being really tired by early morning and a bit panic-stricken each time the contractions peaked so fast. I was feeling fed up with this contraction business! I told them at one point I couldn't go on, knowing of course that I could. I did regain control again and again with the help of Pat and Bill.

Soon after the doctor announced that I could push, I couldn't comfortably do anything else! So I pushed—*some* nice long strong ones—and it didn't seem long before I was wheeled into the delivery room and my legs were in stirrups (a very comfortable position, I found) and we were really engaged in delivering that baby! Bill looked professional in his green elf suit but I was more impressed with the marvelous comfort and strength in his arms holding my back up each time I pushed.

Suddenly the baby's head was emerging, then a shoulder and then the most relief-giving slipping out of her whole body! Hillary Campbell Adams officially existed—a bit primordial to look at, lavender pearl grey with some white gobbets about the ears (which, now I think about it, were probably the doctor's gloved fingers)—a very beautiful, brand new human being!

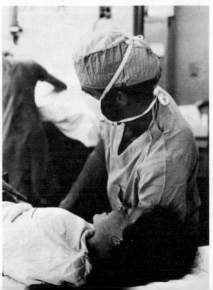

PHOTOGRAPHS BY PAT PETERSON

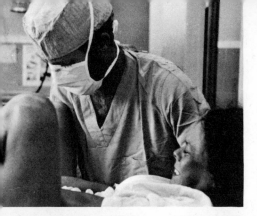

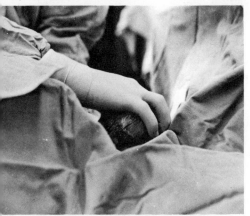

I held her for a few joy-filled seconds before she was whisked off to the nursery. Then Bill and I were alone with our elation and awe, in a new sharing of some very gut-level and joyous responses to what we had enabled each other to do and see. The intellectualizing came later. Everyone in the delivery room echoed our sense of accomplishment and pleasure; removed for a moment from mundane details we could, like children, give ourselves over to the sheer delight of creation and shared love. Then Bill was helping to wheel me back to my room, and I remember being delighted to be on my stomach for the first time since December—once again life's usual mixture of the sublime and the ridiculous!

We still haven't digested the experience. Bits and pieces of what we saw and felt still bob up to consciousness to be wondered at. It's easy to say that the birth of our child was the most profoundly spiritually moving and at the same time physically satisfying event of our life together, that we loved our small daughter with a ferocity and immediacy which astonished us even further. Even today, a month later, we can scarcely believe that what was in is now out; that what was It, is now She! The transition simply does not make sense.

We practiced the exercises and breathing techniques we were taught in the Lamaze classes and they worked! We felt we were well informed and well prepared to truly assist in the delivery of our child, and we were! We would wholeheartedly recommend that all prospective parents take the six-week training course no matter what their intentions for delivery day. We feel very indebted to the people who made the classes possible. We are so glad we were really *there* for our daughter's birth!

SOURCE: Newsletter of the Childbirth Education Association of Rhode Island, October, 1973. By permission of Sara and Bill Adams.

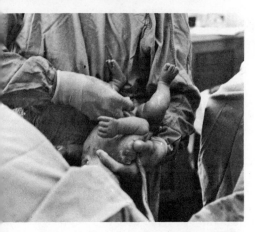

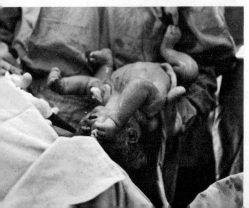

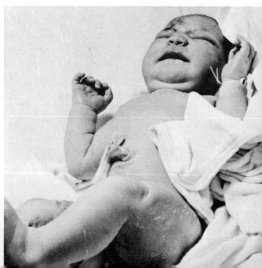

Education and specific experiences are important in setting the mother's expectations of pain and danger and her confidence in her own abilities. The ways in which she handles the fear and pain involved will depend not only on herself, however, but on the support and help she receives during labor. Her husband, the hospital staff, and, most of all, the doctor and midwife have important emotional functions. Directly connected with the mother's fear or confidence, tension or relaxation, pain or easiness, is the amount and type of anesthetic she will receive. A woman who feels confident and in command of herself and who also feels trust in the help she is receiving will most likely need a minimum of drugs. The terrified patient will seek a maximum of drugs, including amnesiacs. (Abnormal physical conditions may require maximum use of drugs too.)

Human beings are not the only living creatures who need help and comfort from their fellow creatures during labor and delivery. A wild elephant was observed giving birth with the assistance of a younger cow, who pushed and massaged with her trunk on the abdomen of the laboring mother [12]. Dolphins gather around a female in labor. As soon as the baby is born, they cooperate in lifting it to the surface of the water, where it takes its first breath.

A growing use of psychological means of relieving and controlling pain in labor is probably the result of two trends. First is an increased interest in having childbirth a positive, rewarding experience for the mother and father instead of a trial to be endured. Second is a growing body of evidence that anesthetics and analgesics given the mother during labor and delivery have more adverse effects upon infants than was previously believed. A review of a large number of studies concludes that the results of obstetrical medication include not only the gross physiological signs of delayed onset of respiration, poor muscle tone, and drowsiness but also important behavioral changes, such as depressed sucking, consolability, and visual attention [2]. These behavior inadequacies may handicap the infant in his future interactions with the environment and in building relationships with his caretakers. The author summarizes, "Without denying the great benefits of analgesia and anesthesia, one should consider carefully the alternative of natural childbirth by means of hypnosis or one of the various relaxation techniques, whenever the physical and emotional condition of the mother allows it."

Two well-known methods of preparation for childbirth have brought pain relief, confidence, and often joy to many women in childbirth. Both methods include teaching the processes of labor, exercises, and breathing. Neither excludes anesthetics, but uses them moderately when patient and midwife or doctor consider them as being indicated. The Read method, originated by an English obstetrician, stresses emotional education and relief of fear through relaxation and knowledge. The LaMaze (pronounced LaMahz) method, contributed by a French obstetrician, uses conditioning to eliminate or diminish pain. LaMaze courses are available in many if not most parts of the United States and can be located through the International Childbirth Association. The LaMaze method is used widely in France, the Soviet Union, and China. It is being used with increasing frequency in North America. Research indicates that the LaMaze method results in shorter labor, less pain, more positive attitudes, and more positive concepts of self and husband [45, 53]. The procedure and results of the LaMaze method are explained in *Why Natural Childbirth?*, a popularly written, research-based book [53]. The series of photographs seen here show mother, father, and baby in a LaMaze birth. The account accompanying the photographs was written by the mother, Sara Adams, a few days after her daughter's birth.

THE BABY DURING LABOR

Being born is a difficult and risky experience that has claimed the attention of philosophers and psychiatrists, as well as physicians and lay people. The great obstetrician DeLee believed that babies suffered pain while being born. The fact that babies give little evidence of a skin pain sense in the early postnatal days is not proof that the global experience of birth is without trauma.

The important bones of the baby's head are separated by the sutures, membranous spaces that feel soft to the touch. Where several sutures meet, the space is called a *fontanelle*. Figure 1-18 shows the anterior and posterior fontanelles on the top of a baby's head. During labor, the infant's head adapts by becoming narrower as the bones squeeze closer together. They may even overlap. The molding, or squeezing together, may result in a head that looks misshapen at birth, but within a few days, the head resumes a normal shape.

The fetal heartbeat responds to each uterine contraction by speeding up, slowing down, and then speeding up again. As labor progresses, the fetal heart beats very fast, slowly, or irregularly. During a strong uterine contraction, the fetal

Figure 1-18. The fontanelles, or membranous spaces, on the top of a newborn baby's head.

SOURCE: After N. J. Eastman and L. M. Hellman. *Williams obstetrics.* New York: Appleton-Century-Crofts, 1966. Fig. 5, p. 196.

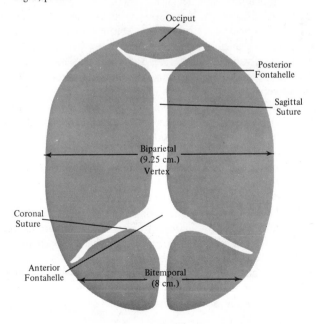

blood cannot get oxygen from the placenta. The increasing concentration of carbon dioxide stimulates the respiratory center and hence the beginning of breathing after birth. Amniotic fluid and mucus escape from the baby's air passages during expulsion of the baby, because of compression of his chest. The attendant may remove excess mucus from the mouth and throat, using a soft rubber ear syringe. Most babies begin breathing by themselves. If an infant does not breathe, slapping, cold water, and other stimulants are no longer used; instead a careful resuscitation is done [18].

The emotional significance of the birth experience on the baby is a matter of conjecture. Some schools of thought hold that birth has a lasting psychological influence, whereas others maintain that the organism is too immature to record experience meaningfully. There is no question that birth is a critical physical experience and no argument with the fact that the newborn needs adequate physical care if he is to survive.

A French obstetrician maintains that the standard methods of treatment of newborns is very harsh and that a gentler transition to extrauterine life benefits the baby physically and emotionally [31]. He delivers the baby into a softly lighted room and places her prone on the mother's bare abdomen where she can feel warmth, softness, and rhythmic movement, the same as before birth. The baby slowly relaxes and extends her limbs. After a gentle, rhythmic massage, the baby is put into a bath that is slightly warmer than body temperature. She moves her hands and feet and may smile. From follow-up observations of individual children born this way, it seems that they thrive and develop smoothly.

BIRTH INJURIES AND DEFECTS

With his big head (a result of his big brain), the human being often has a hard time being born. Kangaroos and bears, born when very tiny, do not run into the same problems. In spite of the wonderful ways in which mothers stretch and babies' heads narrow during the birth process, brain injuries sometimes occur. The infant is equipped to stand some deprivation of oxygen while being born, but when the oxygen deprivation is prolonged, the brain may be damaged. Many such injuries are very slight and their effects may not even be recognized later on. Other brain injuries are very severe, with death the final degree of severity. A multitude of birth injuries fall in between these extremes. From their many studies, Pasamanick and Knobloch [40] conclude that there is a "continuum of reproductive casualty." Some of the more serious results of complications of pregnancy and birth are mental retardation, cerebral palsy, epilepsy, and disorders of behavior, speech, and reading. The associated maternal conditions include toxemias; bleeding; premature birth; difficult, prolonged, or precipitate labor; malpresentation; and major illnesses. Neurological tests on the newborn can often detect minor, as well as major, injuries and can be used to guide caregiving. The degree to which a newborn is *at risk* is estimated by using combinations of tests and observations. An assessment of "at-risk inventories" summarizes the extent to which a great many factors can be expected to affect the infant's health and development [32].

Fetology, the branch of medical science that deals with the fetus, has techniques for diagnosing and treating fetal illnesses and imperfections, thus making it possible to prevent many birth defects. One of its techniques is *amniocentesis,* the drawing off of amniotic fluid through a tube put through the mother's abdominal and uterine walls and into the amniotic sac. Analysis of the fluid can show genetic defects, such as mongolism. The sex of the fetus can be determined, and this may be important in a family that is known to have sex-linked defects, such as hemophilia. The fluid can also show if the fetus is ill and how ill it is from causes such as blood incompatibility. The fetus might be saved by a blood transfusion or a Caesarian delivery. Another diagnostic technique is examination with an *amnioscope,* an instrument for lighting and viewing the inside of the uterus from the birth canal. It is possible to draw a blood sample from the head of the fetus through the birth canal. Fetal surgery is performed by making a small opening in the mother's abdomen and uterus, inserting a catheter into the fetus or giving other treatment, and then closing the incisions in the mother [42]. Research on animals has demonstrated the possibility of much more complicated fetal surgery. Other techniques that have stimulated advances in diagnosis and treatment include *thermography,* a way of mapping the pregnant mother through heat waves, ultrasonics, or mapping of the fetus by sound waves and electrocardiograms of the fetus.

PREMATURITY AND LOW BIRTH WEIGHT

A baby is premature if the gestation period is less than 37 weeks, measured from the mother's last menstrual period. A birth weight of less than 2,500 grams indicates prematurity or inadequate prenatal growth, or both. More babies of low birth weight are born in poor countries than in prosperous ones, and in low socioeconomic groups than in higher ones. Low birth weight is also a danger signal, since 80 to 90 per cent of infant deaths in the United States are of babies who weigh less than 2,500 grams [34]. From one third to one half of low birth-weight babies are probably not premature, but growth-retarded. The survival rate of growth-retarded infants is higher than that of prematures, but the former are more likely to have genetic defects [21]. When handicaps were assessed at 10 years of age, in children whose birth weights were *very* low, under 1,500 grams, severity of handicap was related more strongly to birth weight than to gestation length [35]. In planning care for such infants, it is important to estimate gestation length as accurately as possible.

Growth-Retarded Infants. Infants who are small for their gestational age are also called "small-for-date babies." Whatever term is used, it implies that the fetus did not grow as fast or as much as the average fetus does during gestation.

Growth retardation is often associated with anomalies and mental and neurological impairment. Therefore, it is likely that genetic and early embryonic influences are important, although maternal malnutrition may also contribute to intrauterine growth retardation [34, pp. 110–124]. The mother's long-term prepregnant nutrition may have a greater effect than nutrition during gestation. Small babies usually have small placentas and sometimes defective placentas [21]. The size attained by the fetus is probably limited by the amount of placental tissue serving it. Twins are usually smaller than singletons, because their placentas (if fraternal) or placenta (if identical) do not allow them as much placental tissue as a singleton has. The smaller of a set of twins usually has had the smaller amount of placental tissue. One of the greatest threats to growth-retarded babies is hypoglycemia. Therefore, care includes monitoring of blood sugar levels and injections of glucose when indicated.

Premature Infants. A baby who is premature but not growth-retarded has the development, both physical and behavioral, typical of his *gestational* age. Some of the best criteria used for diagnosing prematurity are evaluation of muscle tone and reflexes; only one or two transverse creases on the ball of the foot; scalp hair that is fine and fuzzy; ear lobes that are pliable and lacking in cartilage; small breast nodules; testes that are not fully descended, and a small scrotum [34]. Additional measures for estimating gestational age are head circumference and changes in the electroencephalogram. A promising new measure is that of measuring visual preferences [19, 39]. The most serious threat to survival of a premature baby is hyaline membrane disease, which makes the lungs unable to expand [21]. In the United States, 25,000 premature infants die early from this disease. Preventive measures for it are being developed.

Causes of prematurity include obstetrical complications and environmental factors of cigarette smoking, high altitudes, toxemia, chronic vascular disease, rubella, syphilis, and malaria [21]. Some cases of intrauterine growth retardation have also involved some of these conditions.

Since earlier studies of low birth-weight children did not distinguish between prematurity and growth retardation, subsequent measures of the progress of these children group the two types together. Older studies found that infants of low birth weight grew into small children who continued to be smaller than average, but later studies showed that infants who weighed at least 2,000 grams at birth were not markedly below average as children [34].

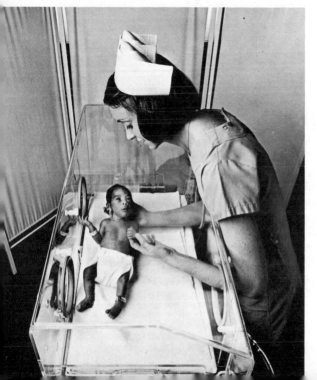

Lying in an incubator, this premature baby gazes at the face of the nurse who is placing him in a position favorable for looking at each other.

COURTESY OF PROCTER & GAMBLE

A careful diagnosis of prematurity was made on the subjects of a longitudinal study in Paris, France, and California [5, 6]. After the evaluation at ten years, reports were made on the significance of prematurity and recommendations for care and education of premature children. One very positive finding was that the delays in mental development seen early in life had often disappeared entirely by 4 years, even in children born very early. There were persistent problems in behavior and emotional life that the authors traced to the basic problem of disturbed bodily-spatial relationships and concepts. A test of imitation of gestures surveyed a child's ability to imitate simple and complex gestures with hands and arms, ability to locate right and left in relation to self and others, body knowledge, and body image. A test of opposite gestures was one of the most highly diagnostic of the premature child. Failure on this test was highly related to IQ, drawing, reading, and speech articulation, all of which are significant for success in school. Remedial education can improve performance in all of these areas, especially if started early.

Prevention of Deficits in Premature Infants. Granted that the premature baby is born with some deficits as compared with full-term infants, much can be done to prevent further problems from developing while the baby completes growth to full-term level, and afterward.

Since the last two months of intrauterine life is the time when the fat is laid down under the skin, a premature baby looks red and wrinkled, as compared with a full-term baby. His head looks extra big for his tiny body. Depending on how immature he is, he may or may not be able to suck and swallow. Feeding him the right nutrients is a problem, even though mechanical devices can put the food into his stomach. Human milk may be even more important for the premature baby than for a mature one. A premature baby may not be able to make *cystine,* an amino acid contained in human milk but not in cow's milk [21]. Even if the infant has to be kept in an incubator, the mother can express her milk, to be given by bottle or tube. By doing so she will not only feed the premature baby essential nutrients but will keep her milk flowing for the time when the baby can nurse. A milk bank may be used if the mother cannot produce her own milk.

The question of adequate stimulation for the premature baby is important. As mentioned earlier, the fetus is constantly stimulated by the mother's movements and the sounds from her interior. The premature baby lies in an incubator or heated crib where there is little change, especially change of a rhythmic nature. Rocking incubators have been devised, but results from them are inconclusive [39]. Since the mother, as well as the infant, is deprived of opportunities for building bonds, new programs are bringing infants and their mothers together. In one successful program, mothers systematically stroked their premature infants for 15 minutes and rocked them for another five minutes, four times a day for 30 days, beginning when the baby came home from the hospital [40a]. Compared with controls, the infants showed greater neurological maturation, higher mental functioning, and greater weight gain.

Anxiety over the premature is one hazard to later development that may be minimized by acquiring expertise in the premature nursery. These parents need counseling and support even more than most new parents. A comprehensive child development service would be ideal in order to meet needs that will arise at later ages, as, for example, the premature child's need for motor education and help in developing bodily orientation to people and the world.

IMPROVING REPRODUCTIVE PERFORMANCE

From the foregoing, it may seem as though having a baby is fraught with peril and problems both for parents and offspring. It might even appear that ignorance is bliss, since people have been having babies for ages without knowing about all the things that can and do go wrong. They have been blaming physical and mental handicaps on chance, nature, or even God's will, rather than upon the biological and environmental processes that are really responsible. A great deal is now known about how to produce healthy, well-developed children and competent parents. The problem is how to implement the knowledge. If it can be put into practice, the quality of human life will be greatly enhanced.

Poverty is one of the basic bars to excellence in childbearing. Poor countries show poor performance in childbearing as compared with prosperous countries, just as do the poor in a given country as compared with the well-to-do. Low birth weights occur in 4 per cent of Scandinavian births, 7 or 8 per cent of British, 7 per cent of white American, 10 per cent of black American, 18 per cent of South African Indian, and 35 per cent of Indian births in Madras [41].

American studies show relationships between mortality and skin color that is highly related to socioeconomic conditions. In Scotland, fetal loss and stillbirths have been higher for semiskilled and unskilled laborers than for professionals and managers ever since statistics have been recorded [30]. When death rates have gone down, the ratio between the classes has been maintained. In the United States,

Figure 1-19. Maternal mortality rates in selected nations for the latest available year.

SOURCE: United Nations Department of Economic and Social Affairs. *Demographic Yearbook 1973.* New York: United Nations, 1974.

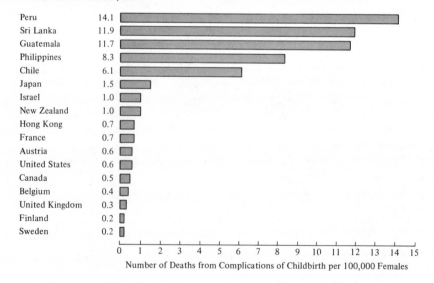

Peru	14.1	
Sri Lanka	11.9	
Guatemala	11.7	
Philippines	8.3	
Chile	6.1	
Japan	1.5	
Israel	1.0	
New Zealand	1.0	
Hong Kong	0.7	
France	0.7	
Austria	0.6	
United States	0.6	
Canada	0.5	
Belgium	0.4	
United Kingdom	0.3	
Finland	0.2	
Sweden	0.2	

0 1 2 3 4 5 6 7 8 9 10 11 12 13 14 15

Number of Deaths from Complications of Childbirth per 100,000 Females the color difference in perinatal mortality is strong in favor of whites. The ratio has increased in recent years. Maternal mortality figures reflect the between-country economic differences seen in the statistics for infants. Figures 1-14, and 1-19 illustrate these differences.

Poorly developed infants result from too many pregnancies and pregnancies that are too closely spaced. To avoid this problem, a variety of effective birth control services should be genuinely available to all women. Heredity counseling should be available and articulated with birth control services.

Summary

A mature ovum in a Fallopian tube, during the middle of the menstrual cycle, is penetrated by a spermatazoon of either male or female type. The fertilized ovum is propelled to the uterus, where it implants itself into the lining and becomes an embryo. The basic forms of tissues and organs develop during the embryonic period. At eight weeks of age, the organism is called a fetus, since its appearance makes it more recognizable as human. Structure and functions differentiate further. The head end is more advanced in development than is the tail. The fetus moves freely.

Pregnancy can be diagnosed through laboratory tests soon after the first missed menstrual period. The first three months of pregnancy is a time of physiological reorganization that usually involves fatigue. New feelings and emotions go along with the pervasive bodily changes that affect all the systems. Adjustment to pregnancy is affected by whether the mother wants the baby, by cultural interpretations of pregnancy, by the mother's physical adequacy, and by her care and experiences during pregnancy. Expectant fathers tend to react like their partners. The role of expectant father is often very demanding emotionally.

Among the many important prenatal influences, nutrition ranks high. The lifetime nutritional history of the mother is salient, as well as her nutritional intake during pregnancy. Barriers to adequate prenatal nutrition include poverty, ignorance, and maladaptive cultural beliefs. The fetus responds to stimulation in all sensory modalities, but the significance of sensory experience is a topic of conjecture. The noxious effects of maternal emotional stress are well established. The ovum, embryo, and fetus can be damaged by physical stress on the mother, radiation, virus diseases, parasites, and many drugs, including cigarette smoke, tranquilizers, barbiturates, psychedelics, and heroin. Hormonal problems and blood incompatibilities pose threats to the fetus, but can usually be managed medically. The mother's age from 20 to 35 are safest for childbearing, for both mother and baby. Risks are increased by many pregnancies and by closely spaced pregnancies.

Labor proceeds in three stages, the opening of the cervix, the expulsion of the fetus, and the expulsion of the placenta. Education for childbirth promotes relaxation in the first stage and controlled relaxation and action in the second stage. Self-confidence and trust in the assistants help to produce a positive emotional state. Some women, and some couples, experience tremendous joy in childbirth. Attention is also directed to the emotional state of the newborn baby.

Through knowledge and techniques from fetology, obstetrics, and child development, many defects can be prevented and others diagnosed and treated early. Some of the birth problems caused by the tremendous development of the human brain can be solved by using that brain. Low birthweight babies are premature and/or growth-retarded. Careful diagnosis facilitates appropriate treatment. Prevention of deficits at first, includes adequate feeding, stimulation, and emotional reactions in the family and throughout childhood, monitoring of development, support and education for parents, and psychomotor education.

References

1. Abraham, S., F. W. Lowenstein, and C. L. Johnson. *Preliminary findings of the first health and nutrition examination survey, United States, 1971–72: Dietary intake and biochemical findings.* DHEW Publication No. (HRA) 74–1219–1. Washington, D.C.: U.S. Government Printing Office, 1974.
2. Aleksandrowicz, M. K. The effect of pain relieving drugs administered during labor and delivery on the behavior of the newborn: A review. *Merrill-Palmer Quarterly,* 1974, **20**, 121–141.
3. Anonymous. Heroin addiction in the newborn. *World Medical Journal,* 1972, **19**:3, 57.
4. Belmont, L., and F. A. Marolla. Birth order, family size, and intelligence. *Science,* 1973, **104**, 1096–1101.
5. Berges, M., I. Lezine, A. Harrison, and F. Boisselier. The "syndrome of the post-premature child": A study of its significance, Part I. *Early Child Development and Care,* 1972, **1**, 239–284.
6. Berges, M., E. Lezine, A. Harrison, and F. Boisselier. The "syndrome of the post-premature child": A study of its significance, Part II. *Early Child Development and Care,* 1973, **2**, 61–94.
7. Berrill, N. J. *The person in the womb.* New York: Dodd, Mead & Co., 1968.
8. Birch, H. Research issues in child health IV: Some philosophic and methodological issues. In E. Grotberg (ed.). *Critical issues in research related to disadvantaged children.* Princeton, N.J.: Educational Testing Service, 1969.
9. Butler, N. R., and H. Goldstein. Smoking in pregnancy and subsequent child development. *British Medical Journal,* 1973, 5892, 573–575.
10. Chess, S. The influence of defect on development in children with congenital rubella. *Merrill-Palmer Quarterly,* 1974, **20**, 255–274.
11. Collis, W. F. R., and M. Janes. Multifactorial causation of malnutrition and retarded growth and development. In N. S. Scrimshaw and J. E. Gordon (eds.). *Malnutrition, learning and behavior.* Cambridge, Mass.: M.I.T. Press, 1967, pp. 55–80.
12. Copans, S. A. A comparative perspective on perinatal maternal and infant effects. Paper presented at meetings of the American Psychological Association, New Orleans, 1974.
13. Coursin, D. B. Nutrition and brain development. *Merrill-Palmer Quarterly,* 1972, **18**, 177–202.
14. Coursin, D. B. Maternal nutrition and the offspring's development. *Nutrition Today,* 1973, **8**:2, 12–18.
15. Cravioto, J. Malnutrition in early childhood and some of its consequences for the individual and community. General Foods Distinguished International Lectures on Nutrition. Toronto, April 10, 1975.

16. Dairy Council Digest. *Nutritional needs during pregnancy.* Chicago: National Dairy Council, 1974, **45**:4, 19–22.

16a. Dobbing, J. Human brain development and its vulnerability. In *Biological and clinical aspects of brain development.* Mead Johnson Symposium on Perinatal and Developmental Medicine No. 6. Evansville, Indiana: Mead, Johnson and Co., 1975.

17. Dodge, J. A. Psychosomatic aspects of infantile pyloric stenosis. *Journal of Psychosomatic Research,* 1972, **16**, 1–5.

18. Eastman, N. J., and L. M. Hellman. *Williams obstetrics* 13th ed. New York: Appleton-Century-Crofts, 1966.

19. Fantz, R. L., and J. F. Fagan, III. Visual attention to size and number of pattern details by term and preterm infants during the first six months. *Child Development,* 1975, **46**, 3–18.

20. Gelles, R. J. Violence and pregnancy: A note on the extent of the problem and needed services. *Family Coordinator,* 1975, **24**, 81–86.

21. General Clinical Research Centers Branch, National Institutes of Health. *How children grow.* DHEW Publication No. (NIH) 72–166. Washington, D.C.: U.S. Government Printing Office. 1972.

22. Grimm, E. R. Psychological and social factors in pregnancy, delivery and outcome. In S. A. Richardson and A. F. Guttmacher (eds.). *Childbearing—Its social and psychological aspects,* Baltimore: The Williams & Wilkins Co., 1967, pp. 1–52.

23. Gunther, M. *Infant feeding.* Chicago: Henry Regnery Co., 1970.

23a. Havemann, E. *Birth control.* New York: Time, Inc., 1967.

24. Heinstein, M. I. Expressed attitudes and feelings of pregnant women and their relations to physical complications of pregnancy. *Merrill-Palmer Quarterly,* 1967, **13**, 217–236.

24a. Hetzel, A. M., and M. Cappetta. *Teenagers: Marriages, divorces, parenthood, and mortality.* National Center for Health Statistics. Series 21. No. 23. DHEW Publication No. (HRA) 74–1901. Washington: U.S. Government Printing Office, 1973.

25. Higgins, A. C., E. W. Crampton, and J. E. Moxley. *A preliminary report of a nutrition study of public maternity patients.* Montreal Diet Dispensary, 1973 (Mimeo).

26. Holden, R. H., E. B. Man, and W. P. Jones. Maternal hypothyroxinemia and developmental consequences during the first year of life. Paper presented at the meetings of the Society for Research in Child Development, Santa Monica, California, March 27, 1969.

27. Holley, W. L., A. L. Rosenbaum, and J. A. Churchill. Effects of rapid succession of pregnancy. In *Perinatal factors affecting human development.* Pan American Health Organization, Pan American Sanitary Bureau, Regional Office of World Health Organization, 1969, pp. 41–45.

28. Honeyman, M. C., and M. A. Menor. Ethnicity is a significant factor in the epidemiology of rubella and Hodgkin's disease. *Nature,* 1974, **251**, 441–442.

29. Hurley, L. S. The consequences of fetal impoverishment. *Nutrition Today,* 1968, **3**(4), 2–10.

30. Illsley, R. The sociological study of reproduction and its outcome. In S. A. Richardson and A. F. Guttmacher (eds.). *Childbearing—Its social and psychological aspects.* Baltimore: The Williams & Wilkins Co., 1967, pp. 75–141.

30a. Lader, L. *Abortion.* New York: Bobbs Merrill, 1966.

31. Leboyer, F. *Birth without violence.* New York: Alfred A. Knopf, Inc., 1975.

32. Levine, M. D. *An assessment of medical predisposition to educational dysfunction:*

A progress report on the development of early life "at-risk inventories." Brookline, Mass.: Brookline Early Education Project, 1973.

33. Liley, A. W. The foetus as a personality. *Australian and New Zealand Journal of Psychiatry,* 1972, **6:**2, 99–105.

34. Lowrey, G. H. *Growth and development of children.* New York: Year Book Medical, 1973.

35. Lubchenco, L. O., M. Delivoria-Papadopoulos, and D. Searls. Long-term follow-up studies of prematurely born infants. II. Influence of birth weight and gestational age on sequelae. *Journal of Pediatrics,* 1972, **80,** 509–512.

36. Mead, M., and N. Newton. Cultural patterning of perinatal behavior. In S. A. Richardson and A. F. Guttmacher (eds.). *Childbearing—Its social and psychological aspects,* Baltimore: The Williams & Wilkins Co., 1967, pp. 142–244.

37. Milkovich, L., and B. J. van den Berg. Effects of meprobamate and chlordiazepoxide on human embryonic and fetal development. *New England Journal of Medicine,* 1974, **291,** 1268–1271.

38. Ounsted, M. Fetal growth. In D. Gairdner and D. Hull (eds.). *Recent advances in paediatrics.* London: Churchill, 1971.

39. Parmelee, A. H., C. B. Kopp, and M. Sigman. Selection of developmental assessment techniques for infants at risk. *Merrill-Palmer Quarterly,* 1976, **22,** 177–199.

40. Pasamanick, B. and H. Knobloch. Epidemiologic studies on the complication of pregnancy and the birth process. In S. Harrison, (ed.). *Childhood psychopathology.* New York: International Universities Press, 1972.

40a. Rice, R. D. Premature infants respond to sensory stimulation. *APA Monitor,* 1975, **6:**11, 8–9.

41. Richardson, S. A., and A. F. Guttmacher, (ed.). *Childbearing: Its social and psychological aspects.* Baltimore: The Williams & Wilkins Co., 1967.

42. Rorvik, D. M. *Brave new baby.* New York: Doubleday & Co., Inc., 1971.

43. Sabry, Z. I., J. Campbell, M. E. Campbell, and A. L. Forbes. Nutrition Canada. *Nutrition Today,* 1974, **9:**1, 5–13.

44. Shank, R. E. A chink in our armor. *Nutrition Today,* 1970, **5:**2, 2–11.

45. Shapiro, H. I., and L. G. Schmitt. Evaluation of the psychoprophylactic method of childbirth in the primigravida. *Connecticut Medicine,* 1973, **37,** 7, 341–343.

46. Sharma, T. Marijuana: Recent research and findings, 1972. *Texas Medicine,* 1972, **68:**10, 109–110.

47. Shields, D. Psychology of childbirth. *Canadian Nurse,* 1974, **70:**11, 24–26.

47a. Smith, C. R., and A. Steinschneider. Differential effects of prenatal rhythmic stimulation on neonatal arousal states. *Child Development,* 1975, **46,** 574–578.

48. Soule, A. B., III. The pregnant couple. Paper presented at meetings of the American Psychological Association, New Orleans, 1974.

49. Stott, D. H., and S. A. Latchford. Prenatal antecedents of child health, development and behavior. *Journal of the American Academy of Child Psychiatry,* 1976 (January).

50. Strauss, M. E., R. H. Starr, and J. E. Lessen-Firestone. Influences of prenatal narcotics addiction on behavioral organization of the neonate. Paper presented at meetings of the Eastern Psychological Association, New York, 1975.

51. Subcommittee on Nutrition, Brain Development and Behavior—Food and Nutrition Board, NAS. The relationship of nutrition to brain development and behavior. *Nutrition Today,* 1974, **9:**4, 12–13.

52. Tanner, J. M., and B. Inhelder. *Discussions on Child Development.* vol. 3. New York: International Universities Press, 1958.

53. Tanzer, D., and J. L. Block. *Why natural childbirth?* New York: Doubleday & Company, 1972.
54. Ullbergh, S. Uptake and distribution of drugs in the fetus. *Acta Pharmacologica et Toxicologia,* 1971, **29** (Supplement 4), 81.
55. Walters, C. E. Prediction of postnatal development from fetal activity. *Child Development,* 1965, **36,** 801–808.
56. Yamazaki, J. N. et al. Outcome of pregnancy in women exposed to the atomic bomb in Nagasaki. *American Journal of Diseases of Children,* 1954, **87,** 448–463.
57. Yeung, D. Lecture of University of Guelph, Guelph, Ontario, April 10, 1975.

Readings in
Prenatal Development and Birth

While a single cell is transformed into an embryo, the embryo into a fetus, and the fetus into a baby, that organism interacts with the environment provided by the mother. She, in turn, is influenced in her reproductive performance by her own body and self, her husband (or partner) and family, and the community and world in which she lives. Within the brief space of the following three articles, we have included considerations of fetal development, the influence of the prenatal environment, new ways of conducting the birth process, and the stimulation of development in the premature baby.

In trying to understand what makes for excellent health and optimal development, researchers often study the abnormal, or what happens when growth processes go wrong. Thus, the first article, the title of which states the child's right to be normal, explores genetic abnormality. Positive treatment conditions are the subjects of the other two articles in this chapter.

Modern technology offers the means of assessing the normalcy of the fetus in an early stage of development. Carlo Valenti, a research obstetrician, describes the technique of amniocentesis and discusses its use in preventing the births of abnormal children, as well as its potential for correcting abnormalities. Mongolism is used to exemplify an abnormality detectable by amniocentesis. Every child developmentalist is faced by the philosophical and moral issues raised in this article.

Attitudes toward giving birth have changed as women defined themselves as more competent, and as the dangers of anesthesia have been recognized. While wanting control over their own bodies, women are also acknowledging their need for emotional support during labor and delivery. Although North American women have been getting such support more and more from their husbands, it is more usual throughout the world for women to get help and support from other women. The role of the nurse-midwife is described and discussed in the article by Marion Steinman. The author also gives a vivid description of labor and delivery in the new style.

Premature infants pose problems in development and care. They are also significant in a theoretical sense, in demonstrating a stage of development that is usually hidden. Are prematures more like fetuses or are they more like newborn babies? Are there some ways in which premature infants are equivalent to newborns? Many research studies deal with such questions. The present study by Ruth D. Rice explores the effects of tactile stimulation on weight gain, neurological functioning, and mental functioning. The article includes a discussion of the experiences of the premature baby.

The Child: His Right to Be Normal

Carlo Valenti

DOWNSTATE MEDICAL CENTER, STATE UNIVERSITY OF NEW YORK

In his new classic of modern biology, *The Person in the Womb*, Dr. N. J. Berrill makes this, among other, declarations:

> If a human right exists at all, it is the right to be born with normal body and mind, with the prospect of developing further to fulfillment. If this is to be denied, then life and conscience are mockery and a chance should be made for another throw of the ovarian dice.

In accord with this philosophy, I draw attention to some favorable prospects for "another throw."

About one in fifty babies is born with a greater or less degree of abnormality inherited from its parents. These weaknesses, more than 500 of them severe enough to be classified as diseases (diabetes, for example), are ordered by the genes carried on the chromosomes. No one has ever seen a gene, but we can identify chromosomes under the microscope. Every normal person has a complement of forty-six of them, paired in twenty-three sets. One of the twenty-three pairs determines sex. The determination is made by chance and occurs as follows (see Figure 1).

The female sex chromosomes are paired XX. In any division of the germ cell in preparation for mating with a male sperm, the female half of the marriage will therefore always be X.

The male sex chromosomes are paired XY. When the division of this germ cell occurs, the sperm may be X or it may be Y.

When a female egg is penetrated by an X sperm, the nuclei of the egg and the sperm will fuse XX and the offspring will be female.

When a female egg is penetrated by a Y sperm, the offspring will be XY, or male.

The choice is simple when everything goes well in the reproductive process. However, faulty working of the ovaries or testes sometimes produces fertilized XXX eggs (super-females, not always fertile), XXYs (outwardly male, but without sperm), XOs (outwardly female, but without ovaries and therefore without eggs), XXXXYs (typically defective mentally), and XYY's (typically defective mentally, often aggressive to a criminal extent).

The other twenty-two pairs of chromosomes suffer displacements when parents bring together certain genetic characteristics. The results can be very sad. For example, the chromosome pairs numbered 13-14-15 are catalogued by the letter D. Pairs No. 21 and 22 are catalogued by the letter G. Sometimes one chromosome of these two pairs is displaced in what is called a D/G translocation. What happens is that one of the No. 21 pair crosses over to and joins up with one of the No. 15 pair, riding piggyback as it were and giving that one No. 15 a lopsided appearance.

From *Saturday Review*, December 7, 1968, pp. 75–78. Copyright © 1968 Saturday Review, Inc. Reprinted by permission.

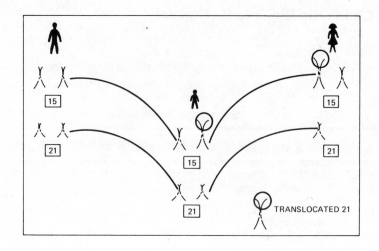

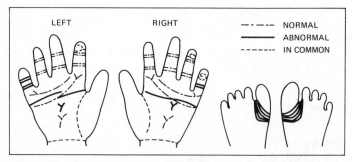

F I G U R E 1.   *How Mongolism is transmitted through a " balanced carrier" to an offspring is demonstrated above. Only two of the twenty-three sets of chromosomes—the No. 15s and the No. 21s—are shown. Note that whereas the father has the normal 21 pair, the mother has one 21 in its normal place and the other upside down on the lopsided No. 15. When chance deals the child the lopsided 15, he has three 21s and is doomed. Palm prints and sole prints of Mongoloid child are below.*

The person who bears this particular pattern of chromosomes is a balanced carrier for Mongolism. We say "balanced" because the total amount of genetic material on the chromosomes is normal, although the number of chromosomes is only forty-five. But the chromosomal pattern is thrown off balance when the balanced carrier's offspring inherits the lopsided chromosome from the carrier along with a 21 from the carrier and a 21 from the other parent. The total inheritance then is three 21s, two in the normal position and one on the lopsided chromosome. The three 21s doom their possessor to Mongolism.

Why focus on the Mongoloid?

A Mongoloid child—in medical terms, he is a victim of "Down's syndrome"—has folded eyes and a flat-rooted nose (the Mongolian-like features from which the popular name of the anomaly derives), small head, fissured protruding tongue, peculiarities in the lines of the palms of the hands and the soles of the feet, retarded intellectual development ranging from idiocy to a maximum prospective mental age of seven years.

Once given life, a Mongoloid is a poignant burden on its parents. For the Mongoloid appeals to all human instincts for companionship. He is cheerful, friendly, imitative, with a good memory for music and for details of situations he has experienced. A Mongoloid's life expectancy averages ten years—a decade of hopelessness, in most cases necessarily spent in a special institution.

Now it has been known for more than a dozen years that before a child is in finished form to leave his mother's womb the chromosomes of the prospective individual can be sampled and analyzed for aberrations. Dr. Fritz Fuchs, Danish-born chief of obstetrics and gynecology at Cornell University Medical College in New York, was able to pioneer such work in his native country because of the liberality of Denmark's laws governing therapeutic abortion.

The method developed by Dr. Fuchs and others is to obtain cells from the amniotic fluid, which is the stuff that every developing fetus floats in. Although the fetus derives almost all of its nourishment from rapidly pulsing blood fed from the placenta by way of the umbilical cord, the fetus before twelve weeks have passed by begins to swallow the amniotic fluid and excrete the fluid through its kidneys and bladder. In growing, the fetus sheds its skin gradually as we living persons shed ours, and other cells are dislodged from the mouth, bronchi, trachea, kidney, and bladder in the course of the swallowing and excreting. The fluid carrying all these cells must be sampled through the wall of the pregnant woman's abdomen by means of a hollow needle similar to those used to draw blood from a vein.

Where the needle enters the womb is of critical importance; if the wrong site were to be chosen, the placenta could be punctured or the fetus itself impaled. Either event could produce serious consequences.

To assure a safe choice, the exact location of the placenta and the floating head of the fetus is determined in the same way that submarines are located when afloat in sea water—that is, by sonar or echo-sounding. The method is feasible as early as the fourteenth week of pregnancy. A tiny portable gun that fires waves at very high speeds is moved across the prospective parent's abdomen in sweeps proceeding successively downward until the entire belly has been scanned. A pattern similar to that seen on a radar screen emerges. With it as a guide, the entry point of the amniocentesis needle is fixed.

After a sample of the amniotic fluid has been removed through the needle, the sample is spun in a centrifuge. The liquid part of the sample is then discarded. A pellet of cells remains. In this pellet is the knowledge we seek.

Two groups of investigators have reported varying success in culturing the cells on nutritive media they have independently developed. Their techniques, described in the medical literature, did not yield good results in our obstetrics and gynecology laboratory here at State University of New York's Downstate Medical Center in Brooklyn. So Edward J. Schutta, Tehila Kehaty, and myself have worked out a culturing method of our own and with it have obtained twenty successes in twenty-four trials. All our failures occurred where the amount of amniotic fluid used was below a certain level. The twenty successful cell cultures yielded seventeen chromosome analyses, or karyotypes. The three failures apparently were due to bacterial contamination.

Two to six weeks of growth are required before the culture is ready to be karyotyped—that is, placed on a glass laboratory slide, dried, stained, and examined microscopically to determine the chromosome pattern.

Last April, a Boston medical colleague familiar with our work referred to us a twenty-nine-year-old mother from Massachusetts who was sixteen weeks pregnant. She knew her grandfather, her mother, her brother, and herself to be balanced carriers of the D/G chromosomal translocation. That is, all four were outwardly normal and healthy, but each carried within himself only one No. 21 chromosome in its normal pairing, while the other 21 was grafted onto one of the No. 15 chromosome pair. In short, although not themselves Mongoloid, three generations of the family carried the genetic threat of Mongolism.

The young New Englander had already experienced a spontaneous abortion, borne a daughter who was also a balanced carrier of the D/G chromosomal translocation, and borne a Mongoloid son who had lived for five months. She wanted another child, and sought our assurance that it would be normal. With the support of her husband, an engineer by profession, she requested a cytogenetic diagnosis on the unborn baby.

Amniocentesis was performed after a sonar sounding on April 15. The amount of amniotic fluid obtained proved inadequate for optimum cell growth. Amniocentesis was performed again on April 29, luxuriant cell cultures were available within two weeks, and satisfactory chromosome preparations were ready for analysis on May 21. The karyotypes showed a male pattern with the D/G chromosomal translocation characteristic of Mongolism. Our hospital's abortion committee authorized a therapeutic interruption of pregnancy on the grounds that, since Mongolism was certain, failure to interrupt could subject the young mother to unjustifiable psychiatric trauma. Notice of the therapeutic abortion was posted routinely on the staff bulletin boards, and the abortion was done on May 31. Autopsy findings and palmprint and soleprint patterns were consistent with our cytogenetic diagnosis.

The young woman who volunteered for this ·experience recovered and returned to her New England home within forty-eight hours. She is still eager for another child if she can have a healthy one. She has requested application of amniocentesis to all future pregnancies.

This woman now has a chance for "another throw of the ovarian dice," as Dr. Berrill put it. The British medical journal, *Lancet*, last July published news of her case in the form of a letter from Schutta, Kehaty, and myself. The *Journal of the American Medical Association* has since notified us that it has accepted for publication a longer formal report of the case. So far as I know, it is the first piece of such news to appear in the medical literature anywhere. It may not be sensational news because D/G chromosomal translocations account for only 2 per cent of all Mongoloid children. But to the individual women involved, it is a promise of release from fear and guilt.

Furthermore, the potential benefits of amniocentesis and karyotyping are applicable to the much greater percentage of Mongolism caused by trisomies. In these there are forty-seven chromosomes, including three No. 21s which appear as triplets in the place of the normal 21 pair (as opposed to the pair of 21s and the 21 contained in the lopsided chromosome of the D/G Mongoloids).

Trisomies are related to aging. Human eggs spoil with time just as other eggs do. . . . Every woman's supply of eggs has been nested in her ovaries since well before she herself was born. All else being equal, she begins releasing them, at the rate of one a month (except during pregnancy and subsequent nursing), when she is about thirteen years old, and continues the process for the forty-odd years that intervene before menopause. Overall, the chance of an American woman giving birth to a Mongoloid child is one in 680. To age twenty-five, the chance is one in 2,000; after age forty-five, one in fifty.

Our laboratory has made cytogenetic diagnoses of two women who feared their pregnancies might produce Mongoloid infants. One of these women was thirty-six years old, the other thirty-seven. Amniocentesis and karyotyping showed no chromosomal aberrations.

The potential of prenatal study of fetal cells obtained by amniocentesis is far greater than we have yet been able to explore. Three broad areas are open to investigation. In the first, a smear of the fetal cells can be made immediately after the cells are collected from the amniotic fluid. The smear shows presence or absence of the sex chromatin body (a condensation of nuclear material), which only female cells possess. The sex of the unborn child can thus be identified and sex-linked hereditary diseases, such as hemophilia and muscular dystrophy, can be diagnosed in the fetus. More than ten years ago, Dr. Fuchs in Denmark demonstrated the value of the technique by screening hemophilic pregnancies and interrupting those that would have resulted in male babies. Only males actually develop hemophilia; females carry the disease without being afflicted by it.

The second field of study of cells obtained by amniocentesis is the analysis of their chromosome complement, as illustrated by the case of the young woman patient described above. Advanced maternal age can cause a number of chromosomal errors in addition to the error that results in Mongolism. Anguish for the mothers involved can be avoided in some cases by interruption of pregnancy. The number of such cases is at the moment still uncertain. The certainty is that in the present state of knowledge we cannot correct chromosomal errors. In the future, however, we may be able to correct the effect of the errors by refining our methods, by applying the principle that each effect is due to a particular enzyme and that each enzyme is ordered by a particular gene. One step in the refinement is to map the locations of the genes on the chromosomes of man, as has already been done with the mouse.

The third area of endeavor in intrauterine medicine (treatment of the fetus in the uterus) is analysis of enzymes produced by the fetal cells that are taken from the amniotic fluid. There are hereditary diseases in which deficiency of given enzymes is known in the adult. Detection of the same deficiencies in the fetal cells may permit diagnosis of diseases in the unborn baby and possibly correction of the deficiencies and thus prevention of the diseases.

For example, one of the signs of Mongolism is flaccid muscles at birth. If the body of a Mongoloid baby is laid prone on the palm of the hand, the baby's head and limbs will flop downward like those of a rag doll. The weakness of the muscles has been attributed to absence of a chemical which can be made only in the presence of a particular enzyme. According to prevailing genetic theory, this enzyme must be missing from Mongoloid cells and the absence must be related to the existence in the cells of three No. 21 chromosomes instead of the normal pair of 21s.

In an English experiment, a chemical named 5-hydroxytryptophan was administered to fourteen Mongoloid babies ranging from a few days to four months in age. Within one to seven weeks later, normal muscle tone was restored to thirteen of these babies, who became able to raise their heads, arms, and legs. Clearly, a missing something had been supplied and had counteracted at least some part of the effect of the abnormal set of three No. 21 chromosomes.

The English researchers were careful to point out that there is yet no evidence that their treatment will improve the mental development of Mongoloid babies. It is conceivable, however, that if Mongolism were diagnosed sufficiently early in the development of the fetus and if the missing chemical could be administered then, the effect on the child might be remarkable.

A great many scientists the world over are now studying enzyme deficiencies in hereditary diseases in the adult human. As their reservoir of knowledge grows, the potential of amniocentesis widens proportionately.

A major determinant of the ultimate effectiveness of intrauterine medicine will be the public attitude on abortion. At present, the laws of many states do not allow therapeutic abortion on genetic grounds.* Genetic grounds are habitually construed as empirical statistical evaluations. Chromosomal analysis is not statistical but is direct and specific evidence of abnormality. As physicians, legislators, and the people come to understand the distinction, they will surely see that the law cannot be interpreted to exclude abortion based on chromosomal analysis. For a law that would compel a mother to give birth to a baby certain to be severely defective would be cruel and uncivilized.

* Note that this article was originally published in 1968. Ed.

Now, the Nurse-Midwife

Marion Steinman

Midwives joke that theirs is the second oldest profession, and most of the world's babies are still delivered by midwives. In the United States, however, in the early part of this century, the medical establishment forced midwives—who were then largely old-fashioned, untrained "grannies"—out of the childbirth business. Maternal and infant mortality was appallingly high in those days. As recently as World War I (according to the National Center for Health Statistics), more than 700 out of every 100,000 women died in childbirth, and 96 out of every 1,000 babies died before the age of 1. As the developing specialty of obstetrics attacked this problem, women were persuaded to have their babies in hospitals, and to be delivered by physicians. Today it is rare for a woman to die in childbirth, and infant mortality is down to 16.5 per 1,000 live births. And today there are only a handful of "granny" midwives left, still legally delivering babies, mostly in rural areas of the South and Southwest.

© 1975 by the New York Times Company. Reprinted by permission.

In the meantime, a different kind of midwife was evolving: the well-educated nurse-midwife. In 1931 the first school for nurse midwives in the United States was started, in New York City, by the Maternity Center Association. A few years later the renowned Frontier Nursing Service started a school for nurse-midwives in rural, mountainous eastern Kentucky. Up through the 1960's, however, there were still only a few hundred nurse-midwives in the country, and they were ministering mostly to the poor, in urban ghettos and in isolated rural areas. Today, there are about 1,200 nurse-midwives in the United States, and there are now 16 schools offering nurse-midwifery training programs (nine of them new since 1972), which turn out 150 new nurse-midwives a year.

More and more middle-class American babies are being delivered by these nurse-midwives. In Springfield, Ohio, a group of nine midwives, working with six back-up physicians, manages the labors and deliveries of 50 or 60 women a month. In Beckley, W. Va., two midwives have recently gone into private practice with two obstetricians. In Minneapolis, at the University of Minnesota hospital, four midwives are delivering a dozen or more babies each month. The United States Air Force now has some 40 midwives working in 15 base hospitals across the country; last year they delivered more than 1,000 women. And in New York City, at Manhattan's Roosevelt Hospital, five young midwives opened a private midwifery service about a year and a half ago which has proved so popular that they expect to do between 180 and 200 deliveries this year. Their clientele is largely educated, professional women: lawyers, nurses, teachers and even one doctor, a pediatrician.

A big step toward wider acceptance of nurse-midwives came in 1971, when the American College of Obstetricians and Gynecologists officially declared that in "medically-directed teams, qualified nurse-midwives may assume responsibility for the complete care and management of uncomplicated maternity patients." The college's statement was prompted by what, at the time, looked like an impending physician shortage. The birth rate was running so high that it seemed as if more midwives would be needed simply to deliver all the expected babies. Since then, the birth rate has fallen, and the college now believes that there are generally enough obstetricians. However, because women are now demanding more health-care services, the American College of Obstetricians and Gynecologists remains "enthusiastic" about nurse-midwives.

In recent years a rift has been developing between many American women and the whole United States system of obstetrical care. Women are vehemently criticizing both obstetricians and hospitals, contending that they are dehumanizing childbirth by viewing it as a disease rather than as a normal physiological process. Specific obstetrical practices—artificial induction of labor, the use of medication, episiotomy (surgical incision of the vagina), the use of forceps, the separation of mother and infant right after birth—have become the subjects of fierce debate between women and doctors. Some critics are even claiming that modern medical technology—such as the heavy use of anesthetics—actually damages babies. The modern nurse-midwives believe that they are uniquely qualified to help bridge this gap.

Today's nurse-midwives are far better educated than the old-time "grannies." To become a nurse-midwife, one must first graduate from a three-year or four-year nursing school and become a registered nurse. Next, one must get a year's experience in obstetrical nursing, and then take a course in nurse-midwifery at one of the 16 schools offering programs recognized by the American College of Nurse-Midwives. (These schools are Columbia and Downstate in New York City, Yale, Johns Hopkins, the Frontier School in Kentucky, Georgetown, Meharry in Tennessee, the Medical Center at Andrews Air Force Base in Maryland, St. Louis University, New Jersey Medical College and the Universities of Illinois, Kentucky, Minnesota, Mississippi, South Carolina and Utah.) The courses of instruction (which may last up to 24 months) include such subjects as normal and abnormal reproductive anatomy and physiology (both male and female), embryology, neonatology and genetics. Student midwives also watch or assist at as many as 40 or 50 labors and deliveries and will themselves manage (under supervision) a minimum of 20. This adds up to at least five years of training after high school. Some programs are open to nurses who do not have bachelor's degrees. An increasing number of nurses, however, who already hold bachelor's degrees, are obtaining master's degrees in midwifery—for a total of six years' training. After graduation, one must take a national certification examination, given since 1971 by the American College of Nurse-Midwives. Upon passing this, one is finally entitled to write the initials C.N.M.—for Certified Nurse-Midwife—after one's name. (Sex is no barrier. There are currently two male C.N.M.'s in the United States—one teaching in Pennsylvania, the other delivering babies in an Army hospital in Kentucky.)

For a long time many states had legal barriers against midwifery, inherited from the days when doctors were trying to drive the "grannies" out of business. Today, the various state laws determining where C.N.M.'s can and cannot practice are changing so rapidly that the College of Nurse-Midwives has a hard time keeping track of them. In the last five years—thanks in part to the statement of the American College of Obstetricians and Gynecologists—nearly half the states (including New York, New Jersey, Pennsylvania, Virginia, Colorado and California, plus the District of Columbia) have changed their laws affecting nurse-midwifery. As of now, nurse-midwives can deliver babies in all but three states: Alabama, Massachusetts and Wisconsin. Yet some strange, extra-legal situations persist. In Alabama, for instance, while "granny" midwives are still legally delivering babies under county-by-county permits, the attorney general has ruled that the practice of nurse-midwifery "violates the present Alabama laws." And in some 20 states without any legal bars against nurse-midwives, there are actually none practicing—because of resistance on the part of hospitals or physicians or nursing groups or simply lack of interest in the communities.

Nurse-midwives handle only normal deliveries, and they always work with an obstetrician backing them up. Midwives can prescribe painkillers, give local (but not general) anesthesia and cut and repair episiotomies. However, they call in the obstetricain whenever a forceps delivery or a cesarean section seems necessary. The midwives' specialty, however, is supporting a woman psychologically, throughout labor and delivery, so as to minimize the amount of medication she needs. "The uniqueness of the midwife," says Dorothea Lang, who is both director of the New York City Health Department's Nurse-Midwifery Service Program and also current president of the American College of

Nurse-Midwives, "is that she knows how to support a mother, minute by minute, and also how to manage her delivery safely at the same time.

"An obstetrician could do this, but he doesn't always have the time. While the midwife's challenge is the normal, the physicians challenge is the abnormal. A normal obstetrical case is only one of his minor problems compared with the serious problems he's got waiting outside his door: complicated obstetrical cases, gynecological surgery, endocrinological problems, breast cancer. That's where his expertise lies. No one else can take care of those women. That's why the obstetrician-midwife team concept is really perfect."

New York City now has about 100 nurse-midwives delivering babies in 18 hospitals. The Roosevelt Hospital program—which was started by Dr. Thomas Dillon, Roosevelt's chief of obstetrics and gynecology, and its chief midwife, Barbara Brennan—is the only one in a private, voluntary hospital offering midwife deliveries to private patients. For a flat fee of $459, a woman gets a package deal covering all prenatal and postpartum visits and, at the time of her delivery, two nights in the hospital. The midwives try to respond to what women want. "Anything that they ask that is reasonable, that won't hurt them or the baby, is fine with us," says Barbara Brennan. Any one person— husband, mother, boyfriend—may stay with a woman throughout labor and delivery. "We don't give our patients anesthesia unless they want it, and if they don't want their legs up in stirrups or they don't want an episiotomy, that's okay."

One young couple, whom I'll call Renée and Sal Smith, recently came to the Roosevelt midwives for the delivery of their firstborn. For the Smiths, the low price was a factor: Sal, 29, teaches literature part-time at a city college while working on his own Ph.D. Renée, 24, a fine-arts major at Hunter, had first gone to an obstetrical clinic at another hospital, but "really hated" it. "The obstetricians weren't personal at all. They were very clinical and just totally medical. I was also afraid. I didn't know who would deliver me, or what they would allow." From Renée's first visit to the midwives, she was "very impressed. The midwife spent an hour with me, explaining things. Doctors some times tend to just say you're fine and not go into the medical details. The midwife would always explain whether my blood pressure was good or not, and what they were testing the urine sample for. It puts the responsibility on you to understand what's going on in your own body." Sal felt that Renée's whole attitude changed with her first visit to the midwives. "I couldn't believe it. Her tension really seemed to come down."

About 8 one Tuesday morning in the early summer, Renée and Sal arrived at the hospital. Renée's uterus was contracting at about five-minute intervals. Throughout her pregnancy, at each appointment, she had seen any one of the five midwives: Barbara Brennan, Eldra Simmons, Jeanne Kobritz, Mary Dowd or Dorinda Dew. This day Renée was greeted by Jeanne Kobritz—a cheerful, outgoing young woman only a few years older than Renée herself— who holds both a B.S. from the University of Maine and an M.S. from Columbia. Jeanne felt Renée's abdomen to determine the baby's position. It was lying head down—the normal way—but facing toward Renée's right side. "That's fine," Jeanne told her. "The head will probably turn to face the rear as it comes down." Jeanne also examined Renée. Wearing a mask and sterile gloves, she reached up into Renée's vagina until she could feel the cervix (the mouth of the uterus). Normally a thick structure, protruding into the vagina, the cervix had thinned and virtually disappeared, and it had also opened to a diameter of a good 6 centimeters (about 2½ inches). It would need to dilate to 10 centimeters (about 4 inches) before the baby's head could pass through. Jeanne and an obstetrical nurse then attached a fetal monitor, strapping two belts, each with an electronic sensor, around Renée's abdomen. One sensor would pick up her unborn baby's heartbeat; the other would detect the frequency and duration of her uterine contractions. The monitor would continuously record this data, throughout Renée's labor, on a long strip of graph paper, and Jeanne would watch it, looking at the relationship of the baby's heartbeat to the stress of Renée's contractions—whether the heart rate dropped, and, if it did, whether and how fast it recovered. As Jeanne and Sal settled down by Renée's bedside in the labor room for the vigil, Sal confided, "We don't care whether the baby is a boy or a girl, but we think it is going to be a boy."

With each contraction, Renée lay back in bed and conscientiously breathed deeply, as she had been taught, to help her relax, while Sal timed the contraction by counting out the seconds, "15 . . . 30 . . . 40 . . . 50 . . ." Jeanne breathed with Renée, picking up her rhythm breath for breath, and Renée sighed gratefully, "It's nice to know that somebody's with me." Jeanne was prepared to spend all day, if necessary, coaching Renée through the unknown ordeal ahead. If all went well this Tuesday morning—if Renée's labor and delivery remained normal—she would have her baby without ever seeing a doctor.

Some women have become so angry at obstetricians and hospitals that they have been taking the extreme step of having their babies at home, attended only by friends or by self-appointed, underground (and illegal) "lay midwives" without any formal training. Women of a number of ethnic groups—Spanish-Americans, Chinese, gypsies—have long preferred, for reasons of modesty, to be delivered by other women and at home. Now the phenomenon is spreading. In a new book, "Immaculate Deception," Suzanne Arms passionately denounces hospitals and physicians and extols the "beauty" and "naturalness" of home birth. The New York City nurse-midwives get calls all the time asking them to do home deliveries—which is against the policy of the American College of Nurse-Midwives. In California, illegal midwifery has become so widespread that last year the state cracked down and arrested several women in Santa Cruz for practicing medicine without a license.

The trouble is, home delivery is risky. While some 95 percent of all births are indeed normal, significant complications can develop after the onset of labor. "A normal delivery is only normal retrospectively," points out Dorothea Lang. "At any minute a normal birth can turn into an abnormal one."

As we shall see.

By 10 a.m., after two hours of labor, Renée's contractions were stronger and coming every two or three minutes, and she was no longer interested in conversation. When Jeanne examined her for the second time, her membranes had ruptured, spilling out the amniotic fluid that surrounds and protects a fetus in the womb. Jeanne routinely checked to make sure that the fluid was not stained with the baby's fecal materal and that the umbilical cord was not appearing ahead of the baby—both signs of trouble. All was well. "You're a good 8 centimeters dilated," Jeanne reported, "and the baby's head seems to be coming down well. Youre moving right along; you went 2 centimeters in an hour and a half. You've got another 2 centimeters to go."

A few minutes later Renée was racked by nausea and threw up repeatedly. Jeanne explained that she had now reached the so-called "transition" stage between early labor and the more active, second stage of labor. "Transition is from about 7 centimeters to fully dilated. You've got all the signs. Your contractions are stronger. You're nauseous, and you probably feel sweaty. Transition is a different type of contraction, different frequency and intensity. And it hurts. It's the part that really bugs you."

11 am. Renée was still not fully dilated, and she was in such agony that she was glassy-eyed and tossing her head from side to side as she tried to breathe deeply through the contractions. "I feel so awful. I can't. I can't. I can't do it anymore."

"Yes, you can. Yes, you can," Jeanne encouraged her. "You're doing remarkably well." Jeanne also asked her if she wanted any medication, and Renée nodded gratefully. Jeanne then rigged an intravenous tube and injected Demerol directly into a blood vessel in Renée's arm so that the drug would work rapidly.

"When women are in transition," Jeanne explained later, "and the contractions come fast and close, they sometimes become almost psychotic. They have these feelings of impending doom, and they often say, 'I can't make it. I'm going to die.'" Renée only said "I can't do it" once or twice, but that's the beginning of a kind of panic that can set in.

"What you have to do is get them out of that right away, because if they get too far into that, it's harder for them to get back under control. If you can just help them with a little medication, to take the edge off the pain, they can do the breathing and relax. And you have to give a lot of encouragement. Renée is doing very well, but even if they aren't, you tell them that they are. Sometimes you're the only thread that they're hanging onto."

About noon, Renée was finally fully dilated, and it was time for her to begin actively pushing the baby out. Jeanne and Barbara Brennan, who had looked in and stayed to help, stood on either side of the bed, supporting Renée's legs while she braced her feet against their sides, as they had her—with each contraction—grab her knees, spread them far apart and bear down hard to try to expel the baby. It was hard work, and Renée screwed up her face each time with the effort. The two midwives kept up a running patter of instruction and encouragement. "Take a deep breath and hold it. Push down hard. Push. Push. Push. A longer push is more effective than a lot of short ones. Take another deep breath and hold it. Hold it. Hold it. Really push that baby's head down as far as you can. Excellent."

Renée had barely begun to push when she sank back on the pillows, exhausted, and moaned, "Please, I can't take any more pain. I don't have any strength left. Can I have something else?" Jeanne dissuaded her, telling her that "whatever you get the baby gets." Just at that point, Barbara was able to tell her, "I can see the baby's head!"

Now, however, ominously, the fetal monitor began showing that the baby's heartbeat was dipping. With each contraction, the heart rate was dropping from a normal 120 to 160 beats a minute to down below 100. The contractions apparently were reducing the blood flow—and thus the oxygen supply—to the baby's brain. The baby was in mild distress.

"I was beginning to sweat a little," Jeanne admitted later. "The fetal heart had been gorgeous throughout the whole labor, so we knew the baby was in good shape. The dip in the heart rate was not significant, really, but it was significant enough that the wheels started to turn. I was concerned enough to start thinking of alternatives."

The cesarean-section room at Roosevelt is only about 50 feet away from the labor rooms, and the midwives can have an obstetrician operating within minutes, if need be, to save a baby's life. "Although an emergency cesarean was in the back of my mind, I didn't really have to think about it with Renée, because she was far enough along that the baby could be delivered with forceps." Jeanne had also just seen the back-up obstetrician in the labor and delivery area, and knew he was already in scrub clothes. "Knowing that it would only be an instant meant that I didn't have to panic that much."

12:20 p.m. Aloud, Jeanne said to Renée, "When you get the next contraction, you've got to push like hell. The baby's heartbeat is a little low. There may be a loop of cord, so that every time you push, it tightens around the baby's neck or an arm or its chest. We want to get the baby out. An obstetrician can deliver it now with forceps, it looks like, if we have to." Jeanne also had the obstetrical nurse give Renée oxygen, to increase the oxygen supply to the baby, and she had Renée roll over on her side, between contractions, to shift the baby's weight. With these maneuvers, the baby's heartbeat picked up as soon as each contraction was over.

"We don't hide things from our patients," Jeanne told me later. "I didn't tell Renée every possible thing that I might be thinking could be going wrong, but I wanted her to be prepared. And that's when you really need to have the patient cooperative and in control, because if they aren't pushing then, you've got more of a problem. Every contraction they don't push means that there is that much more time the baby may be in distress.

"I would have been a lot more nervous if I'd been delivering that baby in somebody's living room. I don't know what I'd do, if I were in somebody's house, and the fetal heart was 60 and going. I just can't imagine how panicky I'd be. You might make it to a hospital, but if you do, what are you giving the parents? You might be giving them a brain-damaged child."

12:38 p.m. "Now don't push!" The midwives and the nurse quickly wheeled Renée out of the labor room and across the hall into the sterile delivery room, where they helped her onto the delivery table and lifted her legs into stirrups. The forceps delivery would not be necessary. Renée's eyes were dark and she was now whimpering with pain. 12:43. "A little teeny push, Renée." Jeanne—in cap, mask, sterile gown and gloves—quickly snipped a small episiotomy to prevent the vagina from tearing. 12:45. As Renée watched in an overhead mirror, the baby's head appeared, face down as predicted. Jeanne expertly slipped her hands down to see if the cord was looped around its neck. It wasn't. Then the rest of the baby slid out. It was a girl. A perfectly normal baby girl, about 6 pounds, letting out a healthy squall.

The tension broke. "I'm not really sure what made the heart go down," Jeanne said. "Maybe head compression." Sal was so excited he kept exclaiming over and over again, "We have a little girl! We have a little girl! I knew we'd have a little girl!"

When the baby was only a minute old, Jeanne laid her on Renée's abdomen and as Renée cradled her newborn, the infant immediately stopped crying and lay peacefully in her mother's arms. Renée's eyes were now luminous with delight. "That wasn't too bad. I was surprised it went so fast."

Premature Infants Respond to Sensory Stimulation

Ruth D. Rice

UNIVERSITY OF TEXAS, DALLAS

The newborn infant is not just a little pink, sleeping, unfeeling glob. Recent psychological findings have made us aware of how intensely the newborn responds to his or her environment.

We now know that each infant at birth has a distinctive personality determined in part by the mother's emotional condition during pregnancy and in the period immediately following birth.

A highly anxious mother subjected to a lot of stress will have a hyperactive, irritable, anxious baby, whose personality development after birth depends largely on minimal stress and maximal gratification of needs.

Failure to meet a baby's specific emotional needs at birth can cause psychosomatic symptoms within a few days or weeks after birth, including colic, hyperactivity, feeding difficulties and sleeping problems.

For premature infants and infants of low birth weight, these things are doubly important, since such infants suffer significantly more handicaps to begin with than do fullterm infants. It is well known that premature babies frequently have neurological, physical and mental defects and impaired motor and social functioning.

Despite numerous advances in scientific knowledge, premature and high-risk births are on the increase. And while new medical techniques have increased the survival rates for premature and high-risk infants, the incidence of morbidity has also increased.

Why is this so? Let's consider how unnatural and abrupt we have made the transition from the womb to life. The intrauterine environment is filled with the rich and varied sensations of the continual and progressive bombardment of activity that continues from the moment of conception to the moment of birth. Tactile-kinesthetic-vestibular stimulation is provided by the movements of the mother, the amniotic fluid, the muscular walls of the uterus, the placenta, and the fetal body itself. The fetus is massaged and stroked with each movement of

From *APA Monitor*, 1975, **6**:11, 8–9. Copyright © 1975 by The American Psychological Association. Reprinted by permission.

the mother as she walks, bends, sits, and moves about. In his dark, watery cradle of amniotic fluid, the fetus swims gracefully about, weightless, as buoyant and active as an astronaut on a spacewalk, capable of free-floating movement and reflexive action. The amniotic fluid creates a whirlpool-like milieu, an environment that at once stimulates and protects the actively developing fetus.

The infant can hear the mother's heartbeat and may be imprinted by it. Other auditory stimulation is provided by the mother's digestive sounds and even by sounds outside the uterus.

The premature infant comes from the rich, close intimacy of the uterus with its constant stimulation to the incubator-isolette where little or no stimulation is provided. Hospital personnel are often reluctant to handle premature babies; many parents take their cues from this model and continue to hold or cuddle their premature infants less than they would a fullterm baby.

Indeed, it is highly probable that the premature child receives less stimulation throughout the entire developmental period than the fullterm child. Not only does this affect his neurophysiological development, but it places in serious jeopardy the mother/infant bonding and attachment relationship. The works by Klaus, Kennell*, Harlow, and others indicate that the attachment bond between mother and infant is based on tactile and sensory stimulation, not merely on feeding or caregiving. Humans are the only mammals that will tolerate the separation of newborn and mother. Other animals uniformly reject newborns from whom they are separated immediately after birth.

There is a significantly high number of premature births among the population of abused children, and the early and prolonged separation of mother and infant, deprived of the sensory bonding and attachment, may be one of the contributing causes.

All newborns need their mothers' close intimacy and frequent touch but the premature infant, cheated of the normal nine months of rich stimulation in the uterus, needs these things the most.

It is a lamentable fact that most hospitals do not allow mothers into their premature nurseries because of the fear of infection. The few studies that have been made in this area show that letting mothers into the nursery does not increase infection. Mothers, using if necessary the same sterile techniques that nurses use, could stroke, cuddle, talk to, feed and care for their babies while they are still in the incubator. Mothers should also be encouraged to provide breast milk for their incubator babies.

The study described below was designed to determine if neurological development and maturation could be facilitated through an increase in myelinization, cortical spacing and Nissl substance, and to determine if other cellular and endocrine functioning could be hastened in the premature infant. The nerve pathways from the skin are among the first to be sufficiently developed to activate and accelerate the rhythms and sequences of development. Since the neonate's responsiveness to tactile stimulation is greater than to other forms of stimulation, a tactile-kinesthetic stimulation treatment was developed to determine the effect on several variables of neurophysiological growth and development. Several variables were examined: (1) nine phylogenetic reflexes which

* See the article by Kennell, Klaus, and others that follows this one.

normally disappear by four months in fullterm infants. The disappearance of these primitive reflexes is a reliable index of maturation. They are: McCarthy, rooting, palmar-mental, crossed extensor, doll's eye, tonic neck, stepping automatic hand grasp and Galant; (2) two reflexes which normally appear with increasing cortical maturation and which normally are present in four-month old fullterm infants, and are also reliable indices of neurological maturation. These reflexes are the labyrinthine head righting reflex and the Landau; (3) weight, length and head circumference gain, and (4) mental and motor functioning.

Thirty prematurely born infants, who were 37 weeks or less in gestational age (determined by the Dubowitz neurological and physical assessment within 48 hours after birth) and whose birth weight was (2500 grams) or less were randomly placed in experimental and control groups. There were no significant differences in any birth variable or in sex. There was an equal distribution of race (Caucasian, black and Mexican-American) between the two groups and each included a set of twins. The infants were all born in a large city-county hospital in Dallas, Texas, and their mothers were all of a low socioeconomic status.

Treatment consisted of a sequential, caudocephalic progression of a precise method of stroking and massaging the infant's entire body. Public health nurses, were taught the treatment and they, in turn, taught the treatment to the mothers. They were instructed to provide the stimulation for 15 minutes, four times a day, for a period of 30 days beginning the day the infant came home from the hospital. Following each stroking treatment, the infant was rocked, held and cuddled for an additional five minutes. Each experimental infant received at least 120 such treatments during the first 30 days after release from the hospital nursery. The average stay of the infants in the hospital was two weeks.

Each mother was visited daily during the 30-day treatment period by a public nurse. Eighteen nurses were used in the study. The mothers were given timers to use with the treatments and weekly charts on which to record her observations about treatments.

When the mother of a control infant went home from the hospital, she received only the usual instructions for infant care given her by the attending physician. Control mothers were also visited by public health nurses, though not as frequently as the experimental mothers.

To insure that all infants, experimental and control, had sufficient nutrition during the experimental period, a four-month supply of formula was provided for each baby.

At four months of age, which was several weeks after treatment had ended, each infants' neurological, physical and mental/motor development was assessed by a pediatrician, a psychologist and a pediatric nurse who did not know which infant was experimental or control.

The results of the assessment indicated that stroking and rocking can accelerate maturation of cellular components insofar as neurological development can be measured by functional behavior. There were significant differences ($p < .05$) in favor of the experimental infants in the assessment of the phylogenetic reflexes. Six of the nine reflexes were not present in the experimental group at four months of age. There were significant differences ($p < .001$) in favor of the experimental infants in the assessment of the labyrinthine and Landau reflexes. A significant difference (p < .04) in weight gain occurred with the experimental infants, indicating an increase in enzymatic and endocrine functioning. And there were significant differences (p < .05) in mental functioning as measured by the Bayley Scales of Infant Development.

There were no significant differences in head circumference, body length or motor development, though the raw scores for each of these variables were greater for the experimental group.

Subjective findings indicated that the infants receiving the stroking and rocking were more socially adaptive and aggressive. Further, the nature of the treatment was such that the mother/infant relationship was enhanced and nurtured. This phenomenon could have far-reaching effects on the infant's continuing development of psycho-social-cognitive development and functioning.

It seems reasonable to predict from the findings of this study that a premature infant who achieves a more robust neurophysiological development would elicit a mother's more confident responsiveness, which in turn would set up a cyclic interaction of stimulus-response behavior. Some evidence of this cyclic interaction was noted when the mothers administered the treatments. Infants quieted, smiled, established eye contact and vocalized. Mothers observed this behavior with interest and pleasure, relating their belief that the "baby likes being stroked and held by me."

In short, the infants who were systematically stroked and rocked by their mothers for 30 days after arriving home from the hospital made significant gains in weight, neurological development and in mental functioning. In addition, it is suggested that they surpassed the rate of growth of normal, fullterm infants by virtue of age adjustment. A baby who was eight weeks premature at birth, and who was 16 weeks at examination date, would have an adjusted age of eight weeks total age. Thus, this infant would have made a 24-week gain in 16 weeks. In other words, at four months, chronological age, not only would this infant have "caught up" with a fullterm infant, but would have accelerated another eight weeks in developmental functioning. This was also evidenced in weight gain. The average weight gain for a fullterm infant is double his birth weight by four months. All the experimental infants more than doubled their birth weight in four months. One infant, who was 32 weeks gestational age and three pounds at birth, weighed over 15 pounds at four months of age—a gain of five times her birth weight.

Chapter 2
Early
Infancy

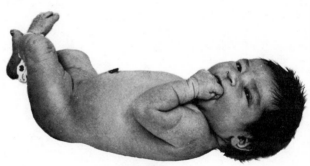

COURTESY OF ARTHUR N. PARMELEE

"Mother, meet your baby. Baby, this is your mother." The two look into each other's eyes, provided both members of the pair have their eyes open. After a normal birth, with minimal use of drugs, the mother and infant are both likely to be awake and alert. It is easy to imagine that the baby is looking with wonder at the world that has suddenly been opened to him. Whether she looks into her baby's eyes immediately, or within a few hours, the mother may feel a sense of wonder and elation.

Films of mother-infant interaction within three hours of birth have revealed a normative pattern of maternal behavior [52]. With her naked infant lying on a heat panel beside her, the mother looked straight at him and began to touch his hands and feet with her fingertips. Gradually, she used her whole fingers, palms, and whole hands, moving from limbs to trunk and head. She touched him all over. She looked into his eyes, placing his face directly in front of hers. If his eyes were closed, she might ask him to open them. "Open your eyes. Oh, come on now, open up your eyes! If you open your eyes, then I will know you are alive."

Structure and Functions of the Newborn

What the mother sees, in her state of elation, may be quite unlike what the nurse and doctor see in their examination. The father and grandparents may describe their new baby as the most beautiful one in the nursery, whereas casual observers see him as ordinary or even ugly. Professional staff will see him in more objective terms.

The infant is usually assessed immediately after birth by means of an Apgar rating, a system of scoring his heart rate, breathing effort, muscle tone, reflex irritability, and color. The Apgar test is useful for predicting survival and indicating infants who need special care [1]. More detailed examinations of the newborn can be done by such tests as the Brazelton Neonatal Assessment Scale [17] and Rosenblith's modification of the Graham Scale [79]. The beautiful newborn baby pictured on these pages was being given the newborn neurological examination chosen for use in the Infant Studies Project, by Dr. Arthur Parmelee and his associates at the University of California at Los Angeles.

Newborn proportions are very different from those at later ages. In comparing the baby shown here with older babies in later chapters the head seems to be large, the trunk small, and the legs short and undeveloped. The top part of the head is large, and the jaws are small. The eyes look big because they really are big in proportion to the rest of the face. The legs are bowed and drawn up, the position making them look even shorter than if they were stretched out.

BIRTH WEIGHT

Weight at birth varies from one ethnic group to another, with geographic location, economic status, and food habits. Table 2-1 illustrates some of these differences.

Birth weight is related to the weight of the mother and even more, to the mother's birth weight, but not to the weight of the father [69]. As mentioned in the previous chapter, the maternal system regulates the quantity of growth of the fetus. The mother's ability to constrain the growth of the fetus represents a safety mechanism for a small woman whose partner is a large man. Their child may be genetically large, but can be kept to a reasonable size before birth. After that, a catch-up mechanism takes over and the baby's growth speeds up to realize his inherited potential [97].

PHYSIOLOGICAL FUNCTIONING

Respiration. The change from being a water-borne parasite to being an air-breathing, independent individual is a complex one, although one that the newborn is ready to make. An example of his fitness to adapt is that he can stand degrees of oxygen deprivation that an adult could not tolerate. The crucial change is in respiration. Breathing begins as he emerges. It may take a day or two for the amniotic fluid and mucus to drain completely from the baby's breathing apparatus. Breathing is irregular, rapid, and shallow, involving the abdomen more than the chest. The neonate is often a noisy breather, wheezing and snuffling in a fashion that can be alarming to first-time parents. During the first five days of life, the average respiration rate was found to be 46 breaths per minute [98].

Table 2-1. Mean Birth Weights (in grams), by Sex, and Sexes Combined.

Country and Ethnicity	Female	Male	Sexes Combined
Brazil			
White	3258	3397	
Black	3204	3325	
Canada	3320	3347	
Eskimo (North American)	3263	3360	
India	2880	2939	
Indonesia	3048	3116	
Israel	3281	3391	
Jamaica	3070	3120	
Navajo (United States)	3166	3242	
Sioux (United States)	3366	3437	
U.S. nonsmoking mothers			
White			3440
Black			3160

SOURCES: M. S. Adams and J. D. Niswander. Birth weight of North American Indians: A correction and amplification. *Human Biology*, 1973, **45**, 351–357; A. M. deAuraújo and F.M. Salzano. Parental characteristics and birthweight in a Brazilian population. *Human Biology*, 1975, **47**, 37–43; S. M. Grantham-McGregor et al. A longitudinal study of infant growth in Kingston, Jamaica. *Human Biology*, 1972, **44**, 549–562; G. A. Harrison et al. *Human biology*. New York: Oxford University Press, 1964; H. V. Meredith. Relation between tobacco smoking of pregnant women and body size of their progeny: A compilation and synthesis of published studies *Human Biology*, 1975, **47**, 451–472; H. Palti and B. Adler. Anthropometric measurements of the newborn, sex differences, and correlations between measurements. *Human Biology*, 1975, **47**, 523–530; Statistics Canada. *Vital Statistics Report*, vol. 1. 1972. Table 15, pp. 80–81.

Breathing reflexes are coordinated with and activated by the oxygen-carbon dioxide balance. The amount of air a baby breathes is regulated thus. Coughing, sneezing, and yawning are all reflexes with important survival value. Coughing and sneezing clear the air passages and lungs. Yawning gives a quick gulp of air when it is needed suddenly.

Circulation. The essential change in circulation immediately follows the change in respiration. Only a small quantity of blood goes to the lungs before birth, since it flows to the placenta to exchange products. After birth, blood is forced into the lungs, and the circulation to the placenta is cut off by the closing of the opening that leads from the fetal heart to the placenta. During fetal life, the right and left ventricles of the heart have an opening between them. Within the first week or ten days of postnatal life, the opening gradually closes. Another important change in the circulatory–respiratory combination is that the lungs expand gradually in the first two weeks. During that time, the blood includes almost twice as many blood cells per cubic millimeter as it does immediately after the lungs are fully expanded. The heart rate decelerates during the birth process and quickly accelerates at birth. A peak heart rate of 174 beats per minute was found at two minutes after birth [103]. Heart rate at 6 weeks was found to be 153.6 when infants were awake and 141.2 when they were sleepy. At 12 weeks, rates were 150.2 while awake and 129.1 when sleepy [75]. Patterns of response become more stable during the first few months suggesting that important changes in control mechanisms take place during the first month of life [62]. Changes in heart rate are often used by experimenters as a means of measuring the infant's response to stimuli. Respiration is also used thus.

Digestion. The newborn changes from taking nutrients in through the placenta to taking food into the mouth and stomach. Hunger contractions and rooting, sucking, and swallowing mechanisms are present at birth. The small lower jaw and the fat pads in the cheeks are equipment for sucking. The mother's breasts first supply colostrum, a highly specialized food adapted to the newborn's needs, not available (as yet) from bottles. Although colostrum looks thin and watery, perhaps yellow, it is a high-protein food that contains immunoglobulin, which protects the infant's intestinal tract [39]. The breasts supply milk from the second or third day, regulating its composition and quantity to the maturity of the baby. Thus, a delicately balanced nutritive relationship continues to exist between the mother and the baby after birth.

The first material evacuated from the colon is meconium, the material accumulated before birth from cellular breakdown, intestinal secretions, bile, mucus, and material swallowed with amniotic fluid. After three days, the stools assume a character that depends on the type of food, those of breast-fed babies differing noticeably from those of bottle-fed babies in appearance. Breast-fed babies usually have several bowel movements a day during the first few weeks, but after age 1, 2, or 3 months they usually change to a pattern of infrequent movements, one a day or every other day. Bottle-fed babies have one to four, or even six a day at first and later the number decreases to one or two [95]. The kidneys excrete small quantities of urine before birth. Frequency of urination increases after the second day to an average of around 20 times a day, with a wide range of individual differences.

Metabolism. The newborn has a higher metabolic rate than the adult, but lower than the preschool child's. Immediately after birth, the temperature drops two to five degrees and then rises to 98 to 99 degrees after about eight hours. Since mechanisms for maintaining a stable body temperature are immature, the neonate's temperature is unstable. Premature babies' temperatures are even more unstable than those of full-term infants. Heat loss is great through the baby's comparatively large surface, which is poorly insulated because skin and fat layers are thin. The newborn shows little diurnal change in temperature [92]. Thus, he gets along best in a controlled temperature, with clothing and bedding carefully regulated to maintain a steady temperature.

Brain Development. The brain continues to grow rapidly after birth, reaching about 90 per cent of adult size by age 3 or 4. The rate of formation of new cells decreases, with an increase in the processes of enlargement and elaboration [27].

A spurt in the growth of glial (supportive) cells begins at 25 weeks. *Myelinization* (laying down of the fatty sheath on nerve cells) follows cell development and proceeds in a definite sequence. Although the whole brain is growing rapidly, some areas mature faster than others. Cells controlling the upper part of the body, the chest and arms, mature and become functional earlier than do the cells controlling the lower parts of the body. Brain development is affected by both nutrition and stimulation.

STATES

As parents well know, infant behavior is different in different states, especially in sleeping, waking, and crying. Then there are different kinds of waking and different kinds of sleeping. Wolff, reporting his classic studies, observed that behavior is *organized* into states [110]. Instead of being a whimsical, unpredictable creature, the newborn infant is quite orderly and consistent in his behavior and makes sense when it is considered in terms of states. Definitions vary somewhat from one investigator to another. Wolff's six definitions are *regular sleep,* breathing smooth and even, little movement of face and body; *irregular sleep,* breathing irregular, movements of body and face, including rapid eye movements; *drowsiness,* less active than in irregular sleep but more active than in regular, eyes open and close, looking glazed, eyelids heavy; *waking activity,* silent or moaning, grunting, whimpering, spurts of diffuse motor activity, face relaxed or pinched, eyes open but not shiny, skin flushed in activity, breathing irregular; *crying,* vocalizing, grimacing, diffuse motor activity, red face; *alert inactivity,* body inactive, face

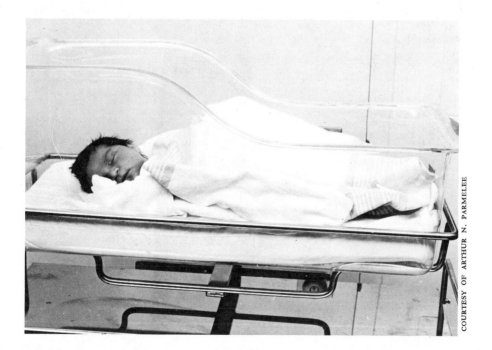

COURTESY OF ARTHUR N. PARMELEE

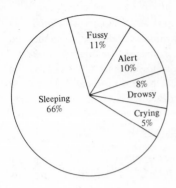

Figure 2-1.   Time spent by newborn babies in five states.

SOURCE: Date from W. K. Berg, C. D. Adkinson, and B. D. Strock. Duration and periods of alertness in neonates. *Developmental Psychology,* 1973, **9,** 434.

relaxed, eyes open, bright and shining, respirations faster and more variable than in regular sleep. In addition to these six states, degree of hunger must be considered [53].

The chemical composition of the blood has been shown to be different in different states [99]. *Cortisol,* a substance associated with stress in adults, was at high level in the blood of 3-day-old infants when they were crying or fussing. Cortisol levels were low during sleep. Thus, behavioral states have physical correlates in blood, as well as in the brain, muscles, and respiratory system.

The infant's response to stimulation depends upon his state and upon the stimulus. For instance, in both kinds of sleep, infants were insensitive to touch; in alert inactivity, response to touch was increased motility; and in waking activity, touch stimuli resulted in decreased motility [110]. In studying the various sense modalities, investigators usually choose the state of alert inactivity for testing the infant's capabilities. It is in this state that he attends most to particular parts of the environment. The amount of time that 1-month-old boy babies spent in alert inactivity was correlated to length of time spent looking at pictures of faces at 3 months [67].

Time spent by 26 newborn infants in five categories of states is represented in Figure 2-1. Regular and irregular sleep have been classified together, and *alert* corresponds to alert inactivity. Wolff's subjects steadily increased the amount of time spent in alert inactivity, the weekly averages of percentage of total time being: first week, 11, second, 17, third, 19, and fourth, 21 [108].

Individual Differences. From the moment of birth, infants differ in the amounts of time they spend in alert inactivity. During the first six hours, some of Wolff's subjects stayed awake and looked for an hour and a half or longer; others fell into a deep sleep as soon as they were cleaned and dressed [109]. Infants vary considerably in the duration of sleep cycles and in the proportion of irregular sleep to other states [78].

Sex Differences. Newborn girls had, on the average, longer periods of alert inactivity than boys [10]. This finding agrees with the general finding that females are more mature at birth than males.

Group Differences. A comparison of newborns of Chinese ancestry with Caucasian newborns showed that the Chinese babies were less likely to change back and forth between states of contentment and upset and that when they cried, they were much more easily consoled by being picked up [37]. In an isolated mountainous region in Mexico, Brazelton and his associates observed and tested Zinacanteco newborns [18]. Compared with American infants, the Zinacantecos stayed in quiet, alert states for long periods, moved slowly and smoothly from one state to another, and did not show deep sleep, intense crying, or intense sucking. What is typical neonatal behavior in the United States may not be the same universally. Reasons for group differences may be genetic or they may be largely environmental, since the newborn infant has had nine months of influences from the environment. The conduct of pregnancy and birth differ widely from one culture to another.

CRYING

Newborn infants cry more than they do later. As they gradually stay awake for longer times, crying decreases and other behaviors such as vocalizing, use of the hands, and social interaction increase.

Several studies have shown that brain-damaged babies cry differently from normal babies, the former having a much higher pitch. A review of these studies concludes that the cry is an indication of the condition of the infant's central nervous system [57].

Influences. Position has been found to influence crying. When fifteen newborn babies were placed on their backs and fifteen on their stomachs, and observed for two hours, the prone (on stomach) babies cried less and slept more [13].

Climate may influence infants' state behavior. Popular opinion holds that babies fuss more in hot weather. In Rhode Island, a study of seasonal variation showed that newborns cried more during the winter than during the summer [90].

Crying and Soothing. Of all changes in state, the change from crying to not crying, be it to sleeping or waking, is the change that parents and caretakers would most like to understand. *Soothability* and *consolability* are terms applied to the infant's responsiveness to attempts to quiet his cries. Considerable research has been done on soothing, although a gifted caretaker could probably console an infant more effectively than could a scholar applying the results of research. The state of alert inactivity is also desired sometimes by parents, and often by researchers, who wish to carry on their experiments at times when the infant will be most responsive to stimuli.

When related to hunger, crying is, of course, soothed by feeding and often, also, when the baby brings her hand to her mouth. Wolff observed, as have most parents of newborns, that crying before meals was rhythmical, with a braying quality and accompanied by tandem kicking. Crying after meals was shrill, not rhythmic, and not accompanied by rhythmic kicking [108].

It is common knowledge that babies are likely to stop crying when fed and when picked up, cuddled, and rocked. The rocking chair and cradle as standard nursery equipment are evidence of this knowledge. Although used infrequently in

North America, swaddling soothes infants in Russia and in other places where it is customary. Pacifiers have long been used to comfort crying babies. In the past decade or two, psychologists have investigated the conditions under which infants are soothed by sucking and being held and rocked. In attempts to soothe a baby, the most frequent methods used by mothers were found to be picking up and rocking. These methods succeeded 85 per cent of the time [9]. Vestibular stimulation (stimulation of the part of the ear that registers movements of the head) occurs when the baby is moved. Rocking results in a rhythmic, strong stimulation. Vertical rocking has been shown to be more effective than horizontal rocking. A fast pace (60 cycles per minute) was more soothing than a slower pace (30 cycles). A high amplitude had more effect than a lower one. By varying the dimensions of rocking, experimenters have concluded that *acceleration* determines the effectiveness of rocking [71]. As the baby was moved through space, a greater acceleration would produce stronger vestibular stimulation and this, the authors hold, is what causes the infant to stop crying. Acceleration may also produce pleasurable sensations in other parts of the body. For example, taking off in a jet plane or a fast start on a motorcycle results in abdominal and chest sensations that are both satisfying and exciting to older individuals.

Further evidence of the enjoyable aspects of rocking was found in a study done in a hospital nursery. Crying infants were rocked until they were quiet, being held upright against the nurse's body while she sat in a rocking chair. In this experiment involving 600 rocking sessions, there were only three occasions when an infant showed any sign of displeasure [106, p. 91]. These studies make one think about the experiences of infants in cultures where babies are carried most of the time. The baby may ride in a string bag on his mother's back, in a shawl under her arm, or even a plastic backpack. In any of these positions, the infant receives vigorous vestibular stimulation as his bearer's walking and bending accelerates his body in one direction and then in another. Contrast this richness with the experience of an infant lying in a stationary crib!

Soothing of crying may result in a change to a sleeping state or to a waking one. When mothers picked up their crying infants and held them to their shoulders, 77.5 per cent of a group of crying infants went into a state of visual alertness. Holding to the shoulder was also somewhat effective in eliciting visual activity in babies who had been sleeping [53].

Continuous stimulation increases the duration of quiet sleep in newborns [84]. Subjects in one study received two-hour sessions of continuous white noise, light, swaddling, and warmth; the control group received softer noise and light, loose clothing, and a cooler temperature [14]. The experimental group cried less, slept more, was less active, and had slower heart rates. The conclusion is that continuous stimulation reduces arousal level, both behavioral and physiological.

SLEEP

Although persons unfamiliar with newborn babies often think that these infants sleep most of the time, the average sleep time of a group of 46 neonates was only between 16 and 17 hours in 24 [70]. By the age of 16 weeks, the average total sleep time had decreased to between 14 and 15 hours. The outstanding developmental changes are not in the number of hours spent in sleep but in the length of sleep periods and their timing during the 24 hours. Babies of 6 weeks sleep as long as five or six hours at a time. By 12 or 16 weeks, they are likely to sleep eight or nine hours at a time and to do so at night. There are occasional young infants, however, who sleep as little as 12 hours out of 24 and others who sleep as much as 21. Parents usually find it easier to take care of a baby who sleeps many hours rather than few. An awake infant, of course, has more varied and stimulating experiences than one who sleeps more.

There are two main types of sleep, *active* or irregular and *quiet* or regular. Active sleep has been described as a "primitive anarchic state" and quiet sleep as a "more mature highly controlled state." As the central nervous system develops inhibiting and controlling mechanisms, quiet sleep increases. One of the distinctive differences between regular and irregular sleep is in the rapid eye movements (REM) that occur during irregular, active sleep. Therefore, the two types of sleep are also called REM and NREM (nonrapid eye movement). Characteristic brain wave (EEG) patterns occur during the two types of sleep. During REM sleep, the EEG is of low voltage and relatively fast; NREM sleep is typified by higher voltage, slower frequency waves [78]. Newborn infants spent a third of their time in REM sleep and another third in quiet NREM sleep. The proportion of REM sleep diminishes as the brain matures. The total REM sleep time decreases from about eight hours in the newborn period to one hour and 40 minutes in the adult. Figure 2-2 shows proportions of quiet and active sleep in a typical newborn sleep cycle. REM sleep in the newborn is different from that of the adult, but changes to an adultlike form at about 3 months of age. During the first 3 months, drowsy REM, fussy REM, and crying REM disappear. Also at 3 months, sleep begins with NREM, whereas in the newborn period, it begins with REM [94].

The sleep of the newborn may be affected by drugs received before or during birth. As mentioned in the previous chapter, infants born to heroin-addicted mothers showed no truly quiet sleep and mostly REM sleep.

Individual differences in sleep patterns are considerable. At 3 weeks of age, a group of infants ranged from 137 to 391 minutes of sleep during eight hours [67]. Girls slept about an hour more than boys. These differences, of course, make a

Figure 2-2. Typical newborn sleep cycle, showing length of time spent in quiet, active, and transitional sleep. The lower line represents a typical cycle at three months, showing longer periods of quiet sleep as compared with the newborn pattern.

Adapted from E. Stern, A. H. Parmelee, Y. Akiyama, M. A. Schultz, and W. H. Wenner. Sleep cycle characteristics in infants. *Pediatrics*, 1969, **43**, Fig. 1, p. 67. Copyright © 1969 by American Academy of Pediatrics.

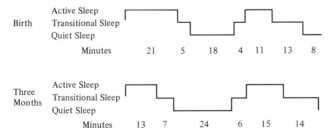

difference to the mother taking care of the baby and also to the baby, in terms of experience.

MOTOR BEHAVIOR AND DEVELOPMENT

The newborn baby has many action patterns ready to use. Some of them need only the appropriate environment in which to emerge full blown, although others are perfected after some practice or repetition. Still others seem to require time more than practice.

Reflexes. Well-integrated behavior patterns that are elicited by a specific stimulus are called *reflexes.* Some of them are protective, such as blinking, withdrawing from painful stimuli, and shivering. Others which may have been protective in the early history of the species include the startle or Moro reflex, the Darwinian or grasp reflex, and the Babkin reflex, in which pressure on the infant's palms causes him to raise his arms, close his eyes, turn his head to the midline, and open his mouth. The baby makes postural adjustments to being held prone and in midair. Sometimes these are called *anti-gravity reflexes.* If not encumbered by clothing and bedding, a new infant will creep, or at least make progress, when prone. Newborns will walk when supported adequately in upright position, with their feet touching a surface. Whether creeping and walking should be called reflexes is debatable, but they are patterns that are ready to work at birth. When lying on his back, the typical newborn posture is the *tonic neck reflex,* in which the head turns to one side, the arm and leg on that side are extended, and the other arm and leg are bent. If the legs or the arms are pressed down to the bed and then suddenly released, they quickly assume the flexed position, as pictured.

The baby is ready at birth to find his food, take it into his mouth, and swallow it. The *rooting reflex* is a response to a touch on the cheek and/or lip. When touched on the cheek, perhaps several times, he opens his mouth and moves his head toward the source of the touch. When touched above the lip, he opens his mouth and moves his head from side to side. These movements are useful for finding the nipple. When touched on the lip, the baby purses his lips or pouts, probably causing erection of the nipple and making it easier to grasp. When the nipple is grasped, it delivers the stimulus to the *sucking* reflex and he sucks, using both *expression* and *suction.* Expression is a lapping movement, whereas suction is a negative pressure, created by increasing the size of the mouth cavity. Even though newborn infants are very skillful in rooting and sucking, sucking behavior is by no means automatic, in the manner of a startle reflex. Sucking is adapted to the pressure of the milk flow [48]. When milk is flowing fast, as it does in the beginning of a breast-feeding or from a bottle whose nipple has big holes, the baby sucks continuously. When the flow is slower, the baby pauses, sucks in a burst of sucks, pauses again, and continues in this pattern. Mothers and caretakers often jiggle the pausing infant, but research shows that it is the milk pressure and not the jiggling that controls the sucking pattern.

Sucking is soothing, and infants will suck on anything in the mouth. Pacifiers are used widely throughout the world, since it is well known that they will help a baby to go to sleep and stay asleep. An experiment on 4-day-old infants demonstrated the power of the pacifier to block responses during sleep [111]. The subjects

During a neurological examination, the newborn baby's legs are pressed down and then released suddenly. The normal response is pictured here. The baby quickly flexes her legs.

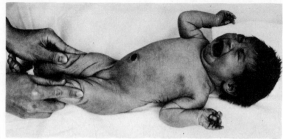

PHOTOGRAPHS COURTESY OF ARTHUR H. PARMELEE

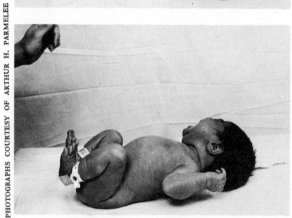

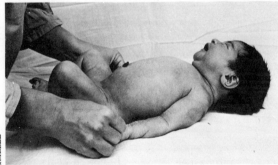

The neurological examination includes this test, in which the arms are pressed down to the baby's sides and then released. The baby immediately raises her arms to a flexed position.

PHOTOGRAPHS COURTESY OF ARTHUR H. PARMELEE

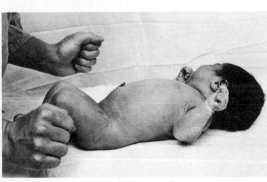

were tickled with a camel's hair brush during regular sleep while sucking and not sucking. They responded less while sucking. While asleep and not sucking, but with the pacifier in the mouth, the baby was likely to respond to tickling with a new burst of sucking.

Sucking is closely related to *looking*. A film analysis showed 2- and 3-day-old infants frequently alerting before and after their hands contacted their mouths [55]. The authors suggested that this pattern may be the early unified behavior from which eye-hand coordination is later differentiated. If so, it is an example of the developmental principle of differentiation and integration. (See Chapter 17 for a discussion of principles of development.)

Bruner points out that at birth and for several days thereafter, the infant sucks with his eyes shut [20, p. 287]. If he looks, he stops sucking. Even by 2 months, when he may appear to be looking and sucking at the same time, recordings show that he is not doing this, but that the two actions are closely coordinated.

Crying. Already mentioned as a state, crying is also motor behavior. It involves the whole body, as well as the vocal apparatus, and varies somewhat in different situations, such as in hunger and satiation.

Posture and Locomotion. On her back, the newborn lies in the tonic-neck-reflex position. When prone, as shown in the series of three photographs, she raises her head to free her nose and turns her head to the side. She also makes crawling movements. When held in a sitting position, she pulls her head forward after it has fallen back, as can be seen in the two photographs. Held upright over a shoulder, she usually alerts, becomes quiet, and looks. Customs of child care are different in regard to holding a baby upright. In North America, it is customary to leave babies lying down except when they cry or give other signs of needing attention. When babies are carried on their mothers' backs, without support to the head, they seem to gain control over their heads quickly, as though only a small amount of practice were needed. When babies are swaddled or tied to cradle boards, of course, they cannot hold their heads up. Yet when they are freed at a later age, they are able to do so.

Grasping. When newborn infants are supported so as to free their arms and hands, they will reach for an object and grasp it. Bower [12, pp. 157–167] has demonstrated reaching at two weeks of age, when infants were presented with an object just out of reach and another object, twice as far away. Subjects reached twice as frequently for the near object as for the far one. They reached with one hand when the object was at one side, and sometimes with both hands when the object was in the midline. The hand opened before contact and closed on contact. There was some accommodation to size and distance of objects. When objects were within reach, they had a hit rate of about 40 per cent. Reaching behavior seems to disappear by 4 weeks of age, to recur at about 20 weeks, with a hit rate of around 80 per cent. Newborn reaching is a unitary reach-grasp pattern that later becomes differentiated into reaching and grasping, two patterns that can then be used separately or combined. Here is another example of the developmental principle of differentiation and integration.

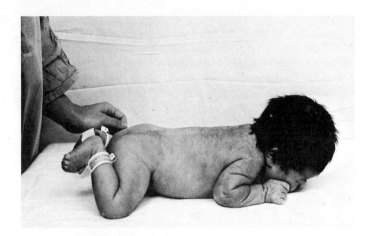

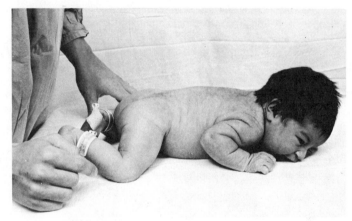

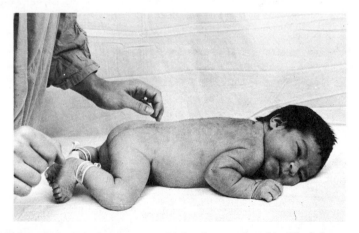

The neurological examiner places the baby prone, with her face on the table. The baby raises her head and turns it to the side.

PHOTOGRAPHS COURTESY OF ARTHUR H. PARMELEE

The space perception that enables the newborn infant to reach-grasp is, according to Bower, built into the visual system through several of its features. Because the two eyes register a slightly different view, their combination gives a third dimension [2, 12]. When the head moves, a near object seems to move farther and faster than a far object. The only spot that does not change place is the one toward which the eyes are directly looking. This place of nonmoving, the center of expansion, becomes larger as the person comes closer to it. Infants, as well as everyone else, use information from these three sources, views from both eyes, movement, and the center of expansion. Information from shading (distribution of light and shadow) was also used for depth perception by infants as young as 2 months [112].

As part of his investigation of newborn reaching, Bower [p. 95] devised a method of showing an intangible, or virtual, object. The object appeared as a solid object in front of a screen, much the way that pictures appear as solid objects in a stereoscopic viewer. The babies reached for the virtual objects just as they had for real ones, and appeared upset when their hands touched nothing. Bower [p. 114] suggests that in infancy there is a unity of the senses, with tactual input expected as part of reaching-grasping, just as the young infant has unity between vision and hearing.

PERCEPTION

How does the world look, feel, smell, and sound to a newborn baby? Even though the infant cannot talk about his experiences, psychologists have found out a great deal about them, through the use of ingenious methods and equipment.

The *orienting reflex* provides a simple way of judging whether an infant is reacting to a stimulus. If the baby stops what he is doing, whether it be sucking,

Postural adjustment is shown in the second picture. As the examiner raises the baby to a sitting position, her head falls backward slightly. She then brings her head forward.

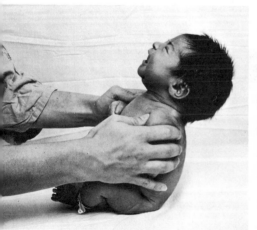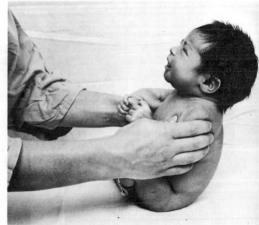

PHOTOGRAPHS COURTESY OF ARTHUR H. PARMELEE

fussing, or moving, then becomes quiet and possibly orients physically to the stimulus, then he is orienting. After several repetitions of a stimulus, the infant adapts and no longer orients. A stimulus perceived as new will result in orienting, indicating that the infant can tell that it is different from the first one.

Since adults and older children show decelerating heart rates when they are orienting, infant heart rates have been monitored to see whether they, too, would decelerate when babies first paid attention to a new stimulus. Results for young infants were puzzling, since newborns have often been found to accelerate their heart rates to a new stimulus [41]. At least one study, however, has found deceleration of the heart rate when newborn infants, in a state of alert inactivity, looked at a checkerboard stimulus [41]. When *variability* of heart rate was taken into consideration, response differences were found [73]. Variability is a beat-by-beat variation in heart rate. Comparing a group with high variability with a group with low variability, it was found that high variability was associated with responsivity. That is, the group with high heart-rate variation responded to stimuli with greater changes in heart rate.

Another method of judging an infant's response to a stimulus is by monitoring electrodermal changes, shown by changes in electric voltage between two parts of the body [3]. This method does not involve applying a current to the infant, but only measuring currents that his body produces.

The object of an infant's gaze can be determined by observing what is reflected in his eyes, either directly or by photography. A baby shows finely graded reactions to taste in the varied patterning of his sucking [59]. Other methods of testing perception are mentioned under discussions of the various sensory modalities.

Tactile Senses. Skin, muscular, and vestibular (inner ear) senses are highly developed before birth, having functioned prenatally longer than the other senses. Sensations from lips, mouth, and other orifices are included in tactile sensations. The skin, being the locus where the individual is in physical contact with his environment, is the place where much interaction occurs. To name the sensations heat, cold, pressure, and pain tells a minimum about tactile experience. Experiments and clinical experiences with infants have led to the conclusion that tactile stimulation is essential for normal development. Patting, caressing, cuddling, carrying, rocking, changing position, washing, drying—all these activities seem to be soothing and to promote well-being in babies. There is a connection between the skin and sympathetic nervous system.

The regular, rhythmic stimulation that the fetus receives from his mother's heartbeat is translated through the amniotic fluid to all of his skin. After birth the baby lying in a crib receives no such stimulation, but a baby carried by a person does, especially if he is in skin-to-skin contact. The concept of his own body, where it stops and where the rest of the world begins, mother and other people, the objects that make up the rest of the world, are all discovered and understood thought tactile senses, with help from vestibular senses and vision.

Taste. Taste buds are well developed in fetal life. The newborn has more taste buds and a wider distribution of them than does an adult. Two studies indi-

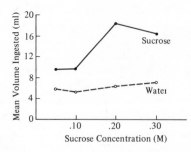 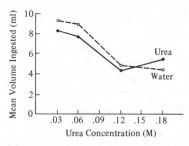

Figure 2-3. Contrast between newborn's acceptance of sucrose and urea solutions, showing preference for sweet and indifference to bitter.

Source: From L. Maller and J. A. Desor. Effect of taste on ingestion by human newborns. In J. Bosma (ed.). *Fourth symposium on oral sensation and perception: development in the fetus and infant.* Fig. 18-1-4, p. 284 and Fig. 18-7, p. 286. Washington, D.C.: U.S. Government Printing Office, 1974.

cate that newborns distinguish between water and a sweet solution, as any baby-nurse knows. After adapting to either water or glucose placed in a drop on the tongue, newborns respond to the other liquid, showing that they distinguished between them [105]. Preference during the first feeding was estimated by measuring the amounts taken of various solutions [63]. It was assumed that preference was the result of taste. The babies drank more sugar solution than water, showing different intakes for the four sugars (sucrose, fructose, glucose, and lactose) at different degrees of concentration. Sucrose was the most preferred, and then fructose. As concentrations increased, the infants drank greater quantities. When tested with bitter, sour, and salty solutions, the infants did not distinguish between these solutions and water. Figure 2-3 contrasts acceptance of the preferred sugar with indifference to the bitter solution.

Further indication that babies really do like sugar came from Lipsitt's [59] findings on sucking patterns of newborns who were given sucrose solution. "Getting excited over savory substances" is how he described it. While taking in sugar, infants slowed down the rate of sucking within each burst of sucks, as though they were savoring the sugar in their mouths. At the same time, heart rate increased.

Smell. Newborn babies react to strong and mild odors by turning away, moving, and showing changes in breathing. Because the two nostrils receive stimuli at slightly different times, location of odors is possible. The ability to locate smells is probably innate [12, p. 19]. During the first few days of life, infants showed discrimination between different odors by habituating to one and then responding to a new one [87]. Some babies were more responsive and more consistent in reactions to odors than were others. For example, oil of lavender elicited a response in one particular infant every day, but no response in two of the other subjects.

Although the olfactory system matures early in life, man does not have as keen a sense of smell as most animals and does not use information from smell as much as from vision and hearing. Perhaps olfaction plays a bigger role in the infant's life than in the adult's, since odors from his mother and other caretakers may be significant to him.

Pain. When a baby cries, adults usually have an urge to make the crying stop and they usually interpret the crying as meaning that the baby is in pain. Gastrointestinal upsets often lead to much crying and hence to many efforts of the caretaker's part to comfort the baby. Until recently, it was commonly believed that circumcision did not hurt a baby very much, because he did not cry a great deal if given something sweet to suck. Changes in sleep patterns after circumcision now suggest that the operation is stressful, as many parents have long suspected [33]. Recent cultural emphasis on sexual fulfillment has also led to questioning the propriety of routine circumcision, since some sexologists hold that sensation is stronger in the intact penis. This concern probably strengthens the position of adults who are eager to protect newborn boys from the pain of circumcision.

Early research on pain in young infants used pinpricks as stimuli, noting how many were necessary before the baby made some withdrawal response. The more modern method is to use mild electric shock up to a level where a withdrawal action is observed. The stimulus can thus be measured exactly. The experiments show that pain sensitivity increases steadily during the first few days of life. A sex difference was found, as well as an age difference, with girls showing more sensitivity than boys, a result in keeping with the generally greater maturity of girls at birth [61]. Tickling has also been used to explore pain responses, since the two types of stimulation have much in common [109]. Newborn babies in all states of rest responded to tickling with vigorous activity. In states of moderate activity, tickling produced moderate increases in activity (51 per cent of trials as compared with 94 per cent in regular sleep). In the state of crying the infant responded with a reduction in activity as often as he did with an increase.

Temperature. Newborn babies increase their muscular activity when the temperature drops. They respond to cold or warm stimuli applied to the skin [74]. Although early studies had suggested that babies preferred lukewarm food, a careful investigation [45] of the use of cold formulas has caused a change in the advice given by pediatricians. Comparisons were made between a group of premature infants fed formulas at the usual lukewarm temperature. There were no significant differences in the feeding behavior, food intake, weight gain, vocal behavior, sleep patterns, or regurgitation of the two groups. Thus research indicates no reason for giving babies warm rather than cold feedings. However, there is no proof that infants cannot distinguish between warm and cold formulas.

Hearing. The newborn baby not only hears but makes fine discriminations in sounds. Sounds have meaning for babies, even before they have learned language.

Infants can distinguish one *pitch* from another, as shown by experiments in which a musical note is played while an infant is sucking. The baby stops sucking, but when the note is repeated several times, he habituates (ceases to respond). A new note is sounded. The baby stops sucking. Change in heart rate can be used instead of sucking to demonstrate discrimination between sounds. Low-pitched sounds soothe crying babies and stimulate motor activity in alert, inactive infants, whereas high frequencies tend to promote distress [32]. Pure tones have been found to be ineffective stimuli, but when pure tones are combined, they act as stimuli. Different combinations of tones resulted in different responses, measured by heartbeat, eye movements, and finger movements [102].

Newborns react differently to different degrees of *loudness*. When white noise was played at 55, 70, and 80 decibels, heart rates and motor responses increased with the level of the sound [96]. The minimal sound that an infant can hear, 35 or 40 decibels, is equivalent to the minimal levels for children and adults [32].

Changes in sound also produce different responses. *Rise* time is the length of time taken by a sound to reach its highest level of loudness. When newborns in the state of alert inactivity heard sounds with slow rise time, they opened their eyes. Sounds with fast rise times were followed by eye-closing and increased head movements. The author concluded that the slow-rise sounds elicited orienting and the fast-rise sounds elicited defensive movements [49].

Lullabies, songs designed especially for babies, combine low pitch, slow rise time, and rhythm, all of which psychologists have demonstrated to be soothing. Another soothing rhythm is the heartbeat sound, which has been the focus of several studies. In a newborn nursery, a group of babies was exposed continuously to a recorded heartbeat sound and compared for crying with a group that did not hear the heartbeat [81]. The infants who heard the heartbeat cried less. Another study [77] confirmed the soothing properties of the heartbeat, but a third study [15] found a metronome and a lullaby sung in a foreign language to be as effective soothers as the heartbeat sound. Although rhythm may be the chief source of the heartbeat effect, it is also likely that the infant's prenatal experience predisposes him to find comfort in the sound of a heartbeat. As a fetus, he heard and felt his mother's heartbeat steadily for many months, while he lived in complete comfort and security. This line of reasoning is also strengthened by the fact that chickens can be imprinted to a rhythmic sound before hatching. That is, newly hatched chicks followed a sound that they had heard regularly while still in their eggs [42].

The human voice is significant to the newborn baby. A variety of studies have shown an overall meaning, a reaction to the sound of crying, and discrimination between phonemes (language sounds). The methods of *kinesics,* using sound-film analysis, have revealed newborn infants showing "interactional synchronies" in relation to adult speech [26]. All 16 of the infants studied showed consistent reactions to human speech, both English and Chinese, no matter whether it came from a present adult or from a tape. Disconnected vowels did not elicit the same response as did natural, rhythmic speech. The author concludes that ". . . the neonate's motor behavior is seen to be entrained by and synchronized with the organized speech behavior of adults in his environment."

Newborn babies cry to the sound of a newborn baby crying. Tested in cribs with constant temperature and constant visual environment, 100 newborns were divided into groups that were exposed to one of these stimuli: no sound, a synthetic cry, a 5-month-old baby crying, and a newborn cry [89]. Crying and heart rate were recorded. Crying occurred in over twice as many of the newborn-crying-tape group as in the no-sound control group. There was not a statistically significant difference between the no-sound group and the other two groups. When duration of crying time was measured, the babies who heard the newborn-crying tape cried

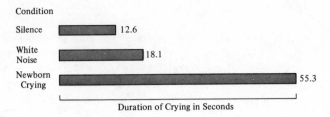

Condition

Silence		12.6
White Noise		18.1
Newborn Crying		55.3

Duration of Crying in Seconds

Figure 2-4. Newborn infants cry longer when they hear the crying of another infant than they do under conditions of silence or white noise.

SOURCE: Data from M. L. Simner. Newborn's response to the cry of another infant. *Developmental Psychology,* 1971, **5,** 136–150.

significantly more than the no-sound and synthetic-cry infants. As Figure 2-4 shows, babies cried longest at the newborn cry, next at the older infant's cry, and least during silence. Heart-rate increases in both the white-noise group and the crying-tape group exceeded those in the silent-control group. Therefore, both sound conditions promoted greater arousal levels, whereas the crying sound stimulated crying. The experiment shows that the newborn infants responded to the vocal properties of the sound of newborn crying. In a subsequent experiment, infants heard recordings of their own crying. Their reactions were compared with those shown when exposed to the crying of another newborn. A baby's own cry was a more powerful stimulus, in terms of heart-rate increases and duration of crying. It seems likely, then, that as the baby hears himself crying, he is stimulated further to crying.

Young infants can perceive small differences between the sounds that make up human language. The difference between *p* and *b* was distinguished by month-old babies, who demonstrated through their sucking behavior that they perceived the sounds as different [31]. Other studies have used heart-rate changes to show that young infants could distinguish between phonemes. Infants between 7 and 20 days of age quieted sooner to their mothers' voices than to the voice of a stranger [45a]. Babies of two months have shown, through changes in their looking behavior, that they can discriminate between different voices, different tone qualities of the same voice, and probably between different statements by the same voice [28]. Young infants also discriminate between certain other categories of sound, perhaps differing rise times [47].

Vision. The typically human parts of the visual system are the most immature at birth; the more ancient parts, which man has in common with even simple animals, are better developed. The older part of the visual system, based on the subcortical part of the brain, serves the peripheral part of the retina and mediates perception of objects and movement in the outer parts of the visual field [19]. Immaturities in the newborn's primary visual system include an underdeveloped central part of the retina (macula and fovea) and probably some of the cells of the cortex of the occipital lobe of the brain. The newborn's eyeball is relatively short, the lens is large and spherical, and the optic nerve is immature [93]. These immaturities result in poor fixation, poor focusing, and poor coordination. Blinking and tear production are limited. Acuity does not increase with increased brightness [30]. Acuity depends upon accommodating by adjusting the thickness of the lens. Because accommodation is very limited during the first month, a baby can focus well on objects held at just the right distance, about seven and one-half inches from his eyes, but cannot focus well on objects held at other distances [44]. Visual pursuit is fairly smooth when a large object is moved from one side to the other,

Figure 2-5. The angular lines, based on photographic records, represent the orientation of a newborn baby's eyes toward a triangle. The point of the triangle offers greater contour than the sides or center, since there is more contrast there between light and dark.

SOURCE: W. Kessen. Sucking and looking: Two organized congenital patterns of behavior in the human newborn. In H. W. Stevenson, E. H. Hess, and H. L. Rheingold (eds.). *Early behavior*. New York: John Wiley & Sons, Inc., 1967, p. 176. By permission.

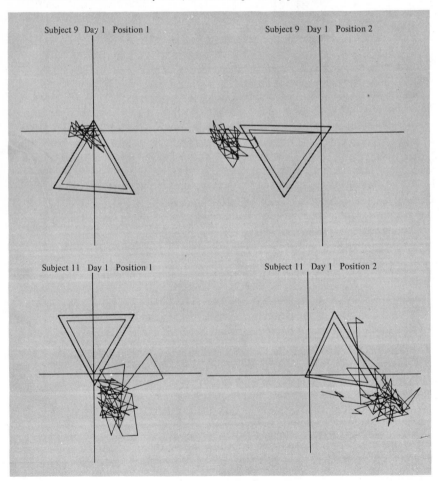

Subject 9 Day 1 Position 1   Subject 9 Day 1 Position 2

Subject 11 Day 1 Position 1   Subject 11 Day 1 Position 2

thus stimulating a large part of, or the entire, retina. When the moving object is small and if it stops in midposition, the infant makes jerky movements and may lose sight of it [19]. At least by two and a half months, infants distinguish between red and green, as shown by an experiment using operant conditioning [83].

Visual preference has been the topic of much research. At all ages, including the earliest days of life, infants can be presented with two targets of different patterns and the object of their gaze recorded. When a baby looks longer or more often at target A than at target B, he is said to prefer target A. Infants will look longer at a checkerboard or bullseye than at a plain target. The reason underlying these preferences is an innate preference for the pattern with the most contour density. *Contour* is the contrast or change between light or dark. Although newborns prefer a larger checkerboard than do infants of two months and older, they are still following the principle of choosing for contour density. The immaturity of the fovea, along with limited acuity, means that widely spaced patterns are more salient for the infant [19, 80]. Although vertical lines have been found to hold the newborn's attention more than horizontal lines [50], there is much evidence to show that contour density is what is most important. Contour density, rather than shape and pattern, determines visual attention at least up to 2 months of age, even though the newborn infant has sufficient acuity to detect geometric forms [80]. Since patterned stimulation is necessary for neural maturation in animals, it seems likely that it is also necessary for humans. The fact that babies seek contour density supports the idea that they need these visual experiences for development. At some

Figure 2-6.   Response times and number of times newborns looked at various targets. Although the face was preferred to other patterns, and patterns to blanks, the results can be explained entirely in terms of contour density.

SOURCE: R. L. Fantz. Visual perception from birth as shown by pattern selectivity. In H. E. Whipple (ed.). *New issues in infant development. Annals of the New York Academy of Sciences,* vol. 118, pp. 793–814, Fig. 7. Copyright © The New York Academy of Sciences, 1965. Reprinted by permission.

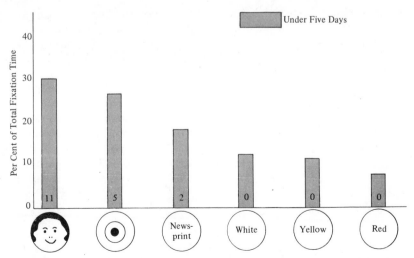

time (as yet unknown) after 2 months, contour and peripheral stimulation becomes less salient and pattern becomes important. Even while the infant's visual attention is controlled by contour density, he is predisposed to behavior that promotes his social-emotional interactions. Faces have much contour, and most of all, eyes are salient. Eyes have dark-light contrasts and they move! Up to 4 months, eyes are more salient than the mouth, but by 5 months, mouths elicit as much attention as eyes [23].

Coordination of Vision and other Senses. What other kinds of visual stimuli could be important to newborn infants? Babies between 2 and 11 weeks showed avoidance responses and upset to shadows that indicate an approaching object [7]. In his book on perception and cognition in infancy, Bower [12] shows a series of photographs of a 10-day-old baby supported upright in a seat, reacting to a big box approaching his face. First, the baby's eyes widened. Then he pulled back his head. As the box came closer, he put his hands between the box and his face. Bower also showed that when newborn infants are supported so as to free their arms and hands, they will reach out and grasp objects in front of them. What was even more surprising, they had some sort of expectation of touching the object. When an unreal or virtual object was projected in place of a real one, the infants reached and cried as their hands met nothing [12, pp. 113–114]. Bower concludes, ". . . in man, there is a primitive unity of the senses, with visual variables specifying tactile consequences."

Coordination of vision and hearing was first conclusively demonstrated on a baby ten minutes after birth, showing that there was an innate ability to look in the direction of a sound. The baby turned her head in the direction of a toy cricket, clicking on one side and then on the other. Later a study on 64 newborns confirmed the experiment [58]. The notion of common visual-auditory space got further affirmation from an experiment in which month-old infants saw their mothers speaking and heard the sound coming first from the mother and then from the side [5]. The babies showed distress when the voice seemed to come from the "wrong" place, struggling, grimacing, and sticking their tongues out. Although a replication experiment [65] failed to find these results, this experiment is consistent with the first two mentioned and with Bower's conclusion that a primitive unity is built into the structure of the nervous system. Bower maintains that perceptual development occurs through differentiation from the original integrated state.

LEARNING

As some of the previous sections have shown, a newborn baby modifies his behavior as a result of experience. Some behavior patterns are ready to operate at birth and require little or no practice. Others emerge only through interaction of infant and environment. Because psychologists have learned how to enable infants to show that they can learn, young babies have proved themselves to be efficient learners.

Habituation studies, such as those used to test discrimination between sounds or visual displays, show that the newborn *learns* a particular stimulus. By not orienting to it, he shows that he has become familiar with it.

Conditioning studies have demonstrated newborns learning by both classical and operant conditioning. In classical conditioning, a new stimulus is paired with the stimulus that elicits a reflex response. After several pairings, the new (conditioning) stimulus alone calls forth the response, without the original (unconditioned) stimulus. For example, a tone was sounded when a nipple was inserted into a baby's mouth. After a number of repetitions, the conditioning stimulus (the tone) elicited the response (sucking) that originally was elicited by the unconditioned stimulus (nipple) [60]. Many other experiments have shown classical conditioning in the young infant, using, in addition to sucking responses, eye-blinking, pupillary reflex, Babkin reflex, heart rate, and electrodermal activity [36]. The *state* of the infant makes a difference in his responses to conditioning procedures [35]. For example, newborn responsiveness to a sound as conditional stimulus was greater in quiet sleep than in active, REM sleep.

In operant conditioning, a response is established by reinforcing it whenever it occurs, or reinforcing a small portion or a beginning of the desired response. Four-day-old infants learned to turn their heads when reinforced by being allowed to suck on a nipple [91]. Another group of infants, just 1 or 2 days old, adjusted their sucking time to shorter duration when stopping their sucking produced music and beginning to suck ended the music [22]. State has been found relevant in operant conditioning, as well as in classical conditioning. Fully awake infants were more responsive to head-turning conditioning than were babies rated low on a scale of wakefulness [24].

These and many other experiments have shown that newborn babies are able to make discriminations and to modify their behavior, that is, to learn. Their capabilities are often underestimated because they can neither talk, sit up, locomote, nor make fine hand movements. When given opportunities to use the behavior patterns they do have, then they can be seen as active, complex, and competent in their own way.

Group and Individual Differences

Every person in the world is unique, even a newborn baby. In some characteristics, the newborn shares similarities with members of one group that is different from other groups, but his particular combination of characteristics is unique. Even identical twins, who share the same genes, have different environments, right from the beginning, and different experiences.

Group differences have been noted between infants in different *cultures,* and, of course, between the *sexes.* Already mentioned under the topic of *states* (see pp. 63–65) are the stability and consolability of Chinese newborns as compared with Americans, and the Zinacanteco babies' smooth transitions and long periods of alert inactivity. Advanced motor development has been reported for African infants [16, 38], although a recent carefully controlled study has shown little difference between African and European newborns and no difference between poor and elite Africans [104]. Afro-Jamaican babies from families of lower socioeconomic status were studied from birth to one year with the Gesell test, which, of course, was standardized on white, United States children of middle status [40].

The Afro-Jamaicans of normal birth weight (2.5 kilograms or more) were advanced at birth in motor development. Those below normal birth weight were average in motor tests.

Sex differences in state behavior were seen at three weeks, when boys fussed and cried more than girls and stayed awake more of the time. When they cried, girls were more easily consoled [66]. In all states, boys tended to startle more than girls, whereas girls were more likely to smile and to show rhythmical mouthing [53]. A review of sex differences suggests that girls are more receptive to stimulation of the mouth and skin and that boys have greater muscular strength [54]. These differences are most probably a result of the action of sex hormones before birth. Girls' greater maturity may also contribute to sex differences at birth.

Individual differences begin with appearance. Newborn babies look different from one another, as anyone who has peered into a hospital nursery can confirm. Behavior patterns are individual too. The following are some of the important ways in which newborn infants differ from one another: time spent in different states, ease of transition, consolability when crying and fussing, tendency to startle, number of erections [53], amount of finger sucking, hand-mouth contacting and mouthing [56], heart rate, level of arousal, depth of sleep, tactile sensitivity and strength [76], and responses to various kinds of sensory stimulation [11].

Caring for Infants

The old-fashioned term, *little stranger* is quite apt. The newborn infant is a stranger in the new world of his family. He is faced with the task of adapting his physiological functioning through interactions with his caretakers, usually primarily his mother. As previous sections have shown, newborn's behavior springs to some extent from within, but he can respond to outside stimulation and he can learn. Successful communication and interaction during the first 2 or 3 months results in regular patterns of eating and sleeping and a feeling on the mother's part that she knows her baby and how to meet his needs. Some babies organize their systems much more easily than do others. A difficult baby, one who fusses and cries inconsolably and shows distress at feeding, needs a skilled caretaker. If his mother is inexperienced and nobody helps her much, then the baby-mother pair has a hard time working out mutual regulation.

Much of the baby's behavior can be explained in terms of *homeostasis,* the maintaining of physiological equilibrium in the organism. Tension is reduced and balance restored by food-seeking, sucking, and swallowing, through breathing, moving, and having baths and dry diapers. To achieve and maintain successive states of equilibrium also requires a certain level of sensory stimulation—enough but not too much of the various kinds. Equilibrium is continually being disturbed and restored on a new level. In its striving for equilibrium, the organism (either baby or adult) gives preference to some needs over others. For example, a certain degree of fatigue takes precedence over a certain degree of hunger and over a certain level of desire for sensory stimulation. As equilibrium is continually disturbed and created, changes occur in the organism's structure and behavior. These changes are growth and development.

Personality is developing while the newborn is reducing his tensions and maintaining homeostasis. The sense of trust is the crucial aspect of personality growth at this time and for at least the first year of life. Erikson [34, pp. 247–251] writes of the feeling of goodness that comes when the baby is helped to cope with his environment. The world must seem like a good place to be and the people in it trustworthy when he is fed before he is overwhelmed by hunger, when he is kept at a comfortable temperature, and when he receives a satisfactory amount of sensory stimulation. As he signals his needs and his caretaker responds, his sense of trust grows.

THE CARETAKING RELATIONSHIP

Caretaker-infant interactions were studied under three conditions of care during the first 8 weeks of life [21]. Groups A and B had been given by their mothers for adoptive placement, whereas the babies in Group C were cared for by their own experienced mothers, both in the hospital and at home. Group A infants were kept on a fixed schedule in the nursery, cared for by regular hospital staff nurses for 10 days, and then were shifted to rooming-in, with one caretaker, on a demand schedule. The babies in Group B were kept on demand schedules with one caretaker but shifted to a second caretaker at 11 days. Subjects were observed and compared for distress in feeding, as shown by crying, fussing, turning away, spitting out the nipple, gagging, and spitting up. During the first 10 days, Group A infants when on fixed schedule with multiple caretakers showed most distress. When the infants in Group B were shifted to another nurse-caretaker, however, they showed greater distress, suggesting that they had, by 11 days, organized their interactions within the caretaking environment. Group C, cared for by their mothers throughout, showed no shifts in distress. The importance of this study is in showing the sensitivity of the newborn infant in communicating and interacting with his caretaker.

The caretaking relationship is a sensitive one from the standpoint of the mother, too. It has been known for some time that interaction immediately after birth between mother and baby animals is important for the development and maintenance of maternal behavior. Because of the use of anesthetics and drugs on human mothers, little was known about their natural behavior with newborn babies. Common hospital practice was to show the baby to the mother right after birth, if she was conscious, then again at six to 12 hours, and then on a four-hour schedule for feeding. Studies of early and prolonged contact have shown some important effects on maternal behavior.

Naked infants (on heat panels) were presented to their mothers about five hours after delivery and photographs were taken at a rate of one per second [52]. As described on the first page of this chapter, a regular sequence of behavior was observed. The mother first poked and picked hesitantly at the baby's extremities with her fingertips. In four or five minutes, she caressed the trunk with her palms, showing mounting excitement. After several minutes, her activity slowed down and sometimes she went to sleep. Usually she positioned the baby directly in front of her face and looked into his eyes, often speaking to him. Several mothers said that after their babies had looked at them, they felt much closer to them.

Mothers who were given extended contact with their infants in hospital (16 hours more than the regular maternity patients) were compared with a control group in strength of attachment to their babies at one month [51]. Interviews showed that the extended-contact mothers were more likely to pick up their babies when they cried and less desirous of going out and leaving the baby. Observations revealed the extended-contact mothers as watching their babies more and as more likely to try to soothe the crying babies. The authors suggest that there may be a period soon after birth, perhaps even the first hour, when the mother is especially sensitive to her baby.

For first-time mothers, self-confidence in caring for premature infants bore a relation to being with the baby in the hospital, rather than being separated from him [86]. Experienced mothers, however, were equally self-confident in both conditions. Although this study does not deal with maternal attachment, it does strengthen the recommendations stemming from attachment studies that mothers and new babies should be with each other.

FEEDING

Normal lactation periods in mammals correspond to the period of rapid infant growth, when the major part of the growth of the nervous system takes place. Satisfactory nutrition ordinarily occurs with breast-feeding and with adequate bottle-feeding during this important period. A statement prepared by the Committee on International Nutrition Programs [25] says that ". . . severe general malnutrition during early postnatal life will affect brain structure and disrupt normal chemical development. . . . Myelination of the brain in the rat, pig and man is also significantly affected by severe early malnutrition. . . ."

Throughout the world, most infants are breast-fed for the first few months. Some continue to receive some breast milk for 2 or 3 years. In the very poor regions of the world, breast-feeding is closely related to survival and growth. Infants in the most economically deprived families who are totally breast-fed tend to grow quite well and resist disease, at least for 3 or 4 months [101]. Even when lactating mothers in poor countries live on relatively poor diets, their babies grow better while nursing than they do after weaning, as Figure 2–7 shows. These

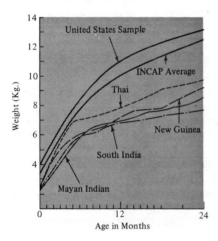

Figure 2-7. The weight curves of babies in four underdeveloped countries fall away from the average standard line just at the age when breast-feeding is stopped. In two of the countries represented here, breast-feeding is stopped around three months. In the other two, around six months is the termination date.

SOURCE: M. Behar. Prevalence of malnutrition among preschool children of developing countries. In N. S. Scrimshaw and J. E. Gordon (eds.). *Malnutrition, learning and behavior.* Cambridge: M. I. T. Press, 1968. Also from R. L. Jackson and H. G. Kelly. Growth charts for use in pediatrics practice. *Journal of Pediatrics,* 1945, **27**, 215–229.

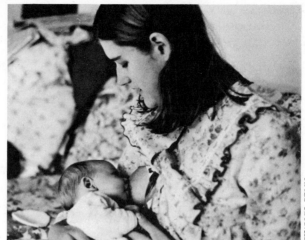

CHARLES BELIN

weight curves, comparing children with an international standard, show a situation that has been demonstrated on many impoverished populations. The baby grows almost normally for the first 3 to 6 months. Then the weight curve drops off throughout the preschool years. The beginning of the depression in the weight curve corresponds with the time when breast milk becomes insufficient, and the total food supply and supplementary foods are inadequate. Although breast-feeding is often prolonged into the second or third year, it does not provide enough food. Supplementary foods are usually unsuitable, insufficient, and late. Contamination from the unsanitary environment increases, immunity from the mother's milk decreases, and the baby becomes ill more and more often. Poor nutrition and disease interact with each other to depress growth [8].

In some socially advanced countries, such as Sweden, breast-feeding is the norm. In a longitudinal study of physical and mental development of 212 Swedish children, only three were not breast-fed. However the mothers of two of these children had tuberculosis and one infant could not suck [72]. The mothers who breast-fed for a longer than average time were older, better educated, and of higher social class. Almost all Chinese mothers breast-feed their babies [88, p. 62]. Donors often supply milk for the few Chinese babies whose mothers cannot do so [4].

Bottle-feeding is most commonly used in the United States, Canada, and other English-speaking countries. Among infants in a sample of lower-income families in New York City, only 17 per cent received any breast-feeding [64]. An English survey showed 28 per cent of infants receiving breast milk for their first food. In most cases, breast-feeding had stopped by one month [29]. Artificial infant feeding predominates in North America because of formulas that approximate human milk, highly developed sanitation, affluence, the reluctance of many women to breast-feed, and a high failure rate among those who have tried. However, when many young women prepare themselves for childbirth, they also learn of the physical and emotional benefits of breast-feeding to themselves and to their children. Information is available in books such as Gunther's *Infant Feeding* [43] and from La Leche League.

Physical Aspects of Breast- and Bottle-Feeding. Human milk, being biochemically different from cow's milk, makes for differences in body composition, physiological reactions, patterns of weight gain, and resistance to disease [6]. Formula-fed babies tend to gain more weight, because feedings are often prepared at too great a concentration [29]. The baby becomes thirsty and if given more formula, becomes dangerously overfed. Extra fat cells acquired in infancy can be the beginning of lifelong obesity [107]. At the same time, the kidneys may be stressed by an overload of materials that must be eliminated.

The fetus receives some immunological protection through the placenta. After birth, more immunological material is obtained from the mother's milk over the early months while the infant is gradually building up his own defenses. The immature gastrointestinal tract, as well as other bodily systems, is thus protected. Cow's milk offers no immunological defenses to the human infant. Babies who receive only breast milk for the first 6 months have the best protection [39].

In England, the Department of Health recommends breast-feeding for at least four to six months, or even two weeks rather than not at all. Breast milk, they say, is sufficient for normal growth. The introduction of solids is unnecessary and possibly harmful [29].

Some dentists maintain that breast-feeding promotes better jaw development than does bottle-feeding. The breast requires a complicated coordination of biting and sucking, whereas the bottle instigates simpler, relatively passive movements.

Although nutritionists generally agree on the superiority of human milk for human infants [46], bottle-feeding can be safe, satisfactory, and convenient. Indeed, it is all this in millions of homes. In all societies, there are some mothers who cannot breast-feed and in affluent societies, some who do not choose to do so. Most of their infants thrive on modified cow's milk, prepared according to a formula. A small proportion of infants have inborn errors of metabolism, which mean that they cannot tolerate certain elements in foods [85]. When screening tests reveal such a disorder, dietary therapy is begun promptly. Help can be had from established genetic centers in both the United States and Canada. A new food bank project in Canada delivers the necessary special foods immediately.

Psychological Aspects of Breast and Bottle. On a sensory level, breast and bottle are very different. From the viewpoint of the baby, the breast is warmer, more flexible, and more responsive and variable. The two milks taste different, and the composition of breast milk changes from the beginning to the end of the nursing period, thus giving some variation in taste. Being closer to his mother's skin, the breast-fed baby probably has more intense tactile and olfactory experiences. The pair are in a face-to-face position, where they look into each other's eyes. A very thorough discussion of the difference between breast- and bottle-feeding is available in an article by Newton [68].

From the mother's viewpoint, breast-feeding is vastly more sensory, an enjoyable experience to some and not to others. Some women choose bottle-feeding because they do not want to be so closely tied to the baby. Many think of bottle-feeding as normal because it is the dominant mode in their culture. A woman's attitudes toward infant feeding are influenced by her feelings about the whole cycle of reproduction and by the ways in which breast-feeding is regarded in her culture and in her family. Possibly because the breast is a powerful sex symbol in their culture, North Americans often feel embarrassment, jealousy, and fear over breast-feeding. These negative emotions inhibit the milk-ejection reflex (let-down mechanism) and spell failure for many would-be nursing mothers.

A movement to promote breast-feeding, headed by La Leche League, has met with some success, especially among families in the upper socioeconomic levels. The majority of North American women, however, feed their babies by bottle. Nutritionists have devised formulas that come close to replicating human milk. Sanitary techniques make infections unlikely. Mothers, fathers, and other caregivers can replicate the natural position by cuddling baby face-to-face while giving the bottle. In breast-feeding, the infant determines how much he will take. With a bottle, the caregiver can see how much remains and is often tempted to urge him to finish or to take just a few more sucks. Such tactics may produce an overweight baby who does not know when he has had enough. Therefore, the caregiver would do well to resist such temptations.

Personality Development through Feeding. The newborn infant does not get many opportunities for controlling her own experiences, but she does know how to eat! She can cry, root, purse her lips, grasp, suck, and swallow. If a breast or

This caregiver is holding the baby in a position that permits the two people to look at each other. Warm personal contact makes bottle feeding more nearly like breast feeding than does a mechanical arrangement.

MARGARET HAMILTON

bottle is offered at the right point in this sequence, the baby has the experience of feeling hungry and doing something that results in feeling full. Through her own powers and efforts, she moves from distress to comfort. A series of such experiences builds toward a sense of trust, an expectation that she can count on her world and herself to bring comfort, to work out well.

The seeds of the sense of autonomy are also in the feeding situation. A conviction of her own individuality and executive power comes from repeated experiences of hunger, finding food, eating as much as she wants, and stopping when she feels like stopping.

Parents and other caregivers develop the sense of generativity through satisfying experiences in feeding the baby. The mother is genetically endowed with the means of cooperating with the baby, both physically and psychologically. With bottle-feeding, however, fathers, grandparents, older children, in fact, anyone who cares, can enjoy personality growth through nurturing an immature being.

HOLDING, CARRYING, CHANGING POSITION

As sections on state behavior and soothing have shown, the caregiver's ways of handling the baby can do much to diminish crying and fussing and to put him to sleep or bring him into a state of quiet alertness. By holding him upright against her warm body, with his eyes able to look, and by talking or singing and rocking, walking or jiggling, she supplies a multitude of stimuli that apparently feel good: warmth, visual stimulation, vestibular stimulation, sound, rhythm, and muscular stimulation. Probably some of the sound and rhythm from her heartbeat and breathing contribute stimuli to the baby's muscles, internal organs, and ears. It feels good to the caregiver, too, not only the satisfaction of soothing and alerting the baby but the cuddliness of his body, his soft skin, clutching fingers, and throaty noises. Mutual regard of eyes and faces is also satisfying.

When a newborn is placed in a crib, he can do little to change his position. As already mentioned, he seems to feel more comfortable prone than supine. Sometimes a change of position will soothe him, as when his caregiver moves him from a prone position to one side or the other.

Although only a mother can breast-feed a baby, anyone can hold, cuddle, and position him. Touching is communication. By being the other person in a touch relationship, the baby affects all who care for him, beginning to build relationships with his father, siblings, grandparents, and others. The resulting tender feelings in children and adults are energizers and growth-promoters.

In most, but not all, non-Western cultures, babies are frequently held close to their mothers and often sleep with them at night. Westerners tend to leave the baby in his crib or playpen unless he indicates a need for care. Each culture has its own way of handling infants and supports it with theories about what is good for them. Some babies are strapped to cradleboards, others swing in hammocks, some are kept vertical, others horizontal. These different methods of handling produce different kinds and degrees of stimulation in the infants. Presumably, different kinds of development would occur in different cultures, and they do. Life and culture are too complex, however, to show a one-to-one relationship between any kind of infant care and a "piece" of adult behavior.

BATHING AND DRESSING

The film *Four Families** shows the activities involved in the physical care of babies in four different cultures. Although the babies are older than newborns, the point is still valid that many different experiences can go under the name of "bath," and that many of those experiences symbolize a cultural attitude toward children. We (the authors) would like to report a personal cross-cultural experience that highlighted for us the different sets of sensations possible in North American and Indian bathing. Laura, our 10-year-old, having fallen in love with the nightwatchman's baby, reported that Umersingh didn't like the way his mother bathed him because he always cried and kicked hard when she put him upside down on her legs, splashed water over him, and rubbed him with her hand. Laura brought Umersingh home for baths in our washbasin, where he never cried, and moved his legs in the most gentle, relaxed way. "Ummy prefers American baths," she concluded. The uniformly warm temperature of our washbasin, in contrast to splashed water that cooled quickly, was probably one point in our favor. Also, having his whole body submerged must have been a more satisfying tactual stimulus than merely being wet. The buoying quality of the water, too, would give muscular stimulation. Our bath was more prolonged, with much sudsy washing, which must have felt smooth, slippery, and soothing. Even so, Umersingh might have preferred the Japanese bath shown in *Four Families* if he could have compared it with American bathing. The Japanese grandmother took the baby into the bath with her, thereby adding all the tactual delights of (and to) her own skin.

Dressing symbolizes and defines attitudes toward the skin and toward activity. The kind and the amount of stimulation and activity possible depend to a large extent on how the baby is clothed. Exposed to the same conditions, a swaddled

* National Film Board of Canada.

An American mother and baby enjoy a bath together. In this family, a social bath is termed "Swedish."

HALVAR LOKEN

baby will not get as much stimulation as a naked baby. Swaddling has been shown to promote calmness and drowsiness, but partial swaddling produces excitement, crying, and activity that looks like outrage [109]. When the surrounding temperature is not ideal, tension reduction is achieved by adding or subtracting clothing and coverings in such a way that the infant's temperature is regulated most comfortably.

Other kinds of physical care can be pleasurably stimulating, such as massage and hair brushing, or of doubtful outcome, such as putting black around the eyes and swabbing the nose. Insofar as the baby's actions initiate care that brings tension reduction, his sense of trust probably increases.

FAMILY-CENTERED HOSPITAL CARE

Psychological health, as well as physical health, is promoted by many modern hospitals. Prenatal care includes education and preparation for childbirth for both parents and preparation for breast-feeding. Fathers are encouraged to participate in childbirth and in caring for the newborn baby. Older siblings are recognized as belonging to the family.

Under the rooming-in plan, mothers and babies are together or within easy access. The baby spends much of the time in a bassinet beside her bed or in a container that can be swung over the bed. Nurses are available to help and teach the mother as she learns to take care of the baby and gets acquainted with him. Experienced nurses can interpret newborns' signals more accurately than first-time mothers [100]. With their skill in feeding, and understanding of young babies, nurses can be tremendously helpful teachers to new mothers, who must learn a great deal in a short time. A nurse takes care of the baby when the mother wants to rest. Fathers, washed and gowned, also hold babies and may learn to give care. Older siblings may visit and perhaps hold the baby. Thus, the family is together and can begin to reorganize to include the new member.

An infant can regulate the timing of his feeding when rooming in, whereas under the old regime of the central nursery, a four-hour schedule may be applied to all babies, whether it suits them or not. Not only does self-regulation help the infant to develop competencies, but it may also be an advantage in establishing the mother's milk flow. Crying has been found to stimulate a let-down reflex in the breasts of the lactating mother who is relaxed [68]. The breasts then feel heavy and ready for suckling, giving her an urge to feed the baby. The mother is likely to receive interested, informed instruction from a nurse who is skilled at helping newborn babies and their mothers to cooperate in breast-feeding. With such assistance, the baby is likely to grasp the nipple in such a way that it will stimulate an adequate sucking reflex and he will avoid the pitfall of getting his nose blocked by his lip. The mother has an excellent chance to feel and be successful from the beginning. A good beginning with breast-feeding can make all the difference between success and failure.

This new, modern family-centered care in North America is neither new nor modern in many other parts of the world, where babies and mothers have always been together. Fifteen years ago, when most North American hospitals maintained strict four-hour schedules, we visited hospitals in India. Bassinets were attached to the beds of mothers in the wards. The mothers handled their babies freely. In a private room, a mother lay surrounded by her whole family while the baby lay on the lap of a nursemaid who sat on the floor. The father was sitting on a chair beside his wife. Her mother, on a sofa, was folding diapers. The brother and sister played on the floor and held the baby when they wished to do so. The warm, informal atmosphere contrasted sharply with what was then the typical scene in North America, where advances in the biological sciences had sterilized the hospitals, physically and psychologically. At present, gains are being made in both areas.

Summary

The new baby is greeted by his mother and assessed by professionals. The head end is large and better developed than the lower body. Birth weight is related to ethnic origin, to the mother's weight, and to prenatal conditions, especially nutrition. Immediate adaptation to extrauterine life includes changes in respiration, circulation, and digestion. Maintenance of body temperature is precarious. The brain is in a stage of rapid growth.

Behavior is organized into states that differ in respect to ongoing behavior, responses to stimuli, and physiological correlates. Individuals, sexes, and ethnic groups show differences in state behavior. Crying behavior gives information about the condition of the central nervous system. When crying, young infants are soothed by various kinds of continuous stimulation, including sucking, swaddling, white noise, light, and rocking. As infants mature, they change sleep patterns in the directions of longer sleep periods, as well as longer waking periods. Quiet sleep increases, but active (REM) sleep continues throughout life.

Motor behavior includes many reflexes, well-integrated behavior patterns, many of which are of obvious usefulness. They include postural and feeding reflexes. Sucking, a reflex, is coordinated with looking. Sucking also acts as a soother. A unitary reach-grasp pattern is coordinated with vision.

Infants' perceptual behavior is explored by observing the orienting reflex, monitoring heart rate and electrodermal changes, by noting what is reflected in his eyes, and by analyzing changes in sucking. Tactile and vestibular senses are well developed at birth and constitute avenues for communication with infants. Prenatal experience probably influences the salience of postnatal stimulation. Not only do newborns discriminate tastes, but they give evidence of lingering over pleasant ones. Responses to odors and pain have also been observed. Temperature changes affect muscular activity. Newborns make fine discriminations in sounds and among categories of sounds, especially those basic to speech. In spite of considerable immaturity in the visual system, the newborn infant looks longer at certain stimuli than at others, contour, or change between light and dark being the salient property. Vision and hearing seem coordinated, possibly as one aspect of a primitive unity of the senses.

Learning is demonstrated in habituation experiments. Young infants have been classically conditioned and operantly conditioned.

An individual infant is different from all others, since his combination of characteristics is unique. Important individual differences include appearance and state behavior, both of which have significance for relating to family and care-takers. Sex differences occur but they are not great. Cultural and genetic group differences have also been established.

Caring for infants involves a mutual regulation between mother (caregiver) and infant, and contributes to personality development of both members of the partnership. New mothers, having much to learn about their infants and about caretaking skills, need guided experiences. Quality of nutrition is important in the infant's growth, development, and health. Human milk is more adequate in meeting all these requirements than is cow's milk. Breast-feeding also offers psychological advantages to mother and infant, but cultural obstacles have resulted in bottle-feeding for the majority of North American infants. Caregiving also includes attention to the position of the baby, as well as bathing and dressing. Family-centered hospital care can help a family to reorganize optimally so as to integrate a new baby into itself.

References

1. Apgar, V. Perinatal problems and the central nervous system. In U.S. Dept. of Health, Education, and Welfare. Children's Bureau, *The child with central nervous system deficit*. Washington, D.C.: U.S. Government Printing Office, 1965.
2. Appel, M. A. Binocular parallax in the eight-week-old infant. Paper presented at meetings of the Society for Research in Child Development, Philadelphia, 1973.
3. Appel, M. A., J. J. Campos, S. Z. Silverman, and E. Conway. Electrodermal responding of the human infant. Paper presented at meetings of the Society for Research in Child Development, Minneapolis, 1971.
4. Arena, J. M. China's children. *Nutrition Today*, 1974, **9**:5, 20–25.
5. Aronson, E. and S. Rosenbloom. Space perception in early infancy: Perception within a common auditory-visual space. *Science*, 1971, **172**, 1161–1163.
6. Bakwin, H. Current feeding practices for infants. *Nutrition News*, 1965, **28**:3.
7. Ball, W., and E. Tronick. Infant responses to impending collision: Optical and real. *Science*, 1971, **171**, 818–820.
8. Behar, M. Prevalence of malnutrition among preschool children of developing countries. In N. S. Scrimshaw and J. E. Gordon (eds.). *Malnutrition, learning and behavior*. Cambridge, Mass.: M.I.T. Press, 1967, pp. 30–41.
9. Bell, S. M., and M. D. S. Ainsworth. Infant crying and maternal responsiveness. *Child Development*, 1972, **43**, 1171–1190.
10. Berg, W. K., C. D. Adkinson, and B. D. Strock. Duration and periods of alertness in neonates. *Developmental Psychology*, 1973, **9**, 434.
11. Birns, B. Individual differences in human neonates' responses to stimulation. *Child Development*, 1965, **36**, 249–259.
12. Bower, T. G. R. *Development in infancy*. San Francisco: W. H. Freeman and Co. Publishers, 1974.
13. Brackbill, Y. Neonatal posture: Psychophysical effects. *Neuropädiatrie*, 1973, **4**, 145–150.
14. Brackbill, Y. Continuous stimulation reduces arousal level: Stability of effect over time. *Child Development*, 1973, **44**, 43–46.
15. Brackbill, Y., G. Adams, D. H. Crowell, and M. L. Gray. Arousal level in neonates and older infants under continuous auditory stimulation. *Journal of Experimental Child Psychology*, 1966, **4**, 178–188.

16. Brazelton, T. B. Effect of maternal expectations on early infant behavior. *Early Child Development and Care*, 1973, **2**, 259–273.
17. Brazelton, T. B. *Neonatal assessment scale*. Philadelphia: J. B. Lippincott Co., 1973.
18. Brazelton, T. B., J. S. Robey, and G. A. Collier. Infant development in the Zinacanteco Indians of Southern Mexico. *Pediatrics*, 1969, **44**, 274–293.
19. Bronson, G. The postnatal growth of visual capacity. *Child Development*, 1974, **45**, 873–890.
20. Bruner, J. S. *Beyond the information given*. New York: W. W. Norton & Company, Inc., 1973.
21. Burns, P., L. W. Sander, G. Stechler, and H. Julia. Distress in feeding; short-term effects of caretaker environment of the first 10 days. *Journal of the American Academy of Child Psychiatry*, 1972, **11**, 427–439.
22. Butterfield, E. C., and G. N. Siperstein. Influence of contingent auditory stimulation upon non-nutritional suckle. In J. F. Bosma (ed.). *Third symposium on oral sensation and perception: The mouth of the infant*. Springfield, Ill.: Charles C Thomas, Publisher, 1972.
23. Caron, A. J., and R. F. Caron. Infant perception of the structural properties of the face. *Developmental Psychology*, 1973, **9**, 385–399.
24. Clifton, R., E. R. Siqueland, and L. P. Lipsitt. Conditioned head-turning in human newborns as a function of conditioned response requirements and states of wakefulness. *Journal of Experimental Child Psychology*, 1972, **13**, 43–57.
25. Committee on International Nutrition Programs. The relationship of nutrition to brain development and behavior. *Nutrition Today*, 1974, **9**:4, 12–13.
26. Condon, W. S., and L. W. Sander. Synchrony demonstrated between movements of the neonate and adult speech. *Child Development*, 1974, **45**, 456–462.
27. Coursin, D. B. Nutrition and brain development in infants. *Merrill-Palmer Quarterly*, 1972, **18**, 177–202.
28. Culp, R. E. Effect of voice quality and content on the looking behavior of two-month-old infants. Paper presented at meetings of the American Psychological Association, New Orleans, 1974.
29. Department of Health and Social Security. *Report on health and social subjects. No. 9*. London: Her Majesty's Stationery Office, 1974.
30. Doris, J., E. Felzen, and R. Poresky. Brightness and visual acuity in neonates. Cornell University. (Mimeo, undated.)
31. Eimas, P. D., E. R. Siqueland, P. Jusczyk, and J. Vigorito. Speech perception in infants. *Science*, 1971, **171**, 303–306.
32. Eisenberg, R. B. The organization of auditory behavior. *Journal of Speech and Hearing Research*, 1970, **13**, 461–464.
33. Emde, R. N., R. J. Harmon, D. R. Metcalf, K. L. Koenig, and S. Wagonfeld. Stress and neonatal sleep. *Psychosomatic Medicine*, 1971, **33**, 491–497.
34. Erikson, E. H. *Childhood and society*. New York: W. W. Norton & Company, Inc., 1963.
35. Fitzgerald, H. E., and Y. Brackbill. Stimulus-response organization, state and conditionability during early infancy. Paper presented at meetings of The Society for Research in Child Development, Philadelphia, 1973.
36. Fitzgerald, H. E., and S. W. Porges. A decade of infant conditioning and learning research. *Merrill-Palmer Quarterly*, 1971, **17**, 79–117.
37. Freedman, D. G., and N. C. Freedman. Behavioral differences between Chinese-American and European-American newborns. *Nature*, 1961, **224**, 1227.

38. Geber, M., and R. F. A. Dean. The state of development of newborn African children. *Lancet,* 1957, **1,** 1216–1219.

39. Gerrard, J. W. Breast-feeding: Second thoughts. *Pediatrics,* 1974, **54,** 757–764.

40. Grantham-McGregor, S. M., and E. H. Black. Gross motor development in Jamaican infants. *Developmental Medicine and Child Neurology,* 1971, **13,** 79–87.

41. Gregg, C., R. Clifton, and M. Haith. Heart rate change as a function of visual stimulation in the newborn. Paper presented at meetings of the Society for Research in Child Development, Philadelphia, 1973.

42. Griet, J. B., S. A. Counter, and W. M. Shearer. Prenatal auditory imprinting in chickens. *Science,* 1966, **155,** 1692–1693.

43. Gunther, M. *Infant feeding.* Chicago: Henry Regnery Co., 1971.

44. Haynes, H., B. L. White, and R. Held. Visual accommodation in human infants. *Science,* 1965, **148,** 528–530.

45. Holt, L. E., Jr., E. A. Davies, E. G. Hasselmeyer, and A. O. Adams. A study of premature infants fed cold formulas. *Journal of Pediatrics,* 1962, **61,** 556–561.

45a. Hulsebus, R. C. Latency of crying cessation measuring infants' discimination of mothers' voices. Paper presented at meetings of the American Psychological Association, Chicago, 1975.

46. Jelliffe, D. B., and E. F. P. Jelliffe (eds.). Symposium on the uniqueness of human milk. *American Journal of Clinical Nutrition,* 1971, **24,** 968–1024.

47. Jusczyk, P. W., B. S. Rosner, J. E. Cutting, C. Foard, and L. Smith. Categorical perception of nonspeech sounds in the two-month-old infant. Paper presented at meetings of the Society for Research in Child Development, Denver, 1975.

48. Kaye, K. Milk pressure as a determinant of the burst-pause pattern in neonatal sucking. *Proceedings,* 80th Annual Convention of the American Psychological Association, 1972, 83–84.

49. Kearsley, R. B. The newborn's response to auditory stimulation: A demonstration of orienting and defensive behavior. *Child Development,* 1973, **44,** 582–590.

50. Kessen, W., P. Salapatek, and M. Haith. The visual responses of the human newborn to linear contour. *Journal of Experimental Child Psychology,* 1972, **13,** 9–20.

51. Klaus, M. H., R. Jerauld, N. C. Kreger, W. McAlpine, M. Steffa, and J. H. Kennell. Maternal attachment: Importance of the first post-partum days. *New England Journal of Medicine,* 1972, **286,** 460–463.

52. Klaus, M. H., B. S. Kennell, N. Plumb, and S. Zuehlke. Human maternal behavior at the first contact with her young. *Pediatrics,* 1970, **46,** 187–192.

53. Korner, A. F. State as a variable, as obstacle and as mediator of stimulation in infant research. *Merrill-Palmer Quarterly,* 1972, **18,** 74–94.

54. Korner, A. F. Sex differences in newborns with special reference to differences in the organization of oral behavior. *Journal of Child Psychology and Psychiatry,* 1973, **14,** 19–29.

55. Korner, A. F., and L. M. Beason. The association of two congenitally organized behavior patterns in the newborn: Hand-mouth coordination and looking. *Perceptual and Motor Skills,* 1972, **35,** 115–118.

56. Korner, A. F., B. Chuck, and S. Dontchos. Organismic determinants of spontaneous oral behavior in neonates. *Child Development,* 1968, **39,** 1145–1157.

57. Lester, B. M. Spectrum analysis of the cry sounds of well-nourished and malnourished infants. *Child Development,* 1976, **47,** 237–241.

58. Leventhal, A. S., and L. P. Lipsitt. Adaptation, pitch discrimination, and sound localization in the neonate. *Child Development,* 1964, **35,** 759–767.

59. Lipsitt, L. P. Infant sucking and heart rate: Getting excited over savory sub-

stances. Paper presented at meetings of the Society for Research in Child Development, Denver, 1975.

60. Lipsitt, L. P., and H. Kaye. Conditioned sucking in the human newborn. *Psychonomic Science,* 1964, **1,** 29–30.

61. Lipsitt, L. P., and N. Levy. Electrotactual threshold in the neonate. *Child Development,* 1959, **30,** 547–554.

62. Lipton, E. L., A. Steinschneider, and J. B. Richmond. Autonomic function in the neonate. VII: Maturational changes in cardiac control. *Child Development,* 1966, **37,** 1–16.

63. Maller, O., and J. A. Desor. Effect of taste on ingestion by human newborns. In J. Bosma (ed.). *Fourth symposium on oral sensation and perception: Development in the fetus and infant.* Washington, D.C.: U.S. Government Printing Office, 1974, pp. 279–291.

64. Maslansky, E., C. R. Cowell, R. Caral, S. N. Berman, and M. Grussi. Survey of infant feeding practices. *American Journal of Public Health,* 1974, **64,** 780–785.

65. McGurk, H., and M. Lewis. Space perception in early infancy: Perception within a common auditory-visual space? *Science,* 1974, **186,** 649–650.

66. Moss, H. A. Sex, age, and state as determinants of mother-infant interaction. *Merrill-Palmer Quarterly,* 1967, **13,** 19–36.

67. Moss, H. A., and K. S. Robson. The relation between the amount of time infants spend at various states and the development of visual behavior. *Child Development,* 1970, **41,** 509–517.

68. Newton, N. Psychologic differences between breast- and bottle-feeding. *American Journal of Clinical Nutrition,* 1971, **24,** 993–1004.

69. Ounsted, M. Fetal growth. In D. Gairdner and D. Hull (eds.). *Recent advances in pediatrics.* London: Churchill, 1971.

70. Parmelee, A. H., and E. S. Stern. Development of states in infants. In C. Clemente, D. Purpura, and F. Mayer (eds.). *Sleep in the maturing nervous system.* New York: Academic Press, Inc., 1972.

71. Pederson, R., and D. Ter Vrugt. The influence of amplitude and frequency of vestibular stimulation on the activity of two-month-old infants. *Child Development,* 1973, **44,** 122–128.

72. Playfair, M. Child development in a Swedish town. *Developmental Medicine and Child Neurology,* 1969, **11,** 801–802.

73. Porges, S. W. Heart rate indices of newborn attentional responsivity. *Merrill-Palmer Quarterly,* 1974, **20,** 231–254.

74. Pratt, K. C., A. K. Nelson, and K. H. Sun. *The behavior of the newborn infant.* Ohio State University Studies, Contributions to Psychology, No. 10, 1930.

75. Rewey, H. H. Developmental change in infant heart rate response during sleeping and waking states. *Developmental Psychology,* 1973, **8,** 35–41.

76. Richmond, J., and E. L. Lipton. Some aspects of the neurophysiology of the newborn and their implications for child development. In L. Jessner and E. Pavenstedt (eds.). *Dynamic psychopathology in childhood.* New York: Grune & Stratton, Inc., 1959.

77. Roberts, B., and D. Campbell. Activity in newborns and the sound of a human heart. *Psychonomic Science,* 1967, **9,** 339–340.

78. Roffwarg, H. P., J. N. Muzio, and W. C. Dement. Ontogenetic development of the human sleep-dream cycle. *Science,* 1966, **152,** 604–617.

79. Rosenblith, J. K. Manual for behavioral examination of the neonate. Workshop conducted at meetings of the American Psychological Association, Montreal, 1973.

80. Salapatek, P. Visual investigation of geometric pattern by the human infant.

Paper presented at meetings of the Society for Research in Child Development, Philadelphia, 1973.

81. Salk, L. Mother's heartbeat as an imprinting stimulus. *Transactions of the New York Academy of Science,* Serial II, 1962, **24,** 753–763.

82. Sameroff, A. J., T. F. Cashmore, and A. C. Kykes. Heart rate deceleration during visual fixation in human newborns. *Developmental Psychology,* 1974, **8,** 117–119.

83. Schaller, M. J. Chromatic vision in human infants: Conditioned operant fixation to 'hues' of varying intensity. *Bulletin of the Psychonomic Society,* 1975 (in press).

84. Schmidt, K. The effect of continuous stimulation on the behavioral sleep of infants. *Merrill-Palmer Quarterly,* 1975, **21,** 77–88.

85. Scriver, C. R. Inborn errors of metabolism. *Nutrition Today,* 1974, **9:5,** 4–13.

86. Seashore, M. J., A. D. Leifer, C. R. Barnett, and P. H. Leiderman. The effects of denial of early mother-infant interaction on maternal self-confidence. *Journal of Personality and Social Psychology,* 1973, **26,** 369–378.

87. Self, P. A., F. D. Horowitz, and L. Y. Paden. Olfaction in newborn infants. *Developmental Psychology,* 1972, **7,** 349–363.

88. Sidel, R. *Women and child care in China.* Baltimore: Penguin Books, 1973.

89. Simner, M. L. Newborn's response to the cry of another infant. *Developmental Psychology,* 1971, **5,** 136–150.

90. Simner, M. L. Seasonal variation in reflexive and spontaneous crying in newborns. Paper presented at meetings of the Society for Research in Child Development, Minneapolis, 1971.

91. Siqueland, E. R. Reinforcement patterns and extinction in human newborns. *Journal of Experimental Child Psychology,* 1968, **6,** 431–442.

92. Smith, C. A. *The physiology of the newborn infant.* Springfield, Ill.: Charles C Thomas, Publisher, 1959.

93. Spears, W. C., and R. H. Hohle. Sensory and perceptual processes in infants. In Y. Brackbill (ed.). *Infancy and early childhood.* New York: The Free Press, 1967, pp. 49–121.

94. Spitz, R. A., R. N. Emde, and D. R. Metcalf. Further prototype of ego formation: a working paper from a research project on early development. In L. J. Stone, H. T. Smith and L. B. Murphy (eds.). *The competent infant.* New York: Basic Books, Inc., 1973, pp. 558–566.

95. Spock, B. *Baby and child care.* New York: Pocket Books, 1968.

96. Steinschneider, A., E. L. Lipton, and B. Richmond. Auditory sensitivity in the infant: Effect of intensity on cardiac and motor activity. *Child Development,* 1966, **37,** 233–252.

97. Tanner, J. M. The regulation of human growth. *Child Development,* 1963, **34,** 828–830.

98. Tarlo, P. A., I. Valimaki, and P. M. Rautaharju. Quantitative computer analysis of cardiac and respiratory activity in newborn infants. *Journal of Applied Physiology,* 1971, **31,** 70–74.

99. Tennes, K., and D. Carter. Plasma cortisol levels and behavioral states in early infancy. *Psychosomatic Medicine,* 1973, **35:2,** 121–128.

100. Thoman, E. B. Some consequences of early infant-mother interaction. *Early Child Development and Care,* 1974, **3,** 249–261.

101. Thomson, A. M. Historical perspectives of nutrition, reproduction and growth. In N. S. Scrimshaw and J. E. Gordon (eds.). *Malnutrition, learning and behavior.* Cambridge, Mass.: M.I.T. Press, 1968, pp. 17–28.

102. Turkewitz, G., H. G. Birch, and K. K. Cooper. Patterns of response to different

auditory stimuli in the human newborn. *Developmental Medicine and Child Neurology,* 1972, **14,** 487–491.

103. Vallbona, C. et al. Cardiodynamic studies in the newborn II. Regulation of heart rate. *Biologia Neonatorum,* 1963, **5,** 159–199.

104. Warren, N., and J. M. Parkin. A neurological and behavioral comparison of African and European newborns in Uganda. *Child Development,* 1974, **45,** 966–971.

105. Weiffenbach, J. M., and B. T. Thach. Taste receptors on the tongue of the newborn human: Behavioral evidence. Paper presented at meetings of the Society for Research in Child Development, Denver, 1975.

106. White, B. L. *Human infants: Experience and psychological development.* Englewood Cliffs, N.J.: Prentice-Hall, Inc., 1971.

107. Winick, M. Childhood obesity. *Nutrition Today,* 1974, **9,** 6–12.

108. Wolff, P. H. Observations on newborn infants. *Psychosomatic Medicine,* 1959, **21,** 110–118.

109. Wolff, P. H. The development of attention in young infants. *Annals of the New York Academy of Science,* 1965, **118,** 815–830.

110. Wolff, P. H. The causes, controls and organization of behavior in the neonate. *Psychological Issues,* 1966, **5:**1.

111. Wolff, P. H., and M. A. Simmons. Nonnutritive sucking and response thresholds in young infants. *Child Development,* 1967, **38,** 631–638.

112. Yonas, A. The development of spatial reference systems in the perception of shading information for depth. Paper presented at meetings of the Society for Research in Child Development, Philadelphia, 1973.

Readings in
Early Infancy

The following articles deal with the competencies of the newborn and very young infant, and the environments in which infants are able to put their competencies to use. Among the most fascinating topics in the field of child development are the recent discoveries of what infants can do in the way of perception, motor behavior, self-regulation, and relating to caregivers. Behavior immediately after birth may set the tone of the first affectional interactions.

Mothers, as well as infants, have resources for interacting very soon after delivery. John H. Kennell and his associates have studied spontaneous behavior of mothers in the first minutes and hours after birth. A follow-up study of mother-infant interaction indicates some lasting effects of these initial contacts.

In the course of mutual regulation of mother and infant, each responds to signals or cues given by the other. Results of research by Padraic Burns, Louis W. Sander, Gerald Stechler, and Harry Julia show that the distress signals of infants are related to the type of care given and to the constancy of the caretaker environment. In a responsive environment, the ability to signal distress is the infant's means of changing the environment.

Lewis P. Lipsitt is justly famous for his elegant experiments with infants, and for his precision and creativity in designing and carrying out research. In the following article, Lipsitt's description of apparatus and procedure serves as an example and explanation of the remarkable ways in which scientists explore response capabilities and the interrelationships between response characteristics.

Maternal Behavior One Year After Early and Extended Post-Partum Contact

John H. Kennell, Richard Jerauld, Harriet Wolfe, David Chesler, Nancy C. Kreger, Willie McAlpine, Meredith Steffa, and Marshall H. Klaus

CASE WESTERN RESERVE UNIVERSITY

INTRODUCTION

In the past decade, extensive observations in animals and a small number of careful studies in the human mother have suggested that the prevailing hospital policies which separate pre-term sick, and even full-term infants from their mothers may change a mother's attachment to her infant, resulting in an alteration of behavior toward her baby months or years after the birth (Leifer et al. 1969, Barnett et al. 1970, Klaus and Kennell 1970). After the long period of separation, usually associated with the care of the preterm or high-risk infant, there has been an increased incidence of mothering disorders which may counteract the beneficial effects of improved hospital care (Klaus and Kennell 1970). There is a disproportionately high incidence of pre-term births, ranging from 21 to 41 per cent, in studies of infants who fail to thrive in the absence of organic disease (Ambuel and Harris 1963, Shaheen et al. 1968). In reports in which the birth history has been recorded, the association of child abuse with either pre-term birth or serious illness, with mother-infant separation in the newborn period, varies from 24 to 39 percent (Elmer and Gregg 1967, Klein and Stern 1971). Since an infant's mental and emotional development is dependent upon his mother's behavior and care, the influence of separation on the mother and infant may be vital.

In certain animals, such as cattle and sheep, immediate separation of the mother and infant after birth for brief periods (one to two hours) may lead to clearly unusual mothering behavior; the mother may neglect her young, butt her own offspring away, or indiscriminately feed her own and other infants (Collias 1956, Hersher et al. 1958). In contrast, if mother and infant animal remain together for the first four days and are separated on the fifth day for the same period of time, the mother quickly resumes the characteristic mothering behavior of her species when she and her young are reunited. Klopfer and coworkers (1964) have shown that goats establish stable and specific mother-infant bonds in the first five minutes after birth. If the kid is in contact with the mother during this short period it will be recognised, accepted, fed, and protected. But if the kid is removed during the initial five-minute period and returned to the mother later, she will often reject it by butting and kicking, and will refuse to nurture or protect it. Thus there is a special attachment period immediately after delivery in some species of animals, and deviant

From *Developmental Medicine and Child Neurology*, 1974, **16**:2, 172–179. Reprinted by permission of Spastics International Medical Publications.

99

behavior may result if the animal mother is separated from her young during this period.

PRESENT STUDY   To test the hypothesis of a special attachment period existing in the human mother, two groups of primiparous mothers were studied. The control group comprised those who had the contact with their babies that is routine in American hospitals (a glance at their baby shortly after birth, a short visit at six to 12 hours after birth for identification purposes, and then 20- to 30-minute visits for feeding every four hours during the day). The extended-contact group consisted of mothers who, in addition to the contact mentioned above, were given their naked babies in bed with a heat panel for a period of one hour within the first three hours after birth and were allowed five extra hours with their babies for each of the first three days—a total of 16 hours more than the control group.

This report describes the differences in maternal behavior at one month and one year in these two groups of mothers, and presents observations which suggest that there may be a period shortly after birth which is of unique importance for mother-to-infant attachment in humans.

MATERIALS AND METHODS

There were 14 mothers in each group. Assignment to the groups depended on the day of delivery. Only mothers who were going to bottle-feed their babies were admitted to the study. The two groups were nearly identical with respect to mean age, social, economic and marital status, color, pre-medication, and days spent in hospital (Table 1). Mean birthweights were similar for both groups of infants.

In order to exclude any influence which might confuse the results, the nurses caring for the mothers adjusted their total daily time spent with them so that it was the same for both groups.

TABLE 1

Clinical Data of Mothers in the Two Groups

	EXTENDED-CONTACT GROUP ($N = 14$)	CONTROL GROUP ($N = 14$)
Black	13	13
White	1	1
Married	4	5
Mean age (years)	18.2	18.6
Days in hospital	3.8	3.7
Nursing time (minutes per day)	13	14
Mean birthweight of babies	3184g	3074g
Male/female infants	6/8	8/6

The first interview with the mothers was conducted 28 to 32 days following delivery and focused on the general well-being of the babies (such as the number of stools passed daily). Two questions about caretaking were scored by independent raters: 0, 1, 2, or 3. (The scores assigned for behavior were chosen arbitrarily to determine whether there were differences between the two groups, not to decide which was "best.")

The first question was: "When the baby has been fed and his diaper is dry and he still cries, what do you do?" Scores were given as follows: 0—mother always let the baby cry it out; 1—mother tended to let the baby cry it out; 2—mother tended to pick up the baby; 3—mother always picked up the baby. The second question was: "Have you been out since your baby was born? How did you feel." The scores were: 0—felt "good" while out; 1—thought about infant while out; 2—worried about infant while out; 3—didn't want to leave infant.

A second measure of maternal behavior was provided during a standardized examination of the infants in the presence of their mothers. Scores were given as follows: 0—mother remained seated and detached during the examination; 1—mother remained seated but watched; 2—mother sometimes stood and watched; 3—mother continuously stood and watched her baby during the examination. When the babies cried, maternal behavior was observed and scores given as: 0—ignored infant; 1—rarely soothed infant; 2—sometimes soothed infant; 3—always soothed infant.

Maternal behavior was also studied by the use of time-lapse films of the mother feeding their infants. All were aware that they were being photographed and they had an unlimited amount of time in which to complete the feeding. The actual filming was performed through a one-way mirror and took 15 minutes, at a speed of 60 frames per minute. The reactions of mothers and babies were then analyzed at one-second intervals. Analysers who did not know to which group the mothers belonged scored each of the first 600 frames for twenty-five specific activities, which varied from caretaking skills (e.g. position of the bottle) to measurements of the mothers' affection and interest (whether the mother's body was touching the infant's, whether she fondled her infant, and the amount of "en face"). "En face" is defined as the position of the mother's face held so that her eyes and those of her infant meet fully in the same vertical plane of rotation. Fondling refers to a spontaneous active interaction, not associated with feeding, initiated by the mother—such as stroking, kissing, bouncing and cuddling.

On finding apparent differences in the maternal behavior of the two groups at one month, we decided to follow-up the mother-infant pairs at one year in order to see whether the differences persisted. At the one-year examination, the mothers were observed by investigators who were not familar with the mothers in the study and none had had contact with the mothers during the 11-month interim.

These observers carefully monitored mother-infant interaction and the movements of the baby through a two-way mirror in seven separate situations: (1) an interview; (2) a physical examination of the infant, with weighing and hematocrit determination; (3) a separation of mother and infant, with the mother going behind a door, then re-entering for a reunion; (4) a picture-taking of the mother and infant; (5) free play; (6) a Bayley developmental testing of the infant; and (7) a filmed feeding of the infant. Verbal utterances were recorded on audiotape. Behavior was recorded by three methods, each of which permitted quantitative and continuous timed observations: (*a*) an analysis of a time-lapse film; (*b*) a direct check-list; and (*c*) a continuous-recording technique using a typewriter.

The standardized interview began with a question about how things were going. The mothers were then asked: "Have you worked or gone to school since the birth of your baby?" 13 mothers (six in the extended contact group, seven in the control group) answered "yes" and were then asked: "How did you feel?"

During the physical examination of the infants, an observer recorded, on a check-list, the location and activities of the mothers every 15 seconds. The mothers' reactions were recorded when their babies cried (for example, whether the mother struck the baby, criticized or scolded, ignored, or soothed her baby). Soothing was defined as three or more active attempts to comfort the baby within a 15-second period. Inter-observer reliability was calculated for individual behaviors. 70 per cent were greater than .85, and 91 per cent were greater than .80 (average = .84).

RESULTS

Analysis of the interview data at one month is shown in Table 2. The extended-contact group had scores of 2 or more, whereas mothers in the control group were at the lower end of the scale. (The chance of this occurrence is less than .05 with the use of the Mann-Whitney U test.)

Mothers in the extended-contact group more often picked up their babies when they cried, and tended to stay at home with their infants.

Observations during the physical examination of the babies revealed different scores for the two groups (Table 3). While no mother in the extended-contact group scored below 3, the scores of the control group ranged 1 to 6

TABLE 2

Maternal Scores from a Standardized Interview at One Month

	NUMBER OF MOTHERS	
MATERNAL SCORES	Control	Extended Contact
0	5	0
1	1	0
2	0	1
3	1	1
4	4	5
5	2	5
6	1	2
Total	14	14

SOURCE OF DATA: Klaus et al., 1972.

TABLE 3

*Scored Observations of the Mothers Made During the Physical
Examination of Their Infants at One Month*

	NUMBER OF MOTHERS	
SCORE	Control	Extended Contact
1	1	0
2	4	0
3	3	1
4	2	1
5	2	4
6	2	3
Total	14	14

SOURCE OF DATA: Klaus et al., 1972.

(p < .02). The mothers in the extended-contact group significantly more often stood beside the examination table and soothed their babies when they cried.

Fondling and "en face" scores for the two groups are shown in Table 4. Although the amount of time the mothers looked at their babies did not significantly differ in the two groups, the extended-contact mothers were observed to have spent significantly more time "en face" and fondling their infants (p < .05).

When their infants were one year of age, the mothers in the two groups also proved to be significantly different in their answers to an interview question and in their behavior during a physical examination of the infants. The scores on the interview questions showed that, of the mothers who had returned to work or school, the extended-contact mothers were more preoccupied with their babies than were the control mothers (Figure 1). Only one of the control mothers said that she missed her baby, while five of the six mothers in the extended-contact group said that they worried about or greatly missed their babies. Six of the seven mothers in the control group did not mention the baby at all, but responded with more self-focused answers, such as "I was happy to be back at work, but I was on my feet all day." This discriminating orientation of the mothers either to their infants or to themselves was similar to the responses observed at the one-month evaluation.

TABLE 4

*Filmed Feeding Analysis at One month, Showing Percentage
of "En Face" and Fondling Times in Mothers of Both Groups*

GROUP	"EN FACE"	FONDLING	TOTAL
Control	3.5	1.6	5.1
Extended Contact	11.6	6.1	17.7

SOURCE OF DATA: Klaus et al., 1972.

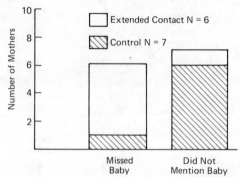

F I G U R E 1.   *Maternal scores from a standardized interview at one year.*

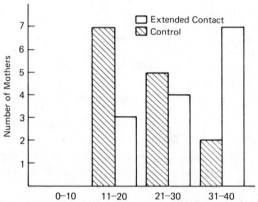

F I G U R E 2.   *Scored observations of the mothers made during the physical examination of their infants at one year. Number of 15-second time periods spent at table-side assisting the physician.*

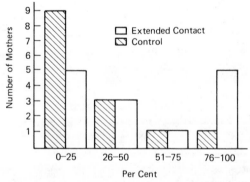

F I G U R E 3.   *Scored observations of the mothers made during the physical examination of their infants at one year. Number of 15-second time periods spent soothing their infants in response to crying.*

Figure 2 shows that, in the 10-minute observation period during the physical examination, seven of the 14 extended-contact mothers spent 31 to 40 of the total 15-second time periods at the tableside assisting the physician, while only two of the mothers in the control group did so (p < .05). Half of the control mothers spent only 11 to 20 of the 15-second time periods assisting.

The mothers' responses to infant crying are seen in Figure 3. Note that six of the extended-contact mothers soothed in response to crying more than 50 per cent of the time, compared with two mothers in the control group. The majority of the control mothers spent less than 25 percent of the time soothing. Over-all, the mothers in the extended-contact group spent more time soothing in response to crying and were more likely to kiss their babies (p = .05).

The mother infant interactions during the developmental examination, interview, picture-taking, and free-play situations showed no significant differences between the two groups. The mean scores of the two groups for the Bayley mean developmental index were 98 for infants of extended-contact mothers and 93 for control infants (p > .05). Observations of the mothers during the feeding and separation studies were confused by the differing motor development of the infants at one year of age and could not be compared.

DISCUSSION

In view of the large number of factors affecting maternal behavior (Klaus and Kennell 1970), such as the mothers' genetic and cultural backgrounds, their relations with their husbands and families, the planning and courses of their pregnancies, their own mothering as infants, and their experiences in their families—the significant differences at one year in response to an interview question for 13 of the mothers, and in maternal behavior during the physical examination for the entire group, were not anticipated. We were surprised at the consistency of the differences over a span of 11 months, and wondered if only a few mothers in one or both groups had accounted for this. However, the ranking of the mothers within each of the two groups showed no significant correlation for the measures at the one-month and one-year examinations (that is, a mother ranking high in a certain activity at one month might be low at one year).

The differences between the two groups that were still present at one month after over 200 feeds, and over the first year after countless other encounters between mother and infant, may have significant effects on the infants. The evidence that differences in maternal attentiveness and responsiveness to the babies' cries continued through the first year assumes additional significance when seen in the light of Rubenstein's (1967) observations that increased maternal attentiveness facilitates later exploratory behavior in infants. A human mother's interaction with her baby, and therefore that baby's ultimate development, may be greatly influenced by early and extended contact.

The only comparable study is that of Leifer et al. (1972) who demonstrated significant differences in attachment behavior between mothers of full-term infants and two groups of mothers of preterm infants at one month. When mothers who were separated from their pre-term babies for the first three to 12 weeks (except for visual contact) were compared with mothers of pre-term infants permitted early tactile contact (two to three days after birth), Leifer and co-workers found no differences in observed behavior at one month. But they did discover that there were more divorces (five compared with none) and more infants relinquished (two compared with none) in the group of mothers with the prolonged separation from their babies.

Even though the social and economic status of the mothers in our study is different from the mothers of the full-term infants in the Leifer study, it is interesting that the same categories of maternal behavior observed during feeding at one month were surprisingly similiar in both studies (*ventral contact*, 77.2 per cent in the Leifer study compared with 64.8 per cent in our extended-contact group and 71.7 in the control group; *mother looks only at her infant*, 75 per cent in Leifer's study compared with 79.5 per cent in our extended-contact group and 72.9 percent in the control mothers).

Leifer noted that a "confluence of factors not all equally influential at any one point in time or over time" are involved in eliciting and maintaining maternal attachment behavior. From our studies, an important factor affecting attachment appears to be the period of time the mother spends in close contact with her baby in the first hours and days of life.

This is a preliminary study, and what appear to be striking findings need to be replicated in a larger study, but those who care for mothers and infants should be aware of the possible long-term effects—both positive and negative—of the early post-partum period.

SUMMARY

The observations of maternal behavior in 28 human mothers of full-term infants reported in this study are consistent with investigations in animals; measurable differences, lasting for as long as one year, are apparent between mothers with early and extended contact and those separated from their infants in the early hours after birth. The awareness of a special attachment period shortly after birth—during which brief periods of partial or complete separation may drastically distort a mother animal's feeding and caring for her infant—would lead a caretaker or naturalist to be extemely cautious about any intervention in the period after birth.

In the human mother, the disproportionately high percentage of mothering disturbances, such as child abuse and deprivation failure-to-thrive, which occur after a mother has been separated from her sick newborn infant, force a thorough review and evaluation of our present perinatal practices.

Acknowledgements   This work is supported in part by the Grant Foundation and the Educational Foundation of America.

References

AMBUEL, J., HARRIS, B. (1963) "Failure to thrive: a study of failure to grow in height or weight." *Ohio Medical Journal*, 59, 997.

BARNETT, C., LEIDERMAN, P., GROBSTEIN, R., KLAUS, M. (1970) "Neonatal separation: the maternal side of interactional deprivation." *Pediatrics*, 45, 197.

COLLIAS, M. (1956) "The analysis of socialization in sheep and goats." *Ecology*, 37, 228.

ELMER, E., GREGG, G. (1967) "Developmental characteristics of abused children." *Pediatrics*, **40**, 596.

HERSHER, L., MOORE, A., RICHMOND, J. (1958) "Effect of post-partum separation of mother and kid on maternal care in the domestic goat." *Science*, **128**, 1342.

KLAUS, M., KENNELL, J. (1970) "Mothers separated from their newborn infants." *Pediatric Clinics of North America*, **17**, 1015.

—— PLUMB, N., ZUEHLKE, S. (1970) "Human maternal behavior at the first contact with her young." *Pediatrics*, **46**, 187.

—— JERAULD, R., KREGER, N., McALPINE, W., STEFFA, M., KENNELL, J. H. (1972) "Maternal attachment: importance of the first post-partum days." *New England Journal of Medicine*, **286**, 460.

KLEIN, M., STERN, L. (1971) "Low birthweight and the battered child syndrome." *American Journal of Diseases of Children*, **122**, 15.

KLOPFER, P. H., ADAMS, D., KLOPFER, M. (1964) "Maternal 'imprinting' in goats." *Proceedings of the National Academy of Science*, **52**, 911.

LEIFER, A. D., LEIDERMAN, P. H., BARNETT, C. R., WILLIAMS, J. A. (1972) "Effects of mother-infant separation on maternal attachment behavior." *Child Development*, **43**, 1203.

RUBENSTEIN, J. (1967) "Maternal attentiveness and subsequent exploratory behavior in the infant." *Child Development*, **38**, 1089.

SHAHEEN, E., ALEXANDER, D., TRUSKOWSKY, M., (1968) "Failure to thrive—a retrospective profile." *Clinical Pediatrics*, **7**, 255.

Distress in Feeding: Short-Term Effects of Caretaker Environment of the First 10 Days*

Padraic Burns, Louis W. Sander, Gerald Stechler, and Harry Julia

BOSTON UNIVERSITY AND FRAMINGHAM STATE COLLEGE

This report is part of an extensive investigation into infant-caretaker adaptation in the first 8 weeks of life. The study involved monitoring of a number of variables involving infants and caretakers, and was designed to investigate the development of regulatory processes in their interaction. The goal of this paper is to illustrate the effect of replacement of the primary caretaker at 11 days of life on a specific aspect of infant behavior, namely, "distress" or discomfort during feeding. This "distress" behavior is viewed as a communication in the interaction process by means of which the infant and caretaker reach a mutually satisfactory adapted state.

From the *Journal of the American Academy of Child Psychiatry*, 1972, **11**, 427–439. Reprinted by permission.

* This research has been supported by USPHS Grants Nos. K5–MH–20, 505, K–MH–18, 521, HDO1766, 1–4, RO3–MH–15, 803–01. Both Dr. Sander and Dr. Stechler are Research Scientists in the Research Development Program of the NIMH.

Acknowledgment is made to Boston Hospital for Women, Lying-In Division, for the extended use of their facilities, without which completion of the study would not have been possible. Acknowledgment is also made to the Booth Memorial Home, and the Crittenton Hastings House, and to their staffs, for their assistance in obtaining subjects. Special appreciation is expressed for the contributions of Davida Pekarsky, M.A., for her help in collecting and preparing these data.

In a previous longitudinal study of early mother-infant interaction, Sander (1962) outlines a sequence of adaptive issues to be negotiated during successive 2–4-month periods in the first year. These are related epigenetically so that the success of one determines to some extent the base on which the next will rest. Successful negotiation of the first issue is achieved when the infant by the age of 2½ months has established regularity in basic life processes such as eating and sleeping, which is coupled with evidence of comfort. This negotiation produces a corresponding feeling of satisfaction in the mother, who may then report that she has come to feel she now "knows" her baby, knows what he needs and how to satisfy him. The successful completion of an initial phase of adaptation readies the infant and mother for a next level of adaptation in the progressive development of social responsiveness and affective communication.

Of particular interest in this previous study was the finding (Pavenstedt and Sander, 1962) that, although there was considerable variation in the speed and success of the negotiation of the various issues, the successful negotiation of the initial adaptation was highly correlated with ratings of outcome of subsequent issues over the first 18 months of life. This observation suggested that the early organization of regulatory processes mediating between infant functions and caretaking activities may be of considerable significance for further development, and this suggested further and more precise investigation.

The conceptual model with which we approach this task includes the infant and primary caretaker (usually the mother) as components of a field or system interacting in an adaptive process, leading to an ever-developing synchronous organization of the field, within each and between the two main partners. A difficulty is generated by the fact that differences in central nervous systems and behavioral organizations are very great between the principals. They begin with a disparate organization and move toward coordination, on the basis of modifications in behavior of each, as their recurrent encounters become stabilized and predictable. For example, the child's sleeping rhythms and patterns only very gradually approximate those of the adult. Over the course of the first months we usually see the gradual development of longer sleep periods during the night and more awakening during the day, with the gradual establishment of a pattern that more or less fits that of the mother and the other family members. The young infant who tends to be wakeful and active at night and to sleep by day can disrupt the schedule of the mother and induce an uncomfortable sense of disorganization in her, or in the rest of the household, if she adapts to the baby. Certainly, asynchronization of interdependent life processes threatens to impose a strain on a family system.

We assume, therefore, that establishment of synchronization between intrinsic infant rhythms and stable regularities of the caretaking system (Sander et al., 1970) is the critical accomplishment of the earliest mother-infant interaction. The research problem is to determine the mechanisms on which synchronization depends. Work to date points to the possibility that the mechanisms may involve highly specific cues (Sander et al., 1970). For example, Wolff (1968) has shown that mothers respond differentially to (tape-recorded) cries of their infants, distinguishing a hungry cry or an exasperated cry from one resulting from a painful stimulus. They appear to differentiate the pain cry by the long rest period following the first long expiratory cry, indicating that "The temporal arrangement of vocalizations thus served an important signaling function even in the newborn period" (p. 5).

The cues used by infants and mothers to regulate interactional behavior have not been extensively studied, and are not well known. Cyclic functions of the infant, such as sleep-wake, hunger-elimination, are generated intrinsically and appear to be relatively independent in the newborn, and in early development become synchronized into regulated behavior. This suggests the need for studies of the specific relation of each major function of the infant to the infant-caretaker interaction. We need clues to specific control links which may regulate the subsystems. This paper will present some data as illustrative evidence bearing on this issue.

METHODS

DESIGN   The study sample consisted of 3 groups of 9 normal[1] infants each (Table 1). Two groups were composed of infants given up by their mothers for adoptive placement and cared for by surrogate mothers. Of these, infants in Group A spent the first 10 days in the newborn nursery being cared for by the usual nursery staff (multiple caretaking) on the usual fixed nursery schedule. These infants were then shifted to an individual rooming-in arrangement in a regular hospital room where each infant was cared for by a single caretaker on a demand schedule 24 hours a day for the next 18 days. At the end of the first 4 weeks, the infant was placed in a regular agency foster home and there followed for a second 4-week period.

The infants in Group B (also going to adoptive placement) went directly into rooming-in (usually 24 hours after delivery) where they had a first single caretaker from day 2 through day 10, and were shifted to a second caretaker

TABLE 1

Group	N	Caretaking Period I (0–10 days)		Caretaking Period II (11–28 days)	Caretaking Period III (29–56 days)
A	9	Nursery		Single Caretaker (X or Y) Rooming-in	Foster Home
B	9	Single Caretaker (X or Y) Rooming-in		Single Caretaker (Y or X) Rooming-in	Foster Home
		0–5 days	6–10 days		
C	9	Natural Mother Rooming-in	Natural Mother At home	Natural Mother At home	Natural Mother At home

[1] Normality was precisely defined and controlled by prenatal history, observation of delivery, and postnatal examination.

from day 11 through day 28. These infants were always on a demand schedule while cared for in the hospital. After the first 4 weeks they also went to foster homes, where we continued to observe them for a second 4 weeks.

Group C was composed of infants of experienced multiparous mothers. These infants were cared for by their own mothers, in rooming-in for 5 days, and then were followed at home for the remainder of the 8-week study period.

Groups A and B were designed to elicit differences in infants cared for *over the first 10 days* by multiple caretakers on a rigid schedule, or by single caretakers on demand schedule, with subsequent (day 11 onward) caretaking conditions being the same. Infant assignment to the 2 groups and to the 2 nurses who did most of the rooming-in surrogate mothering was unbiased. Group C provided a basis for comparison rather than a strict control group. Obviously, home rearing by a mother differs in many ways from hospital and foster home rearing. Group C was designed to provide normative data for the parameters measured, with which to understand the more closely monitored group A and B infant-caretaker pairs.

FEEDING OBSERVATIONS: "DISTRESS IN FEEDING"   During the 8-week period over which each infant was studied, extensive data were collected in areas such as sleep-awake, crying, motility, intervention, perception, and feeding (Sander, 1969; Sander et al., 1970). This paper is concerned with feeding observations, especially the behavior termed "distress in feeding." The findings are based on data from observations of more than 800 feedings of the 27 infants. In Groups A and B, one feeding was observed daily over the 4-week hospital period and twice a week for the foster home period. Group C infants were observed daily for the first 10 days, both in the hospital and at home, 3 times a week for the remainder of the first month, and twice a week thereafter. The single observer sat or stood 4 to 5 feet from the feeding infant, watching carefully and recording a number of variables, such as feeding time, nipple-in time, sucking time, state changes, time looking at caretaker, amount of milk taken, position change, stimulation, and distress, recorded mostly in real time on a portable 4-channel Rustrak recorder.[2] The material described in this paper covers only the small part of the feeding observation data related to distress variables; other of the feeding data have been presented elsewhere (Burns and Sander, 1967) or will be reported more fully in the future.

As we observed feedings, it became clear that some infant-caretaker interactions were smoother and better coordinated than others. This judgment was a complex one and the elements were hard to distinguish and define; the "distress" category served to document the grosser levels of infant disturbance. "Distress during feeding" was defined for this study to include grimacing, turning away from the nipple, spitting out the nipple, gagging, spitting up, fussing, and crying. Each such evidence of distress of disomfort was recorded by the observer, who made a discrimination and judgment as to the nature, quality, and intensity of the behavior. The milder forms of refusal or discomfort (including grimacing, turning away, spitting out the nipple, mild fussing) were

[2] Controlled reliability testing has indicated that the method was extremely reliable, with correlations (Pearson r) for 2 observing 20 feedings ranging from .68 to .99, with 7 out of 9 variables recorded being .9 or better. Correlation for the "distress" measure was .82.

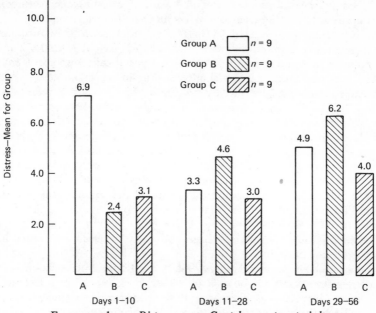

FIGURE 1.   *Distress scores: Caretaker groups x periods.*

given a score of 1 and the more intense (gagging, spitting up, crying) were scored as 2. A "distress" total score was then calculated for each separate feeding. These are the data considered here.

Crying or other distress during feeding is assumed to mean that some instability or incoordination exists in the feeding interaction. The caretaker uses such behavior on the part of the infant to regulate her own actions aimed at restoring him to greater comfort. There is considerable variation from infant to infant in the amount of distress shown. We assume that these variations are strongly influenced by individual differences in the makeup of the organism, as well as by external difference in the infants' environments. However, a distressed baby can usually be quieted by some appropriate comforting behavior by the caretaker. We have not yet been able to deal with the element of individual variation in feeding functions on the basis of initial measures. It is controlled here only by the nonbiased assignment of infants in the sample to the different groups and different caretakers.

FINDINGS

The "distress" measures for the three groups (A, B, C) for each of the 3 time periods (days 1–10, 11–28, 29–56) are shown in Figure 1. It can be seen that in the first time period (days 1–10), as might be expected, the infants in the newborn nursery (Group A), with multiple caretakers and a fixed 4-hour feeding schedule, showed considerably more "distress" events than did infants in rooming-in (Group B) or the Group C infants with their own mothers in the hospital and at home. Thus, it appeared that multiple caretakers and a fixed 4-hour feeding schedule were correlated with more evidence of discomfort and discoordination in the feeding process during the first 10 days.

In the second time period (days 11–28), the Group A infants, now in rooming-in, show a marked decrease in "distress" (t test, $p < .01$, 2 tailed), which appears to follow the shift from the less specifically responsive environment of the newborn nursery to a single rooming-in caretaker.

We were particularly struck by the finding that Group B infants shifted from low "distress" with their first rooming-in caretaker, to significantly higher "distress" with their second rooming-in caretaker (t test, $p < .02$, 2 tailed). Looking at Groups A and B alone in the first 2 time periods (first 4 weeks), an analysis of variance (two-way repeated measures) shows a significant difference between groups ($F = 4.68$, $p < .05$); no difference between time periods ($F = .38$), and a highly significant groups x periods interaction ($F = 11.95$, $p < .005$, df 1/16). This finding indicates that most of the variance is accounted for by the interaction, that is, related not primarily to the structure of the immediate situation (nursery vs. rooming-in), but to the sequence of environments. These findings are based on daily observations under highly uniform external conditions.

In the foster home period (days 29–56), with only 2 observations a week, the "distress" measures for both Groups A and B rose, Group B remaining higher than Group A. These increases are not statistically significant, probably because of both the greater variability in the environments of the foster homes and the relatively fewer observations.

Group C infants maintain a stable course through the 3 time periods with a slight, though not statistically significant rise in the second month, falling between Groups A and B in the first 10 days and slightly below them after day 11.

We were impressed by the increase in "distress" in the second period for Group B infants who had shifted from a first to a second caretaker. This suggested to us that in the first 10 days these infants had already established some organization, some degree of fittedness with the caretaker, in regulation of feeding function which led to distress, when violated by a new caretaker. In support of the idea that the increase is related to caretaker change, we noted that no such increase occurred at this time in Group C. We interpreted this finding as evidence that the degree of specificity of the caretaking environment in the first 10 days had affected the early organization of the infant so that those infants with early specific individual care were (or became) more sensitive to alterations in the caretaking environment.

We were able to pursue this hypothesis further with the same data because most of our sample babies had been cared for by 2 nurses who differed considerably in style of infant care. For Group A these 2 nurses cared for 7 of the 9 babies (over days 11–28), and for Group B cared for 7 of the 9 in days 2–10 (the first rooming-in period), and all 9 over days 11–28. These small groups of infants, although not adequate for statistical analysis, can be studied to see if different caretaking styles may influence "distress" patterns.

The differences in the caretaking styles of the 2 nurses were documented both by strongly agreed-upon clinical impressions and by quantitative difference registered in data on other areas of infant care (Sander, 1969; Sander et al., 1970).

Nurse Y appeared to give the more specifically infant-oriented care. She remained attentive to the infant's behavioral characteristics and insisted on giving priority to discovering individual differences and allowing them to guide her decisions about infant care. This included an ability to manifest her displeasure at interruptions or disruptions caused by the needs of the researchers to awaken or otherwise stimulate the infant in a way or at a time she felt was out of synchrony with the infant's needs.

Nurse X, on the other hand, was much more oriented toward the researcher and regular hospital staff, was very successful in making herself and all concerned comfortable, and even seemed to make the research task easier. At the same time it appeared clear that she did not see the infants so much as separate individuals and would say the same things about each baby.

When we now compare Group A infants with Group B infants first cared for in rooming-in by Nurse X and Nurse Y (Figure 2), it is clear that the infants first cared for by Nurse Y had the lowest "distress" in the first 10 days, followed by the greatest increase in the second period (when cared for by Nurse X), and again the greatest increase in the foster home. The infants first cared for by Nurse X show more "distress" in the first 10 days, but still less than those in the nursery. This score rises relatively less in the second period when they are cared for by Nurse Y, and then remains about the same in the foster home.

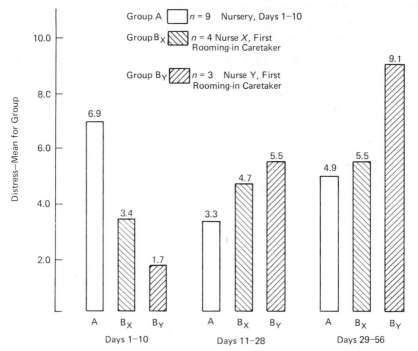

FIGURE 2.   Distress scores: Caretaker groups (initial caretaker).

DISCUSSION

"Distress" behaviors as defined for this study were quite specific infant behaviors which we judged to be evidence of some discomfort or incoordination in the feeding experience.

In our conceptual formulation of the mother-infant interaction and the developmental process, "distress" was viewed not only as a consequence of asynchrony in the interaction, but also as part of the process whereby the infant signals to the caretaker that something is wrong. In response to these signals, the caretaker may alter her behavior, perhaps experimenting with alternate behaviors, until she finds one that most comfortably maintains the infant. We know from the writings of Spitz (1945, 1946) and others (Fineman et al., 1971), and from our own observations of infants with "failure to thrive," that it is possible to "turn off" major aspects of an infant's signaling system. In the extreme examples referred to ("hospitalism," "spasmus nutans," and "failure to thrive"), this condition is generally caused by severe acute or chronic deprivation. The implication of our findings is that very early and what may be considered nonthreatening environmental influences may also significantly affect behavior and communication in the infant-caretaker interaction.

Let us review the findings. First: multiple caretakers and fixed feeding schedules in the newborn nursery result in comparatively high "distress" scores. When the baby is shifted to a single caretaker in rooming-in (days 11–28), this high level is reduced to approximately that of the normative comparison group. Second: a shift from a first single caretaker in the first 10 days to a second single caretaker, with no change in the structure of the rooming-in situation, leads to an increase in "distress" scores. Third: the more individually specific the care in the first 10 days, the more sensitive the infant appears to be to a change in caretaker. We are referring here to the increase in "distress" scores in Group B during the second period, and in particular to the scores of Group B infants initially cared for by Nurse Y.

This evidence indicates that those infants receiving the more individualized and specific care in the first 10 days are more sensitive to ensuing change. This may mean that they are more affected by it, or they may be better prepared to express "distress" in an unfamiliar and presumably asynchronous situation. It is important to note that Group C infants, with more natural mothering and no caretaking shifts, do not show any increase in "distress" over the first 4 weeks and no significant increase over the 8-week study period. We are therefore led to consider the hypothesis that the progressive increases, primarily in Group B infants initally cared for by Nurse Y, are related to the development of an early organization and subsequent interaction with shifting caretaking environments.

We believe that these data point up the importance of the earliest days of life in the establishment of expectations for key environmental features, and in influencing the sensitivity of a "distress signaling system" in its role as a regulating link in the infant-caretaker interaction. However, it is clear that we do not know much about the implications of these findings or their long-term significance. The epigenetic aspect of development implies that any factor with significant effect on early development inevitably affects all subsequent development.

However, it is clear that the question of what this effect will be requires much more information than we now have. It will require continued research, based on a recognition of the infant as a whole organism, and directed at determining how various behavioral systems become related to each other and how they become organized with the environmental context into a regulated total system.

The concept of "distress as a signaling system" within the mother-infant interaction, as discussed here, is one way of regarding the findings and is not demonstrated by these data. Neither do the data as presented elucidate the questions concerning the nature of the specific cues by means of which the infants identify and respond to the specific caretaking environment. We believe that these cues are perceived by the infant as auditory, visual, kinesthetic, and tactile perceptions, and that intensity, timing, pacing, and approach-withdrawal parameters affect the interaction. The feeding observations and other data from the study are being analyzed to see if such variables and their affects can be identified. For example, there is evidence in the feeding data that infants cared for by Nurse Y or by their own mothers spent more time looking at the caretaker during feeding than did infants cared for by Nurse X. We plan to continue these analyses in order to clarify the interrelation of functions, and to dentify more specifically the cues that both infant and mother use to regulate and adjust their mutal adaptation. This study should document the origins of their role and signficance from the point of view of the genesis of a communication system in the dyad.

References

BURNS, P. & SANDER, L. W. (1967), Feeding patterns in early infancy and the assessment of individual differences in their organization. Presented at the Society for Research in Child Development, New York.

FINEMAN, J. B., KUNIHOLM, P., & SHERIDAN, S. (1971), Spasmus nutans: a syndrome of auto-arousal. *Journal of the American Academy of Child Psychiatry*, 10:136–155.

PAVENSTEDT, E. & SANDER, L. W. (1962), Progress report: mother-child interaction during first three years. Submitted to USPHS for Grant #M–3325, Sept., 1960–Dec., 1961, pp. 38–42.

SANDER, L. W. (1962), Issues in early mother-child interaction. *Journal of the American Academy of Child Psychiatry*, 1:141–166.

——— (1969), Regulation and organization in the early infant-caretaker system. In: *Brain and Early Behavior*, ed. R. Robinson. London: Academic Press, pp. 311–332.

——— STECHLER, G., BURNS, P., & JULIA, H. (1970). Early mother-infant interaction and 24-hour patterns of activity and sleep. *Journal of the American Academy of Child Psychiatry*, 9:103–123.

SPITZ, R. A. (1945), Hospitalism: an inquiry into the genesis of psychiatric conditions in early childhood. *The Psychoanalytic Study of the Child*, 1:53–74. New York: International Universities Press.

——— (1946), Hospitalism: a follow-up report. *The Psychoanalytic Study of the Child* 2:113–117. New York: International Universities Press.

WOLFF, P. H. (1968), The role of biological rhythms in early psychological development. In: *Annual Progress in Child Psychiatry and Child Development*, 1968, ed. S. Chess & A. Thomas. New York: Brunner/Mazel, pp. 1–21.

The Synchrony of Respiration, Heart Rate, and Sucking Behavior in the Newborn*

Lewis P. Lipsitt

BROWN UNIVERSITY

In recent years, many advances have been made in the technical aspects of psychobiological recording. This new expertise has found its way into the maternity hospital where it is being used to monitor the condition of the mother and fetus prior to birth. Subsequently, it is used to explore the psychophysiology of the neonate in considerable detail. There is growing disenchantment among child psychologists with the traditional modes of behavioral assessment, especially the developmental test. This has facilitated the migration of developmentalists into the field of infant observation and experimentation with techniques that actually alter the baby's behavior rather than merely assess it. This has occurred in the context of a rising faith in, and indeed numerous demonstrations of, the great sensory capacities and learning proficiencies of the young child. This new appreciation, even of the neonate, has been facilitated by the social and medical interests of developmentalists. They see the possibility of appropriating these experimental techniques to more keenly detect sensory and neurological deficits in infants. Such experimental manipulative procedures can then be used to enhance developmental performance, particularly in those born with, or destined for, physical or social handicaps.

THE POLYGRAPHIC STUDY OF THE NEWBORN

The use of the polygraph for the documentation of infantile responsivity can facilitate the study of processes involving changes in the infant's condition over time, and in response to specific stimulation that may be administered in any sensory modality. Recent studies utilizing polygraphic recording of newborns' responses enable much finer detection of sensory and neurological capability. This is just as one would expect of techniques that are highly sensitive to individual differences. In addition, such procedures enable the simultaneous documentation of multiple responses, yielding a written record of the infant's response. Then the occasion of recording, and the stimulation associated with it, may be rehearsed afterwards to provide the opportunity for further statistical analyses of the episode.

We were concerned in the present studies with the interrelationships among several response characteristics, such as sucking, respiration, and heart rate. In addition, we wished to document the way in which sensory stimulation, taste in this case, serves to alter what might be called the basic congenital responsivity of the infant. In these studies, we have perhaps explored the earliest contributions of the environment to the newborn's response repertoire. The

From *Biologic and Clinical Aspects of Brain Development*. Mead Johnson Symposium on Perinatal and Developmental Medicine, No. 6. Evansville, Ind.: Mead Johnson and Company, 1975, Pp. 67–72. Reprinted by permission.

* Supported by USPHS Grant No. HD 03911.

circumstances in which we have accomplished this do not deviate sharply, of course, from the range of stimulation which infants ordinarily experience within the first few days of life, in the ecological niche which is the normal nursery of the modern maternity hospital. Even so, the techniques are rather exquisitely sensitive to individual differences in newborns. Thus, they enable the documentation both of commonalities among infants with respect to their response to environmental change, and the stability of individual reactions over a period of time.

Testing is done in a special crib, housed in a white sound-attenuated chamber with temperature about 80°F. Ambient light is about 50 ft-candles. Breathing is monitored by a Phipps and Bird infant pneumobelt around the abdomen. Respiratton and body activity are recorded continuously on a Grass polygraph. Hewlett-Packard electrodes are placed on the chest and leg, permitting polygraphic monitoring of the primary heart rate, which is integrated by a Hewlett-Packard cardiotachometer and recorded on another channel. Figure 1 shows a two-day-old child with the pneumobelt attached for the recording of respiration, EKG electrodes for recording of heart rate, and the automatic sucking apparatus in place for recording and for delivery of fluid contingent upon sucking behavior.

Sucking is recorded on another polygraph channel. The "suckometer" consists of a stainless steel housing with a pressure transducer, over which a commercial nipple is pulled. A polyethylene tube runs into the nipple from a pump source and delivers fluid under the control of the experimenter and on demand of the subject. When delivering, the pump ejects into the nipple-end a .02 ml drop contingent upon the execution of a sucking response of preset amplitude.

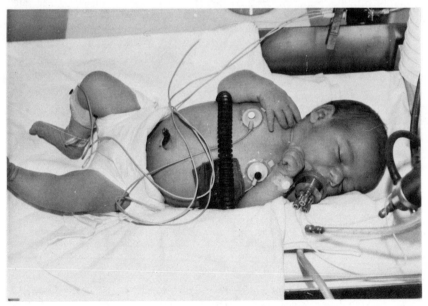

FIGURE 1. *A two-day-old infant in the testing situation.*

In these studies, the situation may be arranged in such a way as to allow the infant to receive no fluid for sucking, or to receive a fluid such as sucrose or dextrose, in any desired concentration, contingent upon sucking, with one drop being ejected onto the tongue for each suck. A polygraph event marker records fluid ejections during fluid delivery periods, or the occurrence of a criterion suck during no-fluid conditions. To insure a constant acoustical environment, a 74 dB background white noise is produced from a noise generator continuously through a speaker enclosed in the infant chamber.

A nurse applies the electrodes and pneumobelt to the infant, who is then swaddled and placed on its left side. The nipple is then inserted, supported by a cushion to enable recording without touching the infant. During the first few sucking bursts on the nipple, no fluid is delivered and the equipment is calibrated. Preamplifier sensitivity is adjusted for each infant so the average sucking amplitude results in a 5 cm excursion of the polygraph pen. The threshold criterion is then set at 2.5 cm, so that only responses causing a pen sweep greater than 2.5 cm meet the criterion of a suck and are counted.

An exemplary polygraph record showing respiration, heart rate, the cardiotachometer transformation of the basic EKG, and sucking can be seen in Figure 2. Newborns characteristically suck in bursts of responses separated by

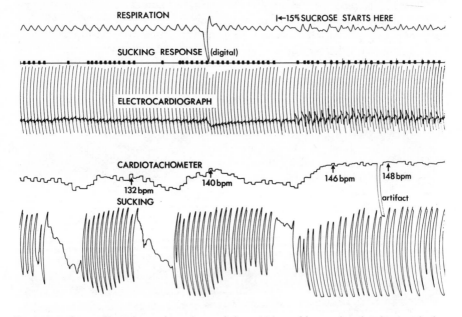

FIGURE 2.   *Exemplary polygraph record from 44-hour-old normal male, showing the last two bursts of no-fluid sucking preceding introduction of the sucrose-sucking condition without interruption. Total polygraph record shown runs for 1 minute. Top channel records respiration, pen marker shows digital representation of criterion sucks, which receive .02 ml drop of fluid during sucrose period. Next operating channel is the electrocardiograph (EKG), then the cardiotachometer transformation of the inter-beat intervals, followed by the sucking record. Long sucking bursts are characteristic of sucrose-sucking. No-fluid sucking occurs in short bursts of more rapid sucks. Heart rate during sucrose may be seen to go to a higher level (and remain there) than during no-fluid sucking.*

rests. The burst lengths and the rest lengths both constitute individual difference variables under no-fluid conditions. But, both of these parameters as well as the sucking rate within bursts (as will be seen later) are importantly influenced by the conditions which are arranged as consequences of the infant's own response. For example, with a change from a no-fluid condition to a fluid-sucking condition, or with a change from sucking for a less sweet solution to a sweeter solution, there is a tendency for the sucking bursts to become longer, for the inter-burst intervals to become shorter, and for the inter-suck intervals to become longer (i.e., for sucking rate within bursts to become slower). Because of these regularities of response in relation to the conditions imposed upon the infants during testing, it is possible to (a) explore the effects of one period of taste experience upon the response of the infant during a subsequent taste experience, and (b) investigate the interrelationships of these various sucking-response parameters with one another and with certain other response measures such as heart rate. The two studies reported here relate to those objectives.

SUCKING FOR SUCROSE, WATER, OR NOTHING

In a study by Kobre and Lipsitt (1972), the infants were first tested for two minutes on the nipple without any fluid delivery whatever. Subjects in this study were rejected for further study if they had a mean sucking rate lower than 30/minute during the two minute period. The 25 subjects remaining were divided into five groups. A total of 20 minutes of responding was recorded for each subject, four successive periods each of five-minutes duration. Between each period the nipple was removed for one minute to allow the tube to be flushed out with water and the child to be picked up.

The 25 infants, most in the third day of life, received one of five reinforcement regimens for the 20-minute period. One group (Suc-Suc) received only sucrose throughout the 20-minute period. A second group (H$_2$O-H$_2$O) received water throughout, and a third group (Suc-H$_2$O) received sucrose and water, alternated twice, in five-minute units. In a second portion of the experiment, one group (NF-NF) received no fluid throughout the four five-minute periods, and a second group (Suc-NF) received sucrose alternated with no fluid in five-minute periods.

It is of interest first to compare the frequency polygons representing the sucking behavior of the three groups which received a constant reinforcement condition throughout the 20-minute sucking period. These are the groups that got either sucrose, or distilled water, or no fluid for that 20 minutes. Figure 3 provides a graphical comparison of the three groups as represented by the computer-generated polygons which threw the inter-suck intervals accumulated during the 20-minute period into bins representing 100-msec intervals. This shows clearly that sucking rate within bursts slows down for a fluid-sucking condition relative to no-fluid sucking, and that sucking rate slows still further for sweet-fluid-sucking relative to sucking for distilled water. Thus there is an orderly progression from no fluid to plain water to 15% sucrose sucking, with the sucking response becoming slower and slower with an apparent increase in the incentive value of the reinforcement delivered consequent upon the response. It may also be noted, parenthetically, that under the sucrose condition the

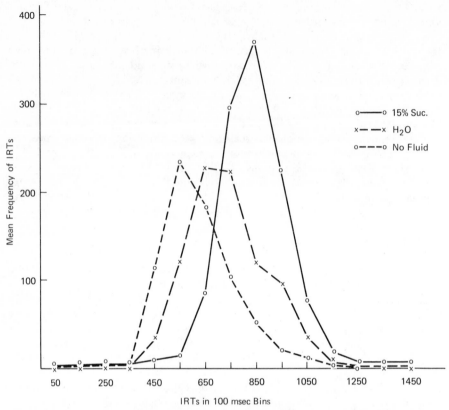

F I G U R E 3.   *Mean incidence of interresponse times (IRTs) for each of the 100 msec bins. Each curve represents the combined IRT distribution for the five subjects in that group (Suc-Suc; H_2O-H_2O; NF-NF) over the 20-minute session. Sucking is slower for sucrose than for water, on average, and slower for water than under the no-fluid condition.*

infants invested a larger number of responses during a comparable period of time than under either the water or no-fluid condition. A somewhat larger number of responses was emitted for water, moreover, than for no fluid.

As has been indicated earlier, rather interesting interplays between various response parameters occur in neonates. For example, while infants suck more slowly within bursts for sweeter fluids, as if to savor them more, it is also the case that when sucking for sweet they tend to take shorter rests. Thus, they suck more times per minute for sweet than for non-sweet. This effect may be seen in Figure 4, wherein the comparison is shown of mean rates per minute for the group which got sucrose throughout with the groups which got water throughout. Then both of these are compared to the group that got sucrose and water alternated in five-minute blocks. Here it may be seen that the sucking rate per minute for the sucrose group is higher than for the water-sucking group. The trend shows that sucking rate over the 20-minute period is remarkably stable, and the difference between the two groups is a reliable one. More

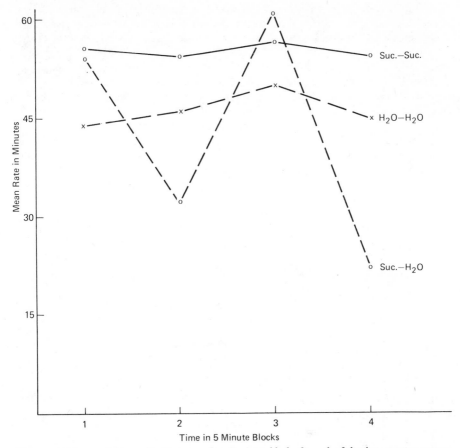

FIGURE 4.   *Mean sucking rate over four 5-minute blocks for each of the three groups; sucrose alone (Suc-Suc), water alone (H_2O-H_2O), and sucrose and water alternated twice (Suc-H_2O). N = 5 in each group.*

important, however, is the obvious indication of an experiental effect in the alternated group. When sucking for sucrose, this group was essentially comparable to the group sucking for sucrose throughout. When switched to water, however, response rate during each of those five minute periods was significantly lower than their counterpart controls in the water-throughout group. Thus, when newborns have experience in sucking for sucrose, an immediately subsequent experience with water "turns them off." They display their apparent "aversion" for the water by a marked reduction in instrumental behavior which would put that fluid in their mouths. As can be seen from the figure, when the response consequent is changed, as from water to sucrose, response rate goes right back up to a normal level. There is even a suggestion there (though not reliable) of a positive contrast effect counterpointing the negative contrast effect shown during the second and fourth blocks (both of which effects are reliable).

The comparable comparison showing a similar effect in the relations between sucking for sucrose and sucking for no fluid is shown in Figure 5. This figure shows the no-fluid group to suck at an essentially constant rate of about 40 sucks per minute throughout the 20-minute testing session. The group alternated between sucrose and no fluid in successive five-minute blocks, however, goes from a sucking rate of almost 60 under sucrose to a rate of about 30 sucks per minute under the no fluid condition. This is a drop to a level significantly below that of the group receiving no fluid throughout. Thus the negative contrast effect occurs under conditions in which the lower-incentive condition involves either no fluid at all, or plain distilled water. There is no reason to suppose at this point that the phenomenon is not widespread throughout the range of incentive conditions and that it would occur whenever the infant is called upon to compare two levels of incentive, such as breast milk versus formula, or formula versus plain water.

More important from the standpoint of the psychologist interested in behavioral changes due to accruing experiences is the fact that the newborn is

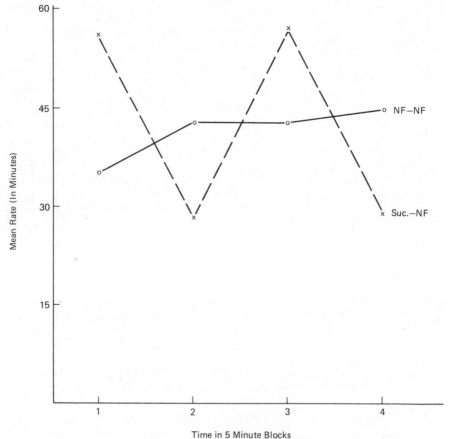

F I G U R E 5.   *Mean sucking rate over four 5-minute blocks for each of two groups; no fluid (NF-NF), and sucrose and no-fluid alternated twice (Suc-NF). N = 5 in each group.*

strikingly affected in his subsequent behavior by his experiences within the immediately previous five minutes. Surely the negative contrast effect demonstrated here is one of the most rudimentary types of behavioral alteration, however temporary, due to experiential circumstances. As in the case of neonatal habituation to olfactory stimulation (Engen and Lipsitt, 1972), there is the strong suggestion that memorial processes are already working during the newborn period, such that there is a lasting impression made, admittedly of unknown duration, of the experience endured. These are the beginnings of learning processes.

RESPIRATION, HEART RATE, AND SUCKING

In a study involving 44 normal full-term newborns, 24 males and 20 females, testing was conducted on two consecutive days, using the polygraph recording techniques previously described. Mean age on initial testing (Day One) was 54 hours (27 to 120 hours) and, on Day Two, 78 hours (51 to 144 hours). All infants, 33 bottle-fed and 11 breast-fed, were seen between 8:30 a.m. and 9:30. Infants in this study were part of a long-term longitudinal study; only some aspects of the newborn data will be considered here. The procedures described here constituted only a portion of the total battery of testing done on each infant but they were administered, under identical standardized contitions, to all infants in the study.

A total of ten minutes of sucking was recorded for each infant immediately following calibration of the apparatus, five successive periods each of two minutes duration. Three of these were sucking for no fluid, followed by two periods of 15% sucrose-sucking. About 35 seconds intervened between periods during which a computer printed out the inter-response time data (IRT) for the preceding period. The nipple was not removed between periods. The infant continued sucking under the same condition as in the preceding period. The beginning of a period following the 35 second print-out was initiated after the infant stopped sucking for at least two seconds after the end of a burst.

At the end of the second sucrose period, the nipple was removed. There then ensued a two-minute period of polygraph recording during a "resting" state, defined as quiescent and with regular respiration, in which the infant neither sucked nor was stimulated in any way.

The results (Lipsitt, Reilly, Butcher, and Greenwood, in press) of this part of the longitudinal study have suggested a very interesting interplay between the sucking response, on the one hand, and heart rate, on the other. They further substantiate a process that suggests a "savoring mechanism" which seems to be present already during the newborn period.

The computer print-out at the end of each two-minute period provided a frequency distribution, for inter-suck intervals under two seconds, of sucking IRTs in 100-msec bins. The mean IRT could be calculated from the print-out, using the midpoint of the bin as its numerical representation. Figure 2, shown earlier, is a polygraph record from this study, showing the final phase of nonnutritive (no-fluid) sucking in comparison with the first phase of sucrose-sucking for an exemplary subject of this experiment.

Table 1 shows the five sucking parameters under the no-fluid and sucrosesucking conditions. The mean and modal IRTs are greater when sucking is for sucrose than when sucking under a no-fluid condition, and the number of responses per burst is twice as large. Also, more rest periods (IRTs > 2 sec) occur under the no-fluid condition. Consequently, despite the faster rate of sucking within bursts under the no-fluid condition, more sucks per minute are emitted under sucrose. All those effects are reliable.

Table 2 compares the heart rate of infants during sucking periods with basal heart rate without the nipple. Very interestingly, the mean heart rate under no-fluid sucking was significantly higher than the basal rate. In turn the mean heart rate under sucrose-sucking was higher than under the no-fluid condition. Although sucking rate within bursts is *reduced* when the infant sucks for sucrose, then, heart rate nevertheless increases reliably.

TABLE 1

Comparison of the means (2-min units) of five sucking parameters under no-fluid and sucrose-sucking conditions over a two-day period, and correlation coefficients (r) comparing Day 1 and Day 2. From the initial group of 44 subjects, 3 failed to suck non-nutritively on Day 1, thus reducing the analyzable records to 41 for both days. In all, 4 subjects had non-analyzable sucrose-sucking records, 2 on Day 1 (these overlapping with the no-fluid failures), reducing the sucrose subjects to 40. The measures are based upon 2 min means, 3 for the no-fluid and 2 for sucrose condition.

	DAY 1		DAY 2		DAY 1/DAY 2	
	MEAN	SD	MEAN	SD	r	p^r
No-fluid sucking (N = 41)						
Total responses	88.3	23.2	96.6	30.9	.62	.001
IRTs 2" (rests)	8.1	2.6	8.7	2.8	.65	.001
Responses/burst	12.9	15.5	11.2	6.1	.79	.001
Mode IRT	620.3	99.0	572.8	61.9	.37	.05
Mean IRT	657.8	81.7	611.9	56.0	.42	.01
15% Sucrose sucking (N = 40)						
Total responses	103.0	28.2	106.2	27.6	.08	—
IRTs 2" (rests)	5.3	2.7	5.9	3.5	.13	—
Responses/burst	29.7	34.2	24.2	21.7	.03	—
Mode IRT	838.1	109.9	771.3	115.7	.63	.001
Mean IRT	855.8	105.3	786.9	85.8	.71	.001

TABLE 2

Heart rate (bpm) during resting and when sucking for no fluid or sucrose, and correlation coefficients (r) comparing Day 1 and Day 2. Failures to suck account for reductions of N from the initial group of 44, except in one case where the heart rate record during sucking was unreadable.

		DAY 1		DAY 2		COMBINED		DAY 1/DAY 2	
	N	Mean	SD	Mean	SD	Mean	SD	r	p^r
Basal	44	113.8	16.7	118.7	18.1	116.3	14.2	.29	.05
No-fluid sucking	40	124.0	14.5	123.4	13.6	123.8	12.2	.46	.01
Sucrose-sucking	39	145.7	15.5	147.4	12.3	146.6	13.1	.71	.001

CONCLUDING REMARKS

The more we study the human neonate under rather precise response-measurement conditions afforded by the polygraph and associated apparatus such as the computer, the more are we impressed, first by the fine interplay between the various congenital responses of the newborn, but secondly, by the extent to which the newborn's behavior and psychophysiological indices are affected by the environmental resources available to the infant at any given moment. Thus, the manual introduction of 10% sucrose into the infant's mouth in the presence of a refusal to suck will almost immediately generate sucking behavior which will persist even upon the subsequent withdrawal of that sucrose incentive. Similarly, and as has been demonstrated in the first experiment reported here, experience in sucking for a sweet substance for a five-minute period will affect the infant's subsequent behavior, at least for the next five minutes, when offered a less sweet incentive.

An important feature of the present experimental techniques is that the infant has been studied not just in the presence of stimulating features of the environment which were under the control of the examiner or experimenter, but also under conditions in which the infant is offered the opportunity to self-regulate. That is, our incentive conditions were such that we simply made available to the infant innocuous but variable reinforcing conditions, to which we studied the infant's response. The newborn through its instrumental or operant activity either made it happen or didn't, or did something in between. We think that we are at the beginning stages of a model for the interaction between an infant and its environment. Involved is not merely a stimulus-response relationship in which the environment or the infant's caretaker serves as stimulus, and the subject responds, or even one in which the infant serves as stimulus, and the environment responds. Rather, it is one in which there is constant reciprocity between the organism and environment, between the infant and the caretaker, in which each serves as a stimulus and each responds. Both operate at least in part according to incentive principles which can and will be discovered. This too simple view of human nature and human development will yield to more complex models as we learn more, but we can learn more only by starting at the beginning.

Finally, the techniques, tools, and results represented in the foregoing should have diagnostic significance in relation to the newborn, inasmuch as such normative findings can be utilized to assess "response deviation" in individual infants subsequently tested by the same techniques. The 24-hour test-retest stabilities of certain of these measures, given in Table 1, lend credibility to the utility of at least some of the measures for tagging the "deviant newborn." Research is in progress presently, involving both high-stress and low-stress newborns. The purpose is to determine the validity of these psychophysiological measures in assessing degree of fetal, obstetrical, or other perinatal distress. Ultimately, longitudinal studies must be done as well, to determine the long-term usefulness of such precise neonatal measures for purposes of assessing prognosis, or at least to determine the utility of these measures in identifying certain newborns for remedial or other special developmental follow-up.

References

ENGEN, T., and LIPSITT, L. P.: Decrement and recovery of responses to olfactory stimuli in the human neonate, Journal of Comparative and Physiological Psychology, 59: 2, 1965.

KOBRE, K. R., and LIPSITT, L. P.: A negative contrast effect in newborns, Journal of Experimental Child Psychology, 14:1, 1972.

LIPSITT, L. P.; REILLY, B. M.; BUTCHER, M. J., and GREENWOOD, M. M.: The stability and interrelationships of newborn sucking and heart rate, submitted for publication, 1974. in press.

Chapter 3
Emerging Resources and Competencies

MARGARET HAMILTON

The basic adjustments to extrauterine life are made by the end of the first three months. A significant turning point occurs at around this time [81, pp. 447–448]. A higher level of brain organization is indicated by type of sleep and other states and by new capabilities in perception, learning, and social interaction. This chapter is concerned with the development that occurs from two or three months to two years, or the end of the neonatal period to the end of infancy. During this period, the individual changes from horizontal to vertical, from stationary to mobile, and from vocal to verbal. Active, like all living creatures, with her powers emerging, like all developing organisms, the infant deals more and more effectively with the inanimate world, people, and herself.

Directions in Personality Development

Infancy encompasses the first critical period in personality growth and part of the second. The development of the sense of trust comes first, laying the groundwork for a feeling of security throughout life. The development of a sense of

127

autonomy is central to personality growth from about 1½ to 3½ or 4 years of age. Most of the infant's behavior and experiences can be understood in the light of these two achievements in personality development [30, pp. 247–254].

TRUST

Successful growth during the first year results in a well-established sense of trust. Begun with the first experience of securing food and skin stimulation, the growth of trust continues through experiences with things, other people, and the self. The good feelings from tension reduction, repeated consistently in good physical care, make the baby confident that he will be fed when hungry, dried when wet, rocked when restless, and stimulated when bored. He is confident also that he can do something toward initiating these satisfying experiences.

People, primarily mother, are part of the good-feeling experiences and come to stand for the whole. Thus, the 4-month baby, crying from hunger, stops crying and even smiles when he sees his mother or hears her footsteps, trusting that she will feed him.

Appreciation of the permanence of objects is a basic ingredient of the sense of trust. Through his interactions with the world during his first year and a half, the baby comes to know that things exist even when he is not perceiving them. As described in greater detail later in the chapter, the first 18 months is the sensori-motor period, in Piaget's series of stages. The two essential achievements of this period are a realization of the permanence of objects and the organization and control of his movements in space. These two achievements go along together. As the baby controls the movements of his body, he deals with the objects of the world, seeing and feeling them, noticing them as they appear and disappear, understanding that events can take place when he is not watching. He comes to trust the world to have certain kinds of order in it, to be dependable. He also comes to know his own powers and how to use them, a beginning of the sense of autonomy.

Establishing trust also involves learning that mother (and others) exists even when she cannot be seen, and that she will come again and again. The game of peekaboo dramatizes mother's disappearance and reappearance. In playing it, the infant lives and relives the frightening situation which has a happy ending, enjoying it throughout the months when trust is growing as he learns that mother continues to exist apart from him. His sense of self begins perhaps from this knowledge and certainly grows as he explores his own body. Fingering his hand and watching it move yield one complex of sensations; fingering the blanket gives another. Reaching, grasping, securing, releasing, touching, mouthing—all tell him what is himself, what are other things and what he can do, or what he can trust his body to do with the world. As a good feeling goes along with the accumulation of knowledge of his body, his power, the objects outside himself, and other people, then the sense of trust grows. Mistrust arises from discomfort; disappointment; anxiety; inability to explore, discriminate, and cope with the world.*

---

* The period of development of trust is the *oral stage* in psychoanalytic theory. The mouth is the site of the most important experiences, feeding and the love relationship associated with feeding. Pain from teething is associated with biting and cruel, harsh experiences. In many psychoanalytic writings the skin senses and other senses, too, are greatly overshadowed by the significance of the mouth.

AUTONOMY

In the previous chapter, we suggested that the newborn baby's abilities are not appreciated by most people, since they do not know how to give the baby a chance to show what she can do. The same is true to some extent through infancy, especially during the first half year. Several experiments give some notion of how eagerly a baby will control her environment if she can, and of how much enjoyment she gets from new and interesting experiences. Infants between 5 and 12 weeks of age adjusted their sucking with the result of sharpening a motion picture when it became blurry [11, pp. 289–291]. In one condition, the film became clear as the infant sucked and blurred when she stopped. In the other condition, sucking caused blurring and stopping sucking resulted in a sharp image. In another experiment, 2-month-olds learned to operate a mobile by pressing their heads on their pillows [84]. After a few days with the mobile, the experimental babies started to smile and coo as they operated it. The control babies, who saw a display that did not respond to their actions, did not smile and coo noticeably. There are few naturally occurring situations in which an infant can reliably cause something to happen. Perhaps the nearest approach to causing a display equal to that of the mobile would be causing an adult to smile and talk. Often a baby can cause smiles and talking when she smiles and coos. If more events were contingent upon her actions, then perhaps the baby would be able to have many more interesting experiences, along with an increasing sense of autonomy. She would have enjoyment and satisfaction as she realized (roughly translated into adult terms), "I can make wonderful things happen. I can put on an interesting show when I want to. I do good work. I decide."

The beginnings of a sense of autonomy may thus be seen in the early weeks and months of life. During the second year the toddler shows more and more concern with doing for herself, choosing, holding on, and letting go.

When the child discovers, through active testing, that there are many situations in which she can choose and live comfortably with her choice, then she feels good about herself. She can decide whether to take a proffered hand or not, whether to play with the truck or the bunny, whether to have a second serving of applesauce or not, whether to sit on grandma's lap or stand on her own feet. Clear and firm restrictions will prevent her from making choices that are beyond her. Frustration and consequent anger are frequent even in older infants who are guided with skill and understanding. Temper outbursts increase in the latter part of infancy, as the child tests herself to find out what she can do and tests her parents and her world to find out what they will let her do. Each successful encounter and choice adds to her sense of autonomy.

Shame and doubt arise when disaster follows choice-making and also when the child is not allowed to make enough choices. Shame, doubt, and inadequacy (lack of autonomy) lead to extremes of behavior—rebellion or oversubmissiveness, hurling or hanging on tight.*

* The period of autonomy is the anal stage in psychoanalytic theory. The central problem is dramatized by the idea of the anal sphincters that open or shut, hanging on or letting go. Depending on the child's experiences with bowel control and control by other people, his personality takes on characteristics like suspicion or confidence, stinginess or generosity, doubt and shame, or autonomy and adequacy.

Physical Development and Health

Development and change are rapid during the first two years of life. This period, as well as the preschool years, is a time when illness is relatively frequent, and careful physical care is consequently very worthwhile.

After the first month, more or less, a baby really looks like a baby, like babies in advertisements and photograph albums, like other babies in the neighborhood —chubby, skin colored pink, golden, brown, or whatever it is destined to be, bumps smoothed out, and nose in shape. New, coarser hair comes in during infancy, replacing the fine black hair of the newborn (if he had it) and showing more and more the color it is going to be. Compared with an older child, a baby has a large forehead, large eyes, small nose, small chin, and plump cheeks. His hands and feet are chubby and his abdomen round; his delicate skin looks soft and fragile.

Babies differ in appearance, from one to another; the older they are, the more obvious the differences. They differ, of course, in coloring, facial features, amount and type of hair, height, and weight. They feel different, too. Firm muscles and good muscle tone give a solid impression, in contrast to the softness of slacker muscles or abundant fat. The baby's reactions to being held also add to the impression, according to whether the infant holds himself erect, pushes away, or yields to the arms that hold him.

PROPORTIONS AND MEASUREMENTS

Changes in shape and proportion continue along the lines charted prenatally, the head regions being most developed, the trunk and legs beginning to catch up, the center of gravity high in the trunk but descending. Birth weight is doubled by 4 or 5 months and tripled at 1 year. Height is doubled by about 4 years. Thus, the child starts life as a slender neonate, fills out to a round, plump infant during the first year, and then in the second year, he again becomes more slender, continuing this trend into middle childhood. A ratio useful for diagnosing malnutrition is that of head to thorax. After 6 months of age, the thorax is larger than the head in normal children. The difference in circumference between thorax and head increases with age. When a child is growing inadequately, his weight deficit is related to the difference between head and thorax [25]. Height and weight percentile tables (Tables 3-1 through 3-4) can be used to compare a white or black baby with others of the same age, sex, and race. These tables are based on repeated measurements of more than 11,000 white infants and 3,700 black infants living in California. Height was measured with the infant lying on his back. The tables can be used to tell how many children (black or white, of either sex) out of 100 will be longer or shorter, heavier or lighter than any given baby. For example, Becky (white) at six months weighs 7.71 kilograms and measures 69.2 centimeters. Tables 3-2 and 3-4 show that she is above the 90th percentile in height (length) and slightly above the 50th percentile in weight. Taller than 90 out of 100 white baby girls, she is very tall. In spite of her chubby face and rounded abdomen, according to Table 3-4 she is average as to weight, since almost 50 out of 100 exceed her in weight.

Height–weight tables that give only averages have little use for the individual,

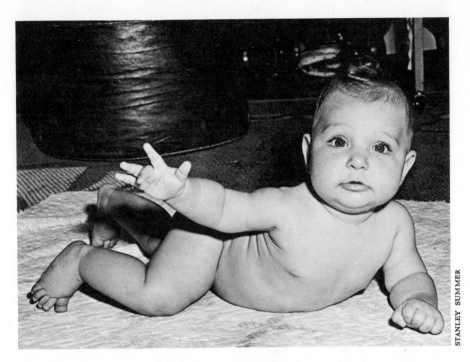

Proportions and posture typical at about 9 months of age.

although they are useful for comparing groups. Percentile tables, such as those shown here, give more information than mere averages. However, they take no account of body build nor do they consider heredity. The ideal weight for a short-legged, long-trunked child such as an Aleutian Islander would obviously be greater than for a white American of the same height. The expected height for the child of tall parents is greater than for the child of short parents. For example, for white Ohio sons of short parents, the average length at 1 year was 73.66 centimeters, at 2, 85.34; for sons of tall parents, the average 1-year length was 77.47, and at 2, it was 88.9 [37]. (The measurements in the article cited were in inches, and have been converted to metric units here.)

Skinfold thickness is a measurement that is useful for detecting suboptimal nutrition in large groups of children, as in national surveys [52]. Accurate scales may not be available for weighing and exact ages may not be known. Exact age is not necessary when skinfold measurements are used between 1 and 5 years of age. Children with protein-calorie malnutrition were usually below the third percentile and almost always below the tenth.

BRAIN DEVELOPMENT

A spurt in brain growth begins before birth and continues during the first 2 years [26a]. Although most of the brain's neurones were formed earlier, during the small growth spurt between 12 and 18 weeks prenatally, most of the large

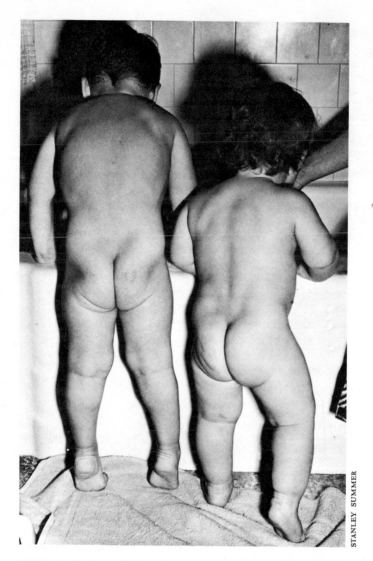

Differences in size and shape between a 1-year-old and a 2-year-old are shown here.

STANLEY SUMMER

growth spurt of the brain occurs postnatally. At this time, the glial cells, which support and serve the neurones, multiply enormously. One of their important functions is the manufacture of myelin sheaths that insulate the nerve fibers. Rapid myelinization takes place during the second half of the brain growth spurt. The neurones develop their dendrites into a complex network. Metabolic patterns mature.

The growth spurt of the cerebellum, which controls coordination and balance,

Table 3-1. Percentile Distribution of Lengths of Males by Race from Age 1 Month Through Age 24 Months: California, 1959–67.

In Centimeters

Age in Months	White							Age in Months	Black						
	Percentile								Percentile						
	3	10	25	50	75	90	97		3	10	25	50	75	90	97
1	49.5	51.2	52.7	54.2	55.7	57.0	58.3	1	48.3	50.0	51.6	53.2	54.7	56.0	57.3
2	53.2	54.9	56.4	57.9	59.4	60.7	62.1	2	52.0	53.8	55.4	57.0	58.6	59.9	61.2
3	56.3	57.9	59.4	61.0	62.5	63.9	65.2	3	55.2	57.0	58.6	60.3	61.8	63.1	64.5
4	58.8	60.5	62.0	63.5	65.1	66.5	67.9	4	58.0	59.8	61.4	63.0	64.6	65.9	67.3
5	61.0	62.7	64.2	65.7	67.3	68.8	70.2	5	60.3	62.1	63.7	65.3	66.9	68.3	69.7
6	62.9	64.5	66.0	67.7	69.3	70.8	72.2	6	62.3	64.1	65.7	67.3	68.9	70.3	71.8
7	64.6	66.2	67.7	69.3	71.0	72.5	74.0	7	64.1	65.8	67.4	69.0	70.7	72.1	73.6
8	66.1	67.6	69.2	70.8	72.5	74.1	75.6	8	65.7	67.3	68.9	70.6	72.2	73.6	75.3
9	67.4	69.0	70.5	72.2	73.9	75.5	77.1	9	67.1	68.7	70.3	72.0	73.6	75.0	76.8
10	68.7	70.2	71.8	73.5	75.2	76.9	78.5	10	68.5	70.0	71.6	73.2	74.9	76.3	78.1
11	69.9	71.4	72.9	74.7	76.4	78.2	79.9	11	69.7	71.2	72.7	74.4	76.1	77.6	79.4
12	71.0	72.5	74.1	75.8	77.6	79.4	81.1	12	70.8	72.3	73.8	75.5	77.2	78.7	80.6
13	72.1	73.6	75.2	76.9	78.8	80.6	82.4	13	71.9	73.3	74.9	76.6	78.3	79.8	81.8
14	73.1	74.6	76.2	78.0	79.9	81.7	83.6	14	73.0	74.4	75.9	77.6	79.3	80.9	83.0
15	74.1	75.6	77.2	79.1	81.0	82.8	84.7	15	74.0	75.3	76.9	78.6	80.4	82.0	84.1
16	75.1	76.6	78.2	80.1	82.0	83.9	85.8	16	74.9	76.3	77.9	79.6	81.4	83.1	85.2
17	76.0	77.5	79.1	81.0	83.0	84.9	86.9	17	75.8	77.2	78.8	80.6	82.4	84.1	86.3
18	76.8	78.4	80.0	82.0	84.0	85.9	87.9	18	76.7	78.1	79.8	81.5	83.3	85.1	87.3
19	77.6	79.2	80.9	82.9	84.9	86.8	88.8	19	77.4	79.0	80.6	82.5	84.3	86.1	88.4
20	78.4	80.0	81.7	83.7	85.8	87.7	89.7	20	78.1	79.8	81.5	83.4	85.2	87.1	89.4
21	79.1	80.8	82.5	84.5	86.6	88.5	90.5	21	78.8	80.6	82.3	84.3	86.1	88.1	90.3
22	79.7	81.5	83.3	85.3	87.4	89.4	91.3	22	79.3	81.4	83.1	85.1	87.0	89.1	91.3
23	80.4	82.2	84.0	86.1	88.2	90.2	92.1	23	79.8	82.1	83.8	86.0	87.9	90.0	92.2
24	81.0	83.0	84.8	86.9	89.1	91.0	92.9	24	80.2	82.8	84.5	86.8	88.8	91.0	93.1

SOURCE: Reprinted by permission from J. Wingerd, E. J. Schoen, and I. L. Solomon. Growth standards in the first two years of life based on measurements of white and black children in a prepaid health care program. *Pediatrics,* 1971, **47**, 818–825.

Table 3-2. Percentile Distribution of Lengths of Females from Age 1 Month Through Age 24 Months: California, 1959–67.

In Centimeters

Age in Months	White Percentile 3	10	25	50	75	90	97	Age in Months	Black Percentile 3	10	25	50	75	90	97
1	49.1	50.6	51.9	53.3	54.7	55.9	57.2	1	47.8	49.7	51.1	52.5	54.0	55.2	56.5
2	52.5	53.9	55.3	56.7	58.1	59.4	60.6	2	51.4	53.2	54.6	56.1	57.6	58.8	60.1
3	55.3	56.7	58.1	59.6	61.0	62.3	63.6	3	54.4	56.2	57.6	59.1	60.6	61.9	63.2
4	57.7	59.1	60.5	62.0	63.5	64.9	66.1	4	57.0	58.7	60.1	61.6	63.2	64.5	65.8
5	59.8	61.2	62.6	64.1	65.7	67.0	68.3	5	59.2	60.8	62.2	63.8	65.4	66.7	68.1
6	61.6	63.0	64.4	66.0	67.5	68.9	70.3	6	61.1	62.7	64.1	65.8	67.4	68.7	70.1
7	63.2	64.6	66.1	67.6	69.2	70.7	72.1	7	62.7	64.4	65.8	67.5	69.1	70.4	71.9
8	64.6	66.1	67.5	69.1	70.8	72.2	73.7	8	64.2	65.9	67.3	69.0	70.6	72.0	73.5
9	66.0	67.4	68.9	70.5	72.2	73.7	75.2	9	65.6	67.3	68.8	70.4	72.1	73.5	75.1
10	67.2	68.7	70.2	71.8	73.5	75.1	76.6	10	66.9	68.6	70.1	71.7	73.4	74.9	76.5
11	68.4	69.9	71.4	73.1	74.8	76.4	78.0	11	68.1	69.8	71.3	73.0	74.7	76.2	77.9
12	69.5	71.0	72.6	74.3	76.1	77.6	79.3	12	69.3	71.0	72.5	74.2	75.9	77.5	79.2
13	70.6	72.1	73.7	75.4	77.2	78.8	80.6	13	70.4	72.1	73.7	75.4	77.1	78.7	80.5
14	71.6	73.2	74.8	76.6	78.4	80.0	81.8	14	71.5	73.2	74.8	76.5	78.3	79.9	81.7
15	72.6	74.2	75.8	77.6	79.5	81.1	83.0	15	72.5	74.2	75.9	77.6	79.3	81.0	82.9
16	73.6	75.2	76.8	78.7	80.5	82.2	84.1	16	73.4	75.2	76.9	78.6	80.4	82.1	84.0
17	74.5	76.1	77.8	79.6	81.5	83.3	85.2	17	74.4	76.2	77.8	79.6	81.4	83.1	85.1
18	75.3	77.0	78.7	80.6	82.5	84.3	86.2	18	75.2	77.0	78.8	80.5	82.4	84.1	86.1
19	76.1	77.8	79.6	81.5	83.4	85.2	87.2	19	76.1	77.9	79.6	81.4	83.3	85.1	87.1
20	76.9	78.6	80.4	82.3	84.3	86.1	88.1	20	76.9	78.7	80.4	82.2	84.3	86.0	88.0
21	77.6	79.3	81.2	83.1	85.1	87.0	88.9	21	77.6	79.5	81.2	83.1	85.2	86.9	88.9
22	78.3	80.0	81.9	83.9	86.0	87.8	89.7	22	78.4	80.3	82.0	83.9	86.1	87.8	89.8
23	79.0	80.8	82.7	84.7	86.8	88.7	90.5	23	79.3	81.1	82.8	84.8	87.1	88.8	90.8
24	79.8	81.5	83.5	85.6	87.7	89.6	91.4	24	80.2	82.0	83.7	85.8	88.1	89.8	91.8

SOURCE: Reprinted by permission from J. Wingerd, E. J. Schoen, and I. L. Solomon. Growth standards in the first two years of life based on measurements of white and black children in a prepaid health care program. *Pediatrics*, 1971, **47**, 818–825.

Table 3-3. Percentile Distribution of Weights of Boys from Age 1 Month Through Age 24 Months: California, 1959–67.

In Kilograms

Age in Months	White Percentile							Age in Months	Black Percentile						
	3	10	25	50	75	90	97		3	10	25	50	75	90	97
1	3.16	3.55	3.91	4.28	4.63	4.93	5.30	1	2.90	3.41	3.76	4.13	4.50	4.82	5.14
2	4.11	4.54	4.92	5.34	5.75	6.11	6.54	2	3.97	4.49	4.89	5.32	5.76	6.18	6.61
3	4.90	5.35	5.77	6.22	6.69	7.11	7.58	3	4.81	5.34	5.79	6.28	6.77	7.27	7.80
4	5.55	6.02	6.47	6.97	7.48	7.95	8.47	4	5.48	6.02	6.51	7.05	7.59	8.16	8.78
5	6.09	6.58	7.06	7.59	8.15	8.67	9.23	5	6.03	6.58	7.10	7.68	8.27	8.89	9.58
6	6.55	7.06	7.56	8.13	8.73	9.29	9.88	6	6.48	7.03	7.59	8.20	8.83	9.50	10.25
7	6.95	7.48	8.00	8.59	9.23	9.82	10.46	7	6.86	7.43	8.01	8.65	9.32	10.02	10.82
8	7.31	7.84	8.38	9.00	9.67	10.30	10.96	8	7.20	7.78	8.38	9.05	9.75	10.48	11.31
9	7.62	8.17	8.73	9.37	10.07	10.73	11.42	9	7.51	8.09	8.72	9.41	10.14	10.88	11.76
10	7.91	8.46	9.04	9.71	10.43	11.12	11.84	10	7.81	8.39	9.03	9.74	10.50	11.26	12.16
11	8.18	8.74	9.34	10.02	10.77	11.47	12.23	11	8.08	8.67	9.33	10.06	10.84	11.60	12.53
12	8.44	9.00	9.61	10.31	11.08	11.81	12.59	12	8.34	8.94	9.62	10.36	11.16	11.93	12.87
13	8.68	9.24	9.87	10.59	11.38	12.12	12.93	13	8.59	9.20	9.89	10.64	11.47	12.23	13.20
14	8.90	9.47	10.12	10.85	11.66	12.42	13.25	14	8.83	9.45	10.15	10.92	11.76	12.52	13.51
15	9.12	9.69	10.35	11.10	11.92	12.70	13.56	15	9.04	9.67	10.39	11.17	12.03	12.79	13.80
16	9.32	9.90	10.57	11.33	12.17	12.97	13.85	16	9.23	9.88	10.62	11.41	12.28	13.04	14.08
17	9.51	10.09	10.78	11.55	12.40	13.22	14.13	17	9.40	10.06	10.82	11.62	12.51	13.27	14.34
18	9.69	10.27	10.98	11.76	12.63	13.47	14.39	18	9.54	10.21	10.99	11.82	12.73	13.49	14.60
19	9.85	10.44	11.16	11.96	12.84	13.70	14.65	19	9.66	10.35	11.15	12.00	12.92	13.69	14.85
20	10.01	10.60	11.34	12.16	13.05	13.93	14.91	20	9.75	10.46	11.29	12.17	13.11	13.88	15.10
21	10.15	10.76	11.51	12.34	13.25	14.16	15.16	21	9.83	10.56	11.43	12.34	13.30	14.08	15.37
22	10.30	10.92	11.69	12.53	13.45	14.40	15.42	22	9.91	10.67	11.57	12.52	13.50	14.31	15.68
23	10.45	11.08	11.87	12.73	13.66	14.65	15.70	23	10.01	10.79	11.74	12.73	13.74	14.57	16.04
24	10.61	11.27	12.07	12.95	13.90	14.93	16.01	24	10.15	10.97	11.96	13.01	14.04	14.91	16.49

SOURCE: Reprinted by permission from J. Wingerd, E. J. Schoen, and I. L. Solomon. Growth standards in the first two years of life based on measurements of white and black children in a prepaid health care program. *Pediatrics*, 1971, **47**, 818–825.

Table 3-4. Percentile Distribution of Weights of Girls from Age 1 Month Through Age 24 Months: California, 1959–67.

In Kilograms

	White								Black						
Age in Months	Percentile							Age in Months	Percentile						
	3	10	25	50	75	90	97		3	10	25	50	75	90	97
1	3.04	3.38	3.70	4.03	4.35	4.65	4.91	1	2.88	3.29	3.60	3.92	4.23	4.55	4.91
2	3.88	4.23	4.58	4.96	5.33	5.68	6.02	2	3.80	4.21	4.56	4.94	5.32	5.72	6.11
3	4.58	4.95	5.33	5.75	6.17	6.58	6.98	3	4.55	4.97	5.35	5.79	6.23	6.69	7.12
4	5.18	5.56	5.97	6.44	6.90	7.35	7.82	4	5.15	5.58	6.01	6.49	7.00	7.51	7.98
5	5.69	6.09	6.52	7.03	7.53	8.03	8.54	5	5.65	6.09	6.55	7.09	7.64	8.21	8.73
6	6.12	6.54	7.00	7.54	8.09	8.62	9.18	6	6.07	6.52	7.01	7.59	8.19	8.81	9.38
7	6.50	6.93	7.41	7.99	8.57	9.14	9.74	7	6.42	6.89	7.41	8.03	8.68	9.33	9.96
8	6.82	7.28	7.79	8.39	9.01	9.61	10.24	8	6.72	7.21	7.76	8.41	9.10	9.79	10.48
9	7.11	7.59	8.12	8.75	9.40	10.03	10.69	9	6.99	7.49	8.08	8.76	9.49	10.20	10.96
10	7.37	7.87	8.42	9.08	9.76	10.41	11.10	10	7.24	7.76	8.37	9.08	9.85	10.58	11.41
11	7.61	8.13	8.70	9.39	10.09	10.77	11.48	11	7.47	8.01	8.65	9.38	10.18	10.94	11.84
12	7.84	8.38	8.97	9.68	10.40	11.10	11.84	12	7.69	8.25	8.92	9.67	10.50	11.28	12.24
13	8.05	8.61	9.22	9.95	10.70	11.42	12.17	13	7.91	8.48	9.17	9.95	10.81	11.61	12.63
14	8.25	8.84	9.47	10.21	10.98	11.72	12.49	14	8.12	8.72	9.42	10.21	11.10	11.92	13.01
15	8.45	9.06	9.70	10.46	11.25	12.01	12.79	15	8.33	8.94	9.67	10.47	11.39	12.22	13.37
16	8.65	9.28	9.93	10.70	11.51	12.29	13.08	16	8.53	9.16	9.90	10.71	11.66	12.51	13.73
17	8.84	9.48	10.16	10.94	11.77	12.56	13.36	17	8.73	9.38	10.13	10.94	11.92	12.79	14.06
18	9.02	9.69	10.37	11.16	12.01	12.82	13.64	18	8.92	9.59	10.34	11.16	12.17	13.06	14.38
19	9.20	9.88	10.58	11.38	12.24	13.07	13.90	19	9.10	9.78	10.54	11.36	12.40	13.32	14.69
20	9.37	10.06	10.77	11.58	12.45	13.31	14.15	20	9.27	9.97	10.73	11.55	12.62	13.56	14.97
21	9.53	10.24	10.96	11.77	12.65	13.53	14.39	21	9.43	10.14	10.90	11.72	12.83	13.79	15.24
22	9.68	10.40	11.12	11.94	12.84	13.73	14.62	22	9.58	10.30	11.05	11.87	13.01	14.01	15.49
23	9.82	10.54	11.27	12.10	13.00	13.92	14.83	23	9.72	10.46	11.20	12.01	13.19	14.23	15.73
24	9.94	10.66	11.40	12.23	13.14	14.09	15.03	24	9.86	10.61	11.33	12.14	13.36	14.44	15.95

SOURCE: Reprinted by permission from J. Wingerd, E. J. Schoen, and I. L. Solomon. Growth standards in the first two years of life based on measurements of white and black children in a prepaid health care program. *Pediatrics,* 1971, **47**, 818–825.

is earlier and faster than that of the other two divisions of the brain, the forebrain and stem. The cerebellum finishes its growth spurt around the end of the first year. Thus it is probably even more vulnerable to growth restriction than is the brain as a whole. The practical implications of the brain growth spurt are the importance of excellent nutrition and appropriate stimulation during the first two years.

ILLNESS

Many kinds of illnesses disrupt the growth process, some slowing it down overall and some making it disproportionate. Infections, especially respiratory infections, are probably the most common type of illness in North American infants, with gastrointestinal upsets second. When parents smoke, their infants have a high incidence of bronchitis and pneumonia during the first year of life [17]. If only one parent smokes, the frequency of these diseases is halfway between the incidence when neither smokes and when both smoke. These findings are from a longitudinal study of 2,205 infants.

Throughout the world, nutrition-related illnesses pose frequent and grave threats to infants and children of all ages. Although protein-calorie malnutrition contributes to the high death rate in poor countries and regions, the majority of malnourished children survive impaired. Another type of nutritional problem results from food-related disorders of the body. For example, 70 per cent of Afro-Americans lack an enzyme required for converting a sugar in cow's milk to a kind that can be absorbed [39]. If an infant lacking the enzyme is fed cow's milk, he is likely to have severe diarrhea, pain, and growth retardation. He may die. Some children react to the gluten of wheat with intestinal changes that interfere with the absorption of nutrients and hence suffer growth retardation. Distorted growth can result from vitamin deficiencies and excesses. Early diagnosis and treatment minimizes growth disturbance. For example, if vitamin D insensitivity (usually inherited) is detected before six months of age, bone deformities can usually be prevented.

Malnutrition. From Appendix A, it can be seen that for the first year a baby needs about three times as many calories and two to three times as much protein per unit of body weight as an adult. Growth in height and weight of well-nourished children is rapid but slowing down in the latter half of the first year. At the same time, the rate of muscle growth increases. If the baby is getting supplementary foods, as most North American children are, a decreasing proportion of calories is coming from milk. If the infant is living in poverty, protein intake is drastically cut as he is weaned on to inadequate foods.

Marasmus and kwashiorkor are two severe diseases that are caused by malnutrition. *Marasmus* is a wasting away of body tissues. When suffering from marasmus, an infant is grossly underweight, with atrophy of muscles and subcutaneous fat but with no clinical edema. Marasmus is caused by undernutrition, resulting from insufficient food or from not utilizing food. It often is the result of early weaning from breast milk to an inadequate food, probably an unsuitable cow's milk formula [3]. Diarrhea frequently contributes to the starvation. A severe emotional disturbance can cause the child not to eat or to be unable to utilize food adequately. A longitudinal study of children with marasmus was done in Chile, where a decline in breast-feeding produced some severe malnutrition in early infancy [66]. These babies were admitted to the hospital at ages 3 to 11 months with acute marasmus that had begun at some time between 1 and 5 months. Most of them weighed little more than they did at birth. They were treated to recovery and sent home with a steady and adequate supply of milk. At ages 3 to 6 years, all were clinically normal, with height far below average (lower than the third percentile) for Chilean children. Their legs were short and their weights were all above the third percentile, many close to the fiftieth percentile. Thus, weights were above normal for heights and some children looked obese. Head circumferences were below normal.

Kwashiorkor occurs most often in 1- to 4-year-olds whose diets are very low in proteins while being not so low in total calories. The biochemical changes in the body are quite different in the two diseases, kwashiorkor having more lasting effects after the acute stage is alleviated. Symptoms of kwashiorkor are swelling of face, legs, and abdomen because of water retention, growth retardation, wasting of muscles with some fat retained, apathy, or whimpering. The hair may be reddish and thin and the skin coarse, spotted, or with a rash or lesions. Liver damage is likely to occur [63]. A frequent beginning for kwashiorkor occurs when a mother weans her baby of a year or more because she has become pregnant [3]. She feeds him starchy foods and little protein.

There are malnourished children in all parts of the world, although nutrition problems are most severe in the poorest countries. Even in North America, where standards of living are generally high, two national nutrition surveys showed

The babies in this picture are 2-year-old twins, both raised at home, the one on the left a girl and the one on the right a boy. The difference in their condition is entirely due to the fact that the boy was nursed and fed first, his sister being fed what little was left over.

UNICEF PHOTO/BALCOMB

Table 3-5.   Number of Calories Received Daily by Young Black and White Children, Above and Below the Poverty Line.

	Poor	*Not Poor*
White	1,592	1,607
Black	1,387	1,507

SOURCE: S. Abraham, F. W. Lowenstein, and C. L. Johnson. Preliminary findings of the first health and nutrition examination survey, United States, 1971–72: Dietary intake and biochemical findings. DHEW Publication No. (HRA) 74–1219–1 Washington, D.C.: U.S. Government Printing Office, 1974.

nutritional defects in children. Clinical assessments of Canadian children from birth to four years found 3.6 per cent of the general population and 9.2 per cent of Eskimo at risk in regard to protein-calorie malnutrition [77]. Biochemical assessments indicated sizable numbers at risk in regard to iron, serum folate, vitamin A, and vitamin C. The United States survey found low caloric intake in 14 per cent of white children between one and five years and in 23 per cent of black children the same age [1]. Table 3-5 shows the number of daily calories received by black and white children above and below the poverty line. Significant deficiencies were also found in amounts of calcium, iron, and vitamins A and C, with black children often showing more severe deficiencies than white. A serious iron shortage was found in New York City infants of low-income families [62]. Some of these babies received too little food, some too much. From one month to one year, there was a steady increase in empty calories.

Malnourished children, including fat ones, are more likely than well-nourished to suffer all sorts of infections and to have more severe cases [87]. Infections add

Figure 3-1.   Average height of young boys from very poor areas contrasted with height of average United States boys of same age.

SOURCE: Reprinted by permission from A. E. Schaefer and O. C. Johnston. Are we well fed? *Nutrition Today*, 4: 1. 2–11. Copyright © 1969 by Enloe, Stalvey and Associates.

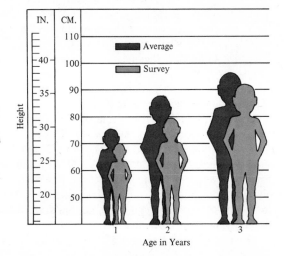

to the state of malnutrition by depressing the appetite and requiring mobilization of nitrogen and other essential nutrients [79]. After the period of stress is over, during convalescence, the normal course of events is the returning of the nutrients to the tissue from which they were drawn, but this process requires extra proteins and vitamins, the very elements most lacking in the diets of the poor. The baby who started an illness as malnourished, then, is in a worse state of nutrition when the infection subsides and is ready to pick up another infection for which his resistance is even lower. Malnutrition depresses the body's manufacture of antibodies. Growth is slowed down, since the nutrients it requires are insufficient.

When the baby is weaned from the breast, or when the mother's milk supply dwindles greatly, the baby loses the immunity-giving benefits of human milk. If the substitute foods are unsanitary and of poor quality, he is exposed to irritants and disease organisms that cause infections, infestations, and diarrhea while he is deprived of nutrients. The depressing effects of low socioeconomic status on height and weight were greatest at one year in a large sample of European children followed from one year until five years of age [45].

Malnutrition and Intelligence. When traditional intelligence tests have been used in many different parts of the world, malnourished children, or children previously malnourished, scored lower than well-nourished children. In Bogotá, Colombia, a typical result of such a study was based on the Griffiths Scale on children under two years [16]. Figure 3-2 contrasts 60 malnourished infants (judged on growth deficits) of lower socioeconomic status with 60 well-nourished infants from the same class and with 30 well-nourished middle-class children. Significant differences are shown between the three groups. Another group of children, hospitalized for severe malnutrition, had an even lower average quotient of 56. The Griffiths Scale, like the Gesell and Bayley tests, includes measure of some tasks where opportunities for learning have influenced the baby. Differences in culture and family would make for differences in quotients. On Piagetian-type tests, however, environmental influences are probably less important. Therefore, differences between groups might be attributed more to differences in nutrition. The Einstein Scale, based on Piaget's work, was used. Up to 10 months of age, there was no difference between malnourished and well-nourished infants, but scores were somewhat lower in the malnourished group between 10 and 24 months. It seems, then, that the most basic aspects of intelligence are most resistant to damage from any sort of deprivation. If true, this finding is reassuring as to the adaptive powers of the human organism, but it is *not* justification for permitting children to receive inadequate food.

From his studies of the role of stimulation and nutrition in the development and treatment of intellectual deficits, Cravioto, the famous Mexican physician-nutritionist, has concluded the following [22]. When a nutritionally deprived child shows mental retardation, he has, in all likelihood, also suffered from lack of emotional and intellectual interaction. His studies have shown the importance of giving loving attention and interesting stimulation along with good food in the treatment of seriously malnourished children. These findings are consistent with the study mentioned previously, and with many other studies that show middle-class children scoring higher in IQ tests than even well-nourished children of lower

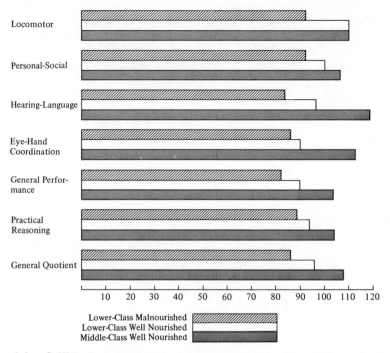

Figure 3-2. Griffiths Scale quotients in three groups of Colombian children, showing differences in socioeconomic status and nutritional status.

SOURCE: Data from L. F. Cobos, M. C. Latham, and F. J. Stare. Will improved nutrition help to prevent mental retardation? *Preventive Medicine*, 1973, **1**, 185–194.

socioeconomic status. A sample of mothers of low educational status gave less appropriate stimulation to their infants, even though they gave affection [82].

Observations of Zambian mothers and infants also showed the growth-promoting effects of stimulation given with abundant food [7]. Born without medication, but in poor condition, probably from poor nutrition in depleted uteruses, these infants were small, limp, and unresponsive, with dry, scaling skin, and little fat. But the mothers *expected* the babies to respond to them, to hold their heads up while carried, and to develop well. The infants were given ample breast milk and much stimulation. By 10 days, the infants were ahead of an American control group in sensory and motor development. They grew more precocious throughout the first year.

Contributions of food and stimulation were analyzed in an enrichment experiment with growth-retarded American children, between 6 and 24 months of age [74]. All subjects were given nutritional treatment, but the experimental group also received a daily hour of home tutoring by a child development specialist. There were no differences in the two groups in that both made large gains in weight and height. However, the tutored group scored higher than the control group on the Bayley Scales of Infant Development, the difference being statistically

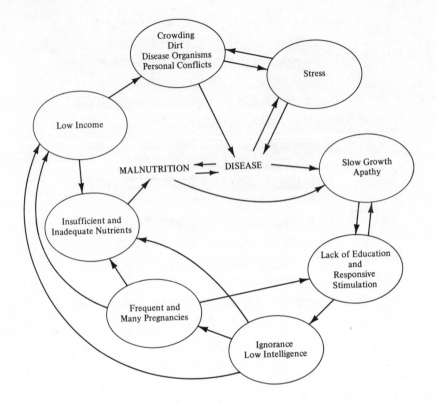

Figure 3-3.　Interacting causes of malnutrition and disease.

significant for psychomotor development, but not for mental development. Thus, whereas feeding did a great deal for the growth-retarded infants, stimulation added a little more to the total gains.

Figure 3-3 summarizes and diagrams the interactions and relationships between malnutrition, disease, and growth.

FEEDING

Although infants are very adaptable in their eating, they soon become creatures of habit, preferring familiar foods as they grow older. It is likely that the toddler who has a varied and diverse diet will grow up with an interest in new foods and an adventurous attitude toward eating, whereas those restricted as to early diet will become conservatives at the table [12].

Introducing New Foods. Low-income families in New York were found to be giving solids to 50 per cent of their month-old babies [62]. There is a widespread custom of adding solids to bottle feedings and of giving solids early. The practice is not confined to low-income families. We have seen college graduates feeding potatoes and gravy to a four-month-old infant and a large piece of iced chocolate cake to a six-month-old. Even well-educated parents need to learn specifically what is good for their infants to eat.

Nutritionists question the value of introducing solids to young infants. Whether the baby is fed human milk or formula, there is no nutritional need to begin solids until three months, or possibly six months [64]. Extra nutrients may place a strain upon the kidneys and other organs. Concern with obesity as a problem has led to awareness that extra fat cells may be laid down by overfeeding in infancy and that these cells remain permanently [87]. There are, however, other causes of obesity, especially insufficient exercise.

When solids are first given, the baby will use the sucking movements that she uses with milk. If the cereal is diluted to a liquid form given in a small spoon as just a taste, she will learn how to cope with the new form of food. Techniques of introducing and increasing solid foods are given in nutrition textbooks, such as McWilliams [63]. Appendix A gives nutrient requirements of infants. Individual needs, of course, vary from these average figures.

Table 3-6 shows the ages at which the deciduous or baby teeth erupt. Before and at the time when teeth are first coming through the gums, amounts of saliva increase and drooling is common. If solids are to be chewed, they have to be mixed with saliva and they must be ground between two teeth. The incisors, good for biting, begin to appear at seven or eight months, whereas molars can be expected at around 15 months. If these physiological indications of readiness for solids are taken seriously, then the offering of foods that need chewing will be delayed until the baby can chew them. However, babies make chewing movements with their gums while teething, and they seem to be comforted by chewing on hard rubber toys and foods that will not break off in pieces, such as a hard biscuit.

Table 3-6. Ages (in months) for Early, Average, and Late Eruption of Deciduous Teeth.

Deciduous Teeth	Early	Average	Late
Lower central incisor	5	7.8	11
Upper central incisor	6	9.6	12
Lower lateral incisor	7	11.5	15
Upper lateral incisor	7	12.4	18
Lower 1st molar	10	15.1	20
Upper 1st molar	10	15.7	20
Lower cuspid	11	18.2	24
Upper cuspid	11	18.3	24
Lower 2d molar	13	26.0	31
Upper 2d molar	13	26.2	31

SOURCE: Data from S. L. Horowitz and E. H. Hixon. *The nature of orthodontic diagnosis*. St. Louis: The C. V. Mosby Co., 1966.

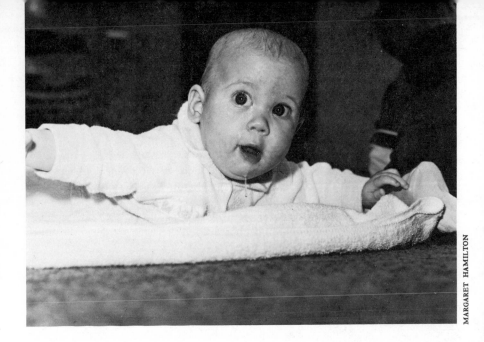

MARGARET HAMILTON

Weaning. Emerging resources include new ways of eating. Instead of getting all of his food as liquids which he sucks, the baby learns to bite and chew solids and to drink liquids from a cup. This particular changeover is called *weaning*. Weaning is also used sometimes to mean any gradual change from immature to mature behavior. In all contexts, weaning usually involves some pushing and encouraging of the child toward more mature behavior. Since an older baby can hold his bottle and carry it with him, he can enjoy sucking and his autonomy at the same time, whereas with breast-feeding, the growing desire for independence may make him accept cup feeding more readily. The timing and techniques of weaning are related to personality development of the child and to cultural prescriptions.

The use of gradualness and gentleness is consistent with what is known about personality development during the first year. While developing his sense of trust, it is most helpful for the baby to be assured that the world and the people in it can be trusted. Traumatic experiences and major readjustments to life are injurious to the sense of trust and hence to the establishment of the foundations of a healthy personality.

An example of another cultural setting shows how weaning can be crucial to the sense of autonomy, rather than to the sense of trust, when weaning occurs at a time when the sense of autonomy is growing rapidly. A group of Zulu babies were studied before, during, and after weaning, which occurred between 15 and 24 months, at the average age of 19 months [2]. The day of weaning was a serious event, fixed months ahead. Bitter juice of the aloe was put on the mother's breast while the child watched and then the breast was offered to him throughout the day. A charm was put around his neck to help him in various ways. On the day of weaning, all but one baby refused the breast after the first encounter with the aloe juice. Behavior changes followed a definite pattern of disintegration, followed by integration on a higher level. During the first two hours, the toddlers became more negativistic, aggressive, and fretful. They sucked their fingers and other objects.

144

Some performed stereotyped actions. After the first day, relationships changed with everyone in the home. With their mothers, they first alternated attacking and ignoring, then tried to gain attention by illness, clinging, fretting, and crying, and finally paid little attention to their mothers, showing no anger and behaving with increasing independence. Sudden increases in mature behavior included helping with housework, imitating others, using new words, talking more distinctly, leaving home more often, and showing hospitality. Children also became more aggressive and mischievous, spilling water, playing with fire, and wasting food. Eating patterns changed, with preferences for adult food and greatly increased appetite.

These behavior changes can be seen as contributing to a growing sense of autonomy. Normal development during the second year, especially the latter half of the second year, involves establishing oneself as a separate individual. All of these six changes in behavior indicate increased independence, power in decision making, differentiation, and reorganization. The weaning experience apparently precipitated the second stage of personality growth. Thus, the method of sudden weaning, conducted differently and timed differently, had a very different result from weaning conducted American-style. Both methods of weaning can be seen to be functional in regard to the stage of personality growth during which they are conducted.

Self-Regulation of Diet in Infancy. Of great practical significance is the question of how competent the child is to select the quantity and quality of his food. "Does the baby know how much he ought to eat?" and "Does the baby know what is good for him?" Probably he would if he had been fed entirely on breast milk for most of the first year and then exposed at each mealtime to a wide selection of simple, nutritionally valuable foods and *no other foods*. Since it is impractical and even impossible to arrange these conditions at home, the baby needs to have a good diet selected for him and presented in small servings at regular times. If the atmosphere is pleasant, and autonomy in feeding encouraged, then most infants will be able to decide how *much* they should eat. If parents and caretakers develop trust in the baby's ability to decide when he has had enough, they will not be tempted to stuff unnecessary calories into him, nor will they set up the dining table as a battleground.

SAFETY

Even newborn infants can move by means of reflex crawling. The first time of turning over is not predictable. Therefore, from the beginning, protection includes never leaving the baby unwatched on a table or bed without sides. When she starts to creep, of course, she needs increased vigilance to prevent injuries. Although a playpen will keep her safe, it may also keep her inactive. Exercise is necessary for bodily fitness, and activity for mental development. Designing the environment for a creeping or toddling infant is an important part of parenting that is discussed in the next chapter. So also will be parental abuse, a type of injury that is increasing, taking the form of neglect and/or direct inflicting of damage.

ESTABLISHING REGULARITY OF BASIC PROCESSES

The body must stay within certain physical and chemical limits if it is to stay alive. In order to function optimally, it must stay within narrower limits. *Homeostasis,* the maintenance of steady states within these limits, is accomplished by integrated control of the nervous and endocrine systems. During the first 3 or 4 months of life, the mechanisms of homeostasis become more and more efficient. The baby settles down to an easier, more automatic supporting of life processes, his energies freed for a wider variety of activities.

Temperature regulation is one of the vital homeostatic processes. A certain constancy has to be kept in spite of heat loss and heat production. The baby regulates his temperature more adequately after the neonatal period than he does in the beginning. For example, the sweat glands become active at about a month of age. Even with temperature regulation improving, infants and young children are still highly susceptible to temperature fluctuation. Bodily temperature is likely to shoot up with active exercise, crying, emotional upset, or rise in surrounding temperature [8, p. 133]. Bodily temperature responds readily to chilling. Infants and young children, when suffering from infections, usually show higher temperatures than do older children. Although the average temperature at 3 months is 37.5° C, about one third of babies this age have temperatures above 37.9 or below 37.1. At 6 months, two thirds of infants have temperatures between 37.8 and 37.2. The corresponding range at 1 year is 37.9 to 37.5. Thus, average temperature and individual variations decrease as the infant grows into childhood. Individual differences continue to exist, though, and it is important to realize that an occasional child may have an unusually high (or low) temperature that is normal for *him* [61].

Heat production increases with age throughout the growth period. The younger the child, the more he is likely to vary from the average and also to vary with himself from time to time [53]. The larger the body, of course, the greater is the absolute amount of heat produced. Taken in terms of heat production per unit of body weight, however, the 6-month-old baby produces more heat than anybody. Heat production builds up from birth to 6 months and then tapers off to adulthood.

Considering what is known about temperature in children, it can be seen that good care includes protection against extremes of temperature and supervision that helps the child to regulate his own temperature. During about the first year a room temperature of between 20 degrees and 22 degrees Celsius is recommended [8, pp. 133–134]. When the baby can run around, 18 degrees to 20 degrees is a good temperature for him. Adequate clothing helps to keep temperature at an optimal level while also providing flexibility. Since infants and young children produce such large amounts of heat, they are likely to become overheated through active play or when wearing heavy clothing. They will show discomfort by a flushed face, perspiration, and perhaps irritability.

Respiration changes considerably during the first year. The rate slows down to about half what it was at birth. After 1 year, it continues to become slower. Breathing becomes deeper, too. At birth, the diaphragm does practically all of the work in breathing. The chest gradually comes into play during infancy, but thoracic breathing is not well established until the end of the preschool period [61]. A young baby's breathing sounds harsh, irregular, and shallow. Gradually his breathing becomes more regular and less noisy as he changes toward thoracic breathing, as his chest grows, and as the tissues covering his chest thicken and insulate the sounds.

The timing of eating, sleeping, and eliminating becomes regularized. By 3 or 4 months, even the baby who has made his own schedule (fed when hungry, allowed to sleep until he wakens) eats and sleeps at fairly predictable times. The newborn sleeps 16 or 17 hours a day, nearly all of the time when he is not eating and receiving care [69]. From age 3 months to 6 months, he gradually stays awake more in the daytime and sleeps longer at night. During the second year, most babies sleep through the night and take one or two naps during the day. Some time during this year, the second nap tends to drop out, with one nap continued until age 4 or 5 years.

As eating and sleeping become regularized, bowel movements also tend to do so. By six months, one or two stools a day are most usual. Wide individual differences occur, however. About half of 2-year-olds have bowel movements at predictable times, and half are unpredictable [76].

LOCOMOTION

The baby's world expands and stimulation increases greatly when he learns to move from one place to another. Much maturation and learning go on before the infant actually creeps, crawls, or hitches.

Growth of the parts of the brain concerned with locomation is indicated as the baby progresses through the locomotor sequence. The *cerebellum,* concerned largely with balance and posture, grows slowly during the first few months and rapidly in size and complexity between 6 and 18 months [20]. The sequence of motor development is shown in the silhouettes presented in Figure 3-4. Here is shown progression from fetal position to walking—in 15 months.

The locomotion of the first year is creeping, of the second year, walking. Each of these patterns of moving can be traced from early beginnings. Considering creeping, you can see its beginning in the early attempts of the baby to raise his head when he is in prone position. Most babies do this momentarily at one month or two months, gradually lifting their heads higher and for longer periods of time. Although some babies actually make progress by crawling during their first weeks, this reflexlike movement fades out, leaving infants stationary until they develop the more purposive kind of creeping movements. Although maturation plays a major role in the achievement of creeping, anyone who watches a baby go through the final stages before creeping sees a great deal of effort and trial and error. For instance, the *swimming stage* is one in which the baby perches on his abdomen and pushes. Any progress at this point is likely to be backward and slight. Shortly afterward comes a stage when babies try out a variety of methods, such as using the stomach as a pivot, hitching by means of head and feet, shoulders and feet, or buttocks and hands, making a bridge by standing on toes and hands and scooting backward. Although some infants retain idiosyncratic ways of creeping, most do it in the usual style, which is shown in Figure 3-4.

Basic to walking are holding the head and shoulders erect, sitting, making stepping movements, and standing. Even in the first three months, most infants

Figure 3-4. The sequence of motor development, with ages at which the average baby achieves each coordination.

SOURCE: Reprinted by permission from M. M. Shirley. *The first two years: a study of twenty-five babies.* Vol. II: *Intellectual development.* Copyright 1933 by University of Minnesota, Minneapolis.

resist with their feet when held in standing position. Gradually more and more of the baby's weight is borne by his feet. Stepping movements (while held) begin in what looks like dancing, standing on the toes, lifting one foot and then the other and putting both feet down in the same place. Later come putting one foot down ahead of the other and bouncing. Before they can pull themselves up into standing position, most babies can stand holding on to helping hands or to the rail of a playpen. Some children, however, learn to pull up before they can remain standing [41, p. 39].

Most children learn to walk during the first three months of the second year. Parents often think that their baby really could walk if he would, since he gets around so quickly and easily with one hand held or with just one hand on a piece of furniture. The stage of cruising or walking with help seems to be a period of perfecting walking skills and gaining confidence before setting out independently. Walking is unsteady at first, gradually improving with maturing and practice. Maturation includes a change in proportions and posture, as well as neuromuscular

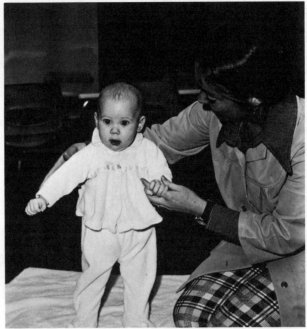

MARGARET HAMILTON

development. The toddler has short legs, a long trunk, large head and abdomen, and consequently a center of gravity high in his trunk. In order to balance himself better, he spreads his feet, walking on a broad base. As his proportions change toward those of childhood, he can afford to place his feet closer together. By the second half of the second year, he can run, covering territory at least twice as fast.

Locomotion includes climbing, too, which looks much like creeping, but begins in the second year, usually in the first three months. Climbing further enlarges the infant's scope of activities, giving him the run of all the floors of his home and access to the sofa, chairs, tabletops, cupboards, drawers.

Because the world expands so enormously with sitting, creeping, walking, running, and climbing, there are a multitude of opportunities for the sense of autonomy to grow. So many choices to make! So many ways in which to test oneself! So many avenues to discovery of powers and limits on powers! It can be very heady or even overwhelming.

Ethnic Differences in Posture and Locomotion. Many studies have compared the motor development of white infants with that of children of other ethnicity. White-black comparisons during the first year have almost always shown black infants to be more advanced posturally than white ones, in both Africa and the United States [4, 24, 35, 40, 42, 54, 83]. The black-white difference decreases and possibly levels out during the second year. The same pattern of differences has been observed in India [70], Mexico and Guatemala [22], and Israel [55], where United States babies have been behind the comparison groups in age of

MARGARET HAMILTON

achieving postural and locomotor milestones during the first year. Many different explanations have been advanced, but none are conclusive. We wonder if the conduct of labor and delivery, especially the liberal use of medication in delivery, might contribute to the slow start of infants in the United States.

EYE-HAND COORDINATION AND MANIPULATION

Gesell's extensive research on United States babies gave a picture of the newborn as having a reflex grasp but as using his eyes more than his hands for contacting and exploring [41]. The United States baby grasps objects that touch his hand, not looking at them until about three months. Grasping advances through a regular sequence, from a primitive, palmar grasp, through using thumb and palm at six months, thumb and fingers at eight months, and the forefinger in precise opposition to the thumb at 11 months. Both hands are active in the early stages of reaching and grasping; using a one-handed grasp and transferring from hand to hand typically occur at six months.

As mentioned in the previous chapter, Bower [6, pp. 150–179] has found that newborn infants readily reach for objects and grasp them if they are alert and supported and held in such a way that their hands and arms are free for action. Their reaches are one-handed unless the object is in the midline. Although most studies of British and North American infants have shown that they do not reach after 4 weeks of age, until about 20 weeks, there was no decline in reaching by infants who had been given objects to reach for daily. Bower has found that infants of 26 weeks can reach and grasp an object without guiding their hands visually. Subsequent refinement of reaching and grasping results from both maturation and experience. As Gesell's sequence shows, arm and hand movements become more controlled and more specific, with fine, precise movements being differentiated out of more general ones. Among the refinements are adapting grasping and lifting to different weights of objects. At six or seven months, a baby grips tightly, with no accommodation to weight. At around nine months, she adjusts her grasp to the weight *after* picking up the object. By about one year, she adjusts her grasp perfectly on picking up an object for the second time. At about 18 months, weight is anticipated by the size of the object.

The topic of eye-hand coordination and manipulation involves both motor development and cognition; the actions put them together. Through acting upon an object, a child *knows* it.

Intellectual Development

As shown in the previous section, the eyes and hands supply stimulation upon which the mind acts. Experience comes from many sources as the infant interacts with people, objects, himself, and his whole environment. He explores through his sensory and motor resources, making some changes in the objects and people

MARGARET HAMILTON

he contacts, changing himself as he receives sensory data and processes them. He communicates with people, rapidly improving his techniques for doing so. As he refines his methods of communicating, he is also developing a tool of thinking.

COGNITION

Cognoscere means "to know." By *cognition* is meant the individual's becoming acquainted with the world and the objects in it, including himself. Cognitive development results in less immediate reaction to stimuli and more application of information and experiences that have been abstracted and stored in memory.

Attention. The first step in taking in information is to attend to a stimulus. Much research is directed to the problems of what determines whether an infant will attend to a given stimulus (fixation), how long he will attend (duration), and what age-related changes occur in attention. The study of attention involves learning and memory, since attending is influenced by previous experience. Most studies on attention have been concerned with *visual* attention. Attention is indicated by cardiac deceleration [65]. It can also be measured by measuring length of visual fixation or number of fixations [9]. When habituation is used for studying attention, a stimulus is shown repeatedly. The subject decreases looking time but looks longer at a new stimulus.

Maturation plays a central role in the changes in visual attention that take place in infancy. It seems that new capabilities emerge as neural networks mature [9]. One new phase begins around the third month, when the gaze is no longer controlled by salient contour and scanning develops. Memory images play a larger and larger part in determining what the baby will look at. As some parts of a visual array are seen as familiar, others that are new are explored.

Of course there are individual differences in attention, just as there are in other areas of development. Some babies fixate stimuli for longer times than do

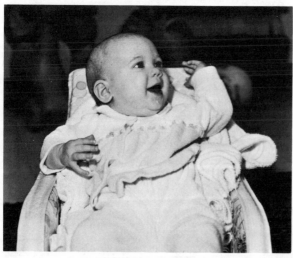

MARGARET HAMILTON

others. The characteristic seems to be quite stable, as an aspect of the temperament of the infant. In a study of year-olds, fixation time was related to the length of time that girls would play with a toy [33].

Visual preferences at various ages have been studied by Fantz and his associates, who measured the duration of fixation upon a particular stimulus and compared it with fixations on other stimuli. The arrays of stimuli varied shape, size, number, and arrangement; for example, the number of squares varied from two to 128 and the size of squares from two inches to one-quarter inch. The experimenters found a regular age-related sequence in which preference for size decreased while preference for number of elements increased [32]. They compared full-term infants with premature infants on their age of reaching steps in the preference sequence. The prematures lagged behind the full-terms when age was measured from the birthdate, but the two groups were virtually the same when age was figured from the date of the mother's last menstrual period. Not only do these experiments tell something of the nature of visual development. They also have a practical application as a method of estimating gestation age in premature babies and very small newborns and for monitoring the development of at-risk infants [68]. Preference for novelty is another dimension that is useful in assessing babies at risk.

A preference for novel rather than familiar visual stimuli was found to emerge in 16 normal infants at about 10 weeks of age [85]. At 4 to 5 months, a group of 89 babies looked longer at the most discrepant or novel stimuli, as compared with stimuli that differed less from the familiar ones [19]. In other words, greater novelty claimed greater attention. Six-month-old infants moved their gaze from one stimulus to another more often than did 3-months infants, showing that the former were looking more vigorously for novelty [46].

Faces are very important in the conduct of human affairs. How and when do they take on meaning for infants? This topic has received much scrutiny from psychologists. Considerable information comes from an elaborate study that used habituation to detect whether at 4 and 5 months, babies could distinguish between a regular face and various distortions [13]. Some of the findings and conclusions follow. At 4 months the eyes, more salient than nose and mouth, are perceived as a unit in the upper half of the face, paired horizontally. The hair and head are salient, more so than the inner face. "Faceness," the configuration of eyes, nose, and mouth, is not recognized. By 5 months, the mouth is as salient as the eyes, the interior face is equal to the head in salience, and facial configuration is recognized. Five and a half months, according to another study, is the age when the ability to discriminate between different faces first appears [31]. Categories of recognition are also building up at this time. Between 5 and 6 months, a group of Guatemalan infants could discriminate between photographs of a man, a woman, and a seven-year-old boy, but not between photographs of two women, two men, or two boys [57].

Another sort of visual behavior that has great practical significance is the patterning of responses to the "visual cliff." Creeping infants stay away from a surface pattern that indicates a dropoff, even though the pattern is only a simulation of an edge. When infants of five months and nine months were placed on the deep or shallow side of the visual cliff, their behavior differed [78]. The younger group showed similar visual attention on both sides and a decelerating heart rate on the deep side. The older group paid more visual attention to the deep side than to the shallow side, and showed an accelerating heart rate. A possible explanation is that the younger infants were merely attentive to the visual patterning, whereas the older ones felt fear. It has survival value for an infant to be interested in a visual pattern that indicates a place where he might get hurt, and for that interest to develop into caution and then fear as he becomes able to move.

Development of Sensorimotor Intelligence. No matter how intelligence is defined, it exists in infants before they can speak, a practical kind of intelligence aimed at solving problems of action [73]. Piaget's work gives valuable insight into what goes on inside babies before they can tell others what they are thinking. The sensorimotor period lasts until the child reorganizes his intelligence on the next level, the period of *preoperational thought*. The changeover usually occurs at between 18 months and 2 years and marks the end of infancy, from a cognitive standpoint.

With no words at its service, sensorimotor intelligence uses percepts and movements, organizing them into action schemas. (A *schema* is a pattern of action or thought that is built up by repetition in similar situations.) The first movements, reflexes, are present at birth. Through his own efforts, experiences, and actions, the child builds his mental structures, or intellectual abilities, and uses them for constructing and restructuring objects.

The achievement of the infancy stage in cognition is to come to know one's immediate environment as permanent objects and background, separate from oneself. *Permanent* means that the object (bottle, mother, rattle, and such) continues to exist even though it is moved, hidden, or placed in a new relationship with other objects (such as mother in a hat). All the parts of an object (such as the nipple on a bottle) must be known to exist even when they cannot be seen.

Understanding some facts about movement is a part of coming to know permanent objects. A child has to find out that when an object is moved, it can be put back again; that when it turns around, it can be turned in the other direction; that when an object is moved away, he can reach it by a path other than the one taken by the object, in fact by many different paths.

Starting with the resources he has for dealing with the world, the baby uses them to develop new patterns of action. For example, he integrates schemas of mouthing, holding, and looking. The result is an examining schema. Using this method of exploration many times with toys, bottles, clothing, and other objects, the infant makes progress toward the conviction that objects are permanent. Other behavior patterns, involving seeing, smelling, tasting, hearing, touching, and manipulating are used in getting knowledge of the world. Locomotion, moving from place to place, gives the baby chances to map out the space in which he lives, getting to truly cognize it, and himself as an object in space.

As experience with reality shows his existing resources to be inadequate or insufficient, the baby develops new schemas through accommodation or improvements in what he has. When the child falls only slightly short of being adequate to cope with an experience, his feeling tone is pleasant and interesting. Growth is

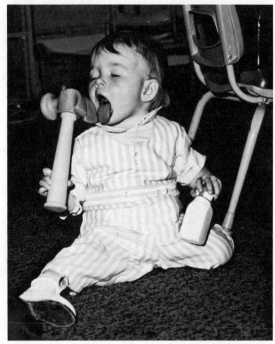

This baby is using schemas
of holding and mouthing to
examine a toy hammer.

MARGARET HAMILTON

stimulated. When he is very inadequate in dealing with the experience, the child is
frightened or he may not even perceive the problem.

Piaget has described six substages of the period of sensorimotor intelligence,
the period during which the infant establishes basic knowledge of the world.
Piaget is not concerned with the exact ages at which children reach the successive
stage of intelligence. He is interested in *how* rather than *when,* and in which structures are invariably built before certain other structures. The substages of sensorimotor intelligence are

1. *The Use of Reflexes.* The reflex action patterns described in Chapter 2,
such as the sucking reflex, are embedded in the whole spontaneous rhythmic action
of the infant. Some of the reflexes develop through use and become differentiated.
The reflex actions and perceptual abilities described in Chapter 2 are the schemas
of the first stage of sensorimotor intelligence. This stage includes approximately
the first month, during which the various abilities improve and consolidate.

2. *The First Habits: Primary Circular Reactions.* Neonatal behavior patterns
begin to change through maturation and experience. The baby learns to bring his
hand to his mouth and to suck on it, most likely his thumb. He touches his hands
together and fingers them, looks at his hands and at objects grasped by his hands.
Objects grasped by the hands are carried to the mouth. He looks at an object
making a noise. He does not know what he can cause and what takes place independently of his own actions. This stage lasts until about 4 months.

3. *Secondary Circular Reactions*. The baby develops ways of prolonging interesting events. When a change in the environment results from his actions, he is likely to repeat those actions. He reaches for the toy suspended from his crib, hits it, watches it move, and hits it again.

He still does not search for an object that has disappeared, suggesting that he still does not conceive of it as existing permanently. However, if all but a small part of an object is covered, as when his bottle sticks out from under his blanket, he recognizes it and can recover it. If an object is made to disappear slowly, he follows it with his eyes and continues the movement of his eyes in the direction in which the object went. If, however, it is jerked away, or quickly screened, he does not look for it. One of Piaget's experiments with his son, Laurent, showed that the baby did not even miss the bottle when it was hidden quickly. Just before a feeding time, when Laurent was hungry, Piaget showed him his bottle, whereupon Laurent cried. Piaget quickly hid the bottle and Laurent stopped crying. This sequence was repeated several times. When Laurent could see a small portion of the bottle, he cried harder than ever [71, p. 30].

Another interesting aspect of substage 3, evident in Laurent's behavior, was failure to realize the existence of the nipple if it did not show. When he saw a small portion of the bottle but not the nipple, he tried to suck the bottle itself, but when the nipple was visible, he turned the bottle around so that he could suck the nipple. Thus, he cognized the bottle as a suckable object, but unless he could see the nipple, he did not deal with the bottle as an object with a specialized suckable portion. Thus, in this stage, objects are becoming endowed with permanence, but the process is not complete. The next stage begins at around 8 months.

4. *Coordination of Secondary Schemas*. Secondary circular reactions become coordinated with each other to form more complex schemas. The new schemas are used definitely as means to ends. This is the earliest age at which the baby shows intention in a definite and unmistakable way. For example, hitting is not just for the sake of hitting, but in order to grasp a new object. Piaget tells how Laurent, at 9½ months, pushed his father's hand and at the same time pulled on the toy that Piaget was holding [72, p. 219].

There is true searching for a vanished object, although still not complete appreciation of the object's permanence. Piaget describes how his daughter Jacqueline searched for a toy parrot. First, Piaget covered it with his hand. Jacqueline raised his hand and grasped the parrot. Piaget slowly took the toy away from her, hid it under a rug, and put his hand on her lap, on the spot where the parrot had first been. Jacqueline raised his hand and looked under it for the parrot. This process was repeated three times [71, p. 51].

5. *Tertiary Circular Reactions*. Instead of merely prolonging or reproducing interesting events, the baby tries to produce new events. He experiments to see what will happen. He appears definitely curious, looking for new experience.

Now the baby looks for a vanished object in the place where it disappeared instead of in the place where he last found it. He demonstrates increased understanding of movements of objects by following a trajectory and looking at its end and by throwing something in back of himself and turning around in the other direction to look for it.

Throwing and dropping toys are common kinds of play at this age, as the infant examines movements of objects, disappearance, and reappearance, building his understanding of the permanence of objects. Piaget watched Laurent using various methods of letting a tin can fall from his hands and then dropping a chunk of bread first as a whole and then in the form of crumbs. Later Laurent dropped toys from different positions. The usual age for this stage is 12 to 18 months.

6. *Invention of New Means through Mental Combinations.* Instead of having to go through a series of sensorimotor explorations and trials, the child can find solutions mentally. He begins this stage by representing objects and actions to himself. Probably the first kind of representing is to act it out. Piaget's daughter, Lucienne, illustrated this behavior when she was trying to get a little chain out of a match box. She looked at the small opening, not knowing how to open it wider, then opened and shut her mouth several times, each time opening it wider [71, pp. 337–338]. After a few quiet moments, she used a new technique to open the box with her finger. Lucienne's opening of her own mouth was a symbolic act, representing the opening of the box, which she desired. This stage, in coping with problems, is midway between trying out solutions in action and thinking them out. When problems are solved by thinking, without any action, the child is representing objects and actions to himself by symbols that are entirely within. He thinks of ways of acting and tries them out by thinking. He can think of objects that are not present, of past events, and of events that might happen.

The toddler shows his new powers by imitation and pretending and by insightful problem solving. When he imitates a past event, he shows that he has a mental image of it. When he pretends, he uses a mental image of a behavior pattern to act out that pattern in a new situation. Feeding a doll, he uses his mental image of his mother's behavior, acting it out at his little table. The achievement of imitation, pretending, and insightful problem solving marks the completion of the stage of sensorimotor development. As with all the stages outlined by Piaget, the average age for beginning and ending a stage is not placed exactly but approximately. The sensorimotor stage, according to Piaget, ends at around 2 years.

Ordering and classifying, cognitive behavior that develops noticeably during the next stage of intellectual development, can be observed in its very beginnings during infancy. Gesell mentions the 1-year-old's sequential play with cubes as being a preliminary to ordering and counting, and his looking at a round hole while holding a matching block as being incipient perception of geometric form [41, p. 65]. Between 12 and 24 months, infants will do some selective ordering and grouping when presented with an array of two different kinds of objects, such as four clay balls with four yellow cubes [75]. Selective ordering and grouping activity increased with age between 12 and 24 months.

Self-Cognition. When and how does the infant come to know herself as a separate, recognizable person? The psychoanalytic hypothesis is that the baby separates her concept of herself from her concept of self-and-mother from the experience of wanting the breast and not receiving it. Other contributions to self-concept come from examining her own body and from contingent action and the realization that she can cause events to occur.

Mirror behavior gives some clues to self-recognition, but infants are not usually able to say who it is that they see in the mirror. Almost all infant tests include items using mirrors. An ingenious procedure yielded information as to whether the baby perceived the image as herself [8a]. Rouge was applied to the noses of infants between the ages of 9 and 24 months. All showed increased interest in their mirror images, but nose-directed behavior increased with age. A quarter of the 15- and 18-month-olds touched their noses and three quarters of the 21- and 24-month-olds did so. The results indicate that there was a gradual increase with age in awareness of whose image was in the mirror.

Parents' Contribution to Development of Sensorimotor Intelligence. Parents provide two essential parts of the world of children's learning, the home base and the field to explore. Shortly before he is able to move around on his own, the infant becomes attached to important people, especially his mother. (The process of attachment is described in the following chapter.) When separated from people to whom he is attached, or threatened with separation, the baby makes efforts to regain contact or nearness, crying, reaching, leaning, looking, and if possible, pursuing. These efforts, attachment behavior, preclude exploratory behavior. When, on the other hand, the mother is present or nearby and available, the baby is free to explore. Studies on both monkeys and humans show clearly that the mother's presence facilitates exploration of the environment.

The second type of contribution made by the mother and other caring people is direct stimulation, and an environment offering optimal stimulation. A mother picks up her baby, cuddles, pats, strokes and kisses him, murmurs words of baby talk, and sings a lullaby to him. She gives him a great rich field of perception: touch sensations on the skin of his body and head; muscle sensations as his muscles are pressed by his mother's hands and as he moves himself; inner ear stimulation as his head swings up from a horizontal to vertical orientation and the balance mechanisms operate; a completely different visual world, full of varied objects instead of walls and ceiling; for his hands to feel, his mother's clothing, her firm shoulder, soft neck and hair; against his cheek, her warm cheek and lips; her voice to listen to. His cognition, his knowing of the world, proceeds through sensory experiences, these and others. Picking him up is only one small act among the many educational acts his mother performs. She props him up, too, so that he can see the world from this angle. He looks at his hands, at toys his mother puts in his lap, at his hands contacting the toys. Babies of 3 or 4 months who have had normal opportunities (for North American culture) strain to sit up and show by their pleasure in being propped that this is welcome experience. A frequent change of position prevents fatigue and enriches the sensory field. Here is one place where resident grandparents and older brothers and sisters can add to a baby's education, since mothers often have many duties in addition to baby teaching, and many fathers are absent all day.

When sitting and examining schemas are sufficiently developed, the normally experienced infant enthusiastically accepts and examines all objects that come his way. For example, here is part of a half hour's observation of an 11-month-old baby.

George pulled himself to his feet and stood watching his mother for a few minutes. He moved around the rail of the playpen by putting one foot out to the side and bringing the other up to it. . . . He squealed, tried to hurry and fell down. . . .

Mrs. MacIntyre gave George a cardboard box with a ball in it. George pounced on the ball and dropped it . . . he crept after it and then put it back in the box. He took it out, dropped it, crept after it, and so on, going through the whole process four times. He sat and watched the adults for a minute. Then he picked up a stuffed cat by the tail. His fingers slipped up and down the tail. He squeezed the cat and touched the fur. He poked its eyes and pulled the whiskers. A red ribbon and bell around the cat's neck came in for a share of fingering and pulling. George dropped the cat and pulled himself up.

George sat down and picked a string of brightly colored beads out of his toy basket. He looked at several of the beads and poked at them with his finger. He shook the string and put it round his neck. Then he tried to get it off by pulling down. The beads worked down over his arm. George roared until his mother pulled them off. He put them on again immediately. . . .

George beat on the saucepan and lid with the spoon, gnawed the spoon, put the lid on the saucepan with a bang, removed the lid. He thumped the pan on the lid and the lid on the pan, put the spoon in the pan and the lid on his head. He put the ball in the saucepan [80, pp. 122–123].

Thus, a baby sought and found many sensations. Visual sensations were combined with touch, giving varieties of shape, texture, size, and color. Touch sensations came from his hands, lips, gums, tongue, knees, feet, and buttocks. He elicited sounds. The whole environment, both physical and social, was responsive to him. He could make things happen and make something happen again!

During the second year, mothers adapt their teaching to their children's growing capacities for understanding. As language becomes more meaningful to toddlers, mothers use it more for teaching. The language behavior of four mothers with their children was examined in terms of the ideas and orientations that they were trying to teach [47]. The children between 15 and 27 months of age had the same mean length of utterance, a measure used for language development (see page 165). The mothers used four contexts for behavior when talking with their children: *physical relationships,* as when one boy said, "put truck in window," his mother replied, "I think that one is too large to go in the window,"; *needs and feelings of the mother and others,* as "I'm too tired to put the truck in the window"; *behavior of others as a model,* as "Betsy keeps her truck in the toy cupboard"; *moral, aesthetic, and cognitive evaluations,* as "That's naughty," or "Let's make things nice and clean." By putting behavior into the first context, a mother would help the child develop concepts of physical reality with laws and regularities independent of human wishes and values.

Most of the time the four mothers spoke in simple, direct sentences to their toddlers, as, for example, "Here comes Daddy" or "Dinner's ready." Occasionally, some spoke in elliptical sentences, as when Dory's mother said "I can't wash your hands unless you put your beads down." This sentence includes an order (put your beads down) and a reason for the order. The reason is not completely spelled out and it is left to Dory to figure out that her hands must be opened in order to be washed, and that in order to open her hands, she must put her beads down. Such an experience is cognitively stimulating. The child who hears such sentences has to be active in solving the problems they present. The child who has little or none of the experience of elliptical statements may be disadvantaged when he goes to school.

Contributions of the home environment in infancy showed a highly significant relationship to performance on intelligence tests, the Bayley Test at 12 months and the Stanford-Binet Test at 36 months [29]. The relationship was even stronger at three years than at one, indicating that the effects of a good environment added up. The variables that were significant in relation to mental test scores were provision of appropriate play materials, maternal involvement with the child, opportunities for variety in daily stimulation, emotional and verbal responsivity of the mother, organization of physical and temporal environment, and avoidance of restriction and punishment.

Communication

From his first moment of life in the world, the infant sends signals to the people close to him and receives signals from them. Baby and mother gaze into each other's eyes. He cries. She holds him. He snuggles and clutches. She offers her breast. He roots and sucks. As he grows, he adds vocalizing that is not crying but cooing, which carries a different meaning. She talks. He listens. Eventually he talks. Communication involves all the senses, since it is nonverbal, as well as verbal. It is more than intellectual, being interpersonal and deeply emotional.

NONVERBAL COMMUNICATION

Babies tell their caregivers a great deal through their behavior, probably unintentionally. Such behavior includes all state behaviors (see pages 63–65), as well as smiling, laughing, looking, vocalizing, snuggling, clinging, and following. Some of these nonverbal behaviors are discussed in the following chapter, in terms of social and emotional relationship.

Caregivers also communicate a great deal, nonverbally and often unintentionally, in their methods and timing of handling babies and in the environments they provide. Facial expression and eye contact may be avenues of communication between infants and adults, just as they are between other people. The patterning and timing of gazing between preverbal infants and adults was found to be the same as the looking that adults do when they converse with each other [50].

Communication gradually takes on a conscious and purposeful quality. The baby cuddles and snuggles in ways that spell love and affection to adults. Perhaps to the baby it means simply a good feeling or a feeling of warmth and closeness. It is a relationship that a baby can choose or reject, since even during the first half of the first year, he will sometimes snuggle close, relaxing and melting his body to conform with the adult's, whereas at other times he will stiffen and push his body upright. During the second year, to cuddle or not to cuddle is a choice that the baby prefers to make. Although he wants and needs loving arms and a hospitable lap, it is important to him to take it or leave it according to how he feels at the moment. He cries and shoves the gushing auntie who snatches him up to hug and kiss him at an inappropriate time, communicating to her clearly.

Stroking, patting, and hugging develop out of early cuddling. Kissing probably comes from the pursing reflex of feeding. During his first two years, the baby takes into himself the acts of love he has experienced, the gestures by which his family have symbolized their love for him. He gives them back, and the expression of love becomes more of a true communication.

Children in the second year often communicate purposefully with their hands, pulling another person to show him something, pushing him away, putting a hand over a mouth that is saying what the child does not want to hear, and pointing at food, toys, and wet pants. Such language of the hands can be very effective in transferring ideas, even without a single word. Insofar as they achieve what the baby wants, these methods of communicating are, to him, adequate ways of coping with the world.

LANGUAGE

Receptive language, or what a person understands, is greater than *productiv*. language, or what he says. A child knows the meaning of many words that he does not produce. Human speech has special significance for a young infant, even though he cannot say a word. And while he is listening, he is getting ready to speak.

Receptive Language Development. The infant perceives human speech more readily than he perceives other kinds of sounds, as though he were especially attuned to the types of sounds upon which languages are built. Considerable evidence supports the idea that infants have innate detectors for the sound patterns that are characteristic of human speech. Newborns seem to respond as much to one language as to another, as did 16 United States infants in their consistent motor reactions to both English and Chinese [18]. Disconnected vowels, however, did not elicit the same response as did real language.

Several experiments using changes in sucking, heart rate, or looking have shown young babies making distinctions between similar sounds in human speech. What is more remarkable, month-old babies who could distinguish between p and b could not tell the difference between pairs of sounds that were equally far apart on a loudness dimension, but not representing differences between units of human speech [28]. Subjects two months of age showed through changes in looking behavior that they could distinguish between different voices, different tone qualities of the same voice, and perhaps between different statements by the same voice [23]. A series of studies by Butterfield shows that newborns will modify the length of sucks in order to hear vocal or instrumental music, that music was more reinforcing than white noise, and that vocal music was more reinforcing than instrumental music [27].

By the time babies are about nine months old, their motor development is advanced enough that they can readily express their listening preferences, provided the experimenter asks his questions in the right form. In order to get answers that would give insight into receptive language development, Friedlander [36] designed a device that he called *Playtest*. Attached to the baby's crib or playpen, *Playtest* is operated by two switches. Each switch operates a channel of an audio tape; an automatic record is kept when the switch is turned on and off. The baby easily turns on the switch of his choice and turns it off when he has had enough or wants to change to the other. The subjects' responses were highly enthusiastic. Some of them used the device for as little as 20 minutes a day, although one 9-month-old girl listened for an average of 50 minutes a day and a year-old boy for over 80 minutes a day. Friedlander studied various types of preferences, including the choice between newness and repetition. For instance, two recordings of a family conversation were paired, one repeating after 20 seconds, the other after 240 seconds. After sampling both tapes thoroughly, the majority of infants chose the short cycle for a few days and then preferred the longer one, the one that gave more information and had less redundancy.

Because children's speech, from its beginning, obeys certain grammatical rules, infants must begin in the second year, or earlier, to extract rules from the speech they hear around them. Just as during the early weeks they are prepared to perceive and extract information from the sounds made by the human voice, so they are later able to learn how to construct meaningful utterances in their own language by operating on information contained in the speech of others. Infants do not know that they are learning rules. Not even an adult can state the grammatical rules of his native language unless he has been formally taught the grammar.

Toward the end of the first year, parents can tell, without experimental equipment, that their babies understand some of the words they say to them. A baby will probably pause in what she is doing when an adult says *no*. She may wave to *bye-bye* and do other little tricks to *peek-a-boo, how big,* and *pat-a-cake.* She knows the name of a special toy, blanket, or food, as well as names of family members and shows that she does by looking at the right person or object, or even going to find one. During the second year, understanding grows at a fast pace, as toddlers respond to whole sentences and show interest in stories and books.

Productive Language Development: Vocalization. The newborn baby makes sounds. The year-old says words. The 2-year-old puts words together. These achievements are typical of all normal children growing up where people are talking. Some children are a little slower, some a little faster in reaching the various milestones of language development, but all learn the language that they hear around them, through an interaction between their own maturing biological equipment and the human language environment. The biological equipment includes brain structures and organs of speech. Although hearing is necessary for ordinary language development, deaf children can be taught to speak through the use of other avenues of reception. Language is related to all of the young child's maturation and learning, especially the maturation of the nervous system, respiratory system, and organs of speech.

Newborns vocalized most when in the active, alert state, and least or not at all in quiet sleep [51]. The state of active sleep included the second largest number of vocalizations, whereas drowsy and alert inactive states involved fewer vocalizations than did active sleep. Figure 3-5 shows percentage of vocalizations in various states by infants of 2 weeks and 3 months of age. The older infants vocalized more during awake states, but no more when drowsy and sleeping. As

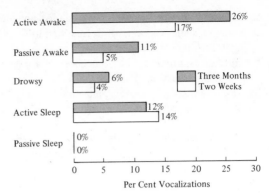

Figure 3-5.   Percentage of vocalizations as a function of age and state.

Source: S. J. Jones and H. A. Moss. Age, state and maternal behavior associated with vocalizations. *Child Development,* 1971, **42**, 1039–1051.

infants mature, they stay awake longer and, of course, hear more language and produce more.

Vocalizations change in predictable ways, from the relatively formless sounds of the newborn to the precise, complex speech of the older child. Just as there is a sequence in motor development, based on maturation, so there is a sequence in the production of sounds, and regularity in the ages at which the sounds are first made. During the first two months, most of the sounds are vowels, mainly the ones made in the front part of the mouth [49]. A new vowel sound appears about every four months during the first year. The first consonant, *h,* is associated with gasping and crying. The early consonants are made in the back of the throat. *Labials* and *dentals* appear last in the sequence.

Cooing, vocal play, and talking back are typical of 2 or 3 months of age, when the baby can hold his head erect and when he has established physiological equilibrium. Infants respond to adults' social approaches by smiling and vocalizing. By 4 months, they make noises that sound like chuckles. *Babbling,* which appears around 6 months, sounds like syllables consisting of consonants and vowels. By 8 or 9 months, the syllables are repeated, as in *gaga.* By 12 months, some of these repetitions are endowed with meaning as real words, such as *mama* and *dada. Expressive jargon,* a kind of speech used in the middle of the second year, is not communication in the sense of expressing ideas through words. The youngster sounds as though he were really talking, but none of it makes sense because there are no real words in it, rather like double-talk. There are rhythmic rises and falls and feeling in the sounds. Expressive jargon is probably an expression of feeling for the child, perhaps of ideas, and it often functions as a contact with another person.

The emotional and biological roots of language are stressed by Lewis [59], who analyzes the early sounds made by infants. *Discomfort cries,* which begin immediately after birth, at first consist of front, narrow vowels, frequently shrill and nasalized, resulting from tension in the whole body including the face. In the second stage of discomfort cries, consonants such as *w, l,* and *h* are added. The third stage of discomfort cries include *m* and *n* sounds. *Comfort sounds* occur in a relaxed state, starting after discomfort cries have begun. The first stage of comfort sounds are vowel-like and indistinct, developing into *a, o,* and *u.* Back consonants, such as *g, k,* and *r,* are added in the second stage and front consonants, *p, b, m, t, d,* and *n,* in the third stage. The almost universal use of *mama* or *nana* for mother or nurse might be accounted for by the fact that if the hungry baby makes anticipatory sucking movements while giving a nasalized discomfort cry, the result is *mama* or *nana. Papa* might be explained as the result of vocalizing in a state of relaxation.

Productive Language Development: Words. During the first half of the second year, the average baby acquires a vocabulary of a few words. Because there is wide variation, the normal vocabulary at 18 months can be said to be more than three and less than 50 [58, p. 128]. Expressive jargon is still used and there is not much effort to communicate, although single words can be comments, questions, or commands. A word may stand for a whole rush of experiences, as did "car, car, car" said by a toddler as she enjoyed an automobile outing. During the middle part of the second year, combinations of words may be functionally one-word utterances, such as *allgone.* When two words are put together, the child has reached the end of infancy, completing the sensorimotor period of development. He has come to realize that words stand for things and actions. Instead of having to go through sensory and motor acts, words can be manipulated in a twinkling. One doesn't even have to be where the problem is. He can think and talk about things that are remote in time and space.

The ability to communicate with language must surely facilitate the sense of autonomy. For instance, saying "drink" can produce water at one's lips, or "out" can transform the whole environment from indoors to outdoors. The extension of the child's powers and control is enormous. As it dawns upon him that everything has a name, that verbal symbols exist and that he can use them, he must have a surge of satisfaction over his expanded powers. One can imagine next a push to discover just how much he can do with these symbols, words, in both understanding and controlling the world and the people in it, including himself.

In Nelson's longitudinal research on language acquisition between the ages of 10 and 25 months, 18 mother–infant pairs were studied [67]. Instead of trying to determine when the babies said their first words, a difficult thing to do, Nelson used ten words as an indicator of speech onset. The average age at which the subjects used ten words was 15.1 months. The range was from 13 to 19 months. Another milestone, the use of 50 words, was achieved at an average age of 19.6 months, with a range of 14 to 24 months. The acquisition rate, or number of words added per month, was 11.1 between the age at ten words and the age at 50 words. Infants varied in acquisition patterns, some starting early, some late, and some accelerating faster than others. The usual course was an initial period of slow growth in word acquisition followed by an increase and then a period of rapid word acquisition during the two months prior to and including the age at which the vocabulary reached 50 words.

Phrase onset was indicated by the child's use of 10 phrases, no matter whether they were used as wholes or constructed from parts. The average age for ten phrases was 19.8 months, with a range from 16 to 24. Thus the age of phrase onset is almost identical with the age of using 50 words. The average number of words used at 2 years was 185.9, with a range from 28 to 436. Mean length of utterance (MLU) at age 2 was 1.9, about two words per utterance. (Mean lengths of utterance is derived from the number of morphemes or meaningful parts of speech used. For example, some morphemes are *dog, baby, s,* as in "dogs," *ed,* as in "chased.") The range of MLU at age 2 was from 1.03 to 3.37. In the stages of language development outlined by Brown [10], an MLU of two represents the achievement of Stage 1 in language development, the stage at which words are combined into sentences.

Early Choice of Vocabulary. Children vary not only in speed of learning language but also in the words they learn and in what they talk about, each baby reflecting her own individual personality and experiences. The particular referent words learned tend to be names of things that the child acts upon (*shoes, bottle,* and *ball,* not *table, window, grass*) or things that he observes doing something (*animals, trucks, clocks*). The words and phrases selected by a certain child reflect what is salient for him in the ways that he is presently organizing his world. Nelson [67] divided her subjects into two groups, according to whether more or less than 50 per cent of each 50-word vocabulary were nominals (things, objects, people) or not. The *referential* group, who used more nominals, talked more about objects, whereas the *expressive* group talked more about self and other people, learning a personal–social language for expressing feelings and needs. During the period before the 50-word vocabulary was achieved, the referential group produced an average of 2.4 different phrases whereas the expressive group averaged 12.6 phrases. Personal–social language includes many phrases that are useful for dealing with people, such as *thank you, give me,* and *go away.* All children, of course, use both referential and expressive language, but individuals vary the proportions they use, according to life experiences that stress one or the other.

Strategies in Early Language Learning. Different life experiences also influence the strategies that children use in learning language. Nelson suggests that the first words are acquired by matching environmental labels with the child's own concepts or schemas. After acquiring a vocabulary of a certain size, she may build a concept to match a word that people use with her. She may now also modify or accommodate old concepts to fit the way in which others use them. The child then makes hypotheses about language and checks them as she gets feedback from other people. Strategies include repetition, imitation, comprehension, and asking questions. An important attitudinal learning is the extent to which the child relies on her own conceptualizations or upon those of other people. If she is persuaded that she should depend upon parents, and later upon other authorities, to define her world, then most likely she is diminished in initiative and creativity

ENVIRONMENTAL INFLUENCES ON LANGUAGE DEVELOPMENT

Most studies of infants' experiences with language have been concerned with what their mothers have done. Most likely the fathers, siblings, grandparents, and neighbors also affect the baby through talking. Although it seems certain that the normal baby will begin to talk if he lives amid ordinary family conversations, preschool children vary considerably in how well they talk and in how much use

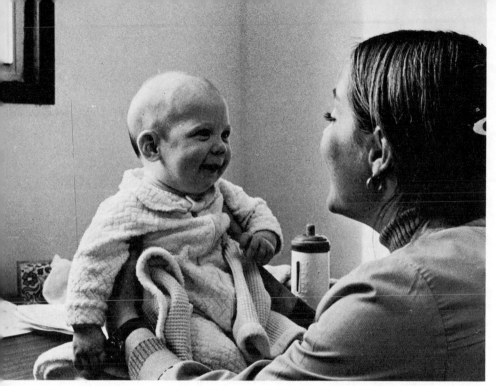

MARGARET HAMILTON

they make of language in solving problems. Since socioeconomic class differences in the latter capacity have been demonstrated at two years of age [43], there must be experiences during infancy that contribute to such differences.

Contingent Vocalization. At around four months of age, when the infant enters Piaget's stage of Secondary Circular Reactions, she "talks back" as she tries to prolong interesting events or to make them happen again. Anyone can confirm for himself the studies that show that infants increase their vocalizing when adults talk to them. Simply say *kitchy-coo* or anything else, and it will sound interesting enough to a baby that she will most likely reply with cooing or babbling.

Mothers vary in how much they vocalize in response to their babies' vocalizations. Mothers from upper middle-class families (professional and executive) were compared with mothers from lower-class families (unskilled laborers) in terms of their interactions with their 12-week-old infants [60]. Although there was no difference in the amount of vocalization of the two groups of mothers, the middle-class mothers vocalized more in response to their infants' vocalizations. The lower-class mothers were more likely to touch their babies in response to vocalizing. Perhaps the contingent vocalization of the middle-class mothers would encourage the babies to use vocalization as a means to an end.

Amount and Quality of Verbal Stimulation. Repeated tests and home observations were made on firstborn infants and their mothers during the time that the babies were from 9 to 18 months old. Children's competence in language was

166

related to the total amount and variety of the mother's speech to the child [15]. The mother's *non*responsive speech was related even more strongly to infant language measures than was her responsiveness to the baby's vocalization. At this stage in language development, therefore, it seems to be more important to have a model of speech than to have one's own vocalizing reinforced. Recalling the likelihood that children abstract rules from the speech they hear, it is reasonable that hearing a large quantity of talking would enable children to build up the structure of language more easily than if they had only a small amount of talking on which to operate.

Although no class difference in amount of verbal stimulation was seen at 12 weeks, girls of 10 months were found to receive more maternal vocalization and to have more verbal interaction with mothers in middle-class families than in working-class families [82]. Perhaps a class difference in children's use of language has some of its roots in a difference in verbal stimulation and interaction.

Stimulation and Acceptance Provided at Home. The influence of a wide range of maternal behavior was shown in a study of 20 mothers and their children between 2 and 6 who were delayed in language development but who had normal IQs [88]. The home environments and mother-child interactions of this group were compared with those of normal children and of children handicapped by Down's syndrome. Home observations were carried out by use of the Caldwell Home Stimulation Inventory. The normal group and Down's syndrome group did not differ from each other. The language-delayed group was different in these categories: less emotional and verbal responsiveness of mother; more restriction and punishment; less provision of appropriate play materials; less maternal involvement with child; fewer opportunities for variety in daily stimulation. The study suggests, but does not prove, that the children's language deficiencies were caused by their inadequate physical, social, and verbal environments. Indeed, most of the mothers had believed for some time that their children were "different" and "difficult." The poor interaction was reciprocal. A sex difference was noted. Eighty per cent of the language-delayed children were boys. Nelson, in her longitudinal study, also observed that rejection slows down the child's learning. The accepting mother facilitated her child's learning of language.

Control and Feedback. Nelson found that a mother may accept or reject what her child says. Through feedback, she lets the baby know what is acceptable and what is not, but if she ignores him, then he cannot tell what is acceptable. If the child's organization of the world is different from hers (he is expressive, she referential, or vice versa), she may try to control him, to "teach" him what is "right." If she accepts what the baby says and interacts warmly, the child is likely to enjoy verbal interchanges and to acquire words rapidly.

Accelerating Language Development. A recent study prompts us to tell of a personal experience. Fowler and Swenson [34] worked with the mothers of three infants to design environments in which language growth would be maximal. One of their purposes was to see how early children could learn to talk. The babies began to imitate words at five and a half months, to speak words spontaneously at 7 months and to put words together at 12 months. One of us (MSS) was psychologist in an infant clinic before our first baby was born. We quite naturally applied at home all we had learned on the job. At seven months, our daughter said "buh" whenever a bus went by the house and "pow" when she saw the talcum powder can. "Buh and "pow" represented two interesting and enjoyable events. Since that time, we have learned that other psychologists' children have spoken words at seven months. Apparently, babies have much greater capacities than most of them have chances to develop.

Measuring Infant Intelligence

Many tests of infant behavior are available. Three widely used tests are the Gesell Development Test [41], Bayley's Scales of Infant Development [5], and the Cattell Infant Intelligence Scale [14]. Uzgiris and Hunt's ordinal scales, based on Piaget's delineation of stages of sensorimotor development, constitute an instrument that is used for research in infant development [48]. There are several dimensions of sensorimotor ability [55].

The Gesell tests consist of four categories of items—motor, adaptive, language, and personal–social behavior—arranged at age levels according to where the average child showed the behavior pattern. In testing an infant, his behavior in each area can be matched to a normative level, giving his developmental age in motor, adaptive, language, and personal–social behavior. Conflicting conclusions have been drawn from studies on the predictive value of the Gesell tests. The tests are helpful in detecting and diagnosing neurological abnormalities.

The Bayley Scales of Infant Development consist of a motor scale and a mental scale, derived from repeated examinations of 1,409 infants in 12 research centers scattered throughout the United States [5]. Norms are given for each half-month level. The Bayley scales have been used in several different parts of the world, since they provide a method for comparing different populations of infants. Bayley mental scale data from Israeli infants have been factor analyzed into different scales, the names of which suggest the main functions included in them: eye–hand, manipulation, object–relation, imitation–comprehension, vocalization–social contact, and active vocabulary [55]. The items of the first two scales can be classified as belonging to Piaget's third stage of sensorimotor development, the third scale to Piaget's fourth stage. All three first scales are similar to Gesell's Adaptive Behavior.

The Cattell Scale was developed as a downward extension of the Stanford–Binet test of intelligence, which is used with preschool and school-age children. Like the Stanford–Binet, the Cattell scale provides a mental age score, which can be converted into an intelligence quotient.

In general, infant tests have not been very good at predicting future IQ, although they do have use in conjunction with clinicians' appraisals. The tests are helpful in finding deviations from normal development and in indicating areas were help is needed.

Programs of Education for Infants

Experiences in providing compensatory education for preschool and school-age children have shown that it is very difficult, if not impossible, to make up completely for deficiencies incurred in infancy. Practically all researchers and practitioners who have worked with infant education have come to the conclusion that mothers must be included if any program is to succeed. Most agree that the *family* should be included. No matter whether babies are cared for at home or in groups in a day-care center, the parents must be part of the program if the babies are to get full benefit. All parents need education and help in bringing up their babies. Some need more than others. Many societies, including North American, are in a state of flux over how to assist parents.

Since parents' feelings about themselves are basic, good programs help them to feel worthwhile as individuals and competent as parents. Competency develops as they learn how children develop, how to design a learning environment, and how to play and teach. Home stimulation programs send trained workers into the home to bring toys, arrange play situations, play with the child, and share with the parents. Group care programs offer observation and discussion, perhaps with films and parent meetings. The philosophy and conduct of such programs is discussed by several authorities in a pamphlet edited by Dittman [26]. Books are also available that tell parents how to educate their children by playing with them [44].

An example of a comprehensive program is the research-based program run by the Children's Center of the University of Syracuse. Its broad services are designed to promote the development of young children and their parents. The Brookline Early Education Program, another example, is based on research on competence [86]. Parents come and go freely in a neighborhood center, where they have meetings, demonstrations, reading materials, films, discussions, and assessments of their children. Here, an ordinary kitchen is set up for safe exploration by toddlers. Parents learn step-by-step about the nature of their children's growth and how to encourage it.

Day-care centers and home day-care programs vary from excellent to very poor. Important as cognitive and language education are, a baby is a whole person who has physical, social, and emotional needs, too. Good care meets all types of needs. Day-care facilities are expanding in North America, but at this writing, they do not meet the needs of all the families who are seeking help in caring for their young children.

Summary

The key to personality development throughout the first year is the sense of trust. Basic experiences include seeking and finding food, comfort, and stimulation. Successful encounters with the world and people in it result in tension reduction and positive contingent stimulation. Thus, the infant learns to trust in regularities in the physical world, in people, especially mother, and in herself.

The sense of autonomy is built upon a sense of trust, as the baby comes to control objects, her own body, and people. She comes to realize that she can cause certain events and that she can choose to do so or not.

Development brings changes in appearance, size, and proportions, as it proceeds in an anterior-to-posterior direction. Growth can be evaluated by using appropriate height and weight tables. Skinfold thickness can give a measure of nutritional status.

Nutrition-related illness is widespread throughout the world, distorting the growth, health, and intelligence of children. Marasmus, a frequent result of early weaning from the breast, is caused by severe calorie deprivation. Kwashiorkor, often a result of inadequate feeding after weaning at a normal time, is caused by protein deprivation. Other deficits result from insufficient intake of the various minerals and vitamins. Gastrointestinal upsets are caused by harsh, rough foods and by various parasites. Malnutrition and infection interact. Malnutrition depresses activity and intelligent behavior, especially when added to deficits in affectionate personal interaction. Many parents do not know what or how to feed their infants. Weaning has significance for personality development as well as for nutrition. Independence in choosing and handling food enhances the sense of autonomy.

Heat production is greater and bodily temperature fluctuates more in the infant than in the older child. Breathing becomes deeper with age; timing of bodily functions becomes regularized. Freedom to move is necessary for the baby to get enough exercise.

Locomotion and manipulation develop in regular sequences, the order of which is determined largely by maturation. The speed may be influenced by opportunities for learning. The sense of autonomy is promoted by growing powers of manipulation and locomotion. The existence of ethnic differences in infant motor development has been demonstrated but not explained. Eye-hand coordination and manipulation are means with which a child acts upon objects and comes to know them. Locomotion also contributes to knowing the world through bodily movements.

Cognitive development involves changes in patterns of taking in information about the world and acting on it. Age-related changes have been charted in attention, especially visual attention. Sensorimotor intelligence, typical of infants, is practical. Piaget has delineated six stages through which the infant establishes basic knowledge about the world, and the objects in it, including himself: the use of reflexes, the first habits, secondary circular reactions, coordination of secondary schemas, tertiary circular reactions, and invention of new means through mental operation. Parents design the environment and take part in the interactions through which the infant develops her intelligence. Communication takes place through those interactions, and language is learned. Human speech is perceived more readily than other kinds of sounds. Infants have listening preferences in regard to speech and music. Some words are understood in the first year, and many in the second. Vocalizations and language production proceed in a predictable sequence but the timing varies. The actual words used and themes of expression vary with the infant's experience. Parents, especially mothers, influence infants' language development through the amount and quality of the verbal stimulation they offer. Contingent response to the baby's vocalizations is stimulating to development. Parental rejection retards language learning.

Infant tests are used to assess motor, mental, and social behavior, and sensorimotor intelligence. Educational programs, a part of any good day-care plan, are being developed throughout the world. Successful education for infants includes the parents in the program, either by going into the home or bringing parents into an outside program.

References

1. Abraham, S., F. W. Lowenstein, and C. L. Johnson. *Preliminary findings of the first health and nutrition survey, United States, 1971–72: Dietary intake and biochemical findings.* DHEW Publication No. (HRA) 74–1219–1. Washington, D.C.: U.S. Government Printing Office, 1974.
2. Albino, R. C., and V. J. Thompson. The effects of sudden weaning on Zulu children. In W. Dennis (ed.). *Readings in child psychology.* Englewood Cliffs, N.J.: Prentice-Hall, Inc., 1963, pp. 128–148.
3. Barnes, R. H. Nutrition and man's intellect and behavior. Proceedings of the First Biological Congress of the American Institute of Nutrition, 1971, **30,** 1429–1433. In S. P. Raman (ed.). *Nutrition, development and learning.* New York: MSS Information Corporation, 1974.
4. Bayley, N. Comparisons of mental and motor test scores for ages 1–15 months by sex, birth order, race, geographic location and education of parents. *Child Development,* 1965, **36,** 379–411.
5. Bayley, N. *Bayley's scales of infant development.* New York: Psychological Corporation, 1968.
6. Bower, T. G. R. *Development in infancy.* San Francisco: W. H. Freeman & Co. Publishers, 1974.
7. Brazelton, T. B. Early effect of maternal expectations on early infant behavior. *Early Child Development and Care,* 1972, **2,** 259–273.
8. Breckenridge, M. E., and M. N. Murphy. *Growth and development of the young child* 8th ed. Philadelphia: W. B. Saunders Company, 1969.
8a. Brooks-Gunn, J., and M. Lewis. Mirror-image stimulation and self-recognition in infancy. Paper presented at meetings of the Society for Research in Child Development, Denver, 1975.
9. Bronson, G. The postnatal growth of visual capacity. *Child Development,* 1974, **45,** 873–890.
10. Brown, R. *A first language: The early stages.* Cambridge, Mass.: Harvard University Press, 1973.
11. Bruner, J. S. *Beyond the information given.* New York: W. W. Norton & Company, Inc., 1973.
12. Capretta, P. J., J. M. Moore, and T. R. Rossiter. Establishment and modification of food and taste preferences: Effects of experience. *Journal of General Psychology,* 1973, **89,** 27–46.
13. Caron, A. J., R. F. Caron, R. C. Caldwell, and S. J. Weiss. Infant perception of the structural properties of the face. *Developmental Psychology,* 1973, **9,** 385-399.
14. Cattell, P. *The measurement of intelligence of infants.* New York: Psychological Corporation, 1940.

15. Clarke-Stewart, K. A. Interactions between mothers and their young children: Characteristics and consequences. *Monographs of the Society for Research in Child Development,* 1973, **38**:6–7.

16. Cobos, F. L., M. C. Latham, and F. J. Stare. Will improved nutrition help to prevent mental retardation? *Preventive Medicine,* 1973, **1**, 185–194.

17. Colley, J. R. T., W. W. Holland, and R. T. Corkhill. Influence of passive smoking and parental phlegm on pneumonia and bronchitis in early childhood. *Lancet,* 1974, November 2, 1031–1034.

18. Condon, W. S., and L. W. Sander. Synchrony between movements of the neonate and adult speech. *Child Development,* 1974, **45**, 456–462.

19. Cornell, E. H. Infants visual attention to pattern arrangement and orientation. *Child Development,* 1975, **46**, 229–232.

20. Coursin, D. B. Nutrition and brain development. *Merrill-Palmer Quarterly,* 1972, **18**, 177–202.

21. Cravioto, J. Nutritional deficiencies and mental performance in childhood. In D. C. Glass (ed.). *Environmental influences.* New York: Rockefeller University Press and Russell Sage Foundation, 1968.

22. Cravioto, J. Malnutrition in early childhood and some of its consequences for the individual and the community. General Foods Distinguished International Lectures on Nutrition. Toronto, April 10, 1975.

23. Culp, R. E. Effect of voice quality and content on the looking behavior of two month old infants. Paper presented at meetings of the American Psychological Association, New Orleans, 1974.

24. Dasen, P. R. Preliminary study of sensorimotor developments in Baoule children. *Early Child Development and Care,* 1973, **2**, 345–354.

25. Dean, R. F. Effects of malnutrition, especially of slight degree, on the growth of young children. *Courrier,* 1965, **15**, 78–83.

26. Dittman, L. L. (ed.). *The infants we care for.* Washington, D.C.: National Association for the Education of Young Children, 1973.

26a. Dobbing, J. Human brain development and its vulnerability. Biological and clinical aspects of brain development. *Mead Johnson Symposium on Perinatal and Developmental Medicine No. 6.* Evansville, Indiana: Mead Johnson and Co., 1975.

27. Doty, D. Infant speech perception. Report of a conference held at the University of Minnesota, June 20–22, 1972. *Human Development,* 1974, **17**, 74–80.

28. Eimas, P. D., E. R. Siqueland, P. Jusczyk and J. Vigorito. Speech perception in infants. *Science,* 1971, **171**, 303–306.

29. Elardo, R., R. Bradley, and B. M. Caldwell. The relation of infants' home environments to mental test performance from six to thirty-six months: A longitudinal analysis. *Child Development,* 1975, **46**, 71–76.

30. Erikson, E. H. *Childhood and society.* New York: W. W. Norton & Company, 1963.

31. Fagan, J. F. Infants' recognition memory for faces. *Journal of Experimental Child Psychology,* 1972, **14**, 453–476.

32. Fantz, R. L., and J. F. Fagan, III. Visual attention to size and number of pattern details by term and preterm infants during the first six months. *Child Development,* 1975, **46**, 3–18.

33. Fenson, L., V. Sapper, and D. G. Minner. Attention and manipulative play in the one-year-old child. *Child Development,* 1974, **45**, 757–764.

34. Fowler, W., and A. Swenson. The influence of early stimulation on language de-

velopment. Paper presented at meetings of the Society for Research in Child Development, Denver, 1975.

35. Frankenburg, W. K., and N. P. Dick. Development of preschool-aged children: Racial-ethnic and social-class comparisons. Paper presented at meetings of the Society for Research in Child Development, Philadelphia, 1973.

36. Friedlander, B. Z. Receptive language development in infancy; Issues and problems. *Merrill-Palmer Quarterly,* 1970, **16,** 7–49.

37. Garn, S. M. The applicability of North American growth standards in developing countries. *Canadian Medical Association Journal,* 1965, **93,** 914–919.

38. Garn, S. M., A. B. Lewis, and R. S. Kerewsky. Genetic, nutritional and maturational correlates of dental development. *Journal of Dental Research,* 1964, **44,** 228–242.

39. General Research Centers Branch, National Institutes of Health. *How children grow.* DHEW Publications No. (NIH) 72–166. Washington, D.C.: U.S. Government Printing Office, 1972.

40. Geber, M. The psychomotor development of African children in the first year and the influence of maternal behavior. *Journal of Social Psychology,* 1958, **47,** 185–195.

41. Gesell, A., and C. Amatruda. *Developmental diagnosis.* New York: Hoeber, 1951.

42. Goldberg, S. Infant care and growth in urban Zambia. *Human Development,* 1972, **15,** 77–89.

43. Golden, M., W. Bridger, and A. Montare. Social class differences in the use of language as a tool for learning in two-year-old children. Proceedings, 80th Annual Convention, APA, 1972, 107–108.

44. Gordon, I. J. *Baby learning through baby play.* New York: St. Martin's Press, Inc., 1970.

45. Graffar, M., and J. Corbier. Contribution to the study of the influence of socio-economic conditions on the growth and development of the child. *Early Child Development and Care,* 1972, **1,** 141–179.

46. Harris, P. L. Eye movements between adjacent stimuli: An age change in infancy. *British Journal of Psychology,* 1973, **64,** 215–218.

47. Holzman, M. The verbal environment provided by mothers for their very young children. *Merrill-Palmer Quarterly,* 1974, **20,** 31–42.

48. Hunt, J. McV. Utility of ordinal scales derived from Piaget's observations. Paper presented at meetings of the American Psychological Association, Montreal, 1973.

49. Irwin, O. C. Infant speech: Vowel and consonant frequency. *Journal of Speech Disorders,* 1946, **11,** 123–125.

50. Jaffe, J., D. N. Stern, and J. C. Perry. "Conversational" coupling of gaze behavior in prelinguistic human development. *Journal of Psycholinguistic Research,* 1973, **2,** 321–329.

51. Jones, S. J., and H. A. Moss. Age, state and maternal behavior associated with vocalizations. *Child Development,* 1971, **42,** 1039–1051.

52. Keet, M. P., J. D. L. Hansen, and A. S. Truswell. Are skinfold measurements of value in the assessment of suboptimal nutrition in young children? *Pediatrics,* 1970, **45,** 965–972.

53. Kelly, V. C., and J. F. Bosma. Basal metabolism in infants and children. In I. McQuarrie (ed.). *Brennemann's practice of pediatrics.* Vol. 1. Hagerstown, Md.: W. F. Prior, 1957.

54. Knobloch, H., and B. Pasamanick. Further observations on the behavioral development of Negro children. *Journal of Genetic Psychology,* 1953, **83,** 137–157.

55. Kohen-Raz, R. Scalogram analysis of some developmental sequences of infant behavior as measured by the Bayley Infant Scale of Mental Development. *Genetic Psychology Monographs*, 1967, **76**, 3–21.
56. Kopp, C. B., M. J. O'Connor, M. Sigman, A. H. Parmelee, and T. G. Marcy. Early cognitive development of pre-term and fullterm infants: Component structure of sensorimotor and developmental examinations. Paper presented at meetings of the Society for Research in Child Development, Denver, 1975.
57. Lasky, R. E., R. E. Klein, and S. Martinez. Age and sex discriminations in five- and six-month-old infants. *Journal of Psychology*, 1974, **88**, 317–324.
58. Lenneberg, E. H. *Biological foundations of language*. New York: John Wiley & Sons, Inc., 1967.
59. Lewis, M. M. *Language, thought, and personality in infancy and childhood*. New York: Basic Books Inc., 1963.
60. Lewis, M., and C. D. Wilson. Infant development in lower-class American families. *Human Development*, 1972, **15**, 112–127.
61. Lowrey, G. H. *Growth and development of children* 6th ed. Chicago: Medical Year Book, 1973.
62. Maslansky, E., C. Cowell, R. Caral, S. N. Berman, and M. Grussi. Survey of infant feeding practices. *American Journal of Public Health*, 1974, **64**, 780–785.
63. McWilliams, M. *Nutrition for the growing years*. 2nd ed. New York: John Wiley & Sons, Inc., 1975.
64. Miles, J. E. Lecture at University of Guelph, Guelph, Ontario, March 14, 1975.
65. Moffit, A. R. Intensity discrimination and cardiac reaction in young infants. *Developmental Psychology*, 1973, **8**, 357–359.
66. Mönckeberg, F. Effect of early marasmic malnutrition on subsequent physical and psychological development. In N. S. Scrimshaw and J. E. Gordon (eds.). *Malnutrition, learning and behavior*. Cambridge, Mass.: M.I.T. Press, 1968, pp. 269–278.
67. Nelson, K. Structure and strategy in learning to talk. *Monographs of the Society for Research in Child Development*, 1973, **38**:1–2.
68. Parmelee, A. H. Selection of developmental assessment techniques for infants at risk. Paper presented at Merrill-Palmer Conference on Research and Teaching of Infant Development, Detroit, 1975.
69. Parmelee, A. H., and E. Stern. Development of sleep states in infants. In C. D. Clemente, D. P. Purpura, and F. E. Mayer (eds.). *Sleep in the maturing nervous system*. New York: Academic Press, 1972.
70. Phatak, P. et al. (eds.). Motor and mental growth of Indian babies of 1 month to 35 months. Research Report No. 1, Baroda, India: Department of Child Development, University of Baroda. Mimeo.
71. Piaget, J. *The construction of reality in the child*. New York: Basic Books, Inc., 1954.
72. Piaget, J. *The origins of intelligence in children*. New York: W. W. Norton & Company, Inc., 1963.
73. Piaget, J., and B. Inhelder. *The psychology of the child*. New York: Basic Books, Inc., 1969.
74. Ramey, C. T., R. H. Starr, J. Pallas, C. F. Whitten, and V. Reed. Nutrition, response-contingent stimulation, and the maternal deprivation syndrome: Results of an early intervention program. *Merrill-Palmer Quarterly*, 1975, **2**, 44–53.
75. Ricciuti, H. N. Object grouping and selective ordering behavior in infants 12 to 24 months old. *Merrill-Palmer Quarterly*, 1965, **11**, 129–148.
76. Roberts, K. E., and J. A. Schoelkopf. Eating, sleeping, and elimination: Practices

of a group of two and a half year old children. *American Journal of Diseases of Children,* 1951, **82,** 121–152.

77. Sabry, Z. I., J. A. Campbell, M. E. Campbell, and A. L. Forbes. Nutrition Canada. *Nutrition Today,* 1974, **9:**1, 5–13.

78. Schwartz, A. N., J. J. Campos, and E. J. Baisel. The visual cliff: Cardiac and behavioral responses on the deep and shallow sides at five and nine months. *Journal of Experimental Child Psychology,* 1973, **15,** 86–99.

79. Scrimshaw, N. S. The effect of the interaction of nutrition and infection on the preschool child. In National Academy of Sciences, *Preschool child malnutrition: Deterrent to human progress.* Washington, D.C.: National Research Council, 1966, pp. 63–73.

80. Smart, M. S., and R. C. Smart. *Living and learning with children.* Boston: Houghton Mifflin Company, 1961.

81. Stone, L. J., H. T. Smith, and L. B. Murphy. *The competent infant.* New York: Basic Books, Inc., 1973.

82. Tulkin, S. R., and J. Kagan. Mother-child interaction in the first year of life. *Child Development,* 1972, **43,** 31–41.

83. Walters, C. E. Comparative development of Negro and white infants. *Journal of Genetic Psychology,* 1967, **110,** 243–251.

84. Watson, J. S., and C. T. Ramey. Reactions to response-contingent stimulation in early infancy. *Merrill-Palmer Quarterly,* 1972, **18,** 219–227.

85. Wetherford, M. J., and L. B. Cohen. Developmental changes in infant visual preferences for novelty and familiarity. *Child Development,* 1973, **44,** 416–424.

86. White, B. L., and J. C. Watts. *Experience and environment: Major influences on the development of competence of the young child.* Vol. 1. Englewood Cliffs, N.J.: Prentice-Hall, Inc., 1972.

87. Winick, M. Childhood obesity. *Nutrition Today,* 1974, **9:**3, 9–12.

88. Wulbert, M., S. Inglis, E. Kriegsmann, and B. Mills. Language play and associated mother-child interactions. *Developmental Psychology,* 1975, **11,** 61–70.

Readings in
Emerging Resources and Competencies

An infant reacts very much as a whole, showing many competencies in an environment favorable to their development and use. From the large number of articles on infant competency, we have chosen one that describes the development of the brain, the organ that directs not only behavior, but growth. The physical and psychological environments are related to behavior and development in the other two articles.

During the first two years of life, brain development is of very special importance, because this is the time of its major growth spurt. John Dobbing describes and explains brain development during the growth spurt and discusses its particular vulnerability at this time. He is cautious in relating brain structure to behavior. Dobbing's clear writing and graphic presentations make a difficult subject understandable to the reader who has little knowledge of this area.

Barry M. Lester's paper documents the wholeness of the infant, showing the effects of malnutrition upon behavior, mediated by the nervous system. By their crying and orienting behavior, infants indicate degrees of well-being. (In the previous chapter, Burns and his associates examined the newborn infant's ability to signal distress and to thereby interact constructively with a caregiver.) No doubt, sensitive parents and nurses interpret such signals intuitively, but research such as Lester's gives an objective basis on which to assess the meaning of behavior.

Psychologists have long believed that mental development was strongly influenced by an infant's experiences at home. But just what are the dimensions of the home learning environment? An instrument for observing and measuring these dimensions has been developed at the Center for Early Development and Education at the University of Arkansas. Using the instrument to measure home environment, mental test performance is related to home experience by Richard Elardo, Robert Bradley, and Bettye M. Caldwell.

Human Brain Development and Its Vulnerability

John Dobbing
UNIVERSITY OF MANCHESTER

THE VULNERABILITY OF THE BRAIN GROWTH SPURT

The growth of all tissues, and indeed of the body as a whole, does not follow a linear course with time. It always proceeds by means of one or more periods of transient rapid growth known as "growth spurts." The brain is no exception. Figure 1 traces the growth in weight of a rat's brain. It is a sigmoid curve, and the growth spurt can be expressed as a velocity curve as shown. There is a similar brain growth spurt in all mammalian species and it always occurs earlier than the general bodily growth spurt.

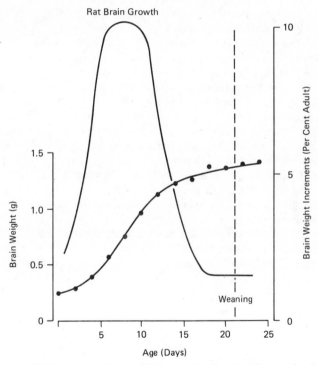

Rat Brain Growth

FIGURE 1. *The brain growth spurt. This occurs in all mammalian species, including man. Its special vulnerability is one of the main topics in this article. Here the brain growth spurt is shown for the rat, with a superimposed first order velocity curve.*

From *Biologic and Clinical Aspects of Brain Development.* Mead Johnson Symposium on Perinatal and Developmental Medicine, No. 6. Evansville, Ind.: Mead Johnson and Company, 1975. Pp. 5–12. Reprinted by permission.

177

The significance of the brain growth spurt for our present discussion is that this transient period of rapid brain growth seems to be one of particular vulnerability to growth restriction. We know this from experiments in animals whose bodily growth rates have been retarded at this time as well as beforehand and afterwards. It could not have been discovered in humans for obvious ethical reasons. However, since we are mainly interested in human children, we must also examine the whole problem of extrapolating experimental results from one animal species to another, including the human animal, and this has already given rise to much confusion.

Another major problem in our enquiry is our total ignorance of what constitutes the physical basis within the brain of higher mental function. We simply do not know how critical it is to have the correct quantity of nerve cells, or of synaptic connections between them, or of myelin or any other structure, nor even whether any of these things matter. Indeed, one is even sometimes left wondering to what extent higher mental function depends at all on the physical brain.

Let us first look at a very much oversimplified scheme of structural brain development, and see which structures are developing during the brain growth spurt which may be the ones whose physical vulnerability is so functionally important. Figure 2 shows such a scheme.

For humans the first three months of fetal life are a period of embryology when the brain is acquiring its adult shape. The same processes in the rat all occur within the first two *weeks* of fetal life. This period, which we can call "embryology" does not concern us here. Then there follows a period when cells which are destined to become nerve cells divide. Let us call this period one of "neuroblast multiplication." This is over by the time of birth in the rat and by about mid-pregancy in the human, except in certain special areas to be mentioned later. At the end of this early period of life we therefore possess our adult *number* of nerve cells, although much more development of them is yet to come.

It is not until about birth in the rat, following the period of neuronal multiplication, that the brain growth spurt begins: so we can assume fairly confidently that restrictions imposed during the growth spurt will not affect *numbers* of neurons except in those exceptional areas where neurogenesis occurs later. It may, however, affect their early development as discussed below.

The next easily measurable event (measured by estimating the increasing quantities of nuclear DNA in the tissue) is a period of tremendous multiplication

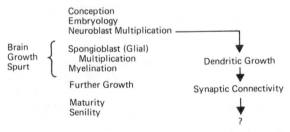

F I G U R E 2.   *A greatly simplified scheme to describe the common mammalian pattern of brain growth.*

of the glial cells of the brain. These cells eventually heavily outnumber nerve cells and their multiplication period is consequently much more conspicuous. It occupies the first half of the brain growth spurt period, from about birth to about 12 postnatal days in the rat. This is the period shown as spongioblast (glial) multiplication in Figure 2. Almost nothing is known about the function of these mysterious glial cells in the adult. The only thing we definitely know about them is that during development many of them are concerned with the manufacture of myelin sheaths, those insulating, laminated, fatty coverings of the nerve fibre which help it to conduct impulses more quickly. Myelination itself can be measured by estimating the increasing quantities of myelin substances in the growing brain at this time, and it is easy to show (as might have been expected) that the most rapid phase of myelination occupies the second half of the brain growth spurt, having awaited the earlier arrival of the glial cells which make the myelin.

Glial cell multiplication, myelination and rapid increase in weight are, however, only three of the most easily measured components of the brain growth spurt, and they are not necessarily the most important from the functional point of view. In structural terms alone, many other things are happening at this time which we cannot so easily measure. Perhaps the most important of these is a very great outgrowth from the nerve cells (which had arrived before the beginning of the growth spurt) of their so-called dendritic tree. Figure 3 shows this process occurring in humans whose brain growth spurt is mainly postnatal, as will be discussed later. The great complexity of the dendritic arborisation is important because it is due to the dendrites that nerve cells are connected together in a very complex electrical circuit by means of the synaptic connections. Any single nerve cell may have as many as 10,000 such connections from other nerve cells. It is indeed much more likely that brain function, and even higher mental function, will be much more seriously affected by a restriction placed on dendritic arborisation during the brain growth spurt than by a moderate deficit in nerve cell number imposed before it begins. Unfortunately these later aspects of neuronal development are much more difficult to measure quantitatively than mere cell multiplication. Figure 3 expresses this difficulty and the fact that dendritic arborisation and developing synaptic connectivity are developmental processes which indeed belong to the brain growth spurt period, alongside the other more easily measured but functionally less important events. In addition at this time there is also a veritable revolution in the developmental metabolism of brain tissue. Radical changes in synthetic and degradative biochemical mechanisms occur, as the metabolic pattern of immaturity subsides, as that required for laying down new structure is transiently developed, and as metabolic preparation is made for maturing adult function. The secrets of the vulnerability of the brain growth spurt could as easily lie in a distortion of these biochemical developments as in disordered structural growth.

We will now consider the evidence for the existence of brain vulnerability during this phase of rapid growth of the organ. First we will describe the very simple experimental designs which have been employed, and then the evidence that quite moderate growth restriction at these times does produce lasting deficits and distortions of brain architecture and function.

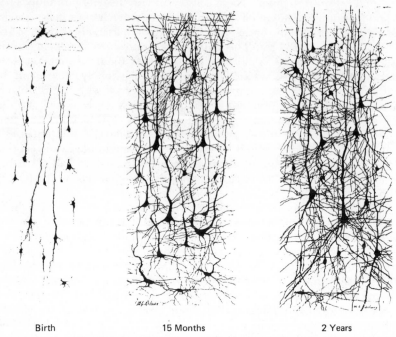

Birth	15 Months	2 Years

FIGURE 3.   *The increase of dendritic complexity in nerve cells of the human cerebral cortex in the first two years of postnatal life. This is the developing circuitry of the brain. Note how poorly developed it is at birth, although the nerve cells themselves are already present. Note also that it is still becoming more complex at two years of age. Adapted from the monographs of J. LeRoy Conel entitled, "The postnatal development of the human cerebral cortex."* (Reference: Conel, J. L. [1939, 1955 & 1959]. *The postnatal development of the human cerebral cortex.* Volumes 1, 5 and 6. Harvard University Press, Cambridge, Mass. Reproduced by kind permission of the publishers.)

EXPERIMENTAL DESIGNS

To test the proposition that the brain growth spurt period is one of enhanced vulnerability of the brain to growth restriction, all we need to do is to identify the timing of these stages in the normal early life of any animal species. We can then arrange to slow down the growth of the animal before, during or after that period, or in any combination of these three.

A convenient method of restricting growth of the fetus and suckling animal experimentally is by mild undernutrition either of the pregnant or lactating mother. Subsequently one can underfeed the weaned offspring. As well as an experimental growth-restricting device, undernutrition will also be directly studied by these methods and that, too, is a pressing world paediatric problem. It will be very important, since it is humans we are ultimately interested in, that the degree of undernutrition is not unrealistically severe compared with common human experience. Too much nonsense has been written by those who have extrapolated experimental results to humans from animal experiments in which the undernutrition has been grossly more severe than occurs even in times of famine in underprivileged human communities.

A convenient animal species is the rat. This is because the brain growth spurt is postnatal, and almost entirely confined to the first three postnatal weeks of life, which is the baby rat's suckling period (Figure 1). In this species birth conveniently occurs between the end of major neuronal multiplication and the beginning of the brain growth spurt (see Figure 2). Thus in the rat our three experimental periods are fetal life (before the growth spurt), the suckling period (during) and the postweaning period of growth by which time the growth spurt is over. Growth restriction in the first, fetal period, is imposed by underfeeding the pregnant mother; in the second by underfeeding the suckling mother; and in the third by directly underfeeding the growing weanling infant. In practice it is usual to foster the offspring at birth to new mothers. Both underfed and normally fed newborns are cross-fostered either to underfed or normally fed lactating foster-mothers. In this way there is a sharper separation at birth between different nutritional regimes.

One important result of such experiments is that growth restriction during the middle suckling period (that of the *brain* growth spurt) permanently affects the future growth of the whole animal although underfeeding during the first and third periods does not. However one tries to refeed or rehabilitate an animal growth restricted at the time of suckling (the first three postnatal weeks), it will always be small. Fetal undernutrition in the rat, provided the newborn is cross-fostered to a well fed lactating mother, and provided the growth restriction is not completely unrealistic in human terms, has little if any effect on subsequent bodily growth. Nor has postweaning growth restriction, in which complete bodily catch-up is available if properly rehabilitated. This last finding is particularly remarkable, since it is not until after weaning that the *bodily* growth spurt occurs, and at this time there is apparently no similar vulnerability of bodily growth. There is something about the successful accomplishment of *brain* growth which is necessary for the programme of proper subsequent *bodily* growth; and the secret is probably in the realms of endocrinology. Finally, in this experimental design, animals reared along these various trajectories of restricted growth are then rehabilitated on a full, *ad libitum* dietary intake until they are fully grown into adulthood, when their brains and their behaviour can be examined for any traces of their early, brain growth spurt restriction.

DEFICITS AND DISTORTIONS IN THE BRAIN FOLLOWING GROWTH RESTRICTION IN THE VULNERABLE PERIOD

We can now list some of the changes which can be found in the adult brain which have persisted since their early growth restriction. These are found only if the underfeeding has been timed to coincide with the brain growth spurt. They are not found following only fetal or postweaning undernutrition in the rat. As will be seen, the changes take the form of quantitative deficits, but there are also structural and functional distortions—and the latter may be the more significant.

Brain size   The adult brain size of previously underfed animals is permanently reduced. In addition it is reduced beyond the point which might have been expected from their reduced body size. Thus there is a permanent distortion of bodily configuration with a true, if slight microcephaly: a brain disproportionately small for the body size. When the brain is examined a little more closely, it is found that the organ is not uniformly reduced. One part of it, for example, the cerebellum, is much more reduced than is the rest of the brain. This has happened because, during the growth spurt of the whole brain, the cerebellum grows much the fastest of any region. And, since vulnerability in the brain appears to be related to speed of growth, the cerebellum suffers most. At all events here is another *distortion*, this time within the brain.

Brain cells   When measured by DNA estimation, the total number of brain cells of all types is reduced in about the proportion one would expect from the reduced brain size. In general it is thought that this deficit is at the expense of glial cells, not neurons, for reasons explained above. However, there is a certain special type of neuron in the cerebellum (the granular neuron) which is known to be an exception to the general rule that adult neuronal number is achieved before the brain growth spurt begins. These particular neurons divide later than the commencement of the brain growth spurt, and, as may have been expected, are found to be differentially deficient in the adult cerebellum following undernutrition at this time. All the other cerebellar neurons, which had already arrived, are present in proper quantity. This is yet another example of a distortion of the brain architecture, this time within the cerebellum which is not, therefore, merely small.

The cerebellar deficit and distortion is a particularly good example of the way in which the vulnerable period hypothesis is found to be justified. All depends on the timing of the growth restriction in relation to developmental events within the growth spurt period. It is also the only example so far discovered of a structural effect having definitely related functional consequences. The cerebellum has an important role in motor coordination: and these animals are found to be permanently clumsy. Perhaps it is significant that there are very large numbers of clumsy human children who are otherwise "normal," even in our own society, and this disorder does have a correlation with previous social disadvantage. This is discussed again later.

Another, somewhat unexpected distortion of cellular architecture has been found in the cerebral cortex. Neurons exist in layers in the cortex, having migrated there during development from their sites of origin. In adult rats who were previously undernourished, there is a small deficit in the deeper layers of the cortex, resulting in another distortion of the histological architecture. The significance of this arbitrary finding is not understood, but the distortion it exemplifies may well be functionally more important than a mere deficit.

Myelination   has already been mentioned as a major brain growth spurt process. Previously undernourished adult brains show a deficit in myelin quantity which is greater than would be accounted for by the reduced brain size: and this is, therefore, yet another example of distortion.

Synaptic Connections   Histological quantitation of brain structures is immensely laborious, since no useful mechanised techniques have yet been devised. Preliminary studies, however, have led to the claim that in some parts of the cerebral cortex there may be as many as *40 per cent* fewer synapses on each individual neuron. If this can be confirmed, we may be getting much nearer to a true physical basis for the distortions of higher mental function following early undernutrition.

Biochemical Distortions   There is already a number of reports that several enzyme systems which catalyse important brain reactions are also distorted. One of these concerns a permanent alteration in the activity of acetylcholinesterase, an enzyme greatly concerned with transmission of impulses at nerve endings. More recently, and perhaps even more significantly, a permanent alteration in the rate of synthesis of 5-hydroxytryptamine has been found in certain brain regions. 5-HT is thought to be one of the important neurotransmitter substances in the brain. Thus there is more than a suspicion that growth restriction permanently affects important brain biochemistry, provided it is correctly timed to the brain growth spurt period.

Permanent Alterations of Behaviour   A very large number of experiments have examined permanent differences in behaviour in animals following early undernutrition and subsequent rehabilitation. Although behavioural measures are ultimately much the most important criteria of whether physical deficits and distortions in the brain have any significance, they will not be discussed in any detail here, mainly because the relevance of such changes to human behaviour is much too large and difficult a discussion. However, permanent changes in animal behaviour which have been found include the clumsiness already mentioned, a tendency of the animals to overreact to stressful situations, and a demonstrable degree of possible "unsociability" in that they have an increase in aggressive and dominance traits. Many scientists have claimed to show deficits in learning ability, problem solving and memory, but although these are fascinating and exciting findings, their strict interpretation is extremely difficult, mixed up as it is with considerations of altered motivation for reward or altered reaction to punishment in the experimental situation.

There is no question whatever that the behaviour of these animals is profoundly and permanently affected. The major difficulty is in discussing these differences in meaningful, human terms.

A Single Opportunity for Brain Growth   Before attempting to extrapolate these findings to the human species, one final point must be discussed which has, of necessity, been discovered in animal experiment. It is that the timing of the brain growth spurt cannot be altered by altering the rate of growth. Whatever the rate of growth, the events within the developing brain which have been described for normal brain growth must occur at certain prescribed ages. Therefore, conditions must be good *at that time* for proper brain growth. There is no possibility of full recovery later if the opportunity to promote good brain growth is missed. This observation could have profound implications for human populations, both in normal times and at times of acute famine and disaster.

EXTRAPOLATION TO HUMANS

The applicability of the above experimental findings in animals to the human species is often seriously misunderstood and misinterpreted. There is no great difference between mammalian species in the pattern of brain development outlined in Figure 2. Even the individual unit structures of which the brain is composed, such as the nerve cells, glia and myelin sheaths, are remarkably similar both in composition and function from one species to another. For the present purposes, however, there is one important interspecies difference: that is in the *timing* of the vulnerable brain growth spurt period in relation to birth. In some precocial species, such as the guinea pig, sheep, cow, or horse, virtually the whole sequence occurs in fetal life, so that the animal is born neurologically very mature. In other species, such as the rat, mouse, and rabbit, the brain growth spurt is virtually entirely postnatal. In a third group, which includes the pig, birth occurs during the growth spurt period, some of it occurring before and some after birth. The important thing to grasp is that it is not important to the present discussion whether growth restriction is prenatal or postnatal. It is only important that it be imposed during the brain growth spurt, whenever that occurs in any particular species, if it is to produce the permanent changes described.

In view of the species' differences in timing, it therefore became vital to know when the human brain growth spurt occurred before we could guess the human implications of our experimental findings, and this has only recently been discovered and published.

About one hundred and forty complete human brains were collected from dead fetuses and children whose brain growth could be presumed to have been normal. By dissecting these into gross regions and analysing some of their constituents, it has been clearly shown that although the human brain growth spurt begins in fetal life, about the middle of gestation, it continues at least until the second birthday and probably beyond. This is in sharp disagreement with previous reports which, on the basis of an inadequate number of specimens inadequately examined, encouraged a text-book dogma that human brain development was virtually over by the fifth postnatal month. The recent finding that the human brain growth spurt occupies a long period of development, *and that most of it is postnatal*, has important practical implications. It is during this period that good brain growth should be actively promoted by ensuring good environmental conditions during its only opportunity to grow properly. It can even be conjectured that growth retarded human brains in babies with fetal growth retardation may be recoverable and compensated by urgent growth promotion after birth throughout at least the first two years. The possible implications for relief operations, as well as the organisation of food supplies in normal times in the Third World are obvious. The prolonged nature of the period of brain cell multiplication is shown in Figure 4, and the evidence that the all important growth of the dendritic tree of human cortical neurons is mainly postnatal has already been illustrated in Figure 4. Scrutiny of Figure 4 shows how little dendritic growth has occurred in humans by birth as well as the great degree of complexity which still has to develop, up to two postnatal years of age.

HUMAN NEURONAL MULTIPLICATION

This survey of human brain growth has also made it possible to determine the timing of the shorter period, before the growth spurt begins, when human

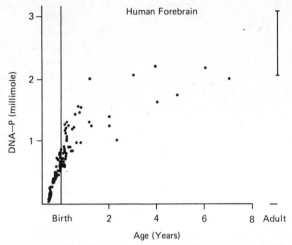

FIGURE 4. *Graph showing the total numbers of cells of all types in the human forebrain from 10 weeks gestation to 7 years of life, and in adults. Each point represents one individual. The cells are 'counted' by chemical estimation of DNA on the assumption that each brain cell nucleus contains an equal quantity of DNA. Note how cell multiplication continues rapidly well into the second postnatal year. For important detail of the fetal period, see Figure 6.* (Reference: Dobbing, J. & Sands, J. [1973]. The quantitative growth and development of the human brain. *Archives of Diseases of Childhood* 48:757–767.)

nerve cells multiply. Figure 5 shows this "mini-growth spurt" to be between 12 and 18 weeks of gestation. The biological importance of this as a period of vulnerability is reduced, however, by the fact that in humans the second trimester is thought to be a time in pregnancy when fetal growth is highly protected due to the smallness of the fetus in relation to the size of the placenta and mother. It is only in the last one third of pregnancy that fetal growth is normally threatened.

Nevertheless, there are hazards from which even the second trimester fetus is not protected. For example, the surprisingly sharp cut-off point between neuronal and glial cell multiplication at 18 weeks shown in Figure 5 bears a surprising resemblance to the cut-off point for producing microcephaly and mental retardation in the survivors of the nuclear attacks on Japan. All who were affected in this way were exposed to irradiation before the eighteenth week. Other examples of fetal hazard at this time which are known or are thought to harm the growing brain are maternal virus infection (for example, rubella), maternal medication, abnormalities of maternal metabolism (e.g., hyperphenylalaninaemia), X-rays, and even maternal fever. It is even possible that the more severe cases of mental retardation which, as mentioned at the beginning, show no damage to the brain except some degree of smallness, may be caused by something in the environment which interfered with this particular neuronal multiplication phase of brain growth between 10 and 18 gestational weeks. Only much more attention to the quantitative aspects of neurohistopathology (which is infinitely laborious) will help to confirm this conjecture.

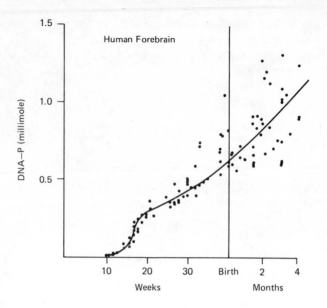

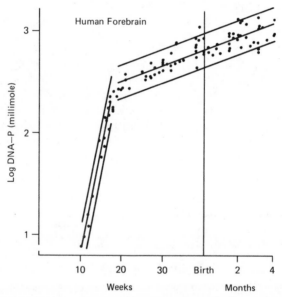

FIGURE 5 A AND 5 B.   *The upper figure shows the increasing numbers of cells in the human forebrain from 10 weeks of gestation to 4 postnatal months. The method of "counting" is explained in the caption to Figure 4. The lower figure plots the logarithm of the individual brain values in the upper figure. Notice the sharp cut-off point at 18 weeks between the earlier phase of nerve cell multiplication and the later phase of glial multiplication.* (Reference: Dobbing, J. & Sands, J. [1973]. The quantitative growth and development of the human brain. *Archives of Diseases of Childhood.* 48:757–767.)

HUMAN CEREBELLAR GROWTH

Figure 6 shows the shapes of the growth curves of cell multiplication in three major regions of the human brain. From this it can be seen that the human cerebellum has growth characteristics which are similar to those in the experimental animal. It grows much faster than the rest of the brain, but at the same time, and its growth spurt period is therefore much shorter. In the animals this led to a differentially much greater vulnerability of the cerebellum to growth restriction, leading to a much larger permanent reduction in cerebellar size and significant distortion of its histological architecture. More importantly it led to motor incoordination, or clumsiness. At the present time it must remain pure conjecture whether some of the very common clumsiness in our own children in Western Europe may be related to an environmentally-induced failure of cerebellar growth. It is possible that about five per cent of our children are clumsy. It is known that its incidence is statistically related to poor socioeconomic circumstances. The question would not be impossible to investigate.

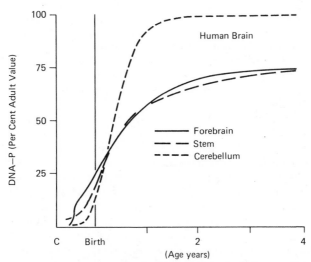

FIGURE 6. *Numbers of brain cells of all types during development in three brain regions. Notice the much more rapid growth spurt in the cerebellum. The article discusses whether clumsiness in children could be due to the differential vulnerability of the cerebellum as occurs in animals.* (Reference: Dobbing, J. & Sands, J. [1973]. The quantitative growth and development of the human brain. *Archives of Diseases of Childhood.* 48:757-767.)

ENVIRONMENTAL EFFECTS ON HUMAN INTELLECT

The suggestion runs right through this article that the new vulnerable-period or growth-restriction pathology of the brain may be involved in a failure of large numbers of human people to reach their full genetic potential, even though their achievement may often be within the normal range. It is important, finally, to examine the possible size of the importance of these environmental restrictions, acting through an effect on physical brain growth.

Certain major considerations must be borne in mind. Firstly, as has repeatedly been stressed, we do not know anything about the physical basis, within the brain, of higher mental function. Secondly, we know quite certainly that the non-physical postnatal environment of the growing child has an enormous part to play in shaping his personality and intellect. Human emotional and intellectual development is astonishingly plastic. Tremendous improvement even in the severely mentally handicapped can be achieved through non-physical means, by increasing the child's experience of external stimulus. Presumably, similar alterations of achievement in normal children accompany comparable alterations of this environmental non-physical input. Indeed, the demonstrable effects of changes in the environment on the psychological development of the normal child are so great, that there seems little need to attach much importance of the comparatively insignificant effects of genetic inheritance.

Enthusiasts in our area of research must be prepared to accept that the intellectual consequences of physical brain growth restriction may also be small, even though the physical effects are clearly demonstrable in the brain. This is especially true of the proposed "deficit and distortion" pathology compared with the better known lesion pathologies. At first sight it may be relevant that the underprivileged world is not obviously populated by idiots. Only the minority whose malnutrition has been severe and clinically evident can be shown to have seriously and permanently diminished intelligence. And, in these children, it is difficult to distinguish between the physical causes of physically disordered brain growth and all the other gross disorders of their non-physical environment to which the malnourished children in a community are commonly exposed.

The following is therefore pure conjecture. Supposing we were able to break down the multitude of different environmental influences on developing intellect. Let us suppose that no single one of them amounted to more than a few per cent contribution (social class would be a much larger factor, but this is really a collection of very many single contributions). If you were then a mother (or a government) wanting to do the best to promote good child development, what would you do? There would be no simple, single factor which you could modify and improve. You would have to promote as many "plus scores" in the algebraic sum of factors contributing to achievement as you could identify. One major factor would presumably be the promotion of good brain growth. This can only be accomplished by achieving good bodily growth; and this in turn demands good socio-economic conditions and, above all, good nutrition. This is surely also true in our own privileged society as well as in the Third World.

It may finally be wondered, why should so much expensive research be necessary in order to come to the quite elementary conclusion that we must feed our children? The answer is that, if that were the whole story, research of this kind would not be necessary. But if, as has been indicated, there exists a particular, vulnerable period, a particular age of development during which the brain has its only opportunity to grow properly, it would be an important and urgent task for the developmental neurobiologist to identify this vulnerable period, so that irrevocably poor brain growth does not occur, and the very best brain growth can be economically promoted. Only when we have succeeded in doing this, by abolishing all forms of environmental restriction at this time, will we be likely to reveal the comparatively small contribution to the variance made by our individual heredity.

Further Reading

1. For a full description of the clinical implications of this subject, see Scientific Foundations of Paediatrics (1974). Edited by John A. Davis and John Dobbing; published by Heinemann, London & Saunders, Philadelphia. This also contains full account of the growth and development of all the other organ systems as well as the brain.
2. For more complete discussion of the behavioural implications, see Dobbing, J. & Smart, J. L. (1974). Undernutrition and the developing brain. Brit. Med. Bull. 30:164–168.

Behavioral Estimates of CNS Integrity in Infantile Malnutrition*

Barry M. Lester

BOSTON CHILDREN'S HOSPITAL MEDICAL CENTER

Abstract

Behavioral processes that have been used to estimate the integrity of the CNS were studied in 20 well-nourished and 20 malnourished 1-year-old male infants. Malnourished infants showed an attenuation of the cardiac-orienting response and an aberrant cry pattern characterized by an initial long sound that is high in pitch, low in intensity, arrhythmical with a long latency to the second cry sound. These results point to behavioral deficits in CNS-mediated processes associated with nutritional insult.

Although animal and human research has found both structural and biochemical abnormalities in malnourished brains[1] the behavioral correlates of these deficits are unclear. Most studies, especially with infants, have been confined to the use of standard developmental scales which provide a gross estimate of psychomotor performance but do not indicate specific behavioral processes that may be affected by nutritional insult.[2] In the present report specific behaviors that have been used to estimate the integrity of the CNS were compared in well-nourished and malnourished infants. Behavior studies were habituation of the cardiac-orienting response (OR) and temporal and acoustic measures of the cry response.

EXPERIMENT I

METHODS   *Subjects*   Twenty well-nourished and 20 malnourished home reared 1-year-old male infants from the lower socioeconomic class of Guatemala City, Guatemala, served as subjects. Consent to participate in the study was

* Supported in part by National Institute of Child Health and Human Development Contract PH43–65–540.

obtained when the mother brought her infant to a government run medical clinic for the indigent for the infant's 1 year checkup. All infants were full term, clinically normal, single births of uneventful pregnancies and had suffered no major illnesses as of the time of testing. Differences in birth weight between the well-nourished ($\bar{X} = 2.52$, $SD = .37$) and malnourished ($\bar{X} = 2.57$, $SD = .38$) groups were not significant. None of the mothers were sedated during the birth of the infant and all infants had been breast-fed. No significant differences were found between the groups with regard to the socioeconomic variables of age or education of the parents or occupation of the father. The age and anthropometric characteristics of the sample are shown in Table 1. The malnourished infants were significantly lighter ($F = 98,44$, $df = 1,38$, $p < .001$), shorter ($F = 23,50$, $df = 1,38$, $p < .001$), and had a smaller head circumference ($F = 14,29$, $df = 1,38$, $p < .001$) than the well-nourished infants. On the Gomez norms[3], based on a sample from Mexico City, the mean per cent of average weight was 66.4% (range of 56%–75%) for the malnourished infants and 94.4% (range of 89%–100%) for the well-nourished infants. According to the nutritional status categories suggested by Gomez, the malnourished infants were suffering from second- and third-degree malnutrition whereas the well-nourished infants were within the expected weight for age.

Procedure   The infants were presented with 20 trials of a pure tone stimulus in a sound-attenuated chamber. Within each nutrition group half of the infants were presented with 10 trials of a 750 Hz tone followed by 5 trials of a 400 Hz tone and 5 trials of the 750 Hz tone. For the other half of the sample this order was reversed. The tones were presented at 90 db for 5 seconds with a randomized intertrial interval having a mean of 20 seconds and a range of 15–25 seconds. All infants were in an awake and alert state when tested. Magnitude of heart rate deceleration was used to measure the OR. Previous work[4] suggests that HR deceleration is a component of the OR facilitating stimulus intake that may reflect the capacity of the nervous system to attend to and process new information.[5] Infant HR was monitored with a set of Beckman biopotential electrodes placed slightly above the infant's nipples and a ground located above the navel. Cardiac responses were recorded in an adjoining room with a Beckman type-R dynograph with cardiotachometer.

T A B L E 1

Age and Anthropometric Characteristics of Well-Nourished and Malnourished Infants

GROUP	AGE (mo)	WEIGHT (kg)	HEIGHT (cm)	HEAD CIRCUMFERENCE
Well-nourished (N = 20)				
$\bar{X}$	12.38	9.44	72.19	45.48
SD	1.30	.87	2.87	1.34
Malnourished (N = 20)				
$\bar{X}$	12.28	7.02	67.77	43.87
SD	1.92	.65	2.89	1.35

Results and Discussion   No significant differences in prestimulus HR were found between the well-nourished and malnourished groups. A repeated measures analysis of variance showed no significant differences due to the order of tone frequency presentation. Accordingly, the order conditions were collapsed resulting in 20 subjects per nutrition cell. Figure 1 presents the mean HR decelerations to the pure tone stimuli for the well-nourished and malnourished infants. A repeated measures analysis of variance for trials 1–10 revealed a significant trials effect ($F = 3,42$, $df = 9,324$, $p < .001$) and a significant nutrition by trials interaction ($F = 5,61$, $df = 9,324$, $p < .001$). These effects were due to the larger mean HR deceleration on trial 1 in the well-nourished than in the malnourished group ($F = 48,99$, $df = 1,38$, $p < .001$). For trials 11–15 the analysis showed a significant trials effect ($F = 3,98$, $df = 4,132$, $p < .001$) and a significant nutrition by trials interaction ($F = 5,52$, $df = 4,132$, $p < .001$). The mean HR deceleration on trial 11 was larger in the well-nourished than in the malnourished infants ($F = 18,85$, $df = 1,38$, $p < .001$). Similarly, the analysis for trials 16–20 revealed significant effects for the trials factor ($F = 3,32$, $df = 4,132$, $p < .025$) and the nutrition by trials interaction ($F = 4,78$, $df = 4,132$, $p < .001$). The mean HR on trial 16 was larger in well-nourished than in malnourished infants ($F = 8,19$, $df = 1,38$, $p < .01$).

These results demonstrate an effect of nutritional status on the infant's ability to respond to and process a novel stimulus. Well-nourished infants showed a classic OR followed by rapid habituation to the repeated presentation of the stimulus. Moreover, qualitative changes in that stimulus produced response recovery or dishabituation which was followed by rapid habituation.

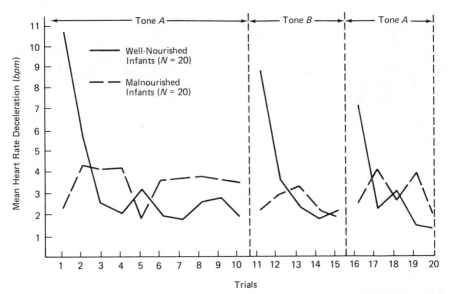

FIGURE 1.   *Mean heart rate deceleration on each trial to pure tone stimuli in well-nourished and malnourished infants. For each trial, heart rate deceleration was calculated by subtracting the mean of the two lowest beats during the 5-second stimulus onset period from the mean of the two lowest beats during the 5 seconds preceding stimulus onset.*

This suggests that the habituation of the OR was due to a neural inhibitory process rather than to peripheral adaptation of the receptor or to fatigue. In contrast, the malnourished infants showed an attentuation of the OR. Neither the repeated presentation of a stimulus nor qualitative changes in that stimulus produced anything but minimal responses in malnourished infants. Since OR evocation is thought to be a necessary precursor to centrally mediated attentional and cognitive processes, OR attenuation in malnourished infants strongly suggests CNS-mediated deficits in these important adaptive functions.

EXPERIMENT II

METHODS   Of the 40 infants, 24 (12 malnourished and 12 well-nourished) cried following the last habituation trial. Since previous studies have shown pathognomic cry patterns to be associated with brain damage[6,7] these cry sounds were subjected to both temporal and acoustic analyses for evidence of aberrant cry patterns. The cry sounds were recorded on a Sony portable tape recorder at a constant recording level at a distance of 1 meter from the mouth of the infant. The cry segment analyzed was the initial spontaneous cry sound following the offset of the last habituation tone. The analysis was performed with the experimenter blind as to the nutritional status of the infant.

Cry signals were analyzed with a model 1510 Real Time Spectrum Analyzer which plots a Fourier transformation of a signal on a cathode ray tube display. Five measures, two temporal and three acoustic, were taken from each cry segment. The temporal measures were the duration of the initial cry sound and the latency to the onset of the next cry sound. The acoustic measures were the fundamental frequency or basic pitch of the initial cry sound, the amplitude or intensity of the fundamental and the number of peaks or major shifts in the frequency of the initial cry sound.

RESULTS AND DISCUSSION   Table 2 summarizes the results of the analysis of variance for the cry measures. The analysis for the temporal measures showed that the duration of the cry and the latency to the next cry sound was longer in malnourished than in well-nourished infants. The analysis for the acoustic measures revealed that the cry of the malnourished infant was of a higher fundamental frequency and lower amplitude than the cry of the well-nourished infant. The number of peaks was also fewer in the malnourished infants than in the well-nourished infants. In other words, the cry of the malnourished infant can be characterized by a long initial sound that is high in pitch, and low in intensity with a long interval to the next cry sound. The malnourished cry also appears arrhythmical as indicated by the number of peaks in the initial cry sound.

Pearson product-moment correlations computed between all of the cry measures are shown in Table 3. Eight of the 10 correlations were significant, and all were in the expected direction. The correlations showed the association between a high fundamental frequency, low amplitude, few number of peaks, long initial cry and long latency to the next cry sound. Thus, both temporal and acoustic attributes of the cry seem to be similarly affected by nutritional insult.

The results from the cry analyses suggest that the cry pattern of malnourished infants is similar to the cry patterns found to be characteristic of some

TABLE 2

Results of Analysis of Cry Measures in Well-Nourished and Malnourished Infants

CRY MEASURE	Well-Nourished ($N = 12$)		Malnourished ($N = 12$)		$F(df = 1.22)$
	$\bar{X}$	SD	$\bar{X}$	SD	
Length of cry (sec)	1.52	.18	2.66	1.15	10.47*
Latency to next cry (sec)	.47	.26	1.8	.69	39.33**
Frequency of fundamental (Hz)	308.00	32.18	479.77	25.61	209.06**
Intensity of fundamental (dB)	50.31	7.0	38.16	5.47	22.48**
Number of peaks	4.5	1.2	2.25	.75	28.74**

*$p < .005$.
**$p < .001$.

brain-damaged infants. In fact, several investigators have pointed to the diagnostic utility of the cry as a sensitive measure of the integrity of the CNS.[8,9] Specifically, studies have found longer initial cry sounds, a longer latency to the second cry sound, higher pitch, and more arrhythmia to be associated with brain damage in infancy.[10,11] If aberrations of the cry pattern are indicative of CNS dysfunction, these findings may suggest that the regulatory function of the CNS is affected by malnutrition.

Finally, the results from the cry analysis can be compared with the HR data from the same subjects reported earlier. Table 4 shows the Pearson product-moment correlations between each cry measure and the magnitude of HR deceleration to the onset of the original stimulus (trial 1) and the two

TABLE 3

Intercorrelations Among Cry Measures

	1	2	3	4	5
1. Length of cry	1.00	—	—	—	—
2. Latency to next cry	.49**	1.00	—	—	—
3. Frequency of fundamental	.56**	.70†	1.00	—	—
4. Intensity of fundamental	−.33	−.50**	−.61**	1.00	—
5. Number of peaks	−.27	−.54**	−.70†	.43*	1.00

*$p < .05$.
**$p < .01$.
†$p < .001$.

TABLE 4

Correlations Between Magnitude of Heart Rate Deceleration and Cry Measures

	STIMULUS ONSET	DISHABITUATION STIMULUS 1	DISHABITUATION STIMULUS 2
Duration of cry	−.45*	−.64**	−.53**
Latency to next cry	−.65†	−.68†	−.52**
Frequency of fundamental	−.70†	−.62**	−.60**
Amplitude of fundamental	.63†	.33	.68†
Number of peaks	.50**	.46*	.46*

* $p < .05$.
** $p < .01$.
† $p < .001$.

dishabituation stimuli (trials 11 and 16). As can be seen in the table, 14 of the 15 correlations were significant and all were in the expected direction. The correlations with the temporal measures showed that longer initial cry sounds and a longer latency to the next cry sound are related to low magnitude HR decelerations on each trial. The correlations with the acoustic measures showed that high frequency, low amplitude, arrhythmical cries are related to low magnitude HR decelerations on each trial. In other words, both temporal and acoustic deviations from the normal cry pattern are associated with a low level OR. On the other hand, infants who evidence normal cry patterns show the expected OR to a novel stimulus.

CONCLUSIONS   This study demonstrates that both orienting and cry behavior are similarly affected by nutritional insult. To the extent that these behaviors mirror the functional integrity of the CNS, the results indicate some of the specific behavioral correlates of CNS dysfunction due to malnutrition. Moreover, it seems reasonable to speculate that nutritional insult is most likely to affect those regions of the CNS responsible for the activation and modulation of behavior.

References

1. DOBBING, J.: Undernutrition and the developing brain. In W. Himwich, editor; *Developmental Neurobiology*, Springfield, Ill., Charles C Thomas. 1970, p. 502.
2. LESTER, B. M.: The consequences of infantile malnutrition. In H. E. Fitzgerald & J. P. McKinney, editors; *Developmental Psychology: Studies in Human Development*, Homewood, Ill., Dorsey Press, in press.
3. GOMEZ, F., CALVAN, R., FRENK, S., CRAVIOTO, J., CHAVEZ, R., & VASQUEZ, J.: Mortality in second and third degree malnutrition. *Journal of Tropical Pediatrics*, September; **77**: 1956.
4. GRAHAM, F. K., & CLIFTON, R. K.: Heart rate change as a component of the orienting response, *Psychological Bulletin*, **65**:305, 1966.
5. SOKOLOV, E. N.: *Perception and the conditioned reflex*. New York, Macmillan, 1963.
6. WASZ-HOCKERT, O., LIND, J., VVORENKOSKI, V., PARTANEN, T. & VALANNE, E.: The infant cry. *Clinics in Developmental Medicine*, **29**: 1968.

7. KARCLITZ, S., & FISICHELLI, V.: The cry thresholds of normal infants and those with brain damage. *Journal of Pediatrics*, **61**:679, 1962.
8. PARMELEE, A.: Infant crying and neurologic diagnosis. *Journal of Pediatrics*, **61**:801, 1962.
9. ILLINGWORTH, R.: Crying in infants and children. *British Medical Journal*, **1**:75, 1955.
10. LIND, J., WASZ-HOCKERT, O., VVORENKOSKI, V., PARTANEN, T., THEORELL, K., & VALANNE, E.: Vocal response to pain stimuli in newborn and young infant. *Ann. Paediat. Fenn.* **10**:122, 1965.
11. WASZ-HOCKERT, O., LIND, J., VVORENKOSKI, V., PARTANEN, T., & VALANNE, E.: The infant cry. *Clinics in Developmental Medicine*, **29**, 1968.

The Relation of Infants' Home Environments to Mental Test Performance from Six to Thirty-six Months: A Longitudinal Analysis*

Richard Elardo, Robert Bradley, and Bettye M. Caldwell
UNIVERSITY OF ARKANSAS

In contrast to the large array of instruments available for the measurement of individual differences in children, there have been almost no techniques available to permit the precise measurement of the child's home learning environment. The present study involved the administration of a home environment inventory to a sample of 77 mothers and infants. Correlations between home inventory data and measures of infant development over a period of 30 months were higher than those typically reported relating infant tests or level of parental education to childhood IQ.

Several investigators (Bloom 1964: Plowden 1967; Walberg & Marjoribanks 1973) have produced evidence attesting to the fact that measures of various characteristics of the home environment contribute more strongly to the prediction of children's abilities than do social status or family structure indices. These studies have been cross-sectional in nature and have focused on children over 10 years of age. Walberg and Marjoribanks (1973), for example, interviewed the mothers and fathers of 185 11-year-old boys with a home environment inventory based on the theorizing of Bloom (1964). They reported that their inventory contributed the most to the prediction of a boy's verbal and numerical abilities, when compared with SES and family structure measures via canonical correlation.

From *Child Development*, 1975, **46**, 71–76. Copyright© 1975 by The Society for Research in Child Development, Inc. Reprinted by permission.

* This investigation was supported by grant SF-500 from the Office of Child Development, Department of Health, Education, and Welfare. A preliminary report was presented at the Southeastern Regional Meeting of the Society for Research in Child Development, Chapel Hill, North Carolina, March 1974. Copies of the Inventory of Home Stimulation may be obtained from Dr. Caldwell. Authors' address: University of Arkansas, Center for Early Development and Education, 814 Sherman Street, Little Rock, Arkansas 72202.

The present study involved the administration of a home environment inventory in infancy (Inventory of Home Stimulation [Caldwell, Heider, & Kaplan 1966]) in order to explore its ability to predict later mental test performance.

METHOD

Subjects   The subjects for this analysis were 77 normal infants, representing part of a larger sample of 135 infants who participated in a longitudinal observation and intervention study (Caldwell, Elardo, & Elardo 1972) which was designed to reveal the effects of different types of environments on infant development.

Excluded from the present sample were infants who received a program of educational intervention in the home and those for whom complete home environment and mental test data were not available. Additional descriptive information about the subjects is contained in Table 1.

Instrumentation   A decade ago, a group of persons working on the Syracuse Early Learning Project (Caldwell & Richmond 1968) began to devote considerable effort to the discovery of ways of assessing the subtle aspects of the young child's home environment in order to determine which specific features of it were most likely to influence development. The staff felt that it was imperative to develop a measure of the home environment that could warn of developmental risk before age 3. Their long-term goal was to produce a valid, reliable, easy-to-administer, observationally based inventory

TABLE 1
Characteristics of the Sample

FAMILY DATA ($N = 77$)

Welfare, 31; nonwelfare, 46
Father absent, 21; father present, 56
Maternal education (average no. of years), 12.1
Paternal education (average no. of years), 12.9
Paternal occupation: wide range of employment, but
on the average skilled labor to sales

CHILD DATA

Black males	$N = 29$,	$\bar{X}DQ^* =$	94.4, SD = 21.7
White males	$N = 15$,	$\bar{X}DQ =$	104.1, SD = 10.7
Black females	$N = 21$,	$\bar{X}DQ =$	104.9, SD = 17.3
White females	$N = 12$,	$\bar{X}DQ =$	102.6, SD = 22.6

* Refers to the average score obtained by the infants when tested at 6 months of age with the Mental Development Index of the Bayley Scales of Infant Development (Bayley 1969).

that would provide an index of the quality and quantity of social, emotional, and cognitive support available to a young child (from birth to 3 years of age) within the home setting.

A survey of empirical data, developmental theory, and expert opinion was conducted for clues to home characteristics that might be associated with favorable development during the early years of life. A list of environmental characteristics likely to foster early development in any setting was compiled and published (Caldwell 1968), and an instrument named the "Inventory of Home Stimulation" was developed and standardized from this list. The current version of the inventory contains 45 items representing the following six subscales: (1) emotional and verbal responsivity of the mother, (2) avoidance of restriction and punishment, (3) organization of the physical and temporal environment, (4) provision of appropriate play materials, (5) maternal involvement with the child, and (6) opportunities for variety in daily stimulation.

Scoring is based partly on observation and partly on answers to a semi-structured interview administered in the home at a time when the child is awake and can be observed in interaction with the mother or primary care giver.

At an early stage of instrument development, consideration was given to the notion of including items based totally on observation of what transpired at the time of the visit. However, in order to cover certain important transactions not likely to occur during the visit, it was necessary to base about one-third of the items on parental report. All items are scored in a binary fashion (yes or no) and are phrased so that the total score equals the number of yes responses marked by the interviewer. The entire procedure takes approximately 1 hour.

At present, extensive standardization data do not exist for the inventory. Data have been gathered from 176 families in central Arkansas, however, and these data indicate that the instrument is sensitive enough to register a wide range of scores for families with identical social status designations.

In terms of reliability, raters can quickly be trained to achieve a 90% level of agreement. Internal consistency (KR-20) coefficients based on 176 cases range from .44 for subscale 6 to .89 for subscale 3. The internal consistency coefficient for the total scale was computed at .89. Using data from assessments made at 6, 12, and 24 months on 91 families, we computed test-retest correlations for each subscale and the total scale. Results indicate that the inventory has a moderate degree of stability across the 18-month period.

With regard to concurrent validity, Inventory of Home Stimulation scores for 91 families were correlated with seven socioeconomic status variables (welfare status, maternal education, maternal occupation, presence of the father in the home, paternal education, paternal occupation, and crowding in the home). Correlations between subscales and maternal education, presence of the father in the home, paternal education, paternal occupation, and crowding were moderate (.25–.55). Correlations between subscales and welfare status and maternal occupation were smaller in magnitude but still positive.

Procedure   Data collected from all subjects include scores on the Mental Development Index (MDI) of the Bayley Scales of Infant Development (Bayley 1969) at 6 and 12 months of age, and scores on the Stanford-Binet scale at 36 months. Each infant's home environment was assessed at 6, 12, and 24 months with the Inventory of Home Stimulation.

Several analyses were performed to determine which aspects of the early home environment were associated with the infants' mental test performance.

RESULTS

The Pearson product-moment and multiple correlation coefficients between home environment scores at 6 months and Bayley MDI scores at 6 and 12 months and Stanford-Binet scores at 36 months are presented in Table 2. An examination of these coefficients indicates that subscale 3 (organization of the physical and temporal environment) and subscale 6 (opportunities for variety in daily stimulation) have the strongest relationship to MDI scores at 6 months, $r = .22$ and .20, respectively. These subscales have a stronger relationship to mental test performance than even the total score on the inventory. The multiple correlation between all six subscales and the 6-month MDI is listed at $R = .31$.

The same general pattern of coefficients obtains between 6-month home environment scores and Bayley MDI scores at 12 months. To be specific, opportunities for variety in daily stimulation and organization of the physical and temporal environment are correlated with the criterion $r = .16$ and .26, respectively. The multiple correlation between all six scores and the 12-month MDI score is calculated at $R = .30$.

Correlations between 6-month home environment scores and 36-month Binet scores are generally higher than correlations between 6 and 12 months,

TABLE 2

Correlations Between 6-month Inventory of Home Stimulation Scores and Mental Test Scores Gathered at 6, 12, and 36 Months

	MENTAL TEST SCORES		
HOME ENVIRONMENT VARIABLES	6-Month Bayley MDI	12-Month Bayley MDI	36-Month Binet
1. Emotional and verbal responsivity of mother	− .008	.093	.254*
2. Avoidance of restriction and punishment	.005	.039	.244*
3. Organization of physical and temporal environment	.224	.263	.402**
4. Provision of appropriate play materials	.146	.067	.408**
5. Maternal involvement with child	.061	−.003	.325**
6. Opportunities for variety in daily stimulation	.204	.158	.305**
Total score	.141	.156	.500**
Multiple correlation†	.313**	.301*	.537**

*$p < .05$
**$p < .0$.
† This represents the correlation of all subscales with mental test scores.

particularly the relationship between the total score and the 36-month Binet score, $r = .50$. In addition, provision of appropriate play materials, $r = .41$, and maternal involvement with child, $r = .33$, seem about as strongly related with 36-month Binet performance as do organization of the physical and temporal environment, $r = .40$, and opportunities for variety in daily stimulation, $r = .31$. The multiple correlation is given at $R = .54$.

Pearson product-moment coefficients and multiple correlation coefficients between 12-month home environment scores and 12-month MDI scores and 36-month Binet scores are shown in Table 3. The 12-month MDI scores seem most strongly related to provision of appropriate play materials, $r = .35$. A moderate relationship is also observed for organization of the physical and temporal environment, $r = .24$, and maternal involvement with child, $r = .22$. A multiple correlation of $R = .40$ was computed for all six subscales for this concurrent analysis.

Correlations ranging from $r = .24$ to $r = .56$ are observed between 12-month home environment scores and 36-month Binet scores, the highest being for provision of appropriate play materials, $r = .56$, and maternal involvement with child, $r = .47$. It is at this level that emotional and verbal responsivity also seems to show a strong relationship to mental test performance, $r = .39$. The correlation between the 36-month Binet score and the total home environment score obtained at 12 months is listed at $r = .55$, while the multiple correlation between the six subscales of the Inventory of Home Stimulation and the 36-month Binet scores is listed at $R = .59$.

In Table 4 the correlations between 24-month home environment scores and 36-month Binet scores are listed. Coefficients range from $r = .41$ for

TABLE 3

Correlations Between 12-Month Inventory of Home Stimulation Scores and Mental Test Scores Gathered at 12 and 36 Months

	MENTAL TEST SCORES	
HOME ENVIRONMENT VARIABLES	12-Month Bayley MDI	36-Month Binet
1. Emotional and verbal responsivity of mother	.176	.387**
2. Avoidance of restriction and punishment	−.008	.241*
3. Organization of physical and temporal environment	.241	.389**
4. Provision of appropriate play materials	.353*	.561**
5. Maternal involvement with child	.218*	.468**
6. Opportunities for variety in daily stimulation	.054	.283*
Total score	.252*	.551**
Multiple correlation†	.400**	.588**

* $p < .05$.
** $p < .01$.
† This represents the correlation of all subscales with mental test scores.

TABLE 4

Correlations Between 24-Month Inventory of Home Stimulation Scores and Mental Test Scores at 36 Months

HOME ENVIRONMENT VARIABLES	MENTAL TEST SCORES, 36-MONTH BINET
1. Emotional and verbal responsivity of mother	.495*
2. Avoidance of restriction and punishment	.406*
3. Organization of physical and temporal enviromnent	.413*
4. Provision of appropriate play materials	.635*
5. Maternal involvement with child	.545*
6. Opportunities for variety in daily stimulation	.499*
Total score	.695*
Multiple correlation**	.718*

$*p < .01.$
** This represents the correlation of all subscales with mental test scores.

avoidance of restriction and punishment to $r = .64$ for provision of appropriate play materials. The total home environment score at 24 months and the Binet score at 36 months share almost 50% common variance, $r = .69$. The multiple correlation between the six subscales and the 36-month Binet scores is computed at $R = .72$. Correlations between Bayley and Binet scores are presented in Table 5.

TABLE 5

Correlations Between 6-Month Bayley MDI, 12-Month Bayley MDI, and 36-Month Stanford-Binet Scores ($N = 77$)

SCALES	MDI-12	IQ-36
MDI-6	.410**	.283*
MDI-12	—	.319**

$*p < .05.$
$**p < .01.$

DISCUSSION

We begin with a note of caution. The analyses presented in this paper are based on only 77 cases. Therefore, it would be presumptuous to assume that highly similar results would be obtained from a more representative group of families. More accurate information may also be obtained by analyzing males and females separately. Nevertheless, the results of our analyses suggest that those aspects of home environment assessed by the Inventory of Home

Stimulation bear an important relationship to cognitive development during the first 3 years of life.

With our sample, the six home inventory subscale scores obtained at 6 months of age yielded a multiple correlation of .54 with the same subjects' Binet at age 3. The home scores obtained at 12 months yielded a multiple correlation of .59 with the Binet at age 3, while the multiple correlation between 24-month home scores and Binet scores at age 3 was .72.

These correlations are quite high; in general, they are higher than those reported in the McCall, Hogarty, and Hurlburt (1972) analysis relating infant tests and parental education to childhood IQ. They are also higher than Bayley-Binet correlations obtained from the same sample (see Table 5). The Inventory of Home Stimulation can thus be of value to those interested in the early identification of environmental factors detrimental to development. The work of Cravioto and DeLicardie (1972), which indicated that the presence of severe malnutrition was significantly associated with home stimulation, is illustrative of this. Cravioto and DeLicardie administered the Inventory of Home Stimulation twice yearly as part of their longitudinal investigation of environmental correlates of severe clinical malnutrition. From a sample of 229 infants, Cravioto and DeLicardie identified 19 infants who suffered from severe clinical malnutrition by the age of 39 months. From their total sample, they then assembled a matched control group for the malnourished infants and examined the distribution of scores on the Inventory of Home Stimulation for both groups. They found that the inventory administered at 6 months of age significantly discriminated between infants who were eventually to become malnourished and those who were not, thus delineating an important relationship between children's social environments and their physiological state.

Also illustrative is the cross-sectional study of Wachs, Uzgiris, and Hunt (1971). They employed the Inventory of Home Stimulation in an investigation designed to relate the home background of infants to the infants' cognitive development, as measured by the Infant Psychological Development Scale (Uzgiris & Hunt 1966). A total of 102 infants were involved in the study, ranging in age from 7 to 22 months. Two kinds of home circumstances were found to be most consistently related to infant development: intensity and variety of stimulation, and opportunities to hear vocal labels for objects, actions, and relationships. The first factor was at several ages negatively correlated with developmental test performance, suggesting the harmful effects of overstimulation or "stimulus bombardment." The second factor, concerned with the infants' verbal environment in the home, revealed several significant positive relationships to development beginning as early as 15 months of age. Wachs et al. (1971) present a convincing argument that certain types of environmental stimulation may be related in a curvilinear rather than a linear manner to psychological development. Their explanation for this type of relationship rests on Hunt's (1961) concept of "Hypothesis of the Match." These researchers see a need for longitudinal research to provide more information for understanding the complex relationships between home circumstances and indices of psychological development.

Our results indicate that home environment, when measured at a time when the infant is approximately 6 months of age, does not relate in any

important fashion to the infant's performance on the Bayley Mental Development Index at 6 or 12 months of age; whereas the correlation between home
environment as measured at 6 months and Binet performance at 3 years
appears to be both significant and important, as do the correlations between
home environment measured at 12 and 24 months of age and Binet performance
at 3 years. These results suggest that the Inventory of Home Stimulation is
measuring a complex of environmental forces which are perhaps prerequisites
to later performance on cognitive tasks, and is measuring those forces at a time
in the infant's life prior to the period in development in which such environmental forces have affected the infant's measured development. During the
first year of life, the subscales dealing with organization of the physical and
temporal environment and, to a lesser extent, opportunities for variety in daily
stimulation seem most strongly related to mental test performance. However,
beginning at 12 months, provision of appropriate play materials and maternal
involvement with the child seem to show the strongest relationships. The
meaning of these findings is uncertain. It may be that different aspects of the
home environment are most salient at certain times in development. It may, on
the other hand, suggest that certain home environment factors interact with
mental capabilities in a complex fashion.

The data obtained after 12 months of age seem to indicate that perhaps the
most enriching environments experienced by the children in our sample may be
characterized as those in which a mother (or some other primary care giver)
provided the infant with a variety of age-appropriate learning materials and
likewise consciously encouraged developmental advances by talking to, looking
at, and otherwise positively responding to and attending to her child.

In this study, as in the case with other correlational studies, several different
hypotheses may be considered as plausible explanations of the results obtained:
(*a*) a stimulating environment produces a bright child, (*b*) a bright child causes
those in the environment to react in a more stimulating fashion, (*c*) some third
factor affects both the child and the child's environment, and (*d*) various types
of children interact differently with certain types of environments. Experimental investigation, or perhaps cross-lagged correlational analysis or path
analysis, must be conducted to determine which of the four is the most plausible
for each of the home environment variables assessed by the inventory.

For the present, for those who are of the opinion that the environmental
forces assessed with the Inventory of Home Stimulation play primarily a causal
role in development, the inventory has the potential for use in the differential
diagnosis of strengths and weaknesses present in an infant's environment, thus
assisting those concerned with prevention and remediation in their task of
designing intervention strategies.

References

BAYLEY, N. *Bayley Scales of Infant Development.* New York: Psychological Corp., 1969.
BLOOM, B. S. *Stability and change in human characteristics.* New York: Wiley, 1964.
CALDWELL, B. M. On designing supplementary environments for early child develop-
    ment. *BAEYC* [*Boston Association for the Education of Young Children*] *Reports*, 1968, **10**
    (No. 1), 1–11.

CALDWELL, B. M.; ELARDO, P.; & ELARDO, R. The longitudinal observation and intervention study: a preliminary report. Paper presented at the meeting of the Southeastern Conference on Research in Child Development, Williamsburg, Va., April 1972.

CALDWELL, B. M.; HEIDER, J.; & KAPLAN, B. The inventory of home stimulation. Paper presented at the meeting of the American Psychological Association, New York, September 1966.

CALDWELL, B. M., & RICHMOND, J. B. The children's center—a microcosmic health, education, and welfare unit. In L. Dittman (Ed.), *Early child care: the new perspectives*. New York: Atherton, 1968.

CRAVIOTO, J., & DELICARDIE, E. Environmental correlates of severe clinical malnutrition and language development in survivors from kwashiorkor or marasmus. In *Nutrition: the nervous system and behavior*. Scientific Publication No. 251. Washington, D.C.: Pan-American Health Organization, 1972.

HUNT, J. McV. *Intelligence and experience*. New York: Ronald, 1961.

McCALL, R. B.; HOGARTY, P. S.; & HURLBURT, N. Transitions in infant sensorimotor development and the prediction of childhood IQ. *American Psychologist*, 1972, 27, 728–748.

PLOWDEN, B. *Children and their primary schools*. London: Her Majesty's Stationery Office, 1967.

UZGIRIS, I. C., & HUNT, J. McV. An instrument for assessing infant psychological development. Mimeographed. Psychological Development Laboratory, University of Illinois, 1966.

WACHS, T.; UZGIRIS, I.; & HUNT, J. McV. Cognitive development in infants of different age levels and from different environmental backgrounds: an explanatory investigation. *Merrill-Palmer Quarterly*, 1971, 17, 283–317.

WALBERG, H., & MARJORIBANKS, K. Differential mental abilities and home environment: a canonical analysis. *Developmental Psychology*, 1973, 9, 363–368.

Chapter 4
Social and Personal Development

ROBERT J. IZZO

The fetus is part of a biological system made up of itself and its mother. Although emergence of the fetus from the mother's body brings about a great change for both persons, they are still bound by biological and psychological ties. They interact with each other, one person's response becoming the other person's cue for the next response. This small social system is the base from which the baby develops as a person and as a member of a family, community, and society.

Family, community, and society, the widening circles of social environment, all have interactions with the infant-mother system. Many fathers are presently claiming the right and duty of relating more meaningfully to their babies. Siblings are recognized as having special relationships with siblings. Day-care centers are scenes of peer interaction, a topic long neglected in the study of North American babies but important in collective societies. Likewise, cross-culture comparisons point to the contributions that can be made to infant well-being when other adults take on some of the responsibility for child care, instead of leaving parents to cope in isolation. The meaning of deprivation is no longer stated in terms of mother absence, or even father absence, but is seen as many-faceted.

The Cultural and Social Environment

The infant's world can be viewed on a large or small scale. A societal perspective helps to clarify the huge variety of behavior patterns seen in families.

CULTURE

Although the infant's first experiences are with his mother and other family members, the culture influences him through them, as well as through the physical environment. The language he hears determines what he will speak and to a large extent, how he will think. The technology of the culture may offer a heated crib, a cradleboard, or a sling to support him, and a hypodermic needle or a string around his waist to keep him safe. The food the baby receives will determine his preferences, along with his health and growth patterns. Health, posture, and activity patterns will be affected by his house, furniture, and grooming equipment. Cognitive and esthetic development will vary with the toys, art, and music available to him. Even the most distant aspects of culture, such as government and law, have important effects on infants. For instance, what supports does the government give to families in the way of nutrition, housing, family planning, and day care of young children? How well do the laws protect children whose parents abuse them?

Stability and Change. The ways in which a family behaves are built on values and roles prescribed by the culture. In a simple, stable society, parents tend to treat their children the way they themselves were treated as children. Such child-rearing methods reflect the ideal patterns of the culture, as expressed in folklore and art. To spank or not to spank, to wean abruptly or gradually, to toilet-train rigorously or permissively—these and similar questions are not really questions to parents who live in an unchanging culture.

An unchanging culture is rare in today's world. In North America, as in much of the world, parents no longer feel comfortable in doing "what comes naturally." Many people have had little or no experience with child-rearing until they have their own babies. Young mothers may have little confidence in their own mothers as baby-experts. Even the advice of child development professionals changes, as can be seen by comparing different editions of government pamphlets, or of Dr. Spock's books. Not only does research continue to give new information about the processes of development, but cultural values change. At present, many North Americans want their children to become independent, assertive, and self-confident, with strong feelings of self-esteem. In the seventeenth century, the Plymouth colonists' ideals were expressed thus, "And surely there is in all children . . . a stubbornness, and stoutness of mind arising from natural pride, which must, in the first place, be broken and beaten down; that so the foundation of their education being laid in humility and tractableness, other virtues may, in their time, be built thereon . . ." [16].

In societies that have changed through revolution, abrupt changes in child-rearing methods have been made, usually with the plan of creating a new kind of adult by starting in infancy. Since leaders speak with great authority in Communist countries, guides to child rearing seem to be clearer than those in the

Children in the nursery of the Shanghai Machine Tool Plant. Two babies share a play pen, and the play pens are close together.

West, leaving parents less likelihood of conflict, confusion, or choice. Makarenko's [39] work, *A Book for Parents,* has guided Soviet parents and teachers ever since the 1930s. Books for Soviet teachers [12, 13] make explicit the Soviet norms of development and the steps to be taken in order to help infants and young children achieve them. Reports on child rearing in China stress the consensus of adults and clarity of goals, values, and commitments stemming from devotion to Mao's works [33, 57, 58]. In China, as in the Soviet Union and in the *kibbutzim* of Israel, there is much emphasis on starting in infancy to learn to love and help one's peers, with the ultimate goal of putting the needs of society ahead of one's personal desires and even ahead of one's family.

Societal Support of Parenthood. When a society needs large numbers of children, it tends to reward those who produce them, by respect, recognition, and material payments. While parents of numerous children are getting gold medals and family pictures in the paper, the unmarried and childless are being punished with extra taxes and public scorn. Only recently has the situation begun to reverse. The world has too many people in it. Many governments are trying to stem the tide of babies. At the same time, it is recognized that after children are born, it is to the advantage of society to see that they are brought up to be healthy, responsible citizens. Therefore, although a lifetime career of motherhood does not receive the social support that used to be its due, there are community and government programs aimed at helping parents to do a good job with the children they have. Socialistic societies, such as New Zealand and Sweden, have long provided substantial aid in the form of medical care, dental care, and education for parenthood.

Some societies have built-in parental support to a greater extent than does

Western society. In the extended family system, common in Asia and Africa, grandmothers, sisters, sisters-in-law, and even cousins may help each other in taking care of infants. In communal societies, there is a general conviction that children are everybody's concern, or more simply, most people like children. A review of a large number of anthropological studies indicates that when mothers and young children are at home all day, with no other company, children are more likely to be rejected [51]. Anyone gets tired and irritated by long-lasting, unrelieved responsibility, and mothers are no exception. Children receive more warmth and acceptance when fathers or others participate in their care at home on a day-to-day basis and also when grandparents are there.

When social change involves a withdrawal of support and/or power from mothers, their roles become extremely difficult. An example is the Akan women of Ghana who have gone from rural matrilineal families to live in cities [44]. As a mother, the Akan woman living with her own mother had the assistance of many of her female relatives. While bringing up her baby, she was also able to work at farming and selling, or in business and thus earned money while rearing children, often many children. Thus she was independent of her husband. With the move to the city, she lost the ready help she had with child rearing and often her financial independence. Newly dependent upon her husband for money and help, shorn of her power, she became a different kind of mother. The shape of family interactions was next modified by the husband's response to the change.

FAMILY MEMBERS

The composition of the family makes a difference. How many persons live together and how many have close connections? Where does this baby come in the lifetime career of this particular family, when parents are young or older, inexperienced or skillful, beginning careers or established financially? How does this child change, or fit into, the established family structure?

The parents, in addition to being shaped by the culture, have been influenced by their own parents and all their experiences in growing up. They have their own unique temperaments, personalities, and modes of expression and interaction. Experiences during pregnancy and delivery, and early interactions have produced certain orientations to this child [68]. The development of parental competencies is influenced by all that the parents are when they start with this child, the opportunities and pressures brought to bear upon them, the characteristics of the infant himself, and the interactions resulting from all this. In reading about average behaviors of parents and infants, the results of studies, it is well to remember the uniqueness of all the individuals, even though there are similarities.

INFANT'S CHARACTERISTICS AND BEHAVIOR

The baby's appearance may be more or less pleasing. Not only is the matter of beauty or good looks involved here but of an appearance that suggests something significant to the parents: a family resemblance causing pride or the expectation that the new baby will act like Aunt Rosa or like her big sister; fragility, including delicate handling, or sturdiness, inciting rough play; a characteristic thought to predict a personality trait, such as red hair indicating temper or a weak chin indicating weak character.

The baby contributes to the social environment that surrounds her, thrusting some persons into new roles and requiring all sorts of accommodations to a new family member. Among animals, as well as humans, the young have certain behavior patterns that elicit certain responses and others that inhibit particular responses in mothers and other members of the species [29]. Examples are crying, looking, smiling, sucking, and clinging. Simply *being* a baby, or appearing as an immature member of the species, has certain effects, such as inhibiting aggression by others toward it.

State Patterns. The particular behavior patterns of an infant exert particular controls on the behavior of her family and caretakers. Even in the first few moments after birth, it makes a difference whether she is alert, looking into her mother's eyes. The *patterning of states* has an important effect on a family. For example, consider the effects of a baby who cries a great deal, one who is easily consoled, one who sleeps a lot, a fussy baby.

Temperament. The behavioral style of the infant affects the ways in which people respond to him. Certain qualities have been defined at 2 or 3 months of age and at subsequent ages throughout childhood through observations of 136 children and interviews with their parents [14]. Nine categories of reactivity emerged. Differing combinations of these categories of reactivity produce children who are different from each other. Although every child is unique, recurring types and generalizations about them can be made. The most usual type shows high rhythmicity, positive approach to new situations, adaptability to change, positive moods, and mild to moderate thresholds of responsiveness. This type is called "the easy child." Such an infant usually fits easily into his family, developing regular sleeping and feeding schedules, accepting new foods, new situations, and strangers.

"The difficult child" is his opposite number, being irregular in biological functions, negative and withdrawing from new experiences, having slow adaptability and intense reactions. About 10 per cent of the children studied were thus. Mothers find such babies difficult to care for and threatening to their feelings of competence, and families are often upset by their fussing, crying, temper tantrums, and protests. These infants need unusually firm, patient, consistent, tolerant handling. When parents are able to meet these needs, the infants usually learn the rules of social living and function energetically and well. When parents cannot give the needed sort of guidance, behavior problems are likely to develop.

Another type is the "slow-to-warm-up" child, who quietly withdraws from new situations and adapts slowly. This kind of baby needs patience, encouragement, and protection from pressure. The "very persistent" type of child becomes extremely absorbed in an activity and resists efforts to divert him. If adults interfere arbitrarily with what he is doing, he is likely to become very angry.

Boy or Girl. Although North Americans are less set in their sex preferences than Asians (who usually want sons more than daughters), most parents want a son if they plan to have only one child and to want a boy and a girl if they are going to have two [43]. Since few parents go to the trouble of trying to produce the gender they prefer, a fair number are disappointed in what they get.

Interactions with Family and Friends

LOVE AND ATTACHMENT

Love has many meanings, differing from one person to another, between cultures and languages, and from one time to another. If we had to describe it, we would say that love includes delight in being with, desire to be with, desire for contact and response from, and tendency to give to the other person. Attachment is a part of love. Because it has been carefully defined and examined by several investigators, especially Bowlby [6] and Ainsworth [2], attachment is easier than love to discuss objectively and precisely.

An *attachment* is an ongoing condition of an individual through which he seeks proximity to and contact with another person or object. Ainsworth says, "An attachment is an affectional tie that one person forms to another specific person, binding them together in space and enduring over time" [2]. Various social-emotional behavioral systems articulate with each other, keeping the individual safe while he is immature and permitting him to gradually expand his powers through interaction with a growing world of persons, places, and objects.

Human attachment behavior includes approaching, embracing, smiling, and calling. Animal babies, as well as human babies, seek the proximity of certain members of their own species, and each species has characteristic attachment behavior patterns. The bond is created as the baby exercises the behavior patterns that are basic to attachment and specific to his species. The time required for establishing the attachment differs with the species and the pertinent behaviors. Geese become attached in no more than 2 hours, perhaps a few minutes, through their inborn tendency to follow the first moving, sound-emitting object they see. Herd animals' babies are on their feet a few minutes after birth, following their mothers and forming attachments within the first 2 or 3 days. Primates take a little longer. Clinging seems to be the most important attachment behavior of monkeys, who require 10 days or 2 weeks to form their bonds. Chimpanzees take about 2 months, and human babies 5 or 6 months. Human beings, born very helpless and with a long infancy to live through, require extensive and long continued protection. They are born with the means for instigating the necessary care and for evoking it, not only from the principal caretaker (mother) but from the father, the rest of the family, and other human beings. A long infancy makes possible a long time for adapting and learning, hence the development of very complex behavior and wide individual variations. The genetic code provides for the beginnings and growth of exploratory behavior in coordination with attachment behavior. The child is protected while he learns.

Bowlby [6, pp. 326–327], a pioneer in the study of attachment, points out that in the second quarter of the first year, an infant is ready to make his first attachment to a specific person. After the first 6 months, an infant can still do so, but the older he grows, the more difficult it is to make his first attachment, and if he has not done so by the second year, the difficulties are very great. An

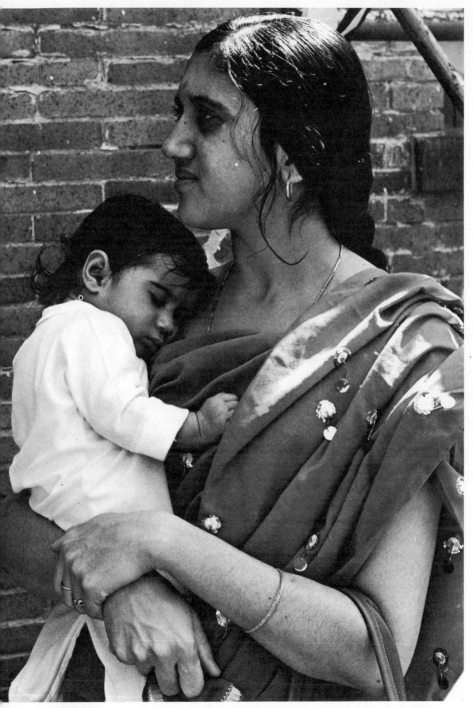

STANLEY SUMMER

established attachment is vulnerable for several years after the first birthday. These facts illustrate the principle of *critical periods in development,* which is discussed in Chapter 5.

Attachment Behavior. The newborn baby and his mother interact with behavior patterns that fit together and through which each person modifies the other one's actions. Through continuous feedback between the two, mutual regulation takes place [63]. More is known about attachment behavior of infants than about attachment behaviors of mothers. Mothers' spontaneous reactions to their infants during the first few hours have been described in Chapter 2, indicating that there is an innate maternal behavior pattern that initiates interaction. The mother puts the baby in a face-to-face position, looks into his eyes, and caresses his limbs and body. The baby may *look* into her eyes, too, since he has a built-in tendency to look at stimuli that move and stimuli that show light-dark contrast. From birth onward, infants tend to look at faces in preference to other stimuli. During the first 6 months, their most vigorous smiles and cooing are in response to faces [65].

Like many other babies, the human newborn elicits his mother's attention and care when he cries. His *crying* is a spontaneous expression of distress, and her response is an anxious feeling that she seeks to relieve by stopping his crying. Thus, crying fulfills the criterion for attachment behavior in that it brings the pair into proximity or contact. *Sucking* also brings the two together and causes pleasant sensations in both mother and baby. The human baby also does an approximation of clinging, although he cannot hang on unaided. He grasps what is put into his hands, which means that when he is held to the shoulder, he may grasp the clothing, skin, or hair of the adult. His body snuggles or bends to fit the body on which it rests. These kinds of contact evoke pleasure in the mother—in fact, in most people. Looking and grasping become integrated into nursing behavior, the infant scanning his mother's face and fingering her person while he sucks.

Following and approaching are attachment behaviors in that they bring the pair closer together or into contact. Until he can crawl or creep, the infant cannot follow bodily, but he can follow with his eyes. The distance receptors, eyes and ears, are also active in the process of making and keeping contact with the object of attachment.

Smiling occurs readily at the sight of a human face by the time the baby is 5 or 6 weeks old. The smile is a very important form of human behavior, having universal meaning of friendliness and cutting across language barriers between adults. Thus, when the infant smiles regularly at his mother and other people, it serves as attachment behavior, bringing people close to him, keeping them with him, and eliciting friendly social behavior in the form of smiles. Cooing and babbling, which often accompany smiling, tie the bonds between baby and others in much the same way that smiling does. Baby babbles. Mother babbles back, nodding and smiling, all quite spontaneously. They scan each other's faces and fixate on each other's eyes.

Familiar objects seem to be pleasurable as the baby recognizes them. He develops schemas or some sort of internal representations with which he can match perceptual experiences. Most likely his mother's face is one of his early schemas. During Piaget's stage of secondary circular reactions, which lasts from about 4 to 8 months, the baby tries to make interesting sights last or to regain perceptual contact with familiar objects. When he succeeds, he shows pleasure by smiling, and when he does not he may cry.

In perceiving stimuli that he himself has caused, an infant experiences contingent stimulation. One of the earliest and most frequent ways in which a baby gets contingent stimulation is for his family members to play with him. Mother makes a noise when Baby makes a noise. Father lifts him high when he puts his hand on Father's face. Sister puffs out her cheeks when Baby opens his mouth. These and other similar interactions have been found to elicit vigorous smiling and cooing as the infant enjoys continuing success in eliciting responses [65]. It is suggested that he feels pleasure as he realizes that he can make something happen and that people become important parts of that pleasurable situation as they play with him. Babies become attached to people who offer them interesting and contingent stimulation. The absence of social play with contingent stimulation may constitute serious deprivation to an infant. Such deprivation may contribute to the failure-to-thrive syndrome, shown by neglected infants and infants in institutions [48].

Growth of Attachment. Before he can become attached to a particular person, the infant must have repeated contact with that person. He also has to be able to tell the difference between that person and everyone else and to have some notion of person permanence [1]. During the neonatal period, mother and baby influence each other, building interaction patterns that become special and unique to both of them. By 1 month of age some infants acted differentially to their mothers, showing excitement and approach movements to them but not to strangers [68]. In the same observational study, 81 per cent of 3-month-old infants showed recognition of their mothers. By 5 months, all did. Confidence in the mother, shown by signs of expecting her to soothe and comfort, was shown by half of the babies at 3 months and by 75 per cent at 5 months.

Smiling and vocalizing become selective, the infant "talking" more to the persons with whom he is building attachments, as they give care and play games. Another sign of attachment is differential crying, when the baby cries if held by someone else and stops crying when his mother takes him. His *looking* shows attachment, when he watches his mother while someone else is holding him. Crying at the mother's departure is further evidence of attachment. Among infants observed throughout the first year of life, 22 weeks was the median age, with a range from 15 to 30 weeks, at which babies cried when left by the mother [60]. Crying when put down by the mother was more frequent than crying when the mother left. These babies cried more frequently when left by the mother than when left by siblings. However, in a study of year-old boys and girls, their mothers, and their fathers, babies cried about as much at their fathers' departures as at their mothers' [67].

Attachment behavior includes making contact over a distance, as well as trying to make and maintain close physical contact. As the infant widens the environment over which he operates, he not only travels through space but also looks and listens to people across space and communicates with them by gesture and vocalizing.

Attachment Figures. Most research on attachment has focused on *mothers* and their infants, but, of course, fathers too are important to babies and vice versa. Ainsworth and others have done many studies on the relationships of various maternal behaviors to the ways in which infants organize their attachment behaviors [2]. The baby's behavior patterns are shaped by the mother's degree of sensitivity and responsiveness to his signals. Babies were likely to show clear-cut, unambivalent attachment to mothers who were very perceptive, responsive, and eager to gratify them socially and in feeding [5]. These infants also showed cognitive behavior associated with maternal perceptive, responsive behavior. They were early in developing a schema of person permanence, followed soon by the appearance of a schema of object permanence. Another related study indicated that infants of such mothers are unusually cooperative and willing to obey their mothers [61]. Mothers of the opposite sort, who were insensitive, inaccessible, and unresponsive, were likely to have babies who showed anxious attachment and ambivalence, defensiveness, and avoidance behavior [1].

Attachment to *fathers* as well as to mothers was studied by placing 1-year-old boys and girls in the "strange situation" (devised by Ainsworth [3]) in which a standard series of episodes is used [67]. The parent and child enter a room with the observer, the observer leaves, the parent puts the baby down, a stranger enters and approaches the baby, the parent leaves, the parent returns, the stranger leaves, the parent leaves the baby alone, the stranger returns, the parent returns, and the stranger leaves. The baby's behavior is observed and analyzed for attachment behaviors, including contact- and proximity-seeking, avoidance, crying, searching, and exploratory behaviors, both visual and locomotive. (While the baby is involved with finding or contacting a parent, of course, she is not exploring toys and the environment, but when the parent is there and available, play and exploration proceed.) The infants in this experiment directed the same sort of behaviors toward both parents. Lack of major mother-father differences was demonstrated in another study using the strange situation [34] and also at home [52]. Most children derived comfort from either parent and made similar responses to the departure and arrival of either. Over 70 per cent of the 144 subjects showed attachment to both parents, 23 per cent to the mother only, and 9 per cent to the father only, whereas 7 per cent did not relate to either parent.

When parent-infant interactions were studied in the home instead of in the laboratory, differences were seen, not in preferences nor in protests, but in modes of behavior [35]. Infants of 7 and 8 months responded more positively to play initiated by fathers. In contrast to mothers, fathers initiated more idiosyncratic play. Games with father were more physical. Apparently, it was more fun to play with father!

A comparison of father-absent and father-present black 5- to 6-months infants demonstrated differences in the boys but not in the girls [46]. The boys with fathers in the home were higher in the Bayley Mental Developmental Index, social responsiveness, and exploratory behavior with a novel stimulus. These results

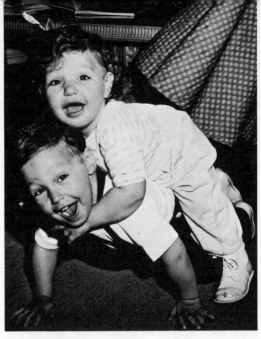

STANLEY SUMMER

should not be taken to mean that fathers make no difference to girl babies, but only that differences were not revealed by the methods used in this research.

Infants usually enjoy watching their *siblings* and playing with them. As part of a study that showed more exploration by babies with siblings than by only children, mothers were interviewed. They confirmed the common impression that older siblings played often with babies. A Scottish study revealed no infants attached solely to siblings, but 12 per cent had siblings among their attachment persons [53]. Family anecdotes often tell of a baby who was much attached to the older sibling who took special care of him. In cultures where children normally care for infants, as in much of Africa and Asia, we would expect to see strong bonds between younger and older siblings. Other family members, especially *grandparents,* become figures of attachment as infants have chances to interact with them and to receive interesting stimulation and sensitive response from them. Attachment to grandparents was seen in 29 per cent of the subjects in the Scottish study.

Babies do not build bonds of attachment solely on the basis of family relationships, but give their affection to those who win it. Twelve per cent of the 6-month-olds were judged attached to a friend or neighbor [53]. Relationships with caregivers in a day nursery were studied from the time the infants were 4 months old until they were 12 months. Using a procedure similar to the strange situation, the babies' affective reactions to mothers and caregivers were compared [50]. *Positive affect* was indicated by smiling, happy vocalizing, and approaching; *negative affect* by facial and vocal expressions of distress and withdrawal or avoidance responses. A sober-attentive facial expression was considered neutral. During the time from 4 to 7 months, the babies showed positive affect to a stranger as well as to a caretaker, but then while responses to the caretaker continued to be positive, the stranger elicited neutral and then slightly negative affect. When the mother departed, leaving the baby with a stranger or caregiver, responses were neutral until almost seven months, when they showed increasing distress with the stranger and none or minimal distress with the caregiver. When the caregiver left the baby with a stranger, negative response was at about the same level as when the mother left the baby with a stranger.

Exploration and Attachment. All young mammals crawl away from their mothers and explore their enviroments as soon as they are able to do so. They return periodically to their mothers and then venture forth again. Mothers retrieve infants who wander too far. Experimenting with rhesus monkeys, Harlow [27] compared exploratory behavior with and without mothers. Alone in a strange place, with strange objects, the baby cowered, crouched, rocked, and sucked his own body. With his mother, real or surrogate, the baby clung to her (or it), then left her to explore the objects in the room, clung again, and explored again. It looked as though he neutralized his fear by contacting her and derived continuing reassurance by seeing her there. Thus are attachment behavior and exploratory behavior articulated in such a way that the baby is kept safe; yet he seeks new experience through which he learns and builds his own competence.

Human babies are more helpless than other primates. They also have more to learn. They spend a long time, 6 to 7 months, in a sedentary condition, in which they cannot move away from their caregivers. As soon as they can creep, they explore. It is at this time that they begin to protest the departure of persons to whom they are attached and to seek contact and proximity vigorously. Using their experimental device, the "strange situation," Ainsworth and Bell studied year-old babies [3]. The largest amount of exploratory behavior, as seen in locomotion, manipulation, and looking, occurred in the beginning of the observation, when the baby was alone with his mother. When the stranger entered, exploration decreased and remained on a low level until the mother returned from her absence. Exploration then gained a bit, but when the mother left, it dropped again and remained depressed. Proximity- and contact-seeking behaviors increased throughout the experiment. When left alone 37 per cent of the babies cried little and searched strongly, 20 per cent cried desperately but searched weakly or not at all, and 32 per cent both cried and searched. As might be expected, crying and exploration were negatively correlated (-0.67 for crying and manipulation). Figure 4-1 shows the amounts of crying and exploratory manipulation throughout the experiment. Other experiments have shown that although infants showed marked distress and almost no locomotion when placed alone in a room, reactions were entirely different when they were permitted to enter an unfamiliar empty room on their own initiative [49]. The latter infants were placed on the floor in front of their mothers in a small room adjoining the large room. Whether the large room contained a toy or not, all the infants left their mothers and went into the other room, with no sign of distress. All returned to their mothers and most re-entered the large room, some several times. Their behavior illustrates using the mother as a secure base for exploration. These experiments offer strong evidence that attachment behavior and exploratory behavior are in dynamic balance in young children and that both kinds of behavior are related to the mother's presence.

Although attachments are usually made to members of the same species, they may involve other species or objects. Babies become attached to blankets.

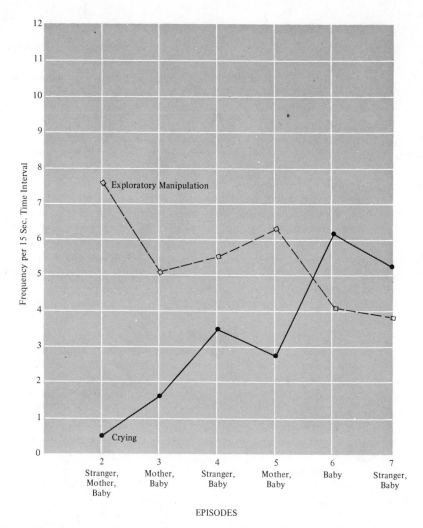

Figure 4-1. Amounts of crying and exploratory behavior of one-year-olds under conditions of mother present and mother absent.

SOURCE: Adapted from M. D. S. Ainsworth and S. M. Bell. Attachment, exploration, and separation: illustrated by the behavior of one-year-olds in a strange situation. *Child Development,* 1970, **41,** 49–67.

Children and pets become attached to each other. Among 2-year-olds who were attached to blankets, exploration and play were facilitated and distress was prevented by the presence of the blanket during the mother's absence. Children not attached to blankets showed more distress and less play and exploration when mothers were absent [45]. These results, which showed that children's comfort and exploration were supported by an attachment object, were in agreement with similar studies on monkeys.

FEAR, WARINESS, AND ANXIETY

When an infant cries, adults almost always interpret the behavior as an indication of distress. *Fear* is probably the universal interpretation when a baby frowns, cries, tries to withdraw, or seeks and clings to a familiar person. The physiological basis for fear reactions is inherited, but its expression is an interaction with the environment. Most specific fears are learned through experience. There are probably inherited physiological reactions that facilitate withdrawal from dangers the young are likely to encounter: strangers, heights, the dark, and excessive stimulation. When left alone or without an attachment figure, babies show a type of fear that Bowlby [7] calls *anxiety*. In a condition of anxiety, a child has a stronger reaction to a fear-producing stimulus. Attachment and fear and affiliation (friendship) are articulated in ways that promote survival of the infant and that permit exploration and growth. When a strange person, object, or situation causes distress and withdrawal, contact through clinging, touching, or even looking at a loved person restores the baby's equilibrium in such a way that he can approach and explore. Loss of support, pain, loud noises, and other intense stimuli also cause distress reactions that look like fear and that can usually be alleviated by holding the baby close. Individual differences in temperament make for more intense reactions in some infants and less in others. Some can be comforted more easily than others.

Separation Anxiety. When separated from his attachment figure and unable to reach her, the infant feels anxious. According to Bowlby [7] the young child's interpretation, or working model, of the world features his attachment figures, how to find them, and how they can be expected to respond to him. The same notion is expressed by Erikson [20, pp. 247–251] in "the sense of trust." The baby has a feeling of comfort and goodness when he feels sure of his mother. This he does when she "combines sensitive care of the baby's individual needs and a firm sense of personal trustworthiness."

When a baby is left by his mother for a long time, as often happens during hospitalization, three phases of behavior usually follow; protest, despair, and detachment [7]. When a child between about 8 months and 3 years is first left by his mother, he is likely to cry and protest, showing acute distress and trying to find and regain the mother. The initial phase gives way to despair, when the child is very quiet. Then comes a more active phase when he pays more attention to the environment and interacts with people and things. When children go home after short hospital separations, they often show angry, contact-resisting behavior along with proximity seeking. Clinging and whining are also very common after hospital separations. It is easy to see how all of these reactions to reunion would be annoying and disturbing to mothers and how they might rebuff or punish the irritating child. A rebuff, however, tends only to intensify the child's attachment behavior. Observations of animal behavior show similar relationships in infant rhesus monkeys, who cling all the harder to "heartless mothers" who ignore, reject, or hurt them. When a child persists in clinging, whining, and/or angry aggressive behavior following a separation, recovery is more likely if his mother gives him extra opportunities for the proximity and contacts he is seeking.

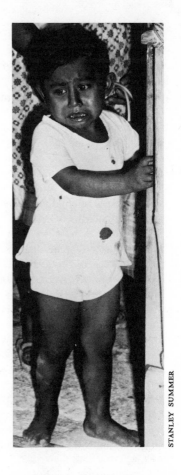

Fear shows in the face and posture of this young child.

From studies of maternal behavior and infant's reactions to brief separations, it was apparent that separation anxiety was related to the baby's confidence in his mother's accessibility and responsiveness [59]. Rather than "spoiling" the baby with attention and making him overdemanding, prompt response to his signals, including his crying, was likely to produce a baby who could accept brief separations easily. Such a baby does not cry when his mother leaves the room, but greets her happily when she comes back. The anxious baby, who does not trust his mother to return or to be accessible, clings, cries when she leaves, and acts negatively when she returns. He may avoid her gaze, refuse to be picked up, or cry to be picked up and then try immediately to get down, and protest when put down. The majority of infants studied in their homes were not anxious in their separation behavior [60]. When the mother left the room, the babies followed twice as often as they cried.

Comparative Studies. Different species of monkeys show different reactions to separation and reunion, suggesting that heredity, as well as social organization, affects the ways in which infant primates organize these behaviors [55]. When a pigtailed monkey infant is left by his mother in a group of monkeys, he is more disturbed than when he is left alone. The pigtailed infant hunched up in a ball for a week, and after reunion with his mother, showed intensified reactions for three months. The bonnet macaque infant showed initial disturbance but quickly attached himself to a substitute mother and apparently had no further ill effects.

Reactions to Strangers. Stranger-avoidance or fear of strangers is commonly seen in the second half of the first year of life. Not only are there individual differences in showing such fear but there are also differences dependent on the age and sex of the baby, the distance of the stranger, what the stranger does, and where the mother or other attachment figure is. A stranger at a distance caused no negative reactions in children under 10 months of age and only a few in babies of 10½ and 12½ months, whereas a close stranger caused some negative behavior in infants from 6½ to 12½ months. Infants at all age levels studied, including 4½ months, showed some disturbance at being held by a stranger [42].

In order to observe the onset and development of fear of strangers, infants were videotaped over a period of 6 months, starting at 3 months of age. The stranger bent over to one-half meter away from the baby, spoke the baby's name, and asked for a smile [9]. The term *wary,* which, in this study, includes fear, was used to describe the infant who cried, frowned, or crawled away. Wariness to a stranger was occasionally shown by 15 of the 32 babies in the fourth month of life. By 6½ months of age, 78 per cent of the subjects had indicated wariness. The number of episodes of wariness also increased, from 20 per cent at 3 to 4 months to 32 per cent at 6 months and 47 per cent at 9 months. The youngest wary babies (9 per cent at 3 months, 4 per cent at 4 months) showed a pattern that suggested tenuousness of the first stages of ability to discriminate a strange face. They first smiled, as young infants typically do to a face. Then they became sober, staring intently for 15 to 30 seconds. Next came frowns, heavy breathing, and crying.

A detailed description and analysis of 106 year-old middle-class infants' responses to strangers was done by Bretherton and Ainsworth [8], using the "strange situation." When the stranger first entered the room where the baby and mother were, all infants looked at her, 58 per cent prolongedly. Then 30 per cent averted their gaze. While looking, the majority had a facial expression intermediate between a smile and cryface, but 18 per cent smiled promptly and 56 per cent smiled during this episode and less than 4 per cent cried. The babies looked more often and for longer times at the stranger than at the mother, although they showed awareness of the mother as she started to leave the room. Most of the babies accepted the stranger's approach and offer of toys. The experiment demonstrated the interplay between two behavioral systems, fear-wariness and affiliation. The first was used when infants cried, withdrew from the stranger, reached for the mother, refused the toy, stared soberly, and averted the eyes from the stranger. Affiliation was shown by smiling, vocalizing, approaching, accepting and offering toys, and touching and playing with the stranger. A combination of fear-wariness and affiliation was seen in the *coy response,* shown by 13 infants, who smiled and averted the gaze, and by 10 who approached the stranger and then immediately retreated. On the whole, the babies showed much more affiliation than fear-wariness.

The *stability* of infants' reactions to strangers was investigated by visiting and testing 51 infants three times within 12 days [56]. Half of the subjects responded consistently in the same way (positive or negative). Twice as many boys as girls were stable (gave the same response over time). As noted in another study [4], boys' reactions were more positive than girls'. As has also been found in other research on infants' reactions to strangers, both boys and girls were more negative toward a male stranger than toward a female stranger. As an explanation of boys being more consistently positive than girls, it is suggested that since mothers tend to touch and handle boy babies less than girls, the boys may be expressing more need for, and pleasure in, physical contact.

Reactions to Strange Objects. Infants show occasional wariness and fear to objects, especially objects that loom. An ethological, or evolutionary-adaptation, point of view holds that during the time when primate species were emerging, the infants who survived were those who avoided looming objects, being alone, especially alone in the dark, and strangers [7]. Fear-wariness was the behavioral system by which the primates, including man, avoided the dangers that threatened them most. The behavioral system survives in modern infants and, to a certain extent, in older children and adults.

When new, stationary objects were shown to infants from 6 to 12 months of age, all showed wariness in looking, but only at 8 months and later did they show hesitancy in touching the object [54]. When first shown an unfamiliar object, the infants looked for a longer time than when seeing it again, the looking time decreasing with each presentation of the object. The younger the infants, the longer they looked on the first trial. Wariness in regard to objects seemed to be a period of immobility in which the baby appraised the situation. By 8 months, the period of wariness and appraisal came before the decision as to whether to approach the situation or to withdraw.

Application of Research Findings. Fears can often be prevented or minimized when the following suggestions are carried out:

1. Avoid separations of the baby from his attachment objects except for brief periods. Since mothers are sometimes necessarily absent, it is wise to encourage the building of other attachments, which the infant is likely to do with anyone who responds to him and who offers him interesting stimulation.
2. Avoid separations and frightening experiences especially at the time when fear of strangers is developing and at its peak. Hospitalization and painful treatments are best postponed if possible. If such experiences are essential, keep the child with a loved person. If the parent is powerless to provide this safeguard to emotional well-being, then provide an object to which the child is attached, such as his blanket, or an object belonging to a person to whom he is attached, such as his mother's purse.
3. Introduce the infant gradually to new situations so as to prevent fears arising from sudden stimulus changes.

4. Provide new situations and gradual changes along with reassurance so as to help the child tolerate novelty and cope with newness.
5. If the baby is afraid of the dark, give him a night light.
6. Use reconditioning, when appropriate. A fear of a specific object or situation may be overcome by experiencing it along with something pleasant and comfortable.

ANGER

Anger is the distress that accompanies being restrained or blocked in progress toward some sort of fulfillment. Anger involves lashing out rather than withdrawing as in fear. The crying and bodily activity of infants under conditions of bodily tension, such as hunger, look like anger. They seem to be reacting similarly to children and adults who are known to be angry. During the first year, babies learn to use anger for solving some of their problems, to a greater or lesser degree, depending on how successful it is.

During the second year, when the desire to establish autonomy is strong, interference with choice making is likely to bring angry resistance, crying, screaming, kicking, perhaps hitting, throwing, and biting. For establishment of a sound sense of autonomy, a baby grows by having many experiences in successful choice making and few in choosing activities where he cannot succeed.

Goodenough's comprehensive and classic study, *Anger in Young Children,*

Figure 4-2. Number of anger outbursts in ten hours by age and sex.

Source: Adapted from F. L. Goodenough. *Anger in young children.* Minneapolis: University of Minnesota Press, 1931.

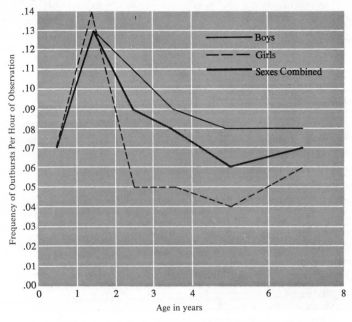

describes and analyzes 1,878 anger outbursts of children in the first 8 years of life [25]. Since the observations were recorded by parents, the cases were necessarily selected from families where parents were unusually cooperative and intelligent. As can be seen in Figure 4-2 there was a marked peak in anger outbursts during the second year and then a rapid decline. Little sex difference appeared in infancy, but during the preschool period, boys had significantly more outbursts than girls. At all ages, however, differences between individuals were greater than differences between the sexes.

Anger behavior changed with age. Most of the outbursts during the first 3 years involved display or undirected energy. Such behavior included crying, screaming, stiffening the body, throwing self on floor, stamping, jumping up and down. With age, such primitive bodily responses tended to be replaced with more directed, less violent, more symbolic expressions. The duration of outbursts changed very little, however.

Physical factors were influential. Anger occurred before mealtimes more than at any other times of day. Children were angry more when ill, even with slight colds or constipation. Outbursts were more frequent among those who had recovered from one or more fairly serious illnesses than among children who had not been ill.

Many psychological factors were shown to be significant. Children who were being toilet trained showed more anger on days following bed-wetting than on days following dry nights. The more adults in the home, the more likely was a child to become angry. When parents shifted from one method of control to another, the child tended to have more outbursts. "Giving the child his own way" was reported more often for children who had many outbursts than for those who had few.

Roots of Violence. All people experience anger, but some express it violently. The roots of violent behavior are in infancy, according to Lourie, a child psychiatrist [37]. When a highly active infant does not receive outside control, but instead is overstimulated, he is likely to break things and hurt people. He feels helpless to control his actions. Especially if other forms of satisfaction are not available, he may come to enjoy being destructive. At the other extreme, if outside controls are very strict, preventing even exploration, inner controls may be stifled. Either situation can lead to violent expression of anger. When the baby is treated violently and cruelly (abused), he is likely to make these forms of behavior part of his own. When given suitable choices within firm limits, and treated with love and respect, even the highly active, aggressive infant can gradually develop his own controls.

SOCIAL DEVELOPMENT AND SOCIALIZATION

As the infant grows older, his social contacts broaden and he interacts with more people. Although many North American babies spend their days at home, with only brief excursions to the store or visiting with parents, more infants are going out of their homes to be cared for during the day with other infants. Day care is common in many other countries. Only 10 per cent of Chinese mothers care for their infants by themselves [57]. At present in North America, day care centers are providing new opportunities for learning about the form and meaning of infants' social interactions outside the family.

Peer Interaction. In a new Canadian day care centre, one of the teachers commented, "The babies are so interested in each other. They watch each other a lot. I am surprised that there is so little conflict between them. They even help each other." Indeed, student observation notebooks contained repeated records of toddlers handing toys to younger babies and trying to comfort them when they cried. The beginnings of sympathy and altruistic behavior can thus be seen in infancy [30]. Even the newborn infant gives indications of rudimentary sympathy by crying more to the sound of a newborn cry than to comparable mechanical sounds [52a].

These observations would not have surprised a *metapelet* (caregiver) in an Israeli *kibbutz,* a teacher in a *yasli sad* in the Soviet Union, or a caregiver in a nursery in China. In all of these collective societies, friendship and cooperation between babies is consciously fostered. Chinese babies are expected to be loving and helpful to one another and to cooperate with adults. They are taught, through example, songs, stories, slides, and direct instruction [33; 57]. For example, if a toddler falls down, the teacher does not pick him up but encourages another child to help him [57, p. 122]. In three films on kibbutz infancy, the Stones show scenes of infants and toddlers playing happily together. When they conflict over a toy or a cookie, a skillful *metapelet* decides which child should have the desired object and then directs the other child's attention in a positive way [62].

Play behavior in American infants from 10 to 24 months was observed by placing together two infant-mother pairs, with infants of like ages [18]. The infants

In a Canadian daycare center, babies of various ages show interest in one another.

MARGARET HAMILTON

were free to contact their mothers, play with toys, and play with each other. The subjects paid little attention to their mothers, much to toys, and interacted an intermediate number of times with the other babies. At all ages, the infants behaved with each other much as infants behave with familiar adults. They smiled, vocalized, gestured, showed and offered toys, imitated each other, and played reciprocally. The ways of playing with toys (physical contact and manipulation) were used only rarely with peers. Play with peers increased with age, the oldest group (22 to 24 months) playing more with their peers than with their mothers. Speculating about why peers become more attractive as playmates than parents, the authors suggest that peers may be more ready to accept playful overtures, their actions may be more novel, and their behavior may be more easily duplicated.

Peer play may have therapeutic value for infants who receive inadequate care and affection from adults. In many areas people find alternative ways of satisfying needs when ordinary paths are blocked. It may be that enrichment in the affiliative system can compensate for deprivation in the attachment behavioral system. As the *kibbutzim* have demonstrated, young children can become strongly attached to one another and cooperative in meeting each other's needs. The necessity for normalcy and compensatory value of peer play have been demonstrated with rhesus monkeys who, having been reared in total isolation for six months, were then placed with younger normal peers [28]. After six months with their peer "therapists," the previous isolates showed almost normal exploration, play, and locomotion. Results of an animal study cannot be taken as valid for humans, or indeed, even for closely related animal species. For example, infant patas monkeys do not initiate peer play as frequently as do rhesus macaques. When patas play together, they do mostly

Although toddler playmates may want the same toy at the same time, they are easily distracted by an offer of something else to do.

STANLEY SUMMER

chasing and little of the contacting and play-fighting typical of macaques [55]. Macaque mothers tolerate little personal aggression from their babies, but permit other babies to come into their cages, whereas patas mothers are permissive with their own infants but intolerant of peer visitors. The effects of various social deprivations and compensations could be expected to differ between the two species.

Behavior with Adults. Babies are not always fearful and wary of strangers, especially when familiar caregivers are present. New people, like new objects and places, provoke curiosity and exploration. Children between 1 and 2½ years of age, at home with their mothers, were observed with male and female strangers [15]. Babies were more positive and playful with more familiar types of people and with responsive, receptive strangers than with passive, ignoring ones, but even with the latter, they made some attempts to initiate interaction.

Social-Cognitive Development. Does an infant realize that other people have experiences and that he shares experiences with them? By the ways in which they show things and point to them, babies give some indication of awareness of the looking behavior of others [36]. When asked to show a toy, most year-olds would hold it up. Over half of them understood pointing by the experimenter. At a year and a half, most babies held up a picture or toy horizontally, letting the experimenter see it while they viewed it also. By 2 years, most children would turn the picture in such a way that only the experimenter could see it. They also moved the experimenter to face an immovable object that they had been asked to show her. Thus, by 2 years, the baby has built up a good understanding of the role of the eyes and of the fact that other people can see what he sees. It is likely that this kind of learning is promoted by parents who show, point, label, play hiding games, read books, and talk about these experiences.

Regulation of Behavior

Before the end of the first year, the infant who has lived in a harmonious relationship is inclined to cooperate with the important people in his life, those to whom he is attached. The origins of socialization can be seen in the baby's obedience to simple commands and prohibitions given by his parents. Studies on infant obedience show how wrong was the old notion of babies as purely selfish creatures who had to be coerced into social acceptability. The attachment bond seems to predispose the infant to comply with requests signaled by loved people [6]. Thus does cooperation grow out of trust.

In their efforts to regulate what a baby does and when, where, and how he does it, parents are influenced by what they believe to be good for the baby and good for the rest of the family and by their own needs. "Good for the baby" involves what is good for him now and what will help him to grow into the right kind of child, adolescent, and adult. "Good for the rest of the family" means considering all the other people in the home and even some beyond the home, perhaps grandparents. Parents' "own needs" include those that they recognize as existing and also needs of which they are unaware or only dimly aware. The behavior influenced by parental guidance includes thinking and feeling as well as overt action.

Family life has many rhythms. The fitting of small rhythms to one another and into larger wholes is a dynamic process. The ways in which infant and family adapt to one another have important outcomes for both.

TIMING

The term *mutual regulation* is perhaps more apt than *scheduling* to describe what ideally happens in a home with a young baby. Since the newborn baby cannot wait for food and comfort, the family has to adjust pretty much to *his* rhythms if he is to be kept comfortable and helped to feel that the world is worth trusting. After 2 or 3 months, however, a baby can wait briefly for food and attention. With the development of physiological stability, some confidence, and some interest in sensorimotor exploration, he can begin to fit into some of the rhythms of the family. Perhaps he'll sit happily on Daddy's lap for five minutes while Mother finishes her dessert, even though he is hungry. In another month or two, the baby can eat larger meals and can last for longer times between meals. Although he may have some preference as to mealtimes, a mother can fit them into convenient times by gradual change and planning the staying qualities of meals and snacks.

In the matter of sleeping, too, a baby accommodates himself more and more to family rhythms as he matures and as he is guided to do so. In the beginning, sleep follows eating, and waking brings a demand for food. Gradually he stays awake for longer periods and sleeps for a longer time at night, when the rest of the family sleeps. In societies where babies are always with other people, going to bed when the family goes to bed, and sleeping when sleepy during the day, there is no problem of scheduling sleep. North American life, especially in the middle class, is tightly scheduled. Infants have to have naps and go to bed early in order to get enough sleep and also for their mothers to get their housework and other jobs done. Parents tend to feel that they need some free, quiet hours without children present, in the evening. Thus, getting the baby to go to sleep at certain times often comes to be a problem. It is usually solved by exerting pressure on the baby's own changing rhythms, waking him from previous sleep in time to have him need sleep appropriately, timing meals, arranging baths, play, and outings to induce just enough fatigue.

Babies often come to resist being put to bed, sometimes because they are put to bed when they really are not tired and sleepy. An infant may feel mistrust and lack of confidence in the family who is overeager to get him out of the way. Fears and excitement can prevent and disturb sleep. Sometimes the most careful attention to schedules and emotional security is not enough, and a tired baby cries when put to bed. In such a case, crying is usually brief.

Scheduling includes planning baths, toileting, and dressing at times that fit both the family and baby. Times for play of different kinds and in different places, walks and rides, visiting and receiving guests—all are part of planning for the baby's well-being and for family living. Thus, the family, especially the mother, structures the infant's life in time and space, in terms of maintaining his life, stimulating his development, and building relationships with him.

Physical well-being hinges on a schedule that fits the baby. Health and optimal growth require adequate nutrition, rest, and exercise. It takes careful planning and management to see that the baby gets all of these while family living goes on to everyone's benefit. What the baby seems to want at the moment is not always what is best in the overall picture, at least as viewed by the adult. A toddler may want to get into the thick of a game with his kindergartner sister and her friends, not realizing that the results for him would be great excitement, frustration, and fatigue. Or he may be hungry and yet refuse to come in for lunch just because it feels so good to be climbing outdoors.

Cognitive development results from good scheduling, too. For the baby too young to sit up by himself, a frequent change of position and scenery is necessary for giving him mental food (visual and tactual stimulation). When he enlarges his own sphere of operations, first by sitting, then by creeping and walking, his family can still enlarge the scene for him by moving him to different rooms and different furniture and taking him places. Scheduling does not mean that the mother has to pick the baby up at 9 and 11 but rather that she carry on a plan of household activity that includes a change of scene and action for the baby at fairly regular intervals. Her management of his toys has a bearing on mental growth, too. He benefits from some system of rotating toys, so that he gets only a few at a time and frequent changes. Thus, a schedule can assure a steady flow of stimulation.

Emotional health is fostered by a suitable schedule. When the infant's physical needs are met before they become overwhelming, he is spared anxiety and frustration. He enjoys the good feeling of trust. Regular holding and cuddling further build up his sense of trust, allaying fears and anxiety and stimulating his senses. Because he trusts, he learns to wait and hope and thus to cooperate as a family member.

CONTROL AND AUTONOMY

Parents everywhere set limits on their infants' behavior. If they did not, there would be no more babies, since babies creep and toddle right into danger, whether it be off the platform of a house built on poles over the sea or under a station wagon parked in the driveway. There are always dangers to be kept from exploring fingers and mouths, too—a dung fire in the corner, incense burning before a household god, an electric socket. Little fingers and mouths have to be prevented from destroying precious objects, such as a threaded loom, a clay water pot, or a piece of Steuben glass.

Cultures vary widely in whether babies are expected to learn self-control from the limits placed on their behavior. In some societies, keeping the baby safe is just that and no more. Somebody is expected to look out for him during his early years to see that he does himself no harm. But in many societies, including the American culture, keeping safe is, of course, a prime motive, but a variety of other aims makes for a wide range of practices.

Parents vary according to how strict or permissive they are with children, or how much autonomy they permit, versus how much they try to control the child. Some parents permit wide autonomy, others a little less; some are very controlling, others somewhat controlling. Parents vary on this dimension within the same culture, and cultures also vary in autonomy-control in adult–child relationships. The teaching manual *Soviet Preschool Education* [12, pp. 24–25] spells out, for example, that the child at 18 months should be taught not to take toys away from others, not to interfere with them, to sit at a table calmly, to obey adults, to feed himself neatly, to wash his hands, to pull up his socks and overalls . . . and more. Probably most North Americans would think that this picture presents a great deal of control and not much permissiveness for autonomy.

Ideals in North America are more diverse than they are in the Soviet Union or China. Individual freedom and self-expression, however, are high on the lists of many people. The development of a strong sense of autonomy, according to Erikson, requires freedom for a toddler to make choices and planning by adults that will ensure a large proportion of successful choices. Thus, the toddler comes to feel, "I can decide" and "What I choose is all right."

Adaptations in the home that make possible the permission of wide limits include the provision of spaces where little damage can result from play and exploration. Fussy, breakable objects can be put away. Furniture can be upholstered or slipcovered in tough, washable fabrics. Floor coverings and draperies can be of relatively indestructible materials. A baby is able to creep in this kind of room without hurting himself or anything else. A toddler climbs, explores, runs cars, and pushes a doll carriage. The bathroom can be arranged so that a toddler can climb steps in front of the washbasin and there enjoy freedom with water play. Some of the cupboards in the kitchen may offer young children freedom to pull out pots and pans and perhaps put them back again.

All societies impose some toilet regulation on children. Toileting is a simple matter for the bare-bottomed babies and toddlers in India and other poor countries with warm climates. Umersingh (whose baths we described in Chapter 2) wore only a shirt until he was about four years old. During his first few months, Leela kept a piece of cloth under him in his little bed. When he was in her arms, she held him aside as he started to urinate or defecate. They spent most of their time outdoors and if Umersingh happened to eliminate in the house, it was only on a mud floor, anyway. When children can walk, they squat down to eliminate, perhaps with assistance at first, but also in imitation of their elders, who are often seen squatting by the roadside or in the field. Thus, neither clothing nor modesty poses any problem for an Indian toddler in a peasant family. The girls must later learn modesty, but the boys remain free to go as and when they feel moved to do so.

In the United States and in many other societies, as well, toilet training can cause problems for mothers and babies. The Soviet manual says, in regard to toileting, "It is extremely important to train a child from the very first year of life to be neat." If a mother feels that way, she will probably begin early to anticipate bowel movements and to put the baby on a toilet seat at the right moment. Some infants tolerate such regulation more easily than others. If the baby does not resist toileting and the mother is eager for it, she may have a healthier relationship with the baby by training him early than by forcing herself to wait. However, when parents are comfortable about allowing the baby a high degree of autonomy, the second half of the second year is the time for easiest learning to use the toilet. By that age most children can perceive signals of imminent elimination, can hang on long enough to get to the toilet, and can release the sphincter muscles at will. The toddler will probably go to the toilet by himself if his clothing is very easy to manage or if he can be left without pants at appropriate times, and if he has a child's toilet chair nearby. One little girl who had recently learned with such arrangements taught a visiting toddler to go to her toilet chair, after the toddler's mother had met only resistance to her efforts in toilet training.

TEACHING ABOUT SEX AND GENDER

Babies learn the names of eyes, nose, mouth, fingers, toes, and many more parts of the body as parents tell them, often playing games such as "This little piggy went to market." A child's concept of self is built as he learns about his physical self in this way. In a happy, affectionate context, he feels good about himself and his body.

When a baby fingers his genitals, as every infant does, there is probably one chance in ten that the mother who lovingly names his toes will exclaim happily, "There's your penis." More likely, she will say nothing to him, possibly removing his hands from his penis and distracting him with a toy or something to look at or listen to. Infants are sensitive to sexual stimulation, showing signs of relaxation and pleasure when their genital areas are touched. Newborn boys have erections of the penis. Both boys and girls learn to stimulate their genitals during infancy, through the process of exploring their bodies.

Although some societies permit expression of infant sexuality, North Americans and many Europeans take a stern attitude toward it. However, parent educators have long believed that it was wise to use the names of organs and functions and to permit babies to explore their bodies. Reasons for this point of view include promoting cognition (increased knowledge of the world, a clear body image), building a positive self-concept, and laying a foundation for good sexual adjustment as an adult.

Gender Role. In all societies, certain behaviors are expected of women and girls, whereas others are expected of men and boys. Some groups also expect behavior differences between male and female infants. In North America, probably everywhere, parents treat boy babies differently from girl babies, and babies treat their fathers differently from their mothers. The universality of sex-based behavior differences is supported by animal studies that show male and female infant monkeys to be different in their interactions with mother and father monkeys. The interweaving of biological, cultural, and cognitive influences on gender-linked behavior make it impossible to say that a given trait is either genetic or learned. Sometimes, however, one sex has a biological base for acquiring a certain behavior more easily. Perhaps these behaviors are more frequently assigned to the sex that can acquire them best. For example, it is well established that the average girl has greater verbal ability than the average boy, that boys are, on the average, more aggressive than girls, and that boys excel in visual–spatial and mathematical performances [38, pp. 351–352]. This sort of knowledge doubtless influences the expectations parents have of their infants and the opportunities they offer them. At any rate, parents and other adults set about teaching masculinity and/or femininity to newborn babies.

By 2 or 3 years, even perhaps by 18 months, a child has some notion of gender, "I am a girl" or "I am a boy." If this conviction is delayed, perhaps from parents' interpreting gender too far out of their own cultural context, the child is likely to have difficulties in his or her gender identity [41, p. 13]. Some parental teaching methods are direct and purposeful, such as smiling and saying, "That's a good girl" or heartily, with a touch of pride, "Ah, he's all boy!" Or the parent dresses the infant so that nobody will make a mistake, pink for girls, blue for boys, and even if both wear overalls, hers has ruffles. She is given a doll, he a truck. Other parental actions may not be so conscious, but nonetheless powerful, since they are expressions of the sex-role stereotypes held by the parents. One of the ways in which mothers are likely to treat boys and girls differently is in proximal and distal activity. That is, they interact more with girls at close range and with boys at a distance. In a series of studies on attachment behavior, Brooks and Lewis [10] did an ingenious study with subjects from a variety of socioeconomic positions, and compared how boys and girls acted with the mother at the same time. The subjects were year-old boy-girl twins and their mothers. The girls touched the mothers more, looked at them more, vocalized to them more, and maintained proximity to them longer than the boys. These results strongly suggest that the mothers had encouraged independent behavior more in their boys than in their girls.

Fathers, as well as mothers (of the middle class), were observed at home with toddlers between 1½ and 2 years of age [22]. Although several of the parents expressed commitment to impartial treatment of boys and girls, there were definite differences. Both parents praised and criticized girls more than boys and joined boys' play more but also left boys alone to play more often than girls. As in the study described in the previous paragraph, independence was encouraged more in boys than in girls. When questioned about what they considered to be gender-appropriate behavior, fathers rated more behaviors as appropriate to only one sex than did mothers. This finding is consistent with many other studies that have shown fathers to be more interested than mothers in having their children behave in gender-appropriate ways, and that girls are permitted a broader range of activities than boys. The behaviors considered proper for boys only were roughhouse play, aggressive behaviors, and dressing up like a man. The behaviors that were rated proper for girls only were playing with dolls, dressing up like a woman, singing, and dancing. In regard to child care, parents of daughters felt that both parents could take part in all aspects of child rearing, but parents of sons thought that mothers and fathers had different duties in respect to bringing up boys.

Thus does the baby learn a gender assignment as an important part of his self-concept, and some of the behavior that the culture deems correct for a boy or a girl. Parents continue their efforts. Other family members add their contributions. Realizing that there are rules about what girls and boys do, the young child tries to figure out what they are and how to obey them. At 20 months, Jason refused to play with a doll that his aunt gave him, although he loved to cuddle toy animals. His father had strong convictions that boys should not play with girls' toys. Somehow, Jason knew.

DEPRIVATION AND NURTURANCE

There are many modes of child rearing, some of them inadequate for health and growth, some questionable and some promising. Several post-revolutionary countries are employing methods that are new and different. What is good for children in North American culture? What could be improved? Having discussed nutritional deprivation in previous chapters, we now focus on other kinds of deprivation.

Abuse and Neglect. Children are deprived of basic human rights when they are physically attacked and when they are not given care necessary for growth and health. *Abuse* is defined as "excessive physical assaults on a child," neglect as "lack of parental provision of basic physical and emotional necessities for a child" [54a]. The word *excessive* makes the definition not very clear, because some people think that it is all right for parents to spank their children, while others believe that any hitting or purposeful infliction of physical pain upon a child is excessive. There is general agreement, however, that abuse is indicated when a child shows physical damage, such as welts, bruises, broken bones and burns and that neglect is related to other types of damage such as severe diaper rash and malnutrition.

According to estimates, over two million children are abused each year in the United States [24]. The problem appears to be growing. The causes are many and complex. The background sources of cruelty to children lie in the culture that permits and even encourages violence and allows parents and sometimes teachers to inflict corporal punishment on children [40]. Abusing and neglecting parents tend to be emotionally upset and aggravated by inability to cope with pressing problems. The infant who soils his diaper may be the last straw to the parent who feels trapped in situational stresses and who has a personal history of violence himself [23]. Often, but not always, abusing parents are poor and were themselves abused children. Often abused children were and are unwanted. The treatment of child abuse must, like its causes, be varied and complex. The elimination of child abuse would require vast social, economic, and educational changes.

In 1974 the United States Congress passed the Child Abuse Prevention and Treatment Act. Preventive and remedial programs are operating in many places, providing facilities for treatment of abused children and abusing parents and opening lines of communication through which anyone can report child abuse [30a]. The act does not, however, provide for much basic research on abuse nor does it acknowledge the social changes that must occur before child abuse can be eliminated [69]. At a national conference on child abuse and neglect, Zigler described these necessary changes:

1. Alleviation of family stress through provision of employment for those who want it.
2. Universal education in child development and parenting in order to teach realistic expectations of children and knowledge of how to care for them.
3. Concerted national efforts to reduce premature births and mental retardation since prematures and retardates are abused more often than normal children. Parents of such children experience extra stress.
4. Family planning programs that will prevent the birth of unwanted children since they are more likely to be abused than wanted children.
5. Homemaker services for families experiencing difficulties.
6. Adequate child care facilities available when families need them.

7. Elimination of corporal punishment in schools as well as in homes.
8. Societal rejection of violence, hostility, and aggression instead of tolerating and even glamorizing it.

Child abuse is rare in societies in which people love and enjoy children in general and in which adults feel responsibility for all children, not just their own. How can North American society move in this direction and close the gap between adults and children? Zigler's suggestions would help. Further help through basic research is needed.

Experiential Deficits and Compensation. A child is deprived when he does not have the experiences necessary for development considered normal in his culture. *Maternal deprivation* and *father absence* are global kinds of deprivation that have been studied extensively. Research has shown that mothers and fathers perform essential functions for children, but that under some circumstances, other people can perform those functions. A finer analysis of developmental deficit is necessary in order to understand the many ways in which children's growth needs can be met. Deficits and deprivations have been studied in institutions and in homes.

Institution-Reared Children. Severe social and intellectual deficits have been observed in children in some institutions (such institutions are now rare, at least in North America). Children in inadequate institutions show what happens when babies live without affectionate interaction and stimulation. A vivid picture of experiential and developmental deficit is painted by Dennis, who has observed children and child-rearing methods in many cultures. He analyzes the environment and development of children who spent their infancy in a crèche for foundlings, in Lebanon [17]. The babies spent their first 3 years in a top-floor room with no view of the outdoors except for the sky. For the first year they lay in bassinets with covered sides, where they were bottle-fed. From 2 to 3 years they were in cribs placed around the wall of a large room and in playpens in the central part. The caretakers, most of them graduates of the crèche, were mechanical and unresponsive in their care of the babies, never talking, never playing. The ratio of caretakers to infants was about 1 to 10, but no assignments of individuals were made. Toys were scarce and limited. There were no mirrors and no household objects. At 2 months, crèche infants were average on tests, but after that, scores dropped. Later tests showed retardation in all areas. One-year-olds could neither sit alone nor creep. Many 2-year-olds could not walk. Developmental Quotients were around 50. Thus, severe experiential deprivation and developmental deprivation prevailed in this institution.

When foundlings from the crèche were adopted into homes before 2 years of age, they soon attained an average IQ of 100 and maintained it. The cognitive interaction and environmental enrichment given by loving parents were sufficient to promote a normal rate of mental growth. For those adopted at between 2 and 4 years, the mean IQ achieved was around 80. The younger adoptees, therefore, had a greater increase in IQ. Two years seemed to be the point beyond which the efforts of normal parents were no longer enough to compensate for developmental deficits because of experiential deprivation. Perhaps the addition of a program of support and education could have pushed up this cutoff point.

Home-Reared Children. Severe deprivation can occur at home, too. Just as institutions like the crèche are rare, extremely depriving homes are also the exception. By assessing the whole home environment, including the mother's behavior toward the baby, certain deficits of experience have been linked to poor development in young children. Intensity of stimulation (too much or too little) and opportunity to hear names of objects are two of these [64]. The Caldwell Home Stimulation Inventory mentioned in the previous chapter, is an instrument for measuring the quality of the home environment [19, 31]. The dimensions it measures relate to the intellectual development of the child.

The social competence of the child, also, is related to the responsiveness of the mother and the environment that she provides [1]. In a series of studies of mother-infant interaction, Ainsworth and her associates have shown interrelationships between quality of mothering and competence of infants. Prompt response to a baby's signals fosters development of communication. Freedom to explore is related to IQ. Quality of attachment is related to quality of exploration and to development of concepts of persons and objects [5].

Enriching the Home Environment. Although most parents might welcome some help in providing an optimal home environment, several programs are oriented to those who need it most. The prevention of developmental deficit at school age is one purpose. Providing a good life for infants and families is another. Infants are at special risk when their parents do not have access to adequate re sources for child rearing, as often happens when they are poor, single, migrant, ill, uneducated, very young, retarded, emotionally disturbed, or otherwise overburdened. Many different programs have been designed to help such families with their children. The two basic kinds are programs carried on within the home and programs outside. Some combine both.

Home-based programs are carried on by visitors who play with and teach the baby, usually sharing the activities and plans with the mother. Thus, the mother learns through encouragement, watching, carrying out new modes of interaction, designing an environment, and understanding the processes of development in her baby. Mothers of high-risk infants often feel helpless and ineffective and have low self-esteem. As they learn how to take better care of their babies and as they see the babies thriving, they begin to feel and be more competent themselves. They feel proud of their babies. Mothering becomes more satisfying. Sometimes these programs include some group meetings, in which mothers have a change away from home, meeting other mothers with whom they can share, and perhaps developing new interests that make life more meaningful. There are hundreds of such programs in the United States. Demonstration projects of home-based education include: Appalachia Educational Laboratory in Charleston, West Virginia; Demonstration and Research Center for Early Education in Nashville, Tennessee; Effectiveness-Training Associates in Pasadena, California; Florida Parent Education Program in Gainesville; and Home Start, administered by the U.S. Office of Education in

This daycare center offers toddlers opportunities to use creative materials freely. This little girl is finding out what she can do with paste and paper.

MARGARET HAMILTON

Washington, D.C. [32]. An example of a book that shows and tells very simply how to educate infants is Gordon's *Baby Learning through Baby Play* [26].

Programs Outside the Home. Most supplementary care programs in North America are for *day care,* either in groups or in another family. For most mothers who have jobs outside the home, especially mothers without husbands, day care is essential. Sometimes grandmothers provide infant care, as many do in China and in the Soviet Union. Day care programs, however, are the help used by most women in the labor force. In China and Russia, most day care centers for infants are located where the women work. Similarly, in the *kibbutzim,* the babies are nearby and the mothers stop in to breast-feed them and play with them, and for reassurance that the babies are all right. Mothers and baby-nurses know each other and can communicate frequently; their values are clear and unified. It must strengthen a baby's sense of trust as she feels that her caretakers at home and at the center know what they are doing and agree on it.

Widespread day care is new in North America. It can and often does supplement the family. However, a wide variety of views on women's role creates conflicts over day care. Many people resent spending public funds on day care because they say mothers should stay home with their babies. These attitudes have, in some places, made it difficult to provide good day care facilities and have made mothers feel guilty and ambivalent about using day care. A review of the effects of maternal employment on children is reassuring [21]. Strength of attachment to the mother seems to be related more to quality of interaction than to amount of time spent with the mother or the father. Infants also become attached to their day care workers, especially when one particular caregiver is responsible for an individual child [50]. When they had become attached to caregivers before six months of age, the infants were generally comfortable when the mothers left them with the caregivers. Several studies showed infants in day care to make more progress in mental development than home-reared children, especially when both groups were at risk developmentally.

As supplements to the home, high-quality day care centers can provide excellent care, links with home, responsive interaction, stability, and opportunities for exploration. They can if they are appropriately planned, constructed, managed, and staffed. (Unfortunately, some are not). The success of a good day-care program was demonstrated by a study that compared mother-infant interaction in three groups, high-risk infants in day care, high-risk infants at home, and a sample of the general population at home [47, 48]. Comparing the two high-risk groups, the day care infants vocalized with their mothers more and interacted more with their mothers. The mothers in the day care group acted more like the mothers in the general population group than did the high-risk home group. Benefits of the program to the high-risk mother-infant pairs were increased responsivity in the infants and increasing concern for optimal child development in the mothers.

Comprehensive Programs. Some programs combine many methods of meeting the needs of children and families. Home-based education may be done in connection with day care, nursery school, or play group. Nutritional counseling and pediatric care may be included. Some of the demonstration centers mentioned previously offer several types of service. Burton White's Harvard Preschool Project has many facets [66].

Daily outdoor exercise is part of the routine of a good day care center.

MARGARET HAMILTON

The Competent Infant-Mother Pair. The Harvard Preschool Project has sought the sources of competence, both social and intellectual, in the young child and has found many of those sources in the interactions between infant and mother. Further purposes of the project are to apply the findings by teaching parents to be competent and by developing the most efficient methods of making the knowledge widely available.

Competent mothers were found at all socioeconomic levels. Some of them had part-time jobs and some did not. The modes of mother-baby interaction that were related to intellectual competence at 30-to-33 months have been analyzed [11]. Intellectual competence was assessed by the Stanford-Binet intelligence test and tests of receptive language and spatial abilities. Before age three, the experiences that correlated best with later tests were those in which the child interacted with another person (usually the mother). The other person created experiences for the child, participated in them, shared and maintained an emotionally warm atmosphere. Responses were tailored to fit the infant's capabilities and interests. Teaching could be direct, as in giving information, through demonstration, pretend play, entertainment or conversation, and often through a blend of several types.

The following excerpt illustrates the sort of playful interaction that stimulates the baby's intellectual development in an atmosphere of approval and enjoyment.

> Mother and Jamie (13 months) are sitting on the floor. Jamie sees a little wooden pig lying on the floor. He picks it up and hands it to Mother calling, "Piggy, piggy." Mother asks, "Shall we hide the piggy?" Jamie smiles. Mother tells him, "I think your piggy is too big to fit under the cup. I'll get something to hide the piggy under." She shows him that the cup is too small. "See, your piggy sticks out. It can't hide under there." Mother goes to the kitchen and returns with pans for a three-tiered cake. Mother hides the pig under the largest pan and places the others on top in a tower. Jamie smiles and laughs and Mother claps, "Terrific." Jamie then covers the pig with the pan, but immediately uncovers it and grins. Mother: "Hey, you found the piggy. Hide him again." Jamie covers the toy pig and looks at Mother. Mother asks, "Well, where did that piggy go?" Jamie takes off the pan and giggles. Mother claps, "There he is. Hurray for Jamie. Jamie found the piggy." [11]

The baby who grows up in a relationship with a competent parent needs no compensatory education, since he develops well. The type of interaction demonstrated by the competent mother-infant pair is the kind of education that will help a child to recover from previous deprivation. Most likely some of these ways of teaching were used by the parents who adopted the babies from the Lebanese crèche and who helped them to achieve normal intellectual development.

Summary

The baby and her family interactions always occur in a cultural setting that influences resources, behavior, and values. The faster the culture changes, the more parents need outside guidance in child rearing. Cultural support of children and parents varies widely. Family composition, characteristics of family members, and the characteristics of the infant herself all influence family interactions.

Babies build bonds of attachment with other people, usually the mother first and then the father. Inborn human behavior patterns provide the base on which to build. Timing of attachment behavior has a large maturational component. Attachment preferences are developed according to interesting and satisfying interactions provided by other people. Exploration behavior is articulated with attachment. Fear and anxiety are likely in the absence of attachment figures and objects and upon separation from them. Wariness and fear of strange people and objects develops gradually.

Anger outbursts reach a peak in the second year, as the baby experiences frustrations in doing and choosing for herself. This time is crucial for developing controls or patterns of violence.

Peer interaction is an important part of social development. When relationships with adults are inadequate, peer play may provide some compensation. During the second year, a toddler develops an understanding of the role of the eyes and of the fact that other people see what she sees.

The infant adapts her rhythms and behavior patterns to those of her family through a process of give and take, in which the parents' planning is very influential. Regulation involves timing and control of eating, sleeping, toileting, exercise, and grooming, all of which have consequences for personality and health. Parents and other significant people also teach gender concepts and gender–appropriate behavior, fathers usually being more interested than mothers in these behaviors.

Deprivation in its most extreme form is abuse. Seriously disturbed parents may attack and/or neglect their infants. Experiential deprivation has been seen in its most extreme form in institutions where infants receive minimal stimulation and little or no responsive social interaction. All types of development are retarded under these circumstances, but intervention by age two can promote normal growth. Depriving homes can be improved through supportive educational programs that involve parents, either at home, outside the home, or both. Day care centers can supplement the home, with benefit to the child and family, but quality of day care is crucial. Comprehensive child development programs serve families in multiple ways that are designed to meet particular needs. Findings on selected competent mother–infant pairs have contributed to programs designed to develop competence in all families.

References

1. Ainsworth, M. D. S. Anxious attachment and defensive reactions in a strange situation and their relationship to behavior at home. Paper presented at meetings of the Society for Research in Child Development, Philadelphia, 1973.
2. Ainsworth, M. D. S. The development of infant-mother attachment. In B. M. Caldwell and H. N. Ricciuti (eds.). *Review of Child Development Research,* vol. 3. Chicago: University of Chicago Press, 1973.
3. Ainsworth, M. D. S., and S. M. Bell. Attachment, exploration, and separation: Illustrated by the behavior of one-year-olds in a strange situation. *Child Development,* 1970, **41,** 49–67.

4. Beckwith, L. Relationships between infants' social behavior and their mothers' behavior. *Child Development,* 1972, **43,** 397–411.

5. Bell, S. M. The development of the object concept as related to mother-infant attachment. *Child Development,* 1970, **41,** 291–311.

6. Bowlby, J. *Attachment and loss.* vol. 1: *Attachment.* London: Hogarth Press, 1969.

7. Bowlby, J. *Attachment and loss.* vol. 2. *Separation: Anxiety and Anger.* London: Hogarth Press, 1973.

8. Bretherton, I., and M. D. S. Ainsworth. *Responses of one-year-olds to a stranger in a strange situation.* Baltimore: Johns Hopkins University, 1973 (Mimeo).

9. Bronson, G. W. Infants' reactions to unfamiliar persons and novel objects. *Monographs of the Society for Research in Child Development,* 1972, **37:**3.

10. Brooks, J., and M. Lewis. Attachment behavior in thirteen-month-old, opposite-sex twins. Paper presented at meetings of the Society for Research in Child Development, Philadelphia, 1973.

11. Carew, J. V., I. Chan, and C. Halfar. Observed intellectual competence and tested intelligence: Their roots in the young child's transactions with his environment. Paper presented at meetings of the Society for Research in Child Development. Denver, 1975.

12. Chauncey, H. (ed.). *Soviet preschool education.* vol. 1: *Program of instruction.* New York: Holt, Rinehart and Winston, Inc., 1969.

13. Chauncey, H. (ed.). *Soviet preschool education.* vol. 2: *Teacher's commentary.* New York: Holt, Rinehart and Winston, Inc., 1969.

14. Chess, S., A. Thomas, and H. G. Birch. Behavior problems revisited: Findings of an anterospective study. In S. Chess and A. Thomas (eds.). *Annual progress in child psychiatry and child development 1968.* New York: Brunner/Mazel, 1968, pp. 335–344.

15. Clarke-Stewart, A. Sociability and social sensitivity: Characteristics of the stranger. Paper presented at meetings of the Society for Research in Child Development, Denver, 1975.

16. Demos, J. Infancy in the Plymouth Colony. In M. Gordon (ed.). *The American family in historical perspective.* New York: St. Martin's Press, 1973.

17. Dennis, W. *Children of the crèche.* New York: Meredith Corporation, 1973.

18. Eckerman, C. O., J. L. Whatley, and S. L. Kutz. Growth of social play with peers during the second year of life. *Developmental Psychology,* 1975, **11,** 42–49.

19. Elardo, R., R. Bradley, and B. M. Caldwell. The relation of infants' home environments to mental test performance from six to thirty-six months: A longitudinal analysis. *Child Development,* 1975, **46,** 71–76.

20. Erikson, E. H. *Childhood and society.* New York: W. W. Norton & Company, 1963.

21. Etaugh, C. Effects of maternal employment on children: A review of recent research. *Merrill-Palmer Quarterly,* 1974, **20,** 71–98.

22. Fagot, B. I. Sex differences in toddlers' behavior and parental reaction. *Developmental Psychology,* 1974, **10,** 554–558.

23. Gelles, R. J. Child abuse as psychopathology: A sociological critique and reformulation. *American Journal of Orthopsychiatry,* 1973, **43,** 611–621.

24. Gil, D. G. Violence against children. *Journal of Marriage and the Family,* 1971, **33,** 644–648.

25. Goodenough, F. L. *Anger in young children*. Minneapolis: University of Minnesota Press, 1931.

26. Gordon, I. J. *Baby learning through baby play*. New York: St. Martin's Press, 1970.

27. Harlow, H. F. The nature of love. *American Psychologist*, 1958, **13**, 673–684.

28. Harlow, H. F., and J. Soumi. Social recovery by isolation reared monkeys. *Proceedings of the National Academy of Science U.S.A.*, 1971, **68**, 1534–1538.

29. Harper, L. V. The young as a source of stimuli controlling caretaker behavior. *Developmental Psychology*, 1971, **4**, 73–78.

30. Hoffman, M. L. Developmental synthesis of affect and cognition and its implications for altruistic motivation. *Developmental Psychology*, 1975, **11**, 607–622.

30a. Hurt, M. *Child abuse and neglect*. DHEW Publication No. (OHD) 74–20. Washington, D.C.: U.S. Government Printing Office, 1975.

31. Kahn, A. J. *Concurrent and longitudinal relationships between mother and child variables*. University of Houston Parent-Child Development Center, Houston, Texas, 1974 (mimeo).

32. Keister, M. E. Practical considerations in the operation of home-based programs for infants, toddlers and their parents. In L. L. Dittman (ed.). *The infants we care for*. Washington, D.C.: National Association for the Education of Young Children, 1973.

33. Kessen, W. (Chairman) Children of China: Report of a visit. Symposium presented at meetings of the American Psychological Association, New Orleans, 1974.

34. Kotelchuck, M. The nature of the infant's tie to his father. *Journal of Genetic Psychology* (in press).

35. Lamb, M. E. Interactions between eight-month-olds and their fathers and mothers. In M. E. Lamb (Ed.), *The role of the father in child development*. New York: John Wiley and Sons, Inc. (in press).

36. Lempers, J. D., E. E. Flavell, and J. H. Flavell. The development in very young children of tacit knowledge concerning visual perception. Paper presented at meetings of the Society for Research in Child Development, Denver, 1975.

37. Lourie, R. S. The roots of violence. *Early Child Development and Care*, 1973, **2**, 1–12.

38. Maccoby, E. E., and C. N. Jacklin. *The psychology of sex differences*. Stanford, Ca.: Stanford University Press, 1974.

39. Makarenko, A. S. *A book for parents*. Moscow: Foreign Languages Publishing House, 1954.

40. Maurer, A. Corporal punishment. *American Psychologist*, 1974, **29**, 614–626.

41. Money, J., and A. A. Ehrhardt. *Man and woman—Boy and Girl*. Baltimore: Johns Hopkins University Press, 1972.

42. Morgan, G. A. Determinants of infant's reaction to strangers: Effects of age and situational differences. Paper presented at meetings of the Society for Research in Child Development, Philadelphia, 1973.

43. Norman, R. D. Sex differences in preference for sex of children: A replication after 20 years. *Journal of Psychology*, 1974, **88**, 229–239.

44. Oppong, C. *Marriage among a matrilineal elite*. Cambridge: Cambridge University Press, 1974.

45. Passman, R. H., and P. Weisberg. Mothers and blankets as agents for promoting play and exploration by young children in a novel environment: The effects of

social and nonsocial attachment objects. *Developmental Psychology,* 1974, **11,** 170–177.

46. Pedersen, F. A., J. Rubenstein, and L. J. Yarrow. Father absence in infancy. Paper presented at meetings of the Society for Research in Child Development, Philadelphia, 1973.

47. Ramey, C. T., and P. J. Mills. Mother-infant interaction patterns as a function of rearing conditions. Paper presented at meetings of the Society for Research in Child Development. Denver, 1975.

48. Ramey, C. T., R. H. Starr, J. Pallas, C. F. Whitten, and V. Reed. Nutrition, response-contingent stimulation, and the maternal deprivation syndrome: results of an early intervention program. *Merrill-Palmer Quarterly,* 1975, **21,** 45–53.

49. Rheingold, H. L., and C. O. Eckerman. The infant's free entry into a new environment. *Journal of Experimental Child Psychology,* 1969, **8,** 271–283.

50. Ricciuti, H. N., and R. Poresky. Development of attachment to caregivers in an infant nursery during the first year of life. Paper presented at meetings of the Society for Research in Child Development, Philadelphia, 1973.

51. Rohner, R. P. *They love me, they love me not.* New Haven: HRAF Press, 1975.

52. Ross, G., J. Kagan, P. Zelazo, and M. Kotelchuck. Separation protest in infants in home and laboratory. *Developmental Psychology,* 1975, **11,** 256–257.

52a. Sagi, A., and M. L. Hoffman. Empathic distress in the newborn. *Developmental Psychology,* 1976, **12,** 175–176.

53. Schaffer, H. R., and P. E. Emerson. The development of social attachments in infancy. *Monographs of the Society for Research in Child Development,* 1964, **29:3.**

54. Schaffer, H. R., A. Greenwood, and M. H. Parry. The onset of wariness. *Child Development,* 1972, **43,** 165–175.

54a. Schmidt, R. What home economists should know about child abuse. *Journal of Home Economics,* 1976, **68:3,** 13–16.

55. Seay, B., and N. W. Gottfried. A phylogenetic perspective for social behavior in primates. *Journal of General Psychology,* 1975, **92,** 5–17.

56. Shaffran, R., and T. G. Decarie. Short term stability of infants' responses to strangers. Paper presented at meetings of the Society for Research in Child Development, Philadelphia, 1973.

57. Sidel, R. *Women and child care in China.* Baltimore: Penguin Books, 1973.

58. Sidel, R. *Families of Fengsheng.* Baltimore: Penguin Books, 1974.

59. Stayton, D. J., and M. D. S. Ainsworth. Individual differences in infant responses to brief, everyday separations as related to other infant and maternal behaviors. *Developmental Psychology,* 1973, **9,** 226–235.

60. Stayton, D. J., M. D. S. Ainsworth, and M. B. Main. Development of separation behavior in the first year of life: Protest, following and greeting. *Developmental Psychology,* 1973, **9,** 213–225.

61. Stayton, D. J., R. Hogan, and M. D. S. Ainsworth. Infant obedience and maternal behavior: The origins of socialization reconsidered. *Child Development,* 1971, **42,** 1057–1069.

62. Stone, J. G. Study guide for three films on kibbutz infancy: Rearing kibbutz babies; Infant development in the kibbutz; Day care for a kibbutz toddler. New York: Institute for Child Mental Health, 1974.

63. Thoman, E. B. Some consequences of early infant-mother-infant interaction. *Early Child Development and Care,* 1974, **3,** 249–261.

64. Wachs, T. D., I. C. Uzgiris, and J. McV. Hunt. Cognitive development in infants of different age levels and from different environmental backgrounds; An exploratory investigation. *Merrill-Palmer Quarterly,* 1971, **17,** 283–317.

65. Watson, J. S. Smiling, cooing and "The Game." *Merrill-Palmer Quarterly,* 1972, **18,** 321–339.

66. White, B., J. Watts, I. Barnett, B. Kaban, J. Marmor, and B. Shapiro. *Experience and environment: Major influences on the development of the young child.* vol. 1. Englewood Cliffs, N.J.: Prentice-Hall, Inc., 1973.

67. Willemsen, E., D. Flaherty, C. Heaton, and G. Ritchey. Attachment behavior of one-year-olds as a function of mother vs. father, sex of child, session and toys. *Genetic Psychology Monographs,* 1974, **90,** 305–324.

68. Yarrow, L. J. Parents and infants: An interactive network. Paper presented at meetings of the American Psychological Association, New Orleans, 1974.

69. Zigler, E. Controlling child abuse—an effort doomed to failure. *Newsletter of the Division on Developmental Psychology, American Psychological Association,* 1976 (February), 17–30.

Readings in
Social and Personal Development

Social behaviors emerge as infants interact with adults and children. Although parents have long been considered the most important influences on children's social and emotional development, new evidence indicates that peers also play a vital role. Other adults are also salient in direct interaction with the baby and in their support to parents.

Prosocial or altruistic behavior in infants and young children is reported by Marion R. Yarrow and Caroline Z. Waxler. Using both mothers' reports and a battery of standard situations, they found infants showing that they observed and interpreted emotional behavior of others. Development of compassion and aggression is discussed.

Toddlers' behavior with one another is the focus of the study by Carol O. Eckerman, Judith L. Whatley, and Stuart L. Kutz. Reactions to a strange peer are different from reactions to a strange adult. Results of the study lead the authors to question what peers offer in contrast to familiar adults.

Day care and other supplements to home care are currently discussed and debated in North America. Many families need such care, and yet it is not universally available. Opponents of day care say that it will weaken the family in general. By learning how supplementary child care is done in other countries, a student gains understanding of alternative ways of meeting human needs.

The Israeli kibbutzim, which have long been of interest to North American child developmentalists, are different from one another, and change with time. Jeanette G. Stone describes and discusses present practices in three kibbutzim in her study guide for viewing films on kibbutz infancy. She refers to earlier practices and their relation to present ones. She makes the reader aware of the unity of the kibbutz culture. Child care practices are made possible, convenient, and even necessary by other practices that are parts of the kibbutz. This article gives a sense of the interdependency of children, parents, community, and nation.

243

The Emergence and Functions of Prosocial Behaviors in Young Children

Marion Radke Yarrow and Carolyn Zahn Waxler
NATIONAL INSTITUTE OF MENTAL HEALTH

The study of children's compassionate feelings and behaviors comprises a complex package for research. Compassion, altruism, prosocial behavior (the label is a problem) involve cognitions, principles, and judgments; they involve feelings and motives. We are well aware that not all of helping, sharing, and sympathizing arise out of identification with the feelings of or concern for the welfare of others, and aware that the phenomena of empathy, compassion, etc. are murky areas—philosophically and empirically. Despite this state of affairs, our research interest is in how compassion (concern for others) is born and bred. Our earlier research used experimental designs with nursery school children. We demonstrated differential changes in prosocial responding as a consequence of different types of modeling and reinforcement. Although these techniques increased the frequency of helping and sympathy (though increase was by no means assured), the helping response was expressed in such a variety of ways as to suggest very different meanings and feelings underlying the response.

The direction of our research program, therefore, shifted to the exploration of the phenomena of compassionate feelings and behaviors more generally. What are the precursors of prosocial inclinations and the very early capabilities of the child in this regard? To get a better grasp of these issues, it seemed important to explore more general questions about the inferential capabilities of young children, of very, very young children, inferences with regard to the affect and thoughts of others. With this kind of knowledge we could more readily ask, how does sensitivity and responsiveness to the needs of others develop? Where and how do they fit into a more general schema of the developing child, both with respect to his cognitive skills and his social behavior?

From three interrelated studies we are attempting to obtain a picture of the emergence and progression of prosocial behaviors, to investigate the cognitions, feelings, and motives involved. The subjects were 128 children, ranging in age from 10 *months* to 7 *years*.

In the first study, with the youngest children, the focus is on the child's emerging sensitivities to affective events in his environment, e.g., a parent's or child's anger or pain or fear or joy or anxiety. Our data are the child's responses to these events and, in turn, responses of others to the child. Three cohorts, of eight children each, were followed for 9 months; the youngest began at 10 months of age, the next cohort at 15 months, and the third cohort at 20 months. Mothers were trained to dictate detailed descriptions of day to day affective events. At three week intervals, investigators visited the home and simulated affective episodes (e.g., pain, anger, joy). Additional data were obtained on the child's development and the home environment.

Presented at meetings of The Society for Research in Child Development, Denver, 1975.
Printed by permission of the National Institute of Mental Health.

The second and third studies began at age 3 with children in nursery school or coming back to the school setting for research purposes. Our purposes were (a) to investigate the development and relations of perspective-taking skills and prosocial behavior; and (b) to investigate the prosocial behavior in the life space of the child: the frequency, circumstances, and generality with which it occurs and its relation to its "opposite," "anti-social" behavior.

Through a battery of standard situations, we assessed the child's perspective-taking skills: That is, was the child able to recognize and identify correctly the perspective of the person in circumstances in which an object or event was encountered or experienced differently by the two of them? One set of tasks dealt with literal perspectives in a visual or tactile perceptual sense; a second set dealt with what we will call cognitive perspectives in the sense of comprehending self-other perspectives deriving from long-term differences in life experiences; and a third set dealt with affective perspective-taking. An example of each follows. Some of the tasks are adapted from Flavell; others are new. An example of literal perceptions is one with a child and another person seated on opposite sides of a table. Can the child indicate that a picture or object appearing upside-down to him would be viewed as right side up to the other, and vice versa? A cognitive perspective-taking task is illustrated by requesting the child to choose gifts for parents and opposite sex peer and for himself. Does his own preference pervade his choices? Emotional perspective-taking was tapped by the child's inability to differentiate between his own and another's immediate affective experiences in situations in which S experienced success and O, failure; S experienced pleasure with one object, but O experienced pleasure with a different object.

Prosocial behaviors (a child's potential helping, sharing, and comforting) were assessed in a series of six standard situations. On two occasions an adult accidentally spilled some materials in the context of play activities. In two other circumstances, there were limited supplies of snack or toys which might be shared. The child also had occasion to witness someone expressing pain (slamming her finger in a drawer) and to see and hear someone crying, ostensibly about a sad story. All of the experimental tasks were interwoven in meaningful contexts of play and interaction. In natural indoor and outdoor play settings, prosocial and aggressive interchanges were recorded. A measure of level of social activity was also obtained.

Our infant subjects supplied very provocative data on sensitivity to affective states of others. Responses were by no means universal. However very young children were often finely discriminative and responsive to others' need states. Children in the youngest cohort showed distress to parental arguments and anger with each other. Responses were sometimes marked: crying, holding hands over ears, comforting a distraught parent, or (punitively) hitting the parent perceived as the guilty one. Parental affection toward each other was equally arousing: Children of 1 to $2\frac{1}{2}$ years tried to join in or to separate the parents—even kicking the mother's leg. One child, from 15 months to 2 years, showed consistently different responses depending on whether mother or father initiated the affectionate hug or kiss. Initiation by the mother aroused no affect in the child, whereas with the father's (or grandfather's) initiation toward the mother, the child would "fall apart" (hitting, glaring, sucking her thumb).

While in the youngest children others' crying tended to elicit contagious crying as well as amusement, crying began to decrease, and as it waned, it was replaced by serious or worried attending. Around one year most of the youngest cohort first showed comfort to a person crying or in pain by patting, hugging, or presenting an object. Among $1\frac{1}{2}$ and 2-year-olds comforting was sometimes sophisticated and elaborate, e. g., fixing the hurt by trying to put a Band-aid on, covering mother with a blanket when she was resting, trying to locate the source of the difficulty. Children also began to express concern verbally, and sometimes gave suggestions about how to deal with the problem. Such precocity on the part of the very young gives one pause. The capabilities for compassion, for various kinds of reaching out to others in a giving sense are viable and effective responses early in life. How such behaviors develop and change in the process of socialization in various cultures and subcultures are issues to which science has addressed little investigation.

Lest one assume that we are ready to reformulate a theory about the innate goodness of man, it should be emphasized too that there were also many, many occasions on which benevolence was *not* forthcoming, and that early aggressions are equally impressive.

If by egocentric one means the translation of the environment in terms of one's own needs and body state in the face of different existing states of others, the data provide such evidence—namely, the child who tries to protect his own possessions when another child is being "robbed" of his, or the child who examines his own old injuries, hurts, and so on when someone else is injured, or verbal self-references—"look at my boo-boo"—as mother ministers to the real needs of an injured child. But the interesting point is that such self-references and self-considerations which have characteristically been conceptualized as the child's inability to take the point of view of the other, or preoccupation with one's own need state, may at times have a quite different function. They may also represent active attempts to *comprehend* (to form hypotheses about) others' affects by "trying them on," in this way trying to master (act positively on) the feelings in themselves which are aroused by others' affects. Support for such an idea is found in our data where it is not uncommon to observe self-referential responses followed by compassionate responses.

In our studies of 3 to 7 year olds, as described earlier, we explored children's perspective-taking (literal physical and psychological) in relation to their helping, sharing, and comforting behaviors. The children's abilities to successfully deal with another's perspective on the perceptual and cognitive tasks increased with age, the most substantial jumps occurring between $4\frac{1}{2}$ and 5 years of age. The prosocial behaviors by the same children showed no systematic developmental changes. Not surprisingly, then, there was no overall relation between perspective-taking abilities and prosocial interventions. This was true also at each given age level.

We expected the two kinds of responding to be related, since both (we assume) involve the capacity to make an inference about someone else's differential experience. Prosocial responding involves also the motivation to act on someone else's behalf. The lack of correspondence was of two kinds: children who succeeded on perspective-taking tests but did not respond prosocially, and children who helped, shared, or comforted, but failed on the perspective-taking tasks. This lack of correspondence raises a number of unsettling questions: Is the conceptualization of a common underlying process of perspective-taking incorrect or simplistic? Are the test-tasks that are presumed to measure self-other perspectives really not measuring these abilities well? Perhaps, especially in young children, the language components in the instructions may have an all-determining influence. In designing perspective-taking tasks for this study and in examining tasks that other investigators have used, we have become very aware of the difficulties in good task-construction. We have the strong impression that the child's capabilities are seriously underestimated by many experimental tasks assessing self-other perspectives.

Our third study extended our information to the functioning of these same children in their peer groups. With what frequency and consistency do they help, share, and comfort? How do these prosocial behaviors relate to aggressive peer interaction?

Prosocial behaviors occurred in almost every child. There was some consistency in relative frequency across natural and experimental settings in sharing and comforting responses. Sharing and comforting were significantly related to each other; neither was reliably associated with helping. Such data provide evidence of limited consistency in behaviors that involve sensitivity to others' feeling states. The relatively impersonal utilitarian "helping" of an inconvenienced person (as measured in our study) seems to tap a different kind of behavior from that involved in responding to the emotional needs, as in reacting to hurt or sadness. The data suggest that prosociality is not a unitary concept. Observations of responding to emotional states of others (here to sadness) documented the complexity in prosocial interventions. Our data indicate that merely tabbing a child as having (or not) shared or comforted another ignores significant variants in these responses: inhibitions, approach-avoidance conflicts, anxieties, sympathy, feelings of relief, success or satisfaction.

Compassion and aggression have long been positively linked in some psychological theories, but data are few. In the present study there were no simple relations between aggressive and prosocial behaviors. There was a single significant positive association (out of eight) only for girls. When level of social interaction is controlled, the significance disappears.

Associations between aggression and prosociality were re-examined, taking into account the absolute *level* of aggression. We reasoned that children with high frequencies of aggressive acts might be expressing qualitative as well as quantitative differences in aggression, e.g., hostile vs. assertive aggression. The sample was divided, therefore, at the mean on frequency of aggression and correlations were computed for each subsample, and data for boys and girls examined separately.

For boys *below* the mean on aggression, there was a significant positive association between aggression and sharing-comforting in peer interaction. In contrast, for boys *above* the mean on aggression the relation was negative. For girls, there was no such pattern. However, since the absolute level of aggression of girls is significantly lower than that of boys, the correlation between aggression and comforting-sharing for girls across the entire range of aggression is consistent with the findings for boys at the lower range of aggression. Controlling on level of social interaction did not materially alter the findings. One might hypothesize that moderately aggressive children are assertive more than hostile and that they are secure and competent in their peer groups. Assertiveness is a quality that might reasonably be expected to go along with the ability to intervene on behalf of another person.

These analyses have emphasized the aggressive behavior *expressed by* the child. There is another element of aggression, that expressed *to* the child. Among the boys and girls who were low to moderate in exhibited aggression, frequency of being the target of aggression and frequency of sharing-comforting behaviors were significantly positively related. In other words, among the relatively non-aggressive children, sensitivity to others' feeling states increased as the frequency of experiences of aggression from others increased. There was no such relation among children high on exhibited aggression. We will hazard a hypothesis: namely, aggressions experienced may contribute to the development of sensitivity to feelings when the child is himself not highly vulnerable and is secure in his relations with others. He may be able to learn from experiencing aggression from others and better understand the feelings and be better able to act empathically.

There is still a very modest accumulation of scientific knowledge regarding the human behaviors that qualify as prosocial. They are not a simple phenomenon. As scientists, we tend to give too little thought to cultural influences on the choice and definition of our research problems. It seems to us that research on prosocial behavior carries many overtones of these influences. In our society, the study of prosocial endeavors has been rather late in coming, compared with studies of aggression (and problems in our society), and compared with individual achievement and intellectual capacities, valued commodities by the society. Theories of prosociality, too, have frequently been formulated with materialistic or economic parallels, for example, cost-accounting theory, which represents a balancing of credit-debit ledgers of human relations. We are suggesting that it might be well to reflect more on our research emphases and theories of child development as products of the cultures and subcultures from which we come.

Growth of Social Play with Peers During the Second Year of Life *

Carol O. Eckerman, Judith L. Whatley, and Stuart L. Kutz
DUKE UNIVERSITY

To assess the social interactions between unfamiliar peers, 30 pairs of home-reared children—10 pairs in each of three age groups, 10–12, 16–18, and 22–24 months of age—were observed in an unfamiliar play setting with their mothers.

From *Developmental Psychology*, 1975, **11**, 42–49. Copyright © 1975 by the American Psychological Association. Reprinted by permission.

* This research was supported in part by a Duke University Research Council Grant. We thank Deborah Hotch for her services as an observer and Gregory E. Kennington for statistical advice.

The children contacted their mothers little and interacted more with toys and one another, exchanging smiles, vocalizations, and toys and imitating each other's actions. Contact of the same objects and involvement in the peer's activities with objects increased reliably with age. By 2 years of age, social play exceeded solitary play and the social partner was most often the peer. The results suggested that children generalize to peers behaviors developed through child–adult interaction, but that peers provide stimulation differing from that of familiar adults.

Scant attention has been paid to the social interactions between children under two years of age, despite the importance attached to early peer interactions by students of nonhuman primates (e.g., Harlow, 1969; Hinde, 1971) and despite repeated observations of human infants exchanging glances, sounds, smiles, and even toys (e.g., Bridges, 1933; Bühler, 1930; Vincze, 1971). Our knowledge of early human sociability remains limited in large measure to child–mother interactions and to children's initial reactions to unfamiliar adults (e.g., Rheingold & Eckerman, 1973; Schaffer, 1971). Yet the interactions between infant peers may mirror the social development occurring through child–adult interaction; and even more important, interactions with peers may contribute in their own right to early social development.

The most comprehensive prior study of interactions between children under 2 years of age is that of Maudry and Nekula (1939), conducted in a foundling home over 30 years ago. Pairs of children 6 to 25 months of age were placed together in a playpen, usually with only a single toy, and prompted into inter-action. Although over 18 types of peer interaction were defined, the data were presented in such molar categories as positive and negative social behavior, precluding a description of what actually went on between the children. Maudry and Nekula (1939) concluded that infants at first fail to distinguish between each other and inanimate objects (6 to 8 months), later treat each other as obstacles to play materials (9 to 13 months), and only when approaching 2 years of age (19 to 25 months) view each other as social partners—a progression that differs markedly from that proposed for infant's interactions with adults (e.g., Schaffer, 1971). Their conclusion, however, was based upon viewing institutionalized children in a single, and probably unusual, setting. Although descriptions of the normally occurring interactions among peers reared together are available (e.g., Bridges, 1933; Bühler, 1930; Vincze, 1971), no such data exist for children reared in a nuclear family.

In the present study, pairs of normal, home-reared children were brought together in a controlled play setting which included their mothers. The children, similar in age and unfamiliar to one another, were left free to interact with several new toys, their mothers, or one another. The goals were (a) to describe the extent and forms of interaction that the children freely engaged in with one another, (b) to assess changes over the second year of life in their interactions, and (c) to compare their behavior with one another to that with their mothers and with novel inanimate objects. Such an examination of interactions among young peers is a prerequisite for reasoning about the role of peers in normal human social development.

METHOD

SUBJECTS   The subjects were 60 normal, home-reared children, drawn on the basis of age from the population of white infants born and residing in

Durham, North Carolina, an industrial city of moderate size. Over 90% of the mothers contacted by telephone agreed to participate.

The subjects were equally divided into three age groups, 10.0 to 12.0, 16.0 to 18.0, and 22.0 to 24.0 months of age, and paired within each group on the basis of age alone. Table 1 summarizes the characteristics of each age group.

Subjects came from homes characterized by above-average levels of education, the equivalent of 2 or 3 years of college for the mothers and 1 or 2 years of post-college training for the fathers; nevertheless, the range in education was considerable. About half of the children had a sibling, and all but 7 spent some time with peers outside the family. Only 4 children, or 7% of the total sample, received 50% or more of their daytime care outside the family.

Two additional pairs were observed at the two younger ages, but their records discarded: in one case, a mother repeatedly interrupted the play, and in the other, one child with a long history of hospitalizations lacked the motor abilities of his age-mates.

STUDY SETTING   The study took place in a room of moderate size (2.8 × 2.9 m), unfurnished except for a few animal pictures on the walls beyond the subjects' reach and several toys on the floor. The toys were a pulltoy with marbles enclosed in a clear plastic ball, a large plastic dump truck, and three 9-cm-square vinyl cubes decorated with pictures and letters; each toy was present in duplicate. Cushions on the floor in opposite corners along the room's

TABLE 1

Characteristics of the Subjects

	AGE GROUP		
ITEM	10–12	16–18	22–24
Age in months			
M	11.4	17.3	23.0
Range	10.4–12.0	16.3–18.0	22.0–23.8
Age difference in months			
M	.6	.6	.5
Range	.1–1.3	.0–1.9	.0–1.0
No. males	12	14	8
No. firstborns	8	13	14
No. having sibling(s)	12	7	9
Years of education			
Father			
M	17.5	18.4	17.3
Range	9–20	12–22	9–22
Mother			
M	14.4	15.3	14.6
Range	10–17	11–17	8–17
Hours/week with peers			
M	5.0	7.6	7.1
Range	0–24	0–45	0–36

length marked the mothers' positions; the toys were spaced along the wall opposite the mothers' positions. A one-way window behind the toys provided visual access: a microphone in the center of the ceiling, auditory access.

PROCEDURE   Each subject and his mother were escorted to a reception room where they met the other mother and child and the female experimenter. For approximately 5 minutes the children were left free to sit on their mothers' laps or to explore the room and the few toys it contained while the experimenter instructed the mothers in their role. They were asked to talk naturally with one another, allowing their children to do as they wished; they could respond with a smile or a word or two to the children's social overtures, but they were not to initiate interaction with them or direct their activities unless intervention was necessary to prevent physical harm.

The mothers carried the subjects into the study room, placed them on the floor before the toys, and sat at their positions on the floor. The experimenter then left the room, closing the door behind her, and the 20-minute session began. At the end of the session, the experimenter obtained from the mothers information about the family and the children's prior exposure to peers.

RESPONSE MEASURES   An observer behind the one-way window systematically sampled each child's behavior. He focused upon one child at a time and alternated 15-second periods of observation with 15 second periods of recording. Every four observation periods, or 2 minutes, the focus shifted from one child to the other. The resulting record thus was based upon 40 observations, 20 of each child. For each observation, the observer recorded whether or not each of 23 behaviors occurred; the frequency of the behavior within the 15-second period was not recorded.

Eighteen behaviors related to the peer's presence or activities were distinguished and defined on the basis of preliminary observations of children in the study setting. These behaviors, grouped into five categories, are defined in Table 2.

Additional measures provided a context for the study of the peer-related activities. Fussing (fretting, whining sounds), crying (loud continuous wailing), smiling (pleasant facial expressions with marked upturning of the corners of the mouth), and laughing (explosive sounds accompanying smiles) provided a measure of the affect engendered by the novel play setting as a whole. Contact of a mother (hugging or any physical contact for at least 3 continuous seconds) and attempts to engage a mother in play with the toys (offering a toy to her, playing with a toy in her lap) provided a measure of the activities directed toward the adults. Solitary play (all contacts with toys that lasted at least 3 seconds and did not involve either the peer or the mothers or qualify as same play) provided a contrast for social play.

A second observer simultaneously and independently recorded the behavior of 27 of the 30 pairs. Percentage of agreement, calculated by dividing the smaller of the two observers' measures by the larger and multiplying by 100, was obtained for each of the pairs on the measures subjected to analyses of variance. Median percentage agreement was above 90% for all measures except that of distant social response, and the lower agreement for this measure ($Mdn = 78\%$) may be attributed to the relative infrequency of the behavior and the slightly

TABLE 2
Behaviors Related to the Presence of Activity of the Peer

CATEGORY	DEFINITION
Watch	Continuous visual regard of the peer or his activities for at least 3 seconds.
Distant social response	One or more of the following six behaviors occurs.
Vocalize	A vocal sound or series of sounds, that may or may not be distinguishable as words, emitted while watching the peer.
Smile	Pleasant facial expression distinguished by a curved mouth with corners upturned, while watching the peer.
Laugh	An explosive sound of joy or amusement, while watching the peer.
Fuss	A fretting, whining, complaining sound emitted while watching the peer.
Cry	Loud continuous wailing while watching the peer.
Gesture	Wave at a peer as in greeting or departure; clap hands while watching the peer.
Physical contact	Touch and/or strike occurs.
Touch	Placing a hand upon the peer in a nonforceful manner, including patting, hugging, rubbing.
Strike	Forceful physical contact with the peer by either hand or foot, including hitting, pushing, or kicking.
Same play materials	Contact of the same toy as the peer or its duplicate for at least 3 continuous seconds without any direct involvement in the activities of the peer.
Direct involvement in peers' play	One or more of the following eight behaviors occurs.
Imitate	Duplication of the peer's activity, preceded by visual regard of the peer's activities. The peer's activity usually involves a toy or some other aspect of the inanimate environment, but it might consist of a distinctive motor response such as jumping.
Show a toy	Hold out a toy toward the peer, but out of his reach, while looking and/or vocalizing to the peer.
Offer a toy	Hold out a toy toward the peer within his reaching distance, while looking and/or vocalizing to the peer.
Accept a toy	Take a toy offered by the peer.
Take over a toy	Contact a toy released by the peer not more than 3 seconds previously.
Take a toy	Take an unoffered toy from the possession of the peer without a struggle.
Struggle over a toy	Both children attempt to gain sole possession of the same toy, including pulling, pushing, whining, etc.
Coordinate play	Act together with the peer to perform a common task, such as building a tower of blocks; or each child repeatedly takes turns performing an activity with attention to the other's activity, as when one child builds a tower of blocks, stands back and laughs as the other kicks it down.

differing perspectives from which the observers viewed the child's face. For three quarters of the pairs, the observers either did not disagree or they disagreed upon only a single instance of a distant social response.

METHODS OF ANALYSIS   The measures for the two children of each pair were summed, and the pair was treated as the unit of replication in analyses of variance. The study was conducted and initially analyzed in two parts. Fourteen of the pairs (Cohort 1) were first observed and predictions of age changes developed from analyses of variance performed on these observations: then the remaining 16 pairs (Cohort 2) were observed to test the predictions. The absence of any reliable cohort effects or Cohort × Age interactions for two-way analyses of variance indicated that the second set of observations replicated the first.

The data presented and analyzed in the present report are those for the total sample of subjects; pooling of the subsamples avoided the complexities involved in two-factor multivariate analyses of variance with unequal Ns and increased the precision with which age comparisons could be made. To assess changes in behavior with age, one-factor multivariate analyses of variance (Cramer, Note 1; further described in Clyde, Cramer, & Sherin, Note 2) were performed on selected related measures, followed by univariate tests.

The data of individual subjects were used to explore the effects of sex, birth order, and amount of prior exposure to peers on selected peer-related behaviors

RESULTS

REACTIONS TO THE NOVEL PLAY SETTING   The subjects of all ages interacted with the toys and their peers, and they contacted their mothers little (see Figure 1). Interactions with the peer included any of the peer-related

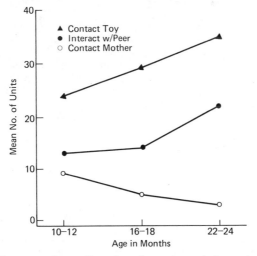

FIGURE 1.   *General reaction to the novel play setting.*

behaviors defined in Table 2 with the exception of the watch category. A multivariate analysis of variance on the three measures indicated a reliable change in behavior with age, $F (6, 50) = 3.42, p < .01$. Both the frequency of interactions with the peer and contact with the toy increased reliably with age, $F (2, 27) = 5.90, p < .01; F (2, 27) = 8.38, p < .001$; in contrast, contact with the mother decreased, $F (2, 27) = 7.73, p < .01$.

Fussing and crying occurred infrequently, during an average of only one of the 40 periods at each age; and at each age, smiling or laughing occurred more frequently ($M = 2.6, 4.7$, and 5.1 periods for the 10–12-, 16–18-, and 22–24-month groups, respectively). Some fussing or crying occurred in 14 pairs; smiling or laughing, in 22 pairs.

NATURE OF THE INTERACTIONS WITH THE PEER   The subjects attended to the peer (i.e., one or more peer-related behaviors occurred) in over 60% of the observations at each age. Table 3 summarizes the results for

TABLE 3

Frequency of Peer-Related Activities

	M for Each Age Group			Range for Each Age Group			
BEHAVIOR	10–12 Months	16–18 Months	22–24 Months	10–12 Months	16–18 Months	22–24 Months	F
Watch	18.3	19.2	15.9	12–26	12–30	7–23	< 1
Distant social response	3.5	3.9	5.2	1–9	0–11	0–14	< 1
Vocalize	1.7	1.5	3.1	0–6	0–5	0–12	
Smile	1.8	2.8	1.9	0–4	0–11	0–12	
Laugh	.0	.3	1.2	—	0–2	0–12	
Fuss	.0	.0	.1	—	—	0–1	
Cry	.0	.0	.0	—	—	—	
Gesture	.0	.1	.0	—	0–1	—	
Physical contact	2.0	.8	1.1	0–7	0–4	0–5	1.14
Touch	2.0	.5	.6	0–7	0–2	0–3	
Strike	.1	.3	.5	0–1	0–3	0–2	
Same play material	6.5	6.8	14.1	0–17	1–15	1–28	4.77*
Direct involvement in play	2.6	4.4	9.9	0–7	0–9	3–20	8.42**
Imitate	.9	1.3	2.0	0–4	0–4	0–8	
Show a toy	.2	.0	.3	0–1	—	0–2	
Offer a toy	.7	.8	.8	0–3	0–4	0–5	
Accept a toy	.3	.5	.2	0–1	0–3	0–1	
Take a toy	.1	.1	.6	0–1	0–1	0–3	
Take over a toy	.4	1.0	.8	0–1	0–6	0–5	
Struggle	.4	.8	3.2	0–2	0–3	0–13	
Coordinate	.0	.0	2.5	—	—	0–8	

* $p < .02$.
** $p < .001$.

each peer-related behavior. A multivariate analysis of variance of the five main categories of peer-related behaviors showed a reliable change with age, F (10, 46) = 2.06, p < .05. At all ages a prominent activity was watching the peer. Distant social responses were more frequent at each age than physical contact, but neither changed reliably with age. Vocalizing and smiling were the most frequent of the distant social responses; touching, the most frequent form of contact, especially at the youngest age. The behaviors related to the peer that changed with age were those that involved the play materials. The frequency of both contact with the same play material and direct involvement in the peer's play increased reliably, F (2, 27) = 4.77, p < .02; F (2, 27) = 8.42, p < .001, respectively.

Contact with the same play material was not simply the result of children playing with a single preferred toy. Analyses of the play material involved, available for the latter 15 pairs of subjects, showed that the pulltoys were involved for 9 pairs, the blocks for 11 pairs, the truck for 9 pairs, and other objects in the room for 3 pairs. Further, all except 2 pairs played with more than one toy in a synchronous manner; 4 played with all three toys synchronously.

Of the behaviors composing direct involvement in the peer's play, four showed orderly increases in frequency with age—imitation of the peer's activity, taking a toy from the peer, struggling over a toy, and coordinating activities with the toys. Five of the behaviors composing direct involvement in the peer's play— offering a toy, accepting a toy, taking a toy, taking over a toy, and struggling over a toy—concern the exchange or attempted exchange of play material between the two children. These exchange activities considered together occurred during an average of 1.9, 3.2, and 5.6 of the 40 intervals at the three ages and thus accounted for the greatest proportion of the activities composing direct involvement in play. Imitation by the focus child was the next most frequent activity across the ages, followed by coordinated play. Note, however, that imitation was recorded only when the focus child imitated the peer and not when the peer imitated him; the best estimate, then, of the frequency of imitation by either child is twice the frequencies tabulated, or 1.8, 2.6, and 4.0 periods at the increasing ages. Taking a toy and struggling—negative social responses according to Maudry and Nekula (1939)—together accounted for far less than half of the direct involvement in the peer's play at all ages.

Most of the peer-related behaviors were divided for purposes of comparison into Maudry and Nekula's (1939) positive and negative social reactions. Smile, laugh, vocalize, gesture, touch, show a toy, imitate, offer a toy, accept a toy, and coordinate toy activities comprise the positive reactions. Watching is excluded here, although included by Maudry and Nekula, since its high frequency at all ages would obscure comparison of the remaining behaviors. Fuss, cry, strike, take a toy, take over a toy, and struggle comprise the negative reactions. The ratio, in mean frequency, of the so-called negative reactions to positive reactions was 1.0 to 7.6, 2.2 to 7.8, and 5.2 to 12.6 for the 10– 12-, 16–18-, and 22–24-month groups, respectively. At all ages, then, positive responses far outweighed negative ones, even when watching the peer was disregarded; and both positive and negative responses increased with age.

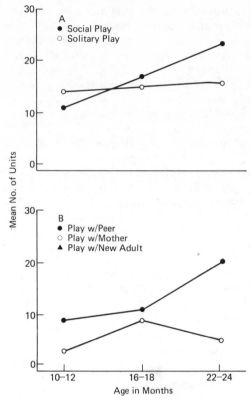

The development of social play. (In social play, the child involves others—peer mother, or new adult—in his activities with nonsocial objects.)

GROWTH OF SOCIAL PLAY　Figure 2 contrasts the subjects' social play with solitary play. Social play includes the prior categories of same play material and direct involvement in play with the peer, as well as play with the mothers. A multivariate analysis of variance of solitary play and social play showed a reliable change in behavior with age. F (4, 52) = 3.78, $p < .01$. Solitary play occurred in slightly more than a third of the periods at all ages; social play, in contrast, increased reliably with age, F (2, 27) = 5.42, $p < .01$, until by 2 years it occurred in 60% of the periods. The increase in social play resulted from the reliable increase in play with the peer (see Figure 2B), $F(2, 27) = 10.86$, $p < .001$. Play with the mother reached a peak at 16 to 18 months. F (2,27) = 3.28, $p = .05$; play with the new adult, that is, the other mother, was rare. By 2 years of age, then, most of the children's activities, with toys also involved a person, and in this novel play setting, that person was more often the peer than the mother.

EFFECTS OF SEX, SIBLINGS, PRIOR EXPOSURE TO PEERS　Sixteen of the 30 pairs were composed of a male and female subject, 6 each in the 22–24- and 10–12-month groups and 4 in the 16–18-month group. In these pairs the effects of sex were examined upon 4 categories of peer-related behavior—watch, distant social response, physical contact, and direct involvement in play. A multivariate analysis of variance with sex as a repeated measures factor and age as an independent groups factor yielded no reliable effects of sex; the F values for univariate tests of the effect of sex were all less than 1.0.

The effects of siblings in the family and the amount of prior exposure to peers outside the family were explored by inspecting the data for pairs showing a contrast in these variables. No suggestive differences were found. Suitable pairs were too few and too irregularly distributed by age group to warrant statistical tests.

DISCUSSION

The results showed that during the second year of life, children in a novel play setting turned less to their mothers and more and more to inanimate objects and their peers. Further, the children increasingly integrated their activities with toys and peers until by 2 years of age, social play predominated. They touched the same objects as their peers, imitated their actions, exchanged toys, and coordinated their play to perform a common task or elaborate a social game.

The current study leads to conclusions about the developmental course of peer interactions quite different from those of Maudry and Nekula (1939). At 10 to 12 months, ages at which Maudry and Nekula characterize infants as treating each other as an obstacle to play material, the children of the present study smiled and vocalized to each other, offered and accepted toys, and imitated each other; only infrequently did they struggle over toys or fuss. Further, rather than episodic, qualitative changes in reactions to peers, the present results suggest an orderly increase in the variety and frequency of social interactions between children—both the so-called negative and positive interactions. Of the numerous differences in methodology that might account for the contrasting pictures of social development, the most salient difference appears to be Maudry and Nekula's prompting of the children into interaction and the accompanying restriction of toy materials and alternative activities. The contrasting conclusions emphasize the need for studying situational and experiential determinants of peer interactions, as has been done for mother–infant interaction. An infant of 10 months faced with a mother holding an attractive object might well pull at that object, directing all attention to obtaining it, but we would hardly conclude that infants of this age characteristically treat their mothers as an obstacle to play materials!

The integration of activities with toys and people during the second year of life highlights a central aspect of development. The responses we call social do not develop in a context devoid of inanimate objects; similarly those responses toward inanimate objects that we label exploration or play occur often in a social context. The mother, or attachment object, provides the setting for the infant's exploration of his inanimate world (e.g., Ainsworth & Wittig, 1969; Rheingold, 1969). Social objects, adults or children, also alter the stimulation that toys offer; they put toys in motion, make them do new things, and place them with other objects in new combinations. A toy on the ground does not equal a toy in the hand of a peer. On the other hand, nonsocial objects are vehicles for many forms of social interaction—for giving and taking, imitating, cooperating, or instructing. Smiling and vocalizing to persons or contacting them may be prominent early social behaviors, but other forms of social interaction require the child's integration of activites with things and people.

Questions remain about the determinants and function of the various forms of early interaction between peers. Are watching a peer's activities, looking, smiling, and vocalizing at him, and offering him toys functionally similar to other behaviors we label exploratory? Is the similarity perceived in matching one's activities to another's reinforcing? Do toy exchanges function to promote imitation and same play? Questions such as these await detailed study of the context in which the peer-related behaviors occur. Still, the present results establish several forms of peer interaction whose origins should be sought in infancy rather than the preschool years, and the behavioral descriptions of these interactions provide the starting point for studies of origins and function.

The children of all ages behaved toward one another not as children do with inanimate objects, but rather more as they do with familiar adults. The physical contact and manipulation characteristic of early activity with toys were minimal with the peer; rather the smiles, vocalizations, and offers of toys to the peer correspond to behaviors seen with mothers (e.g., Rheingold, 1973). A comparison, however, between play with the mother and direct play with the peer (the most nearly comparable categories of play) yields suggestive differences in the developmental course of these activities. At 10 to 12 months both were infrequent; by 16 to 18 months both were more frequent, but play with the mother exceeded that with the peer, and by 22 to 24 months, play with the mother had declined in frequency, while direct play with the peer increased markedly. Both the correspondence in forms of behavior toward the mother and the peer and the initial greater frequency of these behaviors toward the mother suggest that young children generalize to peers' responses developed through interaction with familiar adults.

By 2 years of age, however, the children of the present study interacted more with the peer than with their mothers. The restrictive instructions to the mother and the short duration of the play period may have contributed to this preference, but the fact remains that with increasing age primate young turn progressively more to their peers in play (e.g., Harlow, 1969; Heathers, 1955). The question of what peers offer in contrast to familiar adults is an important one for the fuller understanding of early social behavior. Peers and adults seem to differ in their persistence and affective involvement in children's play and the contrast shifts during the child's development. Mothers and fathers initially invest great persistence, affect, and imagination in attempts to engage their young infants in play, but later in development peers often seem more ready than parents to follow through on a child's playful overtures. Still, peers have two other characteristics that warrant study: Their actions and reactions may be more novel than those of parents, and the activities of peers may be more easily duplicated than those of adults, who only with difficulty behave as a child.

The present study, then, has demonstrated that home-reared children during the second year of life freely engage in a variety of social interactions with unfamiliar peers, interactions that resemble those with familiar adults more than those with inanimate objects. They smile, laugh, vocalize and gesture to one another, show and offer toys, imitate each other, struggle, and engage in reciprocal play. Thus, interactions with peers and with familiar adults appear closely intertwined in development. Yet as more and more of the children's play involved people, the social partner was more often the peer than the mother. This choice of the peer makes still more tenable the speculation that peers—even infant peers—make their own contribution to early human sociability.

Reference Notes

1. CRAMER, E. M. *Revised MANOVA program.* Unpublished manuscript, University of North Carolina at Chapel Hill, Psychometric Laboratory, 1967.
2. CLYDE, D. J., CRAMER, E. M., & Sherin, R. J. *Multivariate statistical programs.* Unpublished manuscript, University of Miami, Biometric Laboratory, Coral Gables, Fla., 1966.

References

AINSWORTH, M. D. S., & WITTIG, B. A. Attachment and exploratory behaviour of one-year-olds in a strange situation. In B. M. Foss (Ed.), *Determinants of infant behaviour IV.* London: Methuen, 1969.

BRIDGES, K. M. B. A study of social development in early infancy. *Child Development,* 1933, **4**, 36–49.

BÜHLER, C. *The first year of life.* New York: John Day, 1930.

HARLOW, H. F. Age-mate or peer affectional system. In D. S. Lehrman, R. A. Hinde, & E. Shaw (Eds.), *Advances in the study of behavior* (Vol. 2). New York: Academic Press, 1969.

HEATHERS, G. Emotional dependence and independence in nursery school play. *Journal of Genetic Psychology,* 1955, **87**, 37–57.

HINDE, R. A. Development of social behavior. In A. M. Schrier & F. Stollnitz (eds.), *Behavior of nonhuman primates: Modern research trends* (Vol. 3). New York: Academic Press, 1971.

MAUDRY, M., & NEKULA, M. Social relations between children of the same age during the first two years of life. *Journal of Genetic Psychology,* 1939, **54**, 193–215.

RHEINGOLD, H. L. The effect of a strange environment on the behaviour of infants. In B. M. Foss (Ed.), *Determinants of infant behaviour IV.* London, Methuen, 1969.

RHEINGOLD, H. L. Independent behavior of the human infant. In *Minnesota Symposia on Child Psychology* (Vol. 7). Minneapolis: University of Minnesota Press, 1973.

RHEINGOLD, H. L., & ECKERMAN, C. O. Fear of the stranger: A critical examination. In H. W. Reese (Ed.), *Advances in child development and behavior* (Vol. 8). New York: Academic Press, 1973.

SCHAFFER, H. R. *The growth of sociability.* Harmondsworth, England: Penguin, 1971.

VINCZE, M. The social contacts of infants and young children reared together. *Early Child Development and Care,* 1971, **1**, 99–109.

The Nature of Kibbutz Child Care

Jeanette G. Stone

Those who view the kibbutz from the outside often perceive its child care as the the mother giving her children over to a sort of institution. Today, kibbutz children are brought up jointly by their parents and by professional caregivers called *metaplot* (metapelet, in the singular). For the young infant, the mother is primary: a full-time mother. Later, she remains the central figure while giving the child less time as she resumes her work by easy stages. The metapelet's job is to provide skillful, affectionate and continuing care to children in the setting of the Children's House. She does not function as a substitute mother; rather she supplements the working parent. In the earlier, more austere days, the metapelet may well have been more dominant.

From earliest infancy through the preschool years, kibbutz children spend the greater part of their days in Children's Houses where they eat, bathe, nap, and where they are educated within the framework of informal learning and play. They also sleep at night in the Children's House, cared for by people on night-watch duty. Somtimes parents take turns sleeping in the Children's Houses. (In some ten percent of the kibbutzim, as in Kibbutz Gesher HaZiv, shown in the film *Day Care for a Kibbutz Toddler*, children sleep in their parents' apartments.)

In all kibbutzim, children spend a long "Children's Hour" with their parents in the family living quarters each day from about 4.00 P.M. on into early evening. Because the working day begins and ends early, and because meals, shopping, and laundry are taken care of by communal services, both parents are free to devote themselves to their children every afternoon—playing with them, swimming or hiking or gardening with them, reading to them, having tea together, feeding them a light supper. Israel works a six-day week. On the Sabbath, kibbutz children spend most of the day with their families.

The younger children are taken back to the Children's House and put to bed (by the parents in some kibbutzim and by metaplot in others) before the parents go to supper in the kibbutz dining hall. Older children may eat supper with their parents; these evening arrangements vary from family to family as well as from kibbutz to kibbutz.

There may be only one or two Children's Houses in a small kibbutz, with small separate age groupings under one roof. In a large settlement, there may be a whole cluster of Children's Houses. The infants and young children are grouped in small units of three to six individuals—each unit with its own metapelet and an assistant; older children are cared for in larger groupings.

Kibbutzim vary in the specific space arrangements and age groups in the Children's Houses. All have separate housing and different metaplot for each age level—babies, preschoolers, school-aged and older children. Some kibbutzim place infants and toddlers under one roof; for example, a House (as in Kibbutz

From *Study Guide for Three Films on Kibbutz Infancy*. New York: Institute for Child Mental Health, 1974. Reprinted by permission.

Ma'agan Mikhail in the film *Rearing Kibbutz Babies*) might have several small babies in one wing, with four or five toddlers in an adjacent wing, each wing with its own metapelet. These two wings usually share a common kitchen, bathroom, and storage area. In another kibbutz (like Kibbutz Dahlia in the film *Infant Development in the Kibbutz*) there would be a shift to a new House for toddlers.

When a newborn baby is brought from the hospital to the kibbutz Infant House, the mother is freed from her job, usually for about six weeks, to devote full time to her baby—to feed and bathe and care for the baby with no other responsibilities. She then resumes work, but on a part-time basis, gradually lengthened.

The mother continues her care for many of the baby's waking hours, all through the first six months, and their mutual attachment becomes strong. During the second six months of the baby's life, the mother gradually adds time to her working day until the end of the first year; by then she will have resumed full-time work and the metapelet will have assumed more care of the infant. (For women full-time work is 7 hours a day; for men it is from 8 to $8\frac{1}{2}$ hours.)

The mother's schedule will be set up, during all of her children's early years and beyond, so that she can take time off every day to visit her children in their Houses. The contemporary kibbutz work schedule is based in part on consideration of children's need for close, continuous contact with their parents.

One often sees fathers (or other relatives) walking or biking through the kibbutz on an errand, stopping to see their children in the Children's Houses. A mother drops in to have a cup of coffee or a bite of fruit and to play with her child during an unscheduled break—this in addition to her scheduled breaks for nursing or visiting. Even after children reach school age, parents continue to visit them during the day.

In the same spirit of joint upbringing, metaplot continue the nurturing of kibbutz children. When the children begin formal schooling—which takes place within the Children's Houses for kindergarten and the first years of elementary education—they are taught by classroom teachers; however, the metaplot assigned to the school-aged children continue to function as general caregivers, and they assist the teachers during school hours, if need be. Before and after classes, the metaplot keep the children clean and fed and supervise their work and play.

Further information on kibbutz care of young children will be found in the references supplied. Very useful—and similar in outlook to our films—are the chapters by Frieda Katz and Gideon Lewin (Early Childhood Education) and Menachem Gerson (Oranim Pedagogical Center of the Kibbutzim) in the newly published volume by A. I. Rabin and Bertha Hazan.

IMPLICATIONS FOR CHILD CARE OUTSIDE THE KIBBUTZ

The films suggest that the kibbutzim have worked out a system of infant and child care in which children thrive with multiple caretakers without, apparently, losing primary connections to their own mothers and their own families. This should not astonish us if we think of such well-established parallel arrangements as the grandmother, or the regular baby-sitter who may care for a child for some hours each day, or the disappearing phenomenon of the amah, ayah, or nanny. So far as we know, such arrangements produce no sundering of the parental relationship.

Since the metapelet may change from time to time when the child shifts to a new Baby House or because the metapelet becomes pregnant or changes jobs, and since substitutes act for her during her various times off, the child's relationship to the metapelet is inherently less fixed than to the mother. And something in the way the metapelet operates—perhaps the presence of other children in her group—keeps the relationship from being as intense as the parental one.

For kibbutz child care (unlike grandmother or sitter or nanny) is *group* care. But in comparing it to other forms of group care, it is important to keep in mind the lavish kibbutz provision for staffing. In Kibbutz Dahlia (*Infant Development in the Kibbutz*) the basic ratio of children to adults is three to one. In Kibbutz Ma'agan Mikhail (*Rearing Kibbutz Babies*) the ratio is four to one; and in Kibbutz Gesher HaZiv (*Day Care for a Kibbutz Toddler*) the ratio is five to one. Even these ratios understate the case, since in each kibbutz, part-time assistants are added at mealtimes, bathtimes, etc. Moreover, as the narration of *Day Care for a Kibbutz Toddler* suggests, the overall size of the group appears to be just as important as the actual ratio in establishing the peaceful and intimate atmosphere of the kibbutz Infant House. For a young child (or for the adult caretaker) maintaining contact with three or four other babies of the same age and with one or two adults at a time is far less of a strain than interacting with, say, fifteen other babies and four or five adults—though the sheer ratio would be the same.

In terms of unit size, therefore, the Infant House arrangement most closely resembles what the United States has termed "family day care." Unlike family day care, however, the metapelet, instead of being on her own all day long, has the built-in institutional supports of other metaplot nearby, of substitute help, of central kitchens and laundries—and of time off during the day to visit her own children or to talk with grownups on an adult level. There is no comparable coffee-break or baby-break in our family day care system. In larger day care settings, separating large groups of children into clusters of four to five within the large group should be feasible. Perhaps as much as anything else, this would make for psychologically manageable family-size, rather than institutional-size, groupings. Note that this recommendation is not made for preschool children but rather for infants and toddlers. The kibbutz, itself, combines the children into larger multiples of the original foursomes as the children grow older.

Many of our child care institutions are marked by difference in status between parents and caregivers, which sometimes causes strain. The metapelet-parent relationship strikes a remarkably even balance: The metapelet is (more or less) professionally trained but she is the mother's equal, neighbor, and permanent co-member in the collective. They are familiar with each other. This may be one reason that the kibbutz appears to function best in its small village format: larger size or urban settings produce anonymity and personal and social distance. The extent to which such social balance can be brought into our own child care facilities needs more exploration. It should be noted, by the way, that the upbringing and schooling of all the children in the kibbutz is supervised by a rotating, elected Education Committee: both mothers and metaplot may be among its members.

Such organizational characteristics of the kibbutz may be hard to transfer to other countries or other kinds of infant and child care. The kibbutz is, after all, a collective which can mobilize such resources as it chooses to assign to child care, and it can deploy its members to those tasks deemed important by the entire community. Truly comparable child care provisions elsewhere would surely be very expensive. At best, we can but try to adapt as many of its important features as possible. What seems most transferable is a *kind* of caring—the metapelet's characteristically warm interest in her charges, knowledgeable interchange, unhurried ministering, and the kind of inventive stimulation caught by our camera in the unrehearsed hours of filming. It may be worth calling the attention of those working directly with children or those who are training such workers to examples in specific sequences in each of the three films discussed in the following sections.

Chapter 5
An Overview of
Human Life
and Growth

STANLEY SUMMER

All of existence is continuous and related. A search for beginnings and causes of life reveals psychological, physiological, biological, biochemical, and physical structures built upon and of each other.

Every organism and its environment have dynamic, reciprocal relationships. Affecting each other and being affected by each other, neither can be understood without the other, nor can either be what it *is* without the other. The cool air under the tree does not exist without the tree, nor would the tree exist without air. An interesting interaction between plants and landscape can be seen in coastal areas where conservation projects are carried out. A beach that was washed away by a hurricane now stretches smoothly into the Atlantic Ocean, backed by sand dunes built by plants. The plants were dead Christmas trees stuck into the sand and then reinforced by living plants which, finding nutrients and moisture enough in the sand, sent down a network of tough roots, which held the sand in the dunes.

More remarkable even than the building of beaches is the interaction of the human baby with his environment, his family. A human baby grows into a human

265

child as he lives in a human family, calling forth maternal and paternal responses from two adults whose behavior could not be parental if he were not there.

Varieties of Interaction Between the Individual and His World

The story of child development begins with the interactions of a small package of DNA and ends with an adult human being living in a complex social network. Everyone has some beliefs and hypotheses as to how these many changes take place. Nobody has explained it all in a comprehensive theory, but many theorists have described and explained parts of it. A theory depends first of all on the point of view from which the observer looks at the human scene and consequently on the phenomena that he observes. Theories of growth and development usually have a biological flavor. Learning experiments may suggest the influence of physics. Research in social relationships often involves sociology and perhaps anthropology. This chapter deals with six types of interactions that represent different ways of looking at human phenomena. They are equilibration, growth and development, learning, maturation, evolutionary adaptation, and heredity.

Equilibration

The organism constantly regulates its life processes so as to maintain physical and mental states within certain limits.

HOMEOSTASIS

Homeostasis is a balance that the organism maintains within itself during the processes of living and as environmental influences affect its internal conditions. Since the balance is continually upset and re-created, through a complex of interactions, it can be called a *dynamic equilibrium*. Through activities that are mostly unconscious, the individual keeps his blood sugar at a definite level, his water content within a given range, his oxygen content just so. Breathing and heartbeat speed up or slow down from their average rates to restore disturbed balances. The mechanisms of homeostasis regulate sleeping and waking states, activity and rest. Pressures and depleted tissues may register consciously as felt needs, leading to such purposeful interactions with the environment as eating, drinking, and eliminating.

Looming large in the life of a newborn infant, the problems of homeostasis dwindle throughout infancy and childhood. By about 3 months of age, basic physiological processes are well controlled. At any time throughout the life span, however, when the balance is seriously threatened, when biological demands become crucial or urgent, the individual drops his higher-order activities, such as giving a lecture or playing tennis, in order to restore the balance within his body.

PSYCHOLOGICAL EQUILIBRIUM

The search for balance occurs in the mental realm as well as in the physical. Equilibration is the process of achieving a state of balance. Sooner or later, the state of equilibrium is upset and a new one must be created. Equilibration includes selecting stimuli from the world, seeking this or that kind, more or less, paying attention to some of them and using some in more complex mental operations. When you consider all the sounds, sights, tastes, and other perceptions available, it follows that a person could not possibly attend to all of them at once. The mother or principal caretaker protects the infant and young child from excessive stimulation, helping the child gradually to take over the functions of selecting and ignoring stimuli [65].

Equilibration is one of Piaget's principles of mental development [50, pp. 5–8]. Action can be provoked when equilibrium is upset by finding a new object, being asked a question, identifying a problem; in fact, by any new experience. Equilibrium is re-established by reaching a goal, answering a question, solving a problem, imitating, establishing an effective tie or any other resolution of the difference between the new factor or situation and the mental organization already existing. Equilibration results in the successive stages of intelligence that Piaget describes.

Equilibration, in Piaget's theory, includes two complementary processes through which the person proceeds to more complex levels of organization— *assimilation,* which is the taking in from the environment what the organism can deal with and *accommodation,* the changing of the organism to fit external circumstances. Just as the body can assimilate foods and not other substances, so the mind can take in certain aspects and events in the external world and not others. Existing structures or *schemas* incorporate experiences that fit them or that almost fit them.

A schema is a pattern of action and/or thought. A baby develops some schemas before he is born and has them for starting life as a newborn. With simple schemas, he interacts with his environment, working toward equilibration. He achieves equilibrium over and over again, by using the schemas available to him at the moment. For example, a baby has a furry toy kitten that he knows as *kitty.* When given a small furry puppy he calls it *kitty,* strokes it and pats it, assimilating the puppy to an existing schema. A new little horse on wheels requires accommodation, since it is too different to be assimilated into the schema for dealing with *kitty.* It looks different; it feels different; it is not good for stroking and patting, but something can be done with the wheels that cannot be done with *kitty.* A new pattern of action is required. The child accommodates by changing and organizing existing schemas to form a schema for dealing with *horsey.* Thus the child grows in his understanding of the world and his ability to deal with his experiences in meaningful ways. Assimilation conserves the structural systems that he has while accommodation effects changes through which he copes more adequately with his environment and behaves in increasingly complex ways.

When homeostasis presents no problems, such as hunger, thirst, or fatigue, a person looks for something to do, something interesting, a new experience. If equilibrium were completely satisfying in itself, then surely he would sit or lie quietly doing nothing. In looking for action, the child seems to be trying to upset his state of equilibrium, as though equilibration were fun! And so it is. Activity is intrinsic in living tissue, brain cells included. The nervous system demands input, just as the digestive system does. Curiosity, exploration, competence, and achievement motivation are all outgrowths of the human propensity for enjoying the process of equilibration. The first stage of the process, perception of a problem, an incongruity or discrepancy, involves tension and a feeling of incompleteness. Something is missing or something is wrong.

The baby pushes himself forward to grasp a toy that is out of reach. The 4-year-old makes a mailbox that is necessary for his game of postman. The first grader sounds out a new word. Each child reduces a feeling of tension as he creates a new equilibrium. The equilibration (achievement of new balance) makes him into a slightly different person from what he has been, a person who can move forward a bit, a person who has made his own mailbox and can therefore make other things, a person who can read another word. Thus, equilibration is a way of describing behavior development. New and more complex behavior occurs as it is demanded by the person's relationship with his surroundings.

When a person's schemas are adequate to deal with the situation in which he finds himself, he reacts automatically. For example, the response of a hungry breast-fed baby of 3 months would be quite automatic when offered his mother's breast. A 10-year-old would automatically answer the question "What is two times two?" When the schemas are not quite adequate to the situation, the child uses what he has, changing them slightly into actions which do solve the problem. For instance, the baby would change his behavior sufficiently to cope with a bottle and the 10-year-old with "$2x = 4$. What does x equal?" The change that takes place at the same time within the child is the development of a new behavior pattern or schema. A pleasant feeling of curiosity and satisfaction accompanies successful adjustments to demands for new behavior.

A person feels uneasy when he encounters a situation in which his resources are very inadequate. In order to provoke uneasiness, the problem must be somewhat similar to those that a person can solve, but not similar enough for him to succeed with. Such a problem for the baby mentioned might be a cup of milk. For the 10-year-old it might be an equation such as $5x - 49/x = 20x/5$. If the situation is so far removed from a person's past experience that his schemas for dealing with it are extremely inadequate, then he will have no reaction to it. He will not notice it. He will not select from the environment the stimuli that would pose the problem. The baby will not try to drink out of a carton full of cans of milk. The child won't attempt to solve:

$$5x + 6y = 145$$
$$12x - 3y = 21$$

Familiar objects in unfamiliar guise produce unpleasantness, uneasiness, or even fear. (Chimpanzees are afraid of the keeper in strange clothes, an anesthetized chimp, or a plaster cast of a chimp's head. Human babies are afraid of strangers.) In order to be frightened or to get the unpleasant feeling, the subject must first have residues of past experience with which to contrast the present experience. Thus does incongruity arise, with its accompanying unpleasant feeling tone. If the individual can cope with the situation successfully, he achieves equilibration and its accompanying pleasant feeling tone. Stimuli preferred and chosen are those that are slightly more complex than the state of equilibrium that the individual has already reached. Thus he moves on to a new state of equilibrium [51].

Growth and Development

The child's body becomes larger and more complex while his behavior increases in scope and complexity. If any distinction is made between the two terms, growth refers to size, and development to complexity. However, the two terms are often used interchangeably, and this is what we have done. The terms *growth* and *development* were borrowed from the physical field, but they are commonly understood in connection with mental and personality characteristics. One can say, "He has grown mentally," or "He has developed mentally." The statement means "He is now functioning on a more complex intellectual level." Or one can speak of growth of personality and development of attitudes. Listening in on second-grade and fifth-grade classrooms in the same school building will reveal differences in subject matter interests and in mode of thinking.

Growth or development can be shown to have taken place either by comparing younger and older individuals at the same moment of time or by comparing the same individuals at two different points of time. When the measures of some characteristic of a number of individuals are averaged by age groups, the averages of the successive age groups show what growth has taken place. If each individual is measured only once, that is, if there are different people at each age, the study is *cross-sectional*. If the same individuals are measured at each successive age, the study is *longitudinal*. If some individuals do not remain available for continued study and new ones are added, the study is called *mixed longitudinal*. In a cross-sectional study, growth status at each age is investigated, and inferences regarding growth are drawn from *differences* between any groups. *Change* in status from age to age can be inferred only if the individuals at the two ages can be assumed to be comparable in all relevant ways. In a longitudinal study both growth status at each age and change in status from age to age can be investigated more precisely, because the same individuals are involved and actual growth patterns are established for individuals.

PRINCIPLES OF GROWTH

There are a number of generalizations about growth that are more apparent with respect to physical growth but that, as far as research can show, are also true for psychological growth. We elaborate on nine such statements about growth at this point, some of them with subheadings.

Variation of Rates. Rates of growth vary from one individual to another, and they vary within one individual. An organism grows at varying rates, from one time to another. The organs and systems grow at varying rates and at different times. There is a sex difference in rates and terminals. Various group differences can be shown. It is no wonder that comparisons of growth require facts obtained by highly controlled methods.

An organism and its parts grow at rates that are different at different times. The body as a whole, as measured by height and weight, shows a pattern of velocity that is fast in infancy, moderate in the preschool period, slow during the school years, and fast in the beginning of adolescence. Figure 5-1 illustrates growth

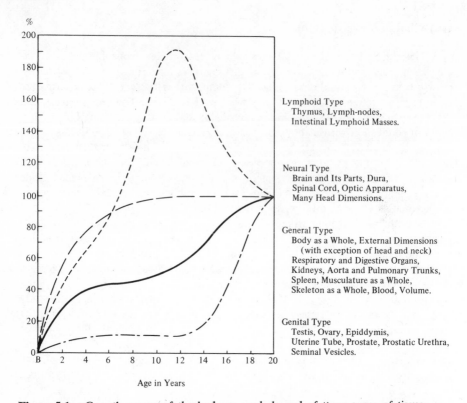

Lymphoid Type
Thymus, Lymph-nodes,
Intestinal Lymphoid Masses.

Neural Type
Brain and Its Parts, Dura,
Spinal Cord, Optic Apparatus,
Many Head Dimensions.

General Type
Body as a Whole, External Dimensions
(with exception of head and neck)
Respiratory and Digestive Organs,
Kidneys, Aorta and Pulmonary Trunks,
Spleen, Musculature as a Whole,
Skeleton as a Whole, Blood, Volume.

Genital Type
Testis, Ovary, Epiddymis,
Uterine Tube, Prostate, Prostatic Urethra,
Seminal Vesicles.

Age in Years

Figure 5-1. Growth curves of the body as a whole and of three types of tissue. Values at each age are computed as percentages of values for total growth.

Source: Reproduced by permission from J. A. Harris, C. M. Jackson, D. G. Paterson, and R. E. Scammon. *The measurement of man.* Minneapolis: University of Minnesota Press, 1930.

of four types of tissue, expressed at each age as percentages of the values for total growth. The general type of growth, which represents not only height and weight but muscles, skeleton, and most of the internal organs, is illustrated by a sigmoid curve, an elongated S. The brain and related tissues grow in a different pattern of velocity, very fast during the first 2 years, moderately until about 6, and very little after that. The growth curve for genital tissue is almost the reverse of that of neural tissue. The genital system grows very little during infancy and childhood and very fast in adolescence. The fourth curve in Figure 5-1 represents the lymph system which grows rapidly throughout infancy and childhood, reaches a peak just before puberty, and then decreases in size throughout adolescence.

Rates of growth vary from one individual to another. Some children are fast growers, some moderate, and some slow in regard to the number of years taken to reach maturity. Periods of fast and slow growth vary as to when they occur and for how long. One child begins the pubescent growth spurt earlier or later than another, grows faster or slower during the spurt, and finishes sooner or later.

There are sex differences in rates. Early in fetal life, girls show evidence of maturing faster than boys, especially in skeletal development. At birth, girls are four weeks ahead of boys skeletally. Boys' skeletal development is about 80 per cent of that of girls' from birth to maturity [59, p. 43]. Girls are ahead of boys in dentition, as measured by eruption of permanent teeth. Although sex differences in height and weight before the preadolescent growth spurt are very slight, favoring boys, sexual maturity and its antecedent growth spurt occur in girls about two years before they do in boys. Therefore, there is a period of about two years when girls are taller and heavier than boys. At all ages, girls are more mature physiologically than boys.

Individual Differences in Terminals. It is obvious, yet it is essential in understanding growth, to recognize that for different people maturity comes at different points. You have only to walk down the street to observe that some people grow until they are over six feet tall, others stop at five feet, and most people stop in between. Measurable mental growth stops at different times for different individuals too. The average girl reaches height and weight terminals before the average boy. Little is known about mental growth terminals.

Dynamic Interrelations in Growth. It would be surprising if different measures of growth were not related to each other. A tremendous number of studies have probed into the question of interrelationships of growth-controlling and regulating mechanisms.

Correlations between measures of growth can be between measures in the same field (physical–physical, mental–mental, and so on), or in different fields (physical–mental, mental–emotional). Skeletal development, assessed by X rays of the wrist, is at present the best indicator of physiological maturity, although if body proportions could be quantified and scaled in some manageable way, this might prove even more useful. Fat thickness in childhood is also a measure of general physiological maturity [24]. Sexual maturity and eventual height can be predicted with good accuracy from measurements of skeletal maturity. A general factor of bodily maturity operating throughout the growth period influences the child's growth as a whole, including his skeleton, size, physiological reactions, and possibly intelligence. Influencing factors of more limited scope operate independently of the general factor and of each other. One of these limited factors controls baby teeth, another permanent teeth, another the ossification centers in the skeleton, and probably several others regulate brain growth. This is why various measures of physical growth have low positive correlations with each other. If there were only one controlling factor, then the different measures would presumably all correlate highly or even perfectly with one another [59].

Studies of the relation between physical and mental growth show a small but consistent positive correlation, bearing out the hypothesis of a general factor that influences all growth processes. This relationship has been documented by a variety of studies [1, 9, 11, 33, 56, 57]. A study of children at the extremes of distributions of mental traits showed gifted boys to be significantly ahead of retarded boys in measures of physical growth [33]. A small positive correlation between mental ability and size is also found in adults [60]. As an example of the relationships between growth and personality, there is evidence that early maturers feel more adequate and more comfortable about themselves than do late maturers [32, 45].

Optimal Tendency. An organism behaves as though it were seeking to reach its maximum potential for development in both structure and function. Even though growth is interrupted, such as in periods of inadequate food supply, the child (or organism) makes up for the lean period as soon as more and better food is available, returning to his characteristic pattern of growth. Only if the deprivation is severe, or if it occurs throughout a critical period, will he show permanent effects from it. During the deprivation period, the organism adapts by slowing growth and cutting down on the use of energy.

All sorts of adaptive arrangements are worked out when there are interferences with the normal course of development, as though the child is determined to reach his best potential by another route when one is blocked. The child with poor eyesight seeks extra information from his other senses. Babies with a tendency toward rickets drink cod liver oil freely if permitted to, selecting their own diets from a wide variety of simple foods [14]. For white children in the northern United States, the characteristics of the home were found to be most important in determining how well the child did at school, but for southern black children the characteristics of the school were more important than those of the home. "It is as if the child drew sustenance from wherever it was available. When the home had more intellectual stimulation to offer, it became more determining; but when the school could provide more stimulation than the home, then the school became the more influential factor." [10, p. 106].

Gesell has stated the principle of optimal tendency as follows. "Every breach in the normal complex of growth is filled through regenerative, substantive, or compensatory growth of some kind. . . . Insurance reserves are drawn upon whenever the organism is threatened. . . . Herein lies the urgency, the almost irrepressible quality of growth" [26, p. 165]. This principle has been recognized as working in physical realms as well as organic, where there seems to be a self-stabilizing or target-seeking property of certain systems [62].

Differentiation and Integration. From large global patterns of behavior, smaller, more specific patterns emerge. Later the small, specific patterns can be combined into new, complicated, larger patterns. For example, a photographic study of human beginnings shows an 11½ weeks' fetus reacting to being stroked on the right cheek [26, p. 25]. The fetus contracted the muscles of its neck, trunk, and shoulder, causing its whole body to bend away from the stimulus and the arms and hands to move backward. When a newborn infant is stroked on the cheek he turns toward the stimulus, pursing his lips and opening his mouth when his lips touch something. Thus, he shows a new, specialized response pattern that involves a small part of his body instead of the whole. As he grows older, the rooting response changes and becomes integrated with other behavior patterns. Instead of turning toward food when he is touched near the mouth, he turns toward the breast or bottle when he sees it. His hands come into play in guiding food toward his mouth. Later he uses a knife and fork. He is integrating behavior patterns of eyes and hands with the rooting pattern, forming a smoothly functioning whole.

Bower analyzes the process of reaching and grasping in terms of differentiation and integration. The newborn baby will reach for a seen object, opening the hand before contact and closing it on contact, but too quickly for hand closure to have been released by the contact. The reaching and grasping is a unitary act. Reaching rarely occurs after 4 weeks, but reappears at around 20 weeks, in a different form. The infant can now reach without grasping and can also combine them. Reaching and grasping are differentiated. Either reaching or grasping can be corrected during the act instead of having to be corrected by starting again. Reaching and grasping are integrated. They are separate but combinable [7, pp. 150–166].

Examples can also be taken from purely intellectual fields, such as mathematics. There is a stage of maturity at the end of infancy when a child knows *one*, *two* and *a-lot-of*. At 5, he has differentiated *three* and *four* out of *a-lot-of*. By 6, numbers up to ten have true meaning. Using these differentiated concepts, the child next combines them in addition and subtraction to form new and more complicated concepts. Conceptual differentiation and integration are at work as the student moves up through algebra and geometry into higher mathematics. There remains an undifferentiated sphere where each person stops in his progress` in mathematics.

Developmental Direction. Certain sequences of development take place in certain directions, in reference to the body. The motor sequence takes two such directions, *cephalocaudal* (head to tail) and *proximodistal* (midline to outer extremities). Like all animals, the child grows a relatively large, complex head region early in life, whereas the tail region or posterior is small and simple. As he becomes older, the region next to the head grows more, and finally, the end region grows. Coordination follows the same direction, the muscles of the eyes coming under control first, then the neck muscles, then arms, chest, and back, and finally the legs. The motor sequence illustrates the proximodistal direction by the fact that the earliest controlled arm movements, as in reaching, are large movements, controlled mostly by shoulder muscles. Later the elbow is brought into play in reaching, then the wrist, and then the fingers.

Normative Sequence. The sequence of motor development has long been noticed and understood as one of the ways of nature. "A child must creepe ere he walke."

As the structures of the body mature in their various sequences, they function in characteristic ways, provided that the environment permits appropriate interaction. The resulting behavior patterns appear in an orderly sequence. Sequences have been described for locomotion, use of hands, language, problem solving, social behavior, and other kinds of behavior [12, 27, 28]. During the decade of the 1930s, the bulk of research in child development was normative, delineating sequences of development and designating average ages for the patterns observed. The classic studies, exemplified by Gesell's work, viewed normative sequences as an unfolding. Although the role of the environment was implicit in these early writings, the focus was on regulation from innate forces. Today interaction between organism and environment is emphasized as basic to development. The change in viewpoint has come about to some extent because of the broadening of areas of child study to include a variety of cultures, at home and abroad. Although child development continues to take place in orderly sequences, exceptions can be found [16]. Hence normative sequences cannot be considered as universal, but must be understood as occurring in particular kinds of environments.

Epigenesis. Growth takes place upon the foundation that is already there. New parts arise out of and upon the old. Although the organism becomes something new as it grows, it still has continuity with the past and hence shows certain consistencies over time. Through interactions with the environment, the organism continues to restructure itself throughout life, being at each moment the product of the interaction that took place in the previous moment between organism and environment. A toddler's body results from interactions of a baby's body with food, water, and air. The motor pattern of walking is derived and elaborated from creeping and standing. Writing is built from scribbling.

Critical Periods. There are certain limited times during the growth period of any organism when it will interact with a particular environment in a specific way. The result of interactions during critical periods can be especially beneficial or harmful. The prenatal period includes specific critical periods for physical growth. The first three months are critical for the development of eyes, ears, and brain, as shown by defects in children whose mothers had rubella during the first three months of pregnancy. Apparently those organs are most vulnerable to the virus of rubella when they are in their periods of rapid growth.

Experiments on vision with human and animal infants reveal critical ages for the development of visual responses, times when the infant will either show the response without experience or will learn it readily [21]. If the visual stimulus is not given at the critical age (as when baby monkeys are reared in darkness), the animal later learns the response with difficulty, or not at all.

Psychological development also shows critical periods in the sense that certain behavior patterns are acquired most readily at certain times of life. Critical periods in personality development include the period of primary socialization, when the infant makes his first social attachments [55] and develops basic trust [18]. A warm relationship with a mother figure is thought to be essential among the experiences that contribute to a sense of trust [8]. This type of critical period is probably not so final and irreversible as is a critical period for the development of an organ in the embryo. If the term *critical period* is applied to the learning of skills such as swimming and reading, then it should be understood that it signifies the most *opportune* time for learning and not the only one [43].

STAGE THEORIES OF DEVELOPMENT

The last three principles of growth are incorporated in theories of child development that present growth occurring in stages. Each stage is created through *epigenesis,* behavior patterns being organized and reorganized or transformed in an orderly sequence. Thus, past, present, and future development are related and can be understood as an ongoing process. Small pieces of behavior can be interpreted in terms of the stage when they occur instead of being invested with one meaning. For example, crying at 1 month of age was seen to be an active attempt to overcome interference with sucking, whereas crying at 1 year of age was found to be a passive mode of response to environmental frustration [36]. Stage theories encourage research that establishes ways of predicting future development [31].

This book is organized in stages of development, leaning heavily on two stage theories: Erikson's theory of personality growth, and Piaget's theory of the growth of intelligence. The ages corresponding with the various stages are only approximations or rough landmarks. Although it is useful to be able to anchor stage concepts to some sort of chronology, it is important to realize that stages are only age-related and not age-determined. The growth principle, *variation of rates,* applies here.

Erikson's Stages. Erikson's theory might be called epigenetic in a double sense. Not only does it portray epigenetic stages but it was built upon Freud's theory and yet is a new organization and a unique creation. Freud proposed psychosexual stages of development, each of which used a certain zone of the body for gratification of the *id* (the unconscious source of motives, strivings, desires, and energy). The *ego,* which mediates between the demands of the id, the outside world, and the superego, "represents what may be called reason and common sense, in contrast to the id, which contains the passions" [23, p. 15]. The *superego* or ego ideal corresponds roughly to *conscience.* Freud's psychosexual stages are *oral,* when the mouth is the main zone of satisfaction, about the first year; *anal,* when pleasure comes from anal and urethral sensations, the second and third years; *phallic,* the third and fourth years, a time of pleasure from genital stimulation; *oedipal,* also genital but now, at 4 and 5 years, the child regards the parent of the opposite sex as a love object and the same-sex parent as a rival; *latency,* from 6 to around 11, when sexual cravings are repressed (made unconscious) and the child identifies with the parent and peers of his own sex; *puberal* when mature genital sexuality begins.

Erikson uses Freud's concepts in his theory of psychosocial development, adding to the complexity of each stage and also adding three stages above the puberal, thus dealing with adulthood as a time for growth. Progress through the stages takes place in an orderly sequence. In making his stages psychosocial as well as psychosexual, Erikson recognizes the interaction between individual and culture as contributing to personal growth. Although Freud's theory has a great deal to say about pathology, Erikson's offers a guide to both illness and health of personality. For each stage, there are problems to be solved within the cultural context. Thus, each stage is a critical period for the development of certain attitudes, convictions, and abilities. After the satisfactory solution of each crisis, the person emerges with an increased sense of unity, good judgment, and capacity to "do well" [19, p. 92]. The conflicts are never completely resolved nor are the problems disposed of forever. Each stage is described with a positive and negative outcome of the crisis involved. The stages are [18, pp. 247–274]:

1. *Basic trust versus basic mistrust.* Similar to Freud's oral stage, the development of a sense of trust dominates the first year. Success means coming to

trust the world, other people, and oneself. Since the mouth is the main zone of pleasure, trust grows on being fed when hungry, pleasant sensations when nursing, and the growing conviction that his own actions have something to do with pleasant events. Consistent, loving care is trust-promoting. Mistrust develops when trust-promoting experiences are inadequate, when the baby has to wait too long for comfort, when he is handled harshly or capriciously. Since life is never perfect, shreds of mistrust are woven into the fabric of personality. Problems of mistrust recur and have to be solved later, but when trust is dominant, healthy personality growth takes place.

2. *Autonomy versus shame and doubt.* The second stage, corresponding to Freud's anal period, predominates during the second and third year. Holding on and letting go with the sphincter muscles symbolizes the whole problem of autonomy. The child wants to do for himself with all of his powers: his new motor skills of walking, climbing, manipulating; his mental powers of choosing and deciding. If his parents give him plenty of suitable choices, times to decide when his judgment is adequate for successful outcomes, then he grows in autonomy. He gets the feeling that he can control his body, himself, and his environment. The negative feelings of doubt and shame arise when his choices are disastrous, when other people shame him or force him in areas where he could be in charge.

3. *Initiative versus guilt.* The Oedipal part of the genital stage of Freudian theory, at 4 and 5 years, is to Erikson the stage of development of a sense of initiative. Now the child explores the physical world with his senses and the social and physical worlds with his questions, reasoning, imaginative, and creative powers. Love relationships with parents are very important. Conscience develops. Guilt is the opposite pole of initiative.

4. *Industry versus inferiority.* Solutions of problems of initiative and guilt bring about entrance to the stage of developing a sense of industry, the latency period of Freud. The child is now ready to be a worker and producer. He wants to do jobs well instead of merely starting them and exploring them. He practices and learns the rules. Feelings of inferiority and inadequacy result when he feels he cannot measure up to the standards held for him by his family or society.

5. *Identity versus role diffusion.* The Freudian puberal stage, beginning at the start of adolescence, involves resurgence of sexual feelings. Erikson adds to this concept his deep insights into the adolescent's struggles to integrate all the roles he has played and hopes to play, his childish body concept with his present physical development, his concepts of his own society, and the value of what he thinks he can contribute to it. Problems remaining from earlier stages are reworked.

6. *Intimacy versus isolation.* A sense of identity is the condition for the ability to establish true intimacy, "the capacity to commit himself to concrete affiliations and partnerships and to develop the ethical strength to abide by such commitments" [18, p. 263]. Intimacy involves understanding and allowing oneself to be understood. It may be, but need not be, sexual. Without intimacy, a person feels isolated and alone.

7. *Generativity versus self-absorption.* Involvement in the well-being and development of the next generation is the essence of generativity. While it includes being a good parent, it is more. Concern with creativity is also part of it. Adults need to be needed by the young, and unless the adults can be concerned and contributing, they suffer from stagnation.

8. *Ego integrity versus despair.* The sense of integrity comes from satisfaction with one's own life cycle and its place in space and time. The individual feels that his actions, relationships, and values are all meaningful and acceptable. Despair arises from remorseful remembrance of mistakes and wrong decisions plus the conviction that it is too late to try again.

Figure 5-2 shows the normal timing of Erikson's stages of psychosocial development. The critical period for each stage is represented by a swelling of the rope that stretches throughout life. The ropes indicate that no crisis is ever solved completely and finally, but that strands of it are carried along, to be dealt with at different levels. As one rope swells at its critical period, the other ropes are affected and interact. Solutions to identity problems involve problems in all the other stages. The metaphor of the rope can also be extended by thinking of the personalities of a family's members as being intertwined ropes. When the parents' Generativity strands are becoming dominant, the infant's Trust strand is dominant. The two ropes fit smoothly together, indicating a complementary relationship between the personalities of infant and parents.

Piaget's Stages. Figure 5-2 shows Piaget's stages in the development of intelligence. Piaget is concerned with the nature of knowledge and how it is acquired. His studies of infants and children have revealed organizations of structures by which the child comes to know the world. The structural units are *schemas,* patterns of action and/or thought. As the child matures, he uses his existing schemas to interact, transforming them through the process of equilibration. Each stage of development is an advance from the last one, built upon it by reorganizing it and adapting more closely to reality. Reorganization and adaptation go on continuously, but from one time to another the results differ from each other. Piaget has broken this series of organizations of structures into units called *periods* and stages. There are three periods, each of which extends the previous one, reconstructs it, and surpasses it [51, pp. 152–159]. Periods are divided into stages that have a constant sequence, no matter whether the child achieves them at a slow or fast pace. Progress through the periods and stages is affected by organic growth, exercise and experience, social interaction or equilibration. The periods are

1. *Sensorimotor.* Lasting from birth until about 2, sensorimotor intelligence exists without language and symbols. Practical and aimed at getting results, it works through action-schemas [51, p. 4]. Beginning with the reflex patterns present at birth, the baby builds more and more complex schemas through a succession of six stages. Figure 5-2 lists the names of the stages. They are described in Chapter 3. During this period the baby constructs a schema of the permanence of objects. He comes to know that things and people continue to exist even when he cannot see them and he realizes that they move when

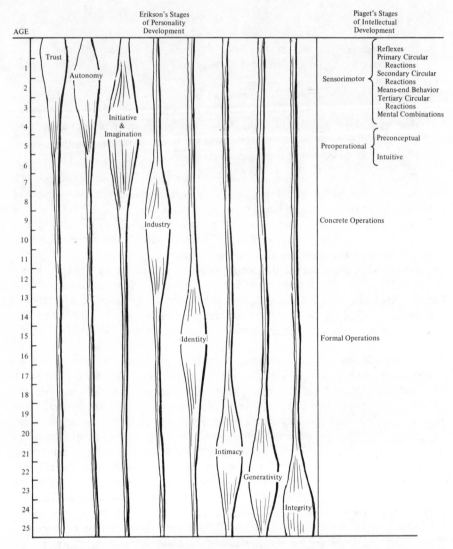

Figure 5-2. Schematic representation of Erikson's stages of psychosocial development, with names of Piaget's stages of the development of intelligence.

he is not looking. He learns control of his body in space. He begins to use language to imitate and to make internal representations of reality.

2. *Preoperational.* Sometimes this period, from about 2 to 7, is considered a subperiod of the whole time from 2 to 11. It is distinctly different, however, from the sensorimotor period and the period that comes around 7, the period of concrete operations. Two stages, preconceptual and intuitive thought, are

included. The preoperational period is marked by the *semiotic* function and imitation. The semiotic function, often called *symbolizing,* is the use of an indicator or sign as distinct from the object or event to which it refers [51, pp. 52–91]. For example, the bell that announces dinner is perceived as distinct from the food but as indicating food. Achievements show much use of his new representational abilities, in deferred imitation (imitation starting after the model has disappeared), symbolic play, drawing, mental images, and verbal representation. The child thinks that names are essential parts of the objects to which they refer. When he gives a reason, it is in terms of how he wants things to be. He sees no need to come to the same conclusions as anyone else because he does not realize the existence of viewpoints other than his own. Throughout this stage the child becomes more flexible in his thinking, more able to use past experience, and to consider more than one aspect of an event at a time.

3. *Concrete operations.* The period from about 7 to 11 years of age is essentially the time when the child can think about real, concrete things in systematic ways, although he has great difficulty in thinking about abstractions. He orders, counts, classifies, and thinks in terms of cause and effect. He develops a new concept of permanence, called *conservation,* through which he realizes that amount, weight, volume, and number stay the same when outward appearances of objects or groups are changed. Although he finds it difficult to change his hypotheses, he learns to take other people's points of view and comes to feel that his reasoning and his solutions to problems should check with other people's. His thinking has become socialized.

4. *Formal operations.* The period of formal operations or logical thought begins at about 11 and continues to develop until about 15, when the individual has the mental operations for adult thinking. Instead of having to think about concrete objects, he can think and reason in purely abstract terms. He can think systematically, combining all factors in a situation so as to exhaust all possibilities. He makes hypotheses and tests them. This type of thinking is basic to logic and to the scientific method. The limitation of this stage is a confusion of what could and should be with what is practically possible. The adolescent resists the imperfections in the world when he can construct ideal arrangements in his mind.

Memory

Both remembering and learning refer to changes in the organism that result from interactions with the environment. In remembering, as in all interactions, the child brings his own resources to bear on the particular environment in which he lives. Some cultures stress memorizing more than others do. Children may be encouraged and assisted in remembering what is considered important to remember. Until recently, it was important for a Maori to be able to recite the names of his ancestors, right back to the one who came to New Zealand in a particular one of the canoes that brought the first Maoris. Because textbooks are scarce in India, college students memorize extensively. In North America, organizing and understanding are often preferred to memorizing.

Memory means the storing of experience within the person, in all likelihood in his brain, in such ways that he can hold it and retrieve it. *Learning* occurs when behavior changes as a result of experience. Therefore, many learning experiments involve memory and many memory experiments involve learning. For many years, psychologists have been exploring the conditions under which children learn everything from swimming to moral behavior. More recently, scientists from different disciplines have been trying to discover the processes by which human beings take in information from their senses, process it, store it, and take it out for use when they need it.

THE STRUCTURES AND PROCESSES OF MEMORY

The *hippocampus,* a deep part of the brain, is a place where memories are made, or, more exactly, the hippocampus is essential for the process of long-term storing of new experience in retrievable form [44]. Biochemical changes occur in the brain as the processes of memory are carried on. One of the mysteries of the process is the form in which the brain stores experience and the method by which it converts perceptual input into items that can be stored and found for later use. Pribram suggests that memory works on the principle of the *hologram* (a construct from physics), a mechanism that codes 10 billion bits of information in the space of about a cubic centimeter [52].

The various sense organs react to stimuli. The processes of attention select certain features. *Perception* involves analyzing stimuli, first in terms of physical or sensory features and later matching them with stored memories and extracting meaning. If processing continues to a deeper level, the material is enriched by associating it with additional stored material. Thus, more meaning is added. A theory of memory holds that the more deeply a stimulus is processed, the longer and more fully it is remembered [13]. Some researchers think that there are different storage structures for long-term and short-term memory, but others think that the same processes are at work and that the level of processing determines how long and how well an experience will be remembered.

The term *control processes* refers to the ways in which an individual uses his perceptual processes, puts material into his memory store (or stores), and finds (retrieves) the stored material when he wants it. The methods of analyzing and coding material and extracting meaning from it will depend, of course, on the type of mental operations used. As Piaget has shown, mental operations are stage-related, depending upon the maturity and experience of the child. Some control processes can be modified by the individual as he adapts to new conditions and learns new techniques [53]. "Learning to learn" includes adopting new patterns of control that improve remembering.

Developmental research deals with age-related changes in the various aspects of memory. Topics include long-term and short-term memory and their connections with each other and with input, response, and control systems. Experimenters vary input, such as visual or verbal, color or form. They require different responses, such as recall or recognition, after different time lags. They consider the effects of intelligence and nutrition, and even of sibling position [13, 53].

Learning

Learning occurs when behavior changes as a result of experience. Behavior includes inner processes as well as actions. Different approaches to the study of learning give different emphases. Some of the terms of behaviorism focus on something being done to the learner. Thus, the learner may be seen as passive. *Behavior shaping,* for example, sounds very much like a "psychosculptor" hewing out a neat set of behavior patterns from a rough bundle of mass activity. (Such is not really the case, as is seen later.) Presently, however, the self is seen as an active shaper of personal destiny, as evaluator, decision-maker, and active learner. The view of self as active is illustrated in the following section on academic learning and in the discussion of social learning. The self can also be seen as active in reinforcement and conditioning.

ACADEMIC LEARNING

A new way of measuring and understanding school learning is offered by Bloom's use of *time* as a yardstick [6]. A child takes a measurable length of time to reach criteria of achievement in reading, mathematics, science, literature, a foreign language, and so on. Bloom reviews studies of the length of time required by children in different countries to reach the same criteria. The average student in the highest-scoring of the developed nations achieved 12 years of learning in 12 years. For children in low-scoring developed nations, the achievement was 8 years in 12 years. The average child in an underdeveloped country achieved 6 years in 12 years. United States research has shown that if the highest 20 per cent of students reach the criterion level one year, 50 per cent will reach it the next year and 80 per cent in 2 years. When mastery teaching is used and students spend extra time during the first year in learning, 80 per cent can reach the same criterion as the upper 20 per cent in one year. (Mastery teaching includes identifying gaps in learning and then using corrective procedures designed especially for the child's particular needs.)

When mastery learning procedures are first offered to students who are not learning fast, the slowest 5 per cent of learners take about five times as long to reach criterion as do the fastest 5 per cent of learners. After achieving several learning units through mastery procedures, the slowest learners reach criterion in three times or less what was required by the fastest. Thus, it pays off to help the slow learners in the early stages. Most likely they will increase in self-esteem and self-confidence as they achieve more and as they learn more effective ways of learning.

Further studies reviewed by Bloom show that the fastest learners spend more time *on task,* or actually learning. From both observation and interviews, the fast learners were found to spend large amounts of time in school actively engaged with the subject matter. Slower learners were likely to spend the first 20 minutes talking, arranging their materials, and fixing their hair and clothing. Then they worked for about 20 minutes. The next 15 or 20 minutes were spent getting ready to leave. *Time on task* explains many of the differences between fast learners and slow learners. In ghetto schools, apathy and hostility depress the amount of time spent on task. Here and in poor countries, hunger and malnutrition contribute to apathy.

Although human beings vary in their initial learning ability, all need to learn basic academic subjects in order to get along in the modern world. Nearly all can learn them if enough time is allowed, but nearly all can learn them much faster and with greater satisfaction if teaching procedures enlist all of their learning potential.

Social Learning

One of the most remarkable features of human beings is that they learn so much and so easily from one another. People learn from the experience of those who lived in the past as well as from face-to-face encounters, learning from others' errors and successes instead of having to try out all kinds of actions. Very often, a person can acquire a new piece of behavior by simply watching another person perform it or by listening to the other person telling how to do it. However, a learner does not imitate everything she sees or hears. She chooses to do what is rewarding, or what she thinks will have positive reinforcement value.

SOCIALIZATION

Children learn by observing their parents and listening to them. Parents teach children through a variety of techniques, as they *socialize* the children. *Socialization* is the teaching done by members of a group or institution in order that the individual will learn to think, feel, and behave as a member of that group. Socialization occurs in people of all ages, but much of it takes place during childhood, as the developing person acquires appropriate values, attitudes, and behavior patterns. Parents are the primary socializers. Siblings and other family members also teach. Teachers and peers are important socializing agents as are, to a lesser extent, other members of the community.

Socialization refers to both the present and the future. The child learns to behave appropriately as the child he now is, but he also learns attitudes, values, and skills that he will use in the future. From interacting with his father, he learns the father role as well as the son role. Similarly, he observes his various socializers as worker, manager, host, citizen, and teacher, and in all the many roles that they play in his society. The child learns some specific information and skills, as well as values and attitudes. Thus, he is gradually socialized into his family, community, and nation through a process that maintains the values and behavior patterns of that group.

MODELING

Infants begin to imitate toward the end of the sensorimotor period. Piaget observes that imitation is always active, never automatic or nonintentional [49]. Imitation is accommodation, a way of modifying present schemas. Imitation is the child's first mode of representing an action. Throughout life, imitation continues to serve as an important mode of learning.

Bandura, who has conducted basic experiments on observational learning, concludes that "virtually all learning phenomena resulting from direct experience can occur on a vicarious basis by observing other people's behavior and its consequences for them" [4]. An action can be learned from one observation. It can be stored for a long time, to be used if and when an appropriate time comes.

Influences on Modeling. Although children will imitate spontaneously, various factors and circumstances have been shown to affect whether they do imitate. Age and developmental level are related to whether children will imitate the ways in which toys are manipulated [22]. The child's past experience with peers affects his tendency to imitate peers [29]. Children who had often been reinforced by peers were more likely to imitate a rewarding peer; children who had seldom been reinforced by peers were more likely to imitate a nonrewarding peer. What happens to the model also has an effect on the child. In one of Bandura's famous experiments, children saw a film of an aggressive model either being punished, rewarded, or having no consequences [3]. Then they were left in a room with the aggressed-against clown and the instruments of aggression, as well as other toys. Those who saw the model being punished did less imitating of his aggressive behavior than did those who saw the model being rewarded or having no consequences. When the children were offered reinforcers for imitating the aggression, the difference between the groups disappeared. Boys imitated more aggressive acts than girls after seeing the model punished, but when rewards were given, the sex difference disappeared. Thus, it seems that children inhibit aggressive imitation when they see the model punished, but they learn the behavior just as readily. Girls are more inhibited than boys by punishment for aggression, but they learn the behavior just as well. Bandura says that one of the most interesting questions in regard to modeling is whether one can keep people from learning what they have seen [4]. Presumably the answer is *no*.

These experiments, and many additional ones, give insight into modeling, but they cannot predict what a given individual will imitate. The situation is analogous to language. One can test a child's level of language development, but one cannot tell just what the child will say. Modeling involves abstracting from what is observed, storing it in memory in some symbolic form, making generalizations and rules about behavior, mentally putting together and trying out different kinds of behavior, and choosing which forms to act out at what times. Thus, other people's behavior is used creatively by the individual in an extraordinarily efficient way of developing new ways of acting that are suited to the particular occasion. Bandura has summarized the component processes of observational learning [4].

Component Processes. First, *attention* regulates the perception of modeled actions. Second, what is observed is transformed into representations that are preserved in *memory*. Coding and symbolic rehearsal make these transformations. Memory keeps the symbolically represented actions available as guides to performance. Third, new response patterns are integrated from *motor* acts. Fourth, *incentive* or *motivational* processes govern the choice of action patterns to be used.

Thus, it is the *person* who actively observes, remembers, judges, decides, and creates a response. The person's own values are the context in which the processes of modeling occur.

CONDITIONING

Conditioning, or learning by association, is the establishing of a connection between a stimulus and a response. In *classical conditioning,* the kind made famous by Pavlov, a neutral stimulus is presented with another stimulus that elicits an innate response. After several such presentations, the neutral stimulus is given without the other stimulus and the response occurs. Pavlov sounded a buzzer when he gave food to his dog. Eventually the dog salivated at the sound of the buzzer.

Operant, or *instrumental,* conditioning is done by rewarding the desired response whenever it occurs. Operant conditioning techniques have been developed for use in a wide variety of situations, with animal and human subjects. By rewarding small pieces of behavior, complex patterns can be built up, thus "shaping" or modifying the behavior of the subject. This technique has proven to be very useful in treating behavior disorders in infants, children, retardates, and the mentally ill.

Conditioning has been used to explore the abilities of infants and to show that newborn babies do learn [37]. Papoušek taught newborn babies to turn their heads to the sound of a buzzer by using a combination of classical and operant conditioning methods [47]. A bell was sounded and if the infant turned to the left, he was given milk. If he did not turn, head turning was elicited by touching the corner of his mouth with a nipple. Then he was given milk. Newborns were slow to condition, taking an average of 18 days, whereas at 3 months, only 4 days were required and by 5 months, 3 days were required. Two-month-old infants learned to operate a mobile by means of pressing their heads on their pillows [63].

REINFORCEMENT

Reinforcements are consequences of events, or so they are seen by the subject. A *positive* reinforcement makes the reoccurrence of the event more likely, a *negative* reinforcement, less likely. Positive reinforcement functions not only through being pleasant or rewarding but because it gives information, such as, "That was right," "You succeeded." Likewise, negative reinforcement is not only unpleasant; it informs the person, "You did wrong." Reinforcement is, therefore, not just a mechanical procedure by which one person manipulates another, but a means by which people can regulate their own behavior [4].

Reinforcement comes from both external and internal sources. People reward themselves when they think they have done well and punish themselves when they fail or do wrong. Or they may try to cheer themselves up after failure, by a reward. The reinforcement may be just a comment to oneself, such as "That was a great job!" Or a person may buy a present for herself or indulge in a fancy dessert. Children's self-rewarding behavior has been studied under various conditions. Although preschool children tend to reward themselves liberally [35], school-age children make complex judgments about giving themselves appropriate reinforcements. School-age children rewarded themselves differently for different types of altruistic behavior [40]. They also apparently considered the length of task and quality of performance in dispensing self-rewards [39]. Thus do children evaluate and direct their own behavior. When children receive inappropriate reinforcement at school, their learning behavior is likely to be depressed [30].

Modern behavior modification programs take account of the individual's capacity for self-regulation rather than simply administering external reinforcements [4]. The person who wants to change his behavior is helped to plan inducements for the desired behavior, to evaluate his own performance, and to dispense the reinforcers.

Successful socialization of children also makes use of children's growing powers of self-regulation. Even if behavior could be controlled by extrinsic rewards and punishments, the result would be a child who could not control herself. And, of course, external rewards and punishments will not give predictable results because the child herself is also active in the process. Experiments with adults have shown that external rewards and punishments sometimes decrease self-motivation [46]. The reason may be that the person sees himself as less self-controlled and with less freedom of choice when someone else is dispensing reinforcements.

Punishment especially is a risky technique of influence. Although punishment is often effective in suppressing behavior, it does not teach new, positive behavior. Parke has summarized the effects of punishment on children as shown by research [48]. Punishment suppressed behavior more effectively when it occurred close in time to the deviation. High-intensity punishment was more effective than low, but when it occurred promptly, high- and low-intensity punishment were equally effective. When the adult withdrew affection or was inconsistent with affection, children were likely to suppress undesired behavior in order to win back the affection. When reasoning and explanation accompanied punishment, light punishment was as effective as severe. Reviewing the deviance had the same effect. Inconsistency delayed the effect. Indiscriminate and harsh punishment may make the child avoid the punisher or may lead to passivity and withdrawal.

Maturation

As the child's bodily structures grow, they change in size and complexity, becoming more and more the way they will be in the mature state. Bodily functions likewise change as the structures do. The whole process is called *maturation.* Although maturation is controlled by hereditary factors, the environment must be adequate to support it. The growth principle of normative sequence is reflected in maturation, since structures and functions mature in an orderly, irreversible sequence. Since maturation is little affected by experience, its effects are the same throughout a species. An impoverished environment slows the process of maturation more than it changes quality or sequence.

Certain behavior patterns are the result of maturation more than of learning because they are relatively independent of experience. Many developmental processes involve both maturation and learning. Examples of processes that are largely maturational are the motor sequence and the emergence of language. In all but the most abnormal environments, infants go through regular sequences of raising the head, raising the chest, sitting, creeping, standing with support, and so on.

Another explanation of maturation is that certain experiences are encountered by everyone and are, therefore, not recognized as experience. Behavior patterns attributed to maturation are really the results of interactions with the universal environment. For instance, everyone makes postural adjustments to gravity, but nobody notices gravity. Another example is that everyone learns to chew food because everyone receives food. The emergence of language is a response to an almost universal experience, the hearing of spoken language.

Some theories of development, such as Gesell's, emphasize the role of maturation in determining behavior. Gesell's descriptions of behavior stages led some parents to think that they could do little to influence their children's behavior and that they must enjoy his good stages and wait patiently while he grew out of unattractive, annoying, or disturbing stages. In contrast, although Piaget recognizes that the body matures, he stresses the necessity for the child to interact, explore, and discover for himself in order to build his mental structures. Mental growth cannot be forced or hurried, however, since its counterpart is physical maturation. "Mental growth is inseparable from physical growth: the maturation of the nervous and endocrine systems, in particular, continues until the age of 16" [51, p. vii].

Evolutionary Adaptation

Evolutionary changes can be considered in terms of behavior patterns or behavior systems.

ETHOLOGY

The behavior patterns that develop through maturation can be traced back in the history of the species or the phylum. These fixed action patterns evolved as the animal adapted to a certain environment. *Ethology,* the study of the relation between animal behavior and environment, has influenced the study of human development, offering insight into certain kinds of behavior that cannot be explained as learning or fully understood as maturation. Lorenz pointed out the implications of ethology for understanding certain forms of human behavior [38]. Bowlby has integrated psychoanalytic theory with ethology [8]. Ainsworth [2] has done extensive research on attachment behavior, a main focus of the ethological approach to human development.

The adaptive behavior pattern becomes fixed in form, appearing as an innate skill in every member of a species, even though he has not had opportunities to learn [17]. A specific stimulus from the environment activates the particular behavior pattern, as though it were a key, unlocking the mechanism. Thus, the behavior is sometimes called an *innate response mechanism,* or IRM. For example, a toad's catching response is released by a small, moving object, a nine-week-old gosling gives an intense fear reaction to his first sight of a hawk, and a stickleback fish will attack a red spot that resembles the red underbelly of another stickleback.

Bowlby points out that the environment to which a species is adapted is the environment in which it evolved into its present form [8, p. 59]. Most likely, when man first emerged as a distinct species, he lived by hunting and gathering in a savannah environment, much like today's most primitive societies and not unlike the ground-dwelling primates [2]. Mother–infant reciprocal behavior was adapted to protecting the infant so as to ensure his survival. The baby's unlearned, spontaneous patterns of crying, clinging, and sucking brought him (and still bring him) into contact with the mother. Other aspects of attachment behavior, maturing a little later, serve to maintain and strengthen the contacts with the mother, who was (and still is) adapted or genetically programmed to respond with specific action patterns. In the urban environment of today, close physical contact of mother and baby is not necessary for protecting the baby from predators, but babies still behave as though it were and mothers still respond to their infants' behavior with innate action patterns. Closeness of mother and baby has other advantages, however, in terms of normal development.

BEHAVIOR SYSTEMS

Ascending the evolutionary scale, the nervous system and brain become more complex. Their first function is to control and integrate the other bodily systems and organs. In the higher animals and most notably in man, the cognitive system has its own needs and demands, in addition to its function as controller and co-ordinator. Curiosity, information seeking, and exploration are modes of obtaining what the cognitive system must have in order to function optimally. Dember maintains that the brain is not like a computer that acts only on demand, but rather it is "an instrument with needs of its own" [15]. Cognitive actions may even result in states that oppose the demands of other systems. Ideas or ideologies can be so strong that the person harms his own body or even kills himself. Such is the case with martyrs, political prisoners resisting torture, and people who accept dares.

Disharmony between behavioral systems is also discussed by Wolff [64]. He points out that different behavioral systems have evolved at different times and with considerable independence between them. Autonomic reactivity appears first followed by organized reflex action and diffuse nonreflex activity. Next, the voluntary behavior system develops and then language. Although all systems influence each other to some extent, there are times when a person's actions do not coincide with her feelings, or words with actions. Many therapies and techniques are presently trying to bring these systems into closer relationships. Such methods include Gestalt techniques, yoga, meditation, brain-wave conditioning, and control of the autonomic system. Wolff suggests that success in these efforts will have survival value for the species and may bring happiness to the individual.

Heredity

Although most students of child development will study the mechanisms of heredity in a biology course, we include a brief account here. After all, the mechanisms of heredity are what start the child developing and guide the course of development.

BIOLOGICAL INHERITANCE

The human being is composed of two main types of cells. By far the larger number of cells are the *body* cells. These are the cells that compose the skeleton, skin, kidneys, heart, and so on. A minority of cells are the *germ* cells. In the male, germ cells are called *spermatazoa* (the singular is *spermatazoon*), usually shortened to *sperm:* in the female, the germ cells are *ova* (the singular is *ovum*).

Each body cell is composed of several different parts, the most important of which for our present discussion are the *chromosomes,* of which there are 46, arranged in 23 pairs. The sizes and shapes of the chromosomes can be determined by viewing a prepared cell through an electron microscope. Twenty-two of the pairs of chromosomes are composed of two highly similar chromosomes, though each pair differs in certain respects from every other pair. These 22 pairs are similar in males and females. In males, the twenty-third pair is composed of two chromosomes that are unequal in size. The larger one is an *X chromosome;* the smaller is a *Y chromosome.* In females, the twenty-third pair is composed of two X chromosomes. When, in the course of growth, a body cell divides to form two

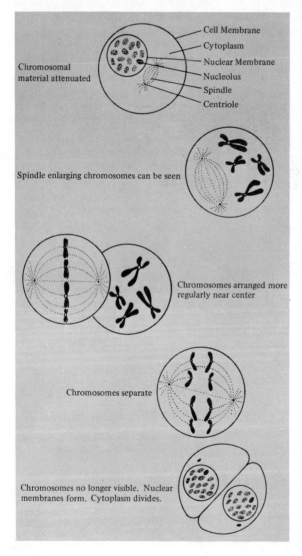

Chromosomal material attenuated

Cell Membrane
Cytoplasm
Nuclear Membrane
Nucleolus
Spindle
Centriole

Spindle enlarging chromosomes can be seen

Chromosomes arranged more regularly near center

Chromosomes separate

Chromosomes no longer visible. Nuclear membranes form. Cytoplasm divides.

Figure 5-3.   Stages in the process of mitosis.

SOURCE: Adapted from P. A. Moody. *Genetics of man.* New York: W. W. Norton & Company, Inc., 1967. Figure 3–2, p. 28.

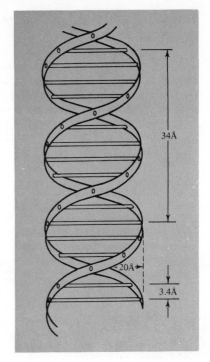

Figure 5-4. DNA takes the form of a double helix.

Source: Adapted from G. W. Burns. *The science of genetics.* New York: Macmillan Publishing Co., Inc. 1969. Figure 14–9, p. 258.

new cells, it goes through the process of *mitosis.* The result of mitosis is that each of the new cells has exactly the same kind and number of chromosomes as the first cell had before it divided. Figure 5-3 shows the process of mitosis.

DNA, a substance in the chromosomes, is the carrier of the genetic code that transmits characteristics from one generation to the next. Figure 5-4 shows a model of the DNA molecule, in the shape of a double helix or spiral ladder. The *genes,* carriers of specific instructions for growth, are arranged in linear order on the spirals. The two spirals can come apart like a zipper. Then each half produces another half.

Dominant and Recessive Genes. A story [58] that might be called *science prediction* rather than *science fiction* went like this: a young couple had been quietly holding hands in a secluded corner of the campus. Then one of them said, "Let's match cards." Each pulled out a printed card containing a few holes. They put one on top of the other. None of the holes matched. They embraced happily. Like most human beings, each carried a few dangerous recessive genes out of the thousand or more that can cause birth defects. Since it takes a recessive gene from each parent to produce a characteristic that does not show in either parent, the young couple could safely plan to have children. Or if not with complete assurance, at least they would know that they were not endangering their future children as far as their own dangerous recessives were concerned. Suppose two of the holes had matched such that each of the couple was carrying a recessive gene for cystic fibrosis. For each conception, chances would be one in four for a child with two recessives and hence having cystic fibrosis, two in four for a child carrying one recessive, like the parents, and not showing the defect, and one in four for a normal child with two normal genes. And suppose they conceived a defective embryo. It could be diagnosed early in pregnancy and aborted, if they so chose.

Although at the moment when this is being written, the story is only prediction, the technology on which it is based is of the present. Many physical characteristics, including a large number of defects, are inherited according to simple Mendelian law, as illustrated in our story. Some other defects, such as color blindness, are sex linked, which means that they are dominant in the male and recessive in the female. A male shows the defect when he carries only one gene for it, but the female does not suffer unless she has two such genes.

Heredity works in more complicated ways, also. Genes work in concert with one another and with the environment. The mechanisms of *crossing over* and *independent assortment* add enormously to the variety of genetic combinations that are possible. Genes "turn on" and off at various times during the life cycle. For example, the control of sexual maturation is considerably influenced by heredity.

Gene Blends. Many characteristics are the results of more than one pair of genes. Skin color in human beings is such a characteristic. It is not determined in all-or-none way, as is seed color in peas. Rather, in spite of popular belief to the contrary, a child's skin color is almost never darker than the skin of the darker parent, nor lighter than the skin of the lighter parent. If the child's skin is darker than either parent's, it is only a shade darker. At least two pairs of genes are considered to be active in determining skin color; there may be three or more.

Standing height is another human characteristic that is the result of many different genes working at least in part in a literally additive way, although blending of the kind that determines skin color may also be operating. A human being's height is the sum of the lengths of many different bones and many pieces of cartilage. Each bone's length is probably determined by one or more genes, and varies somewhat independently of the length of every other bone. Height is, therefore, a *polygenic* trait. (In addition, of course, the variation in heights of a group of individuals is affected by environmental factors such as diet and disease.)

Meiosis. Although each individual receives the chromosomes from germ cells of the parents, the offspring of the same parents do not receive identical chromosomes. The explanation of this difference between brothers and sisters lies in the process of *meiosis,* the formation of germ cells, sperm and ova.

Figure 5-5 shows the development of sperm that contain only two single chromosomes, since to show 23 chromosomes would unnecessarily complicate the diagram. In the diagram the primordial germ cell, the *spermatogonium,* is shown as containing two pairs of chromosomes. In the process of meiosis, the spermatogonium divides into two cells called *secondary spermatocytes,* each of which has one of the members of each pair of chromosomes. Each chromosome is composed of two *chromatids.* Each spermatocyte divides into two *spermatids,* each of which has one of the chromatids from the eight chromatids that are shown to have been in the original spermatogonium. From each spermatid develops a sperm. Therefore,

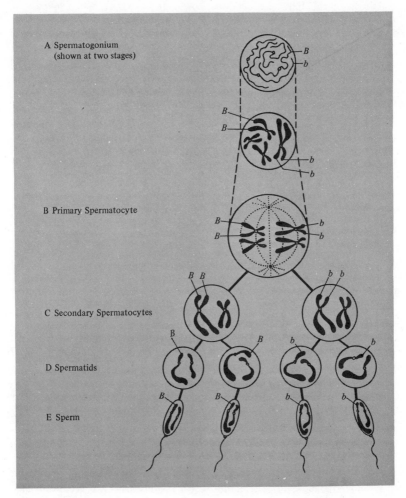

A Spermatogonium
(shown at two stages)

B Primary Spermatocyte

C Secondary Spermatocytes

D Spermatids

E Sperm

Figure 5-5. Meiosis provides the mechanism by which a heterozygous male produces sperm of two kinds: half of them containing the dominant gene, *B,* half of them containing its recessive allele, *b.*

SOURCE: Adapted from P. A. Moody. *Genetics of man.* New York: W. W. Norton & Company, 1967. Figure 3–7, p. 34.

from each male primordial germ cell result four sperm, each containing 23 single chromosomes.

The development of each ovum is similar to the development of each sperm, except that from each female primordial germ cell (called an *obgonium*) there result not four ova, but one. But it, like each sperm, contains 23 chromatids from among the 92 chromatids present in the obgonium. Since the obgonium begins meiosis with two X chromosomes, every ovum contains an X chromosome. The spermatogonium, which begins meiosis with one X and one Y chromosome, results in four sperms, two of which contain an X apiece and two a Y. If an X-bearing sperm fertilizes an ovum, the new individual will have two X chromosomes, and will be female. If a Y-bearing sperm fertilizes an ovum, the new individual will have one Y chromosome and one X chromosome, and will be a male.

In the same way, if one parent has two genes for any trait, each offspring will receive from that parent the same kind of genetic material as any other offspring. But if a parent has unlike genes for a trait, half of the offspring (other things being equal, which they often are not) will receive one kind of gene (for example, the dominant gene) and half will receive the other. The process of meiosis explains part of the genetic difference between brothers and sisters, including the fact that a given father and mother are likely to have both sons and daughters.

BEHAVIOR GENETICS

Not only are body form and coloration inherited from generation to generation but different kinds of functioning are, also. The ability to roll the tongue is one of these functions. One of the authors of this book (MSS) can roll her tongue; RCS cannot. All three of their daughters can. Since this ability is known to be a dominant characteristic, we know that RCS is homozygous recessive. Some of our grandchildren may turn out to be like Grandpa. Our daughters are heterozygous for this characteristic. If their husbands are also heterozygous, we could predict that our grandchildren will be tongue-rollers in the ratio of 3:1.

(Incidentally, the genetic ratios hold only for large populations, not for small samples. Since we expect that the total number of our grandchildren will be no more than six, they might all be tongue-rollers.)

The inheritance of certain defects in mental functioning can be described in terms of chromosomes [42]. Down's syndrome (Mongolism), a type of mental retardation accompanied by distinctive physical anomalies, occurs when an extra chromosome is attached to the chromosome numbered 21, making a total of 47 instead of the normal 46 chromosomes. Klinefelter's syndrome, incomplete sexual development along with lowered intelligence in males, involves two X chromosomes in addition to a Y. Turner's syndrome, in which females have only one X chromosome, includes defective spatial abilities. Males with an XXY condition are more likely than normals to be tall, aggressive, and mentally defective.

The transmission of all-or-none traits, such as tongue-rolling and Down's syndrome, can be explained by basic rules of genetics. When many genes are involved and when the characteristic is highly complex, such as intelligence or emotional stability, *heritability* is studied by *quantitative genetics*. Heritability of a characteristic can be estimated by comparing correlations between groups of known genetic similarity. Since the heredity of animals can be controlled, they can be used for experimental work in heredity. In working with humans, investigators have to use groups that vary in known degrees, from identical twins to unrelated persons. Results of many studies on inheritance of intelligence and personality indicate that there are indeed significant hereditary components in both [61].

Intelligence. Figure 5-6 shows median (average) sizes of correlations between measured intelligence of persons of different degrees of genetic similarity [20]. Unrelated persons living apart show no correlation (−.01). Identical twins

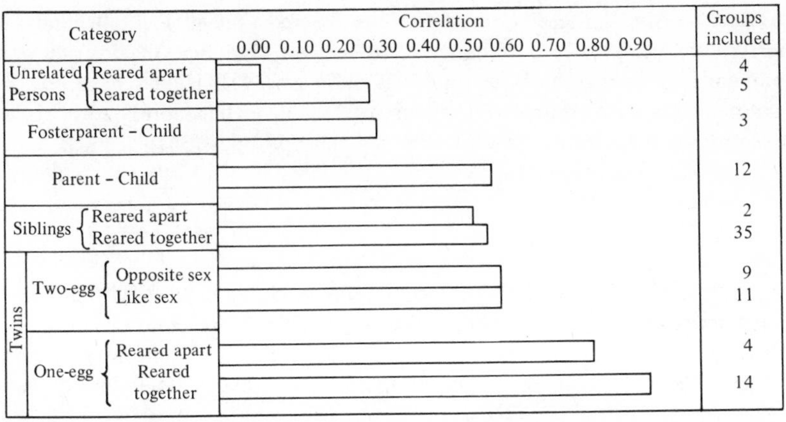

Category	Correlation 0.00 0.10 0.20 0.30 0.40 0.50 0.60 0.70 0.80 0.90	Groups included
Unrelated ⌈ Reared apart		4
Persons ⌊ Reared together		5
Fosterparent – Child		3
Parent – Child		12
Siblings ⌈ Reared apart		2
⌊ Reared together		35
Twins — Two-egg ⌈ Opposite sex		9
⌊ Like sex		11
One-egg ⌈ Reared apart		4
⌊ Reared together		14

Figure 5-6. Median correlation coefficients for intelligence test scores showing degree of similarity between performances of people of varying degrees of relatedness under different and similar environmental conditions.

SOURCE: Data from L. Erlenmeyer-Kimling and L. F. Jervik. *Science,* 1964, **142**, 1477–79.

reared together are very similar (.87). Identical twins reared apart are more closely correlated than those in any other relationship group (.75). Intelligence of parents and children correlates significantly (.50). Heredity components have been found in the following intellectual abilities, listed in order of weight of influence by heredity: word fluency, verbal ability (including spelling and grammar), spatial ability, clerical speed and accuracy, reasoning, number ability, and memory [61]. Sensorimotor intelligence scores were found to be more highly correlated in identical twins than in fraternals [41].

Personality. There is evidence for heritability of several dimensions of personality, the main ones of which are usual activity level; expression of emotions frankly in interpersonal relationships; degree of planning ahead rather than behaving impulsively [61]; extraversion–introversion [54].

Age Trends. Correlations between intelligence of children and parents are low negative in early infancy, zero at around a year, low positive at the end of the second year, and moderate (.5) in early childhood and thereafter [17a]. This pattern is true of children and parents living apart, as well as of those living together. Correlations between stature of parents and children also increase throughout the early preschool years [25].

Sex Differences in Heritability. There is evidence that girls are controlled by heredity more than boys are, most likely because the X chromosome, of which girls have two and boys one, carries more hereditary material than does the Y chromosome. After age 13, measurements of stature correlate more highly for father–daughter than for father–son and for mother–daughter than for mother–son

[25]. Data from the Berkeley Growth Study indicated that girls' intellectual functioning is more genetically determined than is boys, and that the impact of the environment is greater upon boys than it is upon girls [5]. High school boys and girls, studied by a twin control method, showed stronger heritability for girls than for boys on a battery of tests of achievements and aptitudes [34].

Summary

A baby, like all organisms, interacts continuously with the environment. She and her parents influence each other and change each other. Child development is described from different theoretical viewpoints, offering different ways of interpreting and understanding. Six types of interaction are described briefly in this chapter.

Equilibration is a process of regulation that the organism carries on in physical and intellectual modes. Homeostasis is the maintaining of the organism within certain physical limits such as those of chemical content and temperature. Psychological equilibrium involves regulating stimulation to an optimal level and also progressing toward more complex levels of mental organization. Piaget's notion of equilibration includes two complementary processes, accommodation and assimilation. Assimilation is the taking in and using of material from the environment; accommodation is changing the schemas to adjust to reality as it is experienced. Equilibration is enjoyable, as shown by children's curiosity and exploration, looking for problems and incongruities to be solved.

Growth and development, terms that can be used interchangeably, refer to increasing size and complexity of structure and function. The following principles or generalizations hold for many kinds of growth and development: variation in rates between individuals, between sexes, within the organism and of the organism in time; individuals differ in time of reaching maturity; measures of growth are interrelated; organisms behave as though they were seeking to achieve maximum potential, searching for substitute sources of nurture when the usual ones are not available; specific patterns of behavior are differentiated out of larger, global patterns, and then specific patterns are integrated into larger, complex patterns; certain sequences of physical and motor development take place in directions (cephalo-caudal and proximo-distal) in relation to the body; certain behavior patterns mature in orderly sequences; growth is based on a foundation, the organism interacting with the environment to transform itself; critical periods are specific times when the organism will interact with the environment in specific ways that may be harmful or beneficial.

Stage theories, including Erikson's and Piaget's, explain development as proceeding epigenetically, being transformed or reorganized on more and more complex levels that occur in an orderly sequence. Erikson's psychosocial theory uses Freud's psychosexual stages as a base and develops a theory of the healthy personality. The eight stages of man's development involve the development of basic trust versus basic mistrust; autonomy versus doubt and shame; initiative versus guilt; industry versus inferiority; identity versus role diffusion; intimacy versus isolation; generativity versus self-absorption; ego integrity versus despair. Piaget shows how children develop intelligence in the process of dealing with the world and coming to know it. His sensorimotor period, spanning infancy, is subdivided into six stages. The preoperational period, from around 2 to 7, includes the stages of preconceptual and intuitive thought. The period of concrete operations comprises the school years, and the period of formal operations (logical thought) comprises the years of adolescence.

Memory means the storing of experience in such ways that it can be retrieved and used. The process includes perception, attention, coding, and enriching with meaning. Memory performance varies with age, input, and various environmental aspects. Learning is an active process, not something that is done to a person. When academic learning is measured in terms of time, focused aid can help slow learners to achieve more and to increase their self-esteem and motivation. Human beings learn easily from observing one another and hearing or reading of the experiences of others. Through socialization, children and, to some extent, others learn to think, feel, and behave as members of social groups. Selecting among what she sees, hears, and reads, an individual imitates behavior that she expects will be rewarding to her. The components of modeling are attention, symbolic representations in memory, new integrations of motor acts, and control of selection through incentive or motivational processes. Classical conditioning involves linking a new response with an old one, operant conditioning involves strengthening a response when it occurs. Positive reinforcements increase the likelihood of recurrence of an event, negative reinforcements decrease it. Individuals can use reinforcement systematically to change their own behavior. Manipulation of reinforcements is complicated and often does not bring the desired results because not all variables are understood.

Maturation is the growth toward maturity of the body, its structures, and functions—growth that is relatively independent of experience. Most developmental processes involve both maturation and learning.

Evolutionary adaptation accounts for certain behavior patterns that mature quickly into a complex and relatively fixed form. The environment to which a species is adapted is the one in which it emerged in its present form. Attachment behavior in the human infant is most easily understood in terms of evolutionary adaptation. Behavioral systems have also evolved. They are not always in harmony with each other.

Hereditary characteristics in human beings are sometimes the result of single pairs of genes, but often of numbers of genes working together. Most human beings carry several dangerous recessive genes, which will do no harm unless they are matched with the same dangerous genes from the partner in reproduction. Birth defects can be predicted on a chance basis, and some can be predicted with certainty. An ovum contains an X chromosome, a sperm either an X or a Y chromosome. The source of sex differences is in the X and Y chromosomes, including differences in heritability, females being more influenced by heredity. These functions include intelligence and many of its components and also certain personality dimensions. Correlations between physical and mental measurements of parents and children increase during the preschool period.

References

1. Abernathy, E. M. Relationships between physical and mental growth. *Monographs of the Society for Research in Child Development*, 1936, **1**:7.
2. Ainsworth, M. D. S. The development of infant-mother attachment. In B. M. Caldwell and H. N. Ricciuti (eds.). *Review of child development research*, vol. 3. Chicago: University of Chicago Press, 1973.
3. Bandura, A. Influence of models' reinforcement contingencies on the acquisition of imitative responses. *Journal of Personality & Social Psychology*, 1965, **1**, 589–595.
4. Bandura, A. Behavior theory and the models of man. *American Psychologist*, 1974, **29**, 859–869.
5. Bayley, N., and E. S. Schaefer. Correlations of maternal and child behaviors with the development of mental abilities: Data from the Berkeley growth study. *Monographs of the Society for Research in Child Development*, 1964, **29**:6.
6. Bloom, B. S. Time and learning. *American Psychologist*, 1974, **29**, 682–688.
7. Bower, T. G. R. *Development in infancy*. San Francisco: W. H. Freeman & Co., Publishers, 1974.
8. Bowlby, J. *Attachment and loss*. vol. I: *Attachment*. London: Hogarth, 1969.
9. Brenner, A. and L. H. Stott. *School readiness factor analyzed*. Detroit: Merrill-Palmer Institute (undated).
10. Bronfenbrenner, U. *Two worlds of childhood*. New York: Russell Sage Foundation, 1970.
11. Brucefors, A., I. Johannesson, P. Karlberg, I. Klackenberg-Larsson, H. Lichtenstein, and I. Svenberg. Trends in development of abilities related to somatic growth. *Human Development*, 1974, **17**, 152–159.
12. Bühler, C. *The first year of life*. New York: Day, 1930.
13. Craik, F. I. M., and R. S. Lockhart. Levels of processing: A framework for memory research. *Journal of Verbal Learning and Behavior*, 1972, **11**, 671–684.
14. Davis, C. M. Self-selection of diet by newly weaned infants. *American Journal of Diseases of Children*, 1928, **36**, 651–679.
15. Dember, W. N. Motivation and the cognitive revolution. *American Psychologist*, 1974, **29**, 161–168.
16. Dennis, W. *Children of the crèche*. New York: Meredith Corporation, 1973.
17. Eibl-Eibesfeldt, I. Concepts of ethology and their significance in the study of human behavior. In H. W. Stevenson, E. H. Hess, and H. L. Rheingold (eds.). *Early behavior*. New York: John Wiley & Sons, Inc., 1967, pp. 127–146.
17a. Eichorn, D. H. Developmental parallels in the growth of parents and their children. *Newsletter of the Division on Developmental Psychology of the American Psychological Association*, Spring, 1970.
18. Erikson, E. H. *Childhood and society*. New York: W. W. Norton & Company, 1963.
19. Erikson, E. H. *Identity, youth and crisis*. New York: W. W. Norton & Company, 1968.
20. Erlenmeyer-Kimling, L. K., and L. F. Jarvik. Genetics and intelligence: A review. *Science*, 1964, **142**, 1477–1479.
21. Fantz, R. L. The origin of form perception. *Scientific American*, 1961, **204**, 66–72.
22. Fouts, G., and P. Liikanen. The effects of age and developmental level on imitation in children. *Child Development*, 1975, **46**, 555–558.
23. Freud, S. *The ego and the id*, New York: W. W. Norton & Company, 1962.
24. Garn, S. M. Fat thickness and developmental status in childhood and adolescence. *Journal of the American Medical Association*, 1960, **99**, 746–751.

25. Garn, S. M. Body size and its implications. In L. W. Hoffman and M. L. Hoffman (eds.). *Review of child development research*. vol. 2, New York: Russell Sage Foundation, 1966, pp. 529–561.
26. Gesell, A. *The embryology of behavior*. New York: Harper, 1945.
27. Gesell, A. and H. Thompson. *The psychology of early growth*. New York: Macmillan Publishing Co., Inc., 1938.
28. Halverson, H. M. An experimental study of prehension in infants by means of systematic cinema records. *Genetic Psychology Monographs*, 1931, **10**, 107–286.
29. Hartup, W. W., and B. Coates. Imitation of a peer as a function of reinforcement from the peer group and rewardingness of the model. *Child Development*, 1967, **38**, 1003–1016.
30. Havighurst, R. J. Minority subcultures and the law of effect. *American Psychologist*, 1970, **25**, 313–322.
31. Hunt, J. V., and N. Bayley. Explorations into patterns of mental development and prediction from the Bayley scales of infant development. *Minnesota Symposium on Child Psychology*, 1971, **5**, 52–71.
32. Jones, M. C., and P. H. Mussen. Self-conception, motivations, and interpersonal attitudes of early- and late-maturing girls. *Child Development*, 1958, **29**, 492–501.
33. Ketcham, W. A. Relationship of physical and mental traits in intellectually gifted and mentally retarded boys. *Merrill-Palmer Quarterly*, 1960, **6**, 171–177.
34. Klinger, R. Sex differences in heritability assessed by the Washington precollege test battery of achievement/aptitude measures. Paper presented at the meeting of the Society for Research in Child Development, Santa Monica, 1969.
35. Lane, I. M., and R. C. Coon. Reward allocation in preschool children. *Child Development*, 1972, **43**, 1382–1389.
36. Lewis, M. The meaning of a response, or why researchers in infant behavior should be Oriental metaphysicians. *Merrill-Palmer Quarterly*, 1967, **13**, 7–18.
37. Lipsitt, L. P. Learning in the human infant. In H. W. Stevenson, E. H. Hess, and H. L. Rheingold (eds.). *Early behavior*, New York: John Wiley & Sons, Inc., 1967, pp. 225–247.
38. Lorenz, K. *King Solomon's ring*. New York: Thomas Y. Crowell Company, 1952.
39. Masters, J. C., and M. D. Christy. Achievement standards for contingent self-reinforcement: Effects of task length and task difficulty. *Child Development*, 1974, **45**, 6–13.
40. Masters, J. C., and P. A. Pisarowicz. Self-reinforcement and generosity following two types of altruistic behavior. *Child Development*, 1975, **46**, 313–318.
41. Matheny, A. P. Twins: Concordance for Piagetian-equivalent items derived from the Bayley Mental Test. *Developmental Psychology*, 1975, **11**, 224–227.
42. McClearn, G. E. Behavioral genetics: An overview. *Merrill-Palmer Quarterly*, 1968, **14**, 9–24.
43. McGraw, M. B. Major challenges for students of infancy and early childhood. *American Psychologist*, 1970, **25**, 754–756.
44. Milner, B. Memory and the medial regions of the brain. In K. H. Pribram and D. E. Broadbent. *Biology of memory*. New York: Academic Press, Inc., 1970, pp. 29–50.
45. Mussen, P. H., and M. C. Jones. The behavior-inferred motivations of late- and early-maturing boys. *Child Development*, 1958, **29**, 61–67.
46. Notz, W. W. Work motivation and the negative effects of intrinsic rewards: A review with implications for theory and practice. *American Psychologist*, 1975, **30**, 884–891.
47. Papoušek, H. Experimental studies of appetitional behavior in human newborns

and infants. In H. W. Stevenson, E. H. Hess, and H. L. Rheingold (eds.). *Early behavior.* New York: John Wiley & Sons, Inc., 1967, pp. 249–277.

48. Parke, R. D. Some effects of punishment on children's behavior. *Young Children,* 1969, **24,** 225–240.

49. Piaget, J. *Play, dreams and imitation in childhood.* New York: W. W. Norton & Company, 1962.

50. Piaget, J. *Six psychological studies.* New York: Random House, Inc., 1967.

51. Piaget, J., and B. Inhelder. *The psychology of the child.* New York: Basic Books, Inc., 1969.

52. Pines, M. *The brain changers.* New York: Harcourt Brace Jovanovich, Inc., 1973.

53. Reese, H. W. Models of memory and models of development. *Human Development,* 1973, **16,** 397–416.

54. Scarr, S. Social introversion-extraversion as a heritable response. *Child Development,* 1969, **40,** 823–832.

55. Scott, J. P. *Early experience and the organization of behavior.* Belmont, Calif.: Brooks/Cole Publishing Co., 1968.

56. Shuttleworth, F. K. The physical and mental growth of girls and boys age six to 19 in relation to age at maximum growth. *Monographs of the Society for Research in Child Development,* 1939, **4:**3.

57. Stone, C. P., and R. G. Barker. Aspects of personality and intelligence in post-menarcheal and premenarcheal girls of the same chronological age. *Journal of Comparative Psychology,* 1937, **23,** 439–455.

58. Sullivan, W. If we master the gene. *New York Times,* June 14, 1970.

59. Tanner, J. M. *Education and physical growth.* London: University of London Press, 1961.

60. Tanner, J. M. Relation of body size, intelligence test scores and social circumstances. In P. Mussen, J. Langer, and M. Covington (eds.). *Trends and issues in developmental psychology.* New York: Holt, Rinehart and Winston, Inc., 1969.

61. Vandenberg, S. G. Human behavior genetics: Present status and suggestions for future research. *Merrill-Palmer Quarterly,* 1969, **15,** 121–154.

62. Walter, G. Comments. In J. M. Tanner and B. Inhelder (eds.). *Discussions on child development.* vol. I. New York: International Universities Press, 1953.

63. Watson, J. S., and C. T. Ramey. Reactions to response-contingent stimulation in early infancy. *Merrill-Palmer Quarterly,* 1972, **18,** 219–227.

64. Wolff, P. Autonomous systems in human behavior and development. *Human Development,* 1974, **17,** 281–291.

65. Zern, D. S. An interpretation of the effects of stimulation on development: Its role as a resolvable disequilibrator. *Genetic Psychology Monographs,* 1974, **90,** 532–547.

Readings in
An Overview of Human Life and Growth

In an earlier, and possibly in some ways happier, time, man was considered the final and triumphant item of creation, the master and user of other living things. Even the early evolutionary biologists considered that man stood at the apex of evolution; they did not seem aware of the possibility that the process of evolution might continue, resulting in the appearance of new species. They seemed even less aware of the possibility that the evolutionary process of man resulted in a creature who had within him the seeds of his own destruction, like the sabre-toothed tiger, whose overdeveloped canine teeth prevented him from ingesting his prey.

Ecology is the branch of biology that studies the relationship of living things to their environment, including other living things. Recently ecologists have included man as the subject of their study. In general, the results of their investigations have been frightening. Especially in North America man is seen as a fouler of his environment—air, water, and soil—to such an extent that ecologists say that if present trends go unchecked, man may make his continued existence impossible.

In the first article in this chapter, William W. Ballard, a biologist, describes some of the facts about man's evolutionary development and speculates about the future. He makes the important distinction between man as a species and men as individuals who together make up the species. Each individual has characteristics of the species that have arisen during the course of evolution, but each individual has his own personal history, during which he has learned some ways of behaving that may be, in the long run, maladaptive for the species. Ballard's article has been very useful to us in teaching child development courses. We found ourselves referring frequently to his notion of the two computers when we discussed opposing processes or ideas in all sorts of contexts.

Lawrence K. Frank, the author of the second article, gave form, direction, and impetus to the field of child development. Frank's genius provided a flow of ideas for research, education, and theory. He was responsible for establishing child development centers, the parent education movement, and interdisciplinary research. In the article presented here, Frank demonstrates his characteristic warmth and wonder while analyzing the growth processes at work in infants. He describes how the child elaborates his individuality through interaction. In the terms used by Ballard in the first article, Frank shows how the "second computer" begins, based on the beginnings of the "first computer."

Erikson and Piaget, the authors of the third and fourth selections, are also primarily concerned with the development of the "second computer." But both are explicit in their statement that their theories are based on biology. Although both are dealing with psychological material, they start from biological characteristics of man.

299

The epigenetic theory of Erik H. Erikson is represented by the next essay, taken from his book Identity, Youth and Crisis. An artist, teacher, and philosopher thoroughly trained in Freudian psychoanalysis, Erikson has made enormous contributions to the field of child development. His theory is built upon Freudian theory, which he extends and develops into a way of understanding and describing the healthy personality throughout life. Erikson describes stages of personality growth, showing for each one a relation of personality to bodily development and to interaction with the culture. Each stage is derived from and built upon the one preceding it. The organization of this book is shaped by Erikson's stages in childhood and adolescence. The content is influenced by his thinking.

Jean Piaget, the world-famous Swiss psychologist, is the author of the fourth piece in this section. Piaget is primarily a genetic epistemologist, a scientist-philosopher who investigates the production of knowledge. He has developed a comprehensive theory of the mental structures through which human beings build their concept of reality and deal with it. Piaget has stimulated psychological research all over the world. Americans have produced hundreds of studies in response to his theories and findings. Like Erikson's theory of personality development, Piaget's account of the growth of intelligence is epigenetic and interactional. Piaget's theory is very compatible with a child development point of view, because the child's mind is seen as resulting from biologically given beginnings actively engaged with the environment.

The Rise and Fall of Humanity

William W. Ballard

The reading that follows is the last part of a lecture titled " The Rise and Fall of Humanity." In the first part Ballard summarizes the development of living things during the course of four billion years of earth history, the accelerating growth of knowledge in the last few thousand years, and the serious threats to man's continued existence that have stemmed from this knowledge. Basically, Ballard says, the present crisis has arisen because there are too many people on the earth and they are demanding more than the earth can provide. These events have occurred because man as a species of animal is composed of men and women as individuals.

To maximize the amount of life that can be supported in a given ecosystem, a large number of species of plants, animals, and decomposers are brought into balance, each occupying its own niche and following its own instructions to make the best of the things available to it while contributing to the flow of energy and the recycling of materials. If one species in the ecosystem gets out of balance the whole community develops an instability that may either result in an irreversible change in its character, or in the control or rejection of the destabilizing element.

From *Dartmouth Alumni Magazine*, 1970, **62** (6), 60–64. Reprinted by permission of the author, the Dartmouth Alumni College, and the *Dartmouth Alumni Magazine*.

The human species has been manipulating its environment since the invention of agriculture, favoring the plants and animals that serve it for food, repressing or even exterminating others. Where this was overdone—e.g., Mesopotamia, the Near East, Yucatan—ghost cities and records of dead cultures remain to show how powerfully nature can strike back. Quite recently we have begun to use the treasure trove of fossil fuels to grow the food to satisfy the multiplying demands of our own population, and we congratulate ourselves on having temporarily freed ourselves from the normal restrictions of the natural world. It is a dangerous game we are playing.

No good asking why the human *species* takes these risks. A species is an invention of the mind, a generalization. Only human *individuals* actually walk and breathe and make decisions and it is the collection of individuals who have been doing what I say the species has been doing. What went wrong with human individuals, that they have gotten their species and their environment into such a mess? The other face of this question is, what is an indvidual supposed to be doing, and within what limits is he supposed to be held?

THE PRIMARY COMPUTER   To simplify, I shall restrict the latter question to animals rather than plants or decomposers. I shall pick animals that are not on a rampage, animals that have (so far as we can tell) no conscious reasoning ability, no thoughts, loyalties, hopes, or faiths. Some kind of earthworm or some frog will do. I assume that whatever one of these animals does, any choice that it makes, is determined by its inherited computer system. It receives from its ancestors a scanning mechanism which reports what all the circumstances around and inside it are at the moment. This information is checked against an inherited memory encoded in its central nervous system. The computer then not only orders up the strategy and tactics that had met that sort of situation successfully before, but directs what every cell, what every organ, what the whole earthworm or frog must be doing to contribute to that response. (Directions for unsuccessful responses are not encoded in this primary computer, because they simply are not inherited.)

To see what this genetic computer requires the individual worm or frog to do, let us follow his life history, watching him obey and reconstructing from what he does the nature of the commands.

1. As a member of a bisexual species he (or she) starts as a fertilized egg, a single diploid individual with unique heterozygous genic individuality. First, *he develops*. Since the fertilized egg is insulated to a degree from the outside world, his computer works at first mostly on internal information. It refers to the inherited memory in the chromosomes and brings out instructions of various intricate sorts to the ultrastructures of the cell, programmed so that the cell divides into two, then four, then eight cells . . . until the word gets back to the multiplied computers in the multiplied cells that it is time to activate their inherited instructions for differentiation. Tissues and organs are formed, in such sorts and such patterns as have enabled the species to survive so far. The new individual acquires the sensory and neural apparatus for bringing in more and more information from the outside, and this is referred to the more and more specialized computer developing out of the inherited instructions, in a central nervous system (in the case of a frog, a brain and spinal cord). He begins

to move about, respire, feed, excrete, defend himself, in directions and at rates calculated to be appropriate to the sensed state of affairs from moment to moment. This is quite a trick for a self-built computer to bring off, and as an embryologist I wish I understood more of how it is done.

2. The young earthworm or pollywog, having broken loose from its protective envelopes and used up its dowry of yolk, is next under orders to *reach adulthood*. He recognizes dangers and opportunities by continually referring the information flowing in from his sensory apparatus to his inherited memory. He certainly has not learned his behavioral responses from his parents, never having met them. It is the inherited computer which tells him what to do from one millisecond to the next. He survives or not, partly by luck but also partly according to whether his own inherited variant of the species-specific computer will deliver the right answers to the problems of his own day and place. (The *species* survives by offering up enough varieties so that some individuals will have what the new situations demand, the wastage of the other individuals being a necessary part of the cost. No other way has yet been discovered for meeting the demands of an unpredictable future, i.e. winning a game the rules for which have not yet been written.)

3. Our earthworm or frog, if lucky, finds himself a sexually mature individual, with his instructions to reproduce now turned on. These instructions, activated by seasonal or other environmental signals, operate upon particular genes, particular cells, particular organs, and particular behavioral mechanisms set off through the nervous system. Without knowing it, much less knowing why, the animals seeks out a mate, copulates, and shares in the production of fertilized eggs that bring us again to phase 1 of the cycle.

4. Having blindly and without thought followed his instructions to (1) develop, (2) make do, survive, gain strength, and (3) reproduce, our earthworm or frog subsequently (4) *dies*. It is the ancient law. So far as the interests of the individual are concerned, it is absurd.

But now how about man? How unique is he? Does he not learn by experience and education, manage his own life, consciously determine what jobs he shall tackle, what ends he shall serve? My argument that he too is run by an inherited computer program rests partly on the observed fact that (1) he develops, (2) he makes every effort to reach maturity, (3) if lucky enough he sets the cycle going again, and (4) he dies. There is nothing unique about that. Experience, learning, individual preferences serve only for minor embellishments.

I select one case to illustrate that an animal's program is mostly inherited. Four to six weeks after fertilization (depending on temperature) a salamander embryo will have used up its yolk and must by then have acquired an elaborate repertoire of locomotor, hunting-sensory, food-grabbing, and swallowing behavior to keep itself fed and growing. Does the individual learn this behavior by trial and error? No. Starting a day before any of his muscles were mature enough to contract, you can rear him in a dilute anesthetic solution until he has reached the feeding stage. Put him back into pond water, and in twenty minutes the anesthetic will have worn off and he is swimming, hunting, grabbing, and swallowing like a normal tadpole. One is seeing here the computer-controlled maturation of a computer-controlled behavior. No practice, no learning.

The individual within which this remarkable apparatus matures is an expendable pawn, and the apparatus is not for his enjoyment of life, it is to keep the species going.

THE SECONDARY COMPUTER   There is such an inherited program in the human individual, but there is much more. The baby does not so much learn to walk as to develop the inherited capacity to walk; but then he can learn a dance that no man has ever danced before, he can paint a picture with a brush clasped between his toes. During late fetal life and his first six or eight years he gradually matures a second computer system superimposed on, controlling and almost completely masking the ancient frog-type computer. The evolutionary history of this new device is traceable back to, and in some respects beyond, the time of origin of the modern mammals 70 million or more years ago. It has progressed farthest in particular mammalian orders—the carnivores, hoofed animals, bats, whales and primates, and least in the egg-laying mammals and marsupials.

The new trend has worked certain real advantages, and has been kept under reasonable control, in the higher mammals, but it is my strong suspicion that its over-development in man is the root of our trouble. Like the dinosaurs, we contain in our own structure the reason why we will have to go. Robinson Jeffers[1] said it: "We have minds like the fangs of those forgotten tigers, hypertropied and terrible."

Up to a point, the development of brain and spinal cord follows the same course in frog and man. Sense organs, cranial and spinal nerves, principal subdivisions of the brain, basic fiber tract systems, all form in strictly comparable fashion in both. But the adult human brain is a far different thing from the adult frog brain. It continues the multiplication and interconnection of neurons during a far longer growth period, and adds to the elementary or frog-type apparatus two principal complicating tissues that far overshadow the earlier developments. One is often called reticular substance, the other is the cerebral cortex.

The reticular substance is so called because it is an interweaving of small centers of gray substance with short bundles and interspersed mats of axons (the white substance), quite different from the simple contrast between gray and white substance seen in primitive animals and in early embryos. The frog brain is not without this sort of tissue, but in the brains of advanced vertebrates like the teleost fishes, the reptiles, and the birds, it becomes indescribably complex. The modern mammals push this development to still higher orders of magnitude.

Although neurological science is not yet ready with answers to most specific questions about what happens where in the central nervous system, the new techniques of exploration within the brain suggest that in and through the reticular substance the connections for integrating sensory information with the devices for evaluation and for making decisions and coordinated responses are multiplied exponentially.

Thus, an electrode planted within a single neuron in the reticular substance of the hindbrain can give startling evidence that this one cell is receiving and

[1] R. Jeffers, "Passenger Pigeons," in *The Beginning and the End.*

reacting to sensations reported from widely scattered parts of the body, and sending out coded pulses as a calculated response. Your own brain contains hundreds of millions, probably billions of such cells, every one individually a computer.

The neurologists can now stimulate chosen localized areas through implanted electrodes, either hooked up to wires dangling from the cage ceiling or activated through miniaturized transmitters healed in under the scalp and controlled by radio transmission. In such experiments, stimuli delivered to many parts of the reticular substance cause the animal to react as though he were flooded with agreeable sensation. If the cat or rat or monkey learns how to deliver the stimulus to himself by pressing a pedal, he will do so repeatedly and rapidly, until he falls asleep exhausted. As soon as he wakes up, he goes to pounding the pedal again.

There are other reticular areas which have the reverse effect. If the stimulus comes at rhythmical intervals and the animal discovers that he can forestall it by pressing the pedal, he quickly learns to regulate his life so as to be there and step on it just in time. What kind of sensation such a stimulus produces in him can only be guessed by the experimenter. One might suppose that these areas of reticular substance which have such opposite effects are there to add into the computer's analysis of the situation at the moment a go signal or a stop signal for particular alternative choices, or a sense of goodness or badness, satisfaction or distress, urgency or caution, danger or relaxation. A value judgment, in other words.

It is not difficult to see the survival value of such a device. No doubt the basic mechanism exists in the brains of fishes and frogs, though I am not aware that experiments have been done to locate it. In the reticular substance of mammals, however, we see it hugely developed. The result of overdoing this might produce an awareness of the good and bad features of so very many facets of a situation as to delay and perplex the individual in calculating his single coordinated response.

Mammals are also conspicuously good at remembering experiences from their own lives as individuals, and these memories are loaded with value judgments. There is still no clear answer as to where or in what coded form these new personal memories are stored. But an animal with all this added to the ancestral memory, enhanced with perhaps casually acquired and unwisely generalized connotations of goodness and badness, might predictably be endowed with excessive individuality, prone to unnecessarily variable behavior, chosen more often for self-satisfaction than in the interest of species survival.

The other evolutionary development, the formation of the cerebral cortex, is almost unknown in vertebrates other than mammals, and is feeble in some of these. Cerebral cortex is a tissue of awesome complexity, and our techniques for analyzing what happens in it are still highly inadequate. Stimulation of willing human subjects, in chosen spots exposed surgically, or radio stimulation of these areas through permanently installed electrodes operated by healed-in transistor devices, evoke feelings referred to a particular part of the body, or cause normal-appearing localized movements, e.g. the flexion of an arm or a finger, time and again, upon repetition of the signal. Other areas produce more generalized sensory or motor or emotional or physiologic effects. The patient, his brain exposed under local anesthesia, does not know when the stimulus is applied. When the electrode touches a particular spot of his cortex he may report that he is suddenly remembering a scene identifiable as to time and place, but the memory blacks out when the current is cut off. Stimulation of other areas may elicit emotions of sexual attraction or anxiety or rage graded according to the intensity of the signal.

More wide-ranging experiments with cats, monkeys, or barnyard stock, singly or in groups, free to move in large caged areas, show the possibility of turning on and off a great range of complex emotions, behavior, and even personality traits, by local stimulation.[2] The effect produced through a permanently planted electrode is area specific. Though not predictable before the first stimulus is given, the response is repeated with each stimulus, many times a day or over periods of months or years.

In subjective comparison of mammals with greater or less personal individuality one gets the impression that the degrees of freedom of choice, of imaginative recognition of possible ways to react to situations, of storage capacity and retentiveness of memory, and the richness of association, are correlated with the intricacy and amount of the cerebral cortex and reticular substance. Animals highest on both scales include porpoises, elephants, cats and dogs, apes, and people.

One cannot underestimate the effects on the human species of other evolutionary trends that came to a climax in us, for instance the development of upright posture that frees the hands, the reshaping of the fingers for grasping and manipulating, the perfection of binocular vision that can bring into focus either the hands or the far distance at will. Far more significant than these was the development of speech, made possible by and controlled in a particular small area of the new cerebral cortex. This expanded the powers of the human secondary computer by orders of magnitude, even in comparison with that of close relatives like apes.

We no longer communicate with each other by baring teeth, raising hackles and flaunting rumps, but in symbolic language. We can make abstractions and generalizations, and artificial associations. Through speech we can feed into the recording apparatus of each others' secondary computers not only the vast and rather accidental store of individually acquired and long-lasting memories of our own experience, but also the loads of approval or disapproval which we deliberately or unwittingly put upon them. We increasingly remove ourselves into created worlds of our own, calculating our choices by reference to a memory bank of second-hand ghosts of other people's experiences and feelings, prettied up or uglified with value judgments picked up who knows where, by whom, for what reason.

Language gave a fourth dimension to the powers of the secondary computer, and writing a fifth dimension. We can now convince each other that things are good or bad, acceptable or intolerable, merely by agreeing with each other, or by reciting catechisms. With writing we can color the judgments of people unborn, just as our judgments are tailored to the whim of influential teachers in the past.

[2] J. M. R. Delgado, 1969, *Physical Control of the Mind.*

Symbols have given us the means to attach a value judgment to some abstract noun, some shibboleth, and transfer this by association to any person or situation at will. We invent, we practice, we delight in tricks for saying things indirectly by poetry and figures of speech, that might sound false or trite or slanderous or nonsensical if we said them directly. A more normally constructed animal, a porpoise or an elephant, mercifully spared such subtleties, might well look at human beings and see that each one of us has become to some degree insane, out of touch with the actual world, pursuing a mad course of options in the imagined interest of self rather than of species.

The primary computer is still there, programmed in the interest of species survival. With his new powers, man should do better than any other animal at understanding the present crisis and generating an appropriate strategy and tactics. Instead, the effort is drowned out in the noise, the flicker-bicker, the chattering flood of directives from the personalized secondary computer. In pursuit of his own comfort and his own pleasure, man wars against his fellows and against the good earth.

The frame of each person is like a racing shell with two oarsmen in it, back to back, rowing in opposite directions. The one represents the ancient computer system, comparing the personal situation of the moment with an inherited value system and driving the person to perform in such a way that the species will survive, irrespective of how absurd his own expendable life may be. The other represents the secondary computer system, probably located in reticular substance and cerebral cortex, surveying chiefly the memories of childhood and adult life, and deciding how to act according to the value-loaded store of personal experience.

It is this runaway evolutionary development of our superimposed second computer that has produced our inventors, our artists, our saints and heroes, our poets, our thinkers. Our love and hate, ecstasy and despair. The infinite variety of human personalities. It has also atomized the species into a cloud of ungovernable individuals. We split our elections 48 to 52, make laws to break them, and either ignore community priorities or establish them by political blind-man's-buff in frivolous disregard of real emergencies. Six experts will come violently to six different decisions on how to meet a crisis because their personal histories lead them to weigh the same data differently. Each of us can see bad logic and conflicts of interest affecting the judgment of most of our associates; it is more difficult to detect them in ourselves. Our individually acquired prejudices have been built into our secondary computers.

Yet it is a glorious thing to feel the uniqueness, the power of decision, the freedom of being human. Who would prefer to be even so wonderful a creature as a dog, an elephant, a horse, a porpoise? I believe nevertheless that just this ungovernable power of the human individual, the essence of our humanity, is the root of the trouble.

The California biologist Garrett Hardin, in a famous essay called "The Tragedy of the Commons," showed that this accounts for practically all the facets of our apocalyptic crisis, from the population explosion to runaway technology.[3] He is referring to the community pasture where anyone may feed

[3] G. Hardin, 1968, *Science* **162**: 1243. "The Tragedy of the Commons."

his animals. Overgrazing will bring erosion and irreversible deterioration in it. Each herdsman, calculating the advantage and disadvantage to himself of putting out one more animal to graze, balancing his small share of the possible damage against his sole ownership of the extra income, adds another animal in his own interest, and another, and another. All do, and all lose together. The tragedy is the inescapable disaster when each herdsman pursues his own advantage without limit, in a limited commons. This is the tragedy that leaves us with too many human mouths to feed, soil impoverished and washed or blown away, forests skinned off, lakes ruined, plastic bottles and aluminium cans scattered over the countryside, rivers clogged with dead fish, bilge oil spreading on public waters, streets and highways made obscene with advertisements. It is what gives us choking smog, the stink and corruption below paper mills and slaughter houses, the draining of one well by another in a falling water table, the sneaking of radioactive wastes into the air and the oceans.

All these, Hardin makes clear, are problems with *no technological solution*. To be sure, the technology stands ready, but the trouble starts with some individual, you, me, whose response to a situation is to give highest priority to his personal chance of profit, or his family's, or his country's. He has a vivid sense of the value to himself of his own freedom, but the total effects of all such freedoms on the species and on the natural world which supports it is invisible or far out of focus. The technology might just as well not exist.

Some of these problems that will not be solved by technology alone can indeed be brought under control by compacts, treaties, and other agreements between willing groups, or by laws imposed by the majority upon a minority in the common interest. Hardin, however, puts the finger on the population problem as the worst example of the worst class of problems, in which all of us must restrict the freedom of all of us, when none of us want to. He is properly skeptical of conscience or altruism as forces for uniting the community when nearly all of us are still daring to gamble on the continued capacity of the commons to withstand collapse. What is needed, he says, is a fundamental extension of morality.

My way of agreeing with him is to say that human nature is our chief enemy because the species-preserving function of our primary computer has not yet been built into the secondary computer which generates our human nature. It is by now clear that our nature as individuals is not so much inherited as learned by babies as they grow into people, in and from their individual, accidental, and culture-bound experiences. We need to incorporate into the decision-making apparatus that will really control them a new survival morality, a system of values the principal axiom of which is that anything which threatens the welfare of the species is bad, anything that serves to bring the species into harmony with its environment is good. We must, each of us, because of this inner drive, regulate our numbers and our selfish wants as rigorously as the forces of natural selection would have done had we not learned how to set them aside.

Do we know how to create a human nature that can keep the species going without undue sacrifice of the privilege and joy of being human? How much freedom must we give up? Do we want to? Is there time?

Basic Processes in Organisms

Lawrence K. Frank

If we are to understand the infant as a persistent, but ever changing, organism, we need to think in terms that are dynamic, which calls for a recognition of the ongoing processes by which the infant grows, develops, matures, and ages while continually functioning and behaving. As a young mammalian organism, the human infant lives by much the same basic physiological processes as other mammals.

The recognition of process has come with the acceptance of such recently formulated conceptions as that of self-organization, self-stabilization, self-repair, and self-direction which are characteristic not only of organisms but of various man-made machines such as computers and systems designed to operate a planned sequence of activities with the use of positive and negative feedbacks (Wiener 1961; Von Foerster and Zopf 1962). The organism may be said to be "programmed" by its heredity but capable of flexible functioning through the life cycle.

Moreover, it must be re-emphasized that each infant differs to a greater or lesser extent from all other infants, exhibiting not only individual variation but also displaying a considerable range of intra-individual variability, or continually changing functioning and physiological states, especially during the early months of life when the infant is not yet fully organized or capable of adequate self-stabilization.

Since most of our knowledge of infancy and childhood is derived from observations and measurements of selected variables, responses to stimuli, at a given time or a succession of times, we do not gain an adequate conception of the continuous, dynamic processes of living organisms, especially since we tend to focus upon the outcomes, without recognizing the processes which produce them. Accordingly, some account of these basic processes and how they operate may provide a conceptual model for understanding the multidimensional development of infants during the first year of life. Whatever is done to and for the infant, what privations, frustrations and deprivations he may suffer, what demands and coercions he must accept, what spontaneous activity and learning he displays, may be viewed as expressions of his basic functioning processes.

Every experience in the life of an infant evokes some alteration in these organic processes whereby he manages not only to survive but to grow and develop, to learn while carrying on his incessant intercourse with the surrounding world. Thus, by focusing on the organic processes we may discover what is taking place when we speak of adjustment, learning, adaptation, and the transitions encountered at critical stages in his development.

The concept of mechanism indicates or implies a deterministic relationship between antecedent and consequent, usually as a *linear* relationship in which the consequent is proportional to the antecedent. The concept of *process* involves a

From *The Importance of Infancy*, by Lawrence K. Frank. Copyright © 1966 by Random House, Inc. Reprinted by permission of Random House, Inc.

dynamic, *non-linear* operation, whereby the same process, depending upon where, what, how, and in what quantities or intensities it operates, may produce different products which may be all out of proportion to that which initiates or touches off the process. For example the process of fertilization and gestation operates in all mammals to produce the immense variety of mammalian young. But different processes may produce similar or equivalent products, an operation which has been called "equifinality" by Bertalanffy (1950).

A brief discussion of the six basic processes operating in organisms will indicate how the infant organism is able to persist and survive by continually changing and is thereby able to cope with the particular version of infant care and rearing to which he is subjected.

These six processes are: The Growth Process, The Organizing Process, The Communicating Process, The Stabilizing Process, The Directive or Purposive Process, and The Creative Process. (Frank, 1963).

THE GROWTH PROCESS   The infant who has been growing since conception continues, with a brief interruption and often some loss of weight, to grow incrementally, adding gradually to his size and weight. His growth may be slowed down by inadequate or inappropriate feeding, by some difficulties in digesting and assimilating whatever foodstuff he be given, or by a variety of disturbances and dysfunctions. A continuing upward trend in weight is expected as an expression of normal development, although recent cautions have been expressed on the undesirability of too rapid increase in weight and the vulnerability of a fat, waterlogged infant.

This incremental growth in size and weight indicates that the infant is maintaining an excess of growth over the daily losses through elimination of urine and feces, through skin and lungs, and also in the replacement of many cells that are discarded. Thus, millions of blood corpuscles are destroyed and replaced each day, the iron of those destroyed being salvaged and reused. Likewise, cells of the skin and lining of the gastrointestinal tract, of the lungs, kidneys, liver, indeed of almost all organ systems, except the central nervous system and brain, are continually being replaced at different rates.

Probably more vitally significant but less clearly recognized is the continual replacement of the chemical constituents of cells, tissues, and bony structures, like the skeleton and the teeth in which different chemicals are discarded and new materials are selected out of the blood stream to replace them. Here we see a dramatic illustration of the statement that an organism is a configuration which must continually change in order to survive, a conception which is wholly congruous with the recently formulated assumption of the world as an aggregate of highly organized complexes of energy transformations.

Growth, incremental and replacement, is a major functioning process, gradually producing an enlarging infant as the growing cells differentiate, specialize and organize to give rise to the varied tissues and organ systems in the developing embryo and fetus. In this prenatal development the creative process is also operating to produce the unique, unduplicated human infant along with the operation of the organizing process.

THE ORGANIZING PROCESS   Only recently has the process of self-organization been recognized in scientific thinking as basic to all organisms which start with some kind of genetic inheritance and undergo multiplication and duplication of cells with differentation and specialization of components that become organized into a living organism. (Von Foerster and Zopf, 1962). Thus the initial development of an infant takes place through the operation of the growth and the organizing processes which continue to operate throughout its life, maintaining the organism as it undergoes various transitions and transformations and copes with the many discontinuities encountered in its life cycle.

Since the normal infant arrives fully equipped with all the essential bodily components and organ systems, the growth process and the organizing process operate to incorporate the intakes of food, water, and air into its ever changing structure-functioning. Most of the highly organized foodstuffs, proteins, fats, and carbohydrates, are progressively broken down, disorganized, and randomized, and the products of these digestive operations are then circulated through the blood stream from which the constituent cells, tissues, and fluids select out what they need for metabolism and organize these into their specialized structure-functioning components. The recent dramatic findings in molecular biology show how this organizing process operates within the cell as the DNA (the carrier of the genetic information) of the genes directs the production of the various proteins and the utilization of the minerals and vitamins for the growth and multiplication of cells and the maintenance of their functioning.

Also of large significance for the understanding of organic processes are the sequential steps in the utilization of food stuffs for metabolism involving many steps and numerous specialized enzymes and catalysts. Unfortunately some infants suffer from so-called metabolic errors when one or more of these steps in the metabolic sequence is missing or inadequate and therefore his growth and development and healthy functioning are jeopardized.

In the self-organizing organism we encounter circular and reciprocal operations in which every component of the organism by its specialized functioning, gives rise to, and maintains, the total organism of which it is a participant; concurrently, the total organism reciprocally governs when, what, and how each of these components must function and operate to maintain the organized whole. This capacity for self-organizing arises from the autonomy of each component of an organism which over millions of years of evolution has developed its own highly individualized and specialized functioning within the total organic complex but functions according to the requirements of the organism in which it operates.

COMMUNICATION PROCESS   Obviously, these autonomous components which give rise to growth and organization must continually communicate, internally and with the external "surround." The infant has an inherited communication network in his nervous system, his circulatory system, and his lymphatic system. Through these several channels every constituent of an organism continually communicates with all others, directly or indirectly, and with different degrees of speed in communication. Each component continually sends and receives messages whereby its functioning operations are regulated, synchronized, articulated, and related to all others, with greater or less immediacy. The infant is born with most of these internal communications already functioning, having been in operation for varying periods of its prenatal development but with the central nervous system still immature. The infant also has the sensory apparatus for various inputs, of light, of sound, touch, taste and smell, also for pain, heat and cold, and for gravity and for atmospheric pressure changes. But the infant is also initially prepared for dealing with the varying intensities and durations of these intakes and impacts, gradually increasing his capacity for filtering, buffering, mingling, and transducing these inputs whereby he may monitor these sensory communications according to his ever changing internal, physiological states and the kinesthetic and proprioceptive messages by which he continually orients himself and gradually achieves an equilibrium in space.

The infant must carry on this incessant intercourse with the world more or less protected by adults from too severe or hazardous impacts and provided with the food and care required by his helpless dependency. But the infant often must try to defend himself from what his caretakers try to impose on him or compel him to accept, as in feeding, toilet training, etc. Under this treatment much of the infant's energies may be expended in these efforts to maintain his stability and integrity against unwelcomed and uncongenial treatment which may interfere with his normal functioning and compromise his growth and development and learning as a unique organism. Thus we may say that the growth and organizing processes contribute to and are dependent upon the communication process, which operates through the inherited receptors of the infant which may become progressively altered, refined, and increasingly sensitized through learning. Quite early the infant may become receptive to nonverbal communications such as tones of voice, smiling, tactile comforting, or painful treatment.

STABILIZING PROCESS   Since the world presents so many different and continually varying messages and impacts, organisms must be able to cope with the ever changing flux of experience and maintain their integrity and functional capacities by monitoring all their organic functions. While all other organisms have evolved with their species-specific range of sensory awareness and capacity for perception and for living in their ancestral life zones, the human infant, and a few other mammals are able to live in a wide variety of climates and habitations and maintain their internal world within fairly close limitations upon intraorganic variability. This becomes possible through the operation of the stabilizing process.

The stabilizing process operates through a network of physiological feedbacks, both negative and positive, to maintain a dynamic equilibrium and is not limited to the concept of homeostasis which Cannon used to describe the maintenance of the fluid internal environment. The stabilizing process maintains continually changing physiological states. At birth it is not fully developed or operationally effective and hence the infant needs continual care, protection, and appropriate nutrition. But as he grows and develops he increasingly regulates his internal functioning by responding appropriately to the various inputs and outputs, intakes, and outlets. Obviously an infant who must grow, both incrementally and by replacement, cannot tolerate too stable an internal environment which might prevent or limit such growth and adaptive functioning. With his increasing exposure to the world the infant learns to calibrate all his sensory inputs and increasingly to "equalize his thresholds," as Kurt Goldstein (1939) has pointed out.

Not the least significant and often stressful experience under which an infant must maintain his internal stability are the varying practices of child care and feeding, the efforts of parents to regularize his functioning and compel him to conform to whatever regimen of living they wish to establish. Clearly the stabilizing process is essential to the infant's survival and to his continuing growth and development and the variety of learning which he must master. Happily, most infants achieve a progressive enlargement of their capacity for living and for self-regulation and self-stabilization to assume an autonomy expressing their integrity in the face of often uncongenial treatment and surroundings.

THE DIRECTIVE OR PURPOSIVE PROCESS   With the achievement of motor coordination and locomotion, by creeping and crawling, and then assuming an erect posture and learning to walk, the infant enlarges the purposive or goal seeking process which involves continual scanning, probing, and exploring the world and developing his selective awareness and patterned perception, and especially the ability to ignore or to reject what may interfere or distract him in his endeavour to attain remote or deferred goals. Obviously, the purposive process cannot operate effectively until the infant has achieved a considerable degree of internal stabilization and of neuro-muscular coordination, and the ability to cope with a three dimensional, spatial world.

Since the child initially is attracted or impelled by whatever he may become aware of or has an impulse to seek, to handle, to put into his mouth, or otherwise to manipulate, the purposive process is frequently blocked and the child may be severely punished in his attempts to develop his autonomous mastery of his small world. Thus the purposive process operates differentially in each infant who is likely to be attracted by and responsive to different dimensions of his environment at different times; these early explorations provide an endless sequence of learning experiences which involve, not only the actual world of nature, but the wide range of artifacts and of highly individuated personalities with whom he is in contact. With language the infant learns to deal with people and verbal symbols of language for goal seeking.

THE CREATIVE PROCESS   As noted earlier, the creative process begins to operate early in gestation to produce a unique infant as a human organism with the same basic organic functions and similar or equivalent components which, however, are different in each infant. From birth on, therefore, each infant is engaged in creating a highly selective environment or a "life space" that is as congenial and appropriate for his individualized organism, with its peculiar needs and capacities, as is possible under the constraints and coercions imposed by others upon his growth, development, functioning, and learning. In infancy and childhood the individual is more creative than in any other period in his life cycle, but this creativity may be either ignored or discouraged by those who are intent upon making the child conform as nearly as possible to their image or ideal of attainment.

Within recent years the purposive and creative processes have become major foci in the studies of early child growth, development, and education, but it must be remembered that the purposive and creative processes cannot operate independently because they are inextricably related to and dependent upon the other four basic processes which reciprocally contribute to the operation of these two processes.

Most of the training and education of the infant and young child involves curbing, regulating, focusing, and patterning, and also evoking the communicating and stabilizing and directive processes which are more amenable to intervention and control by others. Through supervision and regulation of these processes the child is largely molded, patterned, and oriented into the kind of organism-personality favored by his parents and appropriately prepared for living in his cultural and social order. As he grows older the infant is expected to learn the required conduct for group living and to master the various symbol systems by which he can relate cognitively to the world and negotiate with other people. It appears that learning as an expression of the purposive and the creative processes may be compromised and sometimes severely distorted or blocked when the child is expected or compelled to alter the organizing, communicating, and stabilizing processes, as required by his parents and other more experienced persons.

In the discussion of humanization we will see how the young mammalian organism is transformed into a personality for living in a symbolic cultural world and for participating in a social order, through the various practices of infant care and rearing that are focused upon, and directly intervene in, the operation of these six basic organic processes. But each infant is a highly individualized organism who develops his own idiosyncratic personality through the development and utilization of his basic organic processes.

References

BERTALANFFY, L. VON, "Theory of Open Systems in Physics and Biology," *Science*, CXI, 1950, pp. 27–29. See also Yearbooks of Society for General Systems Research.

FRANK, L. K., "Human Development—An Emerging Discipline," in *Modern Perspectives in Child Development*, In honor of Milton J. E. Senn, Eds. Albert J. Solnit and Sally Provence, New York: International Universities Press, 1963.

———. "Potentiality: Its Definition and Development," in *Insights and the Curriculum*, Yearbook, Association for Supervision and Curriculum Development, Washington, D.C.: National Education Association, 1963.

GOLDSTEIN, KURT, *The Organism*, New York: American Book Company, 1939.

VON FOERSTER, HEINZ, and ZOPF, JR., GEORGE W., Eds., *Principles of Self Organizing Systems*, London: Pergamon Press, 1962.

WIENER, NORBERT, *Cybernetics*, Cambridge and New York: M.I.T. Press and John Wiley and Sons, Inc., 1961.

The Life Cycle : Epigenesis of Identity

Erik H. Erikson

HARVARD UNIVERSITY

Whenever we try to understand growth, it is well to remember the *epigenetic principle* which is derived from the growth of organisms *in utero*. Somewhat generalized, this principle states that anything that grows has a ground plan, and that out of this ground plan, the parts arise, each part having its time of special ascendancy, until all parts have arisen to form a functioning whole. This, obviously, is true for fetal development where each part of the organism has its critical time of ascendance or danger of defect. At birth the baby leaves the chemical exchange of the womb for the social exchange system of his society, where his gradually increasing capacities meet the opportunities and limitations of his culture. How the maturing organism continues to unfold, not by developing new organs but by means of a prescribed sequence of locomotor, sensory, and social capacities, is described in the child-development literature. As pointed out, psychoanalysis has given us an understanding of the more idiosyncratic experiences, and especially the inner conflicts, which constitute the manner in which an individual becomes a distinct personality. But here, too, it is important to realize that in the sequence of his most personal experiences the healthy child, given a reasonable amount of proper guidance, can be trusted to obey inner laws of development, laws which create a succession of potentialities for significant interaction with those persons who tend and respond to him and those institutions which are ready for him. While such interaction varies from culture to culture, it must remain within "the proper rate and the proper sequence" which governs all epigenesis. Personality, therefore, can be said to develop according to steps predetermined in the human organism's readiness to be driven toward, to be aware of, and to interact with a widening radius of significant individuals and institutions.

It is for this reason that, in the presentation of stages in the development of the personality, we employ an epigenetic diagram analogous to the one employed in *Childhood and Society* for an analysis of Freud's psychosexual stages.[1] It is, in fact, an implicit purpose of this presentation to bridge the theory of infantile sexuality (without repeating it here in detail) and our knowledge of the child's physical and social growth.

In Diagram 1 the double-lined squares signify both a sequence of stages and a gradual development of component parts. In other words, the diagram formalizes a progression through time of a differentiation of parts. This indicates (1) that each item of the vital personality to be discussed is systematically related to all others, and that they all depend on the proper development in

From *Identity, Youth and Crisis,* Copyright © 1968 by W. W. Norton & Company, Inc., pp. 92–96. Reprinted by permission of W. W. Norton & Company and Faber and Faber Ltd.

[1] See Erik H. Erikson, *Childhood and Society*, 2nd ed., New York: W. W. Norton & Company, Inc., 1963, Part I.

DIAGRAM 1

	1	2	3	4	5	6	7	8
VIII								INTEGRITY vs. DESPAIR
VII							GENERATIVITY vs. STAGNATION	
VI						INTIMACY vs. ISOLATION		
V	Temporal Perspective vs. Time Confusion	Self-Certainty vs. Self-Consciousness	Role Experimentation vs. Role Fixation	Apprenticeship vs. Work Paralysis	IDENTITY vs. IDENTITY CONFUSION	Sexual Polarization vs. Bisexual Confusion	Leader- and Followership vs. Authority Confusion	Ideological Commitment vs. Confusion of Values
IV				INDUSTRY vs. INFERIORITY	Task Identification vs. Sense of Futility			
III			INITIATIVE vs. GUILT		Anticipation of Roles vs. Role Inhibition			
II		AUTONOMY vs. SHAME, DOUBT			Will to Be Oneself vs. Self-Doubt			
I	TRUST vs. MISTRUST				Mutual Recognition vs. Autistic Isolation			

315

the proper sequence of each item; and (2) that each item exists in some form before "its" decisive and critical time normally arrives.

If I say, for example, that a sense of basic trust is the first component of mental vitality to develop in life, a sense of autonomous will the second, and a sense of initiative the third, the diagram expresses a number of fundamental relations that exist among the three components, as well as a few fundamental facts for each.

Each comes to ascendance, meets its crisis, and finds its lasting solution in ways to be described here, toward the end of the stages mentioned. All of them exist in the beginning in some form, although we do not make a point of this fact, and we shall not confuse things by calling these components different names at earlier or later stages. A baby may show something like "autonomy" from the beginning, for example, in the particular way in which he angrily tries to wriggle his hand free when tightly held. However, under normal conditions, it is not until the second year that he begins to experience the whole critical alternative between being an autonomous creature and being a dependent one, and it is not until then that he is ready for a specifically new encounter with his environment. The environment, in turn, now feels called upon to convey to him its particular ideas and concepts of autonomy in ways decisively contributing to his personal character, his relative efficiency, and the strength of his vitality.

It is this encounter, together with the resulting crisis, which is to be described for each stage. Each stage becomes a crisis because incipient growth and awareness in a new part function go together with a shift in instinctual energy and yet also cause a specific vulnerability in that part. One of the most difficult questions to decide, therefore, is whether or not a child at a given stage is weak or strong. Perhaps it would be best to say that he is always vulnerable in some respects and completely oblivious and insensitive in others, but that at the same time he is unbelievably persistent in the same respects in which he is vulnerable. It must be added that the baby's weakness gives him power; out of his very dependence and weakness he makes signs to which his environment, if it is guided well by a responsiveness combining "instinctive" and traditional patterns, is peculiarly sensitive. A baby's presence exerts a consistent and persistent domination over the outer and inner lives of every member of a household. Because these members must reorient themselves to accommodate his presence, they must also grow as individuals and as a group. It is as true to say that babies control and bring up their families as it is to say the converse. A family can bring up a baby only by being brought up by him. His growth consists of a series of challenges to them to serve his newly developing potentialities for social interaction.

Each successive step, then, is a potential crisis because of a radical change in perspective. Crisis is used here in a developmental sense to connote not a threat of catastrophe, but a turning point, a crucial period of increased vulnerability and heightened potential, and therefore, the ontogenetic source of generational strength and maladjustment. The most radical change of all, from intrauterine to extrauterine life, comes at the very beginning of life. But in postnatal existence, too, such radical adjustments of perspective as lying relaxed, sitting firmly, and running fast must all be accomplished in their own good time.

With them, the interpersonal perspective also changes rapidly and often radically, as is testified by the proximity in time of such opposites as "not letting mother out of sight" and "wanting to be independent." Thus, different capacities use different opportunities to become full-grown components of the ever-new configuration that is the growing personality.

Equilibrium

Jean Piaget
UNIVERSITY OF GENEVA

The psychological development that starts at birth and terminates in adulthood is comparable to organic growth. Like the latter, it consists essentially of activity directed toward equilibrium. Just as the body evolves toward a relatively stable level characterized by the completion of the growth process and by organ maturity, so mental life can be conceived as evolving toward a final form of equilibrium represented by the adult mind. In a sense, development is a progressive equilibration from a lesser to a higher state of equilibrium. From the point of view of intelligence, it is easy to contrast the relative instability and incoherence of childhood ideas with the systematization of adult reason. With respect to the affective life, it has frequently been noted how extensively emotional equilibrium increases with age. Social relations also obey the same law of gradual stabilization.

An essential difference between the life of the body and that of the mind must nonetheless be stressed if the dynamism inherent in the reality of the mind is to be respected. The final form of equilibrium reached through organic growth is more static and, above all, more unstable than the equilibrium toward which mental development strives, so that no sooner has ascending evolution terminated than a regressive evolution automatically starts, leading to old age. Certain psychological functions that depend closely on the physical condition of the body follow an analogous curve. Visual acuity, for example, is at a maximum toward the end of childhood, only to diminish subsequently; and many other perceptual processes are regulated by the same law. By contrast, the higher functions of intelligence and affectivity tend toward a "mobile equilibrium." The more mobile it is, the more stable it is, so that the termination of growth, in healthy minds, by no means marks the beginning of decline but rather permits progress that in no sense contradicts inner equilibrium.

It is thus in terms of equilibrium that we shall try to describe the evolution of the child and the adolescent. From this point of view, mental development is

From *Six Psychological Studies*, by Jean Piaget, translated by Anita Tenzer, edited by David Elkind. Copyright © 1967 by Random House, Inc. Reprinted by permission of Random House, Inc. and Hodder & Stoughton Educational.

a continuous construction comparable to the erection of a vast building that becomes more solid with each addition. Alternatively, and perhaps more appropriately, it may be likened to the assembly of a subtle mechanism that goes through gradual phases of adjustment in which the individual pieces become more supple and mobile as the equilibrium of the mechanism as a whole becomes more stable. We must, however, introduce an important distinction between two complementary aspects of the process of equilibration. This is the distinction between the variable structures that define the successive states of equilibrium and a certain constant functioning that assures the transition from any one state to the following one.

There is sometimes a striking similarity between the reactions of the child and the adult, as, for example, when the child is sure of what he wants and acts as adults do with respect to their own special interests. At other times there is a world of difference—in games, for example, or in the manner of reasoning. From a functional point of view, i.e., if we take into consideration the general motives of behavior and thought, there are constant functions common to all ages. At all levels of development, action presupposes a precipitating factor: a physiological, affective, or intellectual need. (In the latter case, the need appears in the guise of a question or a problem.) At all levels, intelligence seeks to understand or explain, etc. However, while the functions of interest, explanation, etc., are common to all developmental stages, that is to say, are "invariable" as far as the functions themselves are concerned, it is nonetheless true that "interests" (as opposed to "interest") vary considerably from one mental level to another, and that the particular explanations (as opposed to the function of explaining) are of a very different nature, depending on the degree of intellectual development. In addition to the constant functions, there are the variable structures. An analysis of these progressive forms of successive equilibrium highlights the differences from one behavioral level to another, all the way from the elementary behavior of the neonate through adolescence.

The variable structures—motor or intellectual on the one hand and affective on the other—are the organizational forms of mental activity. They are organized along two dimensions—intrapersonal and social (interpersonal). For greater clarity we shall distinguish six stages or periods of development which mark the appearance of these successively constructed structures:

1. The reflex or hereditary stage, at which the first instinctual nutritional drives and the first emotions appear.

2. The stage of the first motor habits and of the first organized percepts, as well as of the first differentiated emotions.

3. The stage of sensorimotor or practical intelligence (prior to language), of elementary affective organization, and of the first external affective fixations. These first three stages constitute the infancy period—from birth till the age of one and a half to two years—i.e., the period prior to the development of language and thought as such.

4. The stage of intuitive intelligence, of spontaneous interpersonal feelings, and of social relationships in which the child is subordinate to the adult (ages two to seven years, or "early childhood").

5. The stage of concrete intellectual operations (the beginning of logic) and of moral and social feelings of cooperation (ages seven to eleven or twelve, or "middle childhood").

6. The stage of abstract intellectual operations, of the formation of the personality, and of affective and intellectual entry into the society of adults (adolescence).

Each of these stages is characterized by the appearance of original structures whose construction distinguishes it from previous stages. The essentials of these successive constructions exist at subsequent stages in the form of substructures onto which new characteristics have been built. It follows that in the adult each stage through which he has passed corresponds to a given level in the total hierarchy of behavior. But at each stage there are also temporary and secondary characteristics that are modified by subsequent development as a function of the need for better organization. Each stage thus constitutes a particular form of equilibrium as a function of its characteristic structures, and mental evolution is effectuated in the direction of an ever-increasing equilibrium.

We know which functional mechanisms are common to all stages. In an absolutely general way (not only in comparing one stage with the following but also in comparing each item of behavior that is part of that stage with ensuing behavior), one can say that all action—that is to say, all movement, all thought, or all emotion—responds to a need. Neither the child nor the adult executes any external or even entirely internal act unless impelled by a motive; this motive can always be translated into a need (an elementary need, an interest, a question, etc.).

As Claparède (1951) has shown, a need is always a manifestation of disequilibrium: there is need when something either outside ourselves or within us (physically or mentally) is changed and behavior has to be adjusted as a function of this change. For example, hunger or fatigue will provoke a search for nourishment or rest; encountering an external object will lead to a need to play, which in turn has practical ends, or it leads to a question or a theoretical problem. A casual word will excite the need to imitate, to sympathize, or will engender reserve or opposition if it conflicts with some interest of our own. Conversely, action terminates when a need is satisfied, that is to say, when equilibrium is re-established between the new factor that has provoked the need and the mental organization that existed prior to the introduction of this factor. Eating or sleeping, playing or reaching a goal, replying to a question or resolving a problem, imitating successfully, establishing an affective tie, or maintaining one's point of view are all satisfactions that, in the preceding examples, will put an end to the particular behavior aroused by the need. At any given moment, one can thus say, action is disequilibrated by the transformations that arise in the external or internal world, and each new behavior consists not only in re-establishing equilibrium but also in moving toward a more stable equilibrium than that which preceded the disturbance.

Human action consists of a continuous and perpetual mechanism of readjustment or equilibration. For this reason, in these initial phases of construction, the successive mental structures that engender development can be considered as so many progressive forms of equilibrium, each of which is an advance upon its predecessor. It must be understood, however, that this functional mechanism, general though it may be, does not explain the content or the structure of the various needs, since each of them is related to the organization of the particular stage that is being considered. For example, the sight of the same object will occasion very different questions in the small child who is still incapable of classification from those of the older child whose ideas are more extensive and systematic. The interests of a child at any given moment depend on the system of ideas he has acquired plus his affective inclinations, and he tends to fulfill his interests in the direction of greater equilibrium.

Before examining the details of development we must try to find that which is common to the needs and interests present at all ages. One can say, in regard to this, that all needs tend first of all to incorporate things and people into the subject's own activity, i.e., to "assimilate" the external world into the structures that have already been constructed, and secondly to readjust these structures as a function of subtle transformations, i.e., to "accommodate" them to external objects. From this point of view, all mental life, as indeed all organic life, tends progressively to assimilate the surrounding environment. This incorporation is effected thanks to the structures of psychic organs whose scope of action becomes more and more extended. Initially, perception and elementary movement (prehension, etc.) are concerned with objects that are close and viewed statically; then later, memory and practical intelligence permit the representation of earlier states of the object as well as the anticipation of their future states resulting from as yet unrealized transformations. Still later intuitive thought reinforces these two abilities. Logical intelligence in the guise of concrete operations and ultimately of abstract deduction terminates this evolution by making the subject master of events that are far distant in space and time. At each of these levels the mind fulfills the same function, which is to incorporate the universe to itself, but the nature of assimilation varies, i.e., the successive modes of incorporation evolve from those of perception and movement to those of the higher mental operations.

In assimilating objects, action and thought must accommodate to these objects; they must adjust to external variation. The balancing of the processes of assimilation and accommodation may be called "adaptation." Such is the general form of psychological equilibrium, and the progressive organization of mental development appears to be simply an ever more precise adaptation to reality.

Reference

CLAPARÈDE, E. *Le développement mental.* Neuchâtel: Delachaux et Niestlé, 1951.

Appendix A
Recommended Daily Nutrients

1. For Canadians

Age (years)	Sex	Weight (kg)	Height (cm)	Energy[a] (kcal)	Protein (g)	Water-Soluble Vitamins						
						Thiamin (mg)	Niacin[e] (mg)	Riboflavin (mg)	Vitamin B6[f] (mg)	Folate[a] (µg)	Vitamin B12 (µg)	Ascorbic Acid (mg)
0-6 mos.	Both	6	—	kg × 117	kg × 2.2 (2.0)[d]	0.3	5	0.4	0.3	40	0.3	20[h]
7-11 mos.	Both	9	—	kg × 108	kg × 1.4	0.5	6	0.6	0.4	60	0.3	20
1-3	Both	13	90	1400	22	0.7	9	0.8	0.8	100	0.9	20
4-6	Both	19	110	1800	27	0.9	12	1.1	1.3	100	1.5	20
7-9	M	27	129	2200	33	1.1	14	1.3	1.6	100	1.5	30
	F	27	128	2000	33	1.0	13	1.2	1.4	100	1.5	30
10-12	M	36	144	2500	41	1.2	17	1.5	1.8	100	3.0	30
	F	38	145	2300	40	1.1	15	1.4	1.5	100	3.0	30
13-15	M	51	162	2800	52	1.4	19	1.7	2.0	200	3.0	30
	F	49	159	2200	43	1.1	15	1.4	1.5	200	3.0	30
16-18	M	64	172	3200	54	1.6	21	2.0	2.0	200	3.0	30
	F	54	161	2100	43	1.1	14	1.3	1.5	200	3.0	30
19-35	M	70	176	3000	56	1.5	20	1.8	2.0	200	3.0	30
	F	56	161	2100	41	1.1	14	1.3	1.5	200	3.0	30
36-50	M	70	176	2700	56	1.4	18	1.7	2.0	200	3.0	30
	F	56	161	1900	41	1.0	13	1.2	1.5	200	3.0	30
51	M	70	176	2300[b]	56	1.4	18	1.7	2.0	200	3.0	30
	F	56	161	1800[b]	41	1.0	13	1.2	1.5	200	3.0	30
Pregnant				+300[c]	+20	+0.2	+2	+0.3	+0.5	+50	+1.0	+20
Lactating				+500	+24	+0.4	+7	+0.6	+0.6	+50	+0.5	+30

[a] Recommendations assume characteristic activity pattern for each age group.
[b] Recommended energy allowance for age 66½ years reduced to 2,000 for men and 1,500 for women.
[c] Increased energy allowance recommended during second and third trimesters. An increase of 100 kcal per day is recommended during the first trimester.
[d] Recommended protein allowance of 2.2 g per kg body weight for infants age 0-2 mos. and 2.0 g per kg body weight for those age 3-5 mos. Protein recommendation for infants, 0-11 mos., assumes consumption of breast milk or protein of equivalent quality.
[e] Approximately 1 mg of niacin is derived from each 60 mg of dietary tryptophan.
[f] Recommendations are based on the estimated average daily protein intake of Canadians.
[g] Recommendation given in terms of free folate.

Age (years)	Sex	Fat-Soluble Vitamins			Minerals					
		Vitamin A (μg RE)[i]	Vitamin D (μg cholcalciferol)[j]	Vitamin E (mg α-tocopherol)	Calcium (mg)	Phosphorus (mg)	Magnesium (mg)	Iodine (μg)	Iron (mg)	Zinc (mg)
0–6 mos.	Both	400	10	3	500[l]	250[l]	50[l]	35[l]	7[l]	4[l]
7–11 mos.	Both	400	10	3	500	400	50	50	7	5
1–3	Both	400	10	4	500	500	75	70	8	5
4–6	Both	500	5	5	500	500	100	90	9	6
7–9	M	700	2.5[k]	6	700	700	150	110	10	7
	F	700	2.5[k]	6	700	700	150	100	10	7
10–12	M	800	2.5[k]	7	900	900	175	130	11	8
	F	800	2.5[k]	7	1000	1000	200	120	11	9
13–15	M	1000	2.5[k]	9	1200	1200	250	140	13	10
	F	800	2.5[k]	7	800	800	250	110	14	10
16–18	M	1000	2.5[k]	10	1000	1000	300	160	14	12
	F	800	2.5[k]	6	700	700	250	110	14	11
19–35	M	1000	2.5[k]	9	800	800	300	150	10	10
	F	800	2.5[k]	6	700	700	250	110	14	9
36–50	M	1000	2.5[k]	8	800	800	300	140	10	10
	F	800	2.5[k]	6	700	700	250	100	14	9
51	M	1000	2.5[k]	8	800	800	300	140	10	10
	F	800	2.5[k]	6	700	700	250	100	9	9
Pregnant		+100	+2.5[k]	+1	+500	+500	+25	+15	+1[m]	+3
Lactating		+400	+2.5[k]	+2	+500	+500	+75	+25	+1[m]	+7

[h] Considerably higher levels may be prudent for infants during the first week of life to guard against neonatal tyrosinemia.

[i] One μg retinol equivalent (1 μg RE) corresponds to a biological activity in humans equal to 1 μg retinol (3.33 IU) and 6 μg β-carotene (10 IU).

[j] One μg cholecalciferol is equivalent to 40 IU vitamin D activity.

[k] Most older children and adults receive enough vitamin D from irradiation but 2.5 μg daily is recommended. This recommended allowance increases to 5.0 μg daily for pregnant and lactating women and for those who are confined indoors or otherwise deprived of sunlight for extended periods.

[l] The intake of breast-fed infants may be less than the recommendation but is considered to be adequate.

[m] A recommended total intake of 15 mg daily during pregnancy and lactation assumes the presence of adequate stores of iron. If stores are suspected of being inadequate, additional iron as a supplement is recommended.

SOURCE: Committee for Revision of the Canadian Dietary Standard. Recommended daily nutrients. Bureau of Nutritional Sciences, Health and Welfare, Canada, 1974.

2. For Americans[a]

		Weight		Height				Vita-min A Activity (RE)[c]	Fat-Soluble Vitamins		
Age (years)		(kg)	(lbs)	(cm)	(in)	Energy (kcal)[b]	Protein (g)		(IU)	Vita-min D (IU)	Vita-min E Activity[e] (IU)
Infants	0.0-0.5	6	14	60	24	kg × 117	kg × 2.2	420[d]	1,400	400	4
	0.5-1.0	9	20	71	28	kg × 108	kg × 2.0	400	2,000	400	5
Children	1-3	13	28	86	34	1,300	23	400	2,000	400	7
	4-6	20	44	110	44	1,800	30	500	2,500	400	9
	7-10	30	66	135	54	2,400	36	700	3,300	400	10
Males	11-14	44	97	158	63	2,800	44	1,000	5,000	400	12
	15-18	61	134	172	69	3,000	54	1,000	5,000	400	15
	19-22	67	147	172	69	3,000	54	1,000	5,000	400	15
	23-50	70	154	172	69	2,700	56	1,000	5,000		15
	51+	70	154	172	69	2,400	56	1,000	5,000		15
Females	11-14	44	97	155	62	2,400	44	800	4,000	400	12
	15-18	54	119	162	65	2,100	48	800	4,000	400	12
	19-22	58	128	162	65	2,100	46	800	4,000	400	12
	23-50	58	128	162	65	2,000	46	800	4,000		12
	51+	58	128	162	65	1,800	46	800	4,000		12
Pregnant						+300	+30	1,000	5,000	400	15
Lactating						+500	+20	1,200	6,000	400	15

[a] The allowances are intended to provide for individual variations among most normal persons as they live in the United States under usual environmental stresses. Diets should be based on a variety of common foods in order to provide other nutrients for which human requirements have been less well defined.
[b] Kilojoules (kJ) = 4.2 × kcal.
[c] Retinol equivalents.
[d] Assumed to be all as retinol in milk during the first six months of life. All subsequent intakes are assumed to be half as retinol and half as β-carotene when calculated from international units. As retinol equivalents, three fourths are as retinol and one fourth as β-carotene.

	Water-Soluble Vitamins							Minerals					
Age (years)	Ascorbic Acid (mg)	Folacin[f] (μg)	Niacin[g] (mg)	Riboflavin (mg)	Thiamin (mg)	Vitamin B_6 (mg)	Vitamin B_{12} (μg)	Calcium (mg)	Phosphorus (mg)	Iodine (μg)	Iron (mg)	Magnesium (mg)	Zinc (mg)
Infants													
0.0–0.5	35	50	5	0.4	0.3	0.3	0.3	360	240	35	10	60	3
0.5–1.0	35	50	8	0.6	0.5	0.4	0.3	540	400	45	15	70	5
Children													
1–3	40	100	9	0.8	0.7	0.6	1.0	800	800	60	15	150	10
4–6	40	200	12	1.1	0.9	0.9	1.5	800	800	80	10	200	10
7–10	40	300	16	1.2	1.2	1.2	2.0	800	800	110	10	250	10
Males													
11–14	45	400	18	1.5	1.4	1.6	3.0	1,200	1,200	130	18	350	15
15–18	45	400	20	1.8	1.5	2.0	3.0	1,200	1,200	150	18	400	15
19–22	45	400	20	1.8	1.5	2.0	3.0	800	800	140	10	350	15
23–50	45	400	18	1.6	1.4	2.0	3.0	800	800	130	10	350	15
51+	45	400	16	1.5	1.2	2.0	3.0	800	800	110	10	350	15
Females													
11–14	45	400	16	1.3	1.2	1.6	3.0	1,200	1,200	115	18	300	15
15–18	45	400	14	1.4	1.1	2.0	3.0	1,200	1,200	115	18	300	15
19–22	45	400	14	1.4	1.1	2.0	3.0	800	800	100	18	300	15
23–50	45	400	13	1.2	1.0	2.0	3.0	800	800	100	18	300	15
51+	45	400	12	1.1	1.0	2.0	3.0	800	800	80	10	300	15
Pregnant	60	800	+2	+0.3	+0.3	2.5	4.0	1,200	1,200	125	18+[h]	450	20
Lactating	80	600	+4	+0.5	+0.3	2.5	4.0	1,200	1,200	150	18	450	25

[e] Total vitamin E activity, estimated to be 80 per cent as α-tocopherol and 20 per cent other tocopherols. See text for variation in allowances.
[f] The folacin allowances refer to dietary sources as determined by *Lactobacillus casei* assay. Pure forms of folacin may be effective in doses less than one fourth of the recommended dietary allowance.
[g] Although allowances are expressed as niacin, it is recognized that on the average 1 mg of niacin is derived from each 60 mg of dietary tryptophan.
[h] This increased requirement cannot be met by ordinary diets; therefore, the use of supplemental iron is recommended.

SOURCE: Food and Nutrition Board, National Research Council. Recommended dietary allowances. Eighth rev. ed., 1974. Washington, D.C.: National Academy of Sciences, 1974.

Appendix B
Height and Weight Interpretation Charts

These charts make it possible to show graphically a child's *status* as to height and weight for any one measurement of size. If two or more measurements are made, separated by a time interval, the child's *progress* will also be shown graphically.

How to Measure Weight and Height Accurately

Use a beam-type platform scale. Weigh the child without shoes, barefoot, or in stockings, wearing minimal clothing, underwear or gym clothes. For children under 24 months, recumbent length is measured between the crown of the head and the bottom of the heel, with the back flat, the knees extended, and the soles of the feet at right angles with the ankles. For children above two, stature is measured as standing height. Without shoes, the feet should be together. Have the child stand normally erect, chin tucked in, eyes looking straight ahead. Stature is the distance between the floor and a horizontal board or bar firmly touching the crown of the head. Up to 36 months, record weight to the nearest quarter kilo (250 grams) and height to the nearest centimeter. At older ages, the nearest kilogram and the nearest centimeter are close enough.

GRAPHING HEIGHT AND WEIGHT STATUS

On the day he was measured, Carl was 7 years and 4 months old. His stature was 122 centimeters and his weight 22 kilograms. To plot his growth status, first find on the age scale of the weight graph a point one third of the way between 7 and 8 years. Imagine a line drawn vertically upward to the point where it intersects with another imaginary horizontal line drawn through a point on the weight scale at 22. Put a dot on the graph at this point. Similarly, find the imaginary vertical line at the bottom of the height scale. Put a dot at the point where that line intersects with an imaginary horizontal line through 122 centimeters. Each of these dots falls just below the 50th percentile line on the graph. These show that Carl is slightly below the average child of 7 years and 4 months, slightly lighter and slightly shorter; he is neither heavy nor light for his height.

GRAPHING HEIGHT AND WEIGHT PROGRESS

On his ninth month birthday Carl weighs 9.75 kilograms and is 72 centimeters tall. As in the earlier measurement, put a pencil dot on the nine-month vertical line where it intersects with the imaginary line through 9.75 kilograms on the weight graph, and the imaginary line through 72 centimeters on the height graph. Lines connecting the two pairs of dots are roughly parallel with the printed 50th percentile lines. In the two months between measurements Carl grew proportionately in height and weight.

EVALUATION OF WEIGHT AND HEIGHT MEASUREMENTS

If the points representing a child's height and weight are not about the same distance above or below the same percentile curve, the difference may indicate that the child is normally slender or normally stocky. If the difference between the stature and weight percentile is more than 25 percentiles, a further check on his or her health should be made.

Normal progress in height and weight gives lines for such a child that stay roughly the same distance from adjacent printed lines on the graph. When the lines go steeply up, or if one goes up and the other is nearly horizontal, a medical investigation of the child's health or nutritional condition is called for. Around the age of 11, a child's lines may cross the printed percentile lines, because there are individual differences in the timing and strength of the puberal growth spurt. A child's lines may go up more steeply for a period of time, or be more horizontal than the printed lines.

Girls' Length and Weight by Age Percentiles: Ages Birth to 36 Months

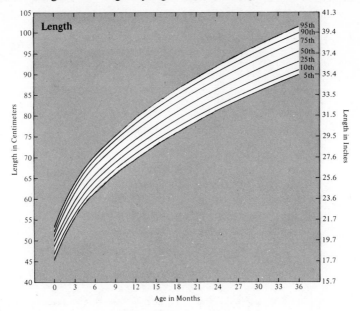

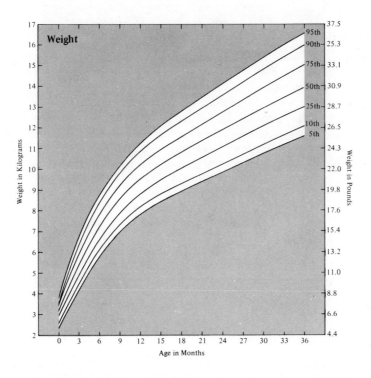

Boys' Length and Weight by Age Percentiles: Ages Birth to 36 Months

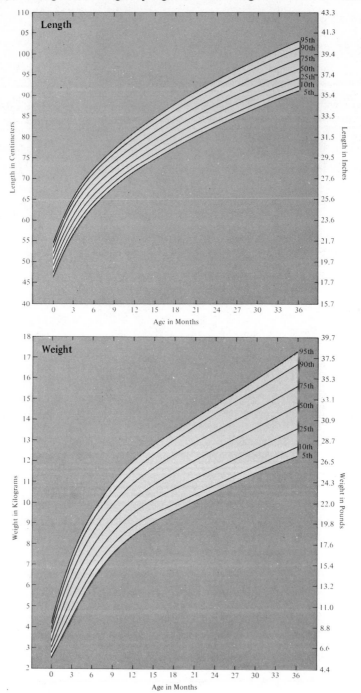

Appendix C
Communicable Diseases of Childhood

	Chickenpox	Diphtheria	Measles	Mumps	Polio
Cause	A virus: Present in secretions from nose, throat and mouth of infected people.	Diphtheria bacillus: Present in secretions from nose and throat of infected people and carriers.	A virus: Present in secretions from nose and throat of infected people.	A virus: Present in saliva of infected people.	3 strains of polio virus have been identified: Present in discharges from nose, throat, bowels of infected people.
How spread	Contact with infected people or articles used by them. Very contagious.	Contact with infected people and carriers or articles used by them.	Contact with infected people or articles used by them. Very contagious.	Contact with infected people or articles used by them.	Primarily, contact with infected people.
Incubation period (from date of exposure to first signs)	13 to 17 days. Sometimes 3 weeks.	2 to 5 days. Sometimes longer.	About 10 to 12 days.	12 to 26 (commonly 18) days.	Usually 7 to 12 days.
Period of communicability (time when disease is contagious)	From 5 days before, to 6 days after first appearance of skin blisters.	From about 2 to 4 weeks after onset of disease.	From 4 days before until about 5 days after rash appears.	From about 6 days before symptoms to 9 days after. Principally at about time swelling starts.	Apparently greatest in late incubation and first few days of illness.
Most susceptible ages	Under 15 years.	Under 15 years.	Common at any age during childhood.	Children and young people.	Most common in children 1 to 16 years.
Seasons of prevalence	Winter.	Fall, winter and spring.	Mainly spring. Also fall and winter.	Winter and spring.	June through September.
Prevention	No prevention.	Vaccination with diphtheria toxoid (in triple vaccine for babies).	Measles vaccine.	Mumps vaccine.	Polio vaccine.
Control	Exclusion from school for 1 week after eruption appears. Avoid contact with susceptibles. Immune globulin may lessen severity. (Cut child's fingernails.) Immunity usual after one attack.	Booster doses (see Appendix D). Antitoxin and antibiotics used in treatment and for protection after exposure. One attack does not necessarily give immunity.	Isolation until 7 days after appearance of rash. Immune globulin between 3 and 6 days after exposure can lighten attack. Antibiotics for complications. Immunity usual after one attack.	Isolation for 9 days from onset of swelling. Immunity usual after one attack but second attacks can occur.	Booster doses (see Appendix D). Isolation for about one week from onset. Immunity to infecting strain of virus usual after one attack.

	Rheumatic Fever	Rubella	Smallpox	Strep Infections	Tetanus	Whooping Cough
Cause	Direct cause unknown. Precipitated by a strep infection.	A virus: Present in secretions from nose and mouth of infected people.	A virus: Present in skin pocks and discharges from mouth, nose and throat of infected people. Rare in U.S.	Streptococci of several strains cause scarlet fever and strep sore throats: Present in secretions from mouth, nose and ears of infected people.	Tetanus bacillus: Present in a wound so infected.	Pertussis bacillus: Present in secretions from mouth and nose of infected people.
How spread	Unknown. But the preceding strep infection is contagious.	Contact with infected people or articles used by them. Very contagious.	Contact with infected people or articles used by them.	Contact with infected people; rarely from contaminated articles.	Through soil, contact with horses, street dust, or articles contaminated with the bacillus.	Contact with infected people and articles used by them.
Incubation period (from date of exposure to first signs)	Symptoms appear about 2 to 3 weeks after a strep infection.	14 to 21 (usually 18) days.	From 8 to 17 (usually 12) days.	1 to 3 days.	4 days to 3 weeks. Sometimes longer. Average about 10 days.	From 7 to 10 days.
Period of communicability (time when disease is contagious)	Not communicable. Preceding strep infection is communicable.	From 7 days before to 5 days after onset of rash.	From 2 to 3 days before rash, until disappearance of all pock crusts.	Greatest during acute illness (about 10 days).	Not communicable from person to person.	From onset of first symptoms to about 3rd week of the disease.
Most susceptible ages	All ages; most common from 6 to 12 years.	Young children, but also common in young adults.	All ages.	All ages.	All ages.	Under 7 years.
Seasons of prevalence	Mainly winter and spring.	Winter and spring.	Usually winter, but anytime.	Late winter and spring.	All seasons, but more common in warm weather.	Late winter and early spring.
Prevention	No prevention, except proper treatment of strep infections. (See Strep Infections.)	Rubella (German measles) vaccine.	Vaccination (no longer given routinely in U.S.).	No prevention. Antibiotic treatment for those who have had rheumatic fever.	Immunization with tetanus toxoid (in triple vaccine for babies).	Immunization with whooping cough vaccine (in triple vaccine for babies).

	Rheumatic Fever	Rubella	Smallpox	Strep Infections	Tetanus	Whooping Cough
Control	Use of antibiotics. One attack does not give immunity.	Isolation when necessary, for 5 days after onset. Immunity usual after one attack.	Vaccinia immune globulin may prevent or modify smallpox if given within 24 hours after exposure. Isolation until all pock crusts are gone. Immunity usual after one attack.	Isolation for about 1 day after start of treatment with antibiotics—used for about 10 days. One attack does not necessarily give immunity.	Booster dose of tetanus toxoid for protection given on day of injury. Antitoxin used in treatment and for temporary protection for child not immunized. One attack does not give immunity.	Booster doses (see Appendix D). Special antibiotics may help to lighten attack for child not immunized. Isolation from susceptible infants for about 3 weeks from onset or until cough stops. Immunity usual after one attack.

SOURCE: *The Control of Communicable Diseases*, American Public Health Association, 1975, and *Report of Committee on Control of Infectious Diseases*, American Academy of Pediatrics, 1974. Courtesy of Metropolitan Life.

Appendix D
Vaccination Schedule

This schedule for first vaccinations is based on recommendations of the American Medical Association and the American Academy of Pediatrics. A first test for TB (tuberculosis) may be recommended at one year. Your physician may suggest a slightly different schedule suitable for your individual child. And recommendations change from time to time as science gains new knowledge.

Disease	No. of Doses	Age for First Series	Booster
Diphtheria Tetanus Whooping Cough	4 doses	2 months 4 months 6 months 18 months	At 4 to 6 years— before entering school. As recommended by physician.
Polio (Oral vaccine)	4 doses	2 months 4 months 6 months 18 months	At 4 to 6 years— before entering school. As recommended by physician.
Rubella (German measles)	1 vaccination	After 1 year	None
Measles	1 vaccination	1 to 12 years	None
Mumps	1 vaccination	1 to 12 years	None

Courtesy of Metropolitan Life.

Author Index

Entries in *italics* refer to pages on which bibliographic references are given. Entries in **boldface** refer to selections by the authors cited.

Subject Index

atmospheric pressure. Some cars have a system which has an expansion chamber, the heating and cooling of the engine causing water transfer between the expansion chamber and the radiator. In these systems the water level need be checked only at long intervals, even up to two years.

Water-Cooled

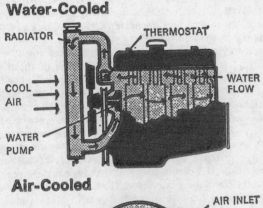

Air-Cooled

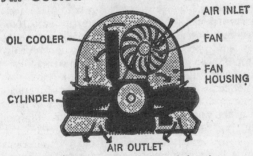

Fig. 48. Water cooled and air cooled engines.

OVERHEATING

Overheating may be due to a fault in the engine and, in a water cooled engine, overheating accompanied by loss of power would generally indicate a fault somewhere other than in the cooling system, such as a weak mixture (see page 105), retarded ignition (see page 47), or binding brakes, possibly the handbrake (see page 69).

Overheating due to a fault in the cooling system could be caused simply by a low water level. A common cause is a broken fan belt. If this is the cause the dynamo (or alternator) will not be running because it is also driven by the fan belt and therefore the charge warning light will go out. (An ammeter, if fitted, will register zero charge). When these two faults occur simultaneously, you can be virtually certain of what has happened without getting out of the car. The wise driver will carry a spare fan belt; it is easily fitted and can save a great deal of trouble. While nylon stockings, tights, ties and other similar things may be used to provide a "get to a garage" repair fan drive, how much better to have the real thing in the boot?

The experienced motorist will know the "hot smell" of an overheating engine and will therefore be aware of the trouble before steam issues from the radiator. Assuming the fan belt was all right the first thing would be to check the radiator water level. In a pressurised system it is dangerous to remove the radiator cap when the engine is hot. The sudden reduction in pressure causes the water to boil violently and results in water and steam spurting out with great risk to hands and face. Radiator caps are now made so that the first part on the releasing movement equalises the pressure before the cap is free and if these caps are removed slowly the violent effect is avoided. However, if the cap must be removed when the engine is hot it is best to place one or two thicknesses of thick cloth over it and to turn it slowly. If the water level has been allowed to become low enough to cause the water in the system to boil, it is better not to top up with cold water. Either top up with hot water or allow the system to cool before topping up with cold water.

Another cause of overheating is restriction of the water flow due to a deposit of "fur" in the system because of the calcium content of the water being high. In some districts this problem does not arise. The deposit may be effectively removed by using one of the proprietary "fur" removers sold by garages and accessory stores. It is unfortunately true, in the case of old cars, that the removal of the lime tends to reveal leaks and when this happens the only remedy is a new radiator.

Occasionally the radiator matrix, especially when it faces the direction of travel, becomes clogged with insects and dirt and its effeciency is in consequence reduced. The remedy is to direct a water jet on the radiator in the opposite direction to the air flow. A fair amount of pressure is needed to dislodge the obstructions. Before doing this take care to cover the engine with a sheet of plastic, to protect the ignition system, or, in curing one trouble, another will be introduced.

THE THERMOSTAT

Failure of the thermostat can cause overheating or overcooling. The thermostat is normally located on the engine below the top outlet hose. Essentially it is a heat operated valve which controls the water flow through the radiator. When the engine is cold the thermostat is closed and it opens gradually as the engine warms to reach the fully open position when the engine is at normal operating temperature.

It is important, from the point of view of fuel consumption, and for other reasons, that the engine should reach its normal operating temperature as soon as possible after it is started. When the engine is first started the water in the cylinder block heats up quickly because the thermostat prevents it from circulating through the radiator. As the water becomes warm some circulation is allowed but the water in the cylinder block is always maintained at a high temperature and it is some time before the whole of the water in the system is at its normal operating temperature.

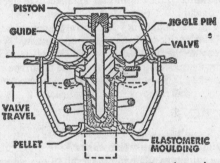

Fig. 49. This is a wax pellet thermostat. When the engine is cold the valve is closed, restricting the water circulation. As the engine heats the wax pellet expands and deforms the elastomeric moulding which causes the valve to open progressively with increase in temperature. The jiggle pin is located in a bleed hole which allows some circulation when the valve is closed and prevents the formation of airlocks. The bleed hole is closed by the pin when the engine is running by the pressure from the water pump.

At one time the thermostat was operated by a bellows which expanded with the increase in temperature and so opened the valve; nowadays the expansion of wax is used because it simplifies manufacture and is more reliable.

You can soon find out if the thermostat is working. When you start the engine from cold and it is just beginning to heat up, place one hand on the cylinder block and the other hand on the radiator header tank. As the engine warms the radiator should remain cold and the engine block warm. Watch out for the fan with the fingers. Even when the engine has been running for some minutes the radiator should be colder to the touch than the cylinder block. If both the radiator and cylinder block heat up at the same rate the thermostat is open all the time. On the other hand if the radiator does not get warm and the engine overheats, the thermostat is *not* opening. With the modern thermostat it is more likely that it will stick open than remain closed.

To remove the thermostat it is necessary to detach the end of the top radiator hose from the cylinder block. The thermostat is normally located in a housing below the hose attachment stub and the cover can be taken off if the fixings are removed; the thermostat can then be lifted out. If it is stuck open you will be able to see this. You can check its operation, supposing it is not stuck, by suspending it in a pan of water and holding a thermometer in the water. If the thermostat commences to open at about 180°F (82°C) and 210°F (99°C) it is not far out.

When re-fitting the thermostat or fitting a new one make sure you place it in position the right side up; it is marked with an arrow to enable this to be done easily. It will be noted when handling the thermostat that there is a loose pin in the valve. This is known as the "jiggle pin" and its purpose is to prevent a pressure difference occurring across the thermostat.

ANTI-FREEZE

In the Winter time anti-freeze *must be used*; water alone will freeze in the coldest weather and the result of this is likely to be a cracked cylinder block. Long life anti-freeze is now obtainable and it is usual to keep it in the system Summer and Winter.

It is best to flush out the system thoroughly before filling with fresh anti-freeze mixture or even if water was previously in the system.

Be guided by the instructions on the anti-freeze container concerning the strength of the mixture to use. A common strength is 25%, or one part anti-freeze to three parts water. Anti-freeze can be used in two ways. One is to mix the anti-freeze and water in the correct proportions in a large container and fill the system from this. It is best to make more than you need so that some will be available for topping up. Alternatively, knowing the water capacity of the cooling system, you find out how much anti-freeze is required and pour this into the drained system and then fill up to the correct level with clean water. If you do it this way you must run the engine until it is hot (after filling up) otherwise the thermostat will prevent the anti freeze from mixing with the water in the water jacket which may therefore freeze even if the rest of the system is protected.

6

Fuel System

THE engine draws in air through the carburettor and the carburettor mixes the correct amount of petrol with the air as it passes through. When the engine is being started from cold a rich mixture (high petrol content) is required and the carburettor is fitted with a device to meet this requirement.

The jet sizes, choke tube and, in the case of the SU and Stromberg carburettors, the jet needle are selected to meet the engine speeds and volume of air intake. An exact determination is made during engine development, and any private owner who thinks he can improve on the recommended setting is something more than an optimist.

The makers may specify more than one setting and may be consulted on this point, but the "normal" setting has been selected as best for normal use, and that is what it is. The alternative settings that are usually available are "economy", or minimum fuel consumption at slightly reduced performance and a "best for power" setting which gives a slight increase in power at the expense of increased fuel consumption. High altitude settings are also normally available.

How Many Carburettors?

The four cylinder engine usually has only one carburettor. This means that all the air is drawn in at one point (carburettor intake). The petrol/air mixture output from the carburettor has to be distributed evenly to the four cylinders. The mixture of petrol with the air is partly vapour and partly minute droplets (a kind of petrol "fog").

The obvious position for the carburettor is in the middle of the cylinder block, but even there it is nearer the two inner cylinders than the two outer ones. Because of the heterogeneous composition of the mixture, the two nearest cylinders tend to receive a richer mixture than the two end cylinders. Therefore it is necessary to set the carburettor to give a correct mixture to the two end cylinders, although this means that the two inner cylinders will then receive a mixture that is too rich.

The only way to ensure that each cylinder receives the correct mixture strength (and will therefore produce maximum power) with carburettors is to have one for each cylinder. This has been done on racing cars but is expensive, and syncronising the operation of the carburettors is difficult. A compromise is to fit one carburettor to each pair of cylinders. The distribution with this arrangement is good, though not quite as good as it would be with one carburettor to each cylinder. This is why some four cylinder engines have two carburettors and six cylinder engines three carburettors. Petrol injection solves the problem in another way, but it is expensive and complicated.

MAINTENANCE

Generally speaking carburettors should not be dismantled; this is likely to do more harm than good. Any filters in the carburettor intake line should be cleaned out occasionally and the operating linkage should be checked to make sure it is working correctly. The float chamber needs to be cleaned out at intervals. Most important, in the case of SU and Stromberg carburettors, is to maintain the correct oil level in the damper.

SLOW RUNNING ADJUSTMENT

The slow running needs to be adjusted occasionally. How to do this will now be explained. Before commencing to adjust the carburettor the following conditions must be fulfilled:

1. The contact breaker points gap must be correctly adjusted. See page 41.
2. The ignition timing must be correct. See page 47.
3. The sparking plug points gap must be correctly adjusted and the plugs must all be firing properly.
4. The tappets must be correctly adjusted. See page 174. In the case of Stromberg and SU carburettors the jet needle must be correctly fitted to the piston.
5. The engine must be at normal operating temperature.

SU CARBURETTOR (Fig. 50)

Unscrew the throttle adjusting screw (5) until the end of the screw is just off its stop. This is to ensure that the throttle is closed to the limit set by the screw. Now open the throttle by turning in the throttle adjusting screw one and a half turns.

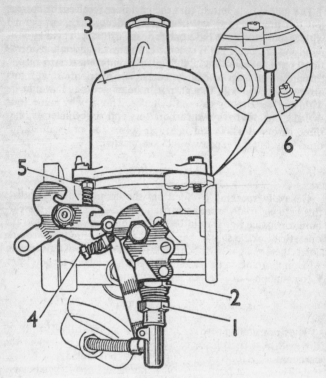

Fig. 50. The HS4 Carburettor.
KEY: 1. Jet adjusting nut; 2. Jet locking nut; 3. Piston/suction chamber; 4. Fast-idle adjusting screw; 5. Throttle adjusting screw; 6. Piston lifting pin.

Remove the suction chamber and piston. Remove the mixture control wire and screw the jet adjustment nut (1) until the jet is flush with the carburettor bridge or, if this condition cannot be obtained, turn the nut up as far as it will go.

Replace the piston and suction chamber. Raise the piston by means of the lift pin (6), then release the pin and allow the piston to fall freely. At the end of its fall it should hit the seat with a click. If there is no click, the needle is either bent or the jet is not centred. See centering the jet needle, page 113.

Turn down the adjusting nut (1) two complete turns and start the engine. Turn the throttle adjusting screw (5), as required to give a good idling speed. Turn the jet adjusting nut up to weaken the mixture or down to make the mixture more rich, as required. Adjust until the fastest idling speed consistent with even running is obtained. While making the adjustments be sure that the jet head is held in contact with the adjusting nut all the time.

As the adjustment is being made the engine speed will probably increase. If this occurs, reduce the speed by carefully unscrewing the throttle adjusting screw (5) Fig. 50 as required to give a good idling speed. Now check the adjustment as described below:

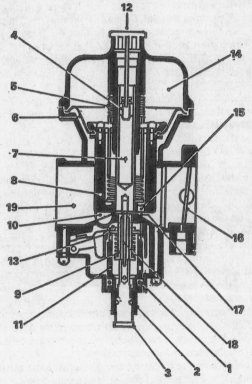

Fig. 51. Stromberg Carburettor.
KEY: 1, "O" ring; 2. Jet assembly; 3, Orifice (throttle) adjusting screw; 4, Damper; 5, Coil spring; 6, Diaphragm; 7, Hollow guide rod; 8, Air valve (equivalent to piston in S.U. carburettor); 9, Orifice; 10, Starter bar; 11, Drilling; 12, Damper cap; 13, Orifice bush; 14, Chamber; 15, Drilling; 16, Throttle; 17, Bridge; 18, Metering needle; 19, Bore.

Lift the piston by approximately $\frac{1}{16}$ in. (1.5 mm) by means of the piston lift pin (6) Fig. 50, then:

1. Mixture too rich: engine R.P.M. (revolutions per minute) increase considerably.
2. Mixture correct: engine R.P.M. increase very slightly.
3. Mixture too weak: engine R.P.M. immediately decrease.

It may be necessary to make a very slight final adjustment to the throttle adjusting screw.

Re-connect the mixture control wire leaving about $\frac{1}{16}$ in. (1.5 mm) free movement of the wire before it starts to pull on the jet lever. Pull the mixture control (choke) out until the linkage is about to move the carburettor jet and adjust the fast idle screw (4) to give an engine speed of about 1,000 R.P.M. when the engine is hot. Check that the idling speed returns to normal when the control is fully in, in the OFF position. Top up the damper.

STROMBERG CARBURETTOR (Figs. 51 and 52)

1. Remove the air cleaner and damper. The damper cap (12) is unscrewed by turning it anti-clockwise.
2. Hold the air valve (8) down on the damper bridge by pressing on it with a pencil, or similar article, inserted through the damper cap opening.
3. Turn the throttle adjusting screw (3) until the jet contacts the underside of the air valve. From this position turn the adjusting screw down three turns.
4. Top-up the damper housing with SAE 20 engine oil (unless some different oil is specified). Raise the piston to the top of its travel and allow it to fall. A spring loaded pin is provided to lift the piston to make this test. If the piston can fall freely it will make a click when it comes to rest. If no click is heard, the jet is out of centre, and this must be corrected. It is assumed that the needle is not bent. See page 113.
5. Fit the damper top cap and screw down securely.
6. Start the engine. Turn the throttle stop screw A to obtain 600/650 R.P.M. Now turn the adjusting screw B slowly in or out to obtain smooth, steady running.
7. To check that the adjustment is correct, lift the piston by about $\frac{1}{16}$ in. (1.5 mm). If this causes the engine speed to increase, the mixture strength is too rich. If the engine stops when the piston is lifted, the mixture is too weak. In either case, further adjustment by means of the adjusting screw is required until, when the piston is lifted as described, the R.P.M. are unaffected or fall slightly.

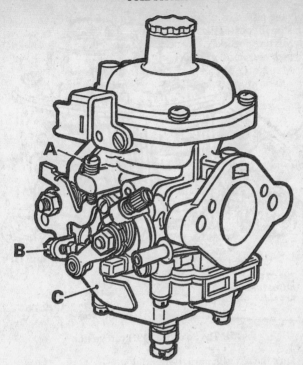

Fig. 52. Stromberg Carburettor. A throttle stop screw. B. Fast/idle screw. C choke lever.

SOLEX CARBURETTOR (Fig. 53)

There are many types of Solex carburettors and the positions of the adjusting screws vary. The throttle adjusting screw or throttle stop is located on the throttle actuating arm; it is fitted with a spring. The slow running adjustment screw is also fitted with a spring and screws into the carburettor body near the bottom.

1. Adjust the throttle adjusting screw until a satisfactory idling speed is obtained.
2. Turn the slow running mixture screw until the engine begins to run unevenly or "hunts". (Engine revs. speed and slow alternately.)

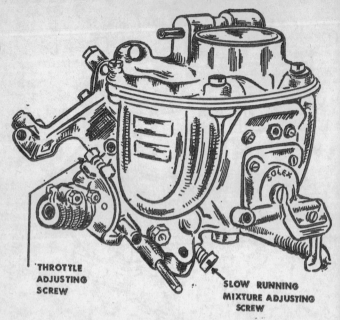

THROTTLE
ADJUSTING
SCREW

SLOW RUNNING
MIXTURE ADJUSTING
SCREW

Fig. 53. The Solex B 32 PIH carburettor.

3. Turn the screw in until the hunting stops.
4. If the idling speed has now become too high, turn out the throttle adjusting screw to reduce idling speed to normal.
5. If the hunting re-appears, turn in the slow running screw very slowly until the hunting disappears.

Ford Carburettor (Figs. 54 and 55)

The locations of the throttle stop and volume control screws on different models are shown in Fig. 55.

1. Turn the throttle stop B until the engine is idling too fast.
2. Slowly turn out the volume control screw A to enrich the mixture until the engine commences to "hunt" or run unevenly, then slowly turn the screw in again (clockwise) until the engine runs evenly.
3. Screw out the throttle stop B very slowly to reduce the idling speed until it is correct. If the engine commences to run unevenly, turn in screw A very slightly.

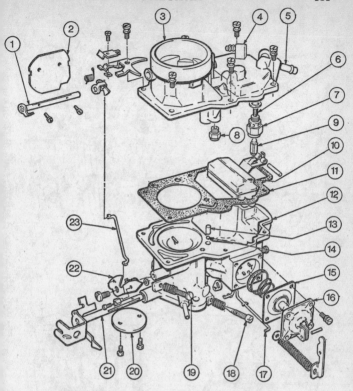

Fig. 54. Showing all the parts of the Ford Carburettor.
KEY: 1. Choke plate shaft; 2. Choke plate; 3. Upper body; 4. External vent; 5. Fuel inlet; 6. Filter; 7. Needle valve housing; 8. Main jet; 9. Needle valve; 10. Float; 11. Gasket; 12. Lower body; 13. Weight; 14. Ball; 15. Accelerator pump diaphragm; 16. Accelerator pump cover; 17. Accelerator pump rod; 18. Volume control screw; 19. Throttle stop screw; 20. Throttle plate; 21. Throttle shaft; 22. Fast idle cam; 23. Choke operating link.

4. Repeat this alternative slight adjustment of the two screws until the engine runs evenly at a satisfactory idling speed. Remember that a gentle "tick over" can't be expected on a modern high compression engine so don't try to obtain too low an idling speed.

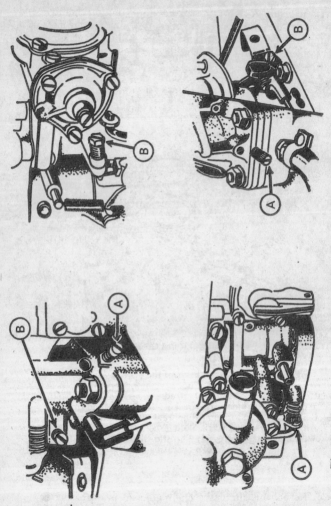

Fig. 55. Adjusting screws on various ford carburettors: A Mixture screw, B Throttle stop.

Jet Centering SU and Stromberg Carburettors

If the piston does not move freely in the suction chamber, and this is not due to the lodgement of an obstruction in the jet, a bent damper rod, or jet needle, or in the case of the SU carburettor to dirt on the suction chamber wall, it is likely that the jet is not correctly centred.

It is very unlikely that the jet will become off-centre unless it is released. Do not release the jet unless it is proved to be off-centre.

To check if the jet is off-centre lift the piston by means of the lift pin. Place the fingers over the bottom of the carburettor and fully lift the jet. With the jet held fully up, release the lift pin and allow the piston to fall. At the end of its fall the piston should make a click as it hits the bridge. If no click is heard the jet is off-centre. Re-centre the jet as explained below.

S.U. Carburettor

1. Remove the jet head screw to release the control linkage.
2. Unscrew the union holding the nylon feed tube into the base of the float chamber and withdraw the tube and jet together. Unscrew the jet adjusting nut (1), Fig. 50, and remove the lock spring. Replace the jet and feed tube.
3. Slacken off the large jet locking nut (2) until the jet bearing is just free to rotate by finger pressure.
4. With the jet damper removed, and using a pencil to press on top of the piston, gently move the piston and needle down on to the jet bridge.
5. Tighten the jet locking nut, keeping the jet hard up against the jet bearing.
6. Lift the piston by means of the piston lift pin, release it and check that it falls freely, hitting the jet bridge with a soft click. Now, fully lower the jet and check to see if there is any difference in the sound of the piston's impact when it is lifted and allowed to fall. If the second test produces a sharper impact sound, the centering operation must be repeated until successful. Finally, re-fit the locking spring and the adjusting nut removed earlier.
7. Before replacing the fuel pipe float chamber connection, fit the end of the plastic pipe so that at least $\frac{3}{16}$ in. (4.8 mm) of the pipe protrudes; after fitting the connection reassemble the controls.

STROMBERG CARBURETTOR (Fig. 51)

1. Lift the air valve (8) and fully tighten the jet assembly (2).
2. Screw up the orifice adjuster (3) until the top of the orifice (9) is just above the bridge (17).
3. Slack off the jet assembly (2) by about half a turn. This will release the orifice bush (13).
4. Lift the air valve (8) and allow it to fall. In falling the air valve needle will centralise the orifice. Make sure the air valve is fully down by removing the damper and pressing down on the air valve with a pencil. Replace the damper.
5. Progressively tighten the jet assembly (2) at the same time checking that the orifice remains centralised to allow the air valve to fall down fully as described in paragraph 4 above. Inability to centralise the jet correctly would indicate a bent jet needle, in which case a new needle would have to be fitted.

DIAPHRAGM RENEWAL, STROMBERG CARBURETTOR

After long service the diaphragm may become perforated and need to be renewed. To do this first scribe a line across the carburettor top cover joint so that the cover can be replaced in the same position from which it was removed, then:

1. Remove the four screws retaining the cover to the body.
2. Lift out the long spring under the cover.
3. Withdraw the air valve from the body.
4. Remove the four screws holding the diaphragm retaining ring in position. This frees the diaphragm, which can now be removed.

To fit the new diaphragm reverse the removal instructions, but be sure that the locating beading on the edge of the diaphragm is properly bedded in the slot provided for it. When re-fitting the cover do not twist it to align the hole(s) for the fixing screws. To do this may distort the diaphragm; therefore align the screw holes properly before pressing the cover into position.

SYNCRONISING TWIN CARBURETTORS

S.U. Carburettors: Refer to Fig. 50. The engine must be at normal operating temperature. Remove the air cleaners. With the

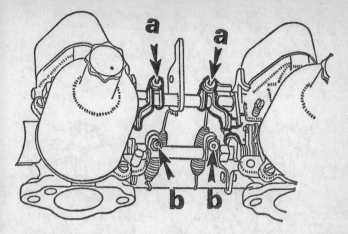

Fig. 56. Tuning Twin S.U. carburettors. aa are the throttle spindle clamping bolts. bb are the jet control interconnection clamping bolts.

engine stopped, unscrew the throttle adjusting screws (5), until the ends of the screws are just off their stops. This is to make sure that the throttles are closed to the limits set by the screws. Now open the throttles by turning in the throttle adjusting screws by one and a half turns.

Slacken both the clamping bolts (aa) Fig. 56 on the throttle interconnections. Disconnect the jet control interconnection by slackening the clamp bolts (bb).

Remove the suction chambers and pistons. Remove the mixture control wire and screw the jet adjustment nuts (1) Fig. 50 on both carburettors until each jet is flush with the carburettor bridge, or if this condition cannot be obtained, turn the nut up as far as it will go.

Replace the pistons and suction chambers. Check that the pistons fall freely on to the jet bridge when lifted by the lift pin (6) and allowed to fall. If a piston will not fall freely the jet needs to be re-centered, see page 113. Turn down the jet adjusting nuts (1) two turns.

Start the engine and adjust the throttle adjusting screws on each carburettor to give the desired idling speed. Compare the intake "hiss" on both carburettors and alter the throttle adjusting screws until the "hiss" is the same.

Turn the jet adjusting nuts (1) on both carburettors up to

Fig. 57. How a piece of plastic tubing can be used to check that the "hiss" is equal at each carburettor intake. The throttle adjusting screws are arrowed.

weaken or down to enrich the mixture, each by the same amount until the fastest idling speed consistent with even running is obtained.

Re-adjust the throttle adjusting screws to obtain correct idling, if necessary.

Check for correct mixture strength by pushing up the lift pin on the front carburettor by $\frac{1}{32}$ in. (0.8 mm) after free movement has been taken up. If the engine speed increases the mixture strength of the front carburettor is too rich. If the engine speed immediately decreases, the mixture strength of the front carburettor is too weak. If the engine speed momentarily increases very slightly the mixture strength of the front carburettor is correct.

Repeat the same procedure at the rear carburettor, then re-check the front carburettor again, since both carburettors are interdependent.

Set the throttle interconnecting clamping levers so that the link pin is 0.006 in. (0.15 mm) away from the lower edge of the fork and tighten the clamp bolts.

With the levers at their lowest position set the jet interconnection clamp bolts so that both jets commence to move at the same time.

Re-connect the mixture control wire with about 1/16 in (1.6mm) free movement before it starts to pull on the jet levers.

Pull the mixture control knob until the linkage is about to move the carburettor jets and adjust the fast idle screws, comparing the intensity of the intake "hiss", to give an equal hiss at an engine speed of about 1000 RPM. Re-fit the air cleaners.

Stromberg Carburettor: The engine must be at its normal operating temperature. Slack off the clamping bolts on the spindle coupling the two carburettors.

Unscrew the throttle stop screws (A Fig. 52) to permit the throttles of both carburettors to close completely. Now screw in the throttle stop screws so that the screw ends just touch the tab on the lever. From this point turn the throttle stop screws 1½ turns each so that the throttles are opened by an equal amount.

Make sure that the fast idle screws B are clear of the levers, or incorrect syncronising will result.

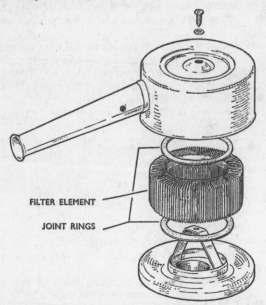

FILTER ELEMENT

JOINT RINGS

Fig. 58. The paper element air cleaner. The filter element should be renewed every 12,000 miles.

Turn the orifice (jet) adjusting screws, (3) Fig. 51, three turns down from the point where the jet orifice comes into contact with the base of the air valve (8).

Check that both cold start levers are fully off against the stops with the dash choke control pushed fully in. Adjust the coupling and control wire as required. Use a piece of plastic tube to check that the hiss is the same at both carburettor intakes. Hold one end of the tube close to the ear and place the other end of the tube alternately in one carburettor intake and then the other to enable the hiss to be compared, See Fig. 57.

Adjust the jet adjusting screws as required to achieve equal hiss. Tighten the clamp bolts on the coupling.

Set the throttle stop screws to give the required idle speed, being careful to turn each screw by the same amount, to obtain a satisfactory idling speed.

FLOAT CHAMBER

Every carburettor has a small petrol reservoir, called the float chamber, which provides the correct level of petrol in relation to the jets.

The float chamber (see Fig. 60) contains a float controlled valve which shuts off the entry of petrol from the fuel pump when the level is correct. The pump which draws petrol from the tank and supplies it to the float chamber may be either mechanical or electrical. These two kinds of pump will be described later.

The petrol entering the fuel pump usually passes through a

Fig. 59. Delco wet air filter. The intake air passes through oil wetted gauze. Dirt in the air sticks to the oil on the gauze. The gauze needs to be cleaned occasionally. See Chapter 10.

filter since if water gains entry to the carburettor the carburettor
will not operate correctly. Dirt has a similar effect and may also
prevent the float operated needle valve from closing thus causing
the float chamber to flood.

TOPPING-UP THE DAMPER

This applies to the SU and Stromberg Carburettors. Unscrew
the cap on top of the suction chamber and add oil as required.
Normally the oil used is SAE 20 engine oil. In odd cases a
different oil may be specified. The level should be about $\frac{1}{2}$ in.
(13mm) above the top of the hollow piston rod (SU carburettor)
or air valve (Stromberg carburettor).

THE FUEL PUMP

The pump fitted may be electrical or mechanical..

The AC Mechanical Fuel Pump

This pump requires little attention. If it is thought that it is not
delivering fuel to the carburettor, it may be checked by disconnecting the pipe from the pump to the carburettor. If the engine is
then turned (preferably by hand with the ignition off), fuel will
be ejected in considerable quantity at each pulse of the pump. If
this does not occur, the pump is at fault. The freed end of the
pipe should be placed in a container to prevent the fuel splashing
over the engine, and to avoid fire risk. If the pump delivers
insufficient fuel the engine will be difficult to start, and when it
starts it will soon stop, as it uses up the fuel that has accumulated
in the float chamber. The engine may continue to run only if a
very high engine speed is maintained. The most likely causes
of such a fault are dirt in the pump, preventing the valves from
working properly, or a punctured diaphragm. The filter may be
choked. The filter is under the metal or glass dome which can be
removed by taking out the top screw. The washer on this screw
and the one round the base of the dome must make leak-proof
joints. On some pumps the glass dome is retained by a wire clip
and screw. It should be noted that an air leak on the suction
side of the pump, that is, between the pump and the fuel tank, will
reduce the pump delivery, or even prevent it altogether. Therefore
check all unions for tightness. If the fuel tank is allowed to run
dry, the pump will take some time to fill the pipes and the float
chamber with fuel. Some of these pumps are fitted with a small

priming lever; by moving the lever up and down the pump may be operated by hand to ensure that the float chamber is filled, and thus prevent unnecessary turning of the engine by the starter. (See Fig. 61).

To dismantle the pump. Disconnect the pipe unions from the pump, and release the fixings holding the pump to the engine. If the pump is dirty it should be cleaned by washing it in paraffin. To prevent dirt entering the pump during this process, it is a good thing to plug up the inlet and outlet openings with small corks or pieces of wood.

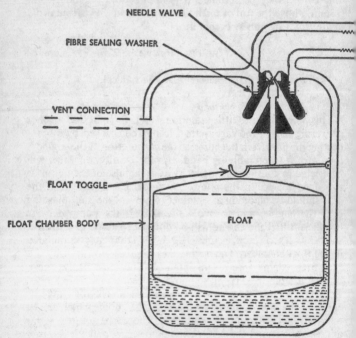

Fig. 60. The float chamber.

First make a light file cut across the edges of the flange so that the two halves can be assembled in the correct relative position. Remove the screws round the joint and lift the top part of the pump away. Remove the diaphragm and pull rod by pressing downwards against the spring and at the same time giving a quarter turn to disengage the pull rod from the fork on the end of the operating arm. The diaphragm and pull rod may then be lifted away.

The valves are small pieces of plastic material, controlled by light springs. They may be removed by taking out the three screws holding the retaining plate in position. The diaphragm and other parts may be renewed individually, but complete replacement kits are available at low cost.

To reassemble the pump proceed thus. Note that the inlet valve fits in the *top part of the pump,* followed by the spring. The outlet valve *fits in the retaining plate* followed by the spring which fits into a small retainer in the top part of the pump.

1. Place the diaphragm pull rod assembly in position, first making sure that the pull rod oil seal is in position in the pump body. Note the locating tab on the diaphragm. This tab must be a quarter turn (90 degrees) to the right of the locating mark on the pump body.

2. Press the diaphragm assembly down, and give a quarter turn to the right, ensuring that the slots in the end of the pull rod engage in the fork end of the operating arm. The location tab on the diaphragm must now correspond with the location mark on the pump body.

3. Place the top of the pump in position, so that the file marks correspond, and press the rocker arm towards the pump so as to compress the spring and allow the two parts of the pump to come together. Maintain the rocker arm in the compressed position until all the fixing screws are in position and are tight. The edge of the diaphragm should be about flush with the edge of the joint all round, if any of it protrudes from the joint, the assembly is incorrect.

If the operating cam in the engine happens to have been in the "lift" position when the pump was removed, it may be found that the pump will not go back on to its seat. To remedy this, turn the engine to alter the position of the cam and allow the pump to seat properly. Do not forget to replace the gasket between the pump and the engine.

While we have given these instructions for servicing the pump, it is better when trouble occurs to fit a fully reconditioned exchange unit, and this is especially true of an old pump where the mechanical linkage is probably worn.

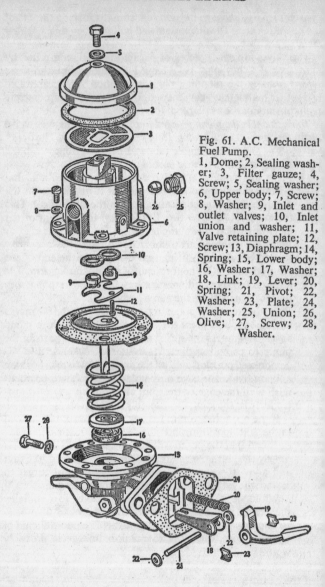

Fig. 61. A.C. Mechanical Fuel Pump.

1, Dome; 2, Sealing washer; 3, Filter gauze; 4, Screw; 5, Sealing washer; 6, Upper body; 7, Screw; 8, Washer; 9, Inlet and outlet valves; 10, Inlet union and washer; 11, Valve retaining plate; 12, Screw; 13, Diaphragm; 14, Spring; 15, Lower body; 16, Washer; 17, Washer; 18, Link; 19, Lever; 20, Spring; 21, Pivot; 22, Washer; 23, Plate; 24, Washer; 25, Union; 26, Olive; 27, Screw; 28, Washer.

The SU Electric Pump:

A number of different types of this pump have been made but all the pumps are basically the same. See Fig. 63.

Cleaning the Filter: On early pumps the filter was a cylindrical piece of gauze closed at one end and could be withdrawn for cleaning if the inlet tube was unscrewed and the pipe adaptor unscrewed from the pump.

On later pumps there is a different arrangement. Refer to Fig. 63.

To clean the Filter. Remove the two screws (35), securing the clamp plate (34), while the pump is held with the screws facing upward. When the clamp plate is removed it is possible to lift inlet and outlet moulded nozzles from the pump. The filter gauze (40), is in the inlet assembly. The gauze should be removed and cleaned with a small quantity of fuel, using a brush to dislodge the dirt from the filter mesh.

When reassembling, replace the parts in the order shown in Fig. 63. Place the outlet valve assembly, tongue side uppermost, in the recess marked 'Outlet'. Place a joint washer on top of the valve assembly and finally add the outlet nozzle.

Place the inlet valve assembly in the recess marked "Inlet" (tongue side of the valve down) and follow this with a joint washer then the filter (dome side uppermost) then another joint washer, completing the assembly with the inlet nozzle.

Make sure that both assemblies nest down evenly into their respective recesses. Place the nozzles so as to line up with inlet and outlet pipes. Fit the clamp plate and screws and tighten down firmly on to the body.

To Clean the Points: Use a piece of strong paper or card, and draw this carefully between the points. If the points are pitted or worn they should be renewed.

TO TEST THE FUEL PUMP

Electric Pump: Disconnect the pipe from the pump to the carburettor and place the end of the pipe in a clear container. *Warning:* There must be no flame or fire of any kind within 20 yards (18.29 m). Switch "On" the ignition. The pump should run continuously, each pulse ejecting considerable quantity of fuel into the container. The fuel pump makers will supply flow rates, but it should be obvious from the rate at which the fuel is ejected if the quantity is sufficient or not. Allow the pump to run until the end of the pipe is submerged in the fuel and observe if any air bubbles are being carried in with the petrol. The presence of air bubbles indicates a leakage on the suction side of the pump, due to loose or faulty unions or connections and will reduce the quantity of fuel the pump can deliver. Make sure, however, that there is sufficient fuel in the tank.

If the pump works satisfactorily during the above test, but not before the pipe to the caruburettor was disconnected, the fault is probably a sticking float needle. If the pump fails to work in the above test, disconnect the pipe from the inlet side of the pump. If the pump now runs, the tank filter is choked, or there is a restriction in the pipe from the pump to the tank. It may be possible to clear this (but possibly only temporarily) by blowing down the pipe using either the mouth or an air line, but do not on any account put compressed air through the pump.

Fig. 62. This is a Delco (AC) fuel pump. It is basically the same as the pump in Fig. 61. The glass dome is removed by releasing the top nut and moving the stirrup sideways.

If the pump still fails to work, disconnect the electric feed wire from the pump (the upper wire, fixed with the larger terminal on the PD pump) and connect it to an earth point via the test lamp. (See fig. 80). If the lamp does not light when the ignition is switched "On", there is a fault in the wiring associated

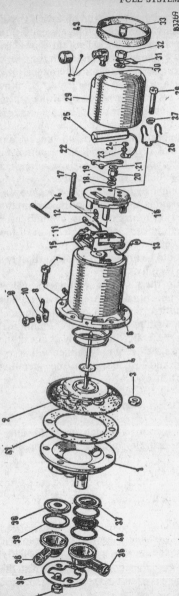

Fig. 63. The SU Fuel Pump Type SP.

KEY: 1. Pump body; 2. Diaphragm and spindle assembly; 3. Roller – armature centralizing; 4. Washer-impact; 5. Spring – armature; 6. Coil housing; 7. Screw securing housing – 2BA; 8. Connector – earth; 9. Screw – 4BA; 10. Washer, spring – 4BA; 11. Tag, terminal – 5BA; 12. Tag terminal – 2BA; 13. Tag, earth 2BA; 14. Pin, rocker pivot; 15. Rocker mechanism; 16. Pedestal; 17. Stud, terminal; 18. Washer, spring; 19. Washer, lead; 20. Nut, terminal; 21. Washer, end cover seal; 22. Contact blade; 23. Washer, 5BA; 24. Screw, pedestal housing – 5BA; 25. Condenser; 26. Clip, condenser; 27. Washer, spring – 2BA; 28. Screw, pedestal housing – 2BA; 29. End cover; 30. Washer, shakeproof; 31. Connector Lucar; 32. Nut, 2BA; 33. Sleeve, insulating; 34. Clamp, plate; 35. Screw, securing, 2BA; 36. Nozzle, inlet and outlet; 37. Valve inlet; 38. Valve outlet; 39. Washer, sealing; 40. Filter; 41. Gasket; 42. Vent, valve.

with the pump or there is a faulty earth. To check the earth connection, connect the metallic base of the pump to a good earth point. If the pump now operates when the ignition is switched "On", the earth connection to the pump is faulty. In the case of the PD pump make the earth check with the small terminal (lower terminal) on the pump. Such a fault, if present, may be either traced and remedied or a new earth provided by fitting a piece of wire between the earth terminal on the pump and a good earth point on the car.

If the pump runs continuously and pumps no fuel or very little fuel and there is no air leak in the inlet side of the pump, it is probable that the valves are not operating properly, a fault which could be due to the presence of dirt on the valve seats.

Mechanical Pump: The pump may be checked by disconnecting either end of the pipe connecting the pump to the carburettor and while it is disconnected operating the hand priming lever. Each time the lever is moved down a considerable spurt of fuel should be ejected from the detached connection. In the absence of a hand lever the engine could be turned over instead. If only a little fuel is ejected the pump is faulty.

Possible faults are, dirt in the pump preventing the valves from seating properly and a punctured diaphragm or air leakage at the dome joint due to a faulty washer, see Fig. 61. The remedies for these faults are obvious. Failure of the pump to pump fuel may be due to air leakage in the intake line, usually at one of the pipe unions. A pump that has seen very long service will necessarily be considerably worn and lost motion in the operating linkage will reduce the pump delivery.

FUEL ECONOMY

Attend to general maintenance, in particular to tyre pressures, contact breaker points gap, sparking plug gaps. Carburettor wear is an important factor in fuel economy. Most manufacturers have an exchange scheme whereby the old carburettor is taken in part exchange for a reconditioned one. The cost is two thirds to half the price of a new carburettor. This is soon recovered in fuel saving.

Driving method is important. To save fuel keep the speed down, use top gear as much as possible, do not accelerate rapidly. When you have accelerated to the speed you require, particularly when climbing, it is possible to throttle back a little without losing power. This should be done.

Difficult Starting – Engine Cold

This may, of course, be due to a mechanical or ignition fault. Check that the engine is receiving fuel from the pump. (See under fuel pump.) Dirt or water in the float chamber will cause difficult starting. Check that the control knob on the dash is operating the rich mixture device on the carburettor properly. If in any doubt operate the device by hand at the carburettor and see if the engine will now start. Make sure that the device is not sticking and that full movement of the operating lever is possible. Dirt in the fuel may cause choked jets. The throttle and starting mixture control interconnection may be incorrectly set. A warm engine will idle from about 500 r.p.m. a cold engine will not; it requires about 1,000 r.p.m. and this fast idle setting is essential for starting from cold, it is obtained automatically by the interconnection, but only if this is correctly adjusted.

Difficult Starting – Engine Hot

This may be due to a mechanical or ignition fault. If however the carburettor is at fault, the trouble is probably an excessively rich mixture due to flooding. If this is so, petrol may be seen dripping from the carburettor. The slow running adjustment may be too rich or the starting carburettor or strangler (choke) may be remaining partially in action. To check by hand that full movement to the off position is obtained at the carburettor, temporarily release the control wire at the carburettor lever to make sure it is not too short. Reconnect with the dash knob fully in and the carburettor lever fully in the off position.

Small drain holes are usually provided in the inlet manifold to allow petrol to drain out and not enter the engine. If the drain is blocked, the excessive fuel will prevent the engine from starting. Pumping the accelerator pedal as the engine is starting will cause the accelerating pump to operate and may stop the engine and make a restart difficult owing to excess petrol. Operating the choke when the engine is warm will prevent the engine from starting. Even if the engine is cold, if the cylinders become flooded with liquid petrol the engine will not start. Often the trouble occurs unexpectedly, through an error, and the engine, which normally starts easily, refuses to start. In such a case continuous operation of the starter, apart from being bad for the battery, will only make matters worse by drawing in still more petrol. The remedy is to depress the accelerator pedal fully, thus putting the carburettor out of action (at such a low engine speed). If the starter is then operated the engine will soon start, as the excess fuel is cleared. Do not close the throttle until this is required to maintain engine speed.

JERKY OR UNEVEN RUNNING – POOR PERFORMANCE

This may be caused by dirt or water in the float chamber, air leaks at the manifold joint or carburettor to manifold joint, blocked or partially blocked jet or jets, badly worn carburettor or simply incorrect adjustment. The fault may of course be in the engine.

If the engine tends to stall when idling and lacks power particularly when accelerating, this may be due to a sticking piston (SU carburettor) or be because of dirt on the suction chamber walls or a punctured diaphragm (Stromberg carburettor). Other possible causes are a bent needle, or out of centre jet. Hesitation at pick-up may be due to low oil level in the damper or to too thin an oil in the damper (SU and Stromberg carburettors.)

7

The Lubricating System

IF an engine were run without any oil at all the metal to metal contact of the rubbing surfaces would produce so much heat that the soft metal in the main and big end bearings would melt and run out. The pistons would expand and seize in the cylinder bores and stop the engine. This, of course, is a very unlikely thing to happen but an engine might run short of oil because of failure of the lubrication system or, more likely, because of neglect on the part of the driver to keep sufficient oil in the sump. Because of the serious consequences of oil starvation, some means of warning the driver of its imminence is always provided.

The oil pump draws oil from the sump or pan on the bottom of the engine and forces it under pressure to all the principle moving parts. The oil delivered by the pump eventually drains back into the sump. The oil therefore is in continual circulation while the engine is running. Although subjected to pressure and extreme heat the oil does not physically deteriorate, as is often stated. The molecular structure of the oil cannot be worn out, but some of the oil is burned and the burning produces substances which contaminate the oil, with undesirable results. Particles of carbon and other debris are also picked up by the oil. Filters are provided in the lubricating system, through which the oil is forced. These filters remove some of the contamination but they cannot remove it all. It is for this reason that all of the oil in the engine has to be drained out at intervals and replaced with fresh oil.

WHICH OIL?

Manufacturers now identify their grades with S.A.E. numbers and the usual range is S.A.E. 20, 30, 40 and 50 for crankcase (engine) oils. The higher the number the thicker the oil. These numbers relate the viscosity to a temperature of 210 degrees F. or about the working temperature of the engine. What the oil does at this temperature clearly is most important. First grade oils contain various additives to improve quality. These are mainly anti-oxidants, which reduce harmful deposits and detergents, which retain some of the products of combustion in suspension where they are harmless. In this way the engine is maintained in a cleaner condition and the gumming up of piston rings and the sticking of valves is avoided. These oils also contain alkali constituents to neutralise the corrosive acids, produced by combustion, which contribute notably to cylinder and piston wear, particularly in engines that are stopped and started frequently.

All manufacturers specify the S.A.E. number of the oil which they consider to be most suited to their engines, and this is the oil the owner should use. Often a lighter oil is recommended for use in winter months than that recommended for summer use. This makes the engine easier to start in very cold weather and gives a slightly reduced fuel consumption. (See list on page 178).

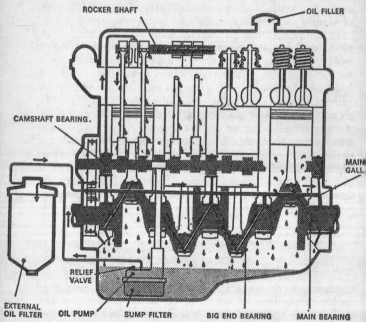

Fig. 64. The Engine Lubrication System.

When oil is heated it thins, or in other words, its viscosity is reduced. An oil that is of just the right viscosity when the engine is hot will be too thick when the engine is cold. Too thin an oil will not give sufficient protection to the bearings. Too thick an oil would make the engine stiff to turn, especially when cold. Oil technicians have succeeded in making oils which do not change viscosity with temperature increase in the same way as ordinary oils. They are thinner when cold and still not too thin when hot. These oils have a double S.A.E. classification such as 10W 30, for example. The W indicating that the viscosity of the oil is related to 0 degrees C.

GRAPHITE

Graphite is a form of carbon, slippery to the feel and graphite and oil mixture are sometimes added to engine oil, gear oil and petrol. It is often specially recommended for use in new and therefore tight engines. If the oil film should momentarily break down the graphite remains to provide a second line of defence.

UPPER CYLINDER LUBRICATION

It is quite a common practice to add a small quantity of oil to the petrol. Ordinary engine oil may be used in the proportion of about two tablespoonfuls to the gallon of petrol, or garages will supply specially compounded oil and dispense it with the petrol. Boxes of tablets may also be purchased, one or more tablets being added to each gallon of petrol. The purpose is to give extra lubrication to parts in the upper part of the engine that tend to receive less oil than they need. Such parts are the valve stems and guides and the top part of the cylinder.

WEAR AND LUBRICATION

Lubrication does not prevent wear and in the course of time the clearances in the cylinders and the bearings become great enough to interfere with the normal running of the engine. The main and big end bearing shells wear and need to be replaced. The bearing areas on the crankshaft wear so that the bearings become oval and need to be ground truly circular once more. The cylinder and pistons wear. The cylinder wears oval and barrel shaped as shown in Fig. 65, most of the wear taking place a little

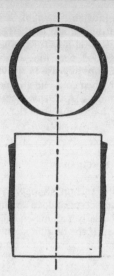

Fig. 65. How the cylinder bore wears. The wear is shown in exaggerated form.

way down from the top of the cylinder. Much wear also takes place on the left-hand side of the cylinder, the side that takes the thrust of the piston. Excessive cylinder wear results in heavy oil consumption and poor compression. The best remedy is to have the cylinders re-ground or re-bored and new oversize pistons fitted. An alternative is to have cylinder liners fitted. Although liners are more expensive than a re-bore they last longer.

OIL PRESSURE TOO LOW

An oil pressure gauge registering the oil pressure in pounds per square inch or an oil indicator light, which goes out when the engine is started, is always provided. Normal gauge readings will vary between about 25 to 50 pounds per square inch with different makes of engine. It is important to note and remember what the normal reading is. The pressure will always be higher when the engine is cold, due to the greater viscosity of the oil, but it will quickly become normal as the engine warms. The pressure should be noted occasionally and if it ever becomes low, or where there is an indicator light, if the light ever comes on when the engine is running, stop the engine. The most likely cause of low oil pressure is insufficient oil in the sump. Check this at once. A broken oil pipe will cause loss of pressure. So will a pressure relief valve that is stuck open, or a leaky pipe union.

If the pressure falls off over a long period, it may be that the sump filter is choked so that the pump is being deprived of oil. Cleaning the filter will cure this trouble.

The oil pump forces oil through the clearances in the main and big end bearings and if these clearances become too large, owing to wear, the oil can escape more easily and therefore the pressure drops. In fact low oil pressure is an indication of worn bearings. Of course, loss of pressure due to this cause would take place over a long period. It should be remembered that using a lighter grade of oil than usual will reduce the pressure, just as using a heavier oil than usual will increase the pressure.

OIL PRESSURE TOO HIGH

This would be due to a blockage in the pressure side of the system and is very unlikely. A more probable cause would be an oil of too high viscosity in the sump. An oil change, using the correct grade oil would cure this trouble. The oil gauge might be faulty.

EXCESSIVE OIL CONSUMPTION

If the cylinders are worn the engine will burn a lot of oil. This will be shown by a smoky exhaust. Oil may also find its way down the valve guides into the cylinders and be burned in this way. The top of the valve stems are often provided with oil sealing washers, which may need to be renewed. The condition of these washers can easily be inspected by removing the tappet cover. This applies only to overhead valve engines.

Oil leaks are a common cause of loss. The best way to trace leaks is to wipe the engine clean and then take the car for a short run. Leaks should then be easily seen. The tappet cover joint often leaks oil; the remedy is to obtain and fit a new washer. The oil sump drain plug or the sump joint are frequent sources of oil

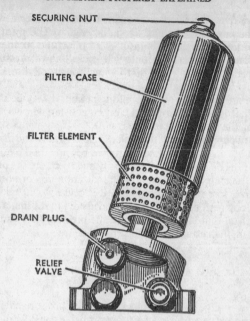

SECURING NUT

FILTER CASE

FILTER ELEMENT

DRAIN PLUG

RELIEF VALVE

Fig. 66. The Tecalemit oil filter. The filter element should be changed every 10,000 miles. Tightening torque on top bolt 20 lbs./ft. maximum, 15 lbs./ft. minimum.

loss, and again the remedy is new washers. Of course, before the sump can be removed all the oil must be drained from it. It is always well worth while to take special care when making joints. Use jointing compound where necessary, and always clean the two surfaces to be joined thoroughly, and be careful not to tear the new washer. A small piece of the old washer left in position by a careless operator may cause a bad leak and result in a lot of trouble before it can be put right. A choked crankcase breather pipe will increase oil consumption. Faulty oil seals on the engine main bearings will allow oil to escape. If the fault is at the clutch end, oil will leak from the drain hole in the bottom of the clutch housing. If at the front end of the engine the oil will leak from behind the pulley. Both these latter faults require a good deal of dismantling to rectify and this is best done by an expert.

In looking for leaks, observe the position of the oil that has dropped onto the floor; obviously it has come from a point immediately above, provided the car is not moved. The amount of oil that drops may not be large as it stops soon after the engine stops. Over a long period with the engine running the loss may be considerable.

Finally, the maximum oil level marked on the dipstick should not be exceeded or the engine will use excessive oil. It is better, however, to maintain the oil at the highest level rather than at the minimum one, because then more oil is in circulation and therefore its temperature is lower.

8

The Starter, Lights and Accessories

THE STARTER

FOR many years cars were almost always fitted with the inertia engagement type of starter and these are still widely used, but the pre-engaged type of starter is now often fitted.

In all cases the starter is engaged by moving a spur gear pinion into mesh with similar teeth on the flywheel rim. The pinion on the pre-engaged starter, as the name implies, is engaged with the teeth on the flywheel *before* the motor is energised, the pinion being withdrawn after the engine has started.

The inertia drive starter is energised before the drive pinion is engaged. This starter is a high torque motor and when engaged without a load accelerates very rapidly. The drive pinion is mounted on a spiralled sleeve, which is attached to the motor shaft. The spiral acts as a coarse thread. The pinion is free to move axially on the sleeve and will move if the pinion is held while the shaft is turned.

When the starter motor is energised, the shaft and spiralled sleeve accelerate so rapidly that the pinion, due to its inertia, is "left behind" thus causing it to be screwed along the sleeve and into engagement with the teeth on the flywheel.

Since the pinion engages under power there is a slight shock. Normally engagement is so quick that the arrangement is satisfactory. When the engine starts the drive is reversed, the higher engine speed turning the pinion out of engagement.

The pre-engagement starter on the other hand does not rotate until the pinion is fully engaged with the flywheel teeth. See Fig. 68.

When the starter switch is operated a fork, actuated by a solenoid moves the pinion towards the flywheel teeth. If tooth to tooth abutment takes place, preventing engagement, the pinion is arrested and caused to turn by the action of a spiralled sleeve, on which it is mounted – this turning enabling the teeth to engage.

At the point where engagement is completed a pair of contacts are closed to energise the motor and thus cause it to turn the engine. The starter pinion remains in engagement when the engine starts and is not withdrawn until the starter switch is released.

A roller clutch is incorporated in the starter drive which will transmit drive only from the starter to the engine so that the starter cannot be overspeeded when the engine starts. The pre-engaged starter is smoother than the inertia starter, wear and noise being reduced.

STARTER FAULTS

Starter fails to operate. If there is *no sound whatever* when the starter switch is operated, switch the headlights on. They should light with normal brilliance. Operate the starter switch with the headlamps still switched on. If the lights dim considerably the starter is jammed in engagement. When this happens to an inertia starter it may almost invariably be released by placing the car in 2nd or 3rd gear (ignition off) and rocking the car back and forward a few times. This cure is less likely to be effective with a pre-engaged starter. See "Starter Jams".

If the lights fail to light either the battery is flat or there is a fault at the battery connections. The connections should be removed from the battery, thoroughly cleaned and scraped to ensure a good contact, and then securely replaced. If the lights now operate but the starter fault is still present, check that connections at the ends of the heavy wire between the starter and starter solenoid switch are clean and tight. *Make sure that the battery earth lead is making really good contact with some metallic part of the car, and that the connection on the battery is tight.*

Ensure first that the car is out of gear. Place the ear as close as possible to the starter solenoid switch and have an assistant turn the starter switch to the "start" position once or twice. The solenoid switch should be heard to operate. If switch is heard to operate, this would be an indication that the starter was at fault. Whatever the outcome of this check, connect one of the test lamp (see fig. 80) leads to a good earth on the car and the other lead to the terminal on the starter solenoid switch carrying the light gauge wire (see Fig. 69). The lamp should light when the ignition is switched on. If the lamp does not light there is a fault in the circuit feeding the switch.

If the lamp lights connect the two heavy terminals on the

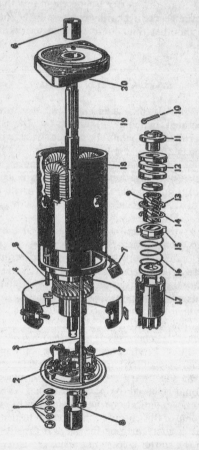

Fig. 67. Lucas M35G Starter Motor.

KEY: 1. Terminal nuts and washers; 2. Brush spring; 3. Through bolt; 4. Band cover; 5. Terminal post; 6. Bearing bush; 7. Brushes; 8. Bearing bush; 9. Sleeve; 10. Split-pin; 11. Shaft nut; 12. Main spring; 13. Retaining ring; 14. Washer; 15. Control nut; 16. Restraining spring; 17. Pinion barrel; 18. Yoke; 19. Armature shaft; 20. Driving end bracket.

switch, with cables still attached, by means of a heavy spanner or with a hammer head. A momentary connection is sufficient. Expect considerable sparking, therefore keep the hands clear. If the starter now operates, the solenoid switch is faulty. If the starter fails to operate it is faulty and should be removed for examination.

If the starter solenoid switch has only two terminals omit the test lamp check and momentarily connect the two terminals as already described.

In the case of a pre-engaged starter the operating solenoid is mounted on the starter and if the hand is placed on it while an attempt is made to operate the starter it will be possible to feel if the solenoid is being energised, since there will be some movement. If there is some movement but the starter does not engage, check the connections; they must be tight and clean. If the trouble is still present, the starter is faulty and should be removed for service or renewal.

If no movement at all is present when the starter switch is operated (ignition switch must, of course, be on) check with the test lamp that one of the starter terminals is alive to earth, if it is not there is a fault in the circuit feeding the starter.

Starter turns engine slowly and then stops. The battery is nearly discharged. In almost every case this is the trouble *but it is possible* that the connections on the battery leads are poor; therefore make sure that all the connections in the starter/battery circuit are clean and tight. In very cold weather the increased viscosity of the oil makes the engine very stiff to turn and a battery that was a bit low might be overtaxed in these circumstances.

Starter engages but jams. This is not an uncommon fault with inertia starters. Excessive wear in the starter, worn pinion and flywheel teeth or a bent starter shaft will contribute to this trouble. Make sure the starter is tight on its fixings; a loose starter will cause jamming. A jammed starter can be released by engaging 2nd or 3rd gear and rocking the car backwards and forwards a few times. There is a square on the end of the starter shaft (often under a cover) which can be turned with a spanner to assist release in bad cases. If the starter will not disengage, slack off the bolts holding it to the engine and repeat the attempts to free it. If the starter still remains engaged it must be removed.

Starter makes a whirring noise when the starter switch is operated but does not turn engine. This is an inertia starter fault. The starter pinion is not moving axially along the shaft. Usually

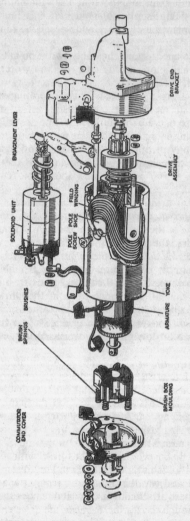

Fig. 68. Starter motor (pre-engagement type).

this is due to dirt on the spiralled sleeve. The remedy is to remove the starter and to thoroughly wash the drive in petrol, rotating the pinion in both directions so that full axial movement is obtained. Finally oil the sleeve slightly using a machine oil (typewriter or sewing machine oil). It may be necessary to dismantle the drive to examine for breakage or excessive wear of the parts.

The method of dismantling the drive varies a little with the make of the starter but all are basically the same. In the recent Lucas starters the drive is dismantled by removing the split pin from the spring cup and then withdrawing all the parts off the shaft. The order in which the parts are fitted must be carefully noted so that they can be correctly re-assembled with any new parts that may be required. Check that the starter shaft is not bent. If you turn the starter while you watch the end of the shaft you will see if the shaft is true. If the shaft is bent a new armature will be required.

DISMANTLING THE STARTER

First remove the inspection band and lift out the brushes. The best way to do this is to use a piece of wire with a hooked end, the hook being used to hold the springs up while the brushes are pulled out of their holders.

Check that the brushes are quite free in the holders; any jamming would be a fault that would need to be cured by rubbing the sides of the brush down a little with a fine file. Brushes should be renewed if their length is reduced to $\frac{7}{16}$ in. (0.49 mm). The brush leads are soldered to their connections on the earthed brush holders and on the ends of the field winding. The old brushes must be unsoldered and the new brushes soldered into position, but note that if the starter has an aluminium field winding it is impossible to solder to the aluminium. In this case the old brush tails must be cut off so as to leave a short length of the copper to which the new brush tails can be soldered.

To renew the brushes it is necessary to dismantle the starter. It is assumed that the inspection band has been removed and the brushes taken out of their holders. Refer to Fig. 67. Unscrew and remove the nuts and washers from the terminal to which the starter lead has been attached. Unscrew and remove the two long bolts passing through the starter. Remove the drive end bracket. The commutator end bracket can now be removed, complete with the armature.

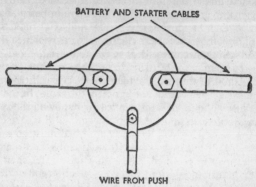

BATTERY AND STARTER CABLES

WIRE FROM PUSH

Fig. 69. Starter Solenoid Switch. The small wire may not be present.

The starter is re-assembled in the reverse order to that in which it was dismantled.

THE LIGHTS

The lights require very little attention, but it is particularly important that they should operate correctly. Keep all lamp glasses clean. Carry the following spare bulbs: stop/tail, indicator and one head lamp bulb, if bulbs are fitted. The bulbs should be carried in a tin box, each bulb being wrapped in a large piece of cloth. The head lights must be properly adjusted.

ADJUSTING THE LIGHTS

It is illegal to drive with incorrectly adjusted lights, and correct adjustment is required to pass the MOT test. The adjusting procedure is explained below.

Place the car so that it is facing a wall and is 25 ft. (7.6 m) from it, on level ground. The car must be square with the wall (both headlamps the same distance from the wall) and normally loaded.

Mark two vertical lines on the wall, the distance between the lines being equal to the distance between the headlamp centres. Draw a horizontal line on the wall at the same height from the ground as the lamp centres. The centreline of the car must correspond with the mid-position between the two vertical lines.

Do one lamp at a time, covering the lamp not being adjusted. Adjust the beam by moving it vertically and/or horizontally, as required, until the light pattern on the wall is as shown in Fig. 70. Two headlight cars and Fig. 71, cars with four headlamps.

Adjusting screws are provided as shown in Fig. 73. In this case access to the screws is obtained by removing the lamp rim. In some cases access holes are provided in the cover or grille. The top screw is used for vertical adjustment of the beam and the side screw for horizontal adjustment.

LIGHTING FAULTS

The most common trouble is that a light will not go on. This may be due to a broken filament in the bulb, in which case a new bulb is required. However if it is found that a headlamp will not light at all, main or dipped beam, this would suggest a wiring fault. If the lamp lights on one filament but not on the other, then this is, almost certainly, a filament failure. This applies to all two filament bulbs. It also applies to light units.

The first thing to suspect in any complete electrical failure is the fuse, if one is fitted. The driving lights (headlamps) are not always fused. If fused, each lamp may be on a separate fuse.

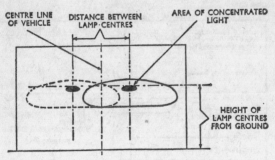

(A) FRONT OF VEHICLE TO BE SQUARE WITH SCREEN

(B) VEHICLE TO BE LOADED AND STANDING ON LEVEL GROUND

(C) RECOMMENDED DISTANCE·FOR SETTING IS AT LEAST 25 FT.

(D) FOR EASE OF SETTING ONE HEADLAMP SHOULD BE COVERED

Fig. 70. Beam setting for two headlamp cars.

If a lamp fails to light and the light unit or bulb is sound, the first thing to do is to clean the bulb contacts in the case of a lamp of this kind. Check that the spring loaded plungers are free to move and are touching the bulb contacts. Check that the lamp is earthed. The lamp shell should be alive to the *unearthed* battery terminal and you can check this with the test bulb, see Fig. 80.

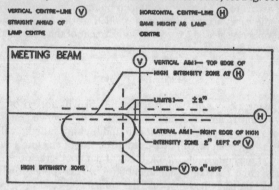

Fig. 71. Beam adjustment, four headlamp cars, main beam single filament bulbs.

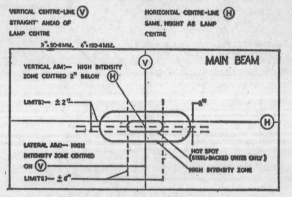

Fig. 72. Beam adjustment, four headlamp cars with dip left light units.

If the bulb will not light check the earth wire and its connection points. If a sealed light unit fails to light at all pull off the socket. Make sure the pins on the light unit are clean, this is best done by scraping them. Replace and remove the socket several times to improve the internal contacts. Using the test bulb, check that the centre hold in the socket is alive to *the unearthed* battery terminal. If it is not there is a fault in the earthing wire or its connections.

If no fault is found, attention must be transferred to the switch. See Chapter 9.

The same sort of tests can be made to any of the other lights if they fail to operate when they should. Look generally for bad earths, and corroded contacts and/or connections.

If all the lights are off, check the battery connections; if these are all right the fault is in the battery.

If you are doubtful about a bulb or light unit you can always check by transferring the bulb or unit to another lamp which is known to work. You can, if you like, check directly on the battery. A double filament bulb, if good, will light if connected directly to the battery.

If one battery terminal is connected to the metal contact on the side of bulb and the other battery terminal is connected to one of the contacts on the bottom of the bulb, a filament should light; if it does not and the battery is charged the bulb is faulty. If the filament does light, try the other contact – the other filament should then light if the bulb is sound.

You can check a sealed light unit by connecting the centre pin to one battery terminal and then alternately connecting each of the remaining pins to the other battery terminal. A filament should light when each outer pin is connected to the battery.

If you have trouble with flickering lights, this is due to a loose connection, usually in the lamp, and should not be difficult to find.

You may buy a car that some immature enthusiast has "loaded" with various fittings, accessories and decorations, often including several extra driving lights. These "added on" lights frequently give trouble because of the poor way they are connected. Look for disconnected wires and poor earths. Generally speaking, the car will be more reliable if you "dump the lot" because they tend to overload the system and may introduce faults.

THE BRAKE LIGHTS

These are operated by a switch in the brake hydraulic lines which is worked by the fluid pressure in the pipes when the brake pedal is depressed. One terminal on the switch should always be alive to earth when the ignition is switched on. You can check this with the test lamp. The second terminal on the switch should only be alive when the brakes are applied. This terminal will light the test lamp if it is connected between it and earth and the brakes are applied. A quicker way of checking the switch is to connect the two terminals together with a piece of wire, or even bridge them with the blade of a screwdriver. If the brake lights now come on, the switch is faulty.

DIRECTION INDICATOR LIGHTS

If an indicator fails to light this is probably due to filament failure in the bulb, therefore check this first. If the bulb is good

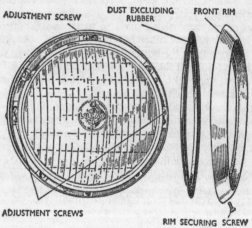

ADJUSTMENT SCREW DUST EXCLUDING RUBBER FRONT RIM

ADJUSTMENT SCREWS

RIM SECURING SCREW

Fig. 73. The beam adjustment screws on a headlamp.

check if the bulb contacts in the lamp are alive to earth, using the test lamp (see Fig. 20). Of course, the ignition must be switched on and the indicator switch moved to operate the lamp while these tests are being made. If no current is reaching the bulb, the flasher unit is probably faulty, but there may be a fault in the wire from the flasher to the lamp. To check for this, connect the terminal marked B or $+$ to the terminal marked L (Lucas flasher unit). If the indicator lamp now lights, there is a fault in the flasher unit and the unit should be renewed. If the indicator lamp does not light there is a fault in the wire, or its connections, between the flasher and the indicator lamp.

If none of the direction indicator lamps will work when the ignition is switched on, first check the fuse. If the fuse is good, check the live terminal on the flasher unit. The terminal marked B or + should always be alive to earth when the ignition is switched on and the fuse is sound. Therefore see if you can light the test lamp when it is connected between this terminal and earth. If the lamp fails to light, there is a fault in the wiring feeding the flasher unit. If the lamp does light check that the wire connections to the flasher are tight and clean. Re-check if the indicator lamps operate, if they do not the flasher unit is faulty and should be renewed.

If an indicator lamp remains on instead of flashing, this usually indicates a faulty flasher unit. It may be that another bulb on the same side of the car has failed. If the flashing rate is too low or too high this is due either to a faulty flasher unit or to the use of a bulb in the indicator lamp that has too low a wattage or too high a wattage.

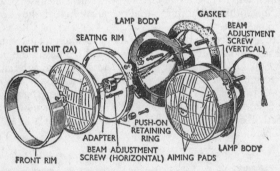

Fig. 74. The beam adjustment screws and other parts of twin headlamps.

Note that if failure of the flasher has been preceded by a blown fuse this could indicate a short circuit at some point in the lamp wiring. If a new flasher unit is fitted with this fault still present it will be destroyed. Therefore be quite sure that there is no short circuit present before fitting the new flasher unit.

WINDSCREEN WIPERS

If the wipers fail to work, check the fuse, then check the switch and wires. Make sure that the feed terminal on the motor is alive when the switch is on. This can be done by connecting the test lamp between this terminal and some earth point. Failure of the lamp to light would indicate a fault in the wiring or switch. If current is reaching the motor, the motor is faulty and should be removed for examination.

The wipers should not be operated when the windscreen is dry. This overloads the motors, and may scratch the screen.

FUEL GAUGE

Most electrical instruments now work off a regulated voltage supply. The voltage in the electrical system varies according to the state of charge of the battery and it is much higher when the alternator or dynamo is charging. This voltage variation would affect the reading of the instruments. The voltage regulator prevents this variation. On older cars the fuel gauge contained two coils, an operating coil and a balancing coil, the combined effect of which was to give a reading that was independent of voltage variation within the normal variation range. Fig. 75 shows such an arrangement.

If the gauge registers "Full" all the time when the ignition is switched on, irrespective of how much fuel there is in the tank, this would indicate a disconnection in the wire between the gauge and the tank unit. Check this wire and its connection to the tank unit and to the gauge. If no fault is apparent, connect a temporary wire from the tank unit to the gauge. If the gauge now works properly the original wire is faulty and should be replaced with a new one.

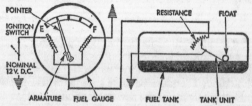

Fig. 75. Petrol gauge. This A.C. Delco gauge has a balancing coil to compensate for varying battery voltage. A single coil meter is now more common, the feed to all the instruments being via a voltage regulator.

The tank unit is earthed to the tank and a break in the earth return will also cause the gauge to give a "Full" reading. To check the earth, connect one test lamp wire to the unearthed battery terminal. With the other test lamp wire touch the fuel tank. The lamp would light showing that the tank is itself earthed. Now transfer the wire from the tank to the tank unit. The bulb should light, showing that the unit is earthed to the tank, and so proving that there is a complete earth return. Should one of the earths be proved faulty it must be corrected. If the earth return is sound the fault must lie in the gauge or in the tank unit, and a replacement of one of these will be required.

If the gauge reads "Empty" all the time there is likely to be a break in the connection between the gauge and the ignition switch, or the auxiliary fuse may be blown. If not, either the tank unit or the gauge is faulty, and of the two the tank unit is the most likely source of the trouble. The only cure would be replacement of the faulty unit.

In the case of a voltage stabilised system the best way to make a check is to have a spare tank unit. Disconnect the wire from the existing tank unit and connect it to the spare unit. Earth the body of the spare unit to some point on the car. As the float arm on the spare unit is moved up and down the gauge should register. If the gauge fails to register it is faulty and should be renewed. If it does register the existing tank unit is faulty and should be renewed.

This method of testing can also be used with the earlier twin coil meter.

Oil Pressure Warning Light

If the light does not go out when the engine is running, even when the oil pressure is normal, the pressure switch contacts may be stuck in the closed position. To check, disconnect the wire from the pressure switch while the engine is running. If the light goes out, the pressure switch is faulty and should be replaced, if the light does not go out there is a short circuit between the wire from the pressure switch to the warning light and earth. The wire should be replaced with a new one.

If the light fails to go on when the ignition is switched on, but before the engine is started, this would indicate a burned out bulb in the warning light. If the bulb is sound hold a screwdriver so that it touches the terminal on the pressure switch and also the engine. If, when the terminal is short circuited in this way, the light remains out, there is a disconnection in the wire to the

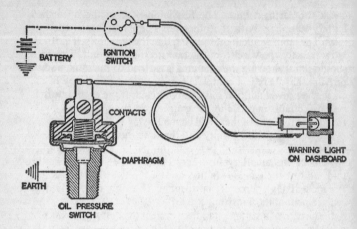

Fig. 76. The circuit of the oil pressure warning light.

ignition switch, to the warning light, or in the wire from the warning light to the pressure switch. If the light does go on, the pressure switch is faulty and should be replaced.

ELECTRIC HORNS

If there is no sound at all when the horn button is pressed there is probably a broken wire or loose connection in the wiring. The horn push may be defective. If a relay is fitted, this may be faulty, or the connections to it broken. The horn may require adjustment. A fuse may be blown. Sometimes twin horns have their own fuse and this may be found inside a bayonet connection in the connecting lead.

If the ear is placed near a horn that will not sound when the push is pressed a slight sound, perhaps a click, may be heard. In this instance the horn probably requires adjustment, or there might be a loose connection in the wiring. A horn that has become full of dirt or mud will cease to operate correctly.

If the horn gives a poor note it is probably either full of dirt or mud or requires adjustment. There may be a loose connection or the horn may be loose on its mounting. A horn that has been wired with the wrong gauge wire (wire too thin) will not sound properly.

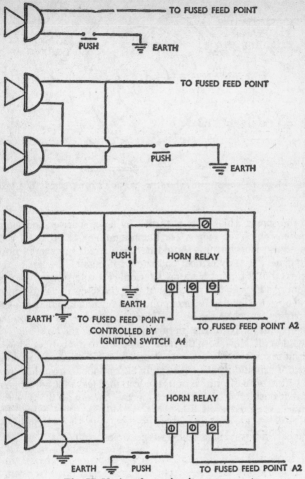

Fig. 77. Various horn circuit arrangements.

HORN ADJUSTMENT

Most horns are fitted with an adjusting screw, this may be on the outside of the horn or inside. In the latter instance the rear cover, or top cover sometimes must be removed to gain access

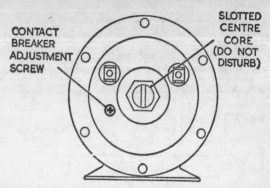

Fig. 78. Horn adjustment, showing the adjustment screw. See text.

to the screw. This screw is turned by a screwdriver and alters the tension on the points. The diaphragm may be provided with an adjustment, but this should not be altered. In general, horn adjustment is very critical and should if possible be left to the expert, but if it must be done, alter only the adjusting screw first mentioned. It will be found that turning the screw in one direction will open the contact breaker points and turning it in the opposite direction will close the points. Turn the screw so as to close the points and turn it further in this direction until the horn will not sound at all. Now, with the horn connected to the battery, slowly turn the screw in the opposite direction. While this is being done the horn should commence to sound. Continue to turn the screw as before until the note is at its loudest, then leave the adjustment in that position. The horn takes a heavy current all the time the points are closed, even if there is no sound, and it is not desirable to keep the horn connected to the battery for long. Therefore make the adjustment as quickly as possible.

9

The Electric Circuit

An electric current can only flow from a battery, or any other source, if it can return to it. There must be a complete "circuit". If we connect three or more bulbs to a battery as shown in Fig. 79A. The bulbs will light. The current will leave the battery at the terminal (1) and return at the terminal (2).

The wires on the (1) side of the bulbs are known as the feed wires; the wires on the (2) side of the bulbs are known as the return wires. If we cut the wire at (3) the bulbs will go out. They will also go out if we break the circuit at (4).

If we cut any of the wires to any bulb, above or below the bulb, the bulb will go out. This is the way the switch works, it simply breaks (and makes) the circuit.

In a car there is not only one circuit but many circuits but all are basically the same as that shown in Fig. 79A. In a car however the body, and chassis if there is one, is connected to the battery and all the return wires from the bulbs or other electrical devices are connected to the body so that these wires are very short or even none existant – the car body itself acting as the circuit return. The body is referred to as "earth". The idea of the system is shown in Fig. 79B.

In the circuits shown in Fig. 79 A, B and C the bulbs are said to be connected in parallel and must all be the same voltage as the battery.

If we clearly understand the electric circuit it becomes quite easy to find any faults that develop in it.

When electricity passes through a wire the wire offers resistance to its passage. The thinner the wire the greater the resistance. Thick wires give an easy path to the current. Electrical pressure is measured in volts; therefore it is the volts which push the current along the wire. If there are sufficient volts the current can be pushed through anything, even an insulator. The rate at which the current is flowing is measured in amperes, often just called amps. The way to get a heavy current is to have plenty of volts, or to provide very low resistance. Resistance is measured in ohms. All wires heat up when a current passes through them. If the current is a very heavy one the covering on the wires may

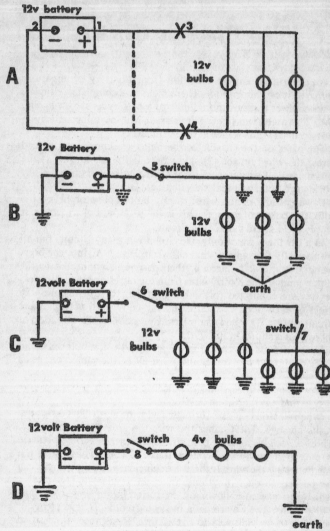

Fig. 79. The Electric Circuit.

burn and the wires may melt. A fuse wire is made just the right thickness to carry a certain maximum current and no more. If more tries to pass, the fuse wire melts, opens the circuit and prevents a fire. The lamps and other equipment in the electric circuit all present considerable resistance to the electric current, but electricity will always take the path of least resistance if it can.

If a connection were to be made, as shown by the broken line in Fig. 79A, or to any of the broken line earth points shown in Fig 79B, the current would take the easier path, or shorter path. This is called a short circuit. It could happen by the wearing through of the covering of the feed wires allowing them to touch the chassis. It could happen by the two wires to any of the bulb holders touching. As the resistance to the current would now be very low, the current would be very heavy and would burn the wires. Of course, when a short circuit happens in a car the fuse blows. If we replace the fuse it blows again. We must find and cure the short circuit. Apart from short circuits, we often get what for short are called disconnections. These may be broken wires or the ends of wires that have become detached from their point of fixing. This results in an open circuit, the current cannot pass, and whatever operates in the circuit is put out of action. If it happens in the ignition circuit the engine will stop, if it is running, and it will not be possible to start it until the fault is cleared.

In Fig. 79B opening the switch 5 will put all the lights out. In Fig. 79C if switches 6 and 7 are closed all the bulbs will be on. If only switch 7 is opened the three right hand bulbs will go out, leaving the three left hand bulbs still on. If switch 6 is opened all the lights will go out whether switch 7 is opened or not. Switch 6 is therefore a master switch. All the circuits in a car that are controlled by the ignition switch are like this – indicators, windscreen wipers and so on; they have their own switches but will only work if the ignition switch is on.

Fig. 79D shows a series circuit with three bulbs. The thing to note here is that the current passing through any bulb has to pass through all the other bulbs. If switch 8 is opened all the bulbs will go out. If the filament of any bulb breaks all the bulbs will go out, because the circuit has been interrupted. In a series circuit the voltage of each bulb must add up to the battery voltage. In the example illustrated there are three 4 volt bulbs and three fours equal 12, which is the battery voltage. The voltages do not need to be the same for each bulb, but their total must equal the battery voltage. *The current that each bulb takes must be the same.*

Series circuits are rare on cars. A series circuit has been used for the direction indicators. Failure of any bulb then puts the indicator warning bulb out and shows that a fault is present.

FAULT TRACING

The great difficulty in finding faults in electrical wiring is that there is nothing to show where they are. All we know for certain is that they are there. In the case of a gas or water pipe we can find the fault easily, but there is no leakage of electricity if there is an open circuit. Often expensive meters are specified and recommended for use in fault finding. They are convenient, but they are not necessary. We can do all we want to do with what we shall call the test lamp, see Fig. 80. This is made by connecting two pieces of wire, each about a yard long to an S.B.C. (Small Bayonet Cap) bulb holder, that is a two contact bulb holder of suitable size to take a bulb with an S.B.C. cap. All the older cars are fitted with this type of bulb. Twin plastic covered lighting flex is ideal for the wire, if the two wires are unwound. In fact, any bulb and bulb holder may be used, but the one mentioned is easily obtainable from electrical suppliers, in both thermosetting plastic and brass. A 12 volt bulb should be used, to suit the car battery voltage.

If you have a battery inspection lamp this will make an ideal test lamp, because some protection will be provided for the bulb, which otherwise is easily broken. The ends of the wires should be fitted with small crocodile clips so that we can connect them easily. A small plastic handled screwdriver is also very useful, we can fix one of the crocodile clips to it, just below the handle, and then use the screwdriver as a test prod. By means of such a test lamp we can trace the current from point to point in a circuit so that a break can be located. By using a battery in conjunction with the test lamp we can check leads for continuity and find out if earth connections are good or bad. The battery we use can be the car battery. We shall explain how to use the test lamp in a moment, but first a word about switches.

SWITCHES

The important thing to know about switches is that every switch has a feed point or input terminal. A simple on/off switch will simply have a feed point and an output point, but some switches have, as well as the feed point, many output points. All

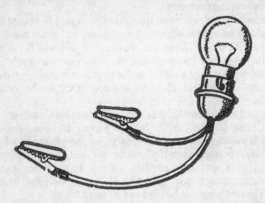

Fig. 80. The test lamp used for tracing electrical faults. The wires should be at least a yard long. Use a 12 volt bulb. It is an advantage to have bulbs of high and low wattage.

the switch does is to connect the output points to the feed point, but it may do this in a certain way, depending upon the position to which it is turned. An off/on switch of the simple kind just connects the feed point to the output point and when it does this the circuit is completed.

Some switches have more than one on position. The ignition/starter switch is one of these. When turned to the first position from off, the ignition circuit is completed, the fuel gauge is energised (and sometimes the fuel pump) and the switches controlling other circuits such as the windscreen wipers, indicators, horns and so on are rendered operative. When the switch is turned further against spring pressure the starter circuit is completed and the starter operates. This switch is key operated so that it can be locked in the off position.

Whether the switch be a multiple one or not, so long as there is no previous over-ride switch in the wire from the battery, one terminal on the switch will always be alive to earth and we can find it quite easily with the test lamp. Clip one of the test lamp wires to any earth point and touch the switch terminals, one after the other with the free test lamp wire when the switch is off. The terminal that lights the lamp is the feed terminal.

If we now turn the switch on and touch the other terminal (if there is only one) with the test lamp wire the lamp should now light showing that the switch has completed the circuit and is therefore working correctly.

If the switch controls more than one circuit and has more than one position we now select another position and again check the terminals with the test lamp and we can find which of the output terminals the second movement of the switch has made alive. By doing this we not only check that the switch is working properly but we can identify which wires are connected to the various terminals.

If we find, for example, that the output terminal carrying the ignition wire on the ignition/starter switch is alive when the ignition is switched on, we can then go to the other end of this wire which is connected to the ignition coil and check if that also is alive. If it is not, there must be a break in the wire. We can check right through any circuit in this way until the fault is found. The test lamp can be used to find most faults.

WIRING FAULTS

Wiring faults can be broadly divided into three kinds: short circuits, in which fuses blow and there may be burning; broken wires or detached connections, which prevent the components in the circuit operating and finally there are high resistance connections, due to corroded connectors, loose screws and poor earths.

Suppose there is a fault in the ignition circuit. We can locate it this way.

First make sure the contact breaker points are open or, better still, place a piece of thin card between the points. Switch the ignition on. Connect one test lamp lead to the unearthed battery terminal. Now refer to fig. 81. Disconnect the wire from the distributor at test point 1. Touch the terminal on the distributor with the test lamp lead. If the lamp lights the moving contact in the distributor is earthed, due to incorrect assembly or to some other fault. If the lamp does not light, re-connect the wire to the terminal.

Remove the test lamp lead from the unearthed battery terminal and connect it to the *earthed* battery terminal or to some other *earthed* point. Touch the terminal on the distributor, test point 1 again. The lamp should light. If the lamp does not light, connect

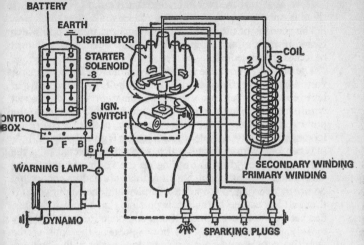

Fig. 81. Ignition circuit check. See text.

the test lamp lead to test point 2 (no need to remove the wire). If the lamp now lights there is a break in the wire from points 1 to 2. If the lamp does not light at point 2, check point 3. If the lamp lights at test point 3 there is a fault in the coil primary windings. Note that the lamp will light more brightly at test point 3 than at point 2.

If the test lamp does not light when the lead is applied to test point 3, check test point 4 (output terminal on ignition switch.) If the lamp lights at 4 but not at 3, there is a break in the wire between these two points.

If the lamp fails to light at test point 4, check test point 5. If it lights at 5 but not at 4 there is a fault in the ignition switch. If the lamp fails to light at test point 5, check test point 6. Now test point 6 may be the B terminal on the control box (as shown) or No. 1 terminal on the fuse box. However a fault any further back than point 5 would affect other circuits as well as the ignition circuit.

Point 8 is normally connected to the starter solenoid and the lead back to point 7 is taken from the same terminal as point 8 lead. All leads to point 6 should be alive to earth. *Remember to remove the card from between the contact breaker points, if it was placed there.*

How To Trace Short Circuits

The position of the short circuit is localized by the fuse which blows. If a fuse blows, is replaced and blows again, the fault must be found and remedied.

The test bulb should be clipped across the fuse holder clips. A voltmeter may be used instead of the test bulb. With the meter or bulb connected, refer to the wiring diagram, and disconnect wires, one by one in the group of circuits affected. Starting at the point furthest from the battery, replacing each one before removing the next. (A sample wiring diagram is given by fig. 82.)

When one wire is found which when disconnected puts the test lamp out or gives no reading on the voltmeter, this is the wire concerned in the fault. Identify this wire and its connecting points by referring to the wiring diagram and the colour code. If the fault has caused burning it is possible that so much damage has been done to other wires that a complete rewire is the only remedy. However, if this has not happened, the ends of the defective wire should be cut off and taped over with insulating tape. Fit a new external wire between the points which the old, faulty wire, connected.

How To Trace Open Circuits

These are caused by wire ends being pulled from their connections, or by terminal screws becoming loose. In rare cases a wire may break. There are two ways of attacking this problem, one is to make a continuity check of the wire suspected. The voltmeter or test lamp has one lead connected to the unearthed battery terminal while the other end is touched on the connection points at the component that is not operating, the switch being "On"; the component may be a windscreen wiper, ignition coil, lamp, or whatever. If current is present, the lamp will light or the voltmeter will show a reading. When testing in this way work back from the component towards the battery, using the wiring diagram as a guide. (See Fig. 82.)

The other method that may be used in tracing such a fault, is to use a loop wire to connect the two points. For example, if it is thought that there may be a break in the wires from the control box to the voltage regulator, check one wire at a time. Reference to the wiring diagram shows that the wire from the D terminal on the dynamo goes to the D terminal on the control box. Disconnect this wire at both ends and replace it by a loop wire, a piece of flex temporarily connected between the two points from which the ends of the other wire have been disconnected. If this clears the fault, then the disconnected wire must be replaced by a new one permanently wired in. If the fault is not cleared, remove the loop wire, reconnect the other wire, then make the same test with the other dynamo wire, which the wiring diagram shows is connected between the F terminal on the dynamo and the F terminal on the control box. Replace all detached wires as soon as possible, otherwise, with a lot of wires detached it may not be easy finding out where they were all connected.

How To Trace Faulty Earths and Other High Resistance Connections

High resistance sometimes occurs in connections, usually in old cars. Wires held by screwed terminals may become loose or corroded. Connections suspected should be unscrewed and examined and cleaned and replaced if they appear to be dirty. Push-in connectors sometimes develop this fault. Simply parting and refitting the connector several times will usually clear the fault. Possibly the most common source of the trouble is the battery connections; it usually occurs after an attempt has been made to use the starter. The starter may not operate or will operate and then will not operate any more; then it is found that the ignition warning light is out and the headlights will not light. If the battery connections are removed, thoroughly cleaned, then replaced and properly tightened the trouble is cured.

Another kind of high resistance connection is the faulty earth. Where the body is used as an "Earth return" such as for the lamps and fuel pump, and so on, it is necessary that the point where the wire is connected to the body should make good metallic contact with it. Sometimes, due to corrosion, the contact is broken and the circuits depending on the contact stop working.

The best check for a faulty earth is to take a loop wire (a piece of single plastic-covered flex will do) and connect one end to a good earth point on the car, or to the earthed battery terminal, and the other end to the wire or terminal or part that is supposed to be earthed. If bridging a suspected bad earth with a good one in this way puts things right then the normal earth point is shown to be faulty and it should be undone, thoroughly cleaned, and remade.

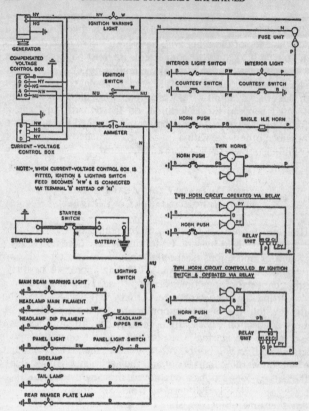

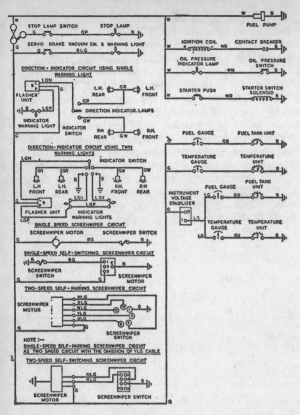

Fig. 82. Lucas wiring diagram showing the usual wiring connections on a variety of circuits. Although the cable colours may not completely conform to those shown, particularly with automatic transmission cars, the key is as follows:

R—Red	W—White	Y—Yellow
N—Brown	G—Green	U—Blue
P—Purple	B—Black	LG—Light Green

CABLE SIZES

A heavy electric current needs a heavy, or thick, wire to carry it. If we use a thin wire to supply, say a headlamp, the lamp will not receive sufficient current and so will give less light than it should do. Spot lamps that have been "added on" are often connected with the wire that reduces the light out-put of the lamp. Cable sizes are usually specified by two numbers divided by a stroke, such as, 37/20 this means that there are in the wire 37 strands of No. 20 S.W.G. (Standard Wire Gauge) wire. The cables listed below are suitable for the purposes indicated.

Side, tail, stop and interior lamps or other light duty circuits: 9/30 or 23/36. Headlamps, spotlamps, horn, and charging circuits, 28/30 or 70/36. The cables are insulated with P.V.C. plastic and protected with an outer covering of glazed material. For starters use: 12 volt circuit, 37/20. The starter relay circuit should be wired with the light duty cable mentioned above, vis. 9/30 or 23/36.

10

Notes on Decarbonising the Engine

CARBON deposit accumulates in the engine due to the burning of petrol in the cylinders. Assuming that a car does 40 miles to the gallon of petrol and covers 40,000 miles per year, 1,000 gallons of fuel will be burned in the engine each year. Obviously this must leave a considerable carbon deposit in the engine.

The effect of this accumulation of carbon is to cause the engine to "pink", to make a high pitched metallic knock when it is pulling hard. Accompanying this excessive tendency to pink is a general falling off in performance. It must be said that almost any engine can be made to pink by incorrect driving. We are here talking about excessive pinking when the car is being driven properly.

In general engines give better service the less they are taken to pieces and therefore it is a mistake to decarbonise the engine at frequent intervals, as some car enthusiasts do, when, in fact, the attention is not required.

To decarbonise the engine one removes the cylinder head as we shall describe. Overhead valve engines are most common, and we shall deal with these first, noting the slightly different procedure required by engines with overhead camshafts. There will be differences in detail from one car to another. Parts may be attached to the cylinder head in one case and not in another. We therefore deal in general with the work. The principal things to do are:

Drain radiator.

Remove valve cover, air cleaner and any other parts which have attachments to the cylinder head.

Disconnect the radiator hose.

Remove the carburettor(s). Sometimes the carburettors or carburettor can be removed while still fixed to the exhaust and inlet manifolds. In either case the petrol feed pipe and other attachments to the carburettor must be removed.

In removing the exhaust and inlet manifolds, these need only be pulled off the studs, so as to rest clear of the head. This is so even if the carburettor(s) are still attached.

Take out the sparking plugs. Mark the leads so that they can be replaced correctly.

Remove the push rods. A good way is to turn the engine until the valves in the cylinder you are dealing with are closed. Fold a piece of cloth into a pad and place it over the rocker end that works on the spring. By pressing heavily the spring is compressed and the end of the rocker over the push rod lifts sufficiently to enable the rod to be pushed sideways and then removed. Each rod must be replaced, on reassembly, *in the same position as it was when removed*. Therefore place all the rods in a safe place in the same order in which they were in the engine, so that no difficulty will arise on replacing.

Remove the rocker shaft.

In the case of an OHC (overhead camshaft) engine there are no rockers. The two types most likely to be encountered are the Hillman Imp and some of the Mark III Ford Cortinas. The camshaft on the Hillman Imp engine is chain driven and the chain must be removed from the chain wheel on the end of the camshaft before the head can be removed.

Once the chain has been released and the cylinder head is off the ends should be placed over the sides of the cylinder block and weights attached to it to hold them there.

On the Ford engine it is necessary to remove the cogged rubber belt, after taking off the guard. The tension roller is released and locked back against its springs. Force the roller fully back against the spring pressure and lock it in that position by tightening the bolt in the slotted hole in the roller mounting bracket. The belt may then be removed.

Warning, Overhead Camshaft Engines: When the drive to them has been disconnected the camshaft(s) must not be rotated or the engine turned, otherwise the valves may be struck by the pistons resulting in serious damage.

Finally, remove the cylinder head itself. Use a ring spanner, and unscrew each nut a little at a time until all are slack. The head remains firmly attached to the block because of the adhesion caused by the high pressure that was exerted by the holding nuts. To break the adhesion, try tapping round the sides with a hammer, but interposing a piece of hardwood between the head and the hammer. The cylinder head may crack if it is struck directly with the hammer. The head may be provided with lugs near the joint, under which the wood may be placed, so that tapping upwards will tend to lift the head. If this fails to get results, replace the plugs and tighten them lightly. Now turn the engine by hand or by using the starter. This should break the joint. The method cannot however be used on the Hillman Imp or similar engines because of the camshaft drive chain. Do not be tempted to drive the blade of a screwdriver, chisel, or any other metal wedge into the joint in order to free the head. This will do damage. Make *quite* sure that all the fixings have been removed.

Lift the head carefully. It is likely that part of the gasket is lifting with the head, the rest being stuck to the cylinder block. Continued lifting of the head in these circumstances will damage the gasket, therefore have an assistant free the gasket from the head by means of a knife. The cylinder head gasket is delicate and easily damaged.

Except for the removal of the valves, all the dismantling has now been completed and the work of removing the carbon can commence. Use an old screwdriver, one with a very blunt end, as a scraper to remove the carbon. Scrape each combustion space in the head completely free from carbon, including the valve heads. The valves are allowed to remain in position to avoid the seats being scratched, as would otherwise happen. Next, the carbon can be removed from the piston crowns. This should be done when the pistons are at the top of the stroke. It is generally considered a good thing to leave a narrow rim of carbon round the edge of the piston, close to the cylinder walls. If this is not done the oil consumption will temporarily rise until a new ridge of carbon has been deposited.

When the work of clearing the carbon is completed the valves are removed. To do this a valve spring compressing tool is required. The forked end of the tool is placed squarely over the valve cup, the end of the valve stem being centrally located in the fork. The screw is placed on the valve head. Tighten the screw. This will compress the springs (there may be two to each valve in an overhead valve engine) and enable the two tapered valve retaining collets to be flicked out with a small screwdriver. If the screw is now released, the valve may be withdrawn. Usually it is found that the spring pressure has caused adhesion between the spring cup and the retaining collets. To try and overcome this with the spring compressing tool may strain it. Therefore break the adhesion before using the tool. Do this by placing the head face down on the bench with a piece of wood under the valve head, so as to prevent it moving downwards, and give the spring cup a light tap with a hammer. This will break the adhesion, and allow the compression tool to work easily. This precaution is not so important if a lever type spring compressor is used. In either case at all times *keep your fingers* WELL CLEAR of parts under spring loaded pressure. Fingers have a nasty habit of getting painfully trapped.

On the Ford OHC engine it is not necessary to take off the camshaft but the cam followers must be removed, after compressing the valve springs. All the followers should be removed before taking out the valves.

On the Hillman Imp engine the camshaft must be taken off before the valves can be removed.

As in the case of the push rods, the valves must be replaced in the same positions from which they were removed. Therefore either place them on a shelf in the same order in which they were removed, or have a length of wood drilled with holes and supported so that the valves may be dropped into the holes and thus retained in the proper order until they are to be replaced. The carbon on the curved portion under the valve head should be removed, and the valve stem should also be cleaned. Do not polish the stem. By placing any of the valves in its own valve guide until it is nearly closed and then trying to move it from side to side any wear between valve and guide may be detected. There should be no movement but an extremely slight movement would be permissible. Worn guides may be withdrawn and new guides replaced by means of a drawbolt arrangement or by using a double diameter brass drift and a hammer.

It is essential to know how far the guide should be inserted, that is, how much of it should be left projecting upwards. This information can be obtained from the makers of the engine, or by measuring the projecting portion of the guide before it is removed. In general a new guide will require a new valve, a wear step probably being present below the valve head on the stem of the old valve. However if the valve is unworn and therefore shows no side play when fitted in the guide it may be refitted. Fitting new guides is not a very easy task and the work may be bypassed by taking the head to a garage and having the guides fitted there. Grinding in the valves must be done *after* new guides have been fitted. After long use the valves tend to leak and require to be reground on their seats to restore the gastight seal they are required to provide.

GRINDING IN THE VALVES

Note that the inlet valves on many Ford engines must NOT be ground in. These valves have an aluminium coating which grinding in would destroy. If grinding is required to remove seat defects in the head, use an old valve.

Grinding in is accomplished by smearing a very small amount of valve grinding paste on the valve seat. The valve is then placed in its position in the cylinder head and rotated first in one direction and then in the other while it is held under light pressure on the seat.

To do this a valve grinding tool is required and takes more than one form. It may be a straight wooden handle about 12 inches long with a rubber sucker fixed to one end. In use the sucker is moistened and attached to the valve head by pressure. The valve is then inserted in its guide and rotated, by rolling the wooden handle between the palms of the hands. This tool can only be used if the valve has a smooth head. Some valves are provided with a slot in the head and in this case a screwdriver may be used to turn the valve on its seat. When the valve is removed from the head it may be found that the seat, instead of being smooth is pitted. Sometimes the seat may be partly burned away, in the case of an exhaust valve, so that a new valve is required. Slight imperfections on the valve seat, and these are most common on the exhaust valve, may be removed in a valve reseating machine, which grinds a small amount off the valve seat. Most garages will do this work for a small sum if the valves are taken to them. It is possible to remove slight pitting by grinding the valve on its seat in the cylinder head, but this is not a good thing to do.

Valve grinding is a wearing process, reducing both the life of the valve and of the cylinder head. Only the minimum amount of grinding to maintain the valves in a gastight condition should be used.

It may be found that the seat on the cylinder head has become pitted. Again, if this is slight, it could be removed by grinding the valve on the seat for a long period, but this is hard on the valve. By far the best method is to use a valve seat cutter to skim just sufficient metal off the seat to remove the damage and then grinding in the valve.

In time the reconditioning of the valve results in the edge of the head becoming very thin or even sharp. When this happens a new valve is required, even if the seat is sound. The eventual result of cutting and grinding the seat on the cylinder head is to lower it below the surrounding surface. This results in the valve being in a pocket so that the effective lift of the valve is reduced. Very old engines or ones that have been "enthusiastically maintained" commonly suffer from this trouble. The seats can be built up by welding and then resurfaced.

Valve trouble can be reduced by decarbonizing the engine as soon as it becomes obvious that it is required. Exhaust valve trouble is usually due to the deposit on the valve head of products derived from the lead dope added to the fuel to increase the anti-knock properties. Tight tappet clearances will lead to valve burning because the valve cannot then seat properly and will leak. An exhaust valve that leaks much will soon burn.

Grinding in of the valves should be continued, using very little fine grinding paste until the seat surface is smooth and even. Generally far too much grinding paste is used. It gets on to the hands. It is not properly removed from the valves before they are inserted. The result is that some of this very damaging material finds its way into the engine and circulates with the oil and causes a considerable amount of rapid wear before it is picked up by the filters. Avoid this by using paraffin and clean rags to clean the valves. Wash the hands thoroughly before handling any engine parts. Pass a piece of clean rag through each valve guide before finally inserting the valve on reassembly. Smear the valve stem with clean engine oil. Use a clean rag to wipe carbon debris from the cylinder walls and piston crowns. Put a teaspoonful of clean engine oil into each cylinder before finally replacing the head.

If the old cylinder head gasket is quite undamaged, it may be used again. It is possible to obtain a complete set of gaskets for cylinder head, manifold, and carburettor, and if this is done there is little use saving the old gasket. Fit the gasket to the cylinder head, making sure it is the right way up. The top surface is usually marked "Top". The gasket should be smeared with grease before it is fitted. Make quite sure that the joint surface on the cylinder block, the cylinder head and the gasket itself are free from any kind of grit or dirt. Even a small piece of carbon in the joint will weaken it and may cause a leak.

When the head, complete with valves, is ready lower it in position. Retightening the holding down nuts is an important operation and should be carefully carried out. Screw all the nuts on their studs until they are finger tight, then tighten a little at a time with a ring spanner. Start with the centre nuts first and work outwards and diagonally. It will be necessary to go round the nuts several times before they are tight. Do not overtighten the nuts. They should be tightened with a torque wrench to the tightness specified by the manufacturers. Since the owner driver is not likely to possess such a wrench, the best he can do is to turn the nuts until they are tight, *not as tight as they will go*.

In the case of the OHC engines previously mentioned the camshaft drive has to be re-connected. Fig. 24 shows how the timing marks must be aligned before replacing the cogged belt on the Ford engines. In the Hillman Imp, the line of the camshaft chainwheel must be parallel to the end of the cylinder block with No. 1 piston at top dead centre before the chain is replaced on the chainwheel.

It may be found that the cylinder head is held by bolts, instead of studs and this makes positioning the gasket difficult when the head is being fitted. In this case pieces of mild steel bar (two will do) threaded at one end with the same thread as in the cylinder holes should be made. They must be long enough to allow for their removal after the cylinder head is back in place.

The tappet clearances must, of course, be reset after decarbonization. (See page 174). A new cylinder head gasket will settle down under the pressure and become slightly thinner. This will reduce the tappet clearances as well as the tightness of the cylinder head nuts. Therefore these items should be checked after the first 50 miles and finally at 200 miles. Side valve engine tappets are not affected by the cylinder head gasket, the valves being in the cylinder block.

This is a necessarily somewhat brief account of the work required to decarbonise the engine. Detailed work has been omitted. For example when I have said "remove the carburettor" I have not said how to remove it. The reader who will be successful at this work will know that as the carburettor is held on by nuts, these will have to be unscrewed, and as there are attachments to the carburettor, throttle, choke, and petrol feed, these must also be removed before the carburettor can be taken off the engine.

II

Maintenance

THERE are two ways to run a motor vehicle. One is to run the
vehicle until something goes wrong, as it inevitably must. The
fault is then put right and you continue as before, until another
fault develops. Once more the fault is rectified and once more
the vehicle proceeds on its way, until the next fault occurs.
Many motorists run their cars on this principle. Some do it
because they do not know of a better way. Some do it because
the car is new, and they will have another new one next year
anyway. This is what puts the risk into buying second-hand
cars. If London's buses were treated in this way, the streets
would be littered with broken down buses. The reason that we
seldom see a broken down bus is because these vehicles are
correctly maintained.

Maintenance keeps running costs down by reducing repairs
and replacements. It also reduces depreciation. Maintenance
does *not* mean taking things to pieces at the week-end "just
to see that everything's all right". Such enthusiastic tinkering
causes trouble. Never take anything to pieces unless this is
necessary to correct a fault known to be present.

All manufacturers supply the essential maintenance information in the instruction book issued with the car, and this of
course should be followed. If this information is not available,
the maintenance schedule given below may be helpful.

Always investigate abnormal noises. If the engine makes
an abnormal noise, check the oil pressure gauge or note if the
oil warning light is on.

DAILY

Check the oil level. Withdraw the dipstick and clean it on a
piece of clean cloth. The dipstick is marked with minimum and
maximum oil levels. The engine must be stopped when the oil
level is checked. Replace the dipstick, push it down as far as it
will go and again withdraw it. You will then be able to see if more
oil is needed or not. The oil level, as shown by the dipstick, must

not be allowed to fall below the minimum level. Over filling will waste oil.

Check water level in radiator. The water should be about an inch below the filler neck. The radiator cannot be too full. Excess water can escape.

Examine the tyres visually. If a tyre has apparently gone soft, it is probably punctured. Inflate it to the correct pressure and re-check pressure after an interval.

WEEKLY

Check tyre pressures with gauge, including the spare wheel. Remove any flints or other objects embedded in tyres. Check that all lights are operating.

MONTHLY

Check battery level, and the levels in the clutch and brake fluid reservoirs.

YEARLY

Flush out the radiator. It is convenient to do this in the late autumn, when anti-freeze is due to be added. The easiest way is to turn on the drain taps and place a water hose in the radiator filler. It may be necessary to push a piece of wire through the taps to clear stoppages, due to sediment. The water is allowed to run through the system until it emerges clear. Alternatively, the top and bottom hoses connecting the radiator to the block may be disconnected. Both the block and the radiator can then be flushed out more quickly and thoroughly. The hoses are then re-connected, but if they are old new ones may be required.

If the radiator honeycomb is choked with mud and insects, as it often is, it should be cleaned by hosing through with a pressure jet, but first the electrical equipment should be thoroughly protected with a plastic sheet of ample size.

EVERY 3,000 MILES

Steering linkage and suspension: Use grease gun on track rod joints, king pins, and other steering parts. Use grease gun on suspension nipples and on universal joints.

Fig. 83. Adjusting the rocker (tappet) clearance. Release the locknut with a ring spanner and turn the adjuster with a screwdriver until the correct clearance is obtained, using a feeler gauge, as shown. The valve which the rocker operates must be fully closed (tappet on back of cam — spring fully expanded). Tighten nut, and re-check clearance. If no lock-nut is provided, turn adjuster as required to obtain correct clearance. The adjuster in this case, being stiff to turn, will retain the clearance. Refer to manufacturers car handbook for appropriate gap for your engine.

Change engine oil. If the car is used in unusually dusty conditions for long periods, dry country lanes or similar conditions abroad, the oil should be changed every 3,000 miles. Change the oil when the engine is thoroughly warm so that the oil will run freely. Unscrew the sump drain plug and have ready at hand a receptacle that is easily large enough to hold all the oil. Normally, oil changes are at 6,000 miles.

Lubrication: Grease all nipples (where fitted).

Accelerator: Oil linkage joints and pedal fulcrum.

Gearbox: Check gearbox oil level.

Clutch: Check clutch pedal clearance. Oil the joints in the operating mechanism. With hydraulically operated clutches, check fluid level, and check for fluid leaks.

Brakes: Test brakes and adjust if this is necessary. Check fluid level in reservoir. Lubricate handbrake.

Steering gearbox: Check oil level (if applicable).

Rear axle: Check oil level.

Air cleaner: If the air cleaner is of the oiled type, remove the gauze and wash it thoroughly in petrol. Note: there should be no fire within 20 yards when this is being done. When clean shake

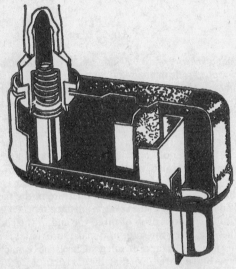

Fig. 84. Crankcase emission valve. When this is fitted it should be removed and cleaned and re-fitted every 6,000 miles. This shows the type fitted to some Ford engines.

the gauze clear of petrol as far as possible. Re-oil the gauze thoroughly with engine oil. If a bath of oil is provided below the filter element, the oil in this should be renewed. The paper elements in other air cleaners need renewal approximately every 12–15 thousand miles.

Fan belt: Check tension.

Body: Oil door hinges, locks, etc. Use machine oil.

General: Check all nuts for tightness. Warning: do not over-tighten, this can cause expensive damage. It is difficult to indicate how tight a nut or bolt should be. It varies with size. But the common idea a nut or bolt is sufficiently tight only when all attempts to tighten it further fail is a very bad one. It is enough when the nut or bolt "feels tight". Special spanners are used to tighten specially important nuts, such as those on the big end bearing caps. Such spanners register the torque, or turning effort applied, on a gauge. The torque to be used is specified by the makers. When properly tightened the nuts are by no means as tight as they could be got. May this serve as a warning to the over enthusiastic owner and save him money.

Every 6,000 Miles

Carry out all checks of a 3,000 mile service and in addition:

Sparking plugs: Clean plugs and reset points gaps.

Distributor: Remove the moulded cover and clean the inside surface by rubbing with a clean fluffless cloth. Pay special attention to the spaces between the brasses, where tracking is likely to take place. Remove the rotor arm and place a few drops of machine oil into the rotor arm spindle. The screw inside the end of the spindle must not be removed. The oil gains access to the spindle bearing through an opening below the screw head. Sparingly smear the cam face with light grease or clean engine oil. Inject a little machine oil through an aperture in the base plate. This will find its way on to the ignition advance/retard mechanism and lubricate it. Add a drop of oil to the end of the rocker arm pivot. When replacing the rotor arm make sure that it is properly keyed, that is down as far as it will go. Check the contact breaker points gap. Make sure also that the distributor cap retaining clips are properly in position. Warning: Take care that no oil or grease gets on to the contact point faces.

Dynamo: (where fitted) Inject a few drops of 30-40 S.A.E. engine oil into the hole marked "Oil" on the end of the dynamo.

Gearbox: Drain and refill. Do this when the oil is warm, after a run.

Back axle: Drain and refill. Do this when the oil is warm.

Fan belt: Check for tension and adjust if necessary. See page 15 or 26.

Fuel system: Clean fuel pump filter.

Toe-in: Have toe-in checked.

Engine: Change engine oil. Renew lubrication oil filter element. Remove, clean and re-fit crankcase emission valve if one is fitted.

Valve Rockers: Check clearances (see fig. 83.)

Brakes: Check disc brake pads for wear. Check brake shoes

for adjustment. Remove the drums and inspect the shoe linings. The linings must not be allowed to wear so thin that the rivet heads come into contact with the drum. Bonded linings, which have no rivets must not be allowed to wear thinner than $\frac{1}{16}$ in. (1.6 mm).

The friction pads of disc brakes should be inspected through the opening in the caliper assembly. This can be done easily if the wheel is removed. It may be necessary to remove a dust cover. Do not allow the pad linings to wear thinner than $\frac{1}{16}$ in. The pads should, preferably be renewed before the linings are as thin as this.

Always road test brakes after adjustment.

Clutch: Check adjustment. See p. 84.

12,000 MILES (ADDITIONAL WORK)

Wheels: Check nuts for tightness and have front wheel toe-in checked.

Sparking plugs: Fit new set of plugs.

Suspension: Examine spring and U bolts. Check nuts for tightness.

Exhaust system: Check fixings for tightness.

Contact breaker points: Renew.

24,000 MILES (ADDITIONAL WORK)

Dynamo and Starter: Renew brushes. Clean commutator. Check bearings for slackness. Carefully check all brake hoses and renew, if necessary.

Ignition timing: Check, and adjust if necessary.

Carburettor: Check and adjust idling, if required.

Oil filler cap filter: (if fitted), clean.

If only small mileages are covered, regard 3,000 miles as 3 months, 6,000 miles as 6 months and so on.

At about 40,000 miles (65,000 km.) nearly all the car makers now urge that the brake hoses should be carefully examined. In general, at this mileage it is advisable to renew all the rubbers in the braking system and to fill the system with new fluid. Refer to a reputable garage for advice if you are in doubt.

MAKE & MODEL	ENGINE Summer/Winter	Sump capacity plus filter [1] Pints	GEAR BOX	Capacity Pints	REAR AXLE	Capacity Pints
AUSTIN						
1959–69 Mini Cooper & Mini Cooper Mk II	Castrol GTX	$8\frac{1}{2}$ [27]	—	—	—	—
1967–69 Mini 850 Mk II, 1000 Mk II, & Mini Cooper "S" Mk II	Castrol GTX	$8\frac{1}{2}$ [27]	—	—	—	—
1961–64 A 110 Mk 1 (Synchro)	Castrol GTX	$12\frac{3}{4}$	Castrol GTX	$4\frac{1}{2}$	Castrol Hypoy	$3\frac{1}{4}$
1961–64 A 110 Mk I (Automatic)	Castrol GTX	$12\frac{3}{4}$	Castrol TQF	$13\frac{1}{2}$	Castrol Hypoy	$3\frac{1}{4}$
1964–69 A 110 Mk II (Synchro)	Castrol GTX	$12\frac{3}{4}$ [61]	Castrol GTX	$5\frac{1}{2}$	Castrol Hypoy	$3\frac{1}{4}$
1964–69 A 110 Mk II (Automatic)	Castrol GTX	$12\frac{3}{4}$ [61]	Castrol TQF	$11\frac{1}{4}$	Castrol Hypoy	$3\frac{1}{4}$
1967–71 3 Litre (Synchro)	Castrol GTX	12	Castrol GTX	5	Castrol Hypoy B	$3\frac{1}{2}$
1967–71 3 Litre (Automatic)	Castrol GTX	12	Castrol TQF	8	Castrol Hypoy B	$3\frac{1}{2}$
1963–71 1100, 1100 Mk II, 1300 & 1300 GT	Castrol GTX	$8\frac{1}{2}$ [27]	—	—	—	—
1965–71 1800, 1800 Mk II & 1800 S	Castrol GTX	$10\frac{1}{4}$ [27] [49]	—	—	—	—

1965–71 1800 & 1800 Mk II (Automatic)	Castrol GTX	6½+1¼	Castrol TQF	13	—	—
1966–71 Mini, Mini Mk II, 1100, 1100 Mk II & 1300 (Automatic)	Castrol GTX	13 [27] [59]	—	—	—	—
1969–71 Maxi	Castrol GTX	8½ [27]	—	—	—	—
FORD (British)						
1961–62 Consul Classic 315 & Capri	Castrol GTX	4+½	Castrol Hypoy Lt	1¾	Castrol Hypoy	2
1962–66 Zephyr	Castrol GTX	6 +1½	Castrol Hypoy Lt	4	Castrol Hypoy	2½
1962–66 Zephyr 4 (Automatic)	Castrol GTX	6 +1½	Castrol TQF	11¼	Castrol Hypoy	2½
1966–71 Zephyr Mk IV V4	Castrol GTX	7½	Castrol Hypoy Lt [48]	3¼ [54]	Castrol Hypoy	3
1962–66 Zephyr 6 & Zodiac (Synchro)	Castrol GTX	6½+1½	Castrol Hypoy Lt	4	Castrol Hypoy	2½
1962–66 Zephyr 6 & Zodiac (Automatic)	Castrol GTX	6½+1½	Castrol TQF	14¼	Castrol Hypoy	2½
1966–71 Zephyr & Zodiac Mk IV V6	Castrol GTX	8 +1a	Castrol Hypoy Lt [48]	3¼ [54]	Castrol Hypoy	3
1962–65 Consul Cortina 1200	Castrol GTX	4+½ [46]	Castrol Hypoy Lt	1¾	Castrol Hypoy	2
1962–65 Consul Classic, Capri & Capri GT	Castrol GTX	6+½ [47]	Castrol Hypoy Lt	1½	Castrol Hypoy	2
1963–66 Consul Cortina 1500, Super, GT & Lotus	Castrol GTX	6¼+½ [47]	Castrol Hypoy Lt	1¾	Castrol Hypoy	2
1963–66 Consul Cortina 1500, Super, GT & Lotus (Automatic)	Castrol GTX	6¼+½ [47]	Castrol TQF	11¼	Castrol Hypoy	2

MAKE & MODEL	ENGINE Summer/Winter	Sump capacity plus filter [1] Pints	GEAR BOX	Capacity Pints	REAR AXLE	Capacity Pints
1964–67 Corsair & GT	Castrol GTX	$6\frac{1}{4}+\frac{1}{2}$ [47]	Castrol Hypoy Lt	$1\frac{3}{4}$	Castrol Hypoy	2
1964–67 Corsair & GT (Automatic)	Castrol GTX	$6\frac{1}{4}+\frac{1}{2}$ [47]	Castrol TQF	$11\frac{1}{4}$	Castrol Hypoy	2
1965–70 Corsair V4, 2000, 2000 E & V4 GT	Castrol GTX	$6+1\frac{1}{2}$	Castrol Hypoy Lt [48]	$2\frac{1}{4}$	Castrol Hypoy	2
1966–67 Cortina 1300	Castrol GTX	$5\frac{1}{2}$	Castrol Hypoy Lt [48]	$2\frac{1}{4}$	Castrol Hypoy	2
1967–70 Cortina 1300 (Cross-flow)	Castrol GTX	$6\frac{1}{2}$	Castrol Hypoy Lt [48]	$2\frac{1}{4}$	Castrol Hypoy	2
1966–67 Cortina 1500 & 1500 GT	Castrol GTX	7	Castrol Hypoy Lt [48]	$2\frac{1}{4}$	Castrol Hypoy	2
1968–70 Cortina 1600, 1600 E & GT	Castrol GTX	$7\frac{1}{2}$	Castrol Hypoy Lt [48]	$2\frac{1}{4}$	Castrol Hypoy	2
1967–71 Executive	Castrol GTX	$8+1\frac{1}{2}$	Castrol Hypoy Lt [48]	$3\frac{1}{4}$ [54]	Castrol Hypoy	3
1968–71 Escort, 1100, 1100 Super, 1300 Super & 1300 GT	Castrol GTX	$6\frac{1}{2}$	Castrol Hypoy Lt [48]	$1\frac{1}{2}$	Castrol Hypoy	2
1968–71 Escort Twin Cam	Castrol GTX	$7\frac{1}{2}$	Castrol Hypoy Lt	$1\frac{3}{4}$	Castrol Hypoy	2
1969–71 Capri 1300, 1300 GT, 1600 & 1600 GT	Castrol GTX	$7\frac{1}{4}$	Castrol Hypoy Lt [48]	2	Castrol Hypoy	2
1969–71 Capri 2000 GT	Castrol GTX	$7\frac{1}{2}$	Castrol Hypoy Lt [48]	$2\frac{1}{4}$	Castrol Hypoy	2

1969–71 Capri 3000 GT & 3000 E	Castrol GTX	8	Castrol Hypoy Lt [48]	3¼	Castrol Hypoy	2
1968–70 Cortina Lotus	Castrol GTX	7½	Castrol Hypoy Lt	1¾	Castrol Hypoy	2
1970–71 Escort RS 1600	Castrol GTX	7¼	Castrol Hypoy Lt	1¾	Castrol Hypoy	2
1970–71 Cortina 1300, 1600 & 1600 GT	Castrol GTX	6	Castrol Hypoy Lt [48]	2	Castrol Hypoy	1¾
1970–71 Cortina 2000	Castrol GTX	6	Castrol Hypoy Lt [48]	2½	Castrol Hypoy	2
1970–71 Escort Mexico	Castrol GTX	8	Castrol Hypoy Lt	1¾	Castrol Hypoy	2
HILLMAN						
1960–64 Husky Series II	Castrol GTX	7+1	Castrol GTX	2¾	Castrol Hypoy	1¾
1960–64 Minx IIIb, IIIc, V, Super Minx I & II	Castrol GTX	8	Castrol GTX [21][43]	2¾	Castrol Hypoy	1¾
1963–71, Imp, Imp Mk II & Californian	Castrol GTX	5½	Castrol Hypoy Lt	4½	—	—
1965–67 Minx V, VI, Husky III, Super Minx III & IV	Castrol GTX	8	Caxtrolite [21]	3½ [19]	Castrol Hypoy	1¾
1967–69 Imp Sport	Castrol GTX	6	Castrol Hypoy Lt	4½	—	—
1967–70 Hunter, Hunter II, New Minx & GT	Castrol GTX	7+½	Castrolite [21]	3½ [19]	Castrol Hypoy	1¾
1970–71 Avenger 1250, 1500 & TC	Castrol GTX	6½+½ [44]	Castrol GTX [21]	3	Castrol Hypoy	1½
1970–71 Hunter De Luxe, Super, GL & GT	Castrol GTX	6½+1	Castrol GTX [21]	3½ [19]	Castrol Hypoy	1¾
MORRIS						
1959–69 Mini-Minor, Mini-Cooper & Mini-Cooper "S"	Castrol GTX	8½ [27]	—	—	—	—

MAKE & MODEL	ENGINE Summer/Winter	Sump capacity plus filter [1] Pints	GEAR BOX	Capacity Pints	REAR AXLE	Capacity Pints
1961–71 Oxford Series VI	Castrol GTX [80]	$7\frac{1}{2}$	Castrol GTX	$4\frac{1}{2}$	Castrol Hypoy	$2\frac{1}{4}$
1961–71 Oxford Series VI (Automatic)	Castrol GTX [80]	$7\frac{1}{2}$	Castrol TQF	$11\frac{1}{4}$	Castrol Hypoy	$2\frac{1}{4}$
1957–71 Minor 1000	Castrol GTX	$6\frac{1}{2}$	Castrol GTX	$2\frac{1}{4}$	Castrol Hypoy	$1\frac{1}{2}$
1962–71 1100, 1100 Mk II, 1300 & 1300 GT	Castrol GTX	$8\frac{1}{2}$ [27]	—	—	—	—
1966–69 Mini, Mini Mk Mk II, Mini-Cooper, 1100, 1100 Mk II & 1300 (Automatic)	Castrol GTX	13 [27] [59]	—	—	—	—
1966–71 1800, 1800 Mk II & 1800 Mk II "S"	Castrol GTX	$10\frac{1}{4}$ [27]	—	—	—	—
1966–71 1800 & 1800 Mk II (Automatic)	Castrol GTX	$7\frac{3}{4}$	Castrol TQF	13	—	—
1971 Marina 1.3	Castrol GTX	7	Castrol Hypoy [119]	$1\frac{1}{2}$	Castrol Hypoy	$1\frac{1}{4}$
1971 Marina 1.8	Castrol GTX	8	Castrol Hypoy [119]	$1\frac{1}{2}$	Castrol Hypoy	$1\frac{1}{4}$
TRIUMPH						
1959–70 Herald Saloon, 12/50, 1200 & Coupe	Castrol GTX	7	Castrol Hypoy	$1\frac{1}{2}$	Castrol Hypoy	1
1967–70 Spitfire 4 Mk III	Castrol GTX	8	Castrol Hypoy	$1\frac{1}{2}$ [91]	Castrol Hypoy	1

1961–67 TR4 / TR4A	Castrol GTX	10+1½	Castrol Hypoy	1½ [41]	Castrol Hypoy	1½
1967–68 TR5 P.I.	Castrol GTX	8	Castrol Hypoy	2 [13]	Castrol Hypoy	2½
1962–66 Vitesse	Castrol GTX	8	Castrol Hypoy	3½ [3]	Castrol Hypoy	1
1964–69 2000	Castrol GTX	8	Castrol Hypoy [21]	2½	Castrol Hypoy	1¾
1966–71 1300 & 1300 TC	Castrol GTX	6¼	Castrol Hypoy	2¼	Castrol Hypoy	1¼
1967–70 GT6 & Mk II	Castrol GTX	8	Castrol Hypoy	1½ [18]	Castrol Hypoy	1
1967–71 Vitesse 2 Litre & Mk II	Castrol GTX	8	Castrol Hypoy	1½ [91]	Castrol Hypoy	1
1968–71 2.5 P.I. & Mk II	Castrol GTX	8	Castrol Hypoy [52]	2½ [19]	Castrol Hypoy	2¼ [116]
1969–71 TR6 P.I.	Castrol GTX	8	Castrol Hypoy	2 [41]	Castrol Hypoy	2¼
1969–71 2000 Mk II	Castrol GTX	8	Castrol Hypoy	2½	Castrol Hypoy	2¼ [116]
1970–71 Toledo 1300	Castrol GTX	7+1	Castrol Hypoy	1½	Castrol Hypoy	1½
1970–71 1500	Castrol GTX	6¼	Castrol Hypoy	2¼	Castrol Hypoy	1¼
1970–71 Stag	Castrol GTX	8+1	Castrol Hypoy [2]	2¼ [117]	Castrol Hypoy	2
1970–71 Spitfire Mk IV	Castrol GTX	7+1	Castrol Hypoy	1½ [91]	Castrol Hypoy	1
1967–71 13/60	Castrol GTX	7½	Castrol Hypoy	1½	Castrol Hypoy	1
1963–67 Spitfire 4 Mk II	Castrol GTX	7	Castrol Hypoy	1½	Castrol Hypoy	1
1967–70 Spitfire 4 Mk III	Castrol GTX	8	Castrol Hypoy	1½ [91]	Castrol Hypoy	1
1961–67 TR4 & TR4A	Castrol GTX	10+1½	Castrol Hypoy	1½ [41]	Castrol Hypoy	1½
1967–68 TR5 P.I.	Castrol GTX	8	Castrol Hypoy	2 [13]	Castrol Hypoy	2½
1962–66 Vitesse	Castrol GTX	8	Castrol Hypoy	3½ [3]	Castrol Hypoy	1
1964–69 2000	Castrol GTX	8	Castrol Hypoy [21]	2½	Castrol Hypoy	1¾
1966–71 1300 & 1300 TC	Castrol GTX	6¼	Castrol Hypoy	2¼	Castrol Hypoy	1¼
1967–70 GT6 / Mk II	Castrol GTX	8	Castrol Hypoy	1½ [18]	Castrol Hypoy	1
1967–71 Vitesse 2 Litre & Mk II	Castrol GTX	8	Castrol Hypoy	1½ [91]	Castrol Hypoy	1

MAKE & MODEL	ENGINE Summer/Winter	Sump capacity plus filter [1] Pints	GEAR BOX	Capacity Pints	REAR AXLE	Capacity Pints
1968–71 2.5 P.I. & Mk II	Castrol GTX	8	Castrol Hypoy [52]	2½ [19]	Castrol Hypoy	2¼ [116]
1969–71 TR6 P.I.	Castrol GTX	8	Castrol Hypoy	2 [41]	Castrol Hypoy	2½
1969–71 2000 Mk II	Castrol GTX	8	Castrol Hypoy	2½	Castrol Hypoy	2¼ [116]
1970–71 Toledo 1300	Castrol GTX	7+1	Castrol Hypoy	1½	Castrol Hypoy	1½
1970–71 1500	Castrol BGTX	6¼	Castrol Hypoy	2¼	Castrol Hypoy	1¼
1970–71 Stag	Castrol GTX	8+1	Castrol Hypoy [2]	2¼ [117]	Castrol Hypoy	2
1970–71 Spitfire Mk IV	Castrol GTX	7+1	Castrol Hypoy	1½ [91]	Castrol Hypoy	1
VAUXHALL						
1957–62 Victor	Castrol GTX	6+1½	Castrol ST	2	Castrol Hypoy	2½
1960–62 Velox & Cresta PAX (Automatic)	Castrol GTX	9½+1½	Castrol TQ Dexron ®	10½	Castrol Hypoy	3¾
1960–62 Velox & Cresta PAX (Synchro)	Castrol GTX	9½+1½	Castrol ST	2 [13]	Castrol Hypoy	3¾
1962–65 Velox & Cresta (Synchro)	Castrol GTX	8+1	Castrol ST	3½ [3]	Castrol Hypoy	3¾
1962–65 Velox & Cresta (Automatic)	Castrol GTX	8+1	Castrol TQ Dexron ®	10½	Castrol Hypoy	3¾
1964–66 Viva & Viva 90	Castrol GTX	5¼+ ½	Castrol ST	1	Castrol Hypoy	1¼
1966–71 Cresta & Cresta De Luxe						
3 Speed	Castrol GTX	8+1	Castrol Hypoy	2 [13]	Castrol Hypoy	4
4 Speed	Castrol GTX	8+1	Castrol Hypoy	2½	Castrol Hypoy	4
Powerglide	Castrol GTX	8+1	Castrol TQ Dexron ®	4	Castrol Hypoy	4

1961–65 Victor & VX 4/90	Castrol GTX	6+½	Castrol ST	2¼	Castrol Hypoy [100]	2½
1965–67 Victor 101 3 Speed	Castrol GTX	6½	Castrol ST	2	Castrol Hypoy [100]	2½
1965–67 VX 4/90 & Victor 101 4 Speed	Castrol GTX	6½	Castrol ST [102]	2½	Castrol Hypoy [100]	2½
1967–70 Viva, Viva De Luxe, Viva 90 De Luxe, Viva SL & Viva 90 SL (Manual)	Castrol GTX	4½+½	Castrol Hypoy	1	Castrol Hypoy	1¼
1967–70 Viva De Luxe, Viva 90 De Luxe, Viva SL & Viva 90SL (Automatic)	Castrol GTX	4½+½	Castrol TQ Dexron ®	4½ [65]	Castrol Hypoy	1¼
1968–70 Viva GT	Castrol GTX	8	Castrol Hypoy	2½	Castrol Hypoy	2½
1967–69 Victor FD 1600 & 2000	Castrol GTX	8¾	Castrol ST [102]	2 [92]	Castrol Hypoy	2½
1968–71 Ventora & Ventora II	Castrol GTX	8¾	Castrol ST [102]	2½ [18]	Castrol Hypoy	4
1967–71 Viscount (Manual)	Castrol GTX	8+1	Castrol Hypoy	2½	Castrol Hypoy	4
1967–71 Viscount (Automatic)	Castrol GTX	8+1	Castrol TQ Dexron ®	4 [65]	Castrol Hypoy	4
1969–71 VX 4/90 (Manual)	Castrol GTX	8	Castrol Hypoy	3 [3]	Castrol Hypoy	4
1969–71 VX 4/90 (Automatic)	Castrol GTX	8	Castrol TQ Dexron ®	4½ [65]	Castrol Hypoy	4
1968–70 Viva 1600 & SL (Manual)	Castrol GTX	7½+½	Castrol Hypoy	2½	Castrol Hypoy	1¼

MAKE & MODEL	ENGINE Summer/Winter	Sump capacity plus filter [1] Pints	GEAR BOX	Capacity Pints	REAR AXLE	Capacity Pints
1968–70 Viva 1600 & SL (Automatic)	Castrol GTX	7½+½	Castrol TQ Dexron ®	4½ [65]	Castrol Hypoy	1¼
1969–71 Victor Super (Manual)	Castrol GTX	8	Castrol Hypoy	2 [92]	Castrol Hypoy	2½
1969–71 Victor Super (Automatic)	Castrol GTX	8	Castrol TQ Dexron ®	4½ [65]	Castrol Hypoy	2½
1969–71 Victor 2000 SL (Manual)	Castrol GTX	8	Castrol Hypoy	2 [92]	Castrol Hypoy	2½
1969–71 Victor 2000 SL (Automatic)	Castrol GTX	8	Castrol TQ Dexron ®	4½ [65]	Castrol Hypoy	2½
1968–71 Victor 3300 SL (Manual)	Castrol GTX	8¾	Castrol Hypoy	2 [92]	Castrol Hypoy	4
1968–71 Victor 3300 SL (Automatic)	Castrol GTX	8¾	Castrol TQ Dexron ®	4½ [65]	Castrol Hypoy	4
1970–71 Viva HC, De Luxe, 90 De Luxe & 90 SL (Manual)	Castrol GTX	5	Castrol Hypoy	1	Castrol Hypoy	1¼
1970–71 Viva HC, De Luxe, 90 De Luxe & 90 SL (Automatic)	Castrol GTX	5	Castrol TQ Dexron ®	—	Castrol Hypoy	1¼
1970–71 Viva 1600 De Luxe & 1600 SL (Manual)	Castrol GTX	8	Castrol Hypoy	2½	Castrol Hypoy	1¼

Model	Engine oil	Capacity	Gearbox oil	Capacity	Rear axle oil	Capacity
1970-71 Viva 1600 De Luxe & 1600 SL (Automatic)	Castrol GTX	8	Castrol TQ Dexron ®	— [106]	Castrol Hypoy	1¼
1961-71 1500	Castrol CRI 30 [85]	4½	Castrol Hypoy B	4½ [106]	—	—
1965-71 1200, 1300 & 1500 (Manual)	Castrol CRI 30 [85]	4½	Castrol Hypoy B	4½ [106]	—	—
1965-71 1200, 1300 & 1500 (Automatic)	Castrol CRI 30 [85]	4½	Castrol TQ Dexron ®	6¼ [110]	Castrol Hypoy B	5¼ [111]
1965-71 1600 (Manual)	Castrol CRI 30 [85]	4½	Castrol Hypoy B	4½ [106]	—	—
1965-71 1600 (Automatic)	Castrol CRI 30 [85]	4½	Castrol TQ Dexron ®	11½ [106]	Castrol Hypoy B	1¾
1968-71 411 (Manual)	Castrol CRI 30 [85]	5¼+1	Castrol Hypoy B	3½ [106]	—	—
1968-71 411 (Automatic)	Castrol CRI 30 [85]	5¼+1	Castrol TQ Dexron ®	10½ [106]	Castrol Hypoy B	1¾

NOTES

1. Capacities of oil filters are shown as a plus (+) quantity alongside sump capacities, where available.
2. When fitted Automatic Transmission – use Castrol TQF – capacity 11½ pints.
3. Includes overdrive.
13. 3½ pints with overdrive.
18. Capacity with overdrive, 3 pints.
19. Capacity with overdrive, 4½ pints from dry.
21. When fitted with automatic transmission, use Castrol TQF. Capacity – 11¼ pints.
27. Includes transmission.
34. Later models capacity 4⅞ pints.
41. Capacity with overdrive 3½ pints.
43. When fitted with Easidrive gearbox, use Castrolite, capacity 2¾ pints.
44. TC Models fitted with engine oil cooler: sump capacity 7½ pints plus 1 pint for filter.
46. 1965 and later models total capacity 5½ pints.
47. 1965 Models total capacity 7 pints.
48. When fitted with automatic transmission, use Castrol TQF. Capacity 10½ pints. Cortina and Corsair ranges capacity 12 pints.
49. Models before engine Nos. 18 AMW-U-L 42259 and 18 AMW-U-H 71232 capacity 12¾ pints.
52. When fitted with automatic transmission, use Castrol TQF, capacity 13½ pints.
54. Capacity with overdrive, 3¾ pints.
57. In winter use Castrolite.
59. Drain and refill capacity 9 pints approx.
61. Cars fitted modified dipstick Part No. 12B 2526 (Standard from Engine No. 29AW/20647) Oil Capacity 11 pints.
65. Automatic Gearbox service refill capacity.
80. When fitted with BMC Diesel Engine use Castrol CR1 20 – capacity 8¼ pints.
85. In winter use Castrol CR1 20. Alternatively – Castrol GTX may be used all year round.
91. Capacity with overdrive 2½ pints.
92. 4-speed Synchro capacity 2½ pints, with overdrive 3 pints.
95. J2M 16 Series, oil capacity 3¾ pints.
100. Where super traction axle fitted use special oil – see Handbook.
102. When fitted Automatic Transmission, use Castrol TQ Dexron ®.
106. Includes final drive.
108. When fitted Automatic Transmission use Castrol TQ Dexron ® Refill capacity 4½ pints.
110. Converter system capacity.
111. Transmission and differential.
116. Estate car rear axle – capacity 1¾ pints.
117. When fitted with overdrive – capacity 3¼ pints.
119. When fitted with Automatic Transmission use Castrol TQF – capacity 9½ pints.

INDEX

189

Uniform with this book

* * *

THE CAR DOCTOR A–Z

by B. C. Macdonald

Symptoms – Causes – Cures

UNIQUE!

This book is an astonishing A.B.C. faultfinder. Look up the symptoms and the book tells you the causes and cures. Precise step-by-step details of the action to take in every circumstance, routine or emergency.

No driver should be without this book.

You can save £££s in garage fees.

Behind the book stands our GUARANTEE:
Return for full money refund if you disagree this is the world's greatest book on the subject.

* * *

ELLIOT RIGHT WAY BOOKS
KINGSWOOD, SURREY, U.K.

B. C. Macdonald's world famous individual models Repairs Series

FORD ESCORT REPAIRS
FORD CORTINA REPAIRS
BLMC MINI REPAIRS
BLMC 1100 AND 1300 REPAIRS
MORRIS MINOR 1000 REPAIRS

B. C. Macdonald, author of the best-seller "THE CAR DOCTOR", now applies all his knowledge and experience for the benefit of owners of the above named models. Each model range has its own book, but for reasons of space, high performance models in the ranges have had to be excluded.

He has evolved an entirely new formula in writing these books, which makes them easy for YOU to understand. The books are divided into ten Chapters, eight of which cover different parts of the car, each written on the same basic plan, i.e.,

Section 1:   General Data
Section 2:   Fault symptoms
Section 3:   Causes and cures. This section consists of the analytical step-by-step approach which has made B. C. Macdonald famous.
Section 4:   and additional sections: special procedures for more complicated repairs and servicing, maintenance, etc.

Particular attention is paid to electrical faults, which without these books are most perplexing. An index allows instant reference to the place in the book where you will find what you want. Chapter 9 in each book deals with general maintenance and 10 gives additional data.

Each of the five books uniform with this volume

ELLIOT RIGHT WAY BOOKS
KINGSWOOD, SURREY, U.K.